THE American Values Reader

Harvey S. Wiener
Marymount Manhattan College

Nora Eisenberg
*LaGuardia Community College of the
City University of New York*

Allyn and Bacon
Boston • London • Toronto • Sydney • Tokyo • Singapore

Vice President: Eben W. Ludlow
Series Editorial Assistant: Tania Sanchez/Linda D'Angelo
Senior Marketing Manager: Lisa Kimball
Editorial–Production Administrator: Donna Simons
Editorial–Production Service: Matrix Productions Inc.
Composition and Prepress Buyer: Linda Cox
Manufacturing Buyer: Suzanne Lareau
Cover Administrator: Linda Knowles
Cover Designer: Studio Nine
Electronic Composition: Omegatype Typography, Inc.

Library of Congress Cataloging-in-Publication Data
Wiener, Harvey S.
    American values reader / Harvey S. Wiener, Nora Eisenberg.
      p.   cm.
    Includes index.
    ISBN 0-205-27381-5
    1. Social values—United States. 2. United States—Social policy.
  3. United States—Social conditions. 4. United States—Moral
conditions. 5. Values—United States. I. Eisenberg, Nora, 1946–   .
II. Title.
HN57.W543   1999
303.3'72'0973–dc21   98-38581
                                                             CIP

The credits for this book begin on page 768, which is an extension of the
copyright page.

Printed in the United States of America
10 9 8 7 6 5 4   RRDV   03 02 01 00

Contents

———— ★ ————

2 *Education*   87

3 *Work and Poverty*   *162*

4 *Health and Health Care*   240

Part II ★ LIBERTY   307

5 *Language and Speech*   311

7 *Rights and Beliefs*   438

Part III ★ The Pursuit of Happiness

8 *Love*

Rhetorical Table of Contents

———— ★ ————

Description

Narration

Illustration

Process

Comparison and Contrast

Classification

Causation

Definition

Argumentation and Persuasion

Preface

──────── ★ ────────

One of the most intense and unresolved—perhaps ultimately unresolvable—discussions in America today revolves around the issue of values and their role in shaping and defining our identity as a people. The debates on morals and values begun by the early writers and philosophers and continued in the contemporary period are still with us. Jonathan Edwards, Thomas Jefferson, Nathaniel Hawthorne, Ralph Waldo Emerson, Frederick Douglass, Elizabeth Cady Stanton, and countless others in earlier centuries labored to define and examine the moral core of our nation. Today, we cannot turn to a newspaper or magazine without finding some reference to the dissolution of society's value system, often in reference to today's youth, but encompassing stock brokers who cheat their clients, public figures who cheat the Internal Revenue Service and abuse taxpayers' money, and elected officials who cheat on their spouses or their constituencies, betraying private or public trust, or both.

Politicians complain about the shredding of the nation's moral fiber. Parents fear the invasion of the home by corrupting agents like movies, television and the Internet, undisciplined children from remote neighborhoods, and books and magazines like *Huckleberry Finn* and *Penthouse*. Religious leaders call for a return to prayer and required values instruction in the classroom as sure ways to move us back on track. The assumption underlying many of these notions is that some absolute code of moral behavior exists for life's situations and dilemmas and that this code, once established, will make our citizens models of American values and right-thinking behavior. Of course, calls for controls over segments of popular culture—revised standards for stricter film rating systems, demands for television rating schemes, the proliferation of banned book lists all over the country—belie our faith in the citizen's ability to choose morally correct actions. But never mind—the society's attention to values as a major element in human behavior moves values to center stage as a teachable, learnable concept.

In education, the conversation about values has taken on a largely political cast, with people on the right and left arguing for a kind of values agenda rooted in political passion. Each group insists on an instructional program based on partisan beliefs. From the left of center we hear politically correct calls for free speech zones and a definition of liberty that would deny free speech to anyone who insults a person's racial, sexual, or ethnic identity. From the right, we hear of a behavioral code that relies on cultural literacy, national performance standards, report cards for schools to highlight the strong and inferior for comparison shopping by educational consumers, and bible reading and flag pledging in the classroom.

Despite the apparent pitfalls, we believe that college freshmen must engage in the values debate and should address the values-laden issues that arise in their studies, in the news, and in their lives. In our experience, few classroom opportunities stimulate deliberation on moral issues; few textbooks explore the notion of values and attendant critical thinking; and, perhaps, not wishing to perpetuate a "here's the right way to think and behave" approach, few institutions face the issue of values at all in the academic curriculum. Yet universities and colleges must help students address values with an openness of mind and diligence of attitude if we are to develop an educated citizenry that can identify and make appropriately reasoned moral choices. Like the rebellious, uncooperative young children Robert Coles identifies in his book *The Moral Intelligence of Children* (see pages 97–102), college students "very much need a sense of purpose and direction in life, a set of values grounded in moral introspection." The key question is: How do we spur this introspection in the college course of study?

We see the freshman writing classroom as fertile ground for the essential exploration. In *The American Values Reader* we offer texts that stimulate thought about values issues; that engage the controversy through penetrating, informed discussion; and that avoid the excesses of partisan politics and religious extremism that have dominated the often passionate discourse. Returning to the three broad areas of self-evident truths and inalienable rights identified by our country's founders—*life, liberty, and the pursuit of happiness*—as the organizing strategy of our book, we make each of these principles a part title. Under each, we propose a series of thematically defined chapters that help explore the larger principle in sharply focused units and from multiple perspectives. The key here, we believe, is our multiple perspectives approach: Chary of a single correct road to eternal truth, we do not prescribe the readings as values gospel or propose them as the core selections in building a moral base. Rather, we provide the readings as touchstones for discussion about values issues and guide our readers in identifying the moral questions raised by a selection and in discussing them thoughtfully, writing about them, and using them as a stimulus for thinking and writing on related issues.

We do not insist on a common cultural or literary base as the only way to provide both intellectual and moral education. Perhaps one cannot argue with William Bennett, a well-known political conservative and former Secretary of Education under George Bush, when he asserts that "planting the ideas of virtue, of good traits in the young comes first" and that "every American child ought to know at least some of the stories and poems" Bennett so faithfully reproduces in his best seller *The Book of Virtues*. Yet the questions in this approach persist: Where are the other voices from other cultures? Whose idea of virtue and good traits define the moral fiber of the nation? How do we confront the reality that large numbers of readers will never have seen the tales and stories Bennett believes define the American character?

We do not favor volumes of "lessons and reminders." Believing in the power of enlightened discourse in the classroom, in the potency of collaborative learning as an educational tool, in the undeniable might of writing as a means of access to new ideas and a way of sharing them publicly, we offer *The American Values Reader* as a primary text for the evolution of values education for freshman students learning to read, write, and think by the academy's guidelines. This book is about the discussion of complex ethical controversies presented by varied writers and thinkers. Never attempting to color an issue one way or the other, we draw widely from an ethnically and geographically diverse group of contributors. Our questioning strategies always ask readers to consider the many facets of the values focus in the text at hand. In Don J. Snyder's "Sorry, the Professional Class Is Full," for example, we concentrate not only on a worker's despair at having lost a job long prepared for but also on the broader issue of "downsizing," now an almost routine procedure in America's work environments, and the wrenching changes it produces in the social fabric. Peggy Fletcher Stack's "Temple Wars," a piece about strong objections to constructing Mormon temples in Massachusetts and Montana residential neighborhoods, leads readers to consider not only the relations between church and state but also the issues of neighborhood sanctity, of religious freedom in general, and of the conflict between demands of the spirit and secular realities.

Relying largely on expository selections, we try to balance historical as well as contemporary views, liberal and conservative outlooks, male and female voices, and multiracial and multiethnic approaches. Early writers whom we include help lay some of the values foundations: Jefferson, Abigail Adams, Paine, Stanton, and others. Among contemporary writers we draw on a wide range of dramatic voices: Malcolm X, Robert Coles, Barbara Ehrenreich. We include some short stories and poems as well: Hawthorne's "The Birthmark," Bret Harte's "The Outcasts of Poker Flat," Dorothy Parker's "The Standard of Living," Poe's "Annabel Lee," and Evans's "When in Rome," to name a few.

We attempt here to make readers sensitive to the values reflected in the readings as well as to their own values as they encounter a selection. We intend a broadly based scheme and do not highlight in each case the political. Rather, we draw on the many elements of the selections to uncover the explicit and implicit values and, through rigorous questioning, engage students in timely debate for classroom conversation or for writing essays.

Our approach sees the potential in every piece for linking past and present values so that any selection can become a mirror to our own culture; *The American Values Reader* through its essays and questioning apparatus reflects the belief in that potential. To encourage readers to join the values conversation embedded in the carefully chosen selections that make up our table of contents, we provide questioning strategies that engage critical thinking in five discussion and writing categories:

- **Meaning and Understanding**: As the first order of business, we provide questions about the literal meaning of the text. Once students understand what the writer is attempting to say, they can examine the ideas embedded in the selection.
- **Techniques and Strategies:** Here our questioning highlights the rhetorical and linguistic strategies the writers use to make their points. We look at issues such as introductions, conclusions, thesis statements, transitions, organizing strategies and the conventional expository modes (description, narration, comparison, definition, and so on), figurative language, and word choice. Teachers can use questioning here to help model effective writing as students produce their own papers about the selections.
- **Speaking of Values**: Under this heading we focus discussion on the values issues suggested by the essay at hand. Questions are designed to encourage critical thinking on the various dimensions of the piece and to present touchpoints for conversation in class. A subcategory here is what we call **Values Conversation,** a collaborative discussion and writing activity. We ask students to form groups to exchange ideas on one of the most salient values issues raised in the reading and to keep a record of the points made. The written work here can serve as an early activity for the drafting of an essay.
- **Writing about Values**: After each essay, we provide a series of prompts that highlight values issues for students to write about. Often a prompt will build on the Values Conversation activity so that students, if they wish, may carry forward to a piece of public writing the discussions initiated in a collaborative setting.
- **Values in Review**: At the end of each chapter, we tie together themes raised by the various selections through writing or discussion prompts designed to have students compare and contrast different perspectives on the values issues. At the end of each section, we ask students to reflect in writing on the inalienable right explored in the chapters.

We believe that readers of this book will benefit immensely from participation in an ongoing discussion about values and beliefs as vital shapers of existence, both private and public. American democracy was and is many things, but it is most importantly an open conversation about life advanced in many forums—town meetings, representative assemblies, and schools. What better place to continue the conversation than in the college composition classroom?

Acknowledgments

As we prepared this text on American values, we carried on extended conversations with teachers, writers, and friends who helped shape the direction of the book and give it much of its energy and focus. Our discussions convinced us of the project's relevance and importance for today's students, and we want to acknowledge publicly all the help and support we received along the way.

Our long-time colleague and friend John Wright encouraged, prodded, and pushed us to bring the project to fruition. Eben Ludlow, our trusted editor and guru at Allyn and Bacon, brought a level of support and enthusiasm to *The American Values Reader* that any author would envy. Linda D'Angelo, Editorial Assistant at Allyn and Bacon, with typical efficiency and care kept us on schedule and helped us through the rough spots of manuscript production. For valuable editorial help early in the project we owe a debt to Brad Beckman. To Christine Timm of Queens College we are grateful for her many contributions to our book.

In addition, we wish to thank the following teacher–scholar–reviewers for offering thoughtful commentary on early drafts and for keeping alive the values conversation: Karen L. Greenberg, Hunter College, CUNY; Dick Harrington, Piedmont Virginia Community College; James C. McDonald, University of Southwestern Louisiana; George Otte, Baruch College and the Graduate Center, CUNY; and David Shimkin, Queensborough Community College, CUNY.

Introduction: Reading and Writing about Values

———— ★ ————

Literacy and Values

Although from the earliest ages much wisdom has flowed from oral traditions, modern societies depend on literate culture for developing and disseminating information, insight, and opinion. Embedded in the American identity is a deep commitment to literacy, words written and read, and a belief in its potential for improving humanity. From the earliest days of the Republic, leading thinkers and thinking leaders like Benjamin Franklin championed the notion of public schools to educate our citizenry.

Today, reading and writing suffuse our lives—whether we're evaluating the ingredients on a cereal box, dashing off a shopping list, pouring our heart out in a letter, reading a novel, developing a report on the job, sending a note to a friend across the country or down the street, or writing a paper for college. Thus, a book like this one, focused on values, rightly begins with one of the quintessential values for America: the complex of communication skills—reading, writing speaking, and listening—that create a literate culture.

Even with the advent of modern technology, text still remains central to our existence. The World Wide Web and an infinite variety of chat rooms (the form is the written word but "chat" means oral *conversation*) connect individuals and communities across the globe in interchange sustained by writing and reading. Virginia Woolf wrote that writing for her was a "voice answering a voice." And this seems true enough, not only for great novelists but also for the rest of us. We write often in response to what we've heard or read. We read to expand our ideas, verify positions, inform our thinking. The pieces in this book took shape as writers reflected on experience, including their experiences in reading and listening. Many voices—written, heard, and remembered—will inform the writing you will do as you work with this book.

When we talk about values, we are talking to a great extent about writing—the vast repository of our beliefs as a culture and people—

1

and reading—the means by which we draw on that repository and in turn enrich it. In sharpening your critical thinking, reading, and writing skills for college, career, and citizenship, perhaps nothing makes more sense than a focus on beliefs and ethics. Here, the stakes of our thinking and communication are nothing less than the terms and forms of our existence. As you read and think about the selections in this book, you will engage in a dynamic conversation about what a broad range of writers represents American values to be, at present and in the past, and what they might be in the future. Critical reading entails an effort not only to understand the meaning of a text but also to explore the values—explicit and implicit—that speak through the words on the page. In what ways does the selection assert a moral position? What ethical system does the writer evince? How do the writer's moral sensibilities match or contradict your own or those of others you have read or heard? And how do the values represented by the various selections in each chapter resonate with or challenge each other? These essential questions should guide your reading and writing. Do you agree with Timothy Harper, for example, who says in Chapter 3 that boys get more attention than girls from teachers in school? And if he is right, what does this suggest about how we as a society value children?

Because we believe our country was founded to a great extent on opinion—about freedom and fairness and opportunity—the conversation about values and opinions is fundamental to our national life.

Reading and Thinking about Values

The special axis of this book places an added burden on the thoughtful reader, as we examine the values implicit in a piece of writing and use them as divining rods for our own individual values as readers and members of social communities. When the subject is the way we live our lives and what we learn from others about how to live our lives with some moral forethought and commitment, reading, writing, and speaking are both challenging and crucial. We will want to bring our best selves to the undertaking. Reading with an outlook that is both critical and fair allows us to get the most out of texts. Reading with a mind that is sharp and open is not always easy, but it is always well worth the bother. An open mind helps us to take in ideas and experiences to which we may not be disposed, and to consider them as we shape our own thinking. A critical mind, one that questions from many angles, helps us to measure the validity of a writer's points and to hone our own thinking about a topic. One approach is more yielding, perhaps, one more oppositional—yin and yang, if you will. The two mentalities represent different human gifts and allow us to bring to a subject a rich, full response.

Certainly, part of what we read helps us learn and accept new values. And we mean more here than just learning about your own existing values or how to gain fuller access to them. Christina Hoff Sommers in "Ethics without Virtue" (Chapter 2) makes the important distinction between merely learning how to respond to a moral act—stealing, in her example—and learning that an act is right or wrong. Be prepared here, then, to learn from what you read not only to clarify your own moral code. You will also learn what some writers believe is right and wrong and what they expect you to adopt as part of that code. Can you change the values that are so much a part of your defining existence? Should you change them? These questions may chafe your conscience, even torment you from time to time, as you confront a stunning new perspective. We do intend the readings presented here to challenge you in ways that you might not have thought possible.

David Blankenhorn, for instance, will force you to reconsider what society should exact from fathers who abandon their families. Yes, these men avoid financial responsibility by not paying child support, and our laws take aim at the pocketbooks of what he calls in Chapter 1 "Deadbeat Dads." But, no, says Blankenhorn, don't exact payments. Exact fatherhood.

How does this point of view measure up to your own? Perhaps in this essay, perhaps in others, you will confront ideas rooted in values that you find alien or may even have abandoned as part of your own growth to knowledge. Key here is not rejecting out of hand some position before you have heard its supporter and analyzed carefully the elements that make the writer speak out. How many of us, for example, would accept the idea of multiple spouses as a valid way to conduct conjugal and family life? Much of our social, cultural, legal, and religious training challenges the notion of polygamy. We look at the idea of harems and the many wives of biblical figures as historical artifacts and at polygamists as weird pariahs of society's mores. Yet Elizabeth Joseph's reasoned, if startling, portrayal of family in "My Husband's Nine Wives" (Chapter 8), filled with religious and familial values bizarre to most readers, surely gives us food for thought. Her essay may convert few of us to her way of life, but she opens a window on our own view of family and brings us to the notion that what we experience every day apparently is not the only way. Much attention goes today to the idea of alternative family structures—single mothers, single fathers, grandparents or aunts or uncles or cousins rearing children. Is a home with one husband and his nine wives simply another acceptable (or unacceptable?) human response to the complexities of our age? These are the kinds of questions that using critical thinking as you read can tease out of an essay. In other words, you want to look at more than what the text says; you want to measure its main points against the values that help define your own life and the lives of those around you;

and you want to look afresh at those values, in some cases for the first time, to see how they bear up under the scrutiny of attack or extreme or renewed support.

Techniques for Reading Openly and Critically

Certain techniques will help you to read value-rich texts so that you get the most out of them as a thinker and writer.

PREVIEWING FOR AN OVERVIEW

Many readers find it useful to review a text before actually reading it. Sometimes called *prereading,* this act will help orient you to the piece and may give you insights into the writer's moral position. Consider the title, first of all. What does it tell you? Then look over the whole. What typographical features of the text assert an organizational scheme? If the piece has headings or boldface words and phrases, what can you gather from them? Can you get a sense of the thesis or main idea—that is, the writer's essential point—from these special features? Look carefully at the beginning and end of the selection and see if these help you identify the essential point. The headnote before the text and the questions after it also can help you identify key elements in advance of your reading.

Returning to the example of Blankenhorn's piece, we see that even before we read the essay, the title, "The Deadbeat Dad," provokes us and suggests a position within a framework of family values. Reflect on the title and many thoughts will explode in your mind even before you look at the first paragraph. Examine the subheading, "The Bad Understudy," that appears on page 48. What does that phrase make you think of? The first sentence of the selection is "The Deadbeat Dad is a bad guy"; the last sentence is "The only solution to the problem of Deadbeat Dads is fatherhood." Reading these apart from the rest of the piece gives valuable insights into the writer's thesis as well as his values. The headnote on page 47 tells you, among other things, that Blankenhorn is chair of the National Fatherhood Initiative, a fatherhood rights activist group. Surely this information provides insights into the writer's preoccupations and gives you a sense of his views before you read about them in his exposition. And the various questions after the selection direct your attention to the essential elements in the argument and to the particular values issues you should consider. Question 3 under "Speaking of Values," for example, tells you of the three categories the writer establishes: the Unnecessary Father, the Old Father, and the New Father. If you examined the question in advance of reading, you'd have another clue to Blankenhorn's assertions well before you examined them in depth.

READING ACTIVELY WITH A PEN OR PENCIL IN HAND

Try to read as actively as possible. You don't need us to tell you that reading is a complex process, and you will want to be in a frame of mind that keeps you open to another's ideas as well as critical and questioning. To take in and respond to the ideas and expression of a piece of writing, notetaking is key. Some people prefer to take notes in the margins of the book. Others find it useful to use a notebook—a reading journal in which to record random thoughts, questions, extraordinary passages copied directly from the text. Some do both, writing in their texts and in a separate reading journal. Whatever method you select, or your teacher requests, your notetaking should help you to organize, remember, and reflect on the selection. Underline or highlight brilliant or provocative or, yes, irritating or even stupid phrases and sentences. Make an index for yourself on the blank back pages of the books you own. Write down a page number and an identifying word or concept that will remind you of why you singled out the passage.

IDENTIFYING THESIS AND DETAILS

As you read, take notes in which you identify the essence of the selection, its *thesis*. Sometimes a writer will state the organizing main idea outright. William Branigin, for example, leaves no doubt about his main point when he makes this assertion in paragraph 6 of his essay "Sweatshops Are Back" (p. 163):

> Despite a ledge of laws against them and periodic pledges by government and business leaders to crack down, sweatshops have made a remarkable comeback in America, evolving from a relative anomaly into a commonplace, even indispensable, part of the U.S. garment industry.

Sometimes the writer will imply the thesis through the accretion of points and details developed as the piece takes shape. In many essays the thesis appears early in the work, but often it is the outgrowth of pages of discussion. Wherever and however the writer has presented the conceptual core of the piece, you as a reader will do well to locate it. Be mindful that identifying the thesis or main idea can be a process requiring careful, attentive examination. If a thesis is not stated outright, you should try to put into words what seems to be the underlying point.

Identify the details that support the main idea. How effective are these in fleshing out the writer's points? Anyone can make an assertion in writing; but to provide some kind of evidence for readers, successful writers know to back up their assertions with details based on sensory observation, statistical information, case studies, expert testimony, or a combination of these devices. When Henry David Thoreau in the selection from *Walden* ("I Borrowed an Axe and Went Down to the Woods," p. 179) wants us to see the "pleasant hillside" where he worked, he shows it to us with a panoply of sensory details: the place is

> covered with pine woods, through which I looked out on the pond, and a small open field in the woods where pines and hickories were springing up. The ice in the pond was not yet dissolved, though there were some open spaces, and it was all dark colored and saturated with water. There were some slight flurries of snow during the days that I worked there, but for the most part when I came out on to the railroad, on my way home, its yellow sand heap stretched away gleaming in the hazy atmosphere, and the rails shone in the spring sun, and I heard the lark and peewee and other birds already come to commence another year with us.

No reader can fail to see the scene as Thoreau sees it. He gives us a delight of sensory images alive with concrete detail—"dark colored and saturated with water," "yellow sand heap stretched away gleaming in the hazy atmosphere," "the lark and peewee." These immediately draw us into the moment with Thoreau and help us understand why in his mind's eye this is indeed such a pleasant hillside.

As you read, then, you should identify powerful details that support the writer's ideas. Also look out for details that you think are unconvincing or that lack specificity.

OBSERVING RHETORICAL STRATEGIES

Read too for the mode or modes of development used to expose the issues. How does the writer build her presentation. Why has she chosen these particular strategies to advance her point? What do the decisions about rhetoric tell you of what the writer values? The writer's dominant approach may rely on description, rendering a phenomenon through sensory details—the face of a sweetheart, possibly, or the quiet features of a Sunday morning schoolyard. Perhaps the central strategy is narrative, building the point largely by telling a story—the birth of a first child, the winning routine in a gymnastics competition, the first day on a new job after twenty years as a homemaker and mother. Perhaps the main mode of development is through illustration, with the writer presenting examples to support a point: the instances of mischief caused over Christmas by a new puppy in the house, for instance. Or perhaps the writer may elucidate a process, limning the steps for a reader to duplicate that process or simply to understand the way it progresses—how to install a program on a computer or how beer is made, for example.

You may find that the writer chooses an analytic strategy rooted in causes, effects, or both—the causes of alcoholism among teenagers, for instance, or the results of AIDS testing on infants, or the causes of poverty and its effects on urban society. Or perhaps the analysis relies on classification, grouping elements in a topic for ease of understanding— the categories of learning disabilities identified among children, say, or the kinds of Supreme Court cases most apt to draw a response from the Justices. Perhaps the strategy for development is comparison and (or) contrast, where the writer shows two or three objects or ideas in the light and shadow of each other—the similarities between a stagecoach ride and a ride in a city bus, the strengths and weaknesses of the three candidates for town dogcatcher, the way a sonnet by Millay and a sonnet by Milton resonate and diverge. Or does the writer, like most of us, combine some of these development strategies for a rich, rounded discussion? Particularly in an argumentative essay, where the writer takes a position on a controversial topic and reasons his way through it, writers will draw on a variety of rhetorical modes. Thus, to argue that HMOs do not provide appropriate service to the sick, a writer, drawing on descriptive and narrative elements, could compare and contrast two patients receiving medical service, one with an HMO physician and one with an unaffiliated physician. The writer then could explain the long-term effects on patient health by HMO guidelines and regulations. Many other options are available, certainly, in such an essay. Writers of argument invariably will draw from an arsenal of rhetorical techniques to light the fire of debate.

Rhetorical strategies organize and advance our thinking, and accomplished writers know, for example, when to tell a story, describe a scene, enumerate examples, compare and contrast issues, explain processes, classify ideas, show causes and effects, define terms, argue a position. The deeper question here is why a writer will chose one strategy over another and what that announces about her values as a thinker and producer of prose or poetry. Reading with an eye to how a selection builds its point makes us aware of the choices we can make ourselves as we write about values issues. The rhetorical strategies reflect the varied human habits of thinking and knowing. Heightening your awareness of them is particularly critical in reading about values, where the full repertoire of thinking means the complex reasoning and response to a complex issue.

WEIGHING AUDIENCE AND PURPOSE

Consider the writer's audience and purpose as you read. This awareness will deepen your sense of the selection and allow you to appreciate and critique ideas more fully. To whom is the piece pitched and to what end? What effect do audience and purpose have on the essay's impact and message? How will the writer's audience respond to the values brought into focus in the writing? A work written for an audience of experts, for example, will require more sophisticated exploration of concepts than a work intended for a general audience. And purposes too help shape a piece. Is the piece simply reflective, or is it argumentative? Does it want the reader to change his thinking, take action, a bit of both? Consider such issues as you read.

ATTENDING TO THE PARTS

Consider and take notes on key sections and moments in the piece. Note the introduction. How effectively does it draw you in and set up the discussion or fictive universe? Do the same for the conclusion. How well does it close the piece, leaving a glow in the reader's mind? Note the transitions, from point to point. Are they effective? Do they advance the logic of the piece? Do the ideas connect logically to each other? Do the ideas relate to a central point that you can determine successfully?

MAKING THE READING PERSONAL

Finally, relate the piece to your own thinking as you read. Consider whether the selection mirrors elements in your own thoughts or challenges them. How has the piece changed your outlook on the issue? In what ways do you agree with the piece? In what ways do you disagree? Why? If you keep a reading journal, you can jot down these ideas and use them as springboards for the essays you will have to write.

As you read the selections in this book, keep in mind the mental qualities that will help you think about values in a deep and meaningful way. Remember to be fair minded so that you can get the best of what the author has to say. Remember too to be questioning and critical so that you can not only embrace ideas, but also discard or refine them—after thorough consideration of all that is there on the page.

Writing about Values

Writing about values requires much of the same carefulness and thoroughness as reading values-rich material. The writing process is an elaborate one as writers plan and replan, draft and redraft, edit and re-edit, and all in all shape an often vague idea into a solid piece of work, giving "to airy nothing," as Shakespeare writes in *A Midsummer Night's Dream*, "a local habitation and a name." Because the issues involved in values and beliefs are both complex and important, you want to support your work by understanding the various phases of writing and practicing the range of activities writers use to inform their work.

Having reached college, you probably have some sense of what helps you to advance, as you write, from confusion to clarity, from fuzziness or emptiness to coherence and complexity—both inside you and on the page. You probably know that your work is stronger when you plan, when you consult, when you take time to rework, edit, and so on. In short, you already know a good deal about the writing process and what it takes to develop a substantial piece of work. Different people have different styles of working as they write. But honoring the various stages of writing—from planning to polishing—will reduce the frustration so common to writing, strengthen your confidence, and build your skills as a thinker and communicator. Indeed, appreciation of the complex process of writing is a value in itself—a set of practices that fosters thoughtfulness. Anyone can write opinionated cant in minutes, but developing an informed and reasoned opinion requires time and care. And moving through all the stages of writing will enable your work to become part of the important and respectful conversation our nation is engaging in around how we live our lives individually and collectively.

Most people who do a good deal of writing—whether they're professional writers or college students—identify a variety of stages and activities for approaching complex writing tasks. Writing, like any activity, involves preparing, planning, doing, usually redoing, consulting, adding final touches. You know this intuitively. Yet the following recommendations will help you to know it better. And awareness of the process will support you through the inevitable frustrations of hard work, and help you fight the sense that something's wrong with you, when you're at times blank, confused or overwhelmed. That's all part of the process. Move through each stage, reaping its benefits. Quickly you'll feel more comfortable, confident, and excited about your abilities as a writer and thinker and your contribution to the values conversation.

GETTING STARTED

Teachers of writing often call the earliest stage of writing *prewriting*. This is the stage when you prepare yourself to meet your task and subject. Most people find a combination of the following useful: read on the subject, talk to people about the subject, jot down ideas, write briefly and informally (often called freewriting) to discover ideas, formulate a thesis, make a plan or outline. In reality, different minds work in different ways. Some people find it very useful to freewrite, some like to list thoughts or pose questions. Most people find reading invaluable, providing information and opinion to respond to in their own work. Some people find it particularly useful to talk to reliable, intelligent friends and colleagues to sharpen a view of the subject. A stirring film, a lively debate on television, a reasoned presentation on radio can provide deep insights into a controversial topic. Some people find formal outlines essential; others like a simpler scratch outline, jotting down a thesis and a few supporting ideas. There are no rules for getting yourself prepared to write. The simple truth is that writers need to search in order to write full, complex pieces. This involves looking outside and inside—to what others know and to what you know, and do not know, about a subject.

Specific prewriting techniques allow you to soak in your subject, important for all writing, but particularly so in writing about values and beliefs, rife with rich argument and information. Often students feel inadequate to a writing task before they start, and often this feeling comes about because they shortchange themselves at this first stage of writing. Thus, we want to spend some time here in more detail about certain phases of prewriting that are bound to enhance your efforts as you explore values—your own and those of others—in the essays you will write in connection with this book.

EXPLORING THE SUBJECT

When you're writing about a complex issue in values, you'll want to get comfortable with the subject. Considering what others have to say will provide you with information and also help you see what you believe about the issue. Reading especially, as we've said, can change your opinion, strengthen your opinion, help you see new ways of viewing things. As we've suggested, take notes as you read: mark down where you agree, disagree, have questions, have insights. The selections in this anthology will open you to new ideas about American values, but you should not stop at the presentations assigned by your instructor. Become intimate with your institution's libraries and, using the automated cataloging system, find subject entries related to the topic you're discussing in class. Look for related films at the video store. Check the television listings in your local newspaper. Surf the Web for an incredible range of insights. With all of these efforts, of course, a lively intelligence will help you separate the wheat from the chaff: there's lots of junk out there, and you have to determine what's useful and what's ridiculous. A plethora of sources can overwhelm you. Make thoughtful choices about how to spend your time checking the opinions of others.

As you will see, we root many of the specific writing assignments included here in library work or in other activities designed to get you to expand your ideas through sources. When you look at the issues swirling about Ann Louise Bardach's piece "Stealth Virus: AIDS and

Latinos" you'll understand why we direct you to do some library research on the history of AIDS—so that you can see and write about the
disease's progress and treatment. Or why we ask you to consider the
films or plays you may have seen about AIDS—to help you uncover a
unity of thought that reflects the artists or society's accepted views on
this medical horror that has so dominated our health policy over the
last decade.

TALKING TO OTHERS

Conversing with people about a topic can often help writers deepen
their knowledge and perceptions. Most writers—professionals and students alike—have special friends that they like to bat ideas around
with. Use these friends or classmates as you approach a piece of writing at the beginning of a project—and at later stages as well.

Interviewing people with special knowledge of the topic also can
provide you with much information, deepening your understanding
and sharpening your point of view. Remember, experts are not only
people who have published on a subject but also people who have
lived through experiences. Thus if you're writing about the issues of
war suggested by Stephen Crane's short story "An Episode of War,"
you might want to interview someone who has fought in Vietnam or
Desert Storm, or lived in a war zone. If you're writing about health care
matters in response to Fred Hechinger's piece "They Tortured My
Mother," you may want to talk to a doctor or nurse, or to a friend or
family member who has been a patient in a hospital. In short, as you
soak in your subject, look around you for resources.

TALKING TO YOURSELF

Talking to yourself at all stages of writing helps you formulate what
you know, don't know, want to know, and want to say. A pen or pencil
or keyboard in hand eases recording and using those private conversations in your mind. Explore different techniques that help you reflect—
and use the one or ones that work best for you. Here spelling and form
don't count. Listing and jotting are for you—to get you into shape to
approach your subject.

LISTING AND (OR) JOTTING

Some people like to put their thoughts in an orderly list; some like to jot
them down, here and there on the page. Some prefer brief notations,
single words. Others need to write more complex ideas. Some people
find asking and answering questions in writing useful. Do whatever

helps you most to prime the pump, whetting your mind on the topic and its complexities.

FREEWRITING

Freewriting is another preparatory writing activity that many find useful in getting the juices going. Generally, when writers freewrite for a particular paper, they establish a set time frame—fifteen minutes, say—and then record on a blank sheet of paper whatever comes to mind about their subject. When you freewrite, just keep writing. Don't censor your thoughts or stop to make corrections. At the end of a few minutes, you'll know more than you knew when you started and, with luck, may have unleashed an exciting insight that will start you on the road to a good paper. Such focused freewriting (sometimes called *timed writing*) takes you wherever your mind travels on the subject. Like listing and jotting, freewriting can help you discover not only information, insights, and questions but also strategies for development, classification of purpose, and so on.

DEVELOPING YOUR THESIS AND PLAN

However you find you like to work, or however your teacher recommends your working, it's useful, by the end of the prewriting stage, to identify a thesis as well as a plan for advancing it. Know that the plan and even the central point may change as you move on. We discover as we write, and it is not uncommon for a writer to reverse or refine her main idea midway through a draft. But after you've primed your mind—reading and talking and jotting and freewriting—state a thesis that will guide your draft, even if you end up trading it in for another one later on.

Your thesis statement should suggest the parameters of your topic. It should also indicate your position on it, your attitude toward or opinion about the subject that you intend to develop. In Chapter 1, when Ruth Gay writes this opening sentence for the second paragraph of her essay "Floors: The Bronx—Then," we know exactly what her topic is and where she intends to take it: "Even in the New World, floors—kitchen floors especially—were sure barometers of a housewife's standards and ability." This is not merely a statement of a topic, floors in people's houses in the New World of the Bronx, New York. It is also a representation of the writer's beliefs about those floors: they indicated the abilities and standards of the woman charged with housewifely duties.

You should know that not every writer will state a thesis directly in a piece of writing. Not only short stories and poems but also many essays leave for the reader alone the delights of inferring the main point and the position the writer takes on it. But for beginning student writers in college, it's always a good idea to write a thesis sentence—whether or not you ultimately include it in your essay. We've said it before, but it's worth repeating: your thesis sentence should and will evolve as you continue thinking and drafting thoughts. Don't be surprised if the thesis that ultimately makes its way into your final copy is vastly different from what you started with.

Hand in glove with your emerging thesis is the need to establish a working plan of development and organization. This plan should include the main and supporting points you will make to advance your thesis. A scratch outline is particularly helpful for many writers at this stage. Particularly for a long paper with details drawn from a variety of sources, your instructor may require a formal outline with roman numerals, upper-case and lower-case letters, and arabic numerals to indicate main headings and subheadings for the various paragraphs. Your outline will help you proceed to your first draft.

And then there is the matter of development. Consider as you plan the panel of strategies writers use as they weigh their approach to a topic—narration, description, exemplification, process, causation, comparison, classification, definition, argumentation, and persuasion. Because these modes reflect entrenched human habits of mind, we often use them in writing without much awareness. But an awareness of our approaches in critical thinking will make for stronger writing and reasoning about the important domain of values and belief in our lives.

As you consider rhetorical development, do so with an awareness of the formal choices available to you—the various development options we named in the section above called "Observe Rhetorical Strategies"—but keep your mind loose as well, allowing yourself to discover the routes that seem to come naturally. Let's say you are trying to plot your development for a paper on marriage or divorce as an outgrowth of the essay you read by Judith S. Wallerstein and Sandra Blakeslee, "The Children of Divorce," in Chapter 1 of this book. One of our proposed writing tasks is "Write an essay about 'the perfect marriage.' Be sure to provide specific details concerning the roles of each spouse as well as what you think their responsibilities should be as parents." As you weigh your thesis and plan, reviewing the rhetorical strategies might help you make the appropriate inroads to the essay. You could describe the physical qualities of members of a perfect marriage or produce a narrative to demonstrate the interactions between two perfect mates. Perhaps you might give a number of examples to show how a husband and wife demonstrate what you consider perfection in a conjugal relation. Perhaps you'll write a "how-to" essay, explaining to your readers the surest pathway to a perfect marriage. Or you could compare one marriage you know with another, thereby arriving at a view of perfection by means of side by side demonstrations. You might also classify marriage behaviors that produce perfection or might write an extended definition of the perfect marriage. You also could argue that a perfect marriage in today's world is impossible; or, as an outgrowth of that perception, you could try to persuade readers never to get married since perfection, in your view, is essential but unachievable. Permutations and combinations of these potential strategies can stimulate further thought on approaches to the essay you're writing

PRODUCING A DRAFT
AND GETTING FEEDBACK

Once you have developed a thesis and a plan for organizing and building your discussion, it's time to write. Most writers need to write several drafts of a piece in order to do their subject and thinking justice. Now and then—rarely, we should add—a writer's first draft will be a final draft, displaying clarity, fullness, and polish. But more often than not a first draft is just that, the first of several attempts, each building on the successes and weaknesses of the one before. Don't think, then, that you have to have everything "perfect" as you write a first draft. Writing, and then reading, your first try can lead you to embrace more fully or reject ideas and positions you laid out in your prewriting, and refine or maintain plans for organization and strategies and details for development. Writing about values, as we've said, requires careful thinking and execution of plans, and writing and reading drafts with both patience and alacrity will be essential to your success in the complex enterprise of values exploration. If you write by hand, leave lots of blank spaces between your written lines. Avoid erasing unwanted words; instead, draw lines or xs through phrases or sentences you reject. You may marvel later on about what you see as their brilliance and might want to retrieve them. If you draft your essay on the computer, double or triple space your sentences and be sure to produce hard copy during the drafting stage. Here too, don't simply cut changes: paste them somewhere that you can retrieve incipient thoughts if you need to later on.

Once you've written a first draft, it's always helpful to show it to others—your teacher, your classmates, your friends. Others' eyes can help you as you look at your draft, identifying strengths and problems. You needn't obey what everyone says, but chances are if there's agreement among readers, you'd do well to pay attention to their remarks as you approach a new draft.

REVISING YOUR DRAFTS

Unless you are particularity lucky with your first draft, you probably need to write an additional draft or drafts to achieve a full, well-developed essay. Don't be discouraged if you find yourself writing many drafts until you and your trusted advisors are satisfied. Keep each draft: often writers find it useful to fuse elements of different drafts as they work. As you review your work with an eye to revision, focus first on the most substantial elements, such as thesis, supporting details, organization, mode of development. Make changes that you think will strengthen your essay. Don't be depressed if your second draft advances a different thesis from the first, or omits some description, replacing it with examples, or vice versa, or reverses the order of your paragraphs. We learn as we write: we discover what we want to say and how we want to say it, as we move through the dialectic of thinking and writing.

Check for structural elements as you revise. You want to be sure that your essay is *unified*—that is, each idea must connect to the main point asserted in your thesis and each point must relate to the other points. You can see why the thesis forms and reforms in the evolution of an essay, if only to maintain the all-important sense of unity as your ideas take shape during successive drafts. Also, you can see that unity requires you to excise stray thoughts and tangents that, interesting though they may be, take your reader afield of the point. You want to be sure too that your essay is *coherent*, that is, each idea must flow logically and smoothly to the next one. As you write and revise, make use of transitional phrases that move the reader along through the complexities of your discussion and subtly link the ideas in as seamless a web as you can spin.

As you develop your drafts, be vigilant about unity and coherence. Through appropriate transitions, pronouns, temporal markers, conjunctive adverbs, and other devices, guide your reader through the parts of the essay, showing where you move on to new points, emphasize existing points, counter thinking, and so on.

You also want to attend to the *introduction* and conclusion of your paper. Introductions generally pull the reader into the essay. They provide a hook and assure the reader that the piece will be of interest. Often, the thesis appears in the introduction, and the paragraph or two that will frame the essay's opening will set the stage for the thesis. If you have defined your main point and planned your essay carefully, the introduction should flow with relative ease as you draft your paper.

Here is the first paragraph of Ruth Gay's essay on floors that we have included in Chapter 1. Note how beautifully it frames the piece and leads so directly to the clear, concise thesis we pointed out earlier as the first sentence of paragraph two in "Floors: The Bronx—Then":

> My mother lived in a house with a beaten earth floor. She never told me this. I only learned it by chance when my father taunted her with it in response to her fine airs and manners. My mother-in-law came from Warsaw, where she had lived in an apartment building made of stone.

The stories of these floors became a talisman of sorts, for one the source of shame, for the other of amusement. My mother-in-law loved to tell the story of how she prepared for her first Sabbath in the New Country. Wanting to wash the kitchen floor, she filled a bucket of water and preparatory to wielding the mop, flung the contents on the floor. Shrieks from her downstairs neighbor, pounding on the door, protests about the *"griner"*—the greenhorn. In Warsaw, she had lived with stone floors, how was she to know that in the New World floors were made of lesser stuff.

    Even in the New World, floors—kitchen floors especially—were sure barometers of a housewife's standards and ability...

This introduction is instructive for many reasons. Note first the use of detail. Concrete images like *beaten earth floor, flung the contents on the floor, shrieks from her downstairs neighbor, pounding on the door*—these immediately draw the reader into the sentient world of the family. Gay makes us read on through her choice of words. Note too how she establishes but does not develop comparative elements—a mother, a mother-in-law—later to be drawn on perhaps. The natural momentum, as we've said before, leads to the thesis statement, which will guide readers through this work.

When it comes to the end of an essay, readers generally expect *conclusions* to contain elements of summary. But the most memorable conclusions do more. Conclusions are the writer's last chance to reach his reader. Treating the subject with a fresh, interesting insight in your conclusion assures the reader that you and your positions have found their exposition in the essay. Look at the last paragraph in George Simpson's piece about a hospital complex, "The War Room at Bellevue," from Chapter 4. Simpson has asserted in this essay that the extraordinary place he writes about is a refuge for those who have a chance for survival after trauma because of the quality of the Adult Emergency Service unit. Does this simple conclusion not make that point indelible?

    So it goes into the morning hours. A Valium overdose, a woman who fainted, a man who went through the windshield of his car. More overdoses. More drunks with split eyebrows and chins. The doctors and nurses work without complaint. "This is nothing, about normal, I'd say," concludes the head nurse. "No big deal."

Take time in writing your conclusion. Can you marshal and refute those who oppose your position in an argument? Can you tell an anecdote to drive the point home? What fresh observation can you make about your thesis that will show that your writing brought you to a new dimension of thought? Ruth Gay uses her conclusion in "Floors: The Bronx—Then" to define the philosophy of life her parents had evolved. A linoleum rug becomes in this final paragraph an emblem of life's rewards for "industry and prudence" and a caution against "excess, showiness, waste."

POLISHING AND PROOFREADING

Once you've addressed the central issues of your piece—what you want to assert in your thesis, which strategies will best develop it, how you want to sequence your discussion—and are satisfied that your latest draft reflects your most complete thinking on the subject, you are ready to do a final draft.

Here is your chance to review your expression and phrasing with exacting care. Check on sentence structure. Does every sentence end where you want it to end? Did you mark the junctures of sentences with appropriate punctuation? Does each sentence express a complete thought? Also, check on your usual errors and problem areas as a writer. Is subject and verb agreement correct? Did you spell *embarrassed* and *occasion* right this time? Do pronouns refer correctly to antecedents? A final polishing edit requires you to look at every word singly and as part of its broader context in a sentence, a paragraph, your essay.

Moving through all stages of writing, from jotting down rough ideas to polishing special phrases, helps writers as they face most any writing task. But when we're writing about issues of values, careful work at every stage enhances the best expression of ideas critical to our lives. The interaction between thought and expression is, perhaps, most profound when we explore matters most rooted in our identity and beliefs. As we look at the development of key writings through the ages, we see evidence of writers engaged in an elaborate process, often reading and conversing to gather ideas, taking notes, writing drafts, gathering commentary, revising, polishing and so on.

One Example: Drafting "The Declaration of Independence"

For our purposes here, perhaps no example from history gives us greater insight into the writing process, especially as it informs writing about values, than the story of the writing of the Declaration of Independence, which we include in its entirety in Chapter 6 of this book.* This seminal document for world democracy, developed to explain and justify America's independence from England, was written by the brilliant Thomas Jefferson, but with the input of a committee of

---

*We want to thank Elaine Maimon and her colleagues for first pointing us to the usefulness of Jefferson's drafts as models for revision and their implications and also to Carl Becker's work, which shows the Declaration in its evolving forms.

colleagues gathered in Philadelphia for the Continental Congress that would found our new nation. On June 11, 1776, the committee of five—Jefferson, Benjamin Franklin, John Adams, Roger Sherman, and Robert Livingston—began work, submitting a final draft on June 28, which Congress adopted on July 4. In a matter of days, then, moving from consultation to drafting, to "peer response," to redrafting and polishing, the document that we look to as the cornerstone of our democracy emerged.

Because of his skill as a stylist, the committee had turned to Jefferson to write the Declaration. We have an early draft—housed today in the Library of Congress—containing Jefferson's words, and the revisions of his colleagues on the committee, particularly Franklin and Adams. (Our source for the excerpt printed here is Carl Becker, *Declaration of Independence: A Study in the History of Political Ideas*, New York: Random, 1958.) A look at the famous second paragraph, which declares the human right to "life, liberty, and the pursuit of happiness," demonstrates the contribution of consultation and revision in transforming both the content and style of the document.

THE ROUGH DRAFT

as it probably read when Jefferson made the 'fair copy' which was presented to Congress as the report of the Committee of Five.

A DECLARATION BY THE REPRESENTATIVES OF THE UNITED STATES OF AMERICA, IN GENERAL CONGRESS ASSEMBLED.

When in the course of human events it becomes necessary for a *one* people to ad-
dissolve the political bands which have connected them with another, and to
~~vance from that subordination in which they have hitherto remained,~~ & to assume
among the powers of earth the *separate and equal* ~~equal & independent~~ station to which the laws of
nature & of nature's god entitle them, a decent respect to the opinions of mankind
requires that they should declare the causes which impel them to *the separation* ~~the~~

We hold these truths to be *self-evident* ~~sacred & undeniable~~; that all men are created equal
~~& independent~~; that *they are endowed by their creator with equal rights, some of which are* ~~from that equal creation they derive in rights~~ inherent & inalienable among *these* ~~which the preservation of~~ life, & liberty, & the pursuit of happiness; that to secure these *rights* ~~ends~~, governments are instituted among men, deriving
their just powers from the consent of the governed; that whenever any form of government ~~shall~~ becomes destructive of these ends, it is the right of the people to alter

or to abolish it, & to institute new government, laying it's foundation on such principles & organizing it's powers in such form, as to them shall seem most likely to effect their safety & happiness. Prudence indeed will dictate that governments long established should not be changed for light & transient causes: and accordingly all experience hath shewn that mankind are more disposed to suffer while evils are sufferable, than to right themselves by abolishing the forms to which they are accustomed. but when a long train of abuses & usurpations, begun at a distinguished period, & pursuing invariably the same object, evinces a design to ~~subject~~ reduce them, ~~to arbitrary power,~~ †*under absolute Despotism* it is their right, it is their duty, to

[†Benjamin Franklin's handwriting—ED.]

All in all, the changes in Jefferson's first effort prune the prose nicely. "Sacred and undeniable" becomes simply "self-evident"; "created equal and independent" becomes simply "created equal." The logic cuts more swiftly and sharply. But "from that equal creation" gets changed to "endowed by their creator," emphasizing for readers the authority of God in the rights of humanity, and invoking that authority in the creation of a new independent nation. The revision here defines one of the essential values of the young nation's founders: from the Godhead, not just from civil law, flow the inalienable rights of people in the new country. No mere stylistic change, this alteration in the draft establishes a precept that to this day undergirds the way we think of ourselves as a people.

Still, as Carl Becker shows, the changes of the committee of five were largely stylistic. When the Declaration goes to Congress, however, the process of consultation wields changes that are of a different order, with profound ethical implications for the nation. (From all reports, Jefferson objected to having his prose fooled with by others, particularly the Congress.)

The rough draft includes, for example, among its list of wrongs committed by the English crown, the wrong of slavery:

> he has waged cruel war against human nature itself, violating its most sacred rights of life & liberty in the persons of a distant people who never offended him, captivating & carrying them into slavery in another hemisphere, or to incur miserable death in their transportation thither.

Yet Congress omits this paragraph as it revises toward the final draft.

The lessons of the Declaration of Independence's evolution are profound. One of the central documents of our nation is the product of a complex drafting process. Individual authorship gives way to authorship by committee, and in turn authorship by Congress. Prose gets polished and ideas get changed. We can only imagine today the fate of the nation had the original committee insisted on the paragraph condemning slavery.

But our purpose here is not to speculate about history; instead, it is to encourage you as writers to take your part in today's lively and critical conversation about values, and at the same time to learn and practice the writer's craft. "Life, liberty, and the pursuit of happiness"—what do they mean to us today? As you read and write, using this book, discover what you think and express it for others to consider in the ongoing democratic debate shaping our nation's future.

Part I
Life

Life, liberty, and the pursuit of happiness—what could the Republic's founders have had in mind when they etched into the Declaration of Independence those three indelible categories that capture the essence of American values? And, perhaps more to the point here, what do those terms, so long in implication and short in precision, mean to Americans today? Our country is so changed from the eighteenth-century world of the Declaration as to be almost unrecognizable. (What would Benjamin Franklin have thought of computerized libraries? What would de Crevecoeur, the cheerleader for agriculture as the basis for our economy, have thought of shopping malls and video buying services? What would Abigail Adams—the articulate early voice of women's rights—have thought of Madeline Albright's service as Secretary of State under President William Jefferson Clinton?)

The founders of our nation, in pleading to the world the case for their separation from England, asserted life, liberty, and the pursuit of happiness as the endowments of "certain inalienable rights." But scholars are still debating what exactly the Declaration's authors meant. Does "certain" mean established beyond doubt? An indefinite but limited number? Does "inalienable" mean given by nature and thus naturally inseparable from humans—men in particular? And if so, which "men"? What did the founders understand as the rights of men who were slaves, or women, who were not men? And what of those particular rights, inalienable and certain, that would make up the endowment—how would the new nation define them, assure them, protect them?

As we begin through readings and conversation to explore these defining concepts of our existence, we turn to the first issue in the trio of rights recorded in the Declaration, *life*. The Republic's founders pledged a person's right to "life"—meaning exactly what? Life as a "duty"—not an uncommon eighteenth-century notion—so that one lives to fulfill an obligation to self and country? Life as a natural force, which society is morally obliged to sustain in the support of humanity— another contemporary notion? Whatever the subtleties of meaning, "life" in the Declaration of Independence was a product of eighteenth-century thinking—Locke, or Rousseau, or Hutcheson, or all of these thinkers and more, depending on our interpretation of prevalent texts and philosophies. Still, Americans in the twentieth century, like those in the century before, hear in the founders' words resounding chords for living and dreaming and defining the essential covenant between citizen and country that makes America special. When we ponder the right to "life," we create our own declarations, asserting our own constructions of rights in both private and public spheres.

As we aim to explore through the readings in Part I the most essential meanings of the word *life* as written by the founders, shaped by their progeny, and brought to our twentieth- (and soon twenty-first) century consciousness, we look to entities and ideas associated with the preservation of life itself.

Chapter 1, Family, considers the source of our individual lives and examines the values at play in the living units and social concepts swirling about our particular existences. Nowhere, perhaps, is the debate on values argued more passionately than in the family arena— more passionately and, one may argue, least thoughtfully. Everyone has or has had a family and everyone has a special image of its shape and form, not always resonating with the images in the minds of others. If you attack traditional family, many on the right proclaim, you attack America. America is the "American family"—though often no more than a romantic blur of father and mother and children. The left, by and large, attacks such fixed concepts of family, legitimizing, if not applauding, single families, gay families, and other arrangements of modern social life. From this perspective, though, pro-family sentiments are often identified as simpleminded and traditional connections devalued.

The writers in Chapter 1 avoid such easy accusation. Still, with considerable energy, each offers an illuminating view of family. In the nostalgic piece "Leave Ozzie and Harriet Alone," for example, Gregory Curtis glances back at the 1950s and that decade's much-criticized cultural images, finding there not hypocrisy but endearing simplicity. We can't go back, the essay says, but don't you want to? As if in answer, Randall Williams looks back through the decades, too, to his own family life—uncovering the degrading poverty that Ozzie and Harriet's thick carpets covered over for a generation of viewers. Through intimate portraits and research and analysis, the writers consider various pictures of parents and family—loving, neglecting, nurturing, suffocating. "Is marriage worth it?" the pieces implicitly and explicitly ask, answering, in turn, as you might suspect, "yes" and "no." Family values—they're killing us, one writer seems to say, while others look to a cluster of beliefs about home and responsibility to reform American life.

Chapter 2, Education, considers another "right" that Americans have come to see as inalienable and essential to democratic life and intrinsic to our value system. "If you complain of neglect of education in sons," Abigail Adams writes to her husband, John, "what shall I say with regard to daughters, who every day experience the want of it?" The selections on education, as if joining this conversation, consider the range of educational "wants"—for sons, daughters, poor, and rich, in turn. And the selections in the chapter ponder not only the "basics" of education but also the moral basics for selfhood and citizenship. Where are these in our society? Christina Hoff Sommers surveys the education scene and finds that virtues have slipped into a swamp of values relativism. Robert Coles, in contrast, talks to children and finds much reflection and wisdom in a rich terrain of "moral moments." Toni Cade Bambara presents a funny yet deadly serious lesson of values that black youngsters learn in an excursion to a high-priced Fifth Avenue toy store. Taken together, the pieces on education reveal Americans learning in prison, in ghettoes, in informal settings, and in youth and old age. In their various ways, the writers challenge educational assumptions and practice, just as their considered phrases reveal the victories of American learning and expression.

As Benjamin Franklin reminded Americans, work and industry ensure the good life. But looking back on our national past or around at our present, thoughtful citizens must scrutinize Franklin's cheerful sentiment. Was it ever true—is it true now—that hard work is the best down payment on the American dream? In Chapter 3, Work and Poverty, we present voices that reflect on the American "work ethic" so long viewed as essential to national and personal well-being. Thoreau narrates his experience in building a house alone in the woods, providing us with a somewhat romantic template for independent initiative and survival. The rest of the selections show experiences and opportunities that one may consider against the moral landscape of Walden Pond. Stephanie Coontz in "A Nation of Welfare Families" argues, through historical examples, that self-reliance is simply a national myth: centuries of "handouts" have given Americans the very ground on which they walk with the swagger of the self made. William Branigin's

"Sweatshops Are Back" and Don Snyder's "Sorry, the Professional Class Is Full" show, in their different ways, dreams snuffed by cruel realities yet, despite this, the persistence of the will to work and succeed. The legacy of economic hardship and poverty, other writers in the chapter suggest, plays havoc with children's lives. Jonathan Kozol's "Children and Poverty" and Frank McCourt's "When Dad Gets a Job" from *Angela's Ashes* paint pictures of the wobbly or crumbling physical and financial foundations on which children must build their lives. Still, facing these challenges, Gary Soto shows us in his story "Looking for Work," children keep hope, holding onto dreams and the energy to work for a new life. Other writers reflect more theoretically on the meaning of modern economic realities for individual lives. In "The Hard Questions: Lost City," Jean Bethke Elshtain looks at new models of work for the next millennium. All in all, the selections in Work and Poverty invite us to identify and investigate the values of work and resourcefulness so fundamental to America and Americans' self-concept.

Finally, in Chapter 4, Health and Healthcare, we gather from the writers' attitudes toward sickness, age, and death much about Americans' values about life. As technology to extend life proliferates, the terms of individual existence change. Fred Hechinger's "They Tortured My Mother" shows through poignant personal experience a medical "machine" organized around saving life at all costs. In the setting of a an old age home, Eudora Welty demonstrates individual and institutional callousness as charity gives way to the thinnest duty. Paul R. McHugh, in examining what he sees as the "illness" and popularity of Dr. Kevorkian—the physician who assists suicide for ill patients—suggests that we are a nation forsaking the natural urge toward life. Ann Louise Bardach explores the AIDS epidemic as the scourge of a Florida Latino community and implies a set of values about life and death that cries out for discussion and analysis. Other writers here consider our views toward doctors and nurses—our idealization of the former, our diminution of the latter—revealing our mentality regarding public roles and private suffering. All in all, the selections in this chapter show healing and healing practices at the heart of our national life.

Life in America today is not simply a biological reality but is also a defining principle of human society. The writers here lay bare the elements of life that they see defining the nation's character and the values at its core.

Chapter 1
Family

Family values

American domestic life

Children of divorce

Deadbeat dads

Family poverty

Family heritage

Fathers and sons, mothers and daughters

Television families

Gregory Curtis

Leave Ozzie and Harriet Alone

Gregory Curtis is the editor of *Texas Monthly* magazine. In this essay he examines the view of American domestic life portrayed by a highly successful television series of the 1950s, *The Adventures of Ozzie and Harriet.*

———————— ★ ————————

1   On a gray morning last August I was riding with David Nelson in the hills just above Sunset Boulevard in Hollywood. We were on our way to see the house where he grew up with his parents, Ozzie and Harriet, and his brother, Rick, the same house shown at the beginning of episodes of *The Adventures of Ozzie and Harriet.* That program, which was on the air from 1952 to 1966, was the original family situation comedy, a television genre that David's father invented. *The Cosby Show, Roseanne* and even *The Simpsons* are direct descendants of *Ozzie and Harriet* and owe their existence to Ozzie's—let's call it what it was—genius.

2   David is the last of the Nelsons. Ozzie died of liver cancer in 1975. Rick died in an airplane crash on New Year's Eve 1985. He was a good rock singer but, after several years of popularity, his success was never again commensurate with his talent. In the end his reputation was unfairly clouded by the discredited report that free-basing cocaine sparking a fire that caused his plane to go down. Harriet died at 85 in 1994.

3   Now David is 60 and has his own company that makes advertisements and promotional films. Except for his broad, athletic frame, he does not look much like the young man on the television show, but the tone of his voice and the cadences of his speech are exactly the same. He is extremely nice and accommodating—taking a morning off to drive me around, among many other courtesies—but also extremely private. He is forthcoming about the show but reticent about his life today, as if he had to expose so much of himself as he grew up that now he wants to take cover whenever possible.

4   The Nelsons' legacy is its own peculiar burden. In the continuing political debate over family values, the phrase "Ozzie and Harriet" has become shorthand for an idyllic America of the past where mothers, fathers and children lived happily together. Social conservatives call for a return to this world. Alan Ehrenhalt wrote in *The Wilson Quarterly:* "America is full of people willing to remind us at every opportunity

that the 1950's are not coming back. Ozzie and Harriet are dead, they like to say, offering an instant refutation to just about anyone who ventures to point out something good about the social arrangement of a generation ago." This is anathema to those who believe that alternative family structures are just as good as the traditional one. Caryl Rivers and Rosalind C. Barnett, two college professors, wrote in Newsday of "a well-financed, well-organized campaign by the right wing to prove the only family system that works is the Ozzie and Harriet family with a breadwinner father and a homemaker mother." They concluded that attempts to "turn back the clock" were doomed to fail. And speaking at Harvard, Barbra Streisand said, "They attacked 'Murphy Brown,' which represents a thoughtful attempt to deal with the reality that Americans now lead lives that, for better or for worse, are very different than the lives of Ozzie and Harriet." Even this newspaper recently said that believing that poor people could live like Ozzie and Harriet in today's world was "cruel."

How can it be that such an important, entertaining and apparently   5
harmless show is at the center of such conflict? Which is it—a reflection of a better world or a model of oppression—or something else entirely?

The Adventures of Ozzie and Harriet was set in an imaginary small   6
town where there is never any politics, any contention, any heartbreak. Everyone is happy. Everyone is well fed and well dressed, lives in a nice house and has the same heart and the same values. At the center of this world are "America's favorite family, the Nelsons," as the show's announcer says. Ozzie plays a character named Ozzie Nelson; Harriet, a character named Harriet Nelson; and so on with David and Ricky. They all live in a virtually unchanging harmony; they love to walk into rooms of the house and greet each other. Scene after scene begins with: "Hi, Mom. Hi, Pop." "Oh, hello, boys." Scene after scene ends with: "Bye, Mom. Bye, Pop." "So long, boys. Have a good time." The plots, such as they are, often concern events or issues from the daily life of the Nelsons. Will Ozzie play Ping-Pong in the father-and-son tournament with David or Ricky? Is David old enough to have his own key to the house? Should Harriet change her hairstyle?

No one would mistake these "problems" for the great social and po-   7
litical dilemmas of our time. But they are exactly the kind of complications that are common in family life. Ozzie makes a happy family, their routine and the minute events of their lives the entire focus of his considerable creative energy. He was close in spirit to P. G. Wodehouse, who also wrote about families, if not exactly about marriage. Like Wodehouse's Bertie Wooster, Ozzie has no visible occupation and nothing of any importance to do except get himself into absurd fixes. He's just around the house, affable, a little bumbling. In Wodehouse the slightest complications are nudged by a gentle but precise hand toward absurdity.

That's how Ozzie wrote as well, so that the slighter the premise the funnier the show. How far, for example, will Ozzie go to satisfy his late-night craving for tutti frutti ice cream?

8   Contrary to what those who damn the show for its old-fashioned values assume, Ozzie is not the wise and all-knowing father. He does not preach to his sons or to Harriet—indeed, there is never any moral lesson to preach about. Everyone in the family is so confident in loving and being loved that nothing needs to be said about it. In one episode, Ozzie mistakenly thinks that Harriet no longer wants to sleep in the same bed with him, and she thinks that he doesn't want to sleep with her. Ozzie camps out on the couch in the den for part of the night until, miserable and lonely, he goes back to Harriet. Here is a plot that goes right to the heart of a marriage. The sexual tension is subtly played; indeed, Ozzie frequently bragged that he and Harriet were the first couple in a television series to be shown sleeping in the same bed. But here Ozzie is hurt and confused and Harriet is hurt and confused, yet neither one confronts the other. The misunderstandings are discovered in a calm conversation, and Harriet welcomes Ozzie back into bed as if he'd done nothing more than get up for a glass of water. Fundamental as the crisis is, it never occurs to either one that the marriage is threatened.

9   This unquestioned harmony makes us think of Ozzie and Harriet as living not only in a different time but also in a phony different time, and that the world the show implied—one of happy husbands and wives and happy children in a land of plenty—was the phoniest thing of all. It ignored all the ugliness that we have now almost obsessively dug up from the society of those days and of our own—oppression of women and minorities, domestic violence, sexual harassment and a host of other abuses and injustices. Today we also have new problems to face, or more vicious versions of the old ones. Last year the high school our daughter and son attend had a racial standoff so intense that the hallways were cleared and patrolled for days. This year there has already been an attempted gang rape of a male student, even the hallways are guarded.

10   When David and Ricky attended Hollywood High in the late 50's, there were no guards in the hallways. Why should they have been so lucky compared with my kids? That's the kind of frustration that politicians are trying to mine with their talk about family, and that's the kind of dismaying change people mean when they say we don't live in an Ozzie and Harriet world anymore. But as I watched hours of old *Ozzie and Harriets* on videotape, I realized that, in spite of the myriad intractable social problems, there is a continuity between *The Adventures of Ozzie and Harriet* and our days, which are supposed to be so different and difficult. That's why the phrase "Ozzie and Harriet" has entered the language and the Nelsons have become the one emblematic family we have.

It gave me a start, I must admit, when I realized that the infinitely   11
small problems the show turned on made it spookily like looking into a
mirror. So many of our family's days sound like plots for the show. The
dog disappears; it turns out he has fallen into a neighbor's sunken garbage can. Our son becomes a vegan. Our daughter gets a job in an ice
cream parlor. Ozzie knew that for a family something as mundane as
buying a car or mother's getting a new hair style is a huge occasion. He
knew something else too. The string that ties a family together is spun
from a series of minute decisions, of routines, of hellos and goodbyes
and hellos again. And there is nothing about these greetings and daily
decisions that depends on wealth or class. "The Adventures of Ozzie
and Harriet," although set in an idealized, gently comic world of
miniscule problems that is now 40 years old, had the exact tone and
rhythm of happy married life.

That gray morning in the car with David, he turned down a short,   12
tree-lined street, parked suddenly and said, "There it is." The familiar
New England-style house was still in gloriously good repair, with shining white shutters by each window. I got out to look more closely, but
to my surprise David stayed in the car. He has been the one to see the
family through its darkest times. He was in the room in this house with
Ozzie when he died. When Harriet died, David was holding her hand.
And he had to battle through the exasperating difficulties of Rick's estate, which was settled only recently after almost 11 years.

After Ozzie died, Harriet lived alone in this house until she finally   13
decided to sell it. On the last day before the new owners moved in, a
friend took Harriet by for a last look inside. She broke down. Seeing the
empty house, she suddenly didn't know where she was or who she
was or why she had lived. Standing there with David waiting for me in
the car, I thought of Harriet panicked and alone in that empty house
and I thought of my wife alone or me alone or our children alone, as
someday they must be, and it made me want to embrace those days
when our lives happen to be a quiet, gentle comedy.

★ Meaning and Understanding

1. What would you say is the main point of this essay?

2. What does the writer say the phrase "Ozzie and Harriet" has come to
   mean in the debate over family values?

3. What are some characteristics of *The Adventures of Ozzie and Harriet*
   shows that were on the air from 1952 to 1966? What role did Ozzie
   himself have in the television family structure?

4. What examples does the writer provide to make the point that "the
   slighter the premise, the funnier the show"?

5. Why does the writer say that the programs, despite their setting in "an idealized, gently comic world of minuscule problems," have "the exact tone and rhythm of happy married life"?

6. Why did Harriet break down on the last day before the new owners moved into the house where her children lived with her and her husband and grew up?

★ *Techniques and Strategies*

1. Where in the selection does the writer come closest to stating what you believe is the thesis of the essay?

2. Only the introduction and conclusion deal with the present-day drive through Hollywood to the Nelson house. Why does the writer frame the essay with those narrative details? How do they engage the reader?

3. Why does the writer provide quotations drawn from commentators on the family values debate? (See paragraph 4.)

4. What is the purpose of paragraph 6, a short series of unanswered questions?

5. How does the writer use the strategy of exemplification? Comparison and contrast? Narration? Argumentation?

★ *Speaking of Values*

1. Why have Ozzie and Harriet "become shorthand for an idyllic America of the past"? Is their lifestyle, in fact, a thing of the past? Explain your answer.

2. How have both conservatives and liberals used the Ozzie and Harriet phenomenon to advance the "political debate over family values"? What is that debate from your point of view? Why should the writer label one argument *conservative* and the other *liberal?*

3. The television family of Ozzie and Harriet and their children was set in an imaginary town where everyone lived "in a virtually unchanging harmony" and where "everyone in the family is so confident in loving and being loved that nothing needs to be said about it." Is such an existence possible in the real world? Why or why not? Do you agree with the writer in his belief that no one would mistake the problems of the television family as great social dilemmas but that these problems "are exactly the kind of complications that are common in family life"? Why or why not?

4. What characteristics of the father as family member do you identify in the portrait of Ozzie as presented in this essay? Is it an accurate portrait? Do you know any fathers who resemble Ozzie Nelson? Why or why not? How does your sense of fatherhood help you react to the character of Ozzie?

5. The writer believes that despite what many see as the phony different world in *The Adventures of Ozzie and Harriet*, there is a continuity between the television series and life in our age. What is that continuity? Do you agree that it exists? Or do you think the writer is reaching too far to make his point? What kinds of "infinitely small problems" as you were growing up, or even now, help you see the television show as a mirror to your own life? From what you have read here, does the television series have "the exact tone and rhythm of happy married life" as you understand it?

★ *Values Conversation*

Form groups and discuss the elements of the idealized Ozzie and Harriet family as compared with real families you know. What similarities and differences do you notice? Make a list of the qualities of the two groups. Can real families behave more like the Ozzie and Harriet family? Should they? Under what conditions?

★ *Writing about Values*

1. Write an essay in which you compare the Ozzie and Harriet family with some other sitcom family currently popular on television—the family of *Roseanne, The Cosby Show,* or *The Simpsons,* for example.

2. Write an essay in which you answer the questions that make up paragraph 5 of the essay.

3. Write an essay called "Leave _____ Alone" in which you fill the blank with the name of a real or television family. Identify and defend the values demonstrated by the people in the family. Or, if you wish to challenge those values, call your essay "Don't Leave _____ Alone." What values emerge from the way the family relates to each other?

Randall Williams

Daddy Tucked the Blanket

Randall Williams, a newspaper reporter, worked for the *Alabama Journal* when he wrote this essay. Drawing on examples and events from his own life, he shows the effects of poverty on people's personal relations.

———— ★ ————

1   About the time I turned 16, my folks began to wonder why I didn't stay home any more. I always had an excuse for them, but what I didn't say was that I had found my freedom and I was getting out.

2   I went through four years of high school in semirural Alabama and became active in clubs and sports; I made a lot of friends and became a regular guy, if you know what I mean. But one thing was irregular about me: I managed those four years without ever having a friend visit at my house.

3   I was ashamed of where I lived. I had been ashamed for as long as I had been conscious of class.

4   We had a big family. There were several of us sleeping in one room, but that's not so bad if you get along, and we always did. As you get older, though, it gets worse.

5   Being poor is a humiliating experience for a young person trying hard to be accepted. Even now—several years removed—it is hard to talk about. And I resent the weakness of these words to make you feel what it was really like.

6   We lived in a lot of old houses. We moved a lot because we were always looking for something just a little better than what we had. You have to understand that my folks worked harder than most people. My mother was always at home, but for her that was a full-time job—and no fun, either. But my father worked his head off from the time I can remember in construction and shops. It was hard, physical work.

7   I tell you this to show that we weren't shiftless. No matter how much money Daddy made, we never made much progress up the social ladder. I got out thanks to a college scholarship and because I was a little more articulate than the average.

8   I have seen my Daddy wrap copper wire through the soles of his boots to keep them together in the wintertime. He couldn't buy new boots because he had used the money for food and shoes for us. We lived like hell, but we went to school well-clothed and with a full stomach.

9   It really is hell to live in a house that was in bad shape 10 years before you moved in. And a big family puts a lot of wear and tear on a new house,

too, so you can imagine how one goes downhill if it is teetering when you move in. But we lived in houses that were sweltering in summer and freezing in winter. I woke up every morning for a year and a half with plaster on my face where it had fallen out of the ceiling during the night.

This wasn't during the Depression; this was in the late 60's and early 70's.   10

When we boys got old enough to learn trades in school, we would try to fix up the old houses we lived in. But have you ever tried to paint a wall that crumbled when the roller went across it? And bright paint emphasized the holes in the wall. You end up more frustrated than when you began, especially when you know that at best you might come up with only enough money to improve one of the six rooms in the house. And we might move out soon after, anyway.   11

The same goes for keeping a house like that clean. If you have a house full of kids and the house is deteriorating, you'll never keep it clean. Daddy used to yell at Mama about that, but she couldn't do anything. I think Daddy knew it inside, but he had to have an outlet for his rage somewhere, and at least yelling isn't as bad as hitting, which they never did to each other.   12

But you have a kitchen which has no counter space and no hot water, and you will have dirty dishes stacked up. That sounds like an excuse, but try it. You'll go mad from the sheer sense of futility. It's the same thing in a house with no closets. You can't keep clothes clean and rooms in order if they have to be stacked up with things.   13

Living in a bad house is generally worse on girls. For one thing, they traditionally help their mother with the housework. We boys could get outside and work in the field or cut wood or even play ball and forget about living conditions. The sky was still pretty.   14

But the girls got the pressure, and as they got older it became worse. Would they accept dates knowing they had to "receive" the young man in a dirty hallway with broken windows, peeling wallpaper and a cracked ceiling? You have to live it to understand it, but it creates a shame which drives the soul of a young person inward.   15

I'm thankful none of us ever blamed our parents for this, because it would have crippled our relationships. As it worked out, only the relationship between our parents was damaged. And I think the harshness which they expressed to each other was just an outlet to get rid of their anger at the trap their lives were in. It ruined their marriage because they had no one to yell at but each other. I knew other families where the kids got the abuse, but we were too much loved for that.   16

Once I was about 16 and Mama and Daddy had had a particularly violent argument about the washing machine, which had broken down. Daddy was on the back porch—that's where the only water faucet was—trying to fix it and Mamma had a washtub out there washing school clothes for the next day and they were screaming at each other.   17

18   Later that night everyone was in bed and I heard Daddy get up from the couch where he was reading. I looked out from my bed across the hall into their room. He was standing right over Mama and she was already asleep. He pulled the blanket up and tucked it around her shoulders and just stood there and tears were dropping off his cheeks and I thought I could faintly hear them splashing against the linoleum rug.

19   Now they're divorced.

20   I had courses in college where housing was discussed, but the sociologists never put enough emphasis on the impact living in substandard housing has on a person's psyche. Especially children's.

21   Small children have a hard time understanding poverty. They want the same things children from more affluent families have. They want the same things they see advertised on television, and they don't understand why they can't have them.

22   Other children can be incredibly cruel. I was in elementary school in Georgia—and this is interesting because it is the only thing I remember about that particular school—when I was about eight or nine.

23   After Christmas vacation had ended, my teacher made each student describe all his or her Christmas presents. I became more and more uncomfortable as the privilege passed around the room toward me. Other children were reciting the names of the dolls they had been given, the kinds of bicycles and the grandeur of their games and toys. Some had lists which seemed to go on and on for hours.

24   It took me only a few seconds to tell the class that I had gotten for Christmas a belt and a pair of gloves. And then I was laughed at— because I cried—by a roomful of children and a teacher. I never forgave them, and that night I made my mother cry when I told her about it.

25   In retrospect, I am grateful for that moment, but I remember wanting to die at the time.

★ *Meaning and Understanding*

1. What is the main point of this essay?

2. What does Williams mean in paragraph 2 when he says he "became a regular guy"?

3. What examples does he provide to demonstrate the poverty of his family?

4. Why does Williams insist in paragraph 7 that his family wasn't "shiftless"?

5. Why does the writer remind the reader that the events he is describing did not take place during the Depression but rather in the 1960s and 1970s?

★ Techniques and Strategies

1. Where does Williams come closest to stating the thesis of the essay?

2. Why does he offer physical details of the various houses he and his family lived in but never describe the members of his family?

3. The writer recounts a violent argument between his mother and father and his father's subsequent remorse. Then (paragraph 19) he offers the simple declaration "Now they're divorced." Why does he frame the information in this way?

4. Williams begins by telling something about himself at 16. Later in the essay he refers to an earlier time when he was in elementary school. What effect does this "reverse chronology" have on your understanding of the narrative?

5. Why does the writer present his essay through a number of comparatively short paragraphs? Does the brevity of these paragraphs serve a distinctive purpose? What is that purpose?

★ Speaking of Values

1. Williams says that he "knew other families where the kids got the abuse, but we were too much loved for that." What does this observation suggest about the relation between poverty and family life?

2. Although his mother and his father frequently yelled at one another, the writer tells us that they never hit one another. Why does he make sure that we understand this point?

3. What were Williams's mother and father like as people? As spouses? As parents? Use examples from the selection to support your points.

4. How does the essay as a whole speak to the issue of "family values"? What are the values that drive this particular family? Again, use examples from the selection to illustrate your points.

5. Why didn't the writer say to his folks, "I found my freedom and I'm getting out"? What values does this reluctance suggest? Do you approve or disapprove of his silence? Why?

★ Values Conversation

Form groups and discuss the ways in which you think families deal with adversity. In other words, how do family members use one another to get through difficult times? Are there any families, other than your own, which you admire? Why or why not? Make a list of characteristics that those families seem to possess.

★ *Writing about Values*

1. Write an essay called "I Had Found My Freedom and I Was Getting Out."

2. How do housing conditions for the poor today compare and contrast with the conditions Williams describes? Draw on research or personal experience to analyze the situation and make recommendations for any changes you believe necessary.

3. Write an essay exploring your own views of the effects of poverty on family and structure. Draw on articles and books you may have read; television, movies, or radio coverage you may have seen; or firsthand observations you may have made.

Ruth Gay

Floors: The Bronx—Then

Born in New York City in 1922, Ruth Gay has been a teacher, a writer, and
an archivist. Her essays have appeared in journals such as *Commentary*
and *Contemporary Judaism*. Among her books are *Jews in America: A Short
History* (1965) and *The Jews of Germany: A Historical Portrait* (1992). Here
she describes the changing sociocultural values of a New York immigrant community from the beginning to the middle of the twentieth century and offers a picture of early immigrant urban life.

★

My mother lived in a house with a beaten earth floor. She never told me 1
this. I only learned it by chance when my father taunted her with it in
response to her fine airs and manners. My mother-in-law came from
Warsaw, where she had lived in an apartment building made of stone.
The stories of these floors became a talisman of sorts, for one the source
of shame, for the other of amusement. My mother-in-law loved to tell
the story of how she prepared for her first Sabbath in the New Country.
Wanting to wash the kitchen floor, she filled a bucket with water and
preparatory to wielding the mop, flung the contents on the floor.
Shrieks from her downstairs neighbors, pounding on the door, protests
about the *"griner"*—the greenhorn. In Warsaw, she had lived with stone
floors; how was she to know that in the New World floors were made
of lesser stuff.

Even in the New World, floors—kitchen floors especially—were 2
sure barometers of a housewife's standards and ability. When I came
home from school on Friday afternoons, it was at the culmination of the
day's and the week's race with the clock to bring the apartment into a
state of perfect cleanliness before Sabbath rest overtook us. I would arrive to find the kitchen chairs stacked in the living room, while the
freshly washed kitchen floor was drying. It would then be covered
with pathways of newspapers, to prevent the marring of the perfect
surface, until finally at some point when the newspapers themselves
created a mass of crumpled debris underfoot, they would be lifted up
to expose the pristine floor. Cleanliness was more than a good in itself.
It was a test of character, a measure of worth, of competence. One of the
most devastating judgments of that time was the whisper that a certain
neighbor was "dirty." Now cleanliness did not have anything to do
with orderliness or repose—in fact, I mostly remember it being

achieved at the cost of immense upheaval, bad temper, and tension about time, since Orthodox Jewish housewives set themselves rigorous standards of work to be accomplished by the end of every Friday—the "end" being measured inexorably by the time that the sun set. And a winter Friday was heart-breakingly short given the amount of work that had to be compressed into it.

3   I would awaken early, early in the morning to the sound of my mother wielding the *hackmesser*—the round-edged chopping knife—as she pounded the gefilte fish mixture. Although the fish had already been ground, the last stages of preparation called for a final reduction by hand in the wooden chopping bowl reserved for this purpose. As I left for school, I would see the parts of the stove dismantled in the sink in some terrible lye solution so strong as to require my mother to use heavy rubber gloves.

4   Then the beds were treated to their weekly dousing of kerosene against bed bugs. Only much later did I realize what a terrible fire hazard was being prepared here in the name of cleanliness. The fear of bed bugs—*vantsen*—organized the housewife's working day. Beds were not made in the morning. It would only encourage the spontaneous generation of these vermin, it was believed, to enclose the warm, breathing air in which we had slept inside tight covers. Instead, the windows were flung open even on the coldest winter days—the mattresses folded in half, and the pillows and featherbeds put out on the windowsill to air. Air and sun were the great panaceas and healers of New York tenement life. They prevented bed bugs; they forestalled tuberculosis; they brought good health. They were the hallmark of respectability. It was the search for air and sun that led to the migration from the Lower East Side, and even from Harlem, to the quiet streets of Brooklyn and the heights of the Bronx.

5   Only in late afternoon was the bedding taken in, the windows closed, and the beds restored to some semblance of normality. Bed bugs were not only in themselves a troublesome and unhealthy plague. More than that, they were a source of shame—and it was shame rather than hygiene, I think, that drove the housewives to scour their apartments and vie with one another in setting absolute standards for their cleanliness.

6   My mother was actually a poor housekeeper—no housekeeper at all by American standards—but she, too, was drawn into its simulacrum by her need to assert her standing as a housewife. In that community to be a *berye*, the Yiddish superlative for housewife, was the highest compliment for a woman. It conveyed skill, shrewdness, accomplishment, a capacity for getting things done. To tell the truth, my mother's gefilte fish was terrible, and we lived all week long in a welter of disorder and makeshift arrangements. But Friday, the climax of the week, the day of preparation for the Sabbath exerted its power even

over her—and no matter how inept she was in her household management, old memories stirred. The atmosphere of our neighborhood, which took on an extraordinary bustle on Friday mornings, also motivated her to take what was largely symbolic, if drastic, action.

My mother had come to this country as little more than a child of 7
thirteen with her sister Chana, who was fifteen months older than she. Traveling with a woman from their village in Galicia, they had crossed the ocean living on their stock of bread and herring brought from home and arrived to be taken in by their oldest brother, Asher now "Harry," and his wife, Feigele, now "Fanny." She was prepared for marvels in the Golden Land. But her first great puzzle came as they were driving in her brother's buggy through the Lower East Side and she saw the high, closely packed tenements. These were understandable. What she couldn't understand were the lines of washing hung out to dry, four and five stories above the ground. How did anyone reach them?

Her bewilderment about the laundry and embarrassment about 8
asking, like my mother-in-law's miscalculation about the floors, marked the beginning of a pattern of confusion and disorientation. What it elicited was a style of caution and withdrawal to safer ground, where the hazard of making mistakes or of being mocked as a *griner* was reduced. But it left a residue of uncertainty, a loss of confidence that stamped their experience with "America." My mother-in-law, after all, arrived as a married woman with two children. She, unlike my mother, could and did remain safely embedded in her family, never learning much English and never needing to, living as she did in an entirely Yiddish-speaking world. There she could be expansive, authoritative, dramatic.

For my mother, however, who arrived in the country as a child, 9
and immediately went to work in a shirt factory, wariness became a way of life. In her shop the other operators at the sewing machines were young Jewish girls like herself, but she went to school at night to learn English. For a long time, however, it remained the language of strangers. In her family, as in the shop, she lived in the self-enclosed world of the immigrant. From moment to moment, her life went on in Yiddish and not only in conversation. New York at that time was rich in its offering of Yiddish newspapers, magazines, cabarets, and theaters—especially theaters. The theater, with its stars and matinee idols, such as Boris Thomashevsky, my mother's favorite, was the magnet of the working girl.

In the years just before the First World War, the Yiddish theater in 10
New York was at its height. Its eager patrons were the shop workers like my mother, the storekeepers, artisans, laborers, and peddlers—the whole immigrant generation, newly arrived and passionate about the theater. It gave them back their lives, heightened, beautified, in elevated language—in a word, dramatized.

11   Of course my mother had never experienced the theater in the tiny shtetl in Galicia from which she came. And certainly her father would never have approved. A Hasid, fervently devoted to the Chortkover Rebbe, he saw each of his five children leave for the Golden Land but stayed behind because for him it was a *treyfe medine*—an unkosher, an unholy, land whose embrace corrupted life itself. His was not the only family that lost its children to the attractions of the New World. The miseries and intermittent pogroms that marked shtetl life—these days so shamelessly sentimentalized—led to an exodus of the young and strong and hopeful that amounted to nearly three million Jews between 1880 and the beginning of the First World War. When my mother sent her father money from her slender earnings, he pleaded with her to desist, since the money, too, was *treyf.*

12   This was a sorrow to my mother, who adored her learned and saintly father. But it did not interfere with her newfound pleasures. In her late teens, as an experienced "operator" she began to specialize in the shop and, at piecework rates, set collars on the body of shirts from morning to night. But this meant high earnings, and, living under her brother's roof, she had money left over for finery on a grand scale. She patronized a dressmaker and ordered elegant evening wear for the theater, for *simchas*—celebrations—for weddings. I saw two of these fantasies that survived into my own childhood: one a heavily beaded, sleeveless, pink satin dance dress, the other an elaborate, full-skirted, full-sleeved confection in black cut velvet—a fabric whose like I have never seen since.

13   It was a hybrid world, of course, where old customs and new opportunities were blended, and in the rich Jewish culture of New York City in the first decades of this century, new rules began to govern the habits of Jewish life. It was understood that the Yiddish theater would not give performances on Friday night or Saturday. But Saturday at sundown and Sundays the box offices opened to great crowds. As my mother told me, people didn't buy tickets in advance—a remnant of Old World fearfulness, where one didn't tempt fate by making advance preparations. So the hubbub and excitement in the lobbies of these theaters before performances were heightened by anxiety over whether one would reach the head of the line before all the tickets were sold.

14   What the public loved above all were the melodramas that reflected the all-too-vivid drama in their own lives: stories of abandoned wives, estranged American children, neglected parents, interspersed with heady musicals and tales from the old country—a mixture that reflected the homesickness already being translated into sugary nostalgia as in the song "Mayn shtetele Belz" and the real problems of immigration.

15   Is it any wonder that Shakespeare's *Lear,* with its theme of the ingratitude of children, was a tremendous hit on Second Avenue? Shakespeare was, in fact, a familiar playwright to Jewish audiences, so familiar that translators took liberties. One announcement for *Hamlet*

advertised that the play had been not only translated but also *improved* for its presentation in Yiddish—*"ibergezetst un farbessert."*

The immigrant audiences of the 1920s were easily reduced to   16
tears—either by happy endings or by tragic ones. This was a young audience, uprooted from "home," anxious about their livelihood, about
staying afloat in the New World, struggling to reconcile what they had
been taught in the Old Country with the unexpected freedoms and
prospects of America. For many who came as young teenagers,
"home" as a place, as a way of life, faded. What remained were the
memories of parents left behind, memories of themselves as children.
But these were rapidly overlaid by the configuration of a totally different society and the wish to enter somehow into that new world.

When they had grown up enough to marry, few of these children   17
had family mementos with which to start a household. At best, like my
mother, they had brought a down quilt—a *perene* covered in a sturdy red
chambray, whose contents were guarded like diamonds. When on occasion the down needed to be cleaned or the cover renewed, like the pearls
that ladies went to Tiffany to have restrung, my mother would take her
quilt to the refurbisher and watch every step of the process to make sure
that *her* down, and only her down, was returned to the new covering.
Having stripped geese herself for the down, she was a connoisseur in
these matters and would sometimes squeeze a doubtful pillow between
her fingers to test whether the little spines were still there. This *perene*
was her sole tangible connection to "home." It was the older ones, the
married couples or the brides, who arrived with firmer remembrances—
their silver candlesticks or even a silver samovar wrapped in their down
quilt. But beyond the essential comforter, the young ones, like my
mother, came without possessions, ready and even anxious to furnish
their lives with the goods of the New World.

What was perhaps unexpected was their hunger for splendor, com-   18
ing as they did from villages where benches were more common at the
table than chairs. Unlike the settlementhouse workers who saw morality in straight lines and recommended plain deal furniture for immigrant homes, my parents and their neighbors invested in curves, high
finishes, ornate carvings, and elaborately patterned linoleum rugs. I
spent many hours of my childhood hanging head down from our
couch, tracing the palmettes and stylized flowers of the linoleum on the
floor with my finger, and it was not until I was nine or ten years old
that I first understood that there were soft woven carpets on which our
replica was based. This discovery came in the living room of a school
friend who lived in the neighborhood, but whose father occupied a
very respected place in our little world. He was the neighborhood
pharmacist, which practically made him a doctor, which was as far as
one's imagination could stretch. Unless it was to a "professor." In dire

medical cases, the victim was sometimes operated on by a "professor"—
a sign of both privilege and despair.

19   Although our pharmacist lived in our neighborhood, he was
clearly much more prosperous than we were, and his apartment had
not only a soft and splendid Chinese rug but, looming over it all (since
that was my perspective), a baby grand piano, which was played in
what seemed to me a dazzling style by my classmate's older sister. In
my imagination, the two, piano and rug, flowed together, conveying as
an ensemble warmth, culture, and luxury. I don't know if my parents
really believed what they said when they criticized the rug's unhy-
gienic nature—how it retained dust, polluting the air and one's lungs.
A linoleum rug, on the other hand, could always be scrubbed, its shining surface a guarantee of its health-giving properties.

20   This dismissive attitude was not entirely convincing to me when I
thought about the pharmacist's world—the softness, the grandness, the
cosmopolitanism of it all. The piano-playing sister eventually married
a German refugee and moved to Pittsburgh—all elements of unthinkable foreignness and distance given our tightly held circle of family. Of
course, our family and their friends and *landsleit* all came from Europe—but from the same part of Europe and were, therefore, known
quantities to one another, speaking in the comforting vernacular of Yiddish. But Germany? That was another world.

21   As for doctors and pharmacists, my parents' attitude toward these
professionals was at the very least one of profound respect. It was a respect based on the same bewilderment that shaped their way of managing in the world. The university and medical education were beyond
their imagining. It was not clear to them how or where one entered the
ladder to such accomplishment. But there was no doubt that these were
men at the apex of humanity who could and did live on the Grand Concourse in the Bronx. This splendid avenue, a miniature Champs
Elysées, with its green center meridian and its handsome apartment
houses, was the culminating point of anyone's aspirations. It even ran
along a ridge, which made it literally the high point of the Bronx, dividing east and west, and like the Champs Elysées, it was a favorite promenade ground on weekends and holidays. Here not only the apartments
but even the lobbies, attended by uniformed doormen, were carpeted in
precious Oriental rugs weighted down by dark, heavily carved Renaissance tables with man-high Chinese vases guarding cavernous corners.

22   Once, when I had broken my arm, I had the occasion to visit one of
these buildings for several Sundays running to see the doctor who had
set my arm and was checking on its progress. I would come in the
morning, pass through the hushed lobby, and take the elevator to the
apartment. Here I would sometimes see the son of the family—a boy
about my age—vanishing down a hallway in what seemed like illimit-
able space, having just picked up the newspaper that had been *delivered*
to the door. It was this whiff of another life that made me think not only

of the carpets—but of the life, the kind of life that was lived with Oriental rugs under foot and with the sort of service that brought a newspaper to the door on a snowy morning.

These glimpses, however brief, showed me a life different from   23
what I knew. I endowed this family with everything that I longed for and found missing at home: the order, repose, and regularity of people who knew their way, who knew how to command the world as my parents did not—who knew, in fact, how to live. Very early I saw my parents as plainly adrift, confident enough at home, but easily intimidated by officials, by authority. My father, who was accustomed to tyrannize over a family of women, could be reduced to silence and submission by a word from a policeman or a government form letter, while my mother, as if arming us for an inevitable struggle, said, "You know who you are, no matter what people say." What went on in the glorious spaces on the Grand Concourse, by contrast, was an existence where people spoke softly, their desires cosseted, their senses indulged. It was something to mull over.

The only carpet that I ever saw that had been brought from the Old   24
Country belonged to a Romanian family. Roughly woven, it did not speak of repose and luxury, but it added depth to the history of the family for whom it was a prized possession. It was large and giddily colored, with a pattern of red and pink roses on a green ground, and it hung on the wall over their couch, not to be profaned by being trodden upon. The Romanians—already unique in a Polish-Russian enclave— seemed even more exotic because they had this substantial talisman from home, as if this carpet held them closer to the old ways than we who traveled with so little baggage.

Despite my parents' acceptance of their linoleum rug, I began to   25
think, secretly, that they were missing something. Did they not know or care about the originals on which this poor cold thing was based? What I did not realize until much later was that this was a perfect example of how they managed the hand that life dealt them. Whatever they had or achieved was good and excellent, a testimony to their industry and prudence. Beyond that was excess, showiness, waste. My father could still remember vividly the hunger of his orphaned childhood, and my mother from her early teens knew the precarious life of a wage earner. A steady job—especially as the Depression deepened—was the utmost limit of one's dreams. It made a linoleum rug an excellent floor covering.

★ Meaning and Understanding

1. Why has Gay's mother never revealed to her daughter that she had lived in "a house with a beaten earth floor"? And why does the author tell us that her mother-in-law "had lived in an apartment building made of stone"?

2. What does the writer mean when she says that "The stories of these floors became a talisman of sorts"? What is a talisman?

3. What is a "greenhorn"? What can you surmise about the powerful use of the word as an epithet—that is, a word used to characterize a person or thing?

4. Why did the immigrants in this essay put such a high premium on cleanliness, actually transforming it into a character trait? Why did Jewish immigrants fear bedbugs so much?

5. What reason does Gay give for the migration from the lower East Side and Harlem to "the quiet streets of Brooklyn and the heights of the Bronx"?

6. Why was "wariness...a way of life" for Gay's mother?

★ Techniques and Strategies

1. Gay peppers the selection with a number of Yiddish words. Why does she use this strategy, even though she provides the translations?

2. Two key images frame Gay's essay: the "beaten earth floor" of her mother's childhood and the "linoleum rug" of her parents' later domestic life. What do these images signify?

3. Who do you think is the intended audience for this selection? How do you know? Give some examples.

4. Where in the selection does Gay state or suggest the thesis of the essay? Why does she rely so heavily upon descriptions of domestic furnishings to support her point?

5. Why does the writer compare the Grand Concourse to the Champs Elysées? Do you think it is a legitimate comparison?

★ Speaking of Values

1. Do you agree with the writer's contention that the material trappings of our lives not only reflect our cultural values but also help to define them? Why or why not?

2. What does the opening few lines of the selection—"My mother lived in a house with a beaten earth floor. She never told me this. I only learned it by chance when my father taunted her with it in response to her fine airs and manners"—tell us about the relation between the writer's mother and father? How do the lines also suggest something about each family's awareness of its own social standing?

3. Gay says that "even in the New World, floors—kitchen floors especially—were sure barometers of a housewife's standards and ability." What does she mean by this? Do we still measure a mother's "standards and ability" by how she cleans her house, even in this new age of the working mother? How do you know? Is it fair to do so? Why or why not?

4. Gay's mother-in-law, because she arrived in America as an already married woman, could live "in an entirely Yiddish-speaking world. There she could be expansive, authoritative, dramatic." What do you think the writer is suggesting about life outside that "Yiddish-speaking world"? What does Gay imply here about language as a symbol of cultural power? How does the writer's father, "who was accustomed to tyrannize over a family of women, [but] could be reduced to silence and submission by a word from a policeman or a government form letter," also reflect the language as power issue?

5. Who seems to have the power in the society described by the author—men or women? Give examples to support your answer. How does today's society reflect a power structure between men and women?

6. What values does the writer associate with the families who occupy the fancy apartments on the Grand Concourse? In what ways does she compare those values with the values of her parents? If the pharmacist was so much richer than Gay's family, why do you think he chose to live in their neighborhood?

7. The writer says that her parents could "manage" the life that was dealt to them by accepting whatever they had achieved as good while rejecting anything more as pure excess. How does this statement reflect or challenge American values today? Is there virtue in simply being satisfied with our lot? Why or why not? How would you define material excess?

★ Values Conversation

Form groups to discuss the particular features in a house or apartment you know that give special insights about the families within and the values they hold. Perhaps it is the kitchen or basement or bedrooms that reveal the family's values. Perhaps it is the garden or the way family members view a particular chair or decorative object.

★ Writing about Values

1. Gay sets forth two value systems in this selection: that of the writer's mother and that of the writer's mother-in-law. Making sure to draw examples and illustrations from the selection, compose an essay in which you compare and contrast these value systems.

2. The writer defines her family's cultural values—and by extension the values of a whole generation—in terms of the kinds of "floors" they walked on. Write an essay in which you define the values of your family or your generation—or both—by some physical element in your house or apartment. You might want to write about the symbolic "floors" you walk on. But perhaps the kitchen or living room or ceilings reveal more of your family and generation's values. Draw on the discussion you held for the Values Conversation activity previously.

3. The Grand Concourse in the Bronx held a particular significance for Jewish immigrants in the early part of the twentieth century. Do some research on the city or town you live in and identify a particular area or part of town that had this same kind of significance for a specific group of people—ethnic, racial, religious, cultural. Write an essay describing this place, the people who inhabited it, and the ways in which it helped define and reflect their cultural values.

David Blankenhorn

The Deadbeat Dad

David Blankenhorn was born in 1955 in Germany and educated in the
United States. He is a writer and the chair of the National Fatherhood Initiative, a fatherhood rights activist group. This essay, which comes from
his book *Fatherless America* (1995), explores the role of fathers in today's
society and offers a perspective on the father who doesn't meet financial
obligations to his family.

————— ★ —————

The Deadbeat Dad is a bad guy. He is morally culpable. He is a criminal   1
and belongs in jail. He is the reigning villain of our contemporary fatherhood script. His visage, framed by a Wanted poster, makes the
cover of *Newsweek*: "Deadbeat Dads: Wanted for Failure to Pay Child
Support." At the Child Guidance Center in Akron, Ohio, a little girl
writes this imaginary letter to her dad:

> Dear Dad,
>
> I wish you the worst Father's Day ever. And if you don't pay, you
> don't get love. Oh yeah, by the way, my mom makes less money than
> you.... I hate you.

The Deadbeat Dad is a bad guy because he refuses to pay. Of course, he   2
has also abandoned his children and the mother of his children. Yet in
contemporary cultural terms that character trait is secondary. The main
issue is not abandonment. The main issue is payment. Accordingly, the
main societal imperative, as Senator Daniel Patrick Moynihan suc-
cinctly puts it, is to "make the daddies pay."

    If we cannot enforce good fatherhood, the script goes, we ought to   3
enforce child-support payments. Besides, for children, money is the
true bottom line. Testifying before the U.S. House Select Committee on
Children, Youth, and Families, Andrew J. Cherlin of Johns Hopkins
University concludes that "the major problem the children have in a
single-parent family is not the lack of a male image, but rather the lack
of a male income."

    In our cultural model of the Deadbeat Dad, the core issue is money   4
absence, not father absence. This belief is widely shared among the experts. In July 1993, for example, the Census Bureau reported a 60 percent increase in out-of-wedlock childbearing since 1982. To the *New*

York Times editorial board, the deeper meaning of this trend was clear: "As the number of unwed mothers grows, so does the number of dead-beat dads." Accordingly, our society's principal response to unwed childbearing must be "a more vigorous effort to track down fathers who refuse to pay support."

5   Meet the Deadbeat Dad of the 1990s: the last traditional breadwin-ner in the experts' story of fatherhood. For him only, fatherhood is mea-sured in dollars. For the New Father, of course, that old breadwinner role is a thing of the past. But for the Deadbeat Dad, the breadwinner role is alive and well: the one role that society demands that he play, even as he resists. For the New Father, breadwinning thwarts father-hood. For the Deadbeat Dad, breadwinning defines fatherhood.

6   In several respects, the Deadbeat Dad and the New Father are op-posites. One is the best, the other is the worst. One lives with his child, the other does not. One repudiates the traditional male role, the other is a caricature of the traditional male role: absent, but expected to pay.

7   Yet underneath these differences, the Deadbeat Dad and the New Father share this fundamental trait: as cultural models, both derive from the idea that fatherhood is superfluous. The essence of the New Father model is the erasure of fatherhood as a gendered social role for men—fatherhood reduced to genderless parenting skills. The essence of the Deadbeat Dad model is that absent fathers can be fathers by writ-ing checks—fatherhood reduced to the size of a wallet. Neither model incorporates fatherhood as a distinctive social role. Both models view men as problems to be overcome. At bottom, both models presuppose an increasingly fatherless society.

8   In this sense, the Deadbeat Dad is less a new departure than a vari-ation on a theme. In cultural terms, he is the next-door neighbor of both the New Father and the Unnecessary Father. Despite the differences, these three guys all recognize one another. Here is the basis of their mu-tual recognition: None of them, as men and fathers, is an irreplaceable caregiver for his children. Indeed, here is the most concise definition of the Deadbeat Dad: the Unnecessary Father who refuses to pay.

The Bad Understudy

9   The Unnecessary Father, the Old Father, and the New Father are the three leading characters of our contemporary fatherhood script. They are the stars. They get most of the attention.

10   The Unnecessary Father is a star because he is the chorus. He com-ments on every scene, he explains all the action. Both the Old Father and New Father are biological fathers. Moreover, both live with their children and thus can perform the daily tasks of fatherhood. In short, they qualify as leading characters in the script largely because both of them combine biological fatherhood with social fatherhood.

The remaining five characters in the script do not meet this threshold test. They are the fatherhood understudies. They are either biological but not social fathers, or social but not biological fathers. They are almost fathers, sort-of fathers. The three biological fathers—the Deadbeat Dad, the Visiting Father, and the Sperm Father—do not live with their children and thus cannot care for them on a routine, daily basis. The Stepfather lives with children, but not his children. The Nearby Guy—the boyfriend, the friend—is not a biological father and he may or may not live with children, though he increasingly finds himself playing what passes for a fatherly social role.

Accordingly, each of these understudy roles represents the growing disembodiment and dispersal of fatherhood in our society. Each embodies the splitting apart of fatherhood from father. More specifically, as cultural models, each of these fathers has lost, or failed to attain, the core prerequisites of good-enough fatherhood. The evidence is overwhelming: To be a good-enough father, a man must reside with his child and sustain a parental alliance with the mother of his child. In cultural terms, these five minor fatherhood roles are understudies, almost-fathers, precisely because their fatherhood is unsupported by these twin foundations.

At the same time, however, all five of these roles are growing in social importance. They characterized increasing proportions of men. With each passing year, these understudy fathers become more present, more vital, in the lives of children. In this sense, they are becoming the fathers in our increasingly fatherless society.

Of these five understudies, the Deadbeat Dad role is by far the thinnest, the most widely known, and the most vilified. It is a small role for bad men. It is a specialty role, defined by minimal expectations and severely limited possibilities. To date, it is not even a speaking role. The point is not to say something but rather to do something: pay. Finally, our culture's view of this role is governed by an assumption of bad faith. As a phrase of speech, a "Deadbeat Dad" is our society's only popular label for parents that is overtly pejorative.

No other family behavior, and no other family policy issue, has generated such an urgent societal consensus on what is to be done. Extracting payments from Deadbeat Dads is now a regnant priority in our society, uniting liberals and conservatives, Republicans and Democrats, elite opinion and popular sentiment. In the 1992 presidential campaign, for example, applause lines about Deadbeat Dads emerged in the stump speeches of both George Bush and Bill Clinton, constituting arguably the only issue in the campaign on which they publicly agreed.

The Deadbeat Dad is also increasingly visible in the popular culture. He is the subject of popular books, magazine features, and made-for-television movies. Even the *National Enquirer,* ever alert to its social responsibilities, has launched a Deadbeat Dad series—"Help find the

cruel louse who deserted his four children"—which enlists the participation of readers in "hunting down and capturing some of the most
wanted deadbeat dads in America."

17   The Deadbeat Dad has emerged as our principal cultural model for
ex-fathers, for obviously failed fathers. As a cultural category, the
Deadbeat Dad has become our primary symbol of the growing failure
of fatherhood in our society. We demonize him in part because he reminds us of our fatherlessness. He represents loss. He forces us to reduce our expectations. Consequently, we vilify him, we threaten him—
we demand that he pay—largely because he so clearly embodies the
contemporary collapse of good-enough fatherhood.

18   Yet the content of our demand illustrates both the depth of our pes-
simism and the lowering of our standards. We do not ask this guy to be
a father. That would be utopian, impossible. We ask him to send a
check. Instead of demanding what is owed, we demand money.

19   We respond to the Deadbeat Dad by denying and pretending. If
only we could get tough with these guys, that would fix what is broken. Get them to pay. That would help the children. That would relieve
the taxpayer. Here, finally, is a family policy we can all agree on.

20   But this strategy is a fantasy. It is based not on evidence but on
wishful thinking. To date, the strategy of tracking down Deadbeat
Dads has failed even on its own terms: It has not improved the economic well-being of the typical fatherless child. Yet the real failure runs
far deeper. From the child's perspective, child-support payments, even
if fully paid, do not replace a father's economic provision. More fundamentally, they do not replace a father.

21   Our current Deadbeat Dad strategy fails even to acknowledge our
society's spreading crisis of family fragmentation and declining child
well-being. For what is broken in our society is not the proper police
procedures to compel small child-support payments from reluctant
men. What is broken is fatherhood.

22   Andrew Cherlin, then, muddles the issue completely. First, he
imagines that, in the home, "a male income" and "a male image" are
two separate things. Fundamentally, they are not. Consequently, his
preference for the former over the latter is all but meaningless. But let
us imagine, with Cherlin, that the two could be separated. He still gets
the issue backward. The "major problem" in fatherless homes is not
"the lack of a male income" (though that certainly is a problem). The
major problem is "the lack of a male image"—that is, the lack of a father. To pretend otherwise is simply to pretend that money is important, but fathers are not.

23   Ultimately, the solution to the growing problem of Deadbeat Dads
is not jail cells, Most Wanted posters, job-training programs, interstate
computer networks, or IRS agents. At best, these are Band-Aids on an
infected wound. At worst, they are a form of denial—a self-defeating

strategy intended to excuse our drift toward fatherlessness. The only solution to the problem of Deadbeat Dads is fatherhood.

★ *Meaning and Understanding*

1. What is the main point of this selection?

2. Why does Blankenhorn divide fatherhood into categories?

3. What characteristics does the writer attribute to the "New Father"? Why is he called "Father" while the Deadbeat Dad is "Dad"?

4. Blankenhorn says that the "Unnecessary Father is a star because he is the chorus." What does the writer mean by this? How does the allusion to Greek theater help you understand the writer's point?

5. What does Blankenhorn mean when he refers to our "cultural script"?

6. Why is the Deadbeat Dad a "bad guy"?

★ *Techniques and Strategies*

1. Where do you think Blankenhorn states the thesis of his essay?

2. What does he hope to accomplish by including the "imaginary letter" from the little girl to her dad?

3. Why does he provide quotations from Senator Moynihan and Mr. Cherlin? And statistics from the Census Bureau?

4. Why does Blankenhorn begin the selection with five simple declarative sentences?

5. Comment on the title of the selection. How does it arouse the reader's interest? Suppose the title were "Fathers Who Don't Pay." How would that title, compared with Blankenhorn's, serve the purposes of the essay?

★ *Speaking of Values*

1. What does the writer suggest is the relation between economics and fatherhood? How, according to Blankenhorn, does society define fatherhood?

2. When the writer suggests that the "essence of the New Father model is the erasure of fatherhood as a gendered social role for men," what point does he make?

3. By breaking down fatherhood into narrowly defined categories, Blankenhorn suggests that our society often sees gender roles as one dimensional. Do you agree? Why or why not?

4. Blankenhorn asserts three categories of fatherhood: the Unnecessary Father, the Old Father, and the New Father. Explain their respective roles and why they "get most of the attention."

5. What does the writer mean when he says that the understudy roles represent "the growing disembodiment and dispersal of fatherhood in our society"?

6. Why is "extracting payment from Deadbeat Dads . . . a regnant priority in our society"? Should we continue to extract payment from deadbeat dads? Why or why not? What does Blankenhorn mean by the last sentence of his essay: "The only solution to the problem of Deadbeat Dads is fatherhood"?

★ Values Conversation

Form groups and lay out what you see are the essential elements of fatherhood. How does the father's role differ from the mother's? Once you have a list of defining qualities, present it to the class at large. Are the elements you've proposed achievable? How does the society support or challenge your assertions? What values do our definitions of fatherhood suggest about us?

★ Writing about Values

1. Write a scene from a play (including dialogue) in which all the Dads mentioned in the selection explain and defend their roles.

2. Write an essay called "The Deadbeat Mom."

3. We live in an age of unparalleled freedom—political, social, sexual—in which social roles are continually being redefined. The writer suggests that there are those in modern society who believe that fatherhood has become "superfluous." Write an essay either defending this idea or refuting it. Draw on your discussions in the previous Values Conversation activity.

E. B. White

Once More to the Lake

E. B. White (1899–1985) was born in Mt. Vernon, New York, and was a widely known, award-winning essayist, whose work appeared for more than 50 years in *The New Yorker.* He also authored several books, including the children's works *Stuart Little* and *Charlotte's Web.* In this essay, written in 1941, White recalls his visits to a Maine lake as a child and a subsequent visit with his son.

——— ★ ———

One summer, along about 1904, my father rented a camp on a lake in Maine and took us all there for the month of August. We all got ringworm from some kittens and had to rub Pond's Extract on our arms and legs night and morning, and my father rolled over in a canoe with all his clothes on; but outside of that the vacation was a success and from then on none of us ever thought there was any place in the world like that lake in Maine. We returned summer after summer—always on August 1 for one month. I have since become a salt-water man, but sometimes in summer there are days when the restlessness of the tides and the fearful cold of the sea water and the incessant wind that blows across the afternoon and into the evening make me wish for the placidity of a lake in the woods. A few weeks ago this feeling got so strong I bought myself a couple of bass hooks and a spinner and returned to the lake where we used to go, for a week's fishing and to revisit old haunts.

I took along my son, who had never had any fresh water up his nose and who had seen lily pads only from train windows. On the journey over to the lake I began to wonder what it would be like. I wondered how time would have marred this unique, this holy spot—the coves and streams, the hills that the sun set behind, the camps and the paths behind the camps. I was sure that the tarred road would have found it out, and I wondered in what other ways it would be desolated. It is strange how much you can remember about places like that once you allow your mind to return into the grooves that lead back. You remember one thing, and that suddenly reminds you of another thing. I guess I remembered clearest of all the early mornings, when the lake was cool and motionless, remembered how the bedroom smelled of the lumber it was made of and of the wet woods whose scent entered through the screen. The partitions in the camp were thin and did not extend clear to the top of the rooms, and as I was always the first up I would dress softly so as not to wake the others, and sneak out into the

1

2

sweet outdoors and start out in the canoe, keeping close along the
shore in the long shadows of the pines. I remembered being very careful never to rub my paddle against the gunwale for fear of disturbing
the stillness of the cathedral.

3   The lake had never been what you would call a wild lake. There
were cottages sprinkled around the shores, and it was in farming country although the shores of the lake were quite heavily wooded. Some of
the cottages were owned by nearby farmers, and you would live at the
shore and eat your meals at the farmhouse. That's what our family did.
But although it wasn't wild, it was a fairly large and undisturbed lake
and there were places in it that, to a child at least, seemed infinitely remote and primeval.

4   I was right about the tar: it led to within half a mile of the shore.
But when I got back there, with my boy, and we settled into a camp
near a farmhouse and into the kind of summertime I had known, I
could tell that it was going to be pretty much the same as it had been
before—I knew it, lying in bed the first morning, smelling the bedroom
and hearing the boy sneak quietly out and go off along the shore in a
boat. I began to sustain the illusion that he was I, and therefore, by simple transposition, that I was my father. This sensation persisted, kept
cropping up all the time we were there. It was not an entirely new feeling, but in this setting it grew much stronger. I seemed to be living a
dual existence. I would be in the middle of some simple act, I would be
picking up a bait box or laying down a table fork, or I would be saying
something, and suddenly it would be not I but my father who was saying the words or making the gesture. It gave me a creepy sensation.

5   We went fishing the first morning. I felt the same damp moss covering the worms in the bait can, and saw the dragonfly alight on the tip
of my rod as it hovered a few inches from the surface of the water. It
was the arrival of this fly that convinced me beyond any doubt that everything was as it always had been, that the years were a mirage and
that there had been no years. The small waves were the same, chucking
the rowboat under the chin as we fished at anchor, and the boat was the
same boat, the same color green and the ribs broken in the same places,
and under the floorboards the same fresh-water leavings and débris—
the dead helgramite, the wisps of moss, the rusty discarded fishhook,
the dried blood from yesterday's catch. We stared silently at the tips of
our rods, at the dragonflies that came and went. I lowered the tip of
mine into the water, tentatively, pensively dislodging the fly, which
darted two feet away, poised, darted two feet back, and came to rest
again a little farther up the rod. There had been no years between the
ducking of this dragonfly and the other one—the one that was part of
memory. I looked at the boy, who was silently watching his fly, and it
was my hands that held his rod, my eyes watching. I felt dizzy and
didn't know which rod I was at the end of.

We caught two bass, hauling them in briskly as though they were 6
mackerel, pulling them over the side of the boat in a businesslike manner without any landing net, and stunning them with a blow on the
back of the head. When we got back for a swim before lunch, the lake
was exactly where we had left it, the same number of inches from the
dock, and there was only the merest suggestion of a breeze. This
seemed an utterly enchanted sea, this lake you could leave to its own
devices for a few hours and come back to, and find that it had not
stirred, this constant and trustworthy body of water. In the shadows,
the dark, water-soaked sticks and twigs, smooth and old, were undu-
lating in clusters on the bottom against the clean ribbed sand, and the
track of the mussel was plain. A school of minnows swam by, each
minnow with its small individual shadow, doubling the attendance, so
clear and sharp in the sunlight. Some of the other campers were in
swimming, along the shore, one of them with a cake of soap, and the
water felt thin and clear and unsubstantial. Over the years there had
been this person with the cake of soap, this cultist, and here he was.
There had been no years.

Up to the farmhouse to dinner through the teeming, dusty field, 7
the road under our sneakers was only a two-track road. The middle
track was missing, the one with the marks of the hooves and the
splotches of dried, flaky manure. There had always been three tracks to
choose from in choosing which track to walk in; now the choice was
narrowed down to two. For a moment I missed terribly the middle alternative. But the way led past the tennis court, and something about
the way it lay there in the sun reassured me; the tape had loosened
along the backline, the alleys were green with plantains and other
weeds, and the net (installed in June and removed in September)
sagged in the dry noon, and the whole place steamed with midday heat
and hunger and emptiness. There was a choice of pie for dessert, and
one was blueberry and one was apple, and the waitresses were the
same country girls, there having been no passage of time, only the illusion of it as in a dropped curtain—the waitresses were still fifteen; their
hair had been washed, that was the only difference—they had been to
the movies and seen the pretty girls with the clean hair.

Summertime, oh, summertime, pattern of life indelible, the fade- 8
proof lake, the woods unshatterable, the pasture with the sweetfern
and the juniper forever and ever, summer without end; this was the
background, and the life along the shore was the design, the cottagers
with their innocent and tranquil design, their tiny docks with the flag-
pole and the American flag floating against the white clouds in the blue
sky, the little paths over the roots of the trees leading from camp to
camp and the paths leading back to the outhouses and the can of lime
for sprinkling, and at the souvenir counters at the store the miniature
birch-bark canoes and the postcards that showed things looking a little

better than they looked. This was the American family at play, escaping the city heat, wondering whether the newcomers in the camp at the head of the cove were "common" or "nice," wondering whether it was true that the people who drove up for Sunday dinner at the farmhouse were turned away because there wasn't enough chicken.

9   It seemed to me, as I kept remembering all this, that those times and those summers had been infinitely precious and worth saving. There had been jollity and peace and goodness. The arriving (at the beginning of August) had been so big a business in itself, at the railway station the farm wagon drawn up, the first smell of the pine-laden air, the first glimpse of the smiling farmer, and the great importance of the trunks and your father's enormous authority in such matters, and the feel of the wagon under you for the long ten-mile haul, and at the top of the last long hill catching the first view of the lake after eleven months of not seeing this cherished body of water. The shouts and cries of the other campers when they saw you, and the trunks to be unpacked, to give up their rich burden. (Arriving was less exciting nowadays, when you sneaked up in your car and parked it under a tree near the camp and took out the bags and in five minutes it was all over, no fuss, no loud wonderful fuss about trunks.)

10   Peace and goodness and jollity. The only thing that was wrong now, really, was the sound of the place, an unfamiliar nervous sound of the outboard motors. This was the note that jarred, the one thing that would sometimes break the illusion and set the years moving. In those other summertimes all motors were inboard; and when they were at a little distance, the noise they made was a sedative, an ingredient of summer sleep. They were one-cylinder and two-cylinder engines, and some were make-and-break and some were jump-spark, but they all made a sleepy sound across the lake. The one-lungers throbbed and fluttered, and the twin-cylinder ones pulled and purred, and that was a quiet sound, too. But now the campers all had outboards. In the daytime, in the hot mornings, these motors made a petulant, irritable sound; at night, in the still evening when the afterglow lit the water, they whined about one's ears like mosquitoes. My boy loved our rented outboard, and his great desire was to achieve single-handed mastery over it, and authority, and he soon learned the trick of choking it a little (but not too much), and the adjustment of the needle valve. Watching him I would remember the things you could do with the old one-cylinder engine with the heavy flywheel, how you could have it eating out of your hand if you got really close to it spiritually. Motorboats in those days didn't have clutches, and you would make a landing by shutting off the motor at the proper time and coasting in with a dead rudder. But there was a way of reversing them, if you learned the trick, by cutting the switch and putting it on again exactly on the final dying revolution of the flywheel, so that it would kick back against

compression and begin reversing. Approaching a dock in a strong following breeze, it was difficult to slow up sufficiently by the ordinary
coasting method, and if a boy felt he had complete mastery over his
motor, he was tempted to keep it running beyond its time and then reverse it a few feet from the dock. It took a cool nerve, because if you
threw the switch a twentieth of a second too soon you would catch the
flywheel when it still had speed enough to go up past center, and the
boat would leap ahead, charging bull-fashion at the dock.

We had a good week at the camp. The bass were biting well and the   11
sun shone endlessly, day after day. We would be tired at night and lie
down in the accumulated heat of the little bedrooms after the long hot
day and the breeze would stir almost imperceptibly outside and the
smell of the swamp drift in through the rusty screens. Sleep would
come easily and in the morning the red squirrel would be on the roof,
tapping out his gay routine. I kept remembering everything, lying in
bed in the mornings—the small steamboat that had a long rounded
stem like the lip of a Ubangi, and how quietly she ran on the moonlight
sails, when the older boys played their mandolins and the girls sang
and we ate doughnuts dipped in sugar, and how sweet the music was
on the water in the shining night, and what it had felt like to think
about girls then. After breakfast we would go up to the store and the
things were in the same place—the minnows in a bottle, the plugs and
spinners disarranged and pawed over by the youngsters from the
boys' camp, the Fig Newtons and the Beeman's gum. Outside, the road
was tarred and cars stood in front of the store. Inside, all was just as it
had always been, except there was more Coca-Cola and not so much
Moxie and root beer and birch beer and sarsaparilla. We would walk
out with the bottle of pop apiece and sometimes the pop would back-
fire up our noses and hurt. We explored the streams, quietly, where the
turtles slid off the sunny logs and dug their way into the soft bottom;
and we lay on the town wharf and fed worms to the tame bass. Everywhere we went I had trouble making out which was I, the one walking
at my side, the one walking in my pants.

One afternoon while we were there at that lake a thunderstorm came   12
up. It was like the revival of an old melodrama that I had seen long ago
with childish awe. The second-act climax of the drama of the electrical
disturbance over a lake in America had not changed in any important respect. This was the big scene, still the big scene. The whole thing was so
familiar, the first feeling of oppression and heat and a general air around
camp of not wanting to go very far away. In mid-afternoon (it was all the
same) a curious darkening of the sky and a lull in everything that had
made life tick; and then the way the boats suddenly swung the other
way at their moorings with the coming of a breeze out of the new quarter, and the premonitory rumble. Then the kettle drum, then the snare,
then the bass drum and cymbals, then crackling light against the dark,

and the gods grinning and licking their chops in the hills. Afterward the calm, the rain steadily rustling in the calm lake, the return of light and hope and spirits, and the campers running out in joy and relief to go swimming in the rain, their bright cries perpetuating the deathless joke about how they were getting simply drenched, and the children screaming with delight at the new sensation of bathing in the rain, and the joke about getting drenched linking the generations in a strong indestructible chain. And the comedian who waded in carrying an umbrella.

13   When the others went swimming, my son said he was going in, too. He pulled his dripping trunks from the line where they had hung all through the shower and wrung them out. Languidly, and with no thought of going in, I watched him, his hard little body, skinny and bare, saw him wince slightly as he pulled up around his vitals the small, soggy, icy garment. As he buckled the swollen belt, suddenly my groin felt the chill of death.

★ *Meaning and Understanding*

1. What do you think is the main point of this selection?

2. Why does White return to the lake? How does it contrast with the sea? What does he think of on the journey over to the lake?

3. What did White and his son do on the first morning?

4. What was "the only thing that was wrong now" at the lake?

5. What is the significance of the thunderstorm White describes near the end of the essay?

★ *Techniques and Strategies*

1. What descriptive elements do you find clearest and (or) most original? Make a list of a few sensory images that give you a good picture of the lake. Note the writer's use of color, sound, and smell to evoke the scene.

2. A subtle shift in perspective occurs in paragraph 9. Identify the nature of this shift and why you think White produces it.

3. The writer opens the essay with the words "One summer, along about 1904. . . ." Why does he identify the year in this manner? What does the anchor in time long past do for the rest of the essay?

4. The essay begins with a reference to an earlier time, slides into the present, and then seems to shift back into time once more. Where do these shifts occur and what impact do they have on your understanding of White's point?

5. Who do you think is the intended audience for this essay? What clues in the selection lead you to your conclusion?

6. The writer refers to the lake as "this holy spot." What makes it "holy"? How does the religious connotation help you to understand the writer's point? What other words and phrases in the selection also suggest mystery or wonder?

7. White opens paragraph 10 by repeating, in different order, words in the second sentence of paragraph 9. Why does he use this strategy? That is, why does he repeat the words but change their order?

★ Speaking of Values

1. In what kind of family did the writer grow up? How do you know? What is your reaction to this kind of family and the values it implies?

2. What is the writer's relation with his son? Give examples to support your point. Again, what values does this connection between son and father suggest? How typical is White's relation with his son when you compare it to relations between sons and fathers you know?

3. Is it common for people as they age to become wistful about their youth in the way that White does in this essay? Why do you believe as you do? To take a different angle on this question, how does our society deal with aging? Do we respect age and maturity or do we fear it? Why do you think this is so?

4. Do you feel at any point in the essay that the writer is envious of his son? Why might he be? Give examples to support your point.

5. In paragraph 12 White says that during the thunderstorm "the joke about getting drenched" linked the generations "in a strong indestructible chain." What does he mean? Why might he think it is so important for the generations to be linked? Do you think it is? Why or why not?

★ Values Conversation

Form groups and have each member of the group identify and describe a place that has a special meaning for his or her family. Then list the reasons why this place is special. How similar are the reasons that group members give? Does this information help you understand the essay better? How so?

★ Writing about Values

1. Choose a place that has significance for you and write a paper about it. First, describe the locale in very objective terms—that is, try to describe

it without injecting into your description any of your own feelings. Then describe the place in subjective terms—that is, describe it in terms of how it makes you feel. Remember that your aim here is to suggest to your audience that it is very difficult to get the true sense of a place from just one kind of description.

2. Write a paper in which you describe an object, a building, or even a location that seems out of place with its surrounding environment. Analyze the values expressed by one of the subjects compared to the values expressed by the other.

3. In this essay the author seems almost suddenly to become aware of his mortality. Write an essay describing a moment when you first became aware of your mortality. That is, when did you first have a sense that you were not going to live forever? Be sure to provide specific details so that your audience understands precisely how you felt at that moment and why the moment was so significant for you.

Alice Walker

Everyday Use

Alice Walker, born in Eatonton, Georgia in 1949, is a poet, short story writer, and novelist. "Everyday Use," from her short story collection *In Love & Trouble: Stories of Black Women* (1973), captures a moment when a mother and her homebound daughter reunite with the third member of the family, a modern sophisticate who returns home for a visit.

———— ★ ————

I will wait for her in the yard that Maggie and I made so clean and wavy yesterday afternoon. A yard like this is more comfortable than most people know. It is not just a yard. It is like an extended living room. When the hard clay is swept clean as a floor and the fine sand around the edges lined with tiny, irregular grooves anyone can come and sit and look up into the elm tree and wait for the breezes that never come inside the house.

Maggie will be nervous until after her sister goes: she will stand hopelessly in corners homely and ashamed of the burn scars down her arms and legs, eyeing her sister with a mixture of envy and awe. She thinks her sister has held life always in the palm of one hand, that "no" is a word the world never learned to say to her.

You've no doubt seen those TV shows where the child who has "made it" is confronted, as a surprise, by her own mother and father, tottering in weakly from backstage. (A pleasant surprise, of course: What would they do if parent and child came on the show only to curse out and insult each other?) On TV mother and child embrace and smile into each other's faces. Sometimes the mother and father weep, the child wraps them in her arms and leans across the table to tell how she would not have made it without their help. I have seen these programs.

Sometimes I dream a dream in which Dee and I are suddenly brought together on a TV program of this sort. Out of a dark and soft-seated limousine I am ushered into a bright room filled with many people. There I meet a smiling, gray, sporty man like Johnny Carson who shakes my hand and tells me what a fine girl I have. Then we are on the stage and Dee is embracing me with tears in her eyes. She pins on my dress a large orchid, even though she has told me once that she thinks orchids are tacky flowers.

In real life I am a large, big-boned woman with tough, man-working hands. In the winter I wear flannel nightgowns to bed and overalls during the day. I can kill and clean a hog as mercilessly as a man. My fat keeps me hot in zero weather. I can work all day, breaking ice to get water for washing. I can eat pork liver cooked over the open fire minutes after it comes steaming from the hog. One winter I knocked a bull calf straight in the brain between the eyes with a sledge hammer and had the meat hung up to chill before nightfall. But of course all this does not show on television. I am the way my daughter would want me to be: a hundred pounds lighter, my skin like an uncooked barley pancake. My hair glistens in the hot bright lights. Johnny Carson has much to do to keep up with my quick and witty tongue.

6   But that is a mistake. I know even before I wake up. Who ever knew a Johnson with a quick tongue? Who can even imagine me looking a strange white man in the eye? It seems to me I have talked to them always with one foot raised in flight, with my head turned in whichever way is farthest from them. Dee, though. She would always look anyone in the eye. Hesitation was no part of her nature.

7   "How do I look, Mama?" Maggie says, showing just enough of her thin body enveloped in pink skirt and red blouse for me to know she's there, almost hidden by the door.

8   "Come out into the yard," I say.

9   Have you ever seen a lame animal, perhaps a dog run over by some careless person rich enough to own a car, sidle up to someone who is ignorant enough to be kind to him? That is the way my Maggie walks. She has been like this, chin on chest, eyes on ground, feet in shuffle, ever since the fire that burned the other house to the ground.

10   Dee is lighter than Maggie, with nicer hair and a fuller figure. She's a woman now, though sometimes I forget. How long ago was it that the other house burned? Ten, twelve years? Sometimes I can still hear the flames and feel Maggie's arm sticking to me, her hair smoking and her dress falling off her in little black papery flakes. Her eyes seemed stretched open, blazed open by the flames reflected in them. And Dee. I see her standing off under the sweet gum tree she used to dig gum out of, a look of concentration on her face as she watched the last dingy gray board of the house fall in toward the red-hot brick chimney. Why don't you do a dance around the ashes? I'd wanted to ask her. She had hated the house that much.

11   I used to think she hated Maggie, too. But that was before we raised the money, the church and me, to send her to Augusta to school. She used to read to us without pity; forcing words, lies, other folks' habits, whole lives upon us two, sitting trapped and ignorant underneath her voice. She washed us in a river of make-believe, burned us with a lot of knowledge we didn't necessarily need to know. Pressed us to her with the serious way she read, to shove us away at just the moment, like dimwits, we seemed about to understand.

Dee wanted nice things. A yellow organdy dress to wear to her   12
graduation from high school; black pumps to match a green suit she'd
made from an old suit somebody gave me. She was determined to stare
down any disaster in her efforts. Her eyelids would not flicker for minutes at a time. Often I fought off the temptation to shake her. At sixteen
she had a style of her own: and knew what style was.

I never had an education myself. After second grade the school   13
was closed down. Don't ask me why: in 1927 colored asked fewer questions than they do now. Sometimes Maggie reads to me. She stumbles
along good-naturedly but can't see well. She knows she is not bright.
Like good looks and money, quickness passed her by. She will marry
John Thomas (who has mossy teeth in an earnest face) and then I'll be
free to sit here and I guess just sing church songs to myself. Although I
never was a good singer. Never could carry a tune. I was always better
at a man's job. I used to love to milk till I was hoofed in the side in '49.
Cows are soothing and slow and don't bother you, unless you try to
milk them the wrong way.

I have deliberately turned my back on the house. It is three rooms,   14
just like the one that burned, except the roof is tin; they don't make
shingle roofs any more. There are no real windows, just some holes cut
in the sides, like the portholes in a ship, but not round and not square,
with rawhide holding the shutters up on the outside. This house is in a
pasture, too, like the other one. No doubt when Dee sees it she will
want to tear it down. She wrote me once that no matter where we
"choose" to live, she will manage to come see us. But she will never
bring her friends. Maggie and I thought about this and Maggie asked
me, "Mama, when did Dee ever *have* any friends?"

She had a few. Furtive boys in pink shirts hanging about on wash-   15
day after school. Nervous girls who never laughed. Impressed with her
they worshiped the well-turned phrase, the cute shape, the scalding
humor that erupted like bubbles in lye. She read to them.

When she was courting Jimmy T she didn't have much time to pay   16
to us, but turned all her faultfinding power on him. He *flew* to marry a
cheap gal from a family of ignorant flashy people. She hardly had time
to recompose herself.

When she comes I will meet—but there they are!   17

Maggie attempts to make a dash for the house, in her shuffling   18
way, but I stay her with my hand. "Come back here," I say. And she
stops and tries to dig a well in the sand with her toe.

It is hard to see them clearly through the strong sun. But even the   19
first glimpse of leg out of the car tells me it is Dee. Her feet were always
neat-looking, as if God himself had shaped them with a certain style.
From the other side of the car comes a short, stocky man. Hair is all
over his head a foot long and hanging from his chin like a kinky mule

tail. I hear Maggie suck in her breath. "Uhnnnh," is what it sounds like. Like when you see the wriggling end of a snake just in front of your foot on the road. "Uhnnnh."

20   Dee next. A dress down to the ground, in this hot weather. A dress so loud it hurts my eyes. There are yellows and oranges enough to throw back the light of the sun. I feel my whole face warming from the heat waves it throws out. Earrings, too, gold and hanging down to her shoulders. Bracelets dangling and making noises when she moves her arm up to shake the folds of the dress out of her armpits. The dress is loose and flows, and as she walks closer, I like it. I hear Maggie go "Uhnnnh" again. It is her sister's hair. It stands straight up like the wool on a sheep. It is black as night and around the edges are two long pigtails that rope about like small lizards disappearing behind her ears.

21   "Wa-su-zo-Tean-o!" she says, coming on in that gliding way the dress makes her move. The short stocky fellow with the hair to his navel is all grinning and he follows up with "Asalamalakim, my mother and sister!" He moves to hug Maggie but she falls back, right up against the back of my chair. I feel her trembling there and when I look up I see the perspiration falling off her chin.

22   "Don't get up," says Dee. Since I am stout it takes something of a push. You can see me trying to move a second or two before I make it. She turns, showing white heels through her sandals, and goes back to the car. Out she peeks next with a Polaroid. She stoops down quickly and lines up picture after picture of me sitting there in front of the house with Maggie cowering behind me. She never takes a shot without making sure the house is included. When a cow comes nibbling around the edge of the yard she snaps it and me and Maggie *and* the house. Then she puts the Polaroid in the back seat of the car, and comes up and kisses me on the forehead.

23   Meanwhile Asalamalakim is going through the motions with Maggie's hand. Maggie's hand is as limp as a fish, and probably as cold, despite the sweat, and she keeps trying to pull it back. It looks like Asalamalakim wants to shake hands but wants to do it fancy. Or maybe he don't know how people shake hands. Anyhow, he soon gives up on Maggie.

24   "Well," I say. "Dee."

25   "No, Mama," she says. "Not 'Dee,' Wangero Leewanika Kemanjo!"

26   "What happened to 'Dee'?" I wanted to know.

27   "She's dead," Wangero said. "I couldn't bear it any longer being named after the people who oppress me."

28   "You know as well as me you was named after your aunt Dicie," I said. Dicie is my sister. She named Dee. We called her "Big Dee" after Dee was born.

29   "But who was *she* named after," asked Wangero.

30   "I guess after Grandma Dee," I said.

"And who was she named after?" asked Wangero.   31

"Her mother," I said, and saw Wangero getting tired. "That's about   32
as far back as I can trace it," I said. Though, in fact, I probably could
have carried it back beyond the Civil War through the branches.

"Well," said Asalamalakim, "there you are."   33

"Uhnnnh," I heard Maggie say.   34

"There I was not," I said, "before 'Dicie' cropped up in our family,   35
so why should I try to trace it that far back?"

He just stood there grinning, looking down on me like somebody   36
inspecting a Model A car. Every once in a while he and Wangero sent
eye signals over my head.

"How do you pronounce this name?" I asked.   37

"You don't have to call me by it if you don't want to," said   38
Wangero.

"Why shouldn't I?" I asked. "If that's what you want us to call you,   39
we'll call you."

"I know it might sound awkward at first," said Wangero.   40

"I'll get used to it," I said. "Ream it out again."   41

Well, soon we got the name out of the way. Asalamalakim had a   42
name twice as long and three times as hard. After I tripped over it two
or three times he told me to just call him Hakim-a-barber. I wanted to
ask him was he a barber, but I didn't really think he was, so I didn't ask.

"You must belong to those beef-cattle peoples down the road," I   43
said. They said "Asalamalakim" when they met you, too, but they
didn't shake hands. Always too busy: feeding the cattle, fixing the
fences, putting up salt-lick shelters, throwing down hay. When the
white folks poisoned some of the herd the men stayed up all night with
rifles in their hands. I walked a mile and a half just to see the sight.

Hakim-a-barber said, "I accept some of their doctrines, but farming   44
and raising cattle is not my style." (They didn't tell me, and I didn't
ask, whether Wangero [Dee] had really gone and married him.)

We sat down to eat and right away he said he didn't eat collards   45
and pork was unclean. Wangero, though, went on through the chitlins
and corn bread, the greens and everything else. She talked a blue streak
over the sweet potatoes. Everything delighted her. Even the fact that
we still used the benches her daddy made for the table when we
couldn't afford to buy chairs.

"Oh, Mama!" she cried. Then turned to Hakim-a-barber. "I never   46
knew how lovely these benches are. You can feel the rump prints," she
said, running her hands underneath her and along the bench. Then she
gave a sigh and her hand closed over Grandma Dee's butter dish.
"That's it!" she said. "I knew there was something I wanted to ask you
if I could have." She jumped up from the table and went over in the
corner where the churn stood, the milk in its clabber by now. She
looked at the churn and looked at it.

47   "This churn top is what I need," she said. "Didn't Uncle Buddy whittle it out of a tree you all used to have?"

48   "Yes," I said.

49   "Uh huh," she said happily. "And I want the dasher, too."

50   "Uncle Buddy whittle that, too?" asked the barber.

51   Dee (Wangero) looked up at me.

52   "Aunt Dee's first husband whittled the dash," said Maggie so low you almost couldn't hear her. "His name was Henry, but they called him Stash."

53   "Maggie's brain is like an elephant's," Wangero said, laughing. "I can use the churn top as a centerpiece for the alcove table," she said, sliding a plate over the churn, "and I'll think of something artistic to do with the dasher."

54   When she finished wrapping the dasher the handle stuck out. I took it for a moment in my hands. You didn't even have to look close to see where hands pushing the dasher up and down to make butter had left a kind of sink in the wood, In fact, there were a lot of small sinks; you could see where thumbs and fingers had sunk into the wood. It was beautiful light yellow wood, from a tree that grew in the yard where Big Dee and Stash had lived.

55   After dinner Dee (Wangero) went to the trunk at the foot of my bed and started rifling through it. Maggie hung back in the kitchen over the dishpan. Out came Wangero with two quilts. They had been pieced by Grandma Dee and then Big Dee and me had hung them on the quilt frames on the front porch and quilted them. One was in the Lone Star pattern. The other was Walk Around the Mountain. In both of them were scraps of dresses Grandma Dee had worn fifty and more years ago. Bits and pieces of Grandpa Jarrell's Paisley shirts. And one teeny faded blue piece, about the size of a penny matchbox, that was from Great Grandpa Ezra's uniform that he wore in the Civil War.

56   "Mama," Wangero said sweet as a bird. "Can I have these old quilts?"

57   I heard something fall in the kitchen, and a minute later the kitchen door slammed.

58   "Why don't you take one or two of the others?" I asked. "These old things was just done by me and Big Dee from some tops your grandma pieced before she died."

59   "No," said Wangero. "I don't want those. They are stitched around the borders by machine."

60   "That's make them last better," I said.

61   "That's not the point," said Wangero. "These are all pieces of dresses Grandma used to wear. She did all this stitching by hand. Imagine!" She held the quilts securely in her arms, stroking them.

62   "Some of the pieces, like those lavender ones, come from old clothes her mother handed down to her," I said, moving up to touch

the quilts. Dee (Wangero) moved back just enough so that I couldn't reach the quilts. They already belonged to her.

"Imagine!" she breathed again, clutching them closely to her bosom.   63

"The truth is," I said, "I promised to give them quilts to Maggie, for   64
when she marries John Thomas."

She gasped like a bee had stung her.   65

"Maggie can't appreciate these quilts!" she said. "She'd probably   66
be backward enough to put them to everyday use."

"I reckon she would," I said. "God knows I been saving 'em for   67
long enough with nobody using 'em. I hope she will!" I didn't want to bring up how I had offered Dee (Wangero) a quilt when she went away to college. Then she had told me they were old-fashioned, out of style.

"But they're *priceless!*" she was saying now, furiously; for she has a   68
temper. "Maggie would put them on the bed and in five years they'd be in rags. Less than that!"

"She can always make some more," I said. "Maggie knows how to   69
quilt."

Dee (Wangero) looked at me with hatred. "You just will not under-   70
stand. The point is these quilts, *these* quilts!"

"Well," I said, stumped. "What would *you* do with them?"   71

"Hang them," she said. As if that was the only thing you *could* do   72
with quilts.

Maggie by now was standing in the door. I could almost hear the   73
sound her feet made as they scraped over each other.

"She can have them, Mama," she said, like somebody used to   74
never winning anything, or having anything reserved for her. "I can 'member Grandma Dee without the quilts."

I looked at her hard. She had filled her bottom lip with checker-   75
berry snuff and it gave her face a kind of dopey, hangdog look. It was Grandma Dee and Big Dee who taught her how to quilt herself. She stood there with her scarred hands hidden in the folds of her skirt. She looked at her sister with something like fear but she wasn't mad at her. This was Maggie's portion. This was the way she knew God to work.

When I looked at her like that something hit me in the top of my   76
head and ran down to the soles of my feet. Just like when I'm in church and the spirit of God touches me and I get happy and shout. I did something I never had done before: hugged Maggie to me, then dragged her on into the room, snatched the quilts out of Miss Wangero's hands and dumped them into Maggie's lap. Maggie just sat there on my bed with her mouth open.

"Take one or two of the others," I said to Dee.   77

But she turned without a word and went out to Hakim-a-barber.   78

"You just don't understand," she said, as Maggie and I came out to   79
the car.

"What don't I understand?" I wanted to know.   80

81   "Your heritage," she said. And then she turned to Maggie, kissed her, and said, "You ought to try to make something of yourself, too, Maggie. It's really a new day for us. But from the way you and Mamma still live you'd never know it."

82   She put on some sunglasses that hid everything above the tip of her nose and her chin.

83   Maggie smiled; maybe at the sunglasses. But a real smile, not scared. After we watched the car dust settle I asked Maggie to bring me a dip of snuff. And then the two of us sat there just enjoying, until it was time to go in the house and go to bed.

★ Meaning and Understanding

1. What do you think is the main point of this story?

2. What is the personality of each of the women? In what ways are they similar? In what ways are they different?

3. Why is Maggie nervous about Dee's visit? What is the significance of Momma's dream about her and Dee being on TV?

4. How does Maggie react to the man who accompanies Dee?

5. How do Momma and Maggie feel about Dee's name change? Why did Dee change her name?

6. Although Wangero (Dee) seems to reject much of her earlier life, she is very willing to take things from Momma's house. What objects in the house interest her?

7. How does Momma finally resolve the issue of who gets the quilts? To whom does she give them? Why does she make the decision she makes?

8. How does Momma feel about Maggie? About Dee? How do you know?

★ Techniques and Strategies

1. This story builds around comparisons and contrasts—between Maggie and Dee, between Momma and each of her daughters, between Momma and a man, between the "new day and the old ways," between "Asalamalakim" and the "beef-cattle peoples down the road." How do these comparisons and contrasts help you understand the characters?

2. Why does the story begin and end in the front yard? We do not get a sense of the inside of the house. Why not?

3. The story begins with Momma saying "I will wait for her in the yard that Maggie and I made so clean and wavy yesterday afternoon." Why doesn't Momma identify Dee by name in the crucial opening of the story? Why do you think Walker uses this technique?

4. Momma often speaks of herself in negatives: "never had an education"; "never was a good singer"; "never could carry a tune"; "was always better at a man's job." How do these self-appraisals help us to know her better?

5. Of what significance is the title of the story? How does it capture the essence of the conflicting personalities?

★ Speaking of Values

1. We read nothing about Momma's husband or Maggie and Dee's father in this story. What do you think of this omission? Has the lack of a male figure in this family had any discernible impact on the women? Why or why not?

2. Much of "Everyday Use" revolves around differing ideas of heritage and tradition. Is it important to preserve family traditions and to pass them on from generation to generation? Why or why not?

3. Near the end of the story Dee asserts that Momma doesn't understand her heritage. Do you agree with Dee? Or is it Dee who does not understand? Support your answer.

4. Dee takes several photographs of the house and yet Momma remarks that Dee had hated the house. Why do you think Dee hated the house? Why did she take all the pictures? What values does the house represent to Dee?

5. Dee asserts that she changed her name because she "couldn't bear it any longer being named after the people who oppress me." What does she mean by this? How can a name be a symbol of oppression? What names that you know might be oppressive to people? Why?

6. Momma says about Dee and Asalamalakim that "They didn't tell me, and I didn't ask, whether Wangero had really gone and married him." Why is this even an issue for Momma? And why doesn't she ask?

★ Values Conversation

Form groups and have each member of the group list some family traditions from his or her own family. Then compare these items. Is any of them roughly similar from family to family? What conclusions can you draw from these similarities?

★ *Writing about Values*

1. Fathers and sons and mothers and daughters often come into conflict with one another. Write an essay about a father and son or mother and daughter you know (you may use yourself!) and discuss and analyze the causes and consequences of the conflict.

2. Cultural traditions and heritage sometimes undergo interesting variations through the passage of time. Identify some traditions or elements of your particular cultural heritage (ethnic, religious, political, etc.) and discuss the ways in which they have changed even during your lifetime.

3. Choose a work of literature that deals with the theme of generational or cultural conflict and discuss and analyze the causes of the conflict and the eventual resolution(s). Some possibilities are *Romeo and Juliet*, *Native Son*, *Invisible Man*, and *All My Sons*.

Mel Lazarus

Angry Fathers

Mel Lazarus was born in New York City in 1927 and, in addition to being the author of numerous books and plays, is also a nationally syndicated cartoonist ("Miss Peach" and "Momma"). Lazarus presents an account of a childhood event that helped shape his life and his relation with his father.

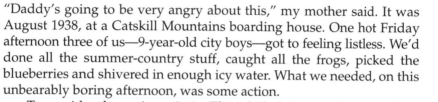

"Daddy's going to be very angry about this," my mother said. It was August 1938, at a Catskill Mountains boarding house. One hot Friday afternoon three of us—9-year-old city boys—got to feeling listless. We'd done all the summer-country stuff, caught all the frogs, picked the blueberries and shivered in enough icy water. What we needed, on this unbearably boring afternoon, was some action. 1

To consider the options, Artie, Eli and I holed up in the cool of the "casino," the little building in which the guests enjoyed their nightly bingo games and the occasional traveling magic act. 2

Gradually, inspiration came: the casino was too new, the wood frame and white Sheetrock walls too perfect. We would do it some quiet damage. Leave our anonymous mark on the place, for all time. With, of course, no thought as to consequences. 3

We began by picking up a long, wooden bench, running with it like a battering ram, and bashing it into a wall. It left a wonderful hole. But small. So we did it again. And again.... 4

Afterward the three of us, breathing hard, sweating the sweat of heroes, surveyed our first really big-time damage. The process had been so satisfying we'd gotten carried away; there was hardly a good square foot of Sheetrock left. 5

Suddenly, before even a tweak of remorse set in, the owner, Mr. Biolos, appeared in the doorway of the building. Furious. And craving justice: When they arrived from the city that night, he-would-tell-our-fathers! 6

Meantime, he told our mothers. My mother felt that what I had done was so monstrous she would leave my punishment to my father. "And," she said, "Daddy's going to be very angry about this." 7

By 6 o'clock Mr. Biolos was stationed out at the driveway, grimly waiting for the fathers to start showing up. Behind him, the front porch was jammed, like a sold-out bleacher section, with indignant guests. They'd seen the damage to their bingo palace, knew they'd have to 8

71

endure it in that condition for the rest of the summer. They, too, craved justice.

9   As to Artie, Eli and me, we each found an inconspicuous spot on the porch, a careful distance from the other two but not too far from our respective mothers. And waited.

10   Artie's father arrived first. When Mr. Biolos told him the news and showed him the blighted casino, he carefully took off his belt and—with practiced style—viciously whipped his screaming son. With the approbation, by the way, of an ugly crowd of once gentle people.

11   Eli's father showed up next. He was told and shown and went raving mad, knocking his son off his feet with a slam to the head. As Eli lay crying on the grass, he kicked him on the legs, buttocks and back. When Eli tried to get up he kicked him again.

12   The crowd muttered: Listen, they should have thought of this before they did the damage. They'll live, don't worry, and I bet they never do that again.

13   I wondered: What will my father do? He'd never laid a hand on me in my life. I knew about other kids, had seen bruises on certain schoolmates and even heard screams in the evenings from certain houses on my street, but they were those kids, their families, and the why and how of their bruises were, to me, dark abstractions. Until now.

14   I looked over at my mother. She was upset. Earlier she'd made it clear to me that I had done some special kind of crime. Did it mean that beatings were now, suddenly, the new order of the day?

15   My own father suddenly pulled up in our Chevy, just in time to see Eli's father dragging Eli up the porch steps and into the building. He got out of the car believing, I was sure, that whatever it was all about, Eli must have deserved it. I went dizzy with fear.

16   Mr. Biolos, on a roll, started talking. My father listened, his shirt soaked with perspiration, a damp handkerchief draped around his neck; he never did well in humid weather. I watched him follow Mr. Biolos into the casino. My dad—strong and principled, hot and bothered—what was he thinking about all this?

17   When they emerged, my father looked over at my mother. He mouthed a small "Hello." Then his eyes found me and stared for a long moment, without expression. I tried to read his eyes, but they left me and went to the crowd, from face to expectant face.

18   Then, amazingly, he got into his car and drove away! Nobody, not even my mother, could imagine where he was going.

19   An hour later he came back. Tied onto the top of his car was a stack of huge Sheetrock boards. He got out holding a paper sack with a hammer sticking out of it. Without a word he untied the Sheetrock and one by one carried the boards into the casino.

20   And didn't come out again that night.

All through my mother's and my silent dinner and for the rest of   21
that Friday evening and long after we had bone to bed, I could hear—
everyone could hear—the steady bang bang bang bang of my dad's
hammer. I pictured him sweating, missing his dinner, missing my
mother, getting madder and madder at me. Would tomorrow be the
last day of my life? It was 3 A.M. before I finally fell asleep.

The next morning, my father didn't say a single word about the   22
night before. Nor did he show any trace of anger or reproach of any
kind. We had a regular day, he, my mother and I, and, in fact, our usual,
sweet family weekend.

Was he mad at me? You bet he was. But in a time when many of his   23
generation saw corporal punishment of their children as a God-given
right, he knew "spanking" as beating, and beating as criminal. And
that when kids were beaten, they always remembered the pain but often forgot the reason.

And I also realized years later that, to him, humiliating me was just   24
as unthinkable. Unlike the fathers of my buddies, he couldn't play into
the conspiracy of revenge and spectacle.

But my father had made his point. I never forgot that my vandal-   25
ism on that August afternoon was outrageous.

And I'll never forget that it was also the day I first understood how   26
deeply I could trust him.

★ Meaning and Understanding

1. What kind of action did the boys produce on the "unbelievably boring" afternoon in 1938?

2. What did Mr. Biolos threaten? How did the writer's mother react?
   What did she say?

3. How did Artie's father react? Eli's father? What did each man do to his
   son?

4. What is the writer's father's initial response to his son's "special kind
   of crime"? Where does he drive off to?

5. What does Lazarus's father do to redress the damage his son did?

★ Techniques and Strategies

1. What is the thesis of this essay?

2. What connection do you see between the "steady bang bang bang
   bang bang of my dad's hammer" and using the battering ram to
   "bash" a hole in the wall? How do the two actions contribute to the selection's coherence?

3. Which sensory images contribute to your ability to see the scene as Lazarus sees it? Indicate the appeals to sight, sound, and touch that create vivid images.

4. What is your reaction to the single sentence as the concluding paragraph of the essay?

5. Who do you think is the intended audience for this piece? On what do you base your decision?

6. The only person who actually speaks in this selection is the writer's mother, who twice says the same thing: "Daddy's going to be very angry about this." Why does Lazarus restrict the dialogue in such a manner?

★ Speaking of Values

1. Both Lazurus's mother and Mr. Biolos suggest that it is the writer's father who must ultimately deal with disciplining his son. What does this suggest about the traditional parenting roles accorded both men and women in our society, especially in the period preceding World War II? How do these roles compare and contrast with roles ascribed to today's parents?

2. This incident takes place during the Depression and yet these people are enjoying their summer at a resort of some kind. What socioeconomic class do you think they belong to? What bearing does this characteristic have on the behavior of the boys, their parents, or the spectators? Explain your answer.

3. Two of the fathers inflict physical punishment on their sons to the approval of the crowd. What do the actions of the fathers and the response of the spectators suggest about the values they hold toward disciplining children? Why might you approve or disapprove of the two fathers' actions? Under what circumstances do you think physical discipline for children is justified? Or do you believe that physical discipline for children is never justified? Explain your answer.

4. The writer suggests that his father never uttered a word throughout the entire proceedings. How does this contrast with the other fathers represented in the selection? Lazarus also says that his father was "strong and principled." How does his silence offer us a clue about his principles?

5. Lazarus concludes the selection by asserting that he would never forget that the day in question "was also the day I first understood how deeply I could trust him." On what is this trust based? How did his father's actions generate trust? Do you think his father acted appropri-

ately? What generalizations can you draw about how a parent can win trust from a child?

★ *Values Conversation*

Anger is often a destructive and terrifying emotion and yet an extremely common one, particularly between parent and child. Form groups and try to come up with a list of situations that made your parents or other relatives angry. Then try to explore the underlying reasons for the anger.

★ *Writing about Values*

1. Write about a time that a parent or other relative punished you. Be sure to explain clearly what you had done and how your parent or relative reacted. Indicate whether or not you thought the punishment inappropriate and why. Try to consider how your parent or relative might have felt both about your deed and about the punishment.

2. "Spare the rod and spoil the child" is an old and often-cited adage. Yet the writer tells us that his father "knew 'spanking' as beating, and beating as criminal. And that when kids were beaten, they always remembered the pain but often forgot the reason." Write an essay to explore your views on whether or not violence is ever justified when adults discipline children in the family. Cite examples from the selection, from your own experience, or from what you have read to support your argument.

3. Vandalism costs the American public millions of dollars each year. What are the underlying causes for vandalism, do you think, and what steps can our society take to overcome it? Write an essay, drawing on local or national statistics, in which you analyze vandalism as a social ill.

Judith S. Wallerstein, Ph.D. and Sandra Blakeslee

The Children of Divorce

Judith S. Wallerstein, who was born in 1921 in New York City, is a psychiatric social worker specializing in the effects of divorce on families. She is the author of many professional articles and co-author of *Surviving the Breakup: How Children and Parents Cope with Divorce* (1980).

Sandra Blakeslee, born in New York City in 1943, is a science writer for the *New York Times*. She is a member of the National Association of Science Writers.

In this selection from their book *Second Chances: Men, Women, and Children a Decade after Divorce* (1989), the writers highlight some of the effects of divorce on children.

1   The experience of divorce is entirely different for parents and for children. Many people have wanted to believe that what is good for adults will be good for their children. It is seductively simple to think that a child's psychological problems are mainly a reflection of family problems—as if children were not people with reactions of their own, separate from those of adults. As a parent puts his or her life together in the post-divorce years, they say, the children will inevitably improve. Because an unhappy woman often has a hard time being a good mother, they argue, it follows that a happy woman will be a good mother.

2   But this argument just does not jibe with my experience. It is often true that an unhappy adult finds it hard to be a nurturing parent for unhappiness can deplete the adult's capacity to provide the care and understanding that children need. But it does not follow that a happy or happier adult will necessarily become a better parent. The "trickle down" theory is not relevant to parent-child relationships. An exciting love affair or a gratifying career advance may make for a much happier adult, but there is no reason to expect that the adult's greater happiness will lead to a greater sensitivity or greater concern for his or her children. To the contrary, circumstances that enrich an adult's life can easily make that adult less available to children. Unfortunately, the genuine love and tenderness between adults in a second marriage is not always shared with the children who come from a previous marriage.

3   Although the decision to divorce is rarely mutual, adults generally do agree about the state of the marriage. It is uncommon—although it

surely happens—for one spouse to be genuinely surprised when the other presses for divorce. Most of the time both adults acknowledge, openly or secretly, that there are flaws and tensions in a marriage on the brink. They may disagree about how to remedy those troubles, but they rarely disagree that the troubles exist. Children, however, can be quite content even when their parents' marriage is profoundly unhappy for one or both partners. Only one in ten children in our study experienced relief when their parents divorced. These were mostly older children in families where there had been open violence and where the children had lived with the fear that the violence would hurt a parent or themselves. Even so, few children truly expect their parents to divorce. When there is fighting in the household, children hope against hope that the fighting will vanish, and they look forward to a more peaceful time. They do not prepare themselves for divorce, and when they are told that a divorce is imminent, many refuse to believe it.

Divorce is a different experience for children and adults because the children lose something that is fundamental to their development—the family structure. The family comprises the scaffolding upon which children mount successive developmental stages, from infancy into adolescence. It supports their psychological, physical, and emotional ascent into maturity. When that structure collapses, the children's world is temporarily without supports. And children, with a vastly compressed sense of time, do not know that the chaos is temporary. What they do know is that they are dependent on the family. Whatever its shortcomings, children perceive the family as the entity that provides the support and protection that they need. With divorce, that structure breaks down, leaving children who feel alone and very frightened about the present and the future. 4

The human newborn is one of the most helpless creatures on earth. Human children need their parents far longer than any other animal species, and children are tragically aware of this fact—they know how absolutely dependent they are on adults. Accordingly, they have a very primitive, very real fear of being left on their own. A child's immediate reaction to divorce, therefore, is fear. When their family breaks up, children feel vulnerable, for they fear that their lifeline is in danger of being cut. Their sense of sadness and loss is profound. A five-year-old enters my office and talks about divorce with the comment "I've come to talk about death." Children grieve over the loss of the family, the loss of the parent who has left home, and the imagined loss of both parents. Their grief may even seem unrelated to the relationship that they had with the parent who left—children cry over parents that they were close to and parents who were distant. 5

Children are profoundly concerned not only for themselves but for the welfare of their parents. It is upsetting to see a parent in tears. A 6 ten-year-old girl says, "Mom thinks no one worries about her. But I do!" Children long intensely for the parent who has left home and worry that he or she might never come back. One seven-year-old was told that his father had moved to Oakland. "Where is Oakland?" wailed the boy. "Is Oakland in Mexico? Where is Mexico?"

7 Children of all ages feel intensely rejected when their parents divorce. When one parent leaves the other, the children interpret the act as including them. "He left Mom. He doesn't care about me." Or "She left Dad. I must not be what she wanted."

8 Children get angry at their parents for violating the unwritten rules of parenthood—parents are supposed to make sacrifices for children, not the other way around. Some keep their anger hidden for years out of fear of upsetting parents or for fear of retribution and punishment; others show it. Little children may have temper tantrums; older children may explode, like the fifteen-year-old girl in our study who put her fist through a wall. Related to the anger is a sense of powerlessness. Children feel that they have no say, no way to influence this major event in their lives. Despite ongoing fantasies that things will magically get better, they cannot prevent divorce, fix it, rescue mom or dad, or rescue the marriage. No one gives priority to their wishes, concerns, and fears.

9 Children feel intense loneliness. It amazes me how little support they get at this time, even from grandparents. Divorce is an acute, painful, long-remembered experience that children must often negotiate with the sense that they are alone in the world. All supports, even their parents, seem to fall away. There may be no one to talk to, nowhere to turn. A child will remember for many years the neighbor down the block who was kind during the divorce. In our study, fewer than 10 percent of the children had any adult speak to them sympathetically as the divorce unfolded.

10 Loyalty conflicts, sometimes flipping from one parent to the other and back again, are a common experience for children of divorce. Many children conceptualize divorce as a fight between two teams, with the more powerful side winning the home turf, and will root for different teams at different times. Even when children are encouraged not to take sides, they often feel that they must. However, when they do take sides to feel more protected, they also feel despair because they are betraying one parent over the other. If they do not take sides, they feel isolated and disloyal to both parents. There is no solution to their dilemma.

11 Many children feel guilty, and some feel that it is their duty to mend the marriage. One seven-year-old believed for five years that she caused her parents' divorce because she failed to deliver a message from one parent to the other. A little boy thought it was his fault because his dog was noisy.

The devastation children feel at divorce is similar to the way they   12
feel when a parent dies suddenly, for each experience disrupts close
family relationships. Each weakens the protection of the family; each
begins with an acute crisis followed by disequilibrium that may last
several years or longer; and each introduces a chain of long-lasting
changes that are not predictable at the outset. But divorce may well be
a more difficult tragedy for the child to master psychologically.

Loss due to death is final; the dead person cannot be retrieved.   13
Only a very young child or someone with a psychotic illness can deny,
for any length of time, the finality of death. Moreover, death always has
an identifiable calendar date and usually a clear cause, no matter how
long and drawn out or unanticipated it might be. The impact of divorce
is different. Finality is not present in the same way as in death, and children logically assume that the divorce can be undone at any time. Divorce is often preceded by several separations, each of which may seem
decisive but turn out not to be final. These can confuse children and
lead them to expect reconciliation, if not immediately, then eventually.
Moreover, divorce is usually a partial loss, and most children tend to
see the departed parent for many years afterward. As a result, children
who experience divorce are more likely to feel a persistent, gnawing
sense that the loss of the intact family is not final; maybe it can be repaired. People who divorce can remarry. People who separate can rejoin. Thus children's capacity to cope with divorce is very much
decreased by the uncertainty of the event itself, by its elusive causes,
and by what children regard and keep alive as its potential reversibil-
ity. Perhaps the most important factor in keeping alive children's hope
for reconciliation is their intense need to think of their parents as mutually affectionate and together.

This feeling can endure for decades. A middle-aged woman whose   14
parents had divorced thirty years earlier sought counseling from a female psychologist on my staff for her periodic depressions. After a
while, she confessed that she was also seeing a male psychologist at another location. Her fervent wish was to bring both psychologists together in one room, to have them hold hands, with her present, so that
they might symbolically restore the intact family that she had lost
when she was five years old. We had a difficult time persuading this intelligent but depressed woman that staging her fantasy would not cure
her depression.

Second chances hold different meanings for parents and for chil-   15
dren. For adults, there is a chance to fall in love, to make a better choice,
and to succeed in another relationship or a second marriage. There is
the chance to achieve new dignity, to undo a mistake, to redefine one's
adulthood, one's goals, and to make use of what was learned during
the first marriage. There is an opportunity for psychological growth
and a chance to be a better parent, with or without a new partner.

16   Children do not perceive divorce as a second chance, and this is part of their suffering. They feel that their childhood has been lost forever. Divorce is a price *they* pay, as forfeiture to their parents' failures, jeopardizing their future lives. But children of divorce do have second chances, in the very futures they are worried about. In the years after divorce, especially in adolescence and later as they enter young adulthood, children have opportunities to negotiate different and better solutions in their own lives and to reinterpret their earlier experiences in light of newfound maturity. They may re-create the kinds of traumatic relationships that they witnessed in their parents' marriage or, as they consciously or unconsciously dredge up past hurts, they may master longstanding fears of repeating their parents' mistakes. They have a chance to choose better and to resolve the unresolved issues of a childhood that included the trauma of divorce. Many children are able to do just this. Sadly, many others fail.

17   I was surprised to discover that the severity of a child's reactions at the time of the parents' divorce does not predict how that child will fare five, ten, and even fifteen years later. All of our programs for children of divorce make the opposite assumption—if we help children acknowledge or recognize their feelings at the time, they'll do better in the years to come. But from what we saw ten and fifteen years later, this is not the case. Some of the most troubled, depressed, and fretful children in our study turned out fine ten years later, while some of the least troubled, seemingly content, and calmest children were in poor shape ten and fifteen years later. *One cannot predict longterm effects of divorce on children from how they react at the outset.* This new finding has important implications for the mental health and legal professions. Much of our energy and effort is focused on the crisis of divorce rather than the long term. But as we talked to our families through the years, we began to think of the postdivorce period as a tapestry made of many threads, with no one thread accounting for all that we saw. As the years went by, we discovered that themes and patterns shifted with each developmental stage. A color that showed little at the outset might later come to dominate the design.

★ Meaning and Understanding

1. What reasons do the writers give for asserting that "the experience of divorce is entirely different for parents and for children"?

2. Why would many people want "to believe that what is good for adults will be good for their children"?

3. Wallerstein and Blakeslee suggest that children rarely expect their parents to divorce, even when divorce is imminent. What reasons do the writers give for this?

4. In paragraph 4, the writer compares the family to a "scaffolding." Do you think this is a legitimate comparison? Why or why not?

5. The writers say that "the devastation children feel at divorce is similar to the way they feel when a parent dies suddenly." What reasons do they give for this observation?

★ Techniques and Strategies

1. The writers present some responses of various children to the divorces of their parents. How do their responses help develop the writers' point?

2. What is the thesis of the selection? Do the writers state it directly? Where?

3. The writers compare the child's experience of death to the child's experience of divorce. How effective is this comparison in helping the writers make their point?

4. Who is the intended audience of this essay? What elements in the essay reveal who this audience is? What purpose is the writer hoping to achieve in this essay?

5. The selection concludes with a metaphor that describes the "postdivorce period as a tapestry of many threads, with no one thread accounting for all that we saw." What point is the writer trying to get across here? How appropriate is this comparison? Explain.

★ Speaking of Values

1. In paragraph 8 the writer refers to the "unwritten rules of parenthood." Do you think there are rules for parenthood? What are they?

2. Marriage is a staple of our social system. And yet it may be that we take the institution for granted. In this age of relative social and sexual freedom, why get married at all, especially when so many marriages end in divorce?

3. If there are "unwritten rules for parenthood," are there also "unwritten rules for childhood"? What might they be?

4. The writer suggests that it is difficult to predict how divorce will affect the subsequent lives of the children involved. What impact could this observation have on the way our society views divorce?

5. Wallerstein and Blakeslee challenge the conventional view that because an unhappy woman often has trouble being a good mother, therefore a happy woman will be a good mother. Do you agree with this challenge? Why or why not?

★ *Values Conversation*

The writers suggest that divorce is often more traumatic for the child than for the adults involved. And yet it is unreasonable to believe that divorce in our society will cease to exist as an option. Form groups and discuss what you think are legitimate reasons for dissolving a marriage in which children are involved and what are not. Remember when you are formulating your criteria to focus on the needs of the children rather than on the parents. Report your findings to the class.

★ *Writing about Values*

1. Do some research on the current divorce laws in your state and write a paper analyzing the criteria for divorce. Do you think the criteria are reasonable? Do they take into account contemporary social standards and beliefs? Are they children oriented or spouse oriented? Both? Neither?

2. Define and analyze the underlying values of a society, like ours, in which divorce is common. After all, the frequency of divorce has risen sharply, and continues at high levels, in our age. What does divorce say about us? About our beliefs and commitments? About our views of family relations?

3. Write an essay describing either the "perfect marriage" or the "perfect divorce." Be sure to provide specific details concerning the roles of each spouse as well as what you think their responsibilities should be. In addition, include the responsibilities, if any, that the children should bear.

Langston Hughes

Mother to Son

Born in Joplin Missouri, Langston Hughes (1902–1967) was a leading poet in the literary movement called the Harlem Renaissance. Like other members of this group, he celebrated African-American culture in his numerous essays, short stories, plays, novels, and poems. In "Mother to Son" Hughes captures a mother's advice to her youngster.

Well, son, I'll tell you:
Life for me ain't been no crystal stair.
It's had tacks in it,
And splinters,
And boards torn up,   5
And places with no carpet on the floor—
Bare.
But all the time
I'se been a-climbin' on,
And reachin' landin's,   10
And turnin' corners,
And sometimes goin' in the dark
Where there ain't been no light.
So, boy, don't you turn back.
Don't you set down on the steps   15
'Cause you finds it kinder hard.
Don't you fall now—
For I'se still goin', honey,
I'se still climbin',
And life for me ain't been no crystal stair.   20

★ *Meaning and Understanding*

1. Who is the person speaking in the poem? To whom is that person speaking?

2. Describe the kind of life that the speaker has lived. What kind of life does she believe her son will live?

3. What is the theme of the poem—the basic point that Hughes is trying to make?

★ Techniques and Strategies

1. What is the basic comparison—here an extended metaphor—underlying the poem? Do you find it effective? Why or why not? What connotations does the phrase "crystal stair" have—especially to someone like the speaker in the poem?

2. What uses of sensory images give this poem its energy and power?

3. Where has Hughes captured with perfect ear the language and diction of one level of African-American experience? Which words and phrases sound particularly credible to you?

4. What is the effect of repeating line 2 as the last line of the poem? Remember that the poem is only twenty lines long.

★ Speaking of Values

1. The mother states through metaphors a variety of tough times in her life. How do you explain her philosophy in light of her life's difficulties? Is she wise, cynical, foolish, a Pollyanna? Explain your point of view.

2. How does the mother feel toward her son? Why do you think she gives him the advice she does? What is the effect of the line, "So, boy, don't you turn back"? What does the line mean?

3. The mother draws on her own life as an example of how her son should behave. How do you think the son might react to this strategy? How do children generally feel about relatives who use their own lives as models of behavior for the young in the family?

4. In what ways does the poem capture a kind of universal exchange between a mother and her child? In what ways is the poem a particularly poignant snapshot of the black experience?

★ Values Conversation

In groups, discuss the family values implicit in this poem. What is the mother's role here? What is the role of the son? Why is the poem not called "Father to Son"? What conclusions can you draw about the African-American family as captured by Hughes in this poem, first published in 1926? What relevance does the poem have to today's families? Do you think that the impact of the poem depends on the racial qualities of the writer and the characters? Why or why not?

★ *Writing about Values*

1. Write an essay in which you explore the family values implied in this poem.

2. Write an essay in which you describe and analyze advice an older person gave to you about life. Did you take the advice? Why or why not?

3. Write an essay—or a poem, if you like—called "Son to Mother" in which you present the son's response to the mother's advice.

Values in Review

1. Several selections in this chapter convey images of the American family and the values inherent in the family structure. Write an essay in which you compare the American family values that emerge from any three pieces in the chapter "Family." Which family values do you find most appropriate for today's society? Why?

2. Mell Lazarus, E. B. White, David Blankenhorn, and Randall Williams offer varying portraits of the American father. What similarities and differences do you note in these portraits? How does the fact that all these writers are males affect their point of view, do you think? Write a definition essay called "The American Father" in which you draw on elements of these essays—as well as your own experiences and observations—to characterize the father in American households.

3. Ruth Gay and Alice Walker portray the mother in the American household from different perspectives. What qualities of the American mother emerge in these two selections? How does the fact that these writers are both female affect their point of view, do you think? Write an essay in which you compare and contrast the portrait of mothers in these pieces—and link that portrait to what you yourself have observed about the mothers you know.

4. Is there such a thing as the "typical American family"? Although many people believe that the typical ("normal" in some observations) family has a loving father and mother at its head, this chapter's selections have presented a wide range of family patterns and relations. Write an essay to explore the elements of family structure that you believe are essential for successful family life today.

Chapter 2
Education

Toni Cade Bambara

The Lesson

Born in New York City, Toni Cade Bambara (1939–1995) had a varied career as a writer, teacher, lecturer, and civil rights activist. Her books include *The Sea Birds Are Still Alive* (1977) and *The Salt Eaters* (1980). In this short story from *Gorilla, My Love* (1972) she shows how a visit to an expensive toy store becomes a lesson in class and economic values.

———— ★ ————

1   Back in the days when everyone was old and stupid or young and foolish and me and Sugar were the only ones just right, this lady moved on our block with nappy hair and proper speech and no makeup. And quite naturally we laughed at her, laughed the way we did at the junk man who went about his business like he was some big-time president and his sorry-ass horse his secretary. And we kinda hated her too, hated the way we did those winos who cluttered up our parks and pissed on our handball walls and stank up our hallways and stairs so you couldn't halfway play hide-and-seek without a goddamn gas mask. Miss Moore was her name. The only woman on the block with no first name. And she was black as hell, cept for her feet, which were fish-white and spooky. And she was always planning these boring-ass things for us to do, us being my cousin, mostly, who lived on the block cause we all moved North the same time and to the same apartment then spread out gradual to breathe. And our parents would yank our heads into some kinda shape and crisp up our clothes so we'd be presentable for travel with Miss Moore, who always looked like she was going to church, though she never did. Which is just one of the things grown-ups talked about when they talked behind her back like a dog. But when she came calling with some sachet she'd sewed up or some gingerbread she'd made or some book, why then they'd all be too embarrassed to turn her down and we'd get handed over all spruced up. She'd been to college and said it was only right that she should take responsibility for the young ones' education, and she not even related by marriage or blood. So they'd go for it. Specially Aunt Gretchen. She was the main gofer in the family. You got some ole dumb shit foolishness you want somebody to go for, you send for Aunt Gretchen. She been screwed into the go-along for so long, it's a blood-deep natural thing with her. Which is how she got saddled with me and Sugar and Junior in the first place while our mothers were in the la-de-da apartment up the block having a good ole time.

So this one day Miss Moore rounds us all up at the mailbox and it's   2
puredee hot and she's knockin herself out about arithmetic. And school
suppose to let up in summer I heard, but she don't never let up. And
the starch in my pinafore scratching the shit outta me and I'm really
hating this nappy-head bitch and her goddamn college degree. I'd
much rather go to the pool or to the show where it's cool. So me and
Sugar leaning on the mailbox being surly, which is a Miss Moore word.
And Flyboy checking out what everybody brought for lunch. And Fat
Butt already wasting his peanut-butter-and-jelly sandwich like the pig
he is. And Junebug punchin on Q.T.'s arm for potato chips. And Rosie
Giraffe shifting from one hip to the other waiting for somebody to step
on her foot or ask her if she from Georgia so she can kick ass, preferably
Mercedes'. And Miss Moore asking us do we know what money is, like
we a bunch of retards. I mean real money, she say, like it's only poker
chips or monopoly papers we lay on the grocer. So right away I'm tired
of this and say so. And would much rather snatch Sugar and go to the
Sunset and terrorize the West Indian kids and take their hair ribbons
and their money too. And Miss Moore files that remark away for next
week's lesson on brotherhood, I can tell. And finally I say we oughta
get to the subway cause it's cooler and besides we might meet some
cute boys. Sugar done swiped her mama's lipstick, so we ready.

So we heading down the street and she's boring us silly about what   3
things cost and what our parents make and how much goes for rent
and how money ain't divided up right in this country. And then she
gets to the part about we all poor and live in the slums, which I don't
feature. And I'm ready to speak on that, but she steps out in the street
and hails two cabs just like that. Then she hustles half the crew in with
her and hands me a five-dollar bill and tells me to calculate 10 percent
tip for the driver. And we're off. Me and Sugar and Junebug and Flyboy hangin out the window and hollering to everybody, putting lipstick on each other cause Flyboy a faggot anyway, and making farts
with our sweaty armpits. But I'm mostly trying to figure how to spend
this money. But they all fascinated with the meter ticking and Junebug
starts laying bets as to how much it'll be when Flyboy can't hold his
breath no more. Then Sugar lays bets as to how much it'll be when we
get there. So I'm stuck. Don't nobody want to go for my plan, which is
to jump out at the next light and run off to the first bar-b-que we can
find. Then the driver tells us to get the hell out cause we there already.
And the meter reads eighty-five cents. And I'm stalling to figure out
the tip and Sugar say give him a dime. And I decide he don't need it
bad as I do, so later for him. But then he tries to take off with Junebug
foot still in the door so we talk about his mama something ferocious.
Then we check out that we on Fifth Avenue and everybody dressed up
in stockings. One lady in a fur coat, hot as it is. White folks crazy.

4   "This is the place," Miss Moore say, presenting it to us in the voice she uses at the museum. "Let's look in the windows before we go in."

5   "Can we steal?" Sugar asks very serious like she's getting the ground rules squared away before she plays. "I beg your pardon," say Miss Moore, and we fall out. So she leads us around the windows of the toy store and me and Sugar screamin, "This is mine, that's mine, I gotta have that, that was made for me, I was born for that," till Big Butt drowns us out.

6   "Hey, I'm going to buy that there."

7   "That there? You don't even know what that is, stupid."

8   "I do so," he say punchin on Rosie Giraffe. "It's a microscope."

9   "Whatcha gonna do with a microscope, fool?"

10   "Look at things."

11   "Like what, Ronald?" asks Miss Moore. And Big Butt ain't got the first notion. So here go Miss Moore gabbing about the thousands of bacteria in a drop of water and the somethinorother in a speck of blood and the million and one living things in the air around us is invisible to the naked eye. And what she say that for? Junebug go to town on that "naked" and we rolling. Then Miss Moore ask what it cost. So we all jam into the window smudgin it up and the price tag say $300. So then she asks how long'd take for Big Butt and Junebug to save up their allowances. "Too long," I say. "Yeh," adds Sugar, "outgrown it by that time." And Miss Moore say no, you never outgrow learning instruments. "Why, even medical students and interns and," blah, blah, blah. And we ready to choke Big Butt for bringing it up in the first damn place.

12   "This here costs four hundred eighty dollars," say Rosie Giraffe. So we pile up all over her to see what she pointin out. My eyes tell me it's a chink of glass cracked with something heavy, and different-color inks dripped into the splits, then the whole thing put into a oven or something. But the $480 it don't make sense.

13   "That's a paperweight made of semi-precious stones fused together under tremendous pressure," she explains slowly, with her hands doing the mining and all the factory work.

14   "So what's a paperweight?" asks Rosie Giraffe.

15   "To weigh paper with, dumbell," say Flyboy, the wise man from the East.

16   "Not exactly," say Miss Moore, which is what she say when you warm or way off too. "It's to weigh paper down so it won't scatter and make your desk untidy." So right away me and Sugar curtsy to each other and then to Mercedes who is more the tidy type.

17   "We don't keep paper on top of the desk in my class," say Junebug, figuring Miss Moore crazy or lyin one.

18   "At home, then," she say. "Don't you have a calendar and a pencil case and a blotter and a letter-opener on your desk at home where you do your homework?" And she know damn well what our homes look like cause she nosys around in them every chance she gets.

"I don't even have a desk," say Junebug. "Do we?"   19

"No. And I don't get no homework neither," say Big Butt.   20

"And I don't even have a home," say Flyboy like he do at school to   21
keep the white folks off his back and sorry for him. Send this poor kid
to camp posters, is his specialty.

"I do," says Mercedes, "I have a box of stationery on my desk and   22
a picture of my cat. My godmother bought the stationery and the desk.
There's a big rose on each sheet and the envelopes smell like roses."

"Who wants to know about your smelly-ass stationery," say Rosie   23
Giraffe fore I can get my two cents in.

"It's important to have a work area all your own so that...."   24

"Will you look at this sailboat, please," say Flyboy, cuttin her off   25
and pointin to the thing like it was his. So once again we tumble all
over each other to gaze at this magnificent thing in the toy store which
is just big enough to maybe sail two kittens across the pond if you strap
them to the posts tight. We all start reciting the price tag like we in assembly. "Handcrafted sailboat of fiberglass at one thousand one hundred ninety-five dollars."

"Unbelievable," I hear myself say and am really stunned. I read it   26
again for myself just in case the group recitation put me in a trance.
Same thing. For some reason this pisses me off. We look at Miss Moore
and she lookin at us, waitin for I dunno what.

Who'd pay all that when you can buy a sailboat set for a quarter at   27
Pop's, a tube of blue for a dime, and a ball of string for eight cents? "It
must have a motor and a whole lot else besides," I say. "My sailboat
cost be about fifty cents."

"But will it take water?" say Mercedes with her smart ass.   28

"Took mine to Alley Pond Park once," says Flyboy. "String broke.   29
Lost it. Pity."

"Sailed mine in Central Park and it keeled over and sank. Had to   30
ask my father for another dollar."

"And you got the strap," laugh Big Butt. "The jerk didn't even have   31
a string on it. My old man wailed on his behind."

Little Q.T. was staring hard at the sailboat and you could see he   32
wanted it bad. But he was too little and somebody'd just take it from
him. So what the hell. "This boat for kids, Miss Moore?"

"Parents silly to buy something like that just to get all broke up,"   33
say Rosie Giraffe.

"That much money it should last forever," I figure.   34

"My father'd buy it for me if I wanted it."   35

"Your father, my ass," say Rosie Giraffe getting a chance to finally   36
push Mercedes.

"Must be rich people shop here," say Q.T.   37

"You are a very bright boy," say Flyboy. "What was your first   38
clue?" And he rap him on the head with the back of his knuckles,
since Q.T. the only one he could get away with. Though Q.T. liable to

come up behind you years later and get his licks in when you half expect it.

39   "What I want to know," I says to Miss Moore though I never talk to her, I wouldn't give the bitch that satisfaction, "is how much a real boat costs? I figure a thousand'd get you a yacht any day."

40   "Why don't you check that out," she says, "and report back to the group?" Which really pains my ass. If you gonna mess up a perfectly good swim day least you could do is have some answers."Let's go in," she say like she got something up her sleeve. Only she don't lead the way. So me and Sugar turn the corner to where the entrance is, but when we get there I kinda hang back. Not that I'm scared, what's there to be afraid of, just a toy store. But I feel funny, shame. But what I got to be shamed about? Got as much right to go in as anybody. But somehow I can't seem to get hold of the door, so I step away for Sugar to lead. But she hangs back too. And I look at her and she looks at me and this is ridiculous. I mean, damn, I have never ever been shy about doing nothing or going nowhere. But then Mercedes steps up and then Rosie Giraffe and Big Butt crowd in behind and shove, and next thing we all stuffed into the doorway with only Mercedes squeezing past us, smoothing out her jumper and walking right down the aisle. Then the rest of us tumble in like a glued-together jigsaw done all wrong. And people lookin at us. And it's like the time me and Sugar crashed into the Catholic church on a dare. But once we got in there and everything so hushed and holy and the candles and the bowin and the handkerchiefs on all the drooping heads, I just couldn't go through with the plan. Which was for me to run up to the altar and do a tap dance while Sugar played the nose flute and messed around in the holy water. And Sugar kept givin me the elbow. Then later teased me so bad I tied her up in the shower and turned it on and locked her in. And she'd be there till this day if Aunt Gretchen hadn't finally figured I was lyin about the boarder takin a shower.

41   Same thing in the store. We all walkin on tiptoe and hardly touchin the games and puzzles and things. And I watched Miss Moore who is steady watchin us like she is waitin for a sign. Like Mama Drewery watches the sky and sniffs the air and takes note of how much slant is in the bird formation. Then me and Sugar bump smack into each other, so busy gazing at the toys, 'specially the sailboat. But we don't laugh and go into our fat-lady bump-stomach routine. We just stare at that price tag. Then Sugar run a finger over the whole boat. And I'm jealous and want to hit her. Maybe not her, but I sure want to punch somebody in the mouth.

42   "Watcha bring us here for, Miss Moore?"

43   "You sound angry, Sylvia. Are you mad about something?" Givin me one of those grins like she tellin a grown-up joke that never turns out to be funny. And she's lookin very closely at me like maybe she plannin to do my portrait from memory. I'm mad, but I won't give her that satisfaction. So I slouch around the store bein very bored and say, "Let's go."

Me and Sugar at the back of the train watchin the tracks whizzin by   44
large then small then gettin gobbled up in the dark. I'm thinkin about
this tricky toy I saw in the store. A clown that somersaults on a bar then
does chin-ups just cause you yank lightly at his leg. Cost $35. I could see
me askin my mother for a $35 birthday clown. "You wanna who that
costs what?" she'd say, cocking her head to the side to get a better view
of the hole in my head. Thirty-five dollars could buy new bunk beds for
Junior and Gretchen's boy. Thirty-five dollars and the whole household
could visit Grandaddy Nelson in the country. Thirty-five dollars would
pay for the rent and the piano bill too. Who are these people that spend
that much money for performing clowns and $1,000 for toy sailboats?
What kinda work they do and how they live and how come we ain't on
it? Where we are is who we are, Miss Moore always pointin out. But it
doesn't necessarily have to be that way, she always adds then waits for
somebody to say that poor people have to wake up and demand their
share of the pie and don't none of us know what kind of pie she talkin
about in the first damn place. But she ain't so smart cause I still got her
four dollars from the taxi and she sure ain't gettin it. Messin up my day
with this shit. Sugar nudges me in my pocket and winks.

Miss Moore lines us up in the front of the mailbox where we   45
started from, seem like years ago, and I got a headache for thinkin so
hard. And we lean all over each other so we can hold up under the
draggy-ass lecture she always finishes us off with at the end before we
thank her for borin us to tears. But she just looks at us like she readin
tea leaves. Finally she say, "Well, what did you think of F.A.O.
Schwartz?"

Rosie Giraffe mumbles, "White folks crazy."   46

"I'd like to go there again when I get my birthday money," says   47
Mercedes, and we shove her out the pack so she has to lean on the mailbox by herself.

"I'd like a shower. Tiring day," says Flyboy.   48

Then Sugar surprises me by sayin, "You know, Miss Moore, I don't   49
think all of us here put together eat in a year what that sailboat costs."
And Miss Moore lights up like somebody goosed her. "And?" she say,
urging Sugar on. Only I'm standin on her foot so she don't continue.

"Imagine for a minute what kind of society it is in which some peo-   50
ple spend on a toy what it would cost to feed a family of six or seven.
What do you think?"

"I think," say Sugar pushing me off her feet like she never done be-   51
fore, cause I whip her ass in a minute, "that this is not much of a democracy if you ask me. Equal chance to pursue happiness means an equal
crack at the dough, don't it?" Miss Moore is beside herself and I am disgusted with Sugar's treachery. So I stand on her foot one more time to see
if she'll shove me. She shuts up, and Miss Moore looks at me, sorrow-
fully I'm thinkin. And somethin weird is goin on, I can feel it in my chest.

52   "Anybody else learn anything today?" lookin dead at me. I walk
away and Sugar has to run to catch up and don't even seem to notice
when I shrug her arm off my shoulder.

53   "Well, we got four dollars anyway," she says.

54   "Uh hunh."

55   "We could go to Hascombs and get half a chocolate layer and then
go to the Sunset and still have plenty money for potato chips and ice-
cream sodas."

56   "Uh hunh."

57   "Race you to Hanscombs," she say.

58   We start down the block and she gets ahead which is O.K. by me
cause I'm going to the West End and then over to the Drive to think this
day through. She can run if she want to and even run faster. But ain't
nobody gonna beat me at nuthin.

★ Meaning and Understanding

1. The speaker, Sylvia, begins the story by remarking that it takes place
back "when everyone was old and stupid or young and foolish." What
does she mean? When does the story take place? What does she mean
by saying "me and Sugar were the only ones just right"?

2. Why does Miss Moore "educate" the children?

3. What is the "lesson" referred to in the title? Where is it most clearly
articulated?

4. At the end of paragraph 3 Sylvia, after watching the people on Fifth
Avenue, concludes, "White folks crazy." What makes her think this?
What is the tone of her statement? Explain.

5. In paragraph 40 the speaker is reluctant to enter the toy store and remarks that she feels "funny, shame." Why does she feel this way?

6. How does the speaker really feel about Miss Moore? How do you
know?

★ Techniques and Strategies

1. Who is the intended audience for this story? How do you know?

2. How does the use of language—the rhythms of speech, the street
slang, the unique comparisons—contribute to the story? Make a list of
unique turns of phrase, paying particular attention to the metaphors
and similes Bambara puts in the mouth of her narrator. How does the
language throughout help reveal Sylvia's character?

3. What does the opening line of the story tell you about the speaker's attitude at the time the story takes place and at the time the story was written?

4. In paragraph 2 the speaker identifies the word "surly" as a "Miss Moore word." What does she mean by this? Can you identify other "Miss Moore words" in the story?

5. How does Bambara introduce the other children in the story? What does this tell us about them?

6. What was Miss Moore's reason for taking the children to the toy store? Where else do you think she had taken them before?

7. In paragraphs 29 and 30 the children name two parks—Alley Pond and Central. Where are these parks? Why does the writer mention them here?

8. A shift occurs in paragraph 12 when the discussion turns to the paperweight. What is the nature of this shift and what is its effect?

★ Speaking of Values

1. What is the neighborhood in the story like? Define some of the community's values. How do you know what these values are?

2. Why does Miss Moore take responsibility for teaching the children? What do you think of her as a teacher? As a person?

3. Why does the price of the sailboat anger the speaker? In that same paragraph (26), what is Miss Moore waiting for?

4. In paragraph 39, why does Sylvia, in spite of her stated feelings about speaking to Miss Moore, ask Miss Moore a question anyway?

5. Miss Moore often says "Where we are is who we are" (paragraph 44). What do you understand this to mean? Do you agree with her? Why or why not?

6. When Sugar makes her assertion about democracy in paragraph 51, the speaker is "disgusted with Sugar's treachery." What is treacherous about Sugar's act and why is the speaker so upset?

7. When Miss Moore asks, "Anybody else learn anything today?" she looks straight at Sylvia—who simply walks away. What is this little dance all about? What does it suggest about the reach of the participants?

8. One of the key issues of this story is class values, particularly the economic gap between the rich and the poor and the way economics

shapes what each group sees as the worth of objects and possessions. How does Bambara explore the issue without lecturing to her readers?

★ *Values Conversation*

Miss Moore says (paragraph 50), "Imagine for a minute what kind of society it is in which some people can spend on a toy what it would cost to feed a family of six or seven. What do you think?" Form groups and answer the question she raises. What consensus do you come to about the economic realities of a democracy as we live it? Are economic gaps between the classes inevitable? Why do you think so? What corrective measures does your group propose—if you think correction desirable?

★ *Writing about Values*

1. Try to recall a neighborhood character who taught you something when you were growing up. Write an essay describing this person and what you might have learned from him or her.

2. Many of us can pinpoint a moment in our lives when we discovered an important truth about life. Write a paper explaining one of these moments from your own life. Be sure to indicate why the event was significant as well as what you actually learned from it.

3. Read another story about learning—Henry James' "The Pupil" or James Joyce's "Araby," for example. Then write a paper comparing and contrasting it to Bambara's "The Lesson."

Robert Coles

A Lesson from History: On Courage

Born in 1929 in Boston, Robert Coles is a well-known psychiatrist and teacher who has spent much of his life illuminating the inner life of children. He was awarded the Pulitzer Prize for his series *Children in Crisis* (1967) and was the recipient of a MacArthur Foundation fellowship in 1981. In this selection from *The Moral Intelligence of Children* (1997), Coles presents his observations on a history lesson he taught to fourth graders.

———— ★ ————

I sit at a desk in a fourth-grade classroom where I am a volunteer teacher and feel the constant curiosity of the children, their evident desire to stretch the boundaries of both knowing and feeling. I ask them to take up our history book so that we can learn together about the founding and exploration of America and, later, the revolutionary war that established our nation's sovereignty. I am anxious that they know facts, dates, the names of the ships, the places where navigators first came ashore. I am anxious that we look at maps, try to know which land was occupied by which nation. I want us to talk about battles, wars, kings and queens who commissioned expeditions. I hope we'll learn as well about the *reasons* various people wanted to come here: their religious convictions; their lives as outcasts, even prisoners, in this or that European country; and of course their desire to start a new life, to strike it rich. Some of the children pay close attention; some of them pretend to do so; some are plainly indifferent or bored. I want to unite them in passionate interest, and so I resort to stories, show pictures, use maps. Suddenly a girl does my work for me with this question: "In those boats [that brought the first settlers here], do you think the people were happy to be there?"

I hadn't really thought about that matter—not ever, or not, certainly, in such a way. I'd thought of *why* the Pilgrims and Puritans, the Quakers and Catholics, had come to these shores, and of course, I knew that the journey was hard and long, that some died en route—but I hadn't tried to put myself in the *minds* of those men, women, and children, as this girl was asking us to do. Telling myself I was being coy, or reacting in the all too predictable manner of my psychiatric kind, I

1

2

reflected the question back to the girl and her classmates: "What do you all think?"

3   Silence greeted all of us, and I got myself ready to ask again in a differently phrased way, or to speculate out loud and myself give an answer—probably say that I didn't think those folks back then thought about happiness so much as other aspects of existence: the right and the wrong. Just as that line of thinking crossed my mind, the girl who had asked the question decided to clarify her intent and, so doing, unwittingly confronted me with my (until then) unwitting condescension: "I was wondering if the Pilgrims, once they were aboard the ships, and once they were out to sea, if they thought to themselves: we did the best thing, we made the right decision."

4   Now the class caught fire—they had all been stymied by that word "happy" as I had been! One girl said *yes*, emphatically, and then explained: "When you do something you know is right to do, you feel glad that you made the right choice, and you're going to be happy, even if the result is a lot of pain and trouble. My mom says, the worst thing, it's when you do something, and you know it's wrong, but you go ahead anyway." A boy across the aisle agrees by nodding as she talks, then picks up after she's stopped, as if he were her alter ego: "You feel worse, even though you've probably made your decision, thinking it would make you feel better! You know what my dad says? He says, 'The easiest way out can end up being the hardest, and vice versa'— you can make a tough choice and then you're so glad, real glad you did it!"

5   Across the room, another voice offered another angle of vision: "The way I look at it, those people were probably scared, real scared. I don't see them sitting there and being happy that they did the right thing. I see them being afraid that they made a mistake, and look what happened: they were going 'nowhere,' you could say! They left this life they had, and they didn't know what to expect, and they were out there on the ocean, and the trip would take forever—we forget how long it took—but even so, they'd made the decision, and they weren't going to turn back: no way. So, they worried, but they knew what they did, and why they did it, and they were 'happy' that way: they'd *decided*."

6   More silence, and I think we've exhausted this subject. I prepare to be the formal teacher and get into details of seventeenth-century American history—but another boy's hand has gone up and I nod to him, and he speaks: "I don't think they thought one way or the other about the rough trip, or the troubles they could have when the ship pulled into some harbor. I think they'd done what they knew they had to do—they were courageous. In Europe, no one complimented them—people criticized them for what they believed. But they knew what they should do; they had this idea of how to worship God, and they weren't going to surrender to other people, their idea of how you should [worship

God]." He stops, and I decide to speak, though as I do I realize he may well have more to say, that I may be interrupting a train of thought: "That's your definition of courage—doing what you have to do?" He is quick to reply: "Courage is when you believe in something, you really do, so you go ahead and try to do what your beliefs tell you [to do], and if you're in danger, that way—well, you're not thinking 'I'm in danger.' You're thinking, this is right, this is important, and I'm going to go ahead, and that is that."

Now there is a flurry of hands raised, not to get permission to spec-   7
ulate on the emotions or beliefs of the Pilgrims and Puritans but to talk about courage, how one behaves in response to one's beliefs or values. These nine-year-old boys and girls are all fired up, ready to declaim, re- ally, about what matters and how a person ought to prove a loyalty to what for him or her does matter. "If you believe something," another boy says, "but you won't risk anything—nothing!—for what you be- lieve, then do you really believe in what you're saying [you do]? I don't think so! I think it's a lot of talk, then; but it's not believing—the person isn't believing." A girl in front of him shakes her head as she talks, and she waves her hand urgently: "It's not fair, to say you have to cross the ocean and you could die in the boat, or when you get there—to prove you're really believing something! I mean, you could believe in some- thing, but that doesn't mean you have to jump over some rope to prove you do. The proof: it's for you to decide, what you'll do to show your belief is—is true. Maybe you don't have to do anything, or show any- one anything. Why should you have to prove yourself by *doing* some- thing? Why not just have your belief, and it's your business, and no one else's?"

Much more discussion as the children attempt to clarify their sense   8
of what a belief is, and how or whether it has truly taken hold in a given life. Another girl defends the boy who spoke of courage as connected to action and brings us back to the Pilgrims by saying this: "Look, it's not whether you do something. It's that those Pilgrims said it meant the whole world to them that they practice their religion the way they wanted to— and if they'd given up on that, wouldn't it mean that they weren't so into their faith? Wouldn't it? With us, here, you can have your ideas, your beliefs, and they're *yours*, so you don't have to prove yourself to anyone. You just have your ideas. But those Pilgrims had to prove themselves to God! I'm not saying you have to go *do* something, if you're going to have beliefs. I guess it depends on what the beliefs are. If the beliefs are—if you have to do something because of the be- liefs, and you don't do it, because you're scared, so you don't practice your religion the way you believe you should, then I think you are not really living up to your beliefs. If you do live up to them, and you have to face a lot of trouble, then you're courageous, that's how you are. I

don't think you believe in courage; I think you become courageous, you act courageous, because you really do believe something, and it's not just a lot of talk; you're not pretending, fooling yourself and other people, too."

9   I am enormously impressed. I glance at my tape recorder to see if the telltale light is on, a sign that I really want what I've just heard to be on the record; a sign, too, that I am so in awe of what I've heard that without that voice on tape I wonder whether I'll be scratching my head in incredulity! An elementary school child shows a capacity for probing moral analysis that encompasses the very nature of a belief, a value as it connects to a lived life. In this case, the value is courage, the capacity to put oneself on the line willingly, with apparent carelessness (no matter what takes place deep within oneself) on behalf of what one believes, what one wants to protect or ensure as possible for oneself and for others. The point, we have been told, is not the establishment of a kind of means test for courage, a rating system; the point is to understand what the issue is for each person—what sets of beliefs or values are at stake, and thus, how a person's courage might be manifested. The Pilgrims, we all agreed, had made their particular daily, weekly, religious practices the heart and soul of their lives, so to cross the ocean in pursuit of such a possibility took courage, that is, a full commitment to a set of ideals, of desired practices as an expression of those ideals. Courage, we were learning, may be defined as a determination, no matter the obstacles or dangers, to live up to one's values rather than a capacity *per se* to face danger with apparent self-assurance. In other words, that girl, and with her the entire class, was intent on going beyond—beneath—the demonstration of a kind of behavior to approach the sources of its inspiration, at least *some* sources.

10   We had not yet gotten into a realm of psychology that would entail discussion of behavior connected to, say, foolhardiness or vengefulness prompted by outrage or loss, states of mind that can prompt what can certainly come across as courageous behavior. When I did ask the class, in a good-bye to the discussion (the clock was running out) what other beliefs or values might prompt courage such as we'd been discussing, a chorus of suggestions, interestingly, descended on us—children speaking out directly, rather than raising their hands, politely waiting their turn: love of parents for children and children for parents came up in various forms of expression, as did love of country, loyalty to friends. These children had in effect declared their conviction that ties to family, friends, and country matter; that such bonds can or ought to or do command enough loyalty to enable the appearance of courage under various sets of circumstances. Put differently, courage became for this class a virtue that is prompted by other virtues—quite a contemplative exercise for all of us to have experienced!

I mention the above to indicate what young school-age children are   11
able to muster collectively and individually in the way of moral reflection—not that we puffed ourselves up by attaching such a phrase to an
informal and unexpectedly vigorous, and rewarding free-for-all. In that
regard, we did well to stumble along, to let the casual, unpredictable
rhythm of a classroom discussion rule the day. My hunch is that if I had
asked more formally for an examination of courage, its antecedents, its
sources in life, in the lives of one or another group of people, the children might have appeased my didacticism, but might also have been
far less forthcoming in their approach to this historical moment, one to
which they managed to find such a personal connection. So many
younger schoolchildren are eager to embrace the imaginary—indeed,
their minds are often afire with it. Given a choice, they will leap into
one or another scenario, be it historical or contemporary, factual or fictional, and bring to it their very own moral or intellectual assumptions.
Teachers have to control and regulate that tendency—help the children
distinguish between themselves (as readers, as discussants) and the
topic at hand. But such distinctions too strongly emphasized or enforced can stifle the willingness of boys and girls in a class to immerse
themselves in, say, the life of seventeenth-century London from which
the Pilgrims were embarking, and their willingness as well to think
personally, confessionally—to level with themselves and others with
respect to their own experiences as they give shape to a particular sense
of what others once did, and why.

All the time, during these first school years, one hopes children are   12
learning what is requested of them, how they must behave, what they
must do, and one hopes, accordingly, that they come to school having
already learned at home what is desirable, what is impermissible, what
is utterly beyond the pale, and why. Under such circumstances, they are
more interested in matters of right and wrong, virtue and vice, than we
sometimes might acknowledge, either as parents or as teachers. They
ache sometimes for a chance to sort out all of that, the mandates and
warnings, the applause and the chastisement they have at various moments received. Moreover, what they have heard read to them, what
they have learned to read, both at home and at school, has only encouraged them to wonder even more about ethical issues. Cinderella, Robin
Hood, David and Goliath, Jack (of the Beanstalk), Goldilocks, the Pied
Piper of Hamelin, Little Red Riding Hood, and those dogs and bunny
rabbits, cats and chickens and frogs whom, anthropomorphically, various storytellers have handed over to young listeners and readers—all of
them struggle for the good, contend with the bad, amid their adventures, the times of danger and peril that confront them. Moreover, parents, especially, make up their own stories to tell children, usually as they
put them to bed, and in so doing commonly draw on family traditions

and anecdotes, with no small resort to a cautionary lesson here, a saga of moral triumph there.

13   All of those times, in a bedroom or dining room or living room or kitchen, in a classroom, out in the playground, are often moral moments, however unacknowledged: opportunities for us adults to make yet again this or that point about how things go in the world, how they might go, how they should go. It is similar with history's moments, as demonstrated above. To offer another example from my classroom teaching (as a parent, I experienced a comparable experience), I still remember how the simple fact that Presidents Abraham Lincoln and John F. Kennedy were assassinated got to my class, to my own children. Both of these American leaders stand for so very much, the former as the one who took on the institution of slavery, the latter as a very young and explicitly hopeful, idealistic president who initiated the Peace Corps and gave national voice yet again to the pain of this nation's more vulnerable people. *Why*, so many children ask, were those two men cut down at the height of their power and influence? What is one to make of such tragedies? For that matter, what is one to think of the assassins, John Wilkes Booth and Lee Harvey Oswald, who almost exactly a century apart did similar deeds: a gun aimed, fired at a president? Here historical fatefulness can become a highly charged drama that deeply engages a child's developing moral sensibility. Here, a parent or a teacher, calling upon his or her own moral interests and, yes, sense of the dramatic can help a child or a group of children think about their own moral situation as they try to understand that of another, a president, an assassin.

★ *Meaning and Understanding*

1. In the first paragraph Coles suggests that he can feel the children's "evident desire to stretch the boundaries of both knowing and feeling." In what way is their desire "evident"? Or do you think he simply assumes this? Explain.

2. In the same paragraph he reminds us that he is "anxious that they know facts, dates, the names of the ships." What is the reason for his anxiety?

3. How will telling stories, and showing pictures and maps "unite [the class] in passionate interest" (paragraph 1)?

4. What is the definition of courage arrived at by one of the boys in the class? Do you agree with it? Why or why not?

5. In paragraph 11, Coles refers to "moral moments." What does he mean by this? What role does he see for parents and other adults in explaining these moments?

★ Techniques and Strategies

1. Coles writes largely in the present tense. Why has he chosen this strategy for his narrative?

2. Do these children speak like any fourth graders you are acquainted with? Are you surprised by the level of their discourse? Is Coles? How does he account for it? How do you?

3. Why does Coles make a point to tell us about his tape recorder? (paragraph 9). How does doing so affect the credibility of his claims?

4. Look at the first sentence of each paragraph in the essay. In what way are they similar? Why do you think Coles uses these kinds of sentences?

5. Where does the writer come closest to stating the thesis of the essay? In what ways is the closing paragraph a fitting conclusion to the selection? How does it relate to the introduction and thesis?

6. Who is the intended audience for this selection? What in the selection leads you to think so?

★ Speaking of Values

1. What philosophy of education does Coles imply in this essay?

2. Why hadn't the author tried to put himself "in the *minds* of those men, women, and children, as this girl was asking us to do" (paragraph 2)? What point is he trying to make here?

3. Coles seems surprised that an elementary school child can show "a capacity for probing moral analysis." Why is he surprised? Are you? How is this observation connected to the main point of the selection?

4. Coles observes in paragraph 12 that children "are more interested in matters of right and wrong, virtue and vice, than we sometimes might acknowledge." Do you agree? Why or why not?

5. What connection does Coles make between a parent's "moral interests" and the capacity of children to "think about their own moral situation" (paragraph 13)?

★ Values Conversation

Form groups and choose a particular historical event familiar to each member of the group. For instance, you might select the crucifixion of Christ, the signing of the Declaration of Independence, the landing of the pilgrims at Plymouth Rock, the stock market crash of 1929, or the first human landing on the moon. Then try to get inside the *minds* of the people involved.

Think about just who would have been involved and what questions you would need to ask to get inside their minds.

★ *Writing about Values*

1. Try to recall a class you have had in which you felt the kind of intellectual excitement that Coles discusses in this selection. Then write a paper describing the class and identifying the reasons why it was exciting.

2. Write your own definition of courage and explain how you might teach the concept to a young child.

3. Choose a single historical figure—Joan of Arc, Thomas Jefferson, Martin Luther King, Charles Lindbergh, Indira Gandhi, for example—and do library research about that person's life. Then write a paper describing what you think might have been in that person's mind at a particularly significant moment in his or her life. Be sure to make clear the connection between what you know about the person's life and the conclusions you are drawing.

Mike Rose

"I Just Wanna Be Average"

Born in 1944, Mike Rose, a writer and teacher, has won awards from the National Academy of Education, the National Council of Teachers of English, and the John Simon Guggenheim Memorial Foundation. In the following essay from his *Lives on the Boundary* (1989), he shares impressions of his secondary school education in South Los Angeles. Rose has also authored *Possible Lives: The Promise of Public Education in America* (1995).

———— ★ ————

It took two buses to get to Our Lady of Mercy. The first started deep in   1
South Los Angeles and caught me at midpoint. The second drifted through neighborhoods with trees, parks, big lawns, and lots of flowers. The rides were long but were livened up by a group of South L.A. veterans whose parents also thought that Hope had set up shop in the west end of the county. There was Christy Biggars, who, at sixteen, was dealing and was, according to rumor, a pimp as well. There were Bill Cobb and Johnny Gonzales, grease-pencil artists extraordinaire, who left Nembutal-enhanced swirls of "Cobb" and "Johnny" on the corrugated walls of the bus. And then there was Tyrrell Wilson. Tyrrell was the coolest kid I knew. He ran the dozens[1] like a metric halfback, laid down a rap that outrhymed and outpointed Cobb, whose rap was good but not great—the curse of a moderately soulful kid trapped in white skin. But it was Cobb who would sneak a radio onto the bus, and thus underwrote his patter with Little Richard, Fats Domino, Chuck Berry, the Coasters,[2] and Ernie K. Doe's mother-in-law, an awful woman who was "sent from down below." And so it was that Christy and Cobb and Johnny G. and Tyrrell and I and assorted others picked up along the way passed our days in the back of the bus, a funny mix brought together by geography and parental desire.

Entrance to school brings with it forms and releases and assess-   2
ments. Mercy relied on a series of tests, mostly the Stanford-Binet, for placement, and somehow the results of my tests got confused with those of another student named Rose. The other Rose apparently didn't do very well, for I was placed in the vocational track, a euphemism for the bottom level. Neither I nor my parents realized what this meant.

[1]*Dozens* is a game in which youngsters try to beat each other's verbal insults.
[2]These were well-known black performers and musicians of the 1950s.

We had no sense that Business Math, Typing, and English-Level D were dead ends. The current spate of reports on the schools criticizes parents for not involving themselves in the education of their children. But how would someone like Tommy Rose, with his two years of Italian schooling, know what to ask? And what sort of pressure could an exhausted waitress apply? The error went undetected, and I remained in the vocational track for two years. What a place.

3   My homeroom was supervised by Brother Dill, a troubled and unstable man who also taught freshman English. When his class drifted away from him, which was often, his voice would rise in paranoid accusations, and occasionally he would lose control and shake or smack us. I hadn't been there two months when one of his brisk, face-turning slaps had my glasses sliding down the aisle. Physical education was also pretty harsh. Our teacher was a stubby ex-lineman who had played old-time pro ball in the Midwest. He routinely had us grabbing our ankles to receive his stinging paddle across our butts. He did that, he said, to make men of us. "Rose," he bellowed on our first encounter; me standing geeky in line in my baggy shorts. "'Rose'? What the hell kind of name is that?"

4   "Italian, sir," I squeaked.

5   "Italian! Ho. Rose, do you know the sound a bag of shit makes when it hits the wall?"

6   "No, sir."

7   "Wop!"

8   Sophomore English was taught by Mr. Mitropetros. He was a large, bejeweled man who managed the parking lot at the Shrine Auditorium. He would crow and preen and list for us the stars he'd brushed against. We'd ask questions and glance knowingly and snicker, and all that fueled the poor guy to brag some more. Parking cars was his night job. He had little training in English, so his lesson plan for his day work had us reading the district's required text, *Julius Caesar,* aloud for the semester. We'd finish the play way before the twenty weeks was up, so he'd have us switch parts again and again and start again: Dave Snyder, the fastest guy at Mercy, muscling through Caesar to the breathless squeals of Calpurnia, as interpreted by Steve Fusco, a surfer who owned the school's most envied paneled wagon. Week ten and Dave and Steve would take on new roles, as would we all, and render a water-logged Cassius and a Brutus that are beyond my powers of description.

9   Spanish I—taken in the second year—fell into the hands of a new recruit. Mr. Montez was a tiny man, slight, five foot six at the most, soft-spoken and delicate. Spanish was a particularly rowdy class, and Mr. Montez was as prepared for it as a doily maker at a hammer throw. He would tap his pencil to a room in which Steve Fusco was propelling spitballs from his heavy lips, in which Mike Dweetz was taunting Billy Hawk, a half-Indian, half-Spanish, reed-thin, quietly explosive boy.

The vocational track at Our Lady of Mercy mixed kids traveling in from South L.A. with South Bay surfers and a few Slavs and Chicanos from the harbors of San Pedro. This was a dangerous miscellany: surfers and hodads and South-Central blacks all ablaze to the metronomic tapping of Hector Montez's pencil.

One day Billy lost it. Out of the corner of my eye I saw him strike out with his right arm and catch Dweetz across the neck. Quick as a spasm, Dweetz was out of his seat, scattering desks, cracking Billy on the side of the head, right behind the eye. Snyder and Fusco and others broke it up, but the room felt hot and close and naked. Mr. Montez's tenuous authority was finally ripped to shreds, and I think everyone felt a little strange about that. The charade was over, and when it came down to it, I don't think any of the kids really wanted it to end this way. They had pushed and pushed and bullied their way into a freedom that both scared and embarrassed them.

Students will float to the mark you set. I and the others in the vocational classes were bobbing in pretty shallow water. Vocational education has aimed at increasing the economic opportunities of students who do not do well in our schools. Some serious programs succeed in doing that, and through exceptional teachers—like Mr. Gross in *Horace's Compromise*[3]—students learn to develop hypotheses and troubleshoot, reason through a problem, and communicate effectively—the true job skills. The vocational track, however, is most often a place for those who are just not making it, a dumping ground for the disaffected. There were a few teachers who worked hard at education; young Brother Slattery, for example, combined a stern voice with weekly quizzes to try to pass along to us a skeletal outline of world history. But mostly the teachers had no idea of how to engage the imaginations of us kids who were scuttling along at the bottom of the pond.

And the teachers would have needed some inventiveness, for none of us was groomed for the classroom. It wasn't just that I didn't know things—didn't know how to simplify algebraic fractions, couldn't identify different kinds of clauses, bungled Spanish translations—but that I had developed various faulty and inadequate ways of doing algebra and making sense of Spanish. Worse yet, the years of defensive tuning out in elementary school had given me a way to escape quickly while seeming at least half alert. During my time in Voc. Ed., I developed further into a mediocre student and a somnambulant problem solver, and that affected the subjects I did have the wherewithal to handle: I detested Shakespeare; I got bored with history. My attention flitted here and there. I fooled around in class and read my books indifferently—the intellectual equivalent of playing with your food. I did what I had to do to get by, and I did it with half a mind.

10

11

12

---

[3]A book by Theodore Sizer about education in America.

13   But I did learn things about people and eventually came into my own socially. I liked the guys in Voc. Ed. Growing up where I did, I understood and admired physical prowess, and there was an abundance of muscle here. There was Dave Snyder, a sprinter and halfback of true quality. Dave's ability and his quick wit gave him a natural appeal, and he was welcome in any clique, though he always kept a little independent. He enjoyed acting the fool and could care less about studies, but he possessed a certain maturity and never caused the faculty much trouble. It was a testament to his independence that he included me among his friends—I eventually went out for track, but I was no jock. Owing to the Latin alphabet and a dearth of *R*s and *S*s, Snyder sat behind Rose, and we started exchanging one liners and became friends.

14   There was Ted Richard, a much-touted Little League pitcher. He was chunky and had a baby face and came to Our Lady of Mercy as a seasoned street fighter. Ted was quick to laugh and he had a loud, jolly laugh, but when he got angry he'd smile a little smile, the kind that simply raises the corner of the mouth a quarter of an inch. For those who knew, it was an eerie signal. Those who didn't found themselves in big trouble, for Ted was very quick. He loved to carry on what we would come to call philosophical discussions: What is courage? Does God exist? He also loved words, enjoyed picking up big ones like *salubrious* and *equivocal* and using them in our conversations—laughing at himself as the word hit a chuckhole rolling off his tongue. Ted didn't do all that well in school—baseball and parties and testing the courage he'd speculated about took up his time. His textbooks were *Argosy* and *Field and Stream*, whatever newspapers he'd find on the bus stop—from the *Daily Worker* to pornography—conversations with uncles or hobos or businessmen he'd meet in a coffee shop, *The Old Man and the Sea.* With hindsight, I can see that Ted was developing into one of those rough-hewn intellectuals whose sources are a mix of the learned and the apocryphal, whose discussions are both assured and sad.

15   And then there was Ken Harvey. Ken was good-looking in a puffy way and had a full and oily ducktail and was a car enthusiast...a hodad. One day in religion class, he said the sentence that turned out to be one of the most memorable of the hundreds of thousands I heard in those Voc. Ed. years. We were talking about the parable of the talents, about achievement, working hard, doing the best you can do, blah-blah-blah, when the teacher called on the restive Ken Harvey for an opinion. Ken thought about it, but just for a second, and said (with studied, minimal affect), "I just wanna be average." That woke me up. Average? Who wants to be average? Then the athletes chimed in with the clichés that make you want to laryngectomize them, and the exchange became a platitudinous melee. At the time, I thought Ken's assertion was stupid, and I wrote him off. But his sentence has stayed with me all these years, and I think I am finally coming to understand it.

Ken Harvey was gasping for air. School can be a tremendously dis-   16
orienting place. No matter how bad the school, you're going to encounter notions that don't fit with the assumptions and beliefs that you
grew up with—maybe you'll hear these dissonant notions from teachers, maybe from the other students, and maybe you'll read them. You'll
also be thrown in with all kinds of kids from all kinds of backgrounds,
and that can be unsettling—this is especially true in places of rich ethnic and linguistic mix, like the L.A. basin. You'll see a handful of students far excel you in courses that sound exotic and that are only in the
curriculum of the elite: French, physics, trigonometry. And all this is
happening while you're trying to shape an identity, your body is
changing, and your emotions are running wild. If you're a working-
class kid in the vocational track, the options you'll have to deal with
this will be constrained in certain ways: you're defined by your school
as "slow"; you're placed in a curriculum that isn't designed to liberate
you but to occupy you, or, if you're lucky, train you, though the training is for work the society does not esteem; other students are picking
up the cues from your school and your curriculum and interacting with
you in particular ways. If you're a kid like Ted Richard, you turn your
back on all this and let your mind roam where it may. But youngsters
like Ted are rare. What Ken and so many others do is protect themselves from such suffocating madness by taking on with a vengeance
the identity implied in the vocational track. Reject the confusion and
frustration by openly defining yourself as the Common Joe. Champion
the average. Rely on your own good sense. Fuck this bullshit. Bullshit,
of course, is everything you—and the others—fear is beyond you:
books, essays, tests, academic scrambling, complexity, scientific reasoning, philosophical inquiry.

The tragedy is that you have to twist the knife in your own gray   17
matter to make this defense work. You'll have to shut down, have to reject intellectual stimuli or diffuse them with sarcasm, have to cultivate
stupidity, have to convert boredom from a malady into a way of confronting the world. Keep your vocabulary simple, act stoned when
you're not or act more stoned than you are, flaunt ignorance, materialize your dreams. It is a powerful and effective defense—it neutralizes
the insult and the frustration of being a vocational kid and, when per-
fected, it drives teachers up the wall, a delightful secondary effect. But
like all strong magic, it exacts a price.

My own deliverance from the Voc. Ed. world began with sopho-   18
more biology. Every student, college prep to vocational, had to take biology, and unlike the other courses, the same person taught all sections.
When teaching the vocational group, Brother Clint probably slowed
down a bit or omitted a little of the fundamental biochemistry, but he
used the same book and more or less the same syllabus across the
board. If one class got tough, he could get tougher. He was young and

powerful and very handsome, and looks and physical strength were high currency. No one gave him any trouble.

19   I was pretty bad at the dissecting table, but the lectures and the textbook were interesting: plastic overlays that, with each turned page, peeled away skin, then veins and muscle, then organs, down to the very bones that Brother Clint, pointer in hand, would tap out on our hanging skeleton. Dave Snyder was in big trouble, for the study of life—versus the living of it—was sticking in his craw. We worked out a code for our multiple-choice exams. He'd poke me in the back: once for the answer under A, twice for B, and so on; and when he'd hit the right one, I'd look up to the ceiling as though I were lost in thought. Poke: cytoplasm. Poke, poke: methane. Poke, poke, poke. William Harvey. Poke, poke, poke, poke: islets of Langerhans. This didn't work out perfectly, but Dave passed the course, and I mastered the dreamy look of a guy on a record jacket. And something else happened. Brother Clint puzzled over this Voc. Ed. kid who was racking up 98s and 99s on his tests. He checked the school's records and discovered the error. He recommended that I begin my junior year in the College Prep program. According to all I've read since, such a shift, as one report put it, is virtually impossible. Kids at that level rarely cross tracks. The telling thing is how chancy both my placement into and exit from Voc. Ed. was; neither I nor my parents had anything to do with it. I lived in one world during spring semester, and when I came back to school in the fall, I was living in another.

20   Switching to College Prep was a mixed blessing. I was an erratic student. I was undisciplined. And I hadn't caught onto the rules of the game: Why work hard in a class that didn't grab my fancy? I was also hopelessly behind in math. Chemistry was hard; toying with my chemistry set years before hadn't prepared me for the chemist's equations. Fortunately, the priest who taught both chemistry and second-year algebra was also the school's athletic director. Membership on the track team covered me; I knew I wouldn't get lower than a C. U.S. history was taught pretty well, and I did okay. But civics was taken over by a football coach who had trouble reading the textbook aloud—and reading aloud was the centerpiece of his pedagogy. College Prep at Mercy was certainly an improvement over the vocational program—at least it carried some status—but the social science curriculum was weak, and the mathematics and physical sciences were simply beyond me. I had a miserable quantitative background and ended up copying some assignments and finessing the rest as best I could. Let me try to explain how it feels to see again and again material you should once have learned but didn't.

21   You are given a problem. It requires you to simplify algebraic fractions or to multiply expressions containing square roots. You know this is pretty basic material because you've seen it for years. Once a teacher

took some time with you, and you learned how to carry out these operations. Simple versions, anyway. But that was a year or two or more in the past, and these are more complex versions, and now you're not sure. And this, you keep telling yourself, is ninth- or even eighth-grade stuff.

Next it's a word problem. This is also old hat. The basic elements 22 are as familiar as story characters: trains speeding so many miles per hour or shadows of buildings angling so many degrees. Maybe you know enough, have sat through enough explanations, to be able to begin setting up the problem: "If one train is going this fast..." or "This shadow is really one line of a triangle..." Then: "Let's see..." "How did Jones do this?" "Hmmmm." "No." "No, that won't work." Your attention wavers. You wonder about other things: a football game, a dance, that cute new checker at the market. You try to focus on the problem again. You scribble on paper for a while, but the tension wins out and your attention flits elsewhere. You crumple the paper and begin daydreaming to ease the frustration.

The particulars will vary, but in essence this is what a number of 23 students go through, especially those in so-called remedial classes. They open their textbooks and see once again the familiar and impenetrable formulas and diagrams and terms that have stumped them for years. There is no excitement here. *No* excitement. Regardless of what the teacher says, this is not a new challenge. There is, rather, embarrassment and frustration and, not surprisingly, some anger in being reminded once again of longstanding inadequacies. No wonder so many students finally attribute their difficulties to something inborn, organic: "That part of my brain just doesn't work." Given the troubling histories many of these students have, it's miraculous that any of them can lift the shroud of hopelessness sufficiently to make deliverance from these classes possible.

Through this entire period, my father's health was deteriorating 24 with cruel momentum. His arteriosclerosis progressed to the point where a simple nick on his shin wouldn't heal. Eventually it ulcerated and widened. Lou Minton would come by daily to change the dressing. We tried renting an oscillating bed—which we placed in the front room—to force blood through the constricted arteries in my father's legs. The bed hummed through the night, moving in place to ward off the inevitable. The ulcer continued to spread, and the doctors finally had to amputate. My grandfather had lost his leg in a stockyard accident. Now my father too was crippled. His convalescence was slow but steady, and the doctors placed him in the Santa Monica Rehabilitation Center, a sun-bleached building that opened out onto the warm spray of the Pacific. The place gave him some strength and some color and some training in walking with an artificial leg. He did pretty well for a year or so until he slipped and broke his hip. He was confined to a wheelchair after that, and the confinement contributed to the diminishing of his body and spirit.

25   I am holding a picture of him. He is sitting in his wheelchair and smiling at the camera. The smile appears forced, unsteady, seems to quaver, though it is frozen in silver nitrate. He is in his mid-sixties and looks eighty. Late in my junior year, he had a stroke and never came out of the resulting coma. After that, I would see him only in dreams, and to this day that is how I join him. Sometimes the dreams are sad and grisly and primal: my father lying in a bed soaked with his suppuration, holding me, rocking me. But sometimes the dreams bring him back to me healthy: him talking to me on an empty street, or buying some pictures to decorate our old house, or transformed somehow into someone strong and adept with tools and the physical.

26   Jack MacFarland couldn't have come into my life at a better time. My father was dead, and I had logged up too many years of scholastic indifference. Mr. MacFarland had a master's degree from Columbia and decided, at twenty-six, to find a little school and teach his heart out. He never took any credentialing courses, couldn't bear to, he said, so he had to find employment in a private system. He ended up at Our Lady of Mercy teaching five sections of senior English. He was a beatnik who was born too late. His teeth were stained, he tucked his sorry tie in between the third and fourth buttons of his shirt, and his pants were chronically wrinkled. At first, we couldn't believe this guy, thought he slept in his car. But within no time, he had us so startled with work that we didn't much worry about where he slept or if he slept at all. We wrote three or four essays a month. We read a book every two to three weeks, starting with the *Iliad* and ending up with Hemingway. He gave us a quiz on the reading every other day. He brought a prep school curriculum to Mercy High.

27   MacFarland's lectures were crafted, and as he delivered them he would pace the room jiggling a piece of chalk in his cupped hand, using it to scribble on the board the names of all the writers and philosophers and plays and novels he was weaving into his discussion. He asked questions often, raised everything from Zeno's paradox to the repeated last line of Frost's "Stopping by Woods on a Snowy Evening." He slowly and carefully built up our knowledge of Western intellectual history—with facts, with connections, with speculations. We learned about Greek philosophy, about Dante, the Elizabethan world view, the Age of Reason, existentialism. He analyzed poems with us, had us reading sections from John Ciardi's *How Does a Poem Mean?*, making a potentially difficult book accessible with his own explanations. We gave oral reports on poems Ciardi didn't cover. We imitated the styles of Conrad, Hemingway, and *Time* magazine. We wrote and talked, wrote and talked. The man immersed us in language.

Even MacFarland's barbs were literary. If Jim Fitzsimmons, hung   28
over and irritable, tried to smart-ass him, he'd rejoin with a flourish
that would spark the indomitable Skip Madison—who'd lost his front
teeth in a hapless tackle—to flick his tongue through the gap and
opine, "good chop," drawing out the single "o" in stinging indictment.
Jack MacFarland, this tobacco-stained intellectual, brandished linguistic weapons of a kind I hadn't encountered before. Here was this *egg-
head*, for God's sake, keeping some pretty difficult people in line. And
from what I heard, Mike Dweetz and Steve Fusco and all the notorious
Voc. Ed. crowd settled down as well when MacFarland took the po-
dium. Though a lot of guys groused in the schoolyard, it just seemed
that giving trouble to this particular teacher was a silly thing to do.
Tomfoolery, not to mention assault, had no place in the world he was
trying to create for us, and instinctively everyone knew that. If nothing
else, we all recognized MacFarland's considerable intelligence and respected the hours he put into his work. It came to this: The trouble-
maker would look foolish rather than daring. Even Jim Fitzsimmons
was reading *On the Road* and turning his incipient alcoholism to literary ends.

There were some lives that were already beyond Jack MacFarland's   29
ministrations, but mine was not. I started reading again as I hadn't
since elementary school. I would go into our gloomy little bedroom or
sit at the dinner table while, on the television, Danny McShane was
paralyzing Mr. Moto with the atomic drop, and work slowly back
through *Heart of Darkness,* trying to catch the words in Conrad's sentences. I certainly was not MacFarland's best student; most of the other
guys in College Prep, even my fellow slackers, had better backgrounds
than I did. But I worked very hard, for MacFarland had hooked me. He
tapped my old interest in reading and creating stories. He gave me a
way to feel special by using my mind. And he provided a role model
that wasn't shaped on physical prowess alone, and something inside
me that I wasn't quite aware of responded to that. Jack MacFarland established a literacy club, to borrow a phrase of Frank Smith's, and invited me—invited all of us—to join.

There's been a good deal of research and speculation suggesting   30
that the acknowledgment of school performance with extrinsic rewards—smiling faces, stars, numbers, grades—diminishes the intrinsic
satisfaction children experience by engaging in reading or writing or
problem solving. While it's certainly true that we've created an educational system that encourages our best and brightest to become cynical
grade collectors and, in general, have developed an obsession with
evaluation and assessment, I must tell you that venal though it may
have been, I loved getting good grades from MacFarland. I now know
how subjective grades can be, but then they came tucked in the back of

essays like bits of scientific data, some sort of spectroscopic readout that said, objectively and publicly, that I had made something of value. I suppose I'd been mediocre for too long and enjoyed a public redefinition. And I suppose the workings of my mind, such as they were, had been private for too long. My linguistic play moved into the world; ... these papers with their circled, red B-pluses and A-minuses linked my mind to something outside it. I carried them around like a club emblem.

31   One day in the December of my senior year, Mr. MacFarland asked me where I was going to go to college. I hadn't thought much about it. Many of the students I teach today spent their last year in high school with a physics text in one hand and the Stanford catalog in the other, but I wasn't even aware of what "entrance requirements" were. My folks would say that they wanted me to go to college and be a doctor, but I don't know how seriously I ever took that; it seemed a sweet thing to say, a bit of supportive family chatter, like telling a gangly daughter she's graceful. The reality of higher education wasn't in my scheme of things: no one in the family had gone to college; only two of my uncles had completed high school. I figured I'd get a night job and go to the local junior college because I knew that Snyder and Company were going there to play ball. But I hadn't even prepared for that. When I finally said, "I don't know," MacFarland looked down at me—I was seated in his office—and said, "Listen, you can write."

32   My grades stank. I had A's in biology and a handful of B's in a few English and social science classes. All the rest were C's—or worse. MacFarland said I would do well in his class and laid down the law about doing well in the others. Still, the record for my first three years wouldn't have been acceptable to any four-year school. To nobody's surprise, I was turned down flat by USC and UCLA. But Jack MacFarland was on the case. He had received his bachelor's degree from Loyola University, so he made calls to old professors and talked to somebody in admissions and wrote me a strong letter. Loyola finally accepted me as a probationary student. I would be on trial for the first year, and if I did okay, I would be granted regular status. MacFarland also intervened to get me a loan, for I could never have afforded a private college without it. Four more years of religion classes and four more years of boys at one school, girls at another. But at least I was going to college. Amazing.

33   In my last semester of high school, I elected a special English course fashioned by Mr. MacFarland, and it was through this elective that there arose at Mercy a fledgling literati. Art Mitz, the editor of the school newspaper and a very smart guy, was the kingpin. He was joined by me and by Mark Dever, a quiet boy who wrote beautifully and who would die before he was forty. MacFarland occasionally invited us to his apart-

ment, and those visits became the high point of our apprenticeship: We'd clamp on our training wheels and drive to his salon.

He lived in a cramped and cluttered place near the airport, tucked 34 away in the kind of building that architectural critic Reyner Banham calls a *dingbat*. Books were all over: stacked, piled, tossed, and crated, underlined and dog eared, well worn and new. Cigarette ashes crusted with coffee in saucers or spilled over the sides of motel ashtrays. The little bedroom had, along two of its walls, bricks and boards loaded with notes, magazines, and oversized books. The kitchen joined the living room, and there was a stack of German newspapers under the sink. I had never seen anything like it: a great flophouse of language furnished by City Lights and Café le Metro. I read every title. I flipped through paperbacks and scanned jackets and memorized names: Gogol, *Finnegan's Wake,* Djuna Barnes, Jackson Pollock, *A Coney Island of the Mind,* F. O. Matthiessen's *American Renaissance,* all sorts of Freud, *Troubled Sleep,* Man Ray, *The Education of Henry Adams,* Richard Wright, *Film as Art,* William Butler Yeats, Marguerite Duras, *Redburn, A Season in Hell, Kapital.* On the cover of Alain-Fournier's *The Wanderer* was an Edward Gorey drawing of a young man on a road winding into dark trees. By the hotplate sat a strange Kafka novel called *Amerika,* in which an adolescent hero crosses the Atlantic to find the Nature Theater of Oklahoma. Art and Mark would be talking about a movie or the school newspaper, and I would be consuming my English teacher's library. It was heady stuff. I felt like a Pop Warner[4] athlete on steroids.

Art, Mark, and I would buy stogies and triangulate from MacFar- 35 land's apartment to the Cinema, which now shows X-rated films but was then L.A.'s premier art theater, and then to the musty Cherokee Bookstore in Hollywood to hobnob with beatnik homosexuals—smoking, drinking bourbon and coffee, and trying out awkward phrases we'd gleaned from our mentor's bookshelves. I was happy and precocious and a little scared as well, for Hollywood Boulevard was thick with a kind of decadence that was foreign to the South Side. After the Cherokee, we would head back to the security of MacFarland's apartment, slaphappy with hipness.

Let me be the first to admit that there was a good deal of adoles- 36 cent passion in this embrace of the avant-garde: self-absorption, sexually charged pedantry, an elevation of the odd and abandoned. Still it was a time during which I absorbed an awful lot of information: long lists of titles, images from expressionist paintings, new wave shibboleths, snippets of philosophy, and names that read like Steve Fusco's misspellings—Goethe, Nietzsche, Kierkegaard. Now this is hardly the stuff of deep understanding. But it was an introduction, a phrase book,

[4]A young people's athletic group nationwide.

a Baedeker[5] to a vocabulary of ideas, and it felt good at the time to know all these words. With hindsight I realize how layered and important that knowledge was.

37 It enabled me to do things in the world. I could browse bohemian bookstores in far-off, mysterious Hollywood; I could go to the Cinema and see events through the lenses of European directors; and, most of all, I could share an evening, talk that talk, with Jack MacFarland, the man I most admired at the time. Knowledge was becoming a bonding agent. Within a year or two, the persona of the disaffected hipster would prove too cynical, too alienated to last. But for a time it was new and exciting: it provided a critical perspective on society, and it allowed me to act as though I were living beyond the limiting boundaries of South Vermont.[6]

★ Meaning and Understanding

1. How does Rose get to school? Why does he call the busload of students "a funny mix" (paragraph 1)?

2. What options are open to "a working class kid in the vocational track"? Why does Rose call it a "dumping ground" (paragraph 11)?

3. Rose refers to Ted Richard as "a street-fighter," and yet also says that Richard loved "to carry on what we would come to call philosophical discussions." What does this point suggest about the relation between physical prowess and intellectual agility? Is it a paradox? (What is a paradox?) Can one be "tough" and "intellectual" at the same time? Explain your point of view.

4. In what way was switching to College Prep "a mixed blessing" (paragraph 19) for Rose?

5. Why was sophomore biology important in Rose's life? How does Brother Clint influence Rose's future?

6. What is a "beatnik"? Why does Rose describe MacFarland as "a beatnik who was born too late"?

★ Techniques and Strategies

1. Where does Rose come closest to stating the thesis of the selection?

2. The writer refers to most of his teachers as "Brother" or "Mister," but introduces MacFarland as "Jack." Why do you think he does this? What is he trying to suggest?

[5]Renowned travel guidebook.
[6]A Los Angeles street in a dejected area.

3. This selection is rich in metaphor. What, for example, is the main metaphor in paragraph 11? How does it help you understand the writer's point? In paragraph 34, Rose refers to MacFarland's apartment as "a great flophouse of language." What is a flophouse and what do you think the writer means here? What other metaphors stand out in the piece?

4. Much of the first half of the selection focuses on Rose's school and classmates. In paragraph 24, however, the writer shifts to a discussion of his father's health. Why do you think he does so at that point? What is the overall effect of this discussion?

5. Rose opens this selection with a catalog of the boys who ride on the bus. Then, near the end of the selection, he provides another catalog, this time of books and authors. What is the purpose of cataloging information as he does? How do you think the catalogs are connected?

6. Rose describes some of his teachers at Our Lady of Mercy: Brother Dill, Mr. Mitropetros, and Mr. Montez. What are the distinguishing features of each man, and how do those features contribute to your understanding of Rose's thesis?

★ Speaking of Values

1. Rose reveals that he was placed in the vocational track at school because of an error and that he remained in that track for two years. What conclusion might you draw from this occurrence in regard to assumptions that educators may sometimes make about students? What incidents of "mistracking" do you know of?

2. Rose makes some strong statements about the purposes and value of vocational education. Identify his ideas about it and discuss his criticisms in light of your own experience and aspirations.

3. Rose implies a general view of the purpose and nature of education in his writing. Try to paraphrase his view. Do you agree with any of his points? Which? Why?

4. How has Rose gained understanding of Ken Harvey's assertion, "I just wanna be average"? What does Rose come to understand about what Ken meant? Would you agree or disagree with the idea that some kids "cultivate stupidity" in order to protect themselves from the "system"? Why or why not?

5. What is it about the teacher MacFarland that makes him successful and worthy of respect? In what ways is he different from Dill, Mitropetros, and Montez? What qualities do you recognize in MacFarland that are similar to qualities in teachers that you hold in high regard?

6. What does Rose have to say about the connection between learning and "extrinsic rewards"? Do you agree with his point of view? Why or why not?

★ *Values Conversation*

Form groups to discuss the various teaching styles of some of your teachers and to evolve a list of qualities you think teachers should have. Report to the class the findings of your group.

★ *Writing about Values*

1. Write a paper about the pros and cons of tracking children into specific school programs. Be sure to include your own opinion about the practice and support your point with concrete illustrations and examples. Speak with teachers, guidance counselors, and school officials to get their ideas about the subject.

2. Rose raises questions about the value of grades—"extrinsic rewards"—in our educational scheme. Do you believe that "smiling faces, stars, numbers, grades" diminish or enhance the intrinsic satisfaction of learning? Write an essay to explore this question.

3. Write a paper about the role of self-esteem in educational achievement. As always, be sure to support your arguments with concrete illustrations and examples.

Abigail Adams

Letter to John Adams (14 August 1776)

Abigail Adams (1744–1818) was born in Massachusetts and was the wife of John Adams, the second President of the United States. From 1774 to 1783, Abigail and John exchanged hundreds of letters. Here she writes to her husband about what he perceived as "the deficiency of education" among his countrymen.

———— ★ ————

Your letter of August 3 came by this day's post. I find it very convenient to be so handy. I can receive a letter at night, sit down and reply to it, and send it off in the morning. 1

You remark upon the deficiency of education in your countrymen. It never, I believe, was in a worse state, at least for many years. The college is not in the state one could wish. The scholars complain that their professor in philosophy is taken off by public business, to their great detriment. In this town I never saw so great a neglect of education. The poorer sort of children are wholly neglected, and left to range the streets, without schools, without business, given up to all evil. The town is not, as formerly, divided into wards. There is either too much business left upon the hands of a few, or too little care to do it. We daily see the necessity of a regular government. 2

You speak of our worthy brother. I often lament it, that a man so peculiarly formed for the education of youth, and so well qualified as he is in many branches of literature, excelling in philosophy and the mathematics, should not be employed in some public station. I know not the person who would make half so good a successor to Dr. Winthrop. He has a peculiar, easy manner of communicating his ideas to youth; and the goodness of his heart and the purity of his morals, without an affected austerity, must have a happy effect upon the minds of pupils. 3

If you complain of neglect of education in sons, what shall I say with regard to daughters, who every day experience the want of it? With regard to the education of my own children, I find myself soon out of my depth, destitute and deficient in every part of education. 4

5   I most sincerely wish that some more liberal plan might be laid and executed for the benefit of the rising generation, and that our new Constitution may be distinguished for encouraging learning and virtue. If we mean to have heroes, statesmen, and philosophers, we should have learned women. The world perhaps would laugh at me and accuse me of vanity, but you, I know, have a mind too enlarged and liberal to disregard the sentiment. If much depends, as is allowed, upon the early education of youth, and the first principles which are instilled take the deepest root, great benefit must arise from literary accomplishments in women.

6   Excuse me. My pen has run away with me. I have no thoughts of coming to Philadelphia The length of time I have and shall be detained here would have prevented me, even if you had no thoughts of returning till December; but I live in daily expectation of seeing you here. Your health, I think, requires your immediate return. I expected Mr. G—— would have set off before now, but he perhaps finds it very hard to leave his mistress. I won't say harder than some do to leave their wives. Mr. Gerry stood very high in my esteem. What is meat for one is not for another. No accounting for fancy. She is a queer dame and leads people wild dances.

7   But hush! Post, don't betray your trust and lose my letter.

★ *Meaning and Understanding*

1. In the first paragraph, Adams remarks that "I find it very convenient to be so handy." What is the "it" she is referring to? And what particular meaning of "handy" is suggested here?

2. At the beginning of the second paragraph she says to her husband: "You remark upon the deficiency of education in your countrymen." Why doesn't she say "our" countrymen? Is this just a slip or do you think she is trying to make a point? If so, what is it?

3. What do you think is the main point of this letter?

4. Speaking of a relative, the writer observes that "he has a peculiar, easy manner of communicating his ideas to youth." What do you think she means by this? Is "peculiar" meant to suggest something odd or does it have another meaning?

5. What "town" is Adams referring to in the second paragraph?

6. The letter is dated "14 August 1776." What is the political situation in the colonies at that time and how might it have affected the content of the letter?

★ Techniques and Strategies

1. Where does Adams come closest to stating the main point of her letter?

2. The audience for the letter is quite apparent—Abigail's husband John. What do the language and sentence structure tell you about the kind of relation that existed between the two people?

3. Abigail Adams signs her letter "Portia." Who was Portia, and why do you think Adams uses a pseudonym?

4. What is the tone of the letter? What words and phrases help you to identify the tone?

5. The long paragraph at the end of the letter makes no reference to education. How do you account for the shift in subject at this point?

★ Speaking of Values

1. What theory of education does Adams imply in this letter?

2. Adams suggests a connection between education and public responsibility. How would you articulate this connection?

3. What qualities does Adams identify as being those of a good teacher? Do you agree with her? Why or why not?

4. The writer makes a plea for better education for young women. What does she suggest about the nature of education for females in colonial society? What specific complaint does she make about her own education? What value does she assign to literacy in women? On what basis does she assert that "great benefit must arise from literary accomplishments in women"?

5. Why might you agree or disagree with the writer's assertion that "if we mean to have heroes, statesmen, and philosophers, we should have learned women"? What is the relation between these roles and education for women? Does anything about the statement reflect the particular values of Adams's time? If so, what are those values?

6. In paragraph 5 Adams suggests that the Constitution should encourage "learning and virtue." What does she mean by "virtue" in this context? Do you accept the connection between learning and virtue as Adams seems to present it?

★ Values Conversation

Form groups to develop a definition, plan, or theory of education that you believe is appropriate to the needs of contemporary American youth.

Don't worry about identifying specific courses. Rather, try to come to some agreement about the following: who should be educated; what kinds of things should people be taught; how, if at all, should learning be assessed; what is the relationship between education and civic duty.

★ *Writing about Values*

1. Do library research to find out what the state of education was in colonial America and write a brief essay about it. Some points to consider are: who was educated and what were people taught; was public education available; what credentials or expertise were required in order to teach.

2. Much contemporary debate concerns the relative learning styles and abilities of males and females. For instance, some observers believe that girls don't do as well in math and science as boys. What do you think? Write a paper expressing your opinion on this subject. Be sure to support your argument with specific examples and illustrations.

3. Education is a controversial issue in America. On one hand, Americans clamor for more and better education for their children; on the other they complain about the high cost of public education. What values do these positions imply? How do you account for this seeming contradiction? Is it unreconcilable? Or is it merely a natural consequence of a democratic society? Write a paper addressing these questions. Before you write your paper, you may find it helpful to find out what the school taxes are in your town, city, or suburb as well as to obtain a copy of the local school budget to see how the tax dollars are actually spent.

Shelby Steele

Indoctrination Isn't Teaching

Born in 1946, Shelby Steele, currently a research fellow at the Hoover
Institute, is a writer and teacher. He won the 1991 National Book Critics
Circle Award for general nonfiction and his essays have appeared in
Harper's, *The American Scholar*, and the *New York Times*. He is also the au-
thor of *The Content of Our Character: A New Vision of Race in America* (1990)
and *The End of Oppression* (1997). In this essay Steele focuses on black En-
glish as a function of "one of the most seductive and dangerous ideas in
American education: self-esteem."

———— ★ ————

At the heart of the furor over black English is one of the most seductive   1
yet dangerous ideas in all of American education: self-esteem.

It is an idea with two parts. The first is the post-60's notion that   2
self-esteem is not only a condition for learning but is also as important
a goal in the education of minority students as academic mastery itself.
The second part is the belief that self-esteem comes as much from
group identity as from individual academic success. Over time, this
link between self-esteem and identity has caused the education of
many minority children, particularly blacks, to be based more on identity enhancement than on high academic expectations.

This idea is the centerpiece of a strategy of racial reform that might   3
be called indirection. By this strategy, minority problems are never directly addressed. Instead, they are understood and approached indirectly through their root causes, which are always said to flow from
America's history of racism.

By forcing the discussion of minority problems into the area of   4
root causes, indirection deflects us away from problem-solving and
into yet another negotiation of who owes what to whom. This is not to
say that black problems don't have root causes or that racism is not
one of them. The point is that indirection is an ingenious opportunism
that makes root causes the only ones with a powerful claim on society's resources.

"Ebonics" is a case in point. It directs us away from the problem—   5
the poor academic performance of black children—by emphasizing
self-esteem and weak racial identity as the root causes of the problem,

the only causes that truly matter. In the interest of self-esteem, of protecting black children from racial shame, ebonics makes broken English the equivalent of standard English. To further bolster identity, it is said that this form of speech has an African origin, despite the lack of evidence.

6   In the world of education, it is assumed that the self-esteem difficulties of black children stem from racial victimization. So, by making poor academic performance a problem of self-esteem and identity, ebonics invokes America's history of racism as the true root cause. Now we no longer have students with academic deficits; we have racial victims, identity victims.

7   Of course it is true that racial victimization—if only its legacy—plays some role in the poor performance of these students. But ebonics seeks to make victimization the only cause that counts. Its purpose is to shift responsibility for the problem away from the people who suffer it and onto society.

8   By seeing racial identity as the main source of the self-esteem of black children, we are left with little more than identity enhancement as a way to improve their performance. So when we find inner-city black children who are in desperate academic shape, we use their very desperation to justify a program of identity enhancement.

9   In Oakland, black English is transformed into a language with African roots. In Los Angeles, there is talk of expanding a small ebonics program to reach all 92,000 African-American students in the school district. In Milwaukee, two schools are devoted to Afrocentric teaching. In Detroit, Baltimore and other cities there are all-black military-style academies and all- male classrooms.

10   Almost everywhere there is an unquestioned belief in role-model theory—matching black students with black teachers, often by sex as well. Now there is the idea that we can match racial identities with "styles of learning."

11   Teaching that is directed primarily as the group identity of at-risk black students offers an imagery of racial glory, which is a kind of propaganda. This puts the black child in a rather absurd position. To garner the self-esteem to do well in school, he must believe that Egyptians flew to work in little gliders or that he has his own racial learning style. He must conform to an ideology in order to be smart.

12   The poor academic performance of black students should be approached directly, with a strong commitment to academic rigor. Nothing special should be done about their self-esteem or their racial identity. The focus of their education should shift from being to doing, from identity to academic mastery. They should be treated with warm human respect, but also with the understanding that high expectations are the only show of respect they will believe in the long run. They don't need rigor as much as they deserve it.

★ *Meaning and Understanding*

1. What is "ebonics"? How was the word coined?

2. Explain Steele's theory of "indirection." What other social issues do people address by indirection?

3. What do you think is the main point of this essay?

4. Many educators talk about "academic rigor." What do you think this means? Give some examples to support your point.

5. In paragraph 2, Steele asserts that to some extent ideas about "self-esteem" are a "post-60's notion." What do you think he means by this? Why might he link ideas about self-esteem to the 1960s?

★ *Techniques and Strategies*

1. How does the introduction engage the reader's attention? Why does Steele call self-esteem a "seductive" idea? What connotations does the word carry?

2. What is the effect of the four cases in the examples Steele provides in paragraph 9? Why has the writer used this rhetorical strategy?

3. In paragraph 5, Steele asserts that certain claims about ebonics lack sufficient evidence and yet people persist in believing them. Does he present any counterevidence, or does he simply assume his audience will agree with him? Do you agree with him? Why or why not?

4. Who is the intended audience for this piece? What evidence is there in the essay that leads you to think so?

5. Steele's essay is an argument that comes to a head in the last paragraph. What is that argument? How has he supported it?

★ *Speaking of Values*

1. Steele says that many people believe that "self-esteem comes as much from group identity as from individual academic success." What do you think about this point? Could his statement account for the popularity of gangs among teenagers? Discuss your reasons for agreeing or disagreeing.

2. What role do you think "racial victimization" plays in students' performance and education?

3. Steele assails "the unquestioned belief in role-model theory"—that is, the idea that students learn better from members of their own sex or race. Do you agree with this point? Why or why not?

4. In the final paragraph, Steele suggests about black students that "the focus of their education should shift from being to doing, from identity to academic mastery." Does this point strike you as an appropriate value for an educational program? Why or why not?

5. Steele's title asserts that "indoctrination isn't teaching." Why might you agree or disagree? What kinds of lessons are, in fact, taught by indoctrination?

⚘ Values Conversation

Form groups to discuss the relations between self-esteem and education. Steele clearly takes issue with the notion that "self-esteem" is a vital ingredient of a person's education. What do you think about the connection between self-esteem and learning? Is it necessary to feel good about oneself in order to learn effectively? Does *not* feeling good about yourself mean you cannot learn? Explain the reasons for your answer.

★ Writing about Values

1. Steele mentions four cities that have attempted to accommodate perceived racial differences in "learning styles." Choose one of the cities and find out what you can about the educational programs there. Then write a paper in which you present the results of your research.

2. Write an essay in which you define education.

3. Is there such a thing as "Standard English"? Or do people in a free society, as someone once suggested, "have a right to their own language"? Write a paper discussing the pros and cons of "having your own language."

Timothy Harper

They Treat Girls Differently, Don't They?

Timothy Harper is a journalist and author who writes on education, technology, and society for a number of popular and professional publications. "Boys get more attention in the classroom than girls," he states.

———— ★ ————

Boys get more attention in the classroom than girls. There's no doubt   1
about it. Reams of studies show that teachers, from preschool to grade
school, interact more with males than with females. Especially in grade
school, boys are called on more often. They get more constructive criticism, and they're asked more challenging questions.

A landmark study by the American Association of University   2
Women found that when science teachers need help with demonstrations in front of their classes, four out of five times they call on a boy
rather than a girl.

Those are the facts. What those facts mean, however, is not so clear.   3
Some parents and teachers believe studies on classroom gender bias
are misleading. Others believe they show that girls are being short-
changed by American education.

An important point to keep in mind from the outset is that gender   4
bias does not start in school. What happens in classrooms, good or bad,
is a reflection of society at large. All of us—parents, teachers, administrators and students—have our baggage. Indeed, one of the remarkable
aspects of the debate over classroom gender bias is the reluctance to
blame anyone, especially teachers. Even the most vocal critics say
teachers typically are not aware of the ways they show their own bias
against girls; when it is pointed out, teachers are surprised and consciously try to treat boys and girls more equally.

While it is not within the scope of this article to suggest how to   5
remedy a centuries-old cultural bias that generally favors males over
females—in school, in the family and on the job—there are some things
that educators, students and parents can do to counteract gender bias
in the classroom.

Critics warn that classroom gender bias hurts girls in very real   6
ways. They argue that when girls enter kindergarten they are just as
outgoing as boys, and almost as interested in math and science. By the

127

end of high school, according to studies, girls are more likely to suffer from low self-esteem and less likely to be taking courses in chemistry, calculus, computers and other science and technology fields that hold such great growth potential in the twenty-first century. Boys gain confidence and competence; girls lose it. Boys learn that school is a place of opportunity. Girls are taught that it is a place of constraints.

7   "I don't think teachers mean for it to happen—they don't realize there's gender bias in their own classrooms," observes Ellen Silber, director of the Institute for the Education of Women and Girls at Marymount College in Tarrytown, New York. Silber, whose research and consulting include teacher training and parent awareness programs, says teachers who are videotaped are surprised to see that they call on boys more often. "But blame is not the point," she notes. "Girls are being conditioned to think that boys are smarter, or that boys need more attention because they're pains in the neck."

8   Indeed, blame is not the issue for those of us who have young children. We don't want to raise boys who think they are automatically in charge, whether in the classroom today or in the boardroom tomorrow. And we don't want to raise daughters who think they must wait to speak until all the boys are finished, or who might have been great scientists if only physics and chemistry hadn't been "boy subjects."

9   David Sadker, a professor of education at American University, did a number of studies with his late wife, Myra, showing gender bias to be deep-rooted in American classrooms. Their studies show that from grade school through graduate school, boys are more likely to shout out answers or otherwise make comments without being called on. Typically, teachers answered the boys who called out, but chastised the girls who called out with comments such as "Please raise your hand if you want to speak." Today, Sadker frets that a cure for cancer might be "locked in the mind" of a girl who never pursued the kind of science education that would unlock it.

10   Not everyone, of course, agrees that classroom gender bias is such a big problem. Diane Ravitch, the former assistant secretary of the U.S. Department of Education and now a research scholar at New York University, says we should instead be celebrating "the successful conquest of American education by girls and women." In 1970, she says, women accounted for barely 40 percent of the college students in the United States; today it's 55 percent. Women earned less than 10 percent of the law and medical degrees awarded in 1970; today, they make up nearly 50 percent of the enrollment in U.S. law schools and colleges of medicine.

11   Yes, boys get more attention than girls, but some say that doesn't mean teachers are biased against girls. David Murray, director of research for the Washington-based Statistical Assessment Service, a private, non-profit think tank that tries to debunk science myths, says, "The reality is that boys are far more disruptive, and what they get is more negative attention."

He says boys are more often found at the extremes of all types of   12
performance, good and bad. Boys score higher on the Scholastic Apti-
tude Test and win more National Merit honors but also are more likely
to have learning disabilities, drug or alcohol problems, and trouble
with the law. Girls get better grades, are less likely to drop out of high
school and are more likely to got to college and get a degree.

Pat O'Reilly, professor of education in the field of developmental   13
psychology and head of educational studies at the University of Cincinnati, agrees that many teachers call on boys more—because they
have shorter attention spans, and the teachers are trying to keep them
involved and interested. (Boys are also three times as likely to receive a
diagnosis of attention-deficit learning disorders.) "How does this affect
girls? They feel less involved and sometimes feel left out," says
O'Reilly. "One of the ways we plan to deal with this issue is to encourage teachers to stop calling on the first person who raises a hand, because boys are more apt to raise their hands—even if it means the
embarrassment and risk of the wrong answer.

"Maybe boys are more confident than girls . . . we're not quite sure.   14
Girls tend to think about an answer before they respond. We are training teachers to be more patient and to wait a minute before they call on
a student. We need to make sure that girls become more confident and
we need to teach boys to think before they speak."

For whatever reason, boys and girls seem to learn differently. Boys   15
are more individualistic and competitive. They create hierarchies and
function well in them. Girls are less competitive and more willing to
cooperate. Instead of creating hierarchies, they find ways to collaborate. For some educators and parents, the answer is to segregate boys
and girls, though single-sex schools or classes may not be constitutional under recent court rulings.

Legal or not, I wouldn't want my daughter to attend special single-   16
sex science classes. What message will that send her about boys? And I
wouldn't want my son to be left in a classroom of boys. Is that going to
teach him to empathize with girls? I want my daughter to be able to
compete with the boys, and my son to be able to collaborate with the
girls. The easy answer, of course, is for us to make education better for
everybody. But how?

From assorted experts and studies, here is a list of recommenda-   17
tions for parents and teachers concerned about gender bias in the classroom.

Parents at Home:

- Ask your daughter (and son) to draw a picture of a scientist. If   18
  she (or he) draws a man—most do—talk about how more and
  more girls are doing well in science studies and growing up to
  become scientists, too.

19 • Listen to your daughter. Girls' voices are naturally softer and girls are often less aggressive about speaking up, so you may have to draw her out. Don't criticize. She should know that her thoughts, feelings, opinions and experiences are valuable both to you and to herself.

20 • Encourage your daughter not to limit herself academically. Find mentors—older girls or women within or outside your family— whose academic and career achievements can serve as role models, and who are willing to talk to your daughter about their experiences and views.

21 • Play sports and engage in other physical activities, such as hiking or cycling, with your daughter. Encourage her to participate in sports—organized community or school teams and neighborhood pickup or playground games. If you put up a hoop for her in the driveway, she'll probably go out to shoot baskets.

22 • Encourage you daughter to keep a journal or diary, and to write and talk about her experiences and reactions to events large and small. Ask her for her opinion and for an explanation or defense of her point of view.

23 • If your daughter thinks a teacher is being unfair, in terms of calling on boys or anything else, encourage her to speak to the teacher. Many kids are too uneasy to do this, but many teachers are too busy to notice slights—real or imagined—unless a student speaks up.

24 • Criticize the media. Talk about the way women are portrayed on television and radio and in movies, magazines, newspapers and elsewhere. Why did that character do or say that? Is anyone really that silly? What would you have done?

Parents, at School:

25 • Talk to teachers. Let them know you're concerned about the issue of gender bias. Ask whether your daughter speaks up in class. How does she respond to teachers' questions? Does she initiate discussions and talk about what she thinks?

26 • Ask teachers what they think of your daughter. If they tend to use words such as "kind," "nice," "quiet," and "conscientious," let teachers know you're just as interested in your daughter's acquiring skills and developing talents as you are in her being a "good girl."

27 • Visit the classroom for an hour or two. Keep track of examples of competitive and collaborative learning and combinations of the two. Count the times teachers address boys vs. girls: responding to them when they call out, answering questions, calling on them, asking them easy or tough questions.

- Grade the teachers' comments: How much of what they say is   28
  disciplinary? Is the criticism constructive? Are the questions
  complex and challenging? Is the praise for girls more about being nice and getting work in on time? Is praise for boys more
  about initiative and ideas? Are boys rewarded for calling out
  while girls are reprimanded?
- Talk to other parents. Compare notes, share concerns. Groups of   29
  parents are more likely to get a positive reaction, whether it's a
  teacher's promise to be more aware of gender bias or a principal's agreement to call a meeting or have a program on gender
  bias.

Teachers:

- Visit each other's classrooms, and talk about gender bias. Keep   30
  track of how other teachers relate to boys and girls, respectively.
  Record each other, either on audio- or videotape, and then go
  back and analyze the tapes.
- Don't always call on the first student to call out or raise a hand.   31
- Make sure to call on the quiet people, boys or girls, even if they   32
  don't raise their hands.
- Recruit role models from the community, both men and women,   33
  willing to come to the classroom and talk about their school and
  work experiences.
- Mix lectures and ask-and-answer reviews with exercises where   34
  students work in teams, collaborating instead of competing.
  Make sure different kids are appointed as the leaders for different team exercises and take turns speaking for the group.
- Give students a chance to speak to you privately about concerns   35
  they may not want to raise in front of the whole class.

★ Meaning and Understanding

1. Do you agree that "what happens in classroom, good or bad, is a reflection of society at large" (paragraph 4)? Why or why not?

2. What evidence does the writer provide to support his point?

3. What do boys learn about school? About girls?

4. Who is the "they" in the title of the essay?

5. Where, according to Harper, does gender bias begin? Do you agree?
   Why or why not? The writer says that "one of the remarkable aspects
   of the debate over classroom gender bias is the reluctance to blame
   anyone." Why does he think it is "remarkable"? Do you think it is?
   Why or why not?

★ Techniques and Strategies

1. What is the writer's tone in this piece? How do you know?

2. Although Harper mentions several researchers and studies, he provides actual statistics from only one (paragraph 10). How does this information contribute to the point he is trying to make?

3. What is your view of the introduction? As for the conclusion, the writer has really provided none. Why do you think he ends the essay with a list? If you were writing a conclusion, what would you include?

4. Clearly the intended audience for this selection is the parents of school-age children. However, do you think the writer is targeting a specific subgroup within that larger group? If so, who might it be?

5. Examine the list of recommendations for parents and teachers that appears at the end of the selection. Is the writer's tone different there from the main body? Explain.

★ Speaking of Values

1. Do you think that "boys get more attention in the classroom than girls"? Explain your reasons for agreeing or disagreeing with this statement.

2. In paragraph 6 the writer states that "boys learn that school is a place of opportunity. Girls are taught that it is a place of constraints." Do you agree? What kinds of constraints might exist for girls? What kinds of opportunities for boys?

3. Do you agree that "boys and girls seem to learn differently"? Why or why not? What reasons does the writer give for believing it?

4. Harper states that while boys are "individualistic and competitive... girls create hierarchies and function well in them." What is a "hierarchy"? Do you agree? Why or why not?

5. What are some reasons critics of gender bias theory give for boys receiving more attention than girls in the classroom? Do they make sense to you? Why or why not?

6. Look at the recommendations for parents and teachers. Which ones do you think are the most useful? Which are least useful? Explain your reasons for thinking so.

★ Values Conversation

Form groups to discuss the issue of gender bias in education. First, make a list of some possible instances of classroom gender bias which you can recall. Why should gender bias exist? Is it still with us or have things changed in schools? How do you know?

★ *Writing about Values*

1. Many scholars cite employment statistics as evidence of gender bias. In other words, they argue that women are underrepresented in certain professions (science, math, and engineering, for example) because of bias. What do you think? Might there be other reasons why women and men pursue some fields of study and not others? What values may career choices imply? How may gender influence these choices? Write a paper to analyze this issue.

2. Write a paper describing a time that you felt discriminated against simply because of your gender. (It does not have to have been in school.) Be sure to explain how you felt at the time of the incident as well as how it may have influenced your future attitudes and behaviors.

3. Many writers argue that textbooks for children show a heavy gender bias toward men. Do you agree? Look at some elementary school textbooks and write a paper about how the writers represent men and women.

Malcolm X

Prison Studies

Born in Omaha, Nebraska, as Malcolm Little, Malcolm X (1925–1965) was a religious activist and civil rights leader as well as a prominent figure in the African-American Muslim community. Imprisoned for robbery in 1961, he educated himself while in prison and chronicles some of his efforts there in this essay. Always a controversial figure, Malcolm X was assassinated in New York City in 1963.

——— ★ ———

1 Many who today hear me somewhere in person, or on television, or those who read something I've said, will think I went to school far beyond the eighth grade. This impression is due entirely to my prison studies.

2 It had really begun back in the Charlestown Prison, when Bimbi first made me feel envy of his stock of knowledge. Bimbi had always taken charge of any conversation he was in, and I had tried to emulate him. But every book I picked up had few sentences which didn't contain anywhere from one to nearly all of the words that might as well have been in Chinese. When I just skipped those words, of course, I really ended up with little idea of what the book said. So I had come to the Norfolk Prison Colony still going through only book-reading motions. Pretty soon, I would have quit even these motions, unless I had received the motivation that I did.

3 I saw that the best thing I could do was get hold of a dictionary—to study, to learn some words. I was lucky enough to reason also that I should try to improve my penmanship. It was sad. I couldn't even write in a straight line. It was both ideas together that moved me to request a dictionary along with some tablets and pencils from the Norfolk Prison Colony school.

4 I spent two days just riffling uncertainly through the dictionary's pages. I'd never realized so many words existed! I didn't know which words I needed to learn. Finally, to start some kind of action, I began copying.

5 In my slow, painstaking, ragged handwriting, I copied into my tablet everything printed on that first page, down to the punctuation marks.

6 I believe it took me a day. Then, aloud, I read back, to myself, everything I'd written on the tablet. Over and over, aloud, to myself, I read my own handwriting.

I woke up the next morning, thinking about those words—im-   7
mensely proud to realize that not only had I written so much at one
time, but I'd written words that I never knew were in the world. Moreover, with a little effort, I also could remember what many of these
words meant. I reviewed the words whose meanings I didn't remember. Funny thing, from the dictionary first page right now, that "aardvark" spring to my mind. The dictionary had a picture of it, a long-
tailed, long-eared, burrowing African mammal, which lives off
termites caught by sticking out its tongue as an anteater does for ants.

I was so fascinated that I went on—I copied the dictionary's next   8
page. And the same experience came when I studied that. With every succeeding page, I also learned of people and places and events from history.
Actually the dictionary is like a miniature encyclopedia. Finally the dictionary's A section had filled a whole tablet—and I went on into the B's. That
was the way I started copying what eventually became the entire dictionary. It went a lot faster after so much practice helped me to pick up handwriting speed. Between what I wrote in my tablet, and writing letters,
during the rest of my time in prison I would guess I wrote a million words.

I suppose it was inevitable that as my word-base broadened, I   9
could for the first time pick up a book and read and now begin to understand what the book was saying. Anyone who has read a great deal
can imagine the new world that opened. Let me tell you something;
from then until I left that prison, in every free moment I had, if I was
not reading in the library, I was reading on my bunk. You couldn't have
gotten me out of books with a wedge. Between Mr. Muhammad's
teachings, my correspondence, my visitors—usually Ella and Reginald—
and my reading of books, months passed without my even thinking
about being imprisoned. In fact, up to then, I never had been so truly
free in my life. . . .

As you can imagine, especially in a prison where there was heavy   10
emphasis on rehabilitation, an inmate was smiled upon if he demonstrated an unusually intense interest in books. There was a sizable
number of well-read inmates, especially the popular debaters. Some
were said by many to be practically walking encyclopedias. They were
almost celebrities. No university would ask any student to devour literature as I did when this new world opened to me, of being able to
read and *understand*.

I read more in my room than in the library itself. An inmate who   11
was known to read a lot could check out more than the permitted maximum number of books. I preferred reading in the total isolation of my
own room.

When I had progressed to really serious reading, every night at   12
about ten P.M. I would be outraged with the "lights out." It always
seemed to catch me right in the middle of something engrossing.

13   Fortunately, right outside my door was a corridor light that cast a glow into my room. The glow was enough to read by, once my eyes adjusted to it. So when "lights out" came, I would sit on the floor where I could continue reading in that glow.

14   At one-hour intervals the night guards paced past every room. Each time I heard the approaching footsteps, I jumped into bed and feigned sleep. And as soon as the guard passed, I got back out of bed onto the floor area of that light-glow, where I would read for another fifty-eight minutes—until the guard approached again. That went on until three or four every morning. Three or four hours of sleep a night was enough for me. Often in the years in the streets I had slept less than that.

15   I have often reflected upon the new vistas that reading opened to me. I knew right there in prison that reading had changed forever the course of my life. As I see it today, the ability to read awoke inside me some long dormant craving to be mentally alive. I certainly wasn't seeking any degree, the way a college confers a status symbol upon its students. My homemade education gave me, with every additional book that I read, a little bit more sensitivity to the deafness, dumbness, and blindness that was afflicting the black race in America. Not long ago, an English writer telephoned me from London, asking questions. One was, "What's your alma mater?" I told him, "Books." You will never catch me with a free fifteen minutes in which I'm not studying something I feel might be able to help the black man. . . .

16   Every time I catch a plane, I have with me a book that I want to read—and that's a lot of books these days. If I weren't out here every day battling the white man, I could spend the rest of my life reading, just satisfying my curiosity—because you can hardly mention anything I'm not curious about. I don't think anybody ever got more out of going to prison than I did. In fact, prison enabled me to study far more intensively than I would have if my life had gone differently and I had attended some college. I imagine that one of the biggest troubles with colleges is there are too many distractions, too much panty-raiding, fraternities, and boola-boola and all of that. Where else but in prison could I have attacked my ignorance by being able to study intensely sometimes as much as fifteen hours a day?

★ *Meaning and Understanding*

1. What do you think is the main point of this selection?

2. What is Malcolm implying when he says that people who come into contact with him "will think I went to school far beyond the eighth grade"?

3. Why does Malcolm answer the question about his alma mater with the single word "Books"?

4. Why were inmates "smiled upon" if they were very interested in books?

5. Why was it "inevitable" that Malcolm began to understand more of what he read?

6. Malcolm refers to his education as "homemade." What do you think he means by this? Does he imply that there is a particular value to this kind of education?

★ Techniques and Strategies

1. The writer says that he "spent two days just riffling uncertainly through the dictionary," and he refers to his "slow, painstaking, ragged handwriting." Why does he characterize his actions and writing in this manner? What effect(s) do you think he is trying to achieve?

2. Malcolm makes a point to tell us about the impact that the "aardvark" entry in the dictionary had on him. Why does he focus on this particular image?

3. Who do you think is the intended audience for this piece? What in the selection leads you to think so?

4. The piece begins and ends with references to celebrity (public speaking, television, "catching a plane"). Considering that much of the body of the selection refers to Malcolm's experience in prison, why do you think he frames the essay in this manner?

5. In paragraph 2 Malcolm offers some of his personal history by mentioning the various prisons he had been in. Why does he do this?

★ Speaking of Values

1. Malcolm tells us that because of his reading, "months passed without my even thinking about being imprisoned. In fact, up to then, I had never been so truly free in my life." In what way is he "truly free"? How can books free people? What does this observation suggest about the value of education?

2. In paragraph 15, Malcolm says that "reading had changed forever the course of my life." How does he suggest that it did so? Refer to specific clues in the selection to support your answer. In what ways can reading change your life or the life of others you know?

3. Obviously there are many kinds of education and clearly Malcolm X was "educated," to some extent, on the street (see paragraph 14) before he went to prison. What connection does he make between reading

and education in general? What is the interrelation between book learning and street learning in producing knowledge?

4. Malcolm says in paragraph 15 that his reading gave him "a little bit more sensitivity to the deafness, dumbness, and blindness that was affecting the black race in America," and in paragraph 16 he refers to "every day battling the white man." What particular definition or purpose of education do these references suggest?

5. In a few places in the selection Malcolm draws a parallel between prison and college. How valid do you think his comparison is? What values does he impart to each institution? Which institution does he prefer? Why? How does his choice affect your way of thinking about education?

★ Values Conversation

Form groups and talk about the value of education in today's world. Discuss why you are actually in school, what you hope to gain by it, and why your relatives and teachers think it is important. Then talk about American society's current view of education. What elements in these views do you find most valid? Why? Consider any differences that you may come up with between your views and the views of your parents and teachers concerning the nature and importance of education.

★ Writing about Values

1. Malcolm makes prison sound almost like a desirable place, certainly different from the picture we often get from firsthand accounts, movies, and TV. Do some research about prison life in America, both as it is today and as it might have been forty or so years ago when Malcolm X was incarcerated. As part of your research, you may wish to view films such as *The Shawshank Redemption* or *Alcatraz*. Then write a paper comparing the picture of prison life that emerges from your research and the kind of existence implied in this selection. Be sure to discuss whether or not you think prison life is conducive to pursuing one's education.

2. In this selection, Malcolm implies that education has a political basis. That is, he says that reading gave him greater insight into the plight of Black Americans and the weaknesses in the collective Black American character. Write a paper discussing what *you* believe to be the value of education. In other words, should education be conservative, radical, transformative, or vocational, to suggest a few possibilities. Could it be all of these? Some of these? Do you have other ideas?

3. In paragraph 10, Malcolm says, "No university would ask any student to devour literature as I did when this new world opened to me, of be-

ing able to read and *understand*." What, in fact, do you think the purpose of a university is? And why does Malcolm believe that one would not require its students to read as he did? Write a paper explaining your understanding of what a university is and what it does. In other words, how might its educational "product" differ from that of a high school's? Or a prison's?

Ellen Tashie Frisina

"See Spot Run": Teaching My Grandmother to Read

In this essay Ellen Tashie Frisina tells about her "secret" project to teach her seventy-year-old grandmother, who came to America from Greece in 1916, to read English.

———— ★ ————

1   When I was 14 years old, and very impressed with my teenage status (looking forward to all the rewards it would bring), I set for myself a very special goal—a goal that so differentiated me from my friends that I don't believe I told a single one. As a teenager, I was expected to have deep, dark secrets, but I was not supposed too keep them from my friends.

2   My secret was a project that I undertook every day after school for several months. It began when I stealthily made my way into the local elementary school—horror of horrors should I be seen; I was now in junior high. I identified myself as a *graduate* of the elementary school, and being taken under wing by the favorite fifth grade teacher, I was given a small bundle from a locked storeroom—a bundle that I quickly dropped into a bag, lest anyone see me walking home with something from the "little kids" school.

3   I brought the bundle home—proudly now, for within the confines of my home, I was proud of my project. I walked into the living room, and one by one, emptied the bag of basic reading books. They were thin books with colorful covers and large print. The words were mono-syllabic and repetitive. I sat down to the secret task at hand.

4   "All right," I said authoritatively to my 70-year-old grandmother, "today we begin our first reading lesson."

5   For weeks afterward, my grandmother and I sat patiently side by side—roles reversed as she, with a bit of difficulty, sounded out every word, then read them again, piece by piece, until she understood the short sentences. When she slowly repeated the full sentence, we both would smile and clap our hands—I felt so proud, so grown up.

6   My grandmother was born in Kalamata, Greece, in a rocky little farming village where nothing much grew. She never had the time to go to school. As the oldest child, she was expected to take care of her brother and sister, as well as the house and meals, while her mother

tended the gardens, and her father scratched out what little he could from the soil.

So, for my grandmother, schooling was out. But she had big plans   7
for herself. She had heard about America. About how rich you could be. How people on the streets would offer you a dollar just to smell the flower you were carrying. About how everyone lived in nice houses—not stone huts on the sides of mountains–and had nice clothes and time for school.

So my grandmother made a decision at 14—just a child, I realize   8
now—to take a long and sickening 30-day sea voyage alone to the United States. After lying about her age to the passport officials, who would shake their heads vehemently at anyone under 16 leaving her family, and after giving her favorite gold earrings to her cousin, saying "In America, I will have all the gold I want," my young grandmother put herself on a ship. She landed in New York in 1916.

No need to repeat the story of how it went for years. The streets   9
were not made of gold. People weren't interested in smelling flowers held by strangers. My grandmother was a foreigner. Alone. A young girl who worked hard doing piecework to earn enough money for meals. No leisure time, no new gold earrings—and no school.

She learned only enough English to help her in her daily business   10
as she traveled about Brooklyn. Socially, the "foreigners" stayed in neighborhoods where they didn't feel like foreigners. English came slowly.

My grandmother had never learned to read. She could make out a   11
menu, but not a newspaper. She could read a street sign, but not a shop directory. She could read only what she needed to read as, through the years, she married, had five daughters, and helped my grandfather with his restaurant.

So when I was 14—the same age that my grandmother was when   12
she left her family, her country, and everything she knew—I took it upon myself to teach my grandmother something, something I already knew how to do. Something with which I could give back to her some to the things she had taught me.

And it was slight repayment for all she taught me. How to cover   13
the fig tree in tar paper so it could survive the winter. How to cultivate rose bushes and magnolia trees that thrived on her little piece of property. How to make baklava, and other Greek delights, working from her memory. ("Now we add some milk." "How much?" "Until we have enough.") Best of all, she had taught me my ethnic heritage.

First, we phonetically sounded out the alphabet. Then, we talked   14
about vowels—English is such a difficult language to learn. I hadn't even begun to explain the different sounds "gh" could make. We were still at the basics.

15   Every afternoon, we would sit in the living room, my grandmother with an afghan covering her knees, giving up her crocheting for her reading lesson. I, with the patience that can come only from love, slowly coached her from the basic reader to the second-grade reader, giving up my telephone gossiping.

16   Years later, my grandmother still hadn't learned quite enough to sit comfortably with a newspaper or magazine, but it felt awfully good to see her try. How we used to laugh at her pronunciation mistakes. She laughed more heartily than I. I never knew whether I should laugh. Here was this old woman slowly and carefully sounding out each word, moving her lips, not saying anything aloud until she was absolutely sure, and then, loudly, proudly, happily saying, "Look at Spot. See Spot run."

17   When my grandmother died and we faced the sad task of emptying her home, I was going through her night-table drawer and came upon the basic readers. I turned the pages slowly, remembering. I put them in a paper bag, and the next day returned them to the "little kids" school. Maybe someday, some teenager will request them again, for the same task. It will make for a lifetime of memories.

★ Meaning and Understanding

1. Why is Frisina so secretive about teaching her grandmother to read?

2. What does she secure from the elementary school?

3. Where was Frisina's grandmother born? What were the family's expectations of her?

4. How did the grandmother get to America? Why did she lie to the passport officials?

5. Why does the speaker undertake to teach her 70-year-old grandmother how to read English? Why does the grandmother, who apparently survived quite well for over half a century without being able to read English, try so hard to learn?

★ Techniques and Strategies

1. What is the writer's thesis?

2. What is the purpose of the essay? Who is the audience?

3. The selection begins in the recent past, shifts to the more distant past of the grandmother's life, and then concludes with the grandmother's death. What does this chronology contribute to your better understanding of the essay?

4. What is the significance of the phrase in quotations in the essay's title?

5. In paragraph 9 the speaker says that there is "no need to repeat the story of how it went for years," and then goes ahead and repeats it. Why do you think she does so?

★ *Speaking of Values*

1. Educating someone may be seen as an act of responsibility, or it may even be seen as an act of love. Which do you think it is in this selection? Explain your answer.

2. What do you think of the fact that the grandmother left her family at the age of fourteen and immigrated alone to America? Why did she do this? How difficult would it be for you to do something similar? In paragraph 13 the speaker remarks that she is grateful to her grandmother for teaching her about her ethnic heritage. What is the relationship between heritage and language? Can you preserve one without the other? Discuss.

3. The phrase "generation gap" implies that people from different generations have difficulty communicating with and understanding each other. Clearly no such gap exists between Frisina and her grandmother. What evidence do you see for a generation gap in America today? What evidence do you see of people who are able to bridge this gap?

4. Educators are now calling for a degree of volunteer work as part of a comprehensive educational program. What volunteer projects, such as teaching illiterate adults to read, could young teenagers undertake, do you think? How would you encourage them to take on these added responsibilities?

★ *Values Conversation*

Sometimes what we learn from older people is invaluable simply because the knowledge they have may well die with them. Form groups and discuss some of the things you may have learned from your grandparents, elderly aunts and uncles, or aged friends of the family, lessons that you probably could not have learned from books.

★ *Writing about Values*

1. Frisina tells us that her grandmother landed in New York in 1916 at the age of fourteen. Do some library research about emigration from Europe at the turn of the century. Then write a paper discussing the reasons

people left their homes to come to America, the kinds of education they may have had in Europe, and how they were educated once they arrived.

2. Read a novel about immigrants—*Call It Sleep, The Rise of David Levinsky, The Joy Luck Club, The Fortunate Pilgrim,* to name a few—and write a paper about the difficulties the characters in the novels have assimilating into American culture. Pay particular attention to the ways in which each author handles the question of language and reading.

3. Write a personal essay describing how you may have taught someone a skill. Remember to explain the difficulties you may have had as well as whatever benefits you believe you may have derived from the act

Christina Hoff Sommers

Ethics without Virtue: Moral Education in America

Christina Hoff Sommers, a philosophy teacher and writer, is the author of *Right and Wrong: Basic Readings in Ethics* (1986), *Vice and Virtue in Everyday Life: Introductory Readings in Ethics* (1987), and *Who Stole Feminism: How Women Have Betrayed Women* (1994). Here she explores the way educational institutions address the issue of values instruction.

─────── ★ ───────

What do students in our nation's schools do all day? Most of them are clearly not spending their time reading the classics, learning math, or studying the physical sciences. It is likely that, along with photography workshops, keeping journals, and perhaps learning about computers, students spend part of their day in moral education classes. But these classes are not, as one might expect, designed to acquaint students with the Western moral tradition. Professional theorists in schools of education have found that tradition wanting and have devised an alternative, one they have marketed in public schools with notable success.

A reform of moral education is not a task to be undertaken lightly. The sincerity and personal integrity of the theorist-reformers is not at issue, but their qualifications as moral educators is a legitimate subject of concern. The leaders of reform do not worry about credentials. They are convinced that traditional middle-class morality is at best useless and at worst pernicious, and they have confidence in the new morality that is to replace the old and in the novel techniques to be applied to this end. In 1970 Theodore Sizer, then dean of the Harvard School of Education, co-edited with his wife Nancy a book entitled *Moral Education*. The preface set the tone by condemning the morality of "the Christian gentleman," "the American prairie," the McGuffey *Reader*, and the hypocrisy of teachers who tolerate a grading system that is "the terror of the young." According to the Sizers, all of the authors in the anthology agree that "the 'old morality' can and should be scrapped."

The movement to reform moral education has its seat in the most prestigious institutions of education. Its theories are seldom contested, and its practice is spreading. Students who have received the new moral instruction have been turning up in freshman college classes in increasing numbers. While giving college ethics courses during the past six years, I have become convinced that the need for a critical appraisal of the claims and assumptions of the movement is urgent. My experience is that the students who received the new teaching have been ill served by their mentors.

4   One gains some idea of the new moral educators from the terminology they use. Courses in ethics are called "values clarification" or "cognitive moral development": teachers are "values processors," "values facilitators," or "reflective-active listeners"; lessons in moral reasoning are "sensitivity modules"; volunteer work in the community is an "action module"; and teachers "dialogue" with students to help them discover their own systems of values. In these dialogues the teacher avoids discussing "old bags of virtues," such as wisdom, courage, compassion, and "proper" behavior, because any attempt to instill these would be to indoctrinate the student. Some leaders of the new reform movement advise teachers that effective moral education cannot take place in the "authoritarian" atmosphere of the average American high school. The teacher ought to democratize the classroom, turning it into a "just community" where the student and teacher have an equal say. Furthermore, the student who takes a normative ethics course in college will likely encounter a professor who also has a principled aversion to the inculcation of moral precepts and who will confine classroom discussion to such issues of social concern as the Karen Ann Quinlan case, recombinant DNA research, or the moral responsibilities of corporations. The result is a system of moral education that is silent about virtue.

5   The teaching of virtue is not viewed as a legitimate aim of a moral curriculum, but there is no dearth of alternative approaches. From the time the values education movement began in the late nineteen sixties, its theorists have produced an enormous number of articles, books, films, manuals, and doctoral dissertations; there are now journals, advanced degree programs, and entire institutes dedicated exclusively to moral pedagogy; and for the past several years, teachers, counselors, and education specialists have been attending conferences, seminars, workshops, and retreats to improve their skills in values-processing. At present, two opposing ideologies dominate moral education: the values clarification movement, whose best-known proponent is Sidney Simon of the University of Massachusetts School of Education; and the cognitive moral development movement, whose chief spokesman is Lawrence Kohlberg, a professor of psychology and education, and director of the Center for Moral Education at Harvard.

6   Values clarification, according to Sidney Simon, is "based on the premise that none of us has the 'right' set of values to pass on to other people's children." Its methods are meant to help students to get at "their own feelings, their own ideas, their own beliefs, so that the choices and decisions they make are conscious and deliberate, based on

their own value system." The success of the values clarification movement has been phenomenal. In 1975 a study from the Hoover Institute
referred to "hundreds perhaps thousands of school programs that employ the clarification methodology" and reported that ten states have
officially adopted values clarification as a model for their moral education programs. Proponents of values clarification consider it inappropriate for a teacher to encourage students, however subtly or indirectly,
to adopt the values of the teacher or the community. In their book,
Readings in Values Clarification, Simon and his colleague Howard Kir-
schenbaum wrote:

> We call this approach "moralizing," although it has also been known
> as inculcation, imposition, indoctrination, and in its most extreme
> form brainwashing. Moralizing is the direct or indirect transfer of a set
> of values from one person or group to another person or group.

The student of values clarification is taught awareness of his preferences and his right to their satisfaction in a democratic society. To help
students discover what it is that they genuinely value, they are asked to
respond to questionnaires called "strategies." Some typical questions
are: What animal would you rather be: an ant, a beaver, or a donkey?
Which season do you like best? Do you prefer hiking, swimming, or
watching television? In one strategy called "Values Geography," the
student is helped to discover his geographical preferences; other lessons solicit his reaction to seat belts, messy handwriting, hiking, wall-
to-wall carpeting, cheating, abortion, hit-and-run drivers, and a mother
who severely beats a two-year-old child.

Western literature and history are two traditional alienating influ- 7
ences that the values clarification movement is on guard against. Simon
has written that he has ceased to find meaning "in the history of war or
the structure of a sonnet, and more meaning in the search to find value
in life." He and his colleagues believe that exposure to one's cultural
heritage is not likely to be morally beneficial to the "average student."

> Because values are complex and because man's thoughts and accom-
> plishments are both abundant and complicated, it is difficult to recom-
> mend that the average student rely on this approach. It takes
> substantial mental stamina and ability and much time and energy to
> travel this road. While the study of our cultural heritage can be de-
> fended on other grounds, we would not expect it to be sufficient for
> value education.

The values clarification theorist does not believe that moral sensibility
and social conscience are, in significant measure, learned by reading
and discussing the classics. Instead Simon speaks of the precious legacy

we can leave to "generations of young people if we teach them to set their priorities and rank order the marvelous items in life's cafeteria."

8   As a college teacher coping with the motley ideologies of high school graduates, I find this alarming. Young people today, many of whom are in a complete moral stupor, need to be shown that there is an important distinction between moral and nonmoral decisions. Values clarification blurs the distinction. Children are queried about their views on homemade Christmas gifts, people who wear wigs, and whether or not they approve of abortion or would turn in a hit-and-run driver as if no significant differences existed among these issues.

9   It is not surprising that teachers trained in neutrality and the principled avoidance of "moralizing" sometimes find themselves in bizarre classroom situations. In a junior high school in Newton, Massachusetts, a teacher put on the blackboard a poster of a Hell's Angel wearing a swastika. The students were asked to react. "He's honest, anyway. He's living out his own feelings," answered one. "He's not fooling," said another. When the students seemed to react favorably to the Hell's Angel, the teacher ventured to suggest that "an alienated person might not be happy."

10   The following conversation took place between a values clarification teacher and her students:

11   *Student:* Does this mean that we can decide for ourselves whether to be honest on tests here?

12   *Teacher:* No, that means that you can decide on the value. I personally value honesty; and although you may choose to be dishonest, I shall insist that we be honest in our tests. In other areas of your life, you may have more freedom to be dishonest.

13   *And another teacher:* My class deals with morality and right and wrong quite a bit. I don't expect them all to agree with me; each has to satisfy himself according to his own conviction, as long as he is sincere, and thinks he is pursuing what is right. I often discuss cheating this way, but I always get defeated because they will argue that cheating is all right. After you accept the idea that kids have the right to build a position with logical arguments, you have to accept what they come up with.

14   The student has values; the values clarification teacher is merely "facilitating" the student's access to them. Thus, no values are taught. The emphasis is on *learning how,* not on *learning that.* The student does not learn *that* acts of stealing are wrong; he learns how to respond to such acts.

15   The values clarification course is, in this sense, contentless. As if to make up for this, it is methodologically rich. It is to be expected that an advocate of values clarification emphasizes method over content in other areas of education, and indeed he does. Many handbooks, strate-

gies, board games, and kits have been developed to help teachers adapt the methods of values clarification to such subjects as English, history, science, math, and even home economics and Spanish. Values clarification guides for girl scout troops and Sunday school classes are also available, as well as manuals to assist parents in clarifying values at the dinner table.

Simon and his colleagues explain that it is useless and anachronistic   16 to teach the student at a "facts level." In a history lesson on the Constitution, for example, the teacher is advised not to waste too much time on such questions as where and when the Constitution was drawn up. Undue attention should also not be given to the "concepts level," where, for example, the teacher discusses the moral origins of the Bill of Rights. When the learning of the subject matter is unavoidable, Simon and his colleagues recommend that it be lifted to a higher and more urgent level where students are asked "you-centered" questions, such as, "What rights do you have in your family?" Or, "Many student governments are really token governments controlled by the 'mother country,' i.e., the administration. Is this true in your school? What can you do about it?" And, "When was the last time you signed a petition?"

The classical moral tradition will not be revived by the practitio-   17 ners of values clarification. Indeed, it is, in their eyes, an alien tradition that is insensitive to the needs and rights of the contemporary student.

II

Lawrence Kohlberg, the leader of the second major movement in moral   18 education, shares with values clarification educators a low opinion of traditional morality. In his contribution to Theodore and Nancy Sizer's anthology, *Moral Education,* he writes, "Far from knowing whether it can be taught, I have no idea what virtue really is." Kohlberg's disclaimer is not a Socratic confession of ignorance; he considers the teaching of traditional virtues to be at best a waste of time and at worst coercive. Like Sidney Simon, he, too, uses the language of conspiracy to characterize the American educational system. He refers often to the "hidden curriculum" and insists that the teacher must not be "an agent of the state, the church, or the social system, [but] rather . . . a free moral agent dealing with children who are free moral agents." Kohlberg cites as an example of covert indoctrination a teacher who yelled at some boys for not returning their books to the proper place. "The teacher would have been surprised to know that her concerns with classroom management defined for her children what she and her school thought were basic values, or that she was engaged in indoctrination." Kohlberg and his disciples are currently busy transforming some of the best school systems in the country into "just communities" where no such indoctrination takes place.

19   Kohlberg's authority derives from his cognitive developmental approach to moral education. Following John Dewey, Kohlberg distinguishes three main stages of moral development (each of which is partitioned into a higher and lower stage, making six in all). The first stage is called the premoral or preconventional reward/punishment level. In the second stage morals are conventional but unreflective. In the third stage moral principles are autonomously chosen on rational grounds. Kohlberg's research applies Piaget's idea that the child possesses certain cognitive structures that come successively into play as the child develops. According to Kohlberg, the latent structures are a cross-cultural fact of cognitive psychology. Kohlberg's more specific thesis on the unfolding of the child's innate moral propensities has received a great deal of deserved attention. The literature on Kohlberg is controversial, and it is far too early to say whether his ideas are sound enough for eventual use in the classroom. Kohlberg himself has urged and already put into practice pedagogical applications of his ideas.

20   From the assumption of innateness, it is but a short step to the belief that the appropriate external circumstances will promote the full moral development of the child. It then becomes the job of the educator to provide those circumstances "facilitating" the child to his moral maturity. The innate structures are essentially contentless, and Kohlberg and his followers do not think it is the job of the moral educator to develop a virtuous person by supplying the content—that is, the traditional virtues. To do that would be, in Kohlberg's contemptuous phrase, to impose on the child an "old bag of virtues." Kohlberg and his associate Moshe Blatt remark in the *Journal of Moral Education*:

> Moral education is best conceived as a natural process of dialogue among peers, rather than as a process of didactic instruction or preaching. The teacher and the curriculum are best conceived as facilitators of this dialogue.

If moral education is to be a dialogue among peers, the relation between teacher and student must be radially transformed. Fully prepared to accept these consequences, Kohlberg, in 1974, founded the Cluster School in Cambridge, Massachusetts. It consisted of thirty students, six teachers, dozens of consultants, and Kohlberg—all of whom had an equal voice in running the school. According to Kohlberg, "The only way school can help graduating students become persons who can make society a just community is to let them try experimentally to make the school themselves." As he soon learned, these student citizens were forever stealing from one another and using drugs during school hours. These transgressions provoked a long series of democratically conducted "town meetings" that to an outsider look very much like EST encounter groups. The students were frequently taken on retreats (Kohlberg and his associates share with the values clarification people a penchant for retreats), where many of them broke the rules against sex and drugs. This provoked more democratic confrontations where, Kohlberg was proud to report, it was usually decided that for the sake of the group the students would police one another on subsequent retreats and turn in the names of the transgressors. Commenting on the rash of thefts at the Cluster School, Kohlberg said "At the moment there is clearly a norm in the Cluster School of maintaining trust around property issues. But there is uncertainty about whether the norm has [fully] developed." Since the Cluster School lasted only five years, this uncertainty will never be resolved.

In turning to the just communities, Kohlberg has consciously aban-   21
doned his earlier goal of developing individual students to the highest stages of moral development. The most he now hopes for is development to stage four, where students learn to respect the new just social order. His reasons are revealing. In 1980 in an anthology edited by Ralph Mosher, *Moral Education: A First Generation of Research and Development*, Kohlberg writes, "Perhaps all stage six persons of the 1960's had been wiped out, perhaps they had regressed, or maybe it was all my imagination in the first place."

The Cluster School has been the subject of a great many articles and   22
doctoral theses. Careers have been advanced just by praising it. In Mosher's anthology one critic writes about the school:

> Cluster School . . . in my judgment, is a unique secondary school environment, characterized by a respect and caring for persons and determination to make the governance structure one in which students can experience the roles necessary for full participation in democracy.

From these remarks—and similar ones by others who visited Cluster School—you would never guess that the school was in shambles and just about to close. The school was racially divided; drugs, sex, and theft were rampant; and Kohlberg was fighting bitterly with the teachers. Here was a school—with thirty students and six exceptionally trained and dedicated teachers—that by any objective standard must be counted a failure. Yet in American professional education nothing succeeds like failure. Having scored their failure at the Cluster School, the Kohlbergians have put their ideas to work in more established schools. (For example, they now exercise a significant influence in such diverse public school systems as Pittsburgh, Pennsylvania; Salt Lake City, Utah; Scarsdale, New York; and Brookline, Massachusetts.)

Brookline High School in Massachusetts provides a particularly   23
sad example of the way the new ideologies can penetrate a fine high school. The school administration has been taken over by Kohlbergians who, with the help of federal funds, are trying to turn it into a "just

community." To this end the governance of the school has been given over to the entire school community—students, teachers, administrators, secretaries, and janitorial staff. To make the process work smoothly, not all students are invited to the weekly "town meetings," just their representatives. But, because many of the two thousand or so students are indifferent, many student representatives are self-appointed. And the big problem is that most of the teachers do not attend (nor, of course, do tired secretaries and maintenances workers).

24   I attended one meeting with thirty students, five teachers, two student visitors from Scarsdale who are working with Kohlberg and studying the Brookline program in hopes of using it in New York, and two observers from the Carnegie-Mellon Foundation, who were there to investigate the possibility of making a film about the Brookline experiment for public television. The kids who participated in the meeting were charming and articulate, and the Carnegie-Mellon people were clearly pleased, and they will make their film. Like many educational experts who admire the Brookline town meetings, these observers are probably unaware that many of the teachers feel harassed and manipulated by the Kohlberg administration. So far, the participants in the town meetings—who are mostly teenagers exercising more power than they will ever be granted in college or graduate school—have voted to rescind a rule against Walkman radios on campus, to prohibit homework assignments for vacation periods, to disallow surprise quizzes, and they have instituted a procedure for bringing teachers who give tests or assignments that are too demanding before a "Fairness Committee." One teacher told me that the students had never asked for the powers they now enjoy. According to the teacher, the school authorities handed these powers over to students "for their own good." Just communities are Kohlberg's answer to the oppression exercised by established authority. Evidently, Kohlberg sees no need to question his assumption that established authority is intrinsically suspect. In any event, it is ironic that now, when teachers with authority are so rare, educational theorists like Kohlberg are proposing that authority itself is the evil to be combated.

25   Ralph Mosher, a Harvard-trained Kohlbergian, is the chief educational consultant to the Brookline High School. In his anthology he writes the following about the standards that have been in place:

> Moral education, all the more powerful because it is "hidden," is embedded in the tacit values of the curriculum and the school. For example, the most worthy/valued student in Brookline High School is the one who achieves early admission to Harvard on a full scholarship. How few can accomplish this is obvious. Yet teachers, counselors, and parents put great, albeit subtle, pressure on the many to do likewise....

What the research [in moral education] has attempted to do is to make some schooling more just.

Mosher's attitude is instructive. Ideals, it seems, are not goals to aim for. They must be attainable by the majority of students. If any goals are set up, they must be ones to which most students can realistically aspire. For Mosher, vigilance against superimposing a hidden agenda with elitist bias is the order of the day.

Kohlberg's ideas have taken hold in the better schools, where one can still find a fair number of parents who can afford to hold attitudes against elitism. Should the public school of Brookline, Cambridge, or Scarsdale fail to provide the education necessary for admission to the best colleges, those parents have recourse to some fine private schools in the neighborhood. In the meantime they can indulge the unexceptionable concept of a just community, whose egalitarian character is welcomed by those who find themselves uncomfortably well-fixed, particularly after the radical views they held in the halcyon sixties. 26

The values clarification and cognitive development reformers are well aware that they are riding a wave of public concern about the need for an effective system of moral education. Thus Mosher writes: 27

> [A] high proportion of Americans (four of five in recent Gallup Polls) support moral education in the public schools. What the respondents mean by moral education is, of course, moot. Probably the teaching of virtues such as honesty, respect for adults, moderation in the use of alcohol/drugs, sexual restraint and so on.... Educators would have to exceed Caesar's wife not to capitalize on an idea whose time appeared to have come.

This last remark about capitalizing on the parent's desire for higher moral standards is disarmingly cynical. Naturally the public wants its "old bag of virtues," but educational theorists such as Mosher are convinced that giving the public what it wants is ineffective and unjust. The traditional moralists have failed (witness Watergate), so now it's their turn. Mosher's attitude to the benighted parents is condescending. No doubt for Mosher and Kohlberg, the morally confident leaders of the reform movement, theirs is the right kind of elitism.

The depreciation of moralizing common to values clarification and cognitive development theory has been effective even in those schools where the reforms have not yet penetrated. Increasingly nowadays, few teachers have the temerity to praise any middle-class virtues. The exception is the virtue of tolerance. But, when tolerance is the sole virtue, students' capacity for moral indignation, so important for moral development, is severely inhibited. The result is moral passivity and confusion and a shift of moral focus from the individual to society. 28

III

29   The student entering college today shows the effects of an educational system that has kept its distance from the traditional virtues. Unencumbered by the "old bag of virtues," the student arrives toting a ragbag of another stripe whose contents may be roughly itemized as follows: psychological egoism (the belief that the primary motive for action is selfishness), moral relativism (the doctrine that what is praiseworthy or contemptible is a matter of cultural conditioning), and radical tolerance (the doctrine that to be culturally and socially aware is to understand and excuse the putative wrongdoer). Another item in the bag is the conviction that the seat of moral responsibility is found in society and its institutions, not in individuals.

30   The half-baked relativism of the college student tends to undermine his common sense. In a term paper that is far from atypical, one of my students wrote that Jonathan Swift's "modest proposal" for solving the problem of hunger in Ireland by harvesting Irish babies for food was "good for Swift's society, but not for ours." All too often one comes up against a grotesquely distorted perspective that common sense has little power to set right. In one discussion in my introductory philosophy class, several students were convinced that the death of one person and the death of ten thousand is equally bad. When a sophomore was asked whether she saw Nagasaki as the moral equivalent of a traffic accident, she replied, "From a moral point of view, yes." Teachers of moral philosophy who are not themselves moral agnostics trade such stories for dark amusement. But it appears that teachers in other disciplines are also struck by the moral perversity of their students. Richard M. Hunt, a professor of government at Harvard University, gave a course on the Holocaust to one hundred Harvard undergraduates. In the course he was disturbed to find that a majority of students adopted the view that the rise of Hitler and the Nazis was inevitable, that no one could have resisted it, and that in the end no one was responsible for what happened. Hunt's teacher assistant remarked to him, "You know, I think if some of our students were sitting as judges at the Nuremberg trials, they would probably aquit—or at least pardon—most of the Nazi defendants." Professor Hunt has dubbed his students' forgiving attitude toward the past "no-fault history."

31   It is fair to say that many college students are thoroughly confused about morality. What they sorely need are some straightforward courses in moral philosophy and a sound and unabashed introduction to the Western moral tradition—something they may never have had before. But few teachers will use that tradition as a source of moral instruction: the fear of indoctrination is even stronger in the colleges than it is at primary and secondary schools. In a recent study of the teaching of ethics prepared by the Hastings Center, a well-respected institute for the study of ethical questions, the authors write:

A major concern about the teaching of ethics has been whether and to what extent it is appropriate to teach courses on ethics in a pluralistic society, and whether it is possible to teach such courses without engaging in unacceptable indoctrination.

And elsewhere in the same report:

No teacher of ethics can assume that he or she has a solid grasp on the nature of morality as to pretend to know what finally counts as good moral conduct. No society can assume that it has any better grasp of what so counts as to empower teachers to propagate it in colleges and universities. Perhaps most importantly, the premise of higher education is that students are at an age where they have to begin coming to their own conclusions and shaping their own view of the world.

It would, however, be altogether incorrect to say that the colleges are ignoring moral instruction. The spread of moral agnosticism has been accompanied by an extraordinary increase in courses of applied ethics. Philosophy departments, isolated and marginal for many years, are now attracting unprecedented numbers of students to their courses in medical ethics, business ethics, ethics for everyday life, ethics for engineers, nurses, social workers, and lawyers. Today there are dozens of journals and conferences, hundreds of books and articles, and—according to the Hastings Center—eleven thousand college courses in applied ethics. 32

The new interest in applied ethics is itself a phenomenon to be welcomed. Public discussions of controversial issues will surely benefit from the contributions of philosophers, and the literature of applied ethics should be read by anyone who seeks a responsible understanding of topical issues. In reading the anthologies of applied ethics, a student encounters arguments of philosophers who take strong stands on important social questions. These arguments often shake a student's confidence in moral relativism. Nevertheless, the literature of applied ethics, like the literature of values clarification and cognitive moral development, has little or nothing to say about matters of individual virtue. The resurgence of moral education in the college thus reinforces the shift away from personal morals to an almost exclusive preoccupation with the morality of institutional policies. After all, most students are not likely to be involved personally in administering the death penalty or selecting candidates for kidney dialysis; and, since most will never do recombinant DNA research, or even have abortions, the purpose of the courses in applied ethics is to teach students how to form responsible opinions on questions of social policy. A strong ethical curriculum is a good thing, but a curriculum of ethics without virtue is a cause for concern. 33

The applied ethics movement in the universities started in the late nineteen sixties when philosophers became interested once again in 34 normative ethics. Between 1940 and 1968 ethics had been theoretical and methodologically self-conscious, to the relative neglect of practical ethics. A large number of philosophers emerged from the sixties eager to contribute to national moral debates. But like Simon, Kohlberg, and their followers, these philosophers were suspicious and distrustful of moralizing and deeply averse to indoctrination. It is no small feat to launch a powerful and influential movement in normative ethics without recourse to the language of vice and virtue and a strong notion of personal responsibility, but that is exactly what is being attempted. The new university moralists, uncomfortable and ideologically at odds with the descredited middle-class ethic, are making their reform movement succeed by addressing themselves, not to the vices and virtues of individuals, but to the moral character of our nation's institutions. Take a look at almost any text used today in college ethics courses—for example, *Ethics for Modern Life*, edited by R. Abelson and M. Friquegnon, *Today's Moral Problems*, edited by R. Wasserstrom, or *Moral Problems* by J. Rachels—and you will find that almost all of the articles consist of philosophical evaluations of the conduct and policies of schools, hospitals, courts, corporations, and the United States government.

35   Inevitably the student forms the idea that applying ethics to modern life is mainly a question of learning how to be for or against social and institutional policies. Appropriately enough, many of the articles sound like briefs written for a judge or legislator. In that sort of ethical climate, a student soon loses sight of himself as a moral agent and begins to see himself as a moral spectator or a protojurist. This is not to deny that many of the issues have an immediate personal dimension. They do, but the primary emphasis is not on what one is to do as a person but on what one is to believe as a member of society—in other words, on ideology and doctrine rather than on personal responsibility and practical decency.

36   The move to issue-oriented courses is hailed as a move back to the days when moral instruction played a significant role in education. Nothing could be further from the truth. Where Aristotle, Aquinas, Mill, and Kant are telling us how to behave, the contemporary university moralist is concerned with what we are to advocate, vote for, protest against, and endorse. Michael Walzer has compared the applied ethics movement to the scholarly activities of the Greek Academicians, the Talmudists, and the medieval Casuists. The comparison is inept, for those earlier moralists were working in a tradition in which it was assumed that the practical end of all moral theory was the virtuous individual. The ancient sophist, with his expertise in rhetoric and politics, is a more convincing analogue to the teachers of issue-oriented ethics, who find little time for the history of ethical theory with its traditional emphasis on the good and virtuous life. One may therefore be wary of the widespread enthusiasm for the "exciting new developments" in the teaching

of ethics. Especially misleading is the frequent observation that the revival of interest in practical ethics is a great advance over the earlier preoccupation with evaluative language (meta-ethics). Admittedly the preoccupation with meta-ethics that characterized the teaching of ethics a decade ago left the student undernourished by neglecting normative ethics. But, in all fairness, neither students nor teachers were under any illusion that meta-ethics was the whole of ethics. Today the student is learning that normative ethics is primarily social policy. This being so, moral action should be politically directed; the individual's task is to bring the right civic institutions (the true moral agents) into place. The student tacitly assumes that ethics is not a daily affair, that it is a matter for specialists, and that its practical benefits are deferred until the time of institutional reform.

The result of identifying normative ethics with public policy is justification for and reinforcement of moral passivity in the student. Even problems that call for large-scale political solutions have their immediate private dimension, but a student trained in a practical ethics that has avoided or de-emphasized individual responsibility is simply unprepared for any demand that is not politically or ideologically formulated. The student is placed in the undemanding role of the indignant moral spectator who needs not face the comparatively minor corruptions in his own life. 37

How, finally, is one to account for the ethics-without-virtue phenomenon? A fully adequate answer is beyond me, but clearly there is a great deal more to the story than the national disenchantment with a system of education that "failed to prevent" moral lapses such as Watergate. A historian of ideas would probably take us back to romantics like Rousseau and to realists like Marx. George Steiner has written of this theme in Rousseau: 38

> In the Rousseauist mythology of conduct, a man could commit a crime either because his education had not taught him how to distinguish good and evil, or because he had been corrupted by society. Responsibility lay with his school or environment for evil cannot be native to the soul. And because the individual is not wholly responsible he cannot be wholly damned.

The values clarification theorists can find little to disagree with in this description.

For social-minded reformers, justice is the principal virtue, and social policy is where ethics is really "at." The assumption is that there is an implicit conflict between the just society and the repressive morality of its undemocratic predecessors. An extreme version of this theme is presented in a little book edited by Trotsky, *Their Morals and Ours*, with its searing attack on the "conservative banalities of bourgeois morality." For Trotsky, of course, social reform requires revolution, but his 39 indictment of the hypocrisies and "brutalities" of "their morals" must sound familiar to the Kohlbergians. The fate of those societies that have actually succeeded in replacing personal morality with social policy is the going price for ignoring the admonition of Max Weber: "He who seeks salvation of the soul—of his own and others—should not seek it along the avenue of politics."

40   An essay on contemporary trends in moral education would be incomplete without mention of the Moral Majority. I have refrained from discussing this movement partly because it receives a great deal of public attention compared to the relative neglect of the movements inspired by the New England professors of education. But I suspect another reason for my silence is my own dismay that at this moment the Moral Majority constitutes the only vocal and self-confident alternative to the ethics-without-virtue movement.

★ Meaning and Understanding

1. In paragraph 2 Sommers remarks that the moral reformers she is writing about "are convinced that traditional middle-class morality is at best useless and at worst pernicious." What do you understand "traditional middle-class morality" to be? What does "pernicious" mean?

2. Sommers talks a great deal about ethics and morality. What is the distinction between them?

3. What point does the example of Brookline High School support?

4. How does Sommers define "values clarification"? What does she mean by distinguishing between "learning how" and "learning that"?

5. The writer refers to the "half-baked relativism of the college student"? What is "relativism" and what does Sommers mean when she says it is "half-baked"?

6. What is "normative ethics"? What is "applied ethics"?

7. What is the "Moral Majority" (paragraph 40)? Why is Sommers dismayed that it "constitutes the only vocal and self-confident alternative to the ethics-without-virtue movement"?

★ Techniques and Strategies

1. Who is the intended audience for this selection? What evidence in the essay supports your point?

2. Why does Sommers inform us in paragraph 15 that "values clarification guides for girl scout troops and Sunday school classes are also available, as well as manuals to assist parents in clarifying values at the dinner table"?

3. What is Sommers's thesis? How do the first few paragraphs prepare readers for it? What is the value of opening the essay with a question?

4. The essay is divided into three distinct sections. Explain how each section works as well as how they are interconnected.

5. What does the "conversation" presented in paragraph 11 add to the essay?

6. Why does Sommers inform us that she is a college philosophy teacher?

7. Make a list of the various educational leaders and philosophers cited in the essay. How do they contribute to Sommers's thesis?

★ *Speaking of Values*

1. In criticizing Kohlberg's ideas, Sommers says that he "sees no need to question his assumption that established authority is intrinsically suspect." Do you think such an assumption should be questioned? Or should established authority always be viewed with suspicion? Explain your point of view.

2. How do you distinguish values from morality? Are they distinguishable? Discuss your response.

3. What is your view of the "values clarification" movement? How do you account for its success? Would you support a values clarification program in your city or hometown school district? Why or why not?

4. What is virtue? Should schools teach virtue? Is it possible to teach it? Sommers asserts that our "system of moral education is silent about virtue." Do you agree? Explain.

5. The writer observes that "many college students are thoroughly confused about morality." Do you agree? Why or why not? Are you or your friends and classmates confused about morality? Why or why not?

★ *Values Conversation*

What is a moral code? Form groups and attempt to develop a statement that suggests a system of behavior and belief that might constitute a moral code. Try to come up with a document that might be used as a guide to helping you make future decisions about moral issues.

★ *Writing about Values*

1. Write a personal statement describing your own "moral system." Explain where your particular beliefs originate, why you adhere to them,

and what inconsistencies or difficulties they may present. Be sure to provide specific examples to demonstrate how your system would help you arrive at moral decisions.

2. If you were designing a curriculum or course of study for moral education of college students, what would you include? Write an essay supporting your ideas.

3. The cluster school movement has gained momentum over the last few years. Do some library research on cluster schools, particularly in your city or state. How have cluster schools succeeded? Failed? Write a paper to explore what you have uncovered.

Values in Review

1. Most of the selections in this chapter imply some theory of education. That is, each author, by critiquing our educational system or
   values, is actually suggesting that the system be reformed in some
   way. Write an essay in which you compare the theories of education
   that emerge from any three pieces in Chapter 2. Which theory do
   you find most appropriate for today's society? Why?

2. Robert Coles, Mike Rose, and Abigail Adams suggest some characteristics of effective teachers. What qualities of a good teacher
   emerge from these selections? Write an essay in which you compare
   and contrast the picture of teachers in these selections and connect
   that picture to what you yourself have observed about the teachers
   you have come into contact with.

3. Shelby Steele, Christina Hoff Sommers, and Timothy Harper discuss
   what they see as "indoctrination" in the classroom. Is education
   without "indoctrination" possible? Drawing on the information and
   perspectives presented in these selections, write an essay in which
   you consider the balance of indoctrination and education that
   should occur in the classroom. Be sure to define what you mean by
   indoctrination.

Chapter 3

Work and Poverty

William Branigin

Sweatshops Are Back

William Branigin was born in 1952. A staff writer for the *Washington Post*, where he was the Southeast Asian correspondent until 1995, Branigin in this essay revisits working conditions long thought to have faded from the American scene.

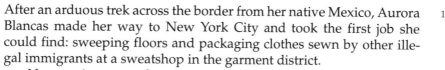

After an arduous trek across the border from her native Mexico, Aurora   1
Blancas made her way to New York City and took the first job she could find: sweeping floors and packaging clothes sewn by other illegal immigrants at a sweatshop in the garment district.

No experience—or documents—necessary.   2

"I started working the same day I asked for the job," she says. "The   3
boss asked me my name and how old I was. Nothing more."

But unlike her fellow workers, Blancas, 28, did not accept quietly   4
the exploitation and abuse that followed when she was hired last summer to work in the dilapidated Eighth Avenue building.

Although her willingness to speak out makes Blancas unusual, the   5
place that employed her and the conditions she found there are not.

Despite a ledger of laws against them and periodic pledges by gov-   6
ernment and business leaders to crack down, sweatshops have made a remarkable comeback in America, evolving from a relative anomaly into a commonplace, even indispensable, part of the U.S. garment industry.

They have also evolved almost entirely into a phenomenon of im-   7
migrants. According to federal investigators and union officials, most such factories are owned by newcomers from Asia, who often exploit other immigrants, many of them illegal, either from Asia or Latin America. Typically, both the workers and the employers see themselves as victims of a system dominated by increasingly powerful major retailers.

In Blancas's case, the owner of the 14th-floor shop in which she   8
worked is a South Korean immigrant whose clothes are sold to suppliers of such stores as Wal-Mart and Kmart. According to Blancas and another former worker, he refused to pay the minimum wage or overtime to his three dozen, mostly female employees. The workers typically toiled at their sewing machines and presses for up to 60 hours a week in a room with wires hanging from the ceiling, three small fans that served as the only source of ventilation and no fire exits. Wages, usually paid in cash to avoid taxes, often were arbitrarily cut or delayed if

163

the owner ran short of funds. Employees who missed a day would be illegally "fined" $30, on top of losing a day's pay.

9   When workers made mistakes, the owner's wife would scream at them, throw garments in their faces and sometimes pull their hair or hit them. One newly arrived young woman was summarily fired for yawning on the job.

10   Last July, after Blancas demanded higher wages and brought the sweatshop to the attention of a garment workers union, she was fired.

11   Whether operating openly in decrepit buildings in New York or Los Angeles or hidden away illegally in people's homes in Dallas, sweatshops violate labor and tax laws amid cutthroat competition for orders that filter down from the retailers.

12   The return of the kind of sweatshops that flourished early this century—and were thought to have been largely eliminated—reflects fundamental changes in the garment industry and, more broadly, in American society. The shops have become part of a vast underground economy, shielded by an overlay of laissez-faire practices and tacit accommodations.

13   Clothing designers and retailers depend on the sweatshops for fast delivery and big profit margins. Unions, hopeful of eventually organizing these workers, appear to be more interested in preserving manufacturing jobs than driving them out of business. Large pools of illegal immigrants are so anxious for work that they accept the shops' meager wages and are often too fearful to complain. Consumers keep gravitating toward the lowest prices they can find. And government agencies do not field enough investigators or cooperate sufficiently with each other to pursue the shops effectively and enforce the laws that would eradicate them.

14   Helping sweatshops to thrive have been technological advances that allow retailers to determine instantly what is selling and to order more of it. This allows stores to limit inventory and avoid getting stuck with large volumes of unpopular apparel. But it also requires quick turnaround, which favors domestic manufacturers. The pressures on these manufacturers to produce garments quickly and still compete with cheap foreign imports have tended to drive down wages and working conditions among the sewing shops that lie at the bottom of the industry.

15   Yet, there is no shortage of workers for these jobs because of a broader change in American society: increasing waves of legal and illegal immigration since the 1970s and growing concentrations of immigrants in cities such as Los Angeles and New York.

16   The sweatshops' revival also reflects a weakening of unions in the garment industry in recent years, in part because of their difficulties in trying to organize workers who are here illegally in the first place. For them, even a sub-minimum wage in the United States generally beats what they could earn in their homelands.

Although the clandestine nature of much of the industry has made   17
it hard to track, recent federal studies point to a rise in the number of
U.S. sweatshops and a worsening of their conditions.

Union and Labor Department officials estimate that minimum   18
wage and overtime violations, two of the basic parameters that define a
sweatshop, prevail in more than half the 22,000 U.S. sewing businesses.
Many also pay their workers "off the books" to avoid various local,
state and federal taxes.

The sweatshop conditions described by Blancas are "typical of the   19
bottom of the industry," says Jeff Hermanson, director of the Garment
Workers' Justice Center, a branch of the Union of Needletrades, Industrial and Textile Employees.

"Physical abuse is unfortunately quite common, and there's al-   20
ways the yelling," he says. The long hours, low wages and lack of benefits often found in Korean-owned sweatshops are also routine in
shops run by Chinese and Latino owners, he says.

In New York, a garment center where much of the industry's chang-   21
ing dynamics play out, Koreans own up to 40 percent of the city's
roughly 4,000 contract sewing shops. Chinese immigrants own almost
all the rest. Yet, the Korean-owned shops have attracted relatively more
attention from labor investigators, mostly because they tend to hire Latino workers, who are less reluctant to complain than Asian employees.

Chinese-owned shops tend to hire only other Chinese, says Maria   22
Echaveste, administrator of the Labor Department's wage and hour division. In some cases, she says, workers have expressed fear for their
lives if they reveal labor violations. Many Chinese sweatshop workers
are believed to be indentured servants toiling under a form of debt
bondage to pay off the heavy cost of being smuggled into the United
States.

"The workers lie to us," one investigator says. "In Chinese shops,   23
the falsification of records is absolutely down to a science. It's almost
impossible to break unless the shop goes out of business. It's only then
that workers tell us those were not the hours and rates they worked."

In the Korean-owned shops, poor working conditions are often ex-   24
acerbated by the lack of a common language between the Koreans and
their mostly young, female Latino employees.

"They [the Korean owners] think they can make themselves under-   25
stood by yelling," says Hermanson of the Garment Workers' Justice
Center, which tries to organize workers and defend them in disputes
with shop owners. The result, especially when owners hit their workers, is an "atmosphere of terror and intimidation," he says.

The Korean Apparel Manufacturers Association says it has been   26
trying to get its 400 member companies in New York to pay at least the
minimum wage. Most now do so, the group says. But these owners are
themselves victims of punishing market forces, the group argues.

27   "The problem for the sewing companies is that the minimum wage goes higher and higher, and the price from manufacturers stays the same or goes down," says a spokeswoman for the association who gave her name only as Hung.

28   She acknowledges that some owners treat their workers harshly but says most do not. As for the illegal aliens among them, she concedes, "That's a problem."

29   For Blancas, trouble started almost immediately after she was hired by a shop called New Young Fashions. The owner, Kim Young Han, paid her less than the $160 a week she says she was promised. She worked six days a week, starting at 7:30 a.m. and finishing at 6 p.m. each weekday. Her pay averaged $2.54 an hour, according to figures compiled by the workers' center.

30   When she found out what the minimum wage was and told her co-workers they should be getting at least $4.25 an hour, "they were astonished," but refused to back her in a confrontation with the owner and his Korean wife, Blancas says.

31   "They were robbing us," she says. "I was very angry.... I said, 'Talk, compañeros, talk,' but they were terrified. The [owner's wife] told me to shut up and leave, and the others just kept quiet."

32   Her co-workers, most of them fellow Mexicans and Ecuadorans, feared being deported as illegal aliens if they complained, Blancas says.

33   Interviewed at his factory, Kim said he had resolved all of his employees' complaints and that he is now complying with labor laws.

34   After Blancas was fired from New Young Fashions, the workers' center helped her recover some of her back wages. She later found work in another garment shop that pays more, though still not the minimum wage. She took a second job in a store.

35   Blancas says she left her home in Mexico City to seek work in the United Sates because her husband had died in a car accident a year earlier and she needed to support her young son. She crossed the border with an uncle, who also works in a sweatshop, and trekked all night over hills to reach a road that would set them on their way to New York.

36   Bertha Morales, a 25-year-old Ecuadoran who worked in another Korean-owned sweatshop, says she was sent by her boss to help out at New Young Fashions one day and was shocked by what she saw. At one point, she said in an interview, the owner's wife struck a worker on the back for sewing buttons incorrectly. Other workers described similar punishment, and one told of an incident in which the boss grabbed her hair and pulled on it.

37   One new employee, a 19-year-old woman from Nicaragua, was summarily fired by the owner's wife for yawning and left the shop in tears, Morales says.

38   Sweatshops such as Kim's lie at the bottom of what the Labor Department describes as a garment industry "food chain" beneath layers

of suppliers, designers and middlemen, who compete fiercely for orders from the big retailers at the top.

It is a system that regulators and union officials say effectively insulates the big-name stores and fashion labels, allowing them to profess shock and ignorance of sweatshop conditions in which their clothes were sewn.   39

Major retailers, such as J.C. Penney, Sears and Wal-Mart, have quality-control inspectors who regularly visit work sites, and they know how much it costs to produce a garment at the minimum wage, a Labor Department official says. But under a 60-year-old law, the retailers can be held liable only if they had "direct knowledge" of labor violations involved in producing their goods.   40

The system also adds markups far in excess of the actual cost of the labor and material that went into the garments.   41

Retailers say too many variables go into the final price of a garment to generalize about any of them, but Labor Department and union officials estimate that labor typically accounts for less than 3 percent of the U.S. retail price of clothing made in domestic sweatshops and as little as one-half of 1 percent for garments sewn abroad.   42

Because of the pressures weighing on those at the low end of the industry, shop owners such as Kim Young Han believe that they, too, are victims of the system.   43

Sitting at his worn desk in a corner of the shop floor, Kim blames his problems on creditors, saying he is owed thousands of dollars by garment manufacturers who had subcontracted several large jobs to him. He produces letters to them demanding payment and threatening "legal action." All are written in longhand; he does not have a typewriter.   44

Wearing jeans and a denim shirt, the lean, craggy-faced Kim, 61, says he had been a lecturer at a junior college in Seoul before coming to the United States years ago to study for a doctoral degree in linguistics under Noam Chomsky. Although that alone makes him a rarity among sweatshop owners, union officials say his violations of labor laws were all too familiar.   45

Asked about the specific allegations against him by the garment workers union, Kim becomes visibly upset and pleads for understanding.   46

"Help me, please," he begs. "I'm in trouble."   47

Seemingly on the verge of tears, Kim complains of having to compete with cheap imports and denies making any windfall profits. "I want to close my factory," he laments over the din of sewing machines and a radio blaring Spanish songs. "The market's no good.... No hope at my age."   48

The National Retail Federation, which represents 2,000 major U.S. retailers, in turn blames sweatshop conditions on subcontractors such as Kim.   49

"The retailers don't employ these workers," says Pamela Rucker, a spokeswoman for the federation. "The retailers many times are at least   50 two or three steps removed from the problem." She asserts, "It's not the retailers who are reaping the benefits from these criminal activities. It's the greedy subcontractors."

51   Shops at the bottom of the industry often go out of business, relocate and open under new names. Some fail altogether, never to reappear. But despite decades of lawmaking against them—and a public campaign by the Clinton administration following the 1995 exposure of a virtual slave-labor garment factory in Los Angeles—the system designed to eradicate the sweatshops has largely failed, union activists say.

52   Local, state and federal agencies charged with enforcing labor, immigration and tax laws have often failed to work together, allowing shop owners and workers to slip through the cracks of the system. Under a directive renewed by Mayor Rudolph W. Giuliani, a strong supporter of immigration, New York authorities are prohibited from sharing information with the Immigration and Naturalization Service.

53   At the direction of the administration and Congress, the INS has thrown the bulk of its resources at the southwestern border to prevent illegal immigrants from crossing into the United States from Mexico. Nationwide, only about 1,700 INS investigators are assigned to the interior of the country, and they spend less than 20 percent of their time enforcing immigration law at work sites of all kinds, according to the agency.

54   In a special effort in New York last year, INS agents arrested 1,824 illegal aliens during inspections of 150 work sites, most of them garment shops. However, because of lack of detention space, almost all were released on their own recognizance and told to return for court hearings.

55   "The percentage that shows up is minute," says Rus Bergeron, an INS spokesman. Most simply find another job in the underground economy, and many return to work at the same shops where they were arrested.

56   Ironically, labor groups such as the Garment Workers Justice Center also play a part in keeping the sweatshops in business. Among the literature the center distributes, for example, are fliers in English, Spanish and Korean that advise shop owners how to fend off searches by INS and Labor Department agents.

57   The fliers encourage employers to challenge inspection on grounds of discrimination and use legal stalling tactics that the INS says often enable them to fabricate employment eligibility records. Fliers in Spanish urge workers to "remain silent" when asked about their nationality, birth place or entry into the United States.

58   The union says its main aim is to protect workers and preserve their jobs, regardless of their immigration status. When faced with la-

bor violations, the justice center usually tries to work out a solution with the employer without government involvement.

Critics call the policy misguided. "If you're trying to defend a liv-   59
ing standard, the minimum wage and Social Security and deal with legitimate companies," one independent labor activist argues, "helping these sweatshops exist would seem to be counterproductive."

For some garment workers, the punishment for exposing sweatshop   60
conditions comes from their employers. After complaining about what she saw at New Young Fashions while filling in there last year, Bertha Morales was fired by her own Korean boss, who was a friend of Kim's.

Others, including two illegal immigrant sisters from Mexico, say   61
workers do not tell authorities about labor violations and physical abuse out of fear that their shops will then be raided by immigration agents.

In the case of another outspoken worker, the consequences of go-   62
ing public—or at least the perception of those effects—became evident after she appeared at a forum on sweatshops in Arlington, Va., last summer. The worker, Nancy Penaloza, 29, said she had labored in Korean-owned sweatshops in New York for nine years, working up to 66 hours a week in filthy conditions. In her current job, she said, she sewed high-quality women's suits, earning $6 apiece for garments that usually sell for $120 or more at stores such as J.C. Penney and Ann Taylor.

"I get paid off the books," Penaloza told the forum. "Even though I   63
am working legally, my boss doesn't pay any taxes or Social Security. . . . I never get a vacation. I never even get a whole weekend off." She said she works in constant fear, not only of her temperamental boss but of the "big rats and mice" that continually crawl over her feet.

A day after she spoke, INS agents raided her factory and arrested   64
most of her co-workers, who were illegal immigrants, Penaloza says. Three days after that, a Labor Department wage inspector showed up. Although she is sure the INS raid was a coincidence, because she did not name her employer at the forum, her co-workers blamed it on her.

A former secretary in Mexico, she says she originally crossed the   65
border as an illegal alien herself, then, "became legal" a couple of years ago.

She says her Korean boss routinely smacks his workers in the head   66
when they make mistakes. He also orders them to tell the Labor Department that they are receiving their proper wages and overtime, she says, and that is what they did during the latest inspection.

"The workers are afraid," Penaloza says. "They don't want to lose   67
their jobs."

And so, she says, "they lied to the inspector," thus perpetuating a   68
cycle that helps the industry to survive.

★ *Meaning and Understanding*

1. What kind of job did Aurora Blancas get in New York? Who owned the business she worked for? Why did she come to America?

2. What is a "sweatshop"? Where does the term come from? Where is the garment district?

3. How do the sweatshops represent "fundamental changes in the garment industry"?

4. Why does sweatshop owner Kim Young Han say he, too, is a victim?

5. How do labor groups keep the sweatshops in business?

★ *Techniques and Strategies*

1. What is Branigin's thesis?

2. Why does Branigin intersperse quotes from various people into his essay?

3. Who is the intended audience for this selection? How do you know?

4. What data do you find most impressive? Why does the writer draw on statistical details in the essay?

5. How does the title of the piece help you understand Branigin's point?

6. Where does the writer use narration? Description? Comparison and contrast? Why does he use these particular strategies?

★ *Speaking of Values*

1. In a capitalistic system, the only objective of business is to make a profit. Do you agree or disagree with this statement? Why?

2. Should illegal aliens in America be protected by labor laws? Why or why not?

3. Branigin indicates that many immigrants are being exploited by other immigrants. Do you think that the immigrant owners of sweatshops have an obligation to take better care of their workers because of their shared experiences? Why or why not?

4. What role do you think unions and the government play in preventing sweatshops from thriving?

★ *Values Conversation*

Have you or anyone you know ever felt exploited by an employer? Form groups and discuss the reasons you felt this way, the actions you may have taken, and the results or consequences of those actions.

★ *Writing about Values*

1. Write an essay about how to eliminate sweatshops from the American scene—or how it is impossible to eliminate them.

2. Write an essay of advice to immigrants coming to America for work.

3. Read either *How the Other Half Lives* by Jacob Riis or *The Jungle* by Upton Sinclair and write an essay on your choice. Be sure to explain what the book reveals about immigrant labor at the turn of the twentieth century and compare it to the picture that Branigin paints of contemporary immigrant labor.

Gary Soto

Looking for Work

Gary Soto was born in Fresno, California in 1952. A college teacher and
an award-winning writer, he has published several volumes of poetry
and short stories and has also written a number of short films. In this
short story from *Living up the Street* (1985), he examines the lure of work
in a young Mexican American's life.

———— ★ ————

1   One July, while killing ants on the kitchen sink with a rolled newspaper, I had a nine-year-old's vision of wealth that would save us from
ourselves. For weeks I had drunk Kool-Aid and watched morning re-
runs of *Father Knows Best,* whose family was so uncomplicated in its
routine that I very much wanted to imitate it. The first step was to get
my brother and sister to wear shoes at dinner.

2   "Come on, Rick—come on, Deb," I whined. But Rick mimicked me
and the same day that I asked him to wear shoes he came to the dinner
table in only his swim trunks. My mother didn't notice, nor did my sister, as we sat to eat our beans and tortillas in the stifling heat of our
kitchen. We all gleamed like cellophane, wiping the sweat from our
brows with the backs of our hands as we talked about the day: Frankie
our neighbor was beat up by Faustino; the swimming pool at the playground would be closed for a day because the pump was broken.

3   Such was our life. So that morning, while doing-in the train of ants
which arrived each day, I decided to become wealthy, and right away!
After downing a bowl of cereal, I took a rake from the garage and
started up the block to look for work.

4   We lived on an ordinary block of mostly working class people:
warehousemen, egg candlers, welders, mechanics, and a union
plumber. And there were many retired people who kept their lawns
green and the gutters uncluttered of the chewing gum wrappers we
dropped as we rode by on our bikes. They bent down to gather our lit-
ter, muttering at our evilness.

5   At the corner house I rapped the screen door and a very large
woman in a muu-muu answered. She sized me up and then asked
what I could do.

6   "Rake leaves," I answered, smiling.

7   "It's summer, and there ain't no leaves," she countered. Her face
was pinched with lines; fat jiggled under her chin. She pointed to the

lawn, then the flower bed, and said: "You see any leaves there—or there?" I followed her pointing arm, stupidly. But she had a job for me and that was to get her a Coke at the liquor store. She gave me twenty cents, and after ditching my rake in a bush, off I ran. I returned with an unbagged Pepsi, for which she thanked me and gave me a nickel from her apron.

I skipped off her porch, fetched my rake, and crossed the street to   8
the next block where Mrs. Moore, mother of Earl the retarded man, let me weed a flower bed. She handed me a trowel and for a good part of the morning my fingers dipped into the moist dirt, ripping up runners of Bermuda grass. Worms surfaced in my search for deep roots, and I cut them in halves, tossing them to Mrs. Moore's cat who pawed them playfully as they dried in the sun. I made out Earl whose face was pressed to the back window of the house, and although he was calling to me I couldn't understand what he was trying to say. Embarrassed, I worked without looking up, but I imagined his contorted mouth and the ring of keys attached to his belt—keys that jingled with each pal-sied step. He scared me and I worked quickly to finish the flower bed. When I did finish Mrs. Moore gave me a quarter and two peaches from her tree, which I washed there but ate in the alley behind my house.

I was sucking on the second one, a bit of juice staining the front of   9
my T-shirt, when Little John, my best friend, came walking down the alley with a baseball bat over his shoulder, knocking over trash cans as he made his way toward me.

Little John and I went to St. John's Catholic School, where we sat   10
among the "stupids." Miss Marino, our teacher, alternated the rows of good students with the bad, hoping that by sitting side-by-side with the bright students the stupids might become more intelligent, as though intelligence were contagious. But we didn't progress as she had hoped. She grew frustrated when one day, while dismissing class for recess, Little John couldn't get up because his arms were stuck in the slats of the chair's backrest. She scolded us with a shaking finger when we knocked over the globe, denting the already troubled Africa. She muttered curses when Leroy White, a real stupid but a great softball player with the gift to hit to all fields, openly chewed his host when he made his First Communion; his hands swung at his sides as he re-turned to the pew looking around with a big smile.

Little John asked what I was doing, and I told him that I was tak-   11
ing a break from work, as I sat comfortably among high weeds. He wanted to join me, but I reminded him that the last time he'd gone door-to-door asking for work his mother had whipped him. I was with him when his mother, a New Jersey Italian who could rise up in anger one moment and love the next, told me in a polite but matter-of-fact voice that I had to leave because she was going to beat her son. She gave me a homemade popsicle, ushered me to the door, and said that I

could see Little John the next day. But it was sooner than that. I went around to his bedroom window to suck my popsicle and watch Little John dodge his mother's blows, a few hitting their mark but many whirring air.

12   It was midday when Little John and I converged in the alley, the sun blazing in the high nineties, and he suggested that we go to Roosevelt High School to swim. He needed five cents to make fifteen, the cost of admission, and I lent him a nickel. We ran home for my bike and when my sister found out that we were going swimming she started to cry because she didn't have the fifteen cents but only an empty Coke bottle. I waved for her to come and three of us mounted the bike—Debra on the cross bar, Little John on the handle bars and holding the Coke bottle which we would cash for a nickel and make up the difference that would allow all of us to get in, and me pumping up the crooked streets, dodging cars and pot holes. We spent the day swimming under the afternoon sun, so that when we got home our mom asked us what was darker, the floor or us? She feigned a stern posture, her hands on her hips and her mouth puckered. We played along. Looking down, Debbie and I said in unison, "Us."

13   That evening at dinner we all sat down in our bathing suits to eat our beans, laughing and chewing loudly. Our mom was in a good mood, so I took a risk and asked her if sometime we could have turtle soup. A few days before I had watched a television program in which a Polynesian tribe killed a large turtle, gutted it, and then stewed it over an open fire. The turtle, basted in a sugary sauce, looked delicious as I ate an afternoon bowl of cereal, but my sister, who was watching the program with a glass of Kool-Aid between her knees, said, "Caca."

14   My mother looked at me in bewilderment. "Boy, are you a crazy Mexican. Where did you get the idea that people eat turtles?"

15   "On television," I said, explaining the program. Then I took it a step further. "Mom, do you think we could get dressed up for dinner one of these days? David King does."

16   "*Ay, Dios,*" my mother laughed. She started collecting the dinner plates, but my brother wouldn't let go of his. He was still drawing a picture in the bean sauce. Giggling, he said it was me, but I didn't want to listen because I wanted an answer from Mom. This was the summer when I spent the mornings in front of the television that showed the comfortable lives of white kids. There were no beatings, no rifts in the family. They wore bright clothes; toys tumbled from their closets. They hopped into bed with kisses and woke to glasses of fresh orange juice, and to a father sitting before his morning coffee while the mother buttered his toast. They hurried through the day making friends and gobs of money, returning home to a warmly lit living room, and then dinner. *Leave It to Beaver* was the program I replayed in my mind:

17   "May I have the mashed potatoes?" asks Beaver with a smile.

"Sure, Beav," replies Wally as he taps the corners of his mouth with 18 a starched napkin.

The father looks on in his suit. The mother, decked out in earrings 19 and a pearl necklace, cuts into her steak and blushes. Their conversation is politely clipped.

"Swell," says Beaver, his cheeks puffed with food. 20

Our own talk at dinner was loud with belly laughs and marked by 21 our pointing forks at one another. The subjects were commonplace.

"Gary, let's go to the ditch tomorrow," my brother suggests. He ex- 22 plains that he has made a life preserver out of four empty detergent bottles strung together with twine and that he will make me one if I can find more bottles. "No way are we going to drown."

"Yeah, then we could have a dirt clod fight," I reply, so happy to be 23 alive.

Whereas the Beaver's family enjoyed dessert in dishes at the table, 24 our mom sent us outside, and more often than not I went into the alley to peek over the neighbor's fences and spy out fruit, apricots or peaches.

I had asked my mom and again she laughed that I was a crazy 25 *chavalo* as she stood in front of the sink, her arms rising and falling with suds, face glistening from the heat. She sent me outside where my brother and sister were sitting in the shade that the fence threw out like a blanket. They were talking about me when I plopped down next to them. They looked at one another and then Debbie, my eight-year-old sister, started in.

"What's this crap about getting dressed up?" 26

She had entered her profanity stage. A year later she would give 27 up such words and slip into her Catholic uniform, and into squealing on my brother and me when we "cussed this" and "cussed that."

I tried to convince them that if we improved the way we looked we 28 might get along better in life. White people would like us more. They might invite us to places, like their homes or front yards. They might not hate us so much.

My sister called me a "craphead," and got up to leave with a stalk 29 of grass dangling from her mouth. "They'll never like us."

My brother's mood lightened as he talked about the ditch—the 30 white water, the broken pieces of glass, and the rusted car fenders that awaited our knees. There would be toads, and rocks to smash them.

David King, the only person we knew who resembled the middle 31 class, called from over the fence. David was Catholic, of Armenian and French descent, and his closet was filled with toys. A bear-shaped cookie jar, like the ones on television, sat on the kitchen counter. His mother was remarkably kind while she put up with the racket we made on the street. Evenings, she often watered the front yard and it must have upset her to see us—my brother and I and others—jump from trees laughing, the unkillable kids of the very poor, who got up unshaken, brushed off, and climbed into another one to try again.

32   David called again. Rick got up and slapped grass from his pants. When I asked if I could come along he said no. David said no. They were two years older so their affairs were different from mine. They greeted one another with foul names and took off down the alley to look for trouble.

33   I went inside the house, turned on the television, and was about to sit down with a glass of Kool-Aid when Mom shooed me outside.

34   "It's still light," she said. "Later you'll bug me to let you stay out longer. So go on."

35   I downed my Kool-Aid and went outside to the front yard. No one was around. The day had cooled and a breeze rustled the trees. Mr. Jackson, the plumber, was watering his lawn and when he saw me he turned away to wash off his front steps. There was more than an hour of light left, so I took advantage of it and decided to look for work. I felt suddenly alive as I skipped down the block in search of an overgrown flower bed and the dime that would end the day right.

★ Meaning and Understanding

1. The narrator kills ants and worms. Why do you think the writer highlights these particular actions?

2. What do you know about *Father Knows Best* and *Leave It to Beaver*? Why are these shows models for the narrator?

3. Why does the narrator decide "to become wealthy, and right away!"? What connection does what his family eats (paragraph 3) have to do with his desire for wealth? What kind of work does he start off to do?

4. How does the teacher treat the narrator and Little John?

5. What kind of soup does the narrator request? Why does he ask for it?

6. What do you think is the main point of this story?

★ Techniques and Strategies

1. Soto frames the story with two images: killing ants at the beginning and skipping down the block looking for work at the conclusion. How do these two images help you understand his point?

2. How effective is the use of dialogue in this story? Explain your answer.

3. Although it is clear that the family in the story is Hispanic, the writer uses only two Spanish constructions—*Ay, Dios,* (paragraph 16) and *chavalo,* (slang for "boy," paragraph 25). Why, since ethnicity is such an

important element in the story, does he so restrict his use of Spanish in this way?

4. Which descriptive details do you find most original and illuminating? Where does Soto's use of sensory language create a vivid picture?

5. Where does the writer use comparison and contrast to advance his theme?

★ Speaking of Values

1. What is the implied relation between television and upward mobility as indicated in this selection? Should we build family values around television presentations? Why or why not?

2. Why do the children think that "white people would like us more" if the children improved the way they looked? What does the statement imply about the treatment of these children by white people? Does appearance affect how we feel about people? Should it?

3. The narrator seems pretty successful in his initial attempts to find work. What is his attitude about work? In what ways does he represent the American work ethic? How does he challenge it?

4. How do you account for the way the teacher treats the narrator and his friends? What values do you think these children learn about education? Why is it important for the narrator to let us know that he and Little John were classified among "the stupids"?

5. What does Soto mean by the phrase "unkillable kids of the very poor"? What does it imply about self-image? about society's view of minorities?

★ Values Conversation

Form groups and discuss the various jobs you had as a young child. What did you do? What were you paid? Did you like working? What values do you think you learned from working as a child?

★ Writing about Values

1. The writer John Hersey once observed that television "is the opiate of the white middle class and the *agent provocateur* of the black working class." What do you think he meant by this? Write a paper in which you try to explain what he is saying about the relation between TV and people's social aspirations. Be sure to include references from "Looking for Work" to help illustrate your points.

2. Although Soto's narrator grew up on shows like *Father Knows Best* and *Leave It to Beaver,* contemporary youths may consume a different diet of TV shows. What TV shows are likely to imbue young children today with values of family and work? What are those values, do you think? Write an essay to demonstrate the values projected by popular television shows about families.

3. American society seems split on the value of work for young children. On one hand we believe that gainful employment builds character at any age. On the other, we construct laws to prevent children from working when they are too young. Where do you stand? Write an essay in which you argue for or against the value of allowing nine-year olds to work for money.

Henry David Thoreau

I Borrowed an Axe and Went Down to the Woods

Living almost all of his life in Concord, Massachusettes, where he was born, Henry David Thoreau (1817–1862) was a social philosopher and naturalist whose ideas on civil disobedience influenced those of Mahatma Gandhi and Martin Luther King, Jr. His best-known works are "Resistance to Civil Government" (1849), *A Week on the Concord and Merrimack Rivers* (1849), and *Walden* (1854). In this excerpt from *Walden,* Thoreau mixes philosophy and house building as he shows readers how he constructed a dwelling in the woods.

Near the end of March, 1845, I borrowed an axe and went down to the woods by Walden Pond, nearest to where I intended to build my house, and began to cut down some tall arrowy white pines, still in their youth, for timber. It is difficult to begin without borrowing, but perhaps it is the most generous course thus to permit your fellow-men to have an interest in your enterprise. The owner of the axe, as he released his hold on it, said that it was the apple of his eye; but I returned it sharper than I received it. It was a pleasant hillside where I worked, covered with pine woods, through which I looked out on the pond, and a small open field in the woods where pines and hickories were springing up. The ice in the pond was not yet dissolved, though there were some open spaces, and it was all dark colored and saturated with water. There were some slight flurries of snow during the days that I worked there; but for the most part when I came out on to the railroad, on my way home, its yellow sand heap stretched away gleaming in the hazy atmosphere, and the rails shone in the spring sun, and I heard the lark and pewee and other birds already come to commence another year with us. They were pleasant spring days, in which the winter of man's discontent was thawing as well as the earth, and the life that had lain torpid began to stretch itself. One day, when my axe had come off and I had cut a green hickory for a wedge, driving it with a stone, and had placed the whole to soak in a pond hole in order to swell the wood, I saw a striped snake run into the water, and he lay on the bottom, apparently without inconvenience, as long as I staid there, or more than a

1

quarter of an hour; perhaps because he had not yet fairly come out of the torpid state. It appeared to me that for a like reason men remain in their present low and primitive condition; but if they should feel the influence of the spring of springs arousing them, they would of necessity rise to a higher and more ethereal life. I had previously seen the snakes in frosty mornings in my path with portions of their bodies still numb and inflexible, waiting for the sun to thaw them. On the 1st of April it rained and melted the ice, and in the early part of the day, which was very foggy, I heard a stray goose groping about over the pond and cackling as if lost, or like the spirit of the fog.

2   So I went on for some days cutting and hewing timber, and also studs and rafters, all with my narrow axe, not having many communicable or scholar-like thoughts, singing to myself,—

> Men say they know many things;
> But lo! they have taken wings,—
> The arts and sciences,
> And a thousand appliances;
> The wind that blows
> Is all that any body knows.

I hewed the main timbers six inches square, most of the studs on two sides only, and the rafters and floor timbers on one side, leaving the rest of the bark on, so that they were just as straight and much stronger than sawed ones. Each stick was carefully mortised or tenoned by its stump, for I had borrowed other tools by this time. My days in the woods were not very long ones; yet I usually carried my dinner of bread and butter, and read the newspaper in which it was wrapped, at noon, sitting amid the green pine boughs which I had cut off, and to my bread was imparted some of their fragrance, for my hands were covered with a thick coat of pitch. Before I had done I was more the friend than the foe of the pine tree, though I had cut down some of them, having become better acquainted with it. Sometimes a rambler in the wood was attracted by the sound of my axe, and we chatted pleasantly over the chips which I had made.

3   By the middle of April, for I made no haste in my work, but rather made the most of it, my house was framed and ready for the raising. I had already bought the shanty of James Collins, an Irishman who worked on the Fitchburg Railroad, for boards. James Collins' shanty was considered an uncommonly fine one. When I called to see it he was not at home. I walked about the outside, at first unobserved from within, the window was so deep and high. It was of small dimensions, with a peaked cottage roof, and not much else to be seen, the dirt being raised five feet all around as if it were a compost heap. The roof was the soundest part, though a good deal warped and made brittle by the sun.

Door-sill there was none, but a perennial passage for the hens under the door board. Mrs. C. came to the door and asked me to view it from the inside. The hens were driven in by my approach. It was dark, and had a dirt floor for the most part, dank, clammy, and aguish, only here a board and there a board which would not bear removal. She lighted a lamp to show me the inside of the roof and the walls, and also that the board floor extended under the bed, warning me not to step into the cellar, a sort of dust hole two feet deep. In her own words, they were "good boards overhead, good boards all around, and a good window,"— of two whole squares originally, only the cat had passed out that way lately. There was a stove, a bed, and a place to sit, an infant in the house where it was born, a silk parasol, gilt-framed looking-glass, and a patent new coffee mill nailed to an oak sapling, all told. The bargain was soon concluded, for James had in the mean while returned. I to pay four dollars and twenty-five cents to-night, he to vacate at five tomorrow morning, selling to nobody else meanwhile: I to take possession at six. It were well, he said, to be there early, and anticipate certain indistinct but wholly unjust claims on the score of ground rent and fuel. This he assured me was the only encumbrance. At six I passed him and his family on the road. One large bundle held their all,—bed, coffee-mill, looking-glass, hens,—all but the cat, she took to the woods and became a wild cat, and, as I learned afterward, trod in a trap set for woodchucks, and so became a dead cat at last.

I took down this dwelling the same morning, drawing the nails, and removed it to the pond side by small cartloads, spreading the boards on the grass there to bleach and warp back again in the sun. One early thrush gave me a note or two as I drove along the woodland path. I was informed treacherously by a young Patrick that neighbor Seeley, an Irishman, in the intervals of the carting, transferred the still tolerable, straight, and drivable nails, staples, and spikes to his pocket, and then stood when I came back to pass the time of day, and look freshly up, unconcerned, with spring thoughts, at the devastation; there being a dearth of work, as he said. He was there to represent spectatordom, and help make this seemingly insignificant event one with the removal of the gods of Troy.   4

I dug my cellar in the side of a hill sloping to the south, where a   5
woodchuck had formerly dug his burrow, down through sumach and blackberry roots, and the lowest stain of vegetation, six feet square by seven deep, to a fine sand where potatoes would not freeze in any winter. The sides were left shelving, and not stoned; but the sun having never shone on them, the sand still keeps its place. It was but two hours' work. I took particular pleasure in this breaking of ground, for in almost all latitudes men dig into the earth for an equable temperature. Under the most splendid house in the city is still to be found the cellar where they store their roots as of old, and long after the superstructure has

disappeared posterity remark its dent in the earth. The house is still but a sort of porch at the entrance of a burrow.

6   At length, in the beginning of May, with the help of some of my acquaintances, rather to improve so good an occasion for neighborliness than from any necessity, I set up the frame of my house. No man was ever more honored in the character of his raisers than I. They are destined, I trust, to assist at the raising of loftier structures one day. I began to occupy my house on the 4th of July, as soon as it was boarded and roofed, for the boards were carefully feather-edged and lapped, so that it was perfectly impervious to rain; but before boarding I laid the foundation of a chimney at one end, bringing two cartloads of stones up the hill from the pond in my arms. I built the chimney after my hoeing in the fall, before a fire became necessary for warmth, doing my cooking in the mean while out of doors on the ground, early in the morning: which mode I still think is in some respects more convenient and agreeable than the usual one. When it stormed before my bread was baked, I fixed a few boards over the fire, and sat under them to watch my loaf, and passed some pleasant hours in that way. In those days, when my hands were much employed, I read but little, but the least scraps of paper which lay on the ground, my holder, or tablecloth, afforded me as much entertainment, in fact answered the same purpose as the Iliad.

7   It would be worth the while to build still more deliberately than I did, considering, for instance, what foundation a door, a window, a cellar, a garret, have in the nature of man, and perchance never raising any superstructure until we found a better reason for it than our temporal necessities even. There is some of the same fitness in a man's building his own house that there is in a bird's building its own nest. Who knows but if men constructed their dwellings with their own hands, and provided food for themselves and families simply and honestly enough, the poetic faculty would be universally developed, as birds universally sing when they are so engaged? But alas! we do like cowbirds and cuckoos, which lay their eggs in nests which other birds have built, and cheer no traveller with their chattering and unmusical notes. Shall we forever resign the pleasure of construction to the carpenter? What does architecture amount to in the experience of the mass of men? I never in all my walks came across a man engaged in so simple and natural an occupation as building his house. We belong to the community. It is not the tailor alone who is the ninth part of a man; it is as much the preacher, and the merchant, and the farmer. Where is this division of labor to end? and what object does it finally serve? No doubt another *may* also think for me; but it is not therefore desirable that he should do so to the exclusion of my thinking for myself.

8   True, there are architects so called in this country, and I have heard of one at least possessed with the idea of making architectural orna-

ments have a core of truth, a necessity, and hence a beauty, as if it were a revelation to him. All very well perhaps from his point of view, but only a little better than the common dilettantism. A sentimental reformer in architecture, he began at the cornice, not at the foundation. It was only how to put a core of truth within the ornaments, that every sugar plum in fact might have an almond or caraway seed in it,—though I hold that almonds are most wholesome without the sugar,—and not how the inhabitant, the indweller, might build truly within and without, and let the ornaments take care of themselves. What reasonable man ever supposed that ornaments were something outward and in the skin merely,—that the tortoise got his spotted shell, or the shellfish its mother-o'-pearl tints, by such a contract as the inhabitants of Broadway their Trinity Church? But a man has no more to do with the style of architecture of his house than a tortoise with that of its shell: nor need the soldier be so idle as to try to paint the precise *color* of his virtue on his standard. The enemy will find it out. He may turn pale when the trial comes. This man seemed to me to lean over the cornice and timidly whisper his half truth to the rude occupants who really knew it better than he. What of architectural beauty I now see, I know has gradually grown from within outward, out of the necessities and character of the indweller, who is the only builder,—but of some unconscious truthfulness, and nobleness, without ever a thought for the appearance; and whatever additional beauty of this kind is destined to be produced will be preceded by a like unconscious beauty of life. The most interesting dwellings in this country, as the painter knows, are the most unpretending, humble log huts and cottages of the poor commonly; it is the life of the inhabitants whose shells they are, and not any peculiarity in their surfaces merely, which makes them *picturesque;* and equally interesting will be the citizen's suburban box, when his life shall be as simple and as agreeable to the imagination, and there is as little straining after effect in the style of his dwelling. A great proportion of architectural ornaments are literally hollow, and a September gale would strip them off, like borrowed plumes, without injury to the substantials. They can do without *architecture* who have no olives nor wines in the cellar. What if an equal ado were made about the ornaments of style in literature, and the architects of our bibles spent as much time about their cornices as the architects of our churches do? So are made the *belles-lettres* and the *beaux-arts* and their professors. Much it concerns a man, forsooth, how a few sticks are slanted over him or under him, and what colors are daubed upon his box. It would signify somewhat, if, in any earnest sense, *he* slanted them and daubed it; but the spirit having departed out of the tenant, it is of a piece with constructing his own coffin,—the architecture of the grave, and "carpenter" is but another name for "coffin-maker." One man says, in his despair or indifference to life, take up a handful of the earth at your feet, and paint your house that color. Is he thinking of his last and narrow house? Toss up a copper for it as well. What an abundance of leisure he must have! Why do you take up a handful of dirt? Better paint your house your own complexion; let it turn pale or blush for you. An enterprise to improve the style of cottage architecture! When you have got my ornaments ready I will wear them.

9   Before winter I built a chimney, and shingled the sides of my house, which were already impervious to rain, with imperfect and sappy shingles made of the first slice of the log, whose edges I was obliged to straighten with a plane.

10   I have thus a tight shingled and plastered house, ten feet wide by fifteen long, and eight-foot posts, with a garrot and a closet, a large window on each side, two trap doors, one door at the end, and a brick fireplace opposite. The exact cost of my house, paying the usual price for such materials as I used, but not counting the work, all of which was done by myself, was as follows; and I give the details because very few are able to tell exactly what their houses cost, and fewer still, if any, the separate cost of the various materials which compose them:—

11

Boards............................	$8 03 ½,	mostly shanty boards.
Refuse shingles for roof and sides......................	4 00	
Laths............................	1 25	
Two second-hand windows with glass	2 43	
One thousand old brick.............	4 00	
Two casks of lime	2 40	That was high.
Hair.............................	0 31	More than I needed.
Mantle-tree iron	0 15	
Nails	3 90	
Hinges and screws	0 14	
Latch............................	0 10	
Chalk............................	0 01	
Transportation.....................	1 40 }	I carried a good part on my back.
In all........................	$28 12 ½	

12   These are all the materials excepting the timber stones and sand, which I claimed by squatter's right. I have also a small wood-shed adjoining, made chiefly of the stuff which was left after building the house.

13   I intend to build me a house which will surpass any on the main street in Concord in grandeur and luxury, as soon as it pleases me as much and will cost me no more than my present one.

14   I thus found that the student who wishes for a shelter can obtain one for a lifetime at an expense not greater than the rent which he now

pays annually. If I seem to boast more than is becoming, my excuse is that I brag for humanity rather than for myself; and my shortcomings and inconsistencies do not affect the truth of my statement. Notwithstanding much cant and hypocrisy,—chaff which I find it difficult to separate from my wheat, but for which I am as sorry as any man,—I will breathe freely and stretch myself in this respect, it is such a relief to both the moral and physical system; and I am resolved that I will not through humility become the devil's attorney. I will endeavor to speak a good word for the truth. At Cambridge College the mere rent of a student's room, which is only a little larger than my own, is thirty dollars each year, though the corporation had the advantage of building thirty-two side by side and under one roof, and the occupant suffers the inconvenience of many and noisy neighbors, and perhaps a residence in the fourth story. I cannot but think that if we had more true wisdom in these respects, not only less education would be needed, because, forsooth, more would already have been acquired, but the pecuniary expense of getting an education would in a great measure vanish. Those conveniences which the student requires at Cambridge or elsewhere cost him or somebody else ten times as great a sacrifice of life as they would with proper management on both sides. Those things for which the most money is demanded are never the things which the student most wants. Tuition, for instance, is an important item in the term bill, while for the far more valuable education which he gets by associating with the most cultivated of his contemporaries no charge is made. The mode of founding a college is, commonly, to get up a subscription of dollars and cents, and then following blindly the principles of a division of labor to its extreme, a principle which should never be followed but with circumspection,—to call in a contractor who makes this a subject of speculation, and he employs Irishmen or other operatives actually to lay the foundations, while the students that are to be are said to be fitting themselves for it; and for these oversights successive generations have to pay. I think that it would be *better than this*, for the students, or those who desire to be benefited by it, even to lay the foundation themselves. The student who secures his coveted leisure and retirement by systematically shirking any labor necessary to man obtains but an ignoble and unprofitable leisure, defrauding himself of the experience which alone can make leisure fruitful. "But," says one, "you do not mean that the students should go to work with their hands instead of their heads?" I do not mean that exactly, but I mean something which he might think a good deal like that; I mean that they should not *play* life, or *study* it merely, while the community supports them at this expensive game, but earnestly *live* it from beginning to end. How could youths better learn to live than by at once trying the experiment of living? Methinks this would exercise their minds as much as mathematics. If I wished a boy to know something about the arts and sciences, for instance, I would not pursue the common course, which is merely to send him into the neighborhood of some professor, where any thing is professed and practised but the art of life;—to survey the world through a telescope or a microscope, and never with his natural eye; to study chemistry, and not learn how his bread is made, or mechanics, and not learn how it is earned; to discover new satellites to Neptune, and not detect the motes in his eyes, or to what vagabond he is a satellite himself; or to be devoured by the monsters that swarm all around him, while contemplating the monsters in a drop of vinegar. Which would have advanced the most at the end of a month,—the boy who had made his own jack-knife from the ore which he had dug and smelted, reading as much as would be necessary for this,—or the boy who had attended the lectures on metallurgy at the Institute in the mean while, and had received a Rodgers' penknife from his father? Which would be most likely to cut his fingers?—To my astonishment I was informed on leaving college that I had studied navigation!—why, if I had taken one turn down the harbor I should have known more about it. Even the *poor* student studies and is taught only *political* economy, while that economy of living which is synonymous with philosophy is not even sincerely professed in our colleges. The consequence is, that while he is reading Adam Smith, Ricardo, and Say, he runs his father in debt irretrievably.

15   As with our colleges, so with a hundred "modern improvements"; there is an illusion about them; there is not always a positive advance. The devil goes on exacting compound interest to the last for his early share and numerous succeeding investments in them. Our inventions are wont to be pretty toys, which distract our attention from serious things. They are but improved means to an unimproved end, an end which it was already but too easy to arrive at; as railroads lead to Boston or New York. We are in great haste to construct a magnetic telegraph from Maine to Texas; but Maine and Texas, it may be, have nothing important to communicate. Either is in such a predicament as the man who was earnest to be introduced to a distinguished deaf woman, but when he was presented, and one end of her ear trumpet was put into his hand, had nothing to say. As if the main object were to talk fast and not to talk sensibly. We are eager to tunnel under the Atlantic and bring the old world some weeks nearer to the new; but perchance the first news that will leak through into the broad, flapping American ear will be that the Princess Adelaide has the whooping cough. After all, the man whose horse trots a mile in a minute does not carry the most important messages; he is not an evangelist, nor does he come round eating locusts and wild honey. I doubt if Flying Childers ever carried a peck of corn to mill.

16   One says to me, "I wonder that you do not lay up money; you love to travel; you might take the cars and go to Fitchburg to-day and see

the country." But I am wiser than that. I have learned that the swiftest traveller is he that goes afoot. I say to my friend, Suppose we try who will get there first. The distance is thirty miles; the fare ninety cents. That is almost a day's wages. I remember when wages were sixty cents a day for laborers on this very road. Well, I start now on foot, and get there before night; I have travelled at that rate by the week together. You will in the mean while have earned your fare, and arrive there some time to-morrow, or possibly this evening, if you are lucky enough to get a job in season. Instead of going to Fitchburg, you will be working here the greater part of the day. And so, if the railroad reached round the world, I think that I should keep ahead of you; and as for seeing the country and getting experience of that kind, I should have to cut your acquaintance altogether.

Such is the universal law, which no man can ever outwit, and with   17 regard to the railroad even we may say it is as broad as it is long. To make a railroad round the world available to all mankind is equivalent to grading the whole surface of the planet. Men have an indistinct notion that if they keep up this activity of joint stocks and spades long enough all will at length ride somewhere, in next to no time, and for nothing; but though a crowd rushes to the depot, and the conductor shouts "All aboard!" when the smoke is blown away and the vapor condensed, it will be perceived that a few are riding, but the rest are run over,—and it will be called, and will be, "A melancholy accident." No doubt they can ride at last who shall have earned their fare, that is, if they survive so long, but they will probably have lost their elasticity and desire to travel by that time. This spending of the best part of one's life earning money in order to enjoy a questionable liberty during the least valuable part of it, reminds me of the Englishman who went to India to make a fortune first, in order that he might return to England and live the life of a poet. He should have gone up garret at once. "What!" exclaim a million Irishmen starting up from all the shanties in the land, "is not this railroad which we have built a good thing?" Yes, I answer, *comparatively* good, that is, you might have done worse; but I wish, as you are brothers of mine, that you could have spent your time better than digging in this dirt.

★ Meaning and Understanding

1. For what purpose does Thoreau borrow an axe? Why does he believe that "it is difficult to begin without borrowing"? What is difficult to begin?

2. What did the hillside where Thoreau worked look like? What are the vital statistics of the house that he ultimately builds? What is the significance of his occupying his house on the "4th of July"?

3. What do you think is the main point of this selection?

4. Thoreau says he returned the axe he borrowed "sharper than I received it." Why does he make it a point to reveal this to us? What did the owner mean when he said the axe "was the apple of his eye"?

5. What is the "division of labor" that the writer refers to in paragraph 14? Why does he make disparaging comments about the building of the railroad?

★ Techniques and Strategies

1. Who is the intended audience for this selection? What is the tone? How do you know?

2. Thoreau compares men to snakes, cowbirds, and cuckoos. What is the point of these comparisons and why does he draw on animal imagery?

3. Among other stylistic techniques, Thoreau often makes use of aphorisms and allusions in his writing. What is an aphorism? An allusion? Find examples of both in the selection and explain them.

4. What is the purpose of the list of expenses in paragraph 11?

5. Thoreau writes a number of paragraphs that are longer than we are used to reading in contemporary writing. Why do you think he uses these long paragraphs?

★ Speaking of Values

1. Thoreau remarks that "it is the most generous course ... to permit your fellow-men to have an interest in your enterprise." What does he mean by this? Is his statement simply an attempt to rationalize his borrowing or does it suggest a legitimate view of the connection between work and society? How much of an interest would "fellow-men" take in an individual's labors today? Why?

2. What does this selection suggest about Thoreau's concept of individualism and self-reliance, two concepts he championed throughout his life and we continue to acknowledge as defining elements of American values?

3. The writer asserts that "there is some of the same fitness in a man's building his own house that there is in a bird's building its own nest." What does he mean by this statement? Do you agree with him? Why or why not?

4. What does Thoreau mean when he says in paragraph 14 that "my excuse is that I brag for humanity rather than for myself"? What is he bragging about? Why does he feel responsible for "humanity"?

5. Why does he raise the issue of a student's dwelling at Cambridge College? (Thoreau means Harvard.) What sense of values is he addressing here?

★ *Values Conversation*

Thoreau seems to celebrate the work that people do with their own hands. Do we still prize manual labor today? Or do we see it as something less than desirable? Form groups and discuss your views on the matter.

★ *Writing about Values*

1. Have you ever built anything by yourself? Write an essay to present your joys and pains in this enterprise. Be sure to indicate what it was you built, how you felt about building it, how others viewed the activity, and why you built it yourself. Did you experience a deep sense of personal satisfaction? Frustration? What, if anything, did the project contribute to your character development, do you think?

2. Thoreau seems to be making a statement about the relation between individual labor and individual freedom. Write a paper analyzing this relation in today's world. Be sure to consider some of the analogies and metaphors Thoreau uses in this selection to help illustrate your points.

3. Thoreau writes, "How could youths better learn to live than by at once trying the experiment of living?" Write a paper giving your views on this point. Which youths would you recommend to follow this course? Why?

Arlie Russell Hochschild

There's No Place like Work

Born in Boston in 1940, Arlie Russell Hochschild is a sociologist specializing in the impact of work on the modern family. Her works include *The Unexpected Community: Portrait of an Old Age Subculture* (1978), *The Managed Heart: Commercialization of Human Feeling* (1983) and *The Second Shift: Working Parents and the Revolution at Home* (1989). Here she explores the relation between work time and family time in American households.

------------ ★ ------------

1 When Cassie Bell, 4, arrives at the Spotted Deer Child-Care Center, her hair half-combed, a blanket in one hand, a fudge bar in the other. "I'm late," her mother, Gwen, a sturdy young woman whose short-cropped hair frames a pleasant face, explains to the child-care worker in charge. "Cassie wanted the fudge bar so bad, I gave it to her," she adds apologetically.

2 "*Pleeese*, can't you take me with you?" Cassie pleads.

3 "You know I can't take you to work," Gwen replies in a tone that suggests that she has been expecting this request. Cassie's shoulders droop. But she has struck a hard bargain—the morning fudge bar—aware of her mother's anxiety about the long day that lies ahead at the center. As Gwen explains later, she continually feels that she owes Cassie more time than she gives her—she has a "time debt."

4 Arriving at her office just before 8, Gwen finds on her desk a cup of coffee in her personal mug, milk no sugar (exactly as she likes it), prepared by a co-worker who managed to get in ahead of her. As the assistant to the head of public relations at a company I will call Amerco, Gwen has to handle responses to any reports that may appear about the company in the press—a challenging job, but one that gives her satisfaction. As she prepares for her first meeting of the day, she misses her daughter, but she also feels relief; there's a lot to get done at Amerco.

5 Gwen used to work a straight eight-hour day. But over the last three years, her workday has gradually stretched to eight and a half or nine hours, not counting the E-mail messages and faxes she answers from home. She complains about her hours to her co-workers and listens to their complaints—but she loves her job. Gwen picks up Cassie at 5:45 and gives her a long, affectionate hug.

6 At home, Gwen's husband, John, a computer programmer, plays with their daughter while Gwen prepares dinner. To protect the dinner

"hour"—8:00–8:30—Gwen checks that the phone machine is on, hears the phone ring during dinner but resists the urge to answer. After Cassie's bath, Gwen and Cassie have "quality time," or "Q.T.," as John affectionately calls it. Half an hour later, at 9:30, Gwen tucks Cassie into bed.

There are, in a sense, two Bell households: the rushed family they   7 actually are and the relaxed family they imagine they might be if only they had time. Gwen and John complain that they are in a time bind. What they say they want seems so modest—time to throw a ball, to read to Cassie, to witness the small dramas of her development, not to speak of having a little fun and romance themselves. Yet even these modest wishes seem strangely out of reach. Before going to bed, Gwen has to E-mail messages to her colleagues in preparation for the next day's meeting; John goes to bed early, exhausted—he's out the door by 7 every morning.

Nationwide, many working parents are in the same boat. More   8 mothers of small children than ever now work outside the home. In 1993, 56 percent of women with children between 6 and 17 worked outside the home full time year round; 43 percent of women with children 6 and under did the same. Meanwhile, fathers of small children are not cutting back hours of work to help out at home. If anything, they have increased their hours at work. According to a 1993 national survey conducted by the Families and Work Institute in New York, American men average 48.8 hours of work a week, and women 41.7 hours, including overtime and commuting. All in all, more women are on the economic train, and for many—men and women alike—the train is going faster.

But Amerco has "family friendly" policies. If your division head   9 and supervisor agree, you can work part time, share a job with another worker, work some hours at home, take parental leave or use "flex time." But hardly anyone uses these policies. In seven years, only two Amerco fathers have taken formal parental leave. Fewer than 1 percent have taken advantage of the opportunity to work part time. Of all such policies, only flex time—which rearranges but does not shorten work time—has had a significant number of takers (perhaps a third of working parents at Amerco).

Forgoing family-friendly policies is not exclusive to Amerco workers.   10 A 1991 study of 188 companies conducted by the Families and Work Institute found that while a majority offered part-time shifts, fewer than 5 percent of employees made use of them. Thirty-five percent offered "flex place"—work from home—and fewer than 3 percent of their employees took advantage of it. And an earlier Bureau of Labor Statistics survey asked workers whether they preferred a shorter workweek, a longer one or their present schedule. About 62 percent preferred their present schedule; 28 percent would have preferred longer hours. Fewer than 10 percent said they wanted a cut in hours.

11   Still, I found it hard to believe that people didn't protest their long hours at work. So I contacted Bright Horizons, a company that runs 136 company-based child-care centers associated with corporations, hospitals and Federal agencies in 25 states. Bright Horizons allowed me to add questions to a questionnaire they sent out to 3,000 parents whose children attended the centers. The respondents, mainly middle-class parents in their early 30's, largely confirmed the picture I'd found at Amerco. A third of fathers and a fifth of mothers described themselves as "workaholic," and 1 out of 3 said their partners were.

12   To be sure, some parents have tried to shorten their hours. Twenty-one percent of the nation's women voluntarily work part time, as do 7 percent of men. A number of others make under-the-table arrange ments that don't show up on surveys. But while working parents say they need more time at home, the main story of their lives does not center on a struggle to get it. Why? Given the hours parents are working these days, why aren't they taking advantage of an opportunity to reduce their time at work?

13   The most widely held explanation is that working parents cannot afford to work shorter hours. Certainly this is true for many. But if money is the whole explanation, why would it be that at places like Amerco, the best-paid employees—upper-level managers and professionals—were the least interested in part-time work or job sharing, while clerical workers who earned less were more interested?

14   Similarly, if money were the answer, we would expect poorer new mothers to return to work more quickly after giving birth than rich mothers. But among working women nationwide, well-to-do new mothers are not much more likely to stay home after 13 weeks with a new baby than low-income new mothers. When asked what they look for in a job, only a third of respondents in a recent study said salary came first. Money is important, but by itself, money does not explain why many people don't want to cut back hours at work.

15   A second explanation goes that workers don't dare ask for time off because they are afraid it would make them vulnerable to layoffs. With recent downsizings at many large corporations, and the well-paying, secure jobs being replaced by lower-paying, insecure ones, it occurred to me that perhaps employees are "working scared." But when I asked Amerco employees whether they worked long hours for fear of getting on a layoff list, virtually everyone said no. Even among a particularly vulnerable group—factory workers who were laid off in the downturn of the early 1980's and were later rehired—most did not cite fear for their jobs as the only, or main, reason they worked overtime. For unionized workers, layoffs are assigned by seniority, and for nonunionized workers, layoffs are usually related to the profitability of the division a person works in, not to an individual work schedule.

Were workers uninformed about the company's family-friendly   16
policies? No. Some even mentioned that they were proud to work for a
company that offered such enlightened policies. Were rigid middle
managers standing in the way of workers using these policies? Sometimes. But when I compared Amerco employees who worked for flexible managers with those who worked for rigid managers, I found that
the flexible managers reported only a few more applicants than the
rigid ones. The evidence, however counterintuitive, pointed to a paradox: workers at the company I studied weren't protesting the time
bind. They were accommodating to it.

Why? I did not anticipate the conclusion I found myself coming to: 17
namely, that work has become a form of "home" and home has become
"work." The worlds of home and work have not begun to blur, as the
conventional wisdom goes, but to reverse places. We are used to thinking that home is where most people feel the most appreciated, the most
truly "themselves," the most secure, the most relaxed. We are used to
thinking that work is where most people feel like "just a number" or "a
cog in a machine." It is where they have to be "on," have to "act,"
where they are least secure and most harried.

But new management techniques so pervasive in corporate life   18
have helped transform the workplace into a more appreciative, personal sort of social world. Meanwhile, at home the divorce rate has
risen, and the emotional demands have become more baffling and
complex. In addition to teething, tantrums and the normal developments of growing children, the needs of elderly parents are creating
more tasks for the modern family—as are the blending, unblending, re-
blending of new stepparents, stepchildren, exes and former in-laws.

This idea began to dawn on me during one of my first interviews   19
with an Amerco worker. Linda Avery, a friendly, 38-year-old mother, is
a shift supervisor at an Amerco plant. When I meet her in the factory's
coffee-break room over a couple of Cokes, she is wearing blue jeans
and a pink jersey, her hair pulled back in a long, blond ponytail.
Linda's husband, Bill, is a technician in the same plant. By working different shifts, they manage to share the care of their 2-year-old son and
Linda's 16-year-old daughter from a previous marriage. "Bill works the
7 A.M. to 3 P.M. shift while I watch the baby," she explains. "Then I work
the 3 P.M. to 11 P.M. shift and he watches the baby. My daughter works at
Walgreen's after school."

Linda is working overtime, and so I begin by asking whether   20
Amerco required the overtime, or whether she volunteered for it. "Oh,
I put in for it," she replies. I ask her whether, if finances and company
policy permitted, she'd be interested in cutting back on the overtime.
She takes off her safety glasses, rubs her face and, without answering
my question, explains: "I get home, and the minute I turn the key, my
daughter is right there. Granted, she needs somebody to talk to about

her day.... The baby is still up. He should have been in bed two hours ago, and that upsets me. The dishes are piled in the sink. My daughter comes right up to the door and complains about anything her stepfather said or did, and she wants to talk about her job. My husband is in the other room hollering to my daughter, 'Tracy, I don't ever get any time to talk to your mother, because you're always monopolizing her time before I even get a chance!' They all come at me at once."

21   Linda's description of the urgency of demands and the unarbitrated quarrels that await her homecoming contrast with her account of arriving at her job as a shift supervisor: "I usually come to work early, just to get away from the house. When I arrive, people are there waiting. We sit, we talk, we joke. I let them know what's going on, who has to be where, what changes I've made for the shift that day. We sit and chitchat for 5 or 10 minutes. There's laughing, joking, fun."

22   For Linda, home has come to feel like work and work has come to feel a bit like home. Indeed, she feels she can get relief from the "work" of being at home only by going to the "home" of work. Why has her life at home come to seem like this? Linda explains it this way: "My husband's a great help watching our baby. But as far as doing housework or even taking the baby when I'm at home, no. He figures he works five days a week; he's not going to come home and clean. But he doesn't stop to think that I work seven days a week. Why should I have to come home and do the housework without help from anybody else? My husband and I have been through this over and over again. Even if he would just pick up from the kitchen table and stack the dishes for me, that would make a big difference. He does nothing. On his weekends off, he goes fishing. If I want any time off, I have to get a sitter. He'll help out if I'm not here, but the minute I am, all the work at home is mine."

23   With a light laugh, she continues: "So I take a lot of overtime. The more I get out of the house, the better I am. It's a terrible thing to say, but that's the way I feel."

24   When Bill feels the need for time off, to relax, to have fun, to feel free, he climbs in his truck and takes his free time without his family. Largely in response, Linda grabs what she also calls "free time"—at work. Neither Linda nor Bill Avery wants more time together at home, not as things are arranged now.

25   How do Linda and Bill Avery fit into the broader picture of American family and work life? Current research suggests that however hectic their lives, women who do paid work feel less depressed, think better of themselves and are more satisfied than women who stay at home. One study reported that women who work outside the home feel more valued at home than housewives do. Meanwhile, work is where many women feel like "good mothers." As Linda reflects: "I'm a good mom at home, but I'm a better mom at work. At home, I get into

fights with Tracy. I want her to apply to a junior college, but she's not interested. At work, I think I'm better at seeing the other person's point of view."

Many workers feel more confident they could "get the job done" at work than at home. One study found that only 59 percent of workers feel their "performance" in the family is "good or unusually good," while 86 percent rank their performance on the job this way.   26

Forces at work and at home are simultaneously reinforcing this "reversal." The lure of work has been enhanced in recent years by the rise of company cultural engineering—in particular, the shift from Frederick Taylor's principles of scientific management to the Total Quality principles originally set out by W. Edwards Deming. Under the influence of a Taylorist world view, the manager's job was to coerce the worker's mind and body, not to appeal to the worker's heart. The Taylorized worker was de-skilled, replaceable and cheap, and as a consequence felt bored, demeaned and unappreciated.   27

Using modern participative management techniques, many companies now train workers to make their own work decisions, and then set before their newly "empowered" employees moral as well as financial incentives. At Amerco, the Total Quality worker is invited to feel recognized for job accomplishments. Amerco regularly strengthens the familylike ties of co-workers by holding "recognition ceremonies" honoring particular workers or self-managed production teams. Amerco employees speak of "belonging to the Amerco," family and proudly wear their "Total Quality" pins or "High Performance Team" T-shirts, symbols of their loyalty to the company and of its loyalty to them.   28

The company occasionally decorates a section of the factory and serves refreshments. The production teams, too, have regular get-togethers. In a New Age recasting of an old business slogan—"The Customer Is Always Right"—Amerco proposes that its workers "Value the Internal Customer." This means: Be as polite and considerate to co-workers inside the company as you would be to customers outside it. How many recognition ceremonies for competent performance are being offered at home? Who is valuing the internal customer there?   29

Amerco also tries to take on the role of a helpful relative with regard to employee problems at work and at home. The education-and-training division offers employees free courses (on company time) in "Dealing With Anger," "How to Give and Accept Criticism," "How to Cope With Difficult People."   30

At home, of course, people seldom receive anything like this much help on issues basic to family life. There, no courses are being offered on "Dealing With Your Child's Disappointment in You" or "How to Treat Your Spouse Like an Internal Customer."   31

If Total Quality calls for "re-skilling" the worker in an "enriched" job environment, technological developments have long been de-skilling   32 parents at home. Over the centuries, store-bought goods have replaced homespun cloth, homemade soap and homebaked foods. Day care for children, retirement homes for the elderly, even psychotherapy are, in a way, commercial substitutes for jobs that a mother once did at home. Even family-generated entertainment has, to some extent, been replaced by television, video games and the VCR. I sometimes watched Amerco families sitting together after their dinners, mute but cozy, watching sitcoms in which television mothers, fathers and children related in an animated way to one another while the viewing family engaged in relational loafing.

33   The one "skill" still required of family members is the hardest one of all—the emotional work of forging, deepening or repairing family relationships. It takes time to develop this skill, and even then things can go awry. Family ties are complicated. People get hurt. Yet as broken homes become more common—and as the sense of belonging to a geographical community grows less and less secure in an age of mobility—the corporate world has created a sense of "neighborhood," of "feminine culture," of family at work. Life at work can be insecure; the company can fire workers. But workers aren't so secure at home, either. Many employees have been working for Amerco for 20 years but are on their second or third marriages or relationships. The shifting balance between these two "divorce rates" may be the most powerful reason why tired parents flee a world of unresolved quarrels and unwashed laundry for the orderliness, harmony and managed cheer of work. People are getting their "pink slips" at home.

34   Amerco workers have not only turned their offices into "home" and their homes into workplaces; many have also begun to "Taylorize" time at home, where families are succumbing to a cult of efficiency previously associated mainly with the office and factory. Meanwhile, work time, with its ever longer hours, has become more hospitable to sociability—periods of talking with friends on E-mail, patching up quarrels, gossiping. Within the long workday of many Amerco employees are great hidden pockets of inefficiency while, in the far smaller number of weekday hours at home, they are, despite themselves, forced to act increasingly time-conscious and efficient.

35   The Avery's respond to their time bind at home by trying to value and protect "quality time." A concept unknown to their parents and grandparents, "quality time" has become a powerful symbol of the struggle against the growing pressures at home. It reflects the extent to which modern parents feel the flow of time to be running against them. The premise behind "quality time" is that the time we devote to relationships can somehow be separated from ordinary time. Relationships go on during quantity time, of course, but then we are only passively, not actively, wholeheartedly, specializing in our emotional ties. We aren't "on." Quality time at home becomes like an office appointment.

You don't want to be caught "goofing off around the water cooler" when you are "at work."

Quality time holds out the hope that scheduling intense periods of togetherness can compensate for an overall loss of time in such a way that a relationship will suffer no loss of quality. But this is just another way of transferring the cult of efficiency from office to home. We must now get our relationships in good repair in less time. Instead of nine hours a day with a child, we declare ourselves capable of getting "the same result" with one intensely focused hour.

Parents now more commonly speak of time as if it is a threatened form of personal capital they have no choice but to manage and invest. What's new here is the spread into the home of a financial manager's attitude toward time. Working parents at Amerco owe what they think of as time debts at home. This is because they are, in a sense, inadvertently "Taylorizing" the house—speeding up the pace of home life as Taylor once tried to "scientifically" speed up the pace of factory life.

Advertisers of products aimed at women have recognized that this new reality provides an opportunity to sell products, and have turned the very pressure that threatens to explode the home into a positive attribute. Take, for example, an ad promoting Instant Quaker Oatmeal: it shows a smiling mother ready for the office in her square-shouldered suit, hugging her happy son. A caption reads: "Nicky is a very picky eater. With Instant Quaker Oatmeal, I can give him a terrific hot breakfast in just 90 seconds. And I don't have to spend any time coaxing him to eat it!" Here, the modern mother seems to have absorbed the lessons of Frederick Taylor as she presses for efficiency at home because she is in a hurry to get to work.

Part of modern parenthood seems to include coping with the resistance of real children who are not so eager to get their cereal so fast. Some parents try desperately not to appease their children with special gifts or smooth-talking promises about the future. But when time is scarce, even the best parents find themselves passing a system-wide familial speed-up along to the most vulnerable workers on the line. Parents are then obliged to try to control the damage done by a reversal of worlds. They monitor mealtime, homework time, bedtime, trying to cut out "wasted" time.

In response, children often protest the pace, the deadlines, the grand irrationality of "efficient" family life. Children dawdle. They refuse to leave places when it's time to leave. They insist on leaving places when it's not time to leave. Surely, this is part of the usual stop-and-go of childhood itself, but perhaps, too, it is the plea of children for more family time, and more control over what time there is. This only adds to the feeling that life at home has become hard work.

Instead of trying to arrange shorter or more flexible work schedules, Amerco parents often avoid confronting the reality of the time

bind. Some minimize their ideas about how much care a child, a partner or they themselves "really need." They make do with less time, less
attention, less understanding and less support at home than they once
imagined possible. They *emotionally downsize* life. In essence, they deny
the needs of family members, and they themselves become emotional
ascetics. If they once "needed" time with each other, they are now increasingly "fine" without it.

42   Another way that working parents try to evade the time bind is to
buy themselves out of it—an approach that puts women in particular
at the heart of a contradiction. Like men, women absorb the work-family speed-up far more than they resist it; but unlike men, they still
shoulder most of the workload at home. And women still represent in
people's minds the heart and soul of family life. They're the ones—
especially women of the urban middle and upper-middle classes—who
feel most acutely the need to save time, who are the most tempted by
the new "time saving" goods and services and who wind up feeling the
most guilty about it. For example, Playgroup Connections, a Washington-
area business started by a former executive recruiter, matches playmates
to one another. One mother hired the service to find her child a French-
speaking playmate.

43   In several cities, children home alone can call a number for
"Grandma, Please!" and reach an adult who has the time to talk with
them, sing to them or help them with their homework. An ad for Kindercare Learning Centers, a for-profit child-care chain, pitches its appeal this
way: "You want your child to be active, tolerant, smart, loved, emotionally stable, self-aware, artistic and get a two-hour nap. Anything else?" It
goes on to note that Kindercare accepts children 6 weeks to 12 years old
and provides a number to call for the Kindercare nearest you. Another
typical service organizes children's birthday parties, making out invitations ("sure hope you can come") and providing party favors, entertainment, a decorated cake and balloons. Creative Memories is a service that
puts ancestral photos into family albums for you.

44   An overwhelming majority of the working mothers I spoke with
recoiled from the idea of buying themselves out of parental duties. A
bought birthday party was "too impersonal," a 90-second breakfast
"too fast." Yet a surprising amount of lunchtime conversation between
female friends at Amerco was devoted to expressing complex, conflicting feelings about the lure of trading time for one service or another.
The temptation to order flash-frozen dinners or to call a local number
for a homework helper did not come up because such services had not
yet appeared at Spotted Deer Child-Care Center. But many women
dwelled on the question of how to decide where a mother's job began
and ended, especially with regard to baby sitters and television. One
mother said to another in the breakroom of an Amerco plant: "Damon
doesn't settle down until 10 at night, so he hates me to wake him up in

the morning and I hate to do it. He's cranky. He pulls the covers up. I put on cartoons. That way, I can dress him and he doesn't object. I don't like to use TV that way. It's like a drug. But I do it."

The other mother countered: "Well, Todd is up before we are, so that's not a problem. It's after dinner, when I feel like watching a little television, that I feel guilty, because he gets too much TV at the sitter's." 45

As task after task falls into the realm of time-saving goods and services, questions arise about the moral meanings attached to doing or not doing such tasks. Is it being a good mother to bake a child's birthday cake (alone or together with one's partner)? Or can we gratefully save time by ordering it, and be good mothers by planning the party? Can we save more time by hiring a planning service, and be good mothers simply by watching our children have a good time? "Wouldn't that be nice!" one Amerco mother exclaimed. As the idea of the "good mother" retreats before the pressures of work and the expansion of motherly services, mothers are in fact continually reinventing themselves. 46

The final way working parents tried to evade the time bind was to develop what I call "potential selves." The potential selves that I discovered in my Amerco interviews were fantasy creations of time-poor parents who dreamed of living as time millionaires. 47

One man, a gifted 55-year-old engineer in research and development at Amerco, told how he had dreamed of taking his daughters on a camping trip in the Sierra Mountains: "I bought all the gear three years ago when they were 5 and 7, the tent, the sleeping bags, the air mattresses, the backpacks, the ponchos. I got a map of the area. I even got the freeze-dried food. Since then the kids and I have talked about it a lot, and gone over what we're going to do. They've been on me to do it for a long time. I feel bad about it. I keep putting if off, but we'll do it. I just don't know when." 48

Banished to garages and attics of many Amerco workers were expensive electric saws, cameras, skis and musical instruments, all bought with wages it took time to earn. These items were to their owners what Cassie's fudge bar was to her—a substitute for time, a talisman, a reminder of the potential self. 49

Obviously, not everyone, not even a majority of Americans, is making a home out of work and a workplace out of home. But in the working world, it is a growing reality, and one we need to face. Increasing numbers of women are discovering a great male secret—that work can be an escape from the pressures of home, pressures that the changing nature of work itself are only intensifying. Neither men nor women are going to take up "family friendly" policies, whether corporate or governmental, as long as the current realities of work and home remain as they are. For a substantial number of time-bound parents, the stripped-down home and the neighborhood devoid of community are simply losing out to the pull of the workplace. 50

51   There are several broader, historical causes of this reversal of realms. The last 30 years have witnessed the rapid rise of women in the workplace. At the same time, job mobility has taken families farther from relatives who might lend a hand, and made it harder to make close friends of neighbors who could help out. Moreover, as women have acquired more education and have joined men at work, they have absorbed the views of an older, male-oriented work world, its views of a "real career," far more than men have taken up their share of the work at home. One reason women have changed more than men is that the world of "male" work seems more honorable and valuable than the "female" world of home and children.

52   So where do we go from here? There is surely no going back to the mythical 1950's family that confined women to the home. Most women don't wish to return to a full-time role at home—and couldn't afford it even if they did. But equally troubling is a workaholic culture that strands both men and women outside the home.

53   For a while now, scholars on work-family issues have pointed to Sweden, Norway and Denmark as better models of work-family balance. Today, for example, almost all Swedish fathers take two paid weeks off from work at the birth of their children, and about half of fathers and most mothers take additional "parental leave" during the child's first or second year. Research shows that men who take family leave when their children are very young are more likely to be involved with their children as they grow older. When I mentioned this Swedish record of paternity leave to a focus group of American male managers, one of them replied, "Right, we've already heard about Sweden." To this executive, paternity leave was a good idea not for the U.S. today, but for some "potential society" in another place and time.

54   Meanwhile, children are paying the price. In her book "When the Bough Breaks: The Cost of Neglecting Our Children," the economist Sylvia Hewlett claims that "compared with the previous generation, young people today are more likely to "underperform at school; commit suicide; need psychiatric help; suffer a severe eating disorder; bear a child out of wedlock; take drugs, be the victim of a violent crime." But we needn't dwell on sledgehammer problems like heroin or suicide to realize that children like those at Spotted Deer need more of our time. If other advanced nations with two-job families can give children the time they need, why can't we?

★ Meaning and Understanding

1. Why, according to Hochschild, are many parents *not* taking the opportunity to reduce their time at work? How does the writer explain the phenomenon, on the other hand?

2. What is Amerco? Why does the writer say that it has "family-friendly" policies? Why does it provide so many free courses to its workers?

3. In what way has the corporate world created a sense of family? What does total quality management contribute to this sense?

4. What are some of the demands and quarrels facing Linda at home? How is the atmosphere at work different? Why does she put in for overtime?

5. How do Amerco parents avoid confronting the "reality of the time bind" (paragraph 39)?

6. How are children "paying the price" of the change in "work-family" balance?

★ Techniques and Strategies

1. What is the advantage of Hochschild's telling us about the marriage and life of Linda and Bill Avery? How do the narrative details contribute to the essay?

2. The selection includes many statistics. How do these numbers help Hochschild establish her point? How did Hochschild collect the data for her study? Do you think her methodology is valid? Why or why not?

3. Who is the intended audience for this selection? How do you know?

4. What is the thesis of the essay? Where does the author state it?

5. Where does the writer use comparison and contrast strategies? Cause and effect?

6. How does the title prepare the reader for the essay?

★ Speaking of Values

1. How is the workplace typical, as described by Hochschild? How is it atypical? When we think of "work," what associations do we normally make?

2. The idea that people would prefer to be at work rather than at home contradicts a basic American value of family centrality in our existence. If Hochschild is right, how do you think Americans evolved this point of work-over-all-else as a key principle of modern life? Do you think we have progressed or regressed to this point? Explain your answer.

3. What obligation does an employer have to be "family friendly"? Is it good business to be so? Why or why not?

4. Do people who opt to spend more time at work than they actually need to compromise their responsibilities as spouses and parents? Why or why not? How do parents that you know weight their time with family and work? Discuss.

★ *Values Conversation*

Form groups to discuss what you see as the appropriate relation between work and family. How much time, energy, or commitment should go to each? Factor in whatever points impressed you in Hochschild's piece as you discuss the issue.

★ *Writing about Values*

1. Write an essay that responds to the question at the start of paragraph 24: "How do Linda and Bill Avery fit into the broader picture of American family and work life?"

2. Identify one or two TV shows that center on the working lives of the characters. Write a paper examining the lives of some of the characters. To what extent do we know about their lives outside work? How important do those lives seem to be? Do they includes spouses, parents, children, and so on?

3. What kind of family life would make mothers and fathers want to spend more time with their families than on the job? Write an essay to explore this point.

Jonathan Kozol

Children and Poverty

Jonathan Kozol was born in Boston in 1936 and has authored several works on the subjects of poverty, race, and education. He has contributed essays to the *New York Times Book Review, Atlantic, Newsweek,* and many other journals and periodicals. Some of his better-known books include *Children of the Revolution* (1977), *Illiterate America* (1985), and *Savage Inequalities: Children in America's Schools* (1991). In this essay from *Amazing Grace* (1995), he explores the lives of "the poorest of the poor."

———— ★ ————

The Number 6 train from Manhattan to the South Bronx makes nine stops in the 18-minute ride between East 59th Street and Brook Avenue. When you enter the train, you are in the seventh richest congressional district in the nation. When you leave, you are in the poorest.   1

The 600,000 people who live here and the 450,000 people who live in Washington Heights and Harlem, which are separated from the South Bronx by a narrow river, make up one of the largest racially segregated concentrations of poor people in our nation.   2

Brook Avenue, which is the tenth stop on the local, lies in the center of Mott Haven, whose 48,000 people are the poorest in the South Bronx. Two thirds are Hispanic, one third black. Thirty-five percent are children. In 1991, the median household income of the area, according to the *New York Times,* was $7,600.   3

St. Ann's Church, on St. Ann's Avenue, is three blocks from the subway station. The children who come to this small Episcopal church for food and comfort and to play, and the mothers and fathers who come here for prayer, are said to be the poorest people in New York. "More than 95 percent are poor," the pastor says—"the poorest of the poor, poor by any standard I can think of."   4

At the elementary school that serves the neighborhood across the avenue, only seven of 800 children do not qualify for free school lunches. "Five of those seven," says the principal, "get reduced-price lunches, because they are classified as only 'poor,' not 'destitute.'"   5

In some cities, the public reputation of a ghetto neighborhood bears little connection to the world that you discover when you walk the streets with children and listen to their words. In Mott Haven, this is not the case. By and large, the words of the children in the streets and schools and houses that surround St. Ann's more than justify the grimness in the words of journalists who have described the area.   6

7   Crack-cocaine addiction and the intravenous use of heroin, which children I have met here call "the needle drug," are woven into the texture of existence in Mott Haven. Nearly 4,000 heroin injectors, many of whom are HIV-infected, live here. Virtually every child at St. Ann's knows someone, a relative or neighbor, who has died of AIDS, and most children here know many others who are dying now of the disease. One quarter of the women of Mott Haven who are tested in obstetric wards are positive for HIV. Rates of pediatric AIDS, therefore, are high.

8   Depression is common among children in Mott Haven. Many cry a great deal but cannot explain exactly why.

9   Fear and anxiety are common. Many cannot sleep

10   Asthma is the most common illness among children here. Many have to struggle to take in a good deep breath. Some mothers keep oxygen tanks, which children describe as "breathing machines," next to their children's beds.

11   The houses in which these children live, two thirds of which are owned by the City of New York, are often as squalid as the houses of the poorest children I have visited in rural Mississippi, but there is none of the greenness and the healing sweetness of the Mississippi countryside outside their windows, which are often barred and bolted as protection against thieves.

12   Some of these houses are freezing in the winter. In dangerously cold weather, the city sometimes distributes electric blankets and space heaters to its tenants. In emergency conditions, if space heaters can't be used, because substandard wiring is overloaded, the city's practice is to pass out sleeping bags.

13   "You just cover up ... and hope you wake up the next morning," says a father of four children, one of them an infant one month old, as they prepare to climb into their sleeping bags in hats and coats on a December night.

14   In humid summer weather, roaches crawl on virtually every surface of the houses in which many of the children live. Rats emerge from holes in bedroom walls, terrorizing infants in their cribs. In the streets outside, the restlessness and anger that are present in all seasons frequently intensify under the stress of heat.

15   In speaking of rates of homicide in New York City neighborhoods, the *Times* refers to the streets around St. Ann's as "the deadliest blocks" in "the deadliest precinct" of the city. If there is a deadlier place in the United States, I don't know where it is.

16   In 1991, 84 people, more than half of whom were 21 or younger, were murdered in the precinct. A year later, ten people were shot dead on a street called Beekman Avenue, where many of the children I have come to know reside. On Valentine's Day of 1993, three more children and three adults were shot dead on the living room floor of an apartment six blocks from the run-down park that serves the area.

In early July of 1993, shortly before the first time that I visited the 17
neighborhood, three more people were shot in 30 minutes in three unrelated murders in the South Bronx, one of them only a block from St.
Ann's Avenue. A week later, a mother was murdered and her baby
wounded by a bullet in the stomach while they were standing on a
South Bronx corner. Three weeks after that, a minister and elderly pa-
rishioner were shot outside the front door of their church, while another South Bronx resident was discovered in his bathtub with his head
cut off. In subsequent days, a man was shot in both his eyes and a ten-
year-old was critically wounded in the brain.

What is it like for children to grow up here? What do they think the 18
world has done to them? Do they believe that they are being shunned
or hidden by society? If so, do they think that they deserve this? What
is it that enables some of them to pray? When they pray, what do they
say to God?

Walking into St. Ann's Church on a hot summer afternoon, one is 19
immediately in the presence of small children. They seem to be everywhere: in the garden, in the hallways, in the kitchen, in the chapel, on
the stairs. The first time I see the pastor, Martha Overall, she is carrying
a newborn baby in her arms and is surrounded by three lively and excited little girls. In one of the most diseased and dangerous communities in any city of the Western world, the beautiful old stone church on
St. Ann's Avenue is a gentle sanctuary from the terrors of the streets
outside.

A seven-year-old boy named Cliffie, whose mother has come to the 20
church to talk with Reverend Overall, agrees to take me for a walk
around the neighborhood. His mother cautions me, "He does tell fibs,"
then gives him a hug and tells him, "Be as interesting as you always
are."

There are children in the poorest, most abandoned places who, de- 21
spite the miseries and poisons that the world has pumped into their
lives, seem, when you first meet them, to be cheerful anyway. Cliffie, as
we set out onto St. Ann's Avenue, seems about as buoyant, and as
lively, and as charmingly mysterious, as seven-year-olds anywhere. He
also seems to feel no shyness and no hesitation about filling the role of
guide that he has been assigned.

Reaching up to take my hand the moment that we leave the 22
church, he starts a running commentary almost instantly, interrupting
now and then to say hello to men and women on the street, dozens of
whom are standing just outside the gateway to St. Ann's, waiting for a
food pantry to open.

At a tiny park in a vacant lot less than a block away, he points to a 23
number of stuffed animals that are attached to the branches of a tree.

"Bears," he says. 24

"Why are there bears in the tree?" I ask. 25

26   He doesn't answer me but smiles at the bears affectionately. "I saw a boy shot in the head right over there," he says a moment later, in a voice that does not sound particularly sad, then looks up at me and asks politely, "Would you like a chocolate chip cookie?"

27   "No, thank you," I say.

28   He has a package of cookies and removes one. He breaks it in half, returns half to the package, and munches on the other half as we are walking.

29   Leading me across the avenue, he hesitates in front of a bodega, looks in both directions up and down the street, then seems to come to a conclusion.

30   "Okay. I think we need to go up here."

31   We head north for a block or two, then turn right and walk a long block to a rutted street called Cypress Avenue.

32   After crossing Cypress, he hesitates again.

33   "Do you want to go down there?" he asks.

34   I say, "Okay," not knowing what he means.

35   "They're burning bodies there," he says.

36   "What kind of bodies?"

37   "The bodies of people!" he says in a spooky voice, as if he enjoys the opportunity to terrify a grown-up.

38   "Is that the truth?"

39   He acts as if he doesn't hear my question and begins to hum.

40   The place that Cliffie is referring to turns out to be a waste incinerator that was put in operation recently over the objections of the parents in the neighborhood. The incinerator, I am later reassured by Reverend Overall, does not burn entire "bodies." What it burns are so-called "redbag products," such as amputated limbs and fetal tissue, bedding, bandages, and syringes that are transported here from 14 New York City hospitals. The waste products of some of these hospitals, she says, were initially going to be burned at an incinerator scheduled to be built along the East Side of Manhattan, but the siting of a burner there had been successfully resisted by the parents of the area because of fear of cancer risks to children.

41   Munching another cookie as we walk, Cliffie asks me, "Do you want to go on Jackson Avenue?"

42   Although I don't know one street from another, I agree.

43   "Come on," he says. "I'll take you there. We have to go around this block."

44   He pauses then, however—"wait a minute"—and he pulls an asthma inhaler from his pocket, holds it to his mouth, presses it twice, and then puts it away.

45   Silent for a while as we walk to Jackson Avenue, he stops when he sees a dog he knows. "That's Princess," he explains. To the dog, he says, "Hi, Princess!" Then, to me: "You see? We're almost there."

He stops again to ask if he can hold my tape recorder. When I hand   46
it to him, he studies the red light to be sure that it is working and then
whispers, "We are going to have a conversation."

As confident and grown-up as he sounds, he has the round face of   47
a baby and is scarcely more than three and a half feet tall. When he has
bad dreams, he tells me, "I go in my mommy's bed and crawl under the
covers." At other times, when he's upset, he says, "I sleep with a picture of my mother and I dream of her."

Unlike many children I have met in recent years, he has an absolutely   48
literal religious faith. When I ask him how he pictures God, he says, "He
has long hair and He can walk on the deep water." To make sure I understand that this is an unusual ability, he adds, "Nobody else can."

He seems to take the lessons of religion literally also. Speaking of a   49
time his mother sent him to the store "to get a pizza"—"three slices,
one for my mom, one for my dad, and one for me"—he says he saw a
homeless man who told him he was hungry. "But he was too cold to
move his mouth! He couldn't talk!"

"How did you know that he was hungry if he couldn't talk?"   50

"He pointed to my pizza."   51

"What did you do?"   52

"I gave him some!"   53

"Were your parents mad at you?"   54

He looks surprised by this. "Why would they be mad?" he asks.   55
"God told us, 'Share!'"

When I ask him who his heroes are, he first says "Michael Jackson"   56
and then "Oprah!"—like that, with an exclamation on the word. I try to
get him to speak about "important" persons as the schools tend to define them. "Have you read about George Washington?"

"I don't even know the man," he says.   57

We follow Jackson Avenue past several boarded buildings and a   58
"flat fix" shop, stop briefly in front of a fenced-in lot where the police of
New York City bring impounded cars, and then turn left in the direction of a highway with an elevated road above it, where a sign says
"Bruckner Boulevard." Crossing beneath the elevated road, we soon
arrive at Locust Avenue.

The medical waste incinerator, a new-looking building, is gunmetal   59
blue on top and cinder block below. From one of its metal sliding-doors,
which is half-open, a sourly unpleasant odor drifts into the street.
Standing in front of the building, Cliffie grumbles slightly but does not
seem terribly concerned. "You sure that you don't want a cookie?"

Again, I say, "No, thank you."   60

"I think I'll have another one," he says and takes another for himself.   61

After we cross Bruckner Boulevard again, he stops to consider the   62
direction we should go. "You want to go the hard way or the easy way
back to the church?"

63   "Let's go the easy way," I say.

64   "Well, actually, they're both the same," he says. "But, if we go up this way, I can show you where my store is."

65   When we get to the grocery that he calls his store, he walks right in and says hello to the man behind the counter, who is friendly to him, then walks out again and sees a young man standing in a doorway who, he tells me, is his cousin, then another man who is, he says, "my other cousin," and to whom he says, "Hi, Woody!" He holds up the tape recorder, which he is still carrying, and asks his cousin, "How old are you?"

66   The man replies, "I'm 32."

67   "Okay," says Cliffie, fiddling with the tape recorder. "I think we can give this thing a rest." He turns it off and hands it back to me.

68   Next to another vacant lot, where someone has dumped a heap of auto tires and some rusted auto parts, he points to a hypodermic needle in the tangled grass and to the bright-colored caps of crack containers, then, for no reason that I can discern, starts puffing up his cheeks and blowing out the air.

69   "The day is coming when the world will be destroyed," he finally announces. "Everyone is going to be burned to crispy cookies."

70   A car stops at that moment so that we can cross a busy street. "See that?" he says. "They let us cross." As we cross, he waves at the driver, who doesn't seem to know him but waves anyway. After we cross, he asks me, "Can I have the tape recorder back?" I hear him whispering into the microphone, "We're out of cookies. I ate a whole bag of cookies. They're all gone."

71   Back again on St. Ann's Avenue, he sees a man he knows close to the church and says hello to him. The man nods. "How you doin', little man?"

72   He holds up the tape recorder to the man. "Say how old you are."

73   The man says, "Sixty-five."

74   "Okay," says Cliffie. "That's enough. So long!"

75   Inside the church, his mother looks at me with some amusement on her face. "Did this child wear you out?"

76   "No," I say. "I enjoyed the walk." I mention, however, that he took me to the waste incinerator and repeats his comment about "burning bodies," to which she responds by giving him a half-sarcastic look, hesitating, and then saying, "Hey! You never know! Maybe this child knows something we haven't heard!"

77   After giving him another pleasantly suspicious look, she leans back in a chair and folds her arms like someone who is getting ready to say something she has planned to tell me all along. "The point is that they put a lot of things into our neighborhood that no one wants," she says. "The waste incinerator is just one more lovely way of showing their affection."

I ask, "Does it insult you?" 78

"It used to," she replies. "The truth is, you get used to the offense. 79
There's trashy things all over. There's a garbage dump three blocks
away. Then there's all the trucks that come through stinking up the air,
heading for the Hunts Point Market. Drivers get their drugs there and
their prostitutes.

"Did he take you down to Jackson Avenue?" 80

When I say he did, she says, "You see a lot of prostitutes down 81
there as well. Further down. By the expressway.... Then we get illegal
dumpers. People who don't live here come and dump things they
don't want: broken televisions, boxes of bottles, old refrigerators, beat-
up cars, old pieces of metal, other lovely things. They do it in the wee
hours of the morning.

"Actually," she says upon reflection, "I've got quite a few nice 82
things that way. Not long ago, somebody dumped a pile of chairs and
tables in the street. Brand-new. I was offended but I was also blessed. I
took two chairs."

A small and wiry woman wearing blue jeans and a baseball cap, a 83
former cocaine addict who now helps addicted women and their children, she tells me that more than 3,000 homeless families have been re-
located by the city in this neighborhood during the past few years, and
she asks a question I will hear from many other people here during the
months ahead. "Why do you want to put so many people with small
children in a place with so much sickness? This is the last place in New
York that they should put poor children. Clumping so many people, all
with the same symptoms and same problems, in one crowded place
with nothin' they can grow on? Our children start to mourn themselves
before their time."

Cliffie, who is listening to this while leaning on his elbow like a 84
pensive grown-up, offers his tentative approval to his mother's words.
"Yes," he says, "I think that's probably true."

He says it with so much thought, and grown-up reservation, that his 85
mother can't help smiling, even though it's not a funny statement. She
looks at him hard, grabs him suddenly around the neck, and kisses him.

In the evening, I go back to look more closely at the corner lot that 86
I had passed with Cliffie, where he pointed out the stuffed bears in the
branches of a tree. In the semidarkness, I can make out several figures,
some of them standing, some squatting on their knees, then many
more, perhaps two dozen people, some of whom are talking to each
other, some apparently transacting business, others who are sleeping. It
is, I later learn, one of many drug parks in the South Bronx that police
sometimes try to shut down but, for the most part, leave in peace for
those who have no other place to shoot their drugs or drink their wine.
The stuffed animals are tied by strings to the branches of the tree, a curious sight, which I later share with a woman cleaning up the kitchen in

the basement of the church, who simply nods at this and says, "They're children's bears," but does not attempt a further explanation.

87   The pastor tells me that the place is known as "Children's Park." Volunteers arrive here twice a week to give out condoms and clean needles to addicted men and women, some of whom bring their children with them. The children play near the bears or on a jungle gym while their mothers wait for needles.

88   At nine P.M., Reverend Overall offers to drive me downtown to Manhattan. Three hungry-looking dogs run past us when she pushes back the gates to the garden of the church to get her car. The dogs disappear into a section of the churchyard where, she says, one of our nation's Founding Fathers, Gouverneur Morris, who wrote the preamble to the U.S. Constitution, has his resting place. His wife, Anne Morris, is buried here beside him.

★ Meaning and Understanding

1. What are some features of the ghetto neighborhood Kozol describes?

2. What are some negative effects of the community on the children who live in Mott Haven? What is a "haven"? How is Mott Haven a cruelly ironic name?

3. Why is the church the center of the community. In what way is it, as Kozol suggests, a "gentle sanctuary"?

4. Although Kozol remarks that this area is "one of the most diseased and dangerous communities in any city in the Western world," he seems to have no fear as Cliffie escorts him around. Why do you think Kozol seems to be unafraid?

5. When Cliffie's mother tells Kozol about picking up some new chairs that someone had discarded, she says, "I was offended but I was also blessed." What does she mean by this?

6. Explain the following statement: "Our children start to mourn themselves before their time."

7. Why is depression common among children in Mott Haven?

★ Techniques and Strategies

1. The selection begins by noting the number of subway stops between East 59th Street in Manhattan and Brook Avenue in the South Bronx. Why is the number of stops important?

2. The first three paragraphs present the reader with statistics of one kind or another. What does Kozol hope to accomplish by presenting this data?

3. What is the thesis of this selection? Find the sentence that best defines it.

4. What details of Cliffie seem most vivid to you? How has Kozol captured the buoyance, liveliness, and mystery of a seven-year-old?

5. Who is the intended audience for this selection? What is the tone? How do you know?

★ Speaking of Values

1. How does the description of Mott Haven and the people who live there affect you? What communities have you lived in or seen or read about that are similar to Mott Haven?

2. What do you make of Cliffie's religious faith? Is it understandable? Why or why not? Does Cliffie seem too grownup or too childish for a seven-year-old? Explain your response.

3. Why do you think the authorities "put so many people with small children in a place with so much sickness"?

4. What do you think is the significance of the stuffed animals attached to the tree branches in the park? And what does the cleaning woman mean when she says simply that they are "children's bears"?

5. In many urban areas poverty and wealth coexist. And certainly dire poverty is not unique to cities. Yet the contrasts seem to be more pronounced in urban environments. What are some of the consequences of this proximity of wealth to poverty in cities? How does it affect the people? The institutions? Discuss.

★ Values Conversation

What community "sanctuaries" do you think can and should play a role in poverty-stricken neighborhoods? Form groups to identify the community groups and discuss what their contributions should be.

★ Writing about Values

1. Write an essay describing a poor community you have seen or lived in and compare it to the portrait Kozol provides here.

2. Write an essay about the coexistence of poverty and wealth in some community you know or can research.

3. Go to your video store and take out a few movies such as *Grand Canyon*, *Boyz 'n the Hood*, *Trading Places*, *Midnight Cowboy*, or any others with similar themes and write an essay to compare and contrast any two of them in their representation of contemporary wealth and poverty.

Jean Bethke Elshtain

The Hard Questions: Lost City

Jean Bethke Elshtain was born in 1941. Her works include *The Family in Political Thought* (1982), *Public Man; Private Woman: Women in Social and Political Thought* (1981), and *Promises to Keep; Decline and Renewal of Marriage in America* (1996). In this essay for the *New Republic*, she highlights a job dilemma facing American society.

———— ★ ————

1   There is a joke making the rounds this election. President Clinton approaches a voter with outstretched arms. After pumping the guy's hand, the president asks for his vote. "Why should I support you?" asks the voter. "Well, because I've created millions of new jobs on my watch," the president answers. "Yeah, I've got *three* of them," the rueful voter shoots back. The joke speaks to the undercurrent of anxiety seething beneath the sunny statistics on low unemployment. This economy is generating low-pay, service sector jobs with few prospects for long-term security, reliable benefits or opportunities to hone crucial career skills.

2   Work has always been central to American identity. The "huddled masses," including my own grandparents, came here in search of the dignity of labor and the recognition and standing that hard, dependable work ought, by rights, to afford. They dreamt about owning a bit of land or, even more improbably, a home; of improving their lives and the lives of their children; of passing something on to their grandchildren. No more. Now you're a sucker if you believe these things, or so those calling the economic shots are, in effect, telling people, and *showing* them in the crassest of ways. What is rewarded now is maximum flexibility, which means, in practice, no particular commitment to a job, a skill or a place. Welcome to the brave new world of the global economy.

3   At one point, not that long ago, people who attained higher learning could look forward to careers—vocations, an earlier generation would have called them—commensurate with their education and abilities. This was always, in part, a prerogative of the middle class. But that class kept growing, incorporating many who had begun life in modest circumstances. As it grew, this professional middle tier was forced to become more inclusive as a result of concrete political struggles. Working-class Americans struck their own kind of deal through

union organization and collective bargaining arrangements. Job security helped families remain stable, communities grow, folks make sense of themselves in relation to work and the wider polity.

But an emerging body of analysis not only shows the ways in 4
which this word is imploding, it demonstrates how profoundly dislocated the human beings affected come to feel. In a study now underway, the distinguished sociologist Richard Sennett is examining what happens to people cut adrift from perduring work and, therefore, from long-term expectations. Without work as a stable frame of reference, given de-skilling, out-sourcing and down-sizing, workers face the prospect of changing jobs some eleven times over the course of a life (as a matter not of choice and upward mobility, but of harsh necessity), and men and women come to see themselves as *dispensable,* in Sennett's distressing language. The old mobility, available to those who could see their work lives in terms of a "career path," is being replaced by a new dislocability. This fuels a corrosive sense of uselessness. It also means that the middle class is shrinking; an underclass is growing; and a smaller, but substantial, overclass of the very successful—those with incomes in constant dollars of over $100,000—has quadrupled since 1950. The shrinking of the middle class is particularly worrisome for those concerned with the fate of democracy, for it is the class that has historically been the backbone of liberal democratic regimes.

At earlier points in our history we had other sources of meaning 5
and purpose. In his beautiful book about Chicago in the years following World War II, *The Lost City,* Alan Ehrenhalt describes a densely textured world of religion, ethnicity, neighborhood, family. As that world was abandoned or disintegrated, work—"the job"—and what it could buy and sustain rose in importance. And now that expectation is harder to meet. What was lost cannot be restored and the promise of what would replace it has been depleted. It is as if a tacit social contract has been broken, yet there is no one to blame, no way to think about this politically. Ghostly corporations that operate outside the purview not only of particular communities but increasingly of the nation-state cannot be held accountable.

In the meantime, sunny publicists for the new order, managerial 6
boosters who prate about the glories of contingency like post-moderns gone daft, unabashedly describe their view of the future as one in which the *entire* work force is replaceable, effaceable, utterly "contingent." These hawkers of new economic realities celebrate doing "more with less," and the "less" are those human beings destined for the vocational scrapheap. Most starkly, Sennett is finding that self-worth founded "on the conviction that one's experience is more than a series of random events" either cannot emerge in the new economic order or comes under terrific pressure to succumb.

7   The implications for civic life are dire. The qualities of mind and habits of the heart that democracy relies on—loyalty, reciprocity, trust, self-discipline—dry up under the harsh lights of shapeless, evanescent, half or part-time or multiflex-time work.

8   Of course, there are those who thrive under the new regime—namely the emergent technocratic elite. But increasingly low-tech work is being "out-sourced" and high-tech work is being automated. What's left? Partial, service sector, temp-work. Man Power, Inc., a temp-agency, is now the largest single private employer in the United States; temp-work; dispensable self. We haven't begun to plumb the depths of these changes and their long-term implications for Americans as citizens, parents and workers. But a story stripped of long-term reference points, including the dignity and recognition conferred by work, is ripe for other sorts of stories, and they may not be democratic ones.

9   As Thomas Hobbes, among others, taught us: fear, should it become the overriding passion, breeds authoritarian solutions. Hobbes, of course, believed that, human passions being what they were, a Leviathan would be needed to forestall descent into the war of all against all. Hobbes overdramatized, surely. But if you try to peer through the dislocating and far-reaching changes of the present, if you shut out the beckoning siren calls of the new elite and their various mouthpieces, it may well be the mordant voice of Hobbes rather than the buoyant tones of democratic thinkers that you recognize blaring at the far end of the line. As economic disparity grows, lines of connection between classes attenuate. An expanding middle class no longer serves as an intermediary between the elites and those left out, the permanent losers. This development could easily fuel antidemocratic movements—nativist populism, brittle nationalism, an expanding security state. Does this seem apocalyptic? Perhaps. But it is better than syrupy evasion, the pre-packaged Pablum of the techno-managerial boosters.

★ Meaning and Understanding

1. What, according to Jean Bethke Elshtain, is the relation between work and American identity? What expectations did people like her grandparents have when they came to the country?

2. How, according to the writer, has the "brave new world" of global economies changed the possibilities for modern American workers? The words in quotation marks come from Shakespeare's The Tempest. Find out the context for the statement in the play. Why has the writer used the quote here?

3. Why is the shrinking of the middle class worrisome? How do part-time workers contribute to the problems the writer sees?

4. In paragraph 6, Elshtain refers to the "sunny publicists for the new order." What does the writer mean by the "new order"? Who are the "sunny publicists"? Who is the "technocratic elite"?

5. Who was Thomas Hobbes? Why does the writer cite him?

6. What does the writer see as fueling antidemocratic movements?

★ *Techniques and Strategies*

1. What is the point of the joke with which the essay begins? How does it establish the groundwork for what follows?

2. Who is the intended audience for this essay? What is the tone? How do you know?

3. What is the thesis of the essay? State it in your own words. How has the writer maintained unity throughout the essay?

4. In addition to Hobbes, the writer cites other external sources. How do they contribute to the essay?

5. Look at the concluding sentence of the essay. Why do you think the writer has chosen the alliterative sequence of p sounds?

6. How does the subtitle, "Lost City," contribute to your understanding of Elshtain's point?

★ *Speaking of Values*

1. The joke at the essay's beginning, of course, belies a profound truth about people's economic needs today, when more than one job per person is often the rule, not the exception. What are the problems you see in multiple jobs for Americans? What advantages, if any, do you see?

2. Elshtain speaks about the shrinking middle class. How would you define the middle class? Does the middle class have social values and beliefs different from other classes? Should our society protect the middle class from shrinking? Why or why not?

3. The writer says that the qualities democracy depends on are "loyalty, reciprocity, trust, self-discipline." Why might you agree or disagree? Why does she believe that these qualities are "drying up"? What is your view on the presence or absence of these qualities in today's America?

4. In the final paragraph Elshtain asserts that "as economic disparity grows, lines of connection between classes attenuate." What do you

understand this statement to mean? Do you agree with it? Is it important that the different economic classes stay "connected"? Why or why not?

5. Do you agree with Richard Sennett (paragraph 4) that "without work as a stable frame of reference...men and women come to see themselves as *dispensable*"? How do part-time jobs contribute to the problem? Why has American industry turned to part- or half-time workers?

★ *Values Conversation*

Elshtain asserts that the present American economy is generating only low-paying service sector jobs. Form groups and see if you can identify the kinds of jobs that she is referring to. Then discuss among yourselves the kinds of jobs that you or people you know may now have and whether or not they fall into this category.

★ *Writing about Values*

1. Write an essay in which you argue for the importance of full-time jobs for American workers. Or, take the opposite point: argue for the importance of part-time jobs.

2. Write an essay to define the middle class. Explain why you think it should (or should not) be preserved.

3. Read Alan Ehrenhalt's *The Lost City* (1995) and write an essay about it.

Frank McCourt

When Dad Gets a Job

Born in 1930, Frank McCourt is a former schoolteacher turned writer after retiring from the classroom. The selection that follows is from his memoir *Angela's Ashes* (1996), McCourt's first published book and winner of the Pulitzer Prize in 1997. McCourt here confronts the effects of work and poverty on a family's life.

——— ★ ———

When Dad gets a job Mam is cheerful and she sings,   1

> Anyone can see why I wanted your kiss,
> It had to be and the reason is this
> Could it be true, someone like you
> Could love me, love me?

When Dad brings home the first week's wages Mam is delighted   2
she can pay the lovely Italian man in the grocery shop and she can hold
her head up again because there's nothing worse in the world than to
owe and be beholden to anyone. She cleans the kitchen, washes the
mugs and plates, brushes crumbs and bits of food from the table, cleans
out the icebox and orders a fresh block of ice from another Italian. She
buys toilet paper that we can take down the hall to the lavatory and
that, she says, is better than having the headlines from the *Daily News*
blackening your arse. She boils water on the stove and spends a day at
a great tin tub washing our shirts and socks, diapers for the twins, our
two sheets, our three towels. She hangs everything out on the clothes-
lines behind the apartment house and we can watch the clothes dance
in wind and sun. She says you wouldn't want the neighbors to know
what you have in the way of a wash but there's nothing like the sweetness of clothes dried by the sun.

When Dad brings home the first week's wages on Friday night we   3
know the weekend will be wonderful. On Saturday night Mam will
boil water on the stove and wash us in the great tin tub and Dad will
dry us. Malachy will turn around and show his behind. Dad will pretend to be shocked and we'll all laugh. Mam will make hot cocoa and
we'll be able to stay up while Dad tells us a story out of his head. All we
have to do is say a name, Mr. MacAdorey or Mr. Leibowitz down the
hall, and Dad will have the two of them rowing up a river in Brazil
chased by Indians with green noses and puce shoulders. On nights like

that we can drift off to sleep knowing there will be a breakfast of eggs, fried tomatoes and fried bread, tea with lashings of sugar and milk and, later in the day, a big dinner of mashed potatoes, peas and ham, and a trifle Mam makes, layers of fruit and warm delicious custard on a cake soaked in sherry.

4   When Dad brings home the first week's wages and the weather is fine Mam takes us to the playground. She sits on a bench and talks to Minnie MacAdorey. She tells Minnie stories about characters in Limerick and Minnie tells her about characters in Belfast and they laugh because there are funny people in Ireland, North and South. Then they teach each other sad songs and Malachy and I leave the swings and see-saws to sit with them on the bench and sing,

> A group of young soldiers one night in a camp
> Were talking of sweethearts they had.
> All seemed so merry except one young lad,
> And he was downhearted and sad.
> Come and join us, said one of the boys,
> Surely there's someone for you.
> But Ned shook his head and proudly he said
> I am in love with two, Each like a mother to me,
> From neither of them shall I part.
> For one is my mother, God bless her and love her,
> The other is my sweetheart.

5   Malachy and I sing that song and Mam and Minnie laugh till they cry at the way Malachy takes a deep bow and holds his arms out to Mam at the end. Dan MacAdorey comes along on his way home from work and says Rudy Vallee better start worrying about the competition.

6   When we go home Mam makes tea and bread and jam or mashed potatoes with butter and salt. Dad drinks the tea and eats nothing. Mam says, God above, How can you work all day and not eat? He says, The tea is enough. She says, You'll ruin your health, and he tells her again that food is a shock to the system. He drinks his tea and tells us stories and shows us letters and words in the *Daily News* or he smokes a cigarette, stares at the wall, runs his tongue over his lips.

7   When Dad's job goes into the third week he does not bring home the wages. On Friday night we wait for him and Mam gives us bread and tea. The darkness comes down and the lights come on along Classon Avenue. Other men with jobs are home already and having eggs for dinner because you can't have meat on a Friday. You can hear the families talking upstairs and downstairs and down the hall and Bing Crosby singing on the radio, Brother, can you spare a dime?

8   Malachy and I play with the twins. We know Mam won't sing Anyone can see why I wanted your kiss. She sits at the kitchen table talking

to herself, What am I going to do? till it's late and Dad rolls up the stairs singing Roddy McCorley. He pushes in the door and calls for us, Where are my troops? Where are my four warriors?

Mam says, Leave those boys alone. They're gone to bed half hun- 9
gry because you have to fill your belly with whiskey.

He come to the bedroom door. Up, boys, up. A nickel for everyone 10
who promises to die for Ireland.

> Deep in Canadian woods we met
> From one bright island flown.
> Great is the land we tread, but yet
> Our hearts are with our own.

Up, boys, up. Francis, Malachy, Oliver, Eugene. The Red Branch 11
Knights, the Fenian Men, the IRA. Up, up.

Mam is at the kitchen table, shaking, her hair hanging damp, her 12
face wet. Can't you leave them alone? she says. Jesus, Mary and Joseph, isn't it enough that you come home without a penny in your pocket without making fools of the children on top of it?

She comes to us. Go back to bed, she says. 13

I want them up, he says. I want them ready for the day Ireland will 14
be free from the center to the sea.

Don't cross me, she says, for if you do it'll be a sorry day in your 15
mother's house.

He pulls his cap down over his face and cries, My poor mother. 16
Poor Ireland. Och, what are we going to do?

Mam says, You're pure stone mad, and she tells us again to go to 17
bed.

On the morning of the fourth Friday of Dad's job Mam asks him if 18
he'll be home tonight with his wages or will he drink everything again? He looks at us and shakes his head at Mam as if to say, Och, you shouldn't talk like that in front of the children.

Mam keeps at him. I'm asking you, Are you coming home so that 19
we can have a bit of supper or will it be midnight with no money in your pocket and you singing Kevin Barry and the rest of the sad songs?

He puts on his cap, shoves his hands into his trouser pockets, sighs 20
and looks up at the ceiling. I told you before I'll be home, he says.

Later in the day Mam dresses us. She puts the twins into the pram 21
and off we go through the long streets of Brooklyn. Sometimes she lets Malachy sit in the pram when he's tired of trotting along beside her. She tells me I'm too big for the pram. I could tell her I have pains in my legs from trying to keep up with her but she's not singing and I know this is not the day to be talking about my pains.

We come to a big gate where there's a man standing in a box with 22
windows all around. Mam talks to the man. She wants to know if she

can go inside to where the men are paid and maybe they'd give her some of Dad's wages so he wouldn't spend it in the bars. The man shakes his head. I'm sorry, lady, but if we did that we'd have half the wives in Brooklyn storming the place. Lotta men have the drinking problem but there's nothing we can do long as they show up sober and do their work.

23   We wait across the street. Mam lets me sit on the sidewalk with my back against the wall. She gives the twins their bottles of water and sugar but Malachy and I have to wait till she gets money from Dad and we can go to the Italian for tea and bread and eggs.

24   When the whistle blows at half five men in caps and overalls swarm through the gate, their faces and hands black from the work. Mam tells us watch carefully for Dad because she can hardly see across the street herself, her eyes are that bad. There are dozens of men, then a few, then none. Mam is crying, Why couldn't ye see him? Are ye blind or what?

25   She goes back to the man in the box. Are you sure there wouldn't be one man left inside?

26   No, lady, he says. They're out. I don't know how he got past you.

27   We go back through the long streets of Brooklyn. The twins hold up their bottles and cry for more water and sugar. Malachy says he's hungry and Mam tells him wait a little, we'll get money from Dad and we'll all have a nice supper. We'll go to the Italian and get eggs and make toast with the flames on the stove and we'll have jam on it. Oh, we will, and we'll all be nice and warm.

28   It's dark on Atlantic Avenue and all the bars around the Long Island Railroad Station are bright and noisy. We go from bar to bar looking for Dad. Mam leaves us outside with the pram while she goes in or she sends me. There are crowds of noisy men and stale smells that remind me of Dad when comes home with the smell of the whiskey on him.

29   The man behind the bar says, Yeah, sonny, whaddya want? You're not supposeta be in here, y'know.

30   I'm looking for my father. Is my father here?

31   Naw, sonny, how'd I know dat? Who's your fawdah?

32   His name is Malachy and he sings Kevin Barry.

33   Malarkey?

34   No, Malachy.

35   Malachy? And he sings Kevin Barry?

36   He calls out to the men in the bar, Youse guys, youse know guy Malachy what sings Kevin Barry?

37   Men shake their heads. One says he knew a guy Michael sang Kevin Barry but he died of the drink which he had because of his war wounds.

38   The barman says, Jeez, Pete, I didn't ax ya to tell me history o' da woild, did I? Naw, kid. We don't let people sing in here. Causes trouble.

Specially the Irish. Let 'em sing, next the fists are flying. Besides, I never hoid a name like dat Malachy. Naw, kid, no Malachy here.

The man called Pete holds his glass toward me. Here, kid, have a   39
sip, but the barman says, Whaddya doin', Pete? Tryina get the kid drunk? Do that again, Pete, an' I'll come out an' break y'ass.

Mam tries all the bars around the station before she gives up. She   40
leans against a wall and cries. Jesus, we still have to walk all the way to Classon Avenue and I have four starving children. She sends me back into the bar where Pete offered me the sip to see if the barman would fill the twins' bottles with water and maybe a little sugar in each. The men in the bar think it's very funny that the barman should be filling baby bottles but he's big and he tells them shut their lip. He tells me babies should be drinking milk not water and when I tell him Mam doesn't have the money he empties the baby bottles and fills them with milk. He says, Tell ya mom they need that for the teeth an' bones. Ya drink water an' sugar an' all ya get is rickets. Tell ya Mom.

Mam is happy with the milk. She says she knows all about teeth   41
and bones and rickets but beggars can't be choosers.

When we reach Classon Avenue she goes straight to the Italian gro-   42
cery shop. She tells the man her husband is late tonight, that he's prob-ably working overtime, and would it be at all possible to get a few things and she'll be sure to see him tomorrow?

The Italian says, Missus, you always pay your bill sooner or later   43
and you can have anything you like in this store.

Oh, she says, I don't want much.   44

Anything you like, missus, because I know you're an honest   45
woman and you got a bunch o' nice kids there.

We have eggs and toast and jam though we're so weary walking   46
the long streets of Brooklyn we can barely move our jaws to chew. The twins fall asleep after eating and Mam lays them on the bed to change their diapers. She sends me down the hall to rinse the dirty diapers in the lavatory so that they can be hung up to dry and used the next day. Malachy helps her wash the twins' bottoms though he's ready to fall asleep himself.

I crawl into bed with Malachy and the twins. I look out at Mam at   47
the kitchen table, smoking a cigarette, drinking tea, and crying. I want to get up and tell her I'll be a man soon and I'll get a job in the place with the big gate and I'll come home every Friday night with money for eggs and toast and jam and she can sing again Anyone can see why I wanted your kiss.

The next week Dad loses the job. He comes home that Friday night,   48
throws his wages on the table and says to Mam, Are you happy now? You hang around the gate complaining and accusing and they sack me. They were looking for an excuse and you gave it to them.

49   He takes a few dollars from his wages and goes out. He comes home late roaring and singing. The twins cry and Mam shushes them and cries a long time herself.

★ *Meaning and Understanding*

1. Why is Mam cheerful when Dad gets a job?

2. How will the weekend be wonderful when Dad brings home the first week's wages (paragraph 2)?

3. Why does Mam sit at the kitchen table talking to herself?

4. What has Dad done with his wages in the third week?

5. What does Dad do for a living?

6. Where does Mam take her family on the fourth Friday? Why does she take them there?

7. How does the bartender react to Francis's request for water and sugar to fill the baby bottles?

★ *Techniques and Strategies*

1. Why does McCourt intersperse song lyrics with the details of this selection?

2. What is the organizational pattern of the piece? Is it effective? Why or why not?

3. What imagery do you find particularly effective?

4. The narrator here is clearly a child. What effect does that narrative voice have on your reaction to the story McCourt tells?

5. Comment on the use of dialogue here. How effective is it? Why does McCourt rely so heavily on dialogue?

6. The piece begins with Mam's singing and concludes with her crying. How do these two events frame the action of the story?

★ *Speaking of Values*

1. What does McCourt suggest about the relation between work and family harmony? Do you accept his viewpoint? Why or why not?

2. McCourt says that "there's nothing worse in the world than to owe and be beholden to anyone." Do you agree with this sentiment? Why or why not? Would most of the people you know agree? Why or why not?

3. What does the selection tell you about the relations between husbands and wives in the period about which McCourt writes? How have relations changed between spouses during our age? How have they remained the same?

4. Children are often the innocent victims of familial problems and tensions. In what ways are the children affected by Dad's behavior? Mam's?

5. What does the reaction of the grocer to Mam's request tell you about Mam's life? What does his reaction and that of the bartender tell you of the community in which the McCourts lived?

6. Dad blames Mam for his losing his job. Do you agree with him? Why or why not?

★ *Values Conversation*

The role of work in a person's life transcends the simple (though important) economic dimension and enters into other major areas of human existence. Form groups and discuss the role of work in the lives of Americans today. Relate your discussion ultimately to the McCourt family and their travails.

★ *Writing about Values*

1. Write a paper about a job that you or someone you know (a family member, perhaps) lost for some reason. Be sure to explain what the job was like, why it was lost, and the effect that it had on the person who was fired.

2. In this piece we learn almost nothing about Dad at work. Write a story about Dad on the job. What is he like? What are his co-workers like? His boss? What are his duties?

3. Alcoholism is a grave problem in our society. Do some library research about alcoholism on the job and then write a paper that analyzes the consequences of alcoholism at the workplace.

Don J. Snyder

Sorry, the Professional Class Is Full

Don J. Snyder, born in 1950 in Lansdale, Pennsylvania, is a former college professor. He now works as a carpenter, house painter, and part-time teacher and is the author of two novels. This essay comes from *The Cliff Walk: A Memoir of a Job Lost and a Life Found* (1997). Snyder exposes in very personal terms the effects of losing a job on the lives of a middle-class family.

———— ★ ————

1   In the spring of 1991, professors were being laid off across the country alongside plumbers, managers and bank tellers, but I was on the inside—in one of those comfortable college teaching jobs where bad news isn't about you. Then word started getting around Colgate University that I had been fired. A student came up to me after class one morning and gave me the lay of the land. "Man, not another baby boomer out of work," he said, shaking his head. "Every time one of you guys loses his real job, you take the jobs at Blockbuster and the mall so I can't even pick up summer work."

2   I was a college professor so far removed from the real world that I just smiled and started back to my office. I was 41, married, with three children under 7 years old and a fourth due in a few months. We were living an unhurried life in upstate New York, in a small town in a big house, where we paid our way each month without much sweat. There was a generous package of benefits that included 5 weeks off at Christmas, 10 days off during spring break and 3 months in the summer. This amounted to roughly 18 weeks of paid vacation per year.

3   It was a dream. There had never been a violent crime in town. We bought a six-bedroom house on a peaceful tree-lined street, an easy walk to the campus ski slope and golf course. Because most of the non-university residents in town earned little more than the minimum wage, my faculty salary enabled us to live like royalty, and Colleen, my wife, was able to fulfill her longstanding desire to stay at home with our children.

4   The best part about the job by far was my students. They were so pleasant and eager to please that I went the extra mile, inviting them to our house for dinner and movies and teaching literature with a no-holds-barred passion that made my classes some of the most popular on campus. I was well paid for my efforts and nominated every spring for "Pro-

fessor of the Year" by the Student Honor Society, which sent me beautiful letters extolling my devotion to bringing literature to life for students.

I received another one of those letters in March 1991, my third year, the same day the dean of faculty wrote to inform me that I was being fired. The terms of my dismissal were as fair as anyone could ask for: I would be allowed to finish the rest of my third year and to return for a fourth with a pay raise and full benefits, and an additional stipend of $3,000 if I wished to serve as adviser to the debate club. Meanwhile, the dean would recommend me highly to other universities with an official letter that said I was being dismissed simply because the English department was already top-heavy with tenured professors.

My first reaction on reading the letter was that some mistake had been made. *They got the wrong guy.* In all the jobs I had held across the years, from the first one picking vegetables when I was 13, I had never been fired. I sat on our back porch and read the letter several times before I walked to campus, climbed the hill to the dean of faculty's office and waited there until he could see me.

I had enough self-confidence then, or maybe it was arrogance or just a long history of successes, to think that I would be able to fix things. I would say the perfect words, would tell him about all my achievements, I would make the right impression and the decision would be recanted.

The dean was gracious and in a hurry. While he was promising that he would write me glorious letters saying how I was loved by my students and respected by my colleagues, I was watching him glance at the big clock on the wall and I was thinking: Wait a second, pal, you're not going to give me the bum's rush here. We're going to take a long time, maybe the rest of the afternoon, because I've got a lot of wonderful things to tell you about myself and about the work I've done here.

I laid it out for him, but I could tell by the way his smile never changed that I was already floating off his screen. I heard my voice climbing a little too high as I explained to him that my father was ill and that we had a new baby coming. When at last he put his hand out for me to shake, I was short of breath. "I'm sorry," he said, showing me to the door.

That night I read "The Littlest Angel" to Nell and Erin at bedtime. When they conked out, I sat down on the floor by their night light and wrote out my first budget on the inside cover of the book. It didn't look bad at all. We had just drained our savings in order to replace the old plumbing in our house, but with 17 more months on the payroll, plus my pension plan that I could convert to cash, we would have more than $15,000 before I would be cut off on Aug. 1, 1992. Then I would begin a new job with a new monthly income kicking in. So as long as we could sell our house for as much as we had paid for it, there was really nothing to worry about.

11   But when it came to telling Colleen that I had been fired, I never could seem to find the right time, or the right room in our house. There was always her with her lovely pregnant belly and her faith in me, and then there was me with my pink slip.

12   Cara was born in June. She was a real beauty, and nothing else mattered for a while as we were all cast into the blissful trance that a newborn baby bestows upon a family. She gazed at us with clear, knowing eyes, and I, like some napping Navy commander who thinks the torpedo that just ripped off the bow of his ship was only a passing school of tuna, told myself that being one of the millions of Americans who had been laid off, passed over, downsized or just plain cheated out of a job was only a temporary setback. "Wow, four kids under 7," one of my more-practical colleagues said to me. To which I gave my stock response, "We're still hoping for a set of twins."

13   The only problem was this: That spring, 14 of the 23 colleges where I had applied rejected me. I had filled myself so full of hot air that I didn't see what this meant. Or maybe I did see, because each time a rejection letter arrived in the mail I was obsessed with getting rid of it. I would read the letter once, bury it at the bottom of the kitchen trash and then take the trash bag with me and drop it in the dumpster behind the Creative Arts House on campus, where I was holding classes that semester.

14   One morning, a few days before graduation, I saw a guy in a white shirt and tie sitting in an unmarked car parked next to the dumpster. I waved to him as I dropped my trash bag in. An hour later came a visit from the head of security. "We've been trying to catch the person all semester," he said. "It was the diapers that made us sure it wasn't student trash."

15   I apologized and told him I would pay whatever fine was required. "I've been fired," I told him. "I'm only here for three more days, and I'm just trying to get out of town without punching anybody."

16   I was as surprised to say such a thing as he was to hear it said by a professor. He stepped away from me. "No, no," I told him. "I'm only kidding." But I don't think I was. For the first time, I acknowledged to myself that I was behaving badly. The part of me that had always longed to be on the inside of the good life and willing to make any concession to get there recognized that my future as an *employed* college professor depended in part upon the impression I left at Colgate. I knew that I should leave gracefully, shaking hands and giving best wishes to the people who had fired me.

17   But the newer part of me—the angry outsider who was just discovering the heady joy of defying authority—was rehearsing my new role in earnest. One night when a few students dropped by the house to say goodbye, I told them about the dumpster incident. It was pretty late and we were standing out on the deck, where we could hear the distant

roar of frat parties. I was holding center stage, telling my little story and hamming it up for the students when the lie just came on suddenly. "Yeah," I said, "you know what Hawthorne said about being an outsider." I made it up on the spot: "Hawthorne said when you're an outsider, every hour you spend trying to get inside is an hour you should have spent learning to survive on the outside."

I began the morning of graduation day by locking myself in the   18
sanctuary of the downstairs bathroom and reading the help-wanted section in The New York Times for the first time in 10 or 12 years. I discovered that while I had been away in the ivory tower, the working world had been divided neatly—computer wizards on one end; nurses, sales clerks and prison guards on the other. "Malls, prisons or hospitals," I muttered. I didn't need the lousy help-wanted page anyway. I would get my next great job from the professional journals. I crushed the pages into basketballs and fired bank shots off the shower stall into the wicker wastebasket. "What is a *systems analyst* anyway?"

"What did you say, Daddy?" came a daughter's voice from another   19
world.

I got down on my hands and knees, crawled quietly to the door   20
and yanked it open. "BOO!"

"Daddy!" Nell cried.   21

I kissed her and said: "Daddy's going to become a systems analyst,   22
sweetheart. He's going to make a lot of money and everyone's going to be happy, happy, happy."

"Do we still have to move?" she asked.   23

I put our house up for sale as casually as if it were a motel we had   24
been staying in. When I was rejected for 30 more teaching jobs over the next year, I moved us back to Maine, where my wife and I are from, fully believing that the telephone would ring at any moment and it would be somebody eager to offer me something.

About the only acknowledgement I made to reality was that the job   25
market might have got a little tougher since I last put my hat in the ring; I knew perfectly well that white male professors in English departments were as plentiful as shopping-mall Santa Clauses and that their security was threatened anew each time a new white male was issued a red suit. But I didn't want to step forward and join the ranks of those pathetic men who hit a middle-age roadblock and immediately start looking around for somebody to blame. All I wanted to do was dump our stuff in a rented house, shake the dust off my shoes, find a way back to the passing lane and floor the accelerator.

I remember the angry days best. In one morning's mail there was a   26
form letter from another college telling me how much they had enjoyed reading my application materials but that they had selected another candidate. What made this rejection different from the others was that it was from a small college marooned on an outpost of northern Michi-

gan. I thought I would get the job hands down and secretly I had been carrying it in my head as the job offer I would happily turn down in favor of something much better.

27   Finally I decided to call and ask why I had not been granted an interview. I got a tape telling me to call back after 8 A.M. I tried a second time and got the same tape. "It's 9:30, you jerk," I said to the recorded voice.

28   I had forgotten that it was Sunday.

29   I was breathing in quick shallow gasps when I finally reached the college the next morning and was passed along to the chairman of the English department. He recognized my name and listened patiently while I went over my seven years of college teaching at two of the finest private universities in the nation and my three published books and prestigious foundation grants. What I expected him to say was that I was overqualified for the job. Then he explained the situation: "When we put this advertisement in the newspapers and journals we never expected to attract anyone with your qualifications. But the truth is, we got over 300 applications and there were nine candidates whose experience exceeded yours. One had been nominated for a Pulitzer Prize. Three were former department heads. It's just so tough. I'm terribly sorry."

30   I was waiting in line at the pharmacy one day when a short, pale-faced man in army fatigues standing next to me told me that his kids all had the chicken pox and he wished he could be at home helping his wife take care of them but he had too much work to do.

31   "What kind of work?" I asked him.

32   "I've got my own company," he said.

33   I was thinking in slightly grander terms than the Jiffy Clean company that was advertised in big blue letters emblazoned across both sides of his van. He had parked right beside me, and before we drove off he told me that he had been in business three years. "The only bad part is the hours," he explained. "I usually go 10 hours every day, then go home, eat supper and sleep for 5 hours, then work all night on the office buildings. What about you?"

34   "Well," I said, "I'm out of work right now." Before I could dazzle him with my employment history, he handed me a business card.

35   "I've got a bid in for a big law firm," he said merrily. "If I get it, I could use you. We don't do windows, but like I said, the hours are long."

36   I took his card, thanked him and stood there in silence for a few seconds before the anger kicked in and I began saying under my breath: *Do I look like a janitor to you, pal? No offense, but I don't think the Jiffy Clean company is in my destiny, I'm a college professor. Can't you tell by looking at me?*

37   In those days, I looked forward to dark when I could put my 3-year-old son to bed and read to him until he fell asleep. Then I would

stay in his room writing out my budget in his copy of "Curious George." It wasn't that I believed these budgets were suddenly going to reveal some truth about how we could salvage our future, but there was a marvelous spiritual high that would come as I divided the final figure by what I estimated it cost us to live each month. There, before my eyes, the dollars would turn into time. How much time we had left to live on the money we had. How much time before Colleen stopped me in the hallway after all the children were asleep and asked me point blank if I was or was not going to continue to support her.

I know that it takes a very weak man to lose his way when he has a   38
beautiful wife and four healthy children living under his roof, with no debt and over $6,000 left in the bank, when he's not in a war or facing anything even close to real peril. But I was so lost over the next year of my life that I could never look at Colleen without setting off an amazing image in my head that had her living with another man and working at the drive-through window of a bank in town. In the fantasy, I would be the first customer every weekday morning, waiting there, just staring at the glass when she raised the curtain to open for business.

One day Colleen came home and told me that she had met the wife   39
of a local contractor who was looking to hire someone through the winter. I walked out of the room. I heard her calling sweetly to me, but I kept on going.

I put on my coat and stood on the back porch smoking a cigarette.   40
I started thinking that maybe I would return to the employment office in the morning, and then I remembered something that had happened there: I had left the line one day to use the men's room. When I opened the door, there was a tiny Vietnamese man standing by the sink. He was running hot water over a Tupperware container that was filled with horrible-looking congealed gravy with chunks of meat sticking in it. It nauseated me. But the little man turned and smiled at me, and gave me a little bow, and said: "Better hot. Very good hot."

It was at that point that I decided to go to the construction site in   41
the morning to see about the job.

The contractor, Larry Wagner, was 10 years younger than I, a rugged,   42
friendly fellow who, with his partner, Billy LeBlond, and a crew of three carpenters, was building a frame of a house that was as big as a hotel. "We'll work all winter," Larry said. "By spring, it'll be finished." When he offered to pay me $15 an hour, I told him I would start the next day.

It was three times as much money as I was worth to him, but Larry   43
held the simple belief that if a person worked hard, he should be paid enough to keep from falling behind in his bills.

We worked 10-hour days together outside. Some mornings it was   44
25 below and the ocean was buried under sea smoke when I walked to work at sunrise. A half-hour into the job, I would start hoping for the day to end. But after a month I began to feel myself gaining strength in

my legs and shoulders. It was a feeling I had not had in the 20 years I had been working in offices. I was always tired; I would fall asleep in whatever chair I sat down in 10 minutes after dinner. But I began getting up two hours earlier in the morning, writing in the journals Colleen and I kept for the children, eager for the sky to lighten so I could go to work.

45   I stayed on the construction job until it was finished. I was out of work only a few days when Colleen met someone who needed his house painted. I found the work restful; there was a steady cadence to it that seemed blessedly to carry over to the rest of my life. I was able to hold my kids again without feeling that I had cast them into darkness, and I could look at my wife without feeling that she would be better off with another man. Over the summer I painted two more houses, charging $15 an hour, not enough to afford health insurance but enough to pay our bills. I patched together a working life the way so many people in America were learning to do: I was hired as a caretaker of a summer mansion, I found rough-carpentry jobs replacing rotten sills and repairing leaking roofs and I landed a temporary teaching job three days a week a hundred miles away.

46   One Saturday morning, I ran into a toy store on the way home from work wearing my paint-spattered clothes. The salesclerk looked at me when I handed him a check and said, "You must be a painter." I guess because they were words I never expected anyone to say to me, I thought they were meant for someone else. Then I looked down at the paint on my hands an said with great satisfaction, "Yeah, I am." I felt something draining out of me then, the velocity of an old life perhaps.

★ Meaning and Understanding

1. Why does Snyder call his job and life a "dream" and say that he was "far removed from the real world"?

2. What happens to Snyder's college position? When he receives a letter from the dean of faculty, why does he initially think *"they got the wrong guy"*?

3. What is a baby boomer? How does the student's comment in paragraph 1 about baby boomers help you understand the point of the essay?

4. How does the birth of a new daughter affect Snyder's view of his situation?

5. Why does he say that he had filled himself "so full of hot air"? How does the quote from Hawthorne affect Snyder after he utters it?

6. What does the chair of the English Department at the college in northern Michigan tell Snyder?

7. What kinds of jobs does Snyder ultimately take? Why does he take them?

★ Techniques and Understanding

1. What is the thesis of this essay?

2. Examine and identify the extended metaphor in paragraph 24. How does it help you understand the point of the essay? How does it relate to the metaphor in the last sentence of the essay?

3. Who is the intended audience for this piece? How do you know?

4. Where does Snyder use transitions to move the narrative along smoothly?

5. Why does the writer italicize the sentences at the end of paragraph 35?

6. Look again at the title of this essay. How effective is it in capturing the main idea of the piece?

★ Speaking of Values

1. Snyder expresses shock when he is fired because he believes that he had done a superior job. What does his situation suggest to you about the relation between job security and doing "a good job"? What factors other than job performance may cause someone to lose a job?

2. Snyder seems to imply that there are different rules for the "professional class." What is the "professional class" and what are these rules? Do you agree with his point? Why or why not?

3. People sometimes closely tie their identities to what they do to earn a living. Clearly, Snyder does the same thing—or at least he did at first. Discuss the consequences of identifying yourself closely with your job. How is work related to our self-image? to our sense of well being?

4. Snyder remarks to his daughter that he is "going to make a lot of money and everyone's going to be happy, happy, happy." He expresses here a familiar American value. Of course money is essential to our material survival. But is money *essential* to happiness? Can people be happy without lots of money? Defend your position.

★ Values Conversation

Cutbacks and downsizing in businesses, government, and universities have become routine. Form groups to discuss these issues. How strongly should "bottom line" management control workers' lives? Do businesses have any obligations to their workers' job stability? Or are shareholders and consumers the only true concern of business?

★ *Writing about Values*

1. Write an essay to give advice to people who lose their job. What specific recommendations can you make? What in Snyder's experience can you generalize to others?

2. Changing careers, as Snyder has, can be both wrenching and rewarding. Write an essay about someone you know who has changed careers. How has the person adjusted? Why did the person change jobs?

3. Interview someone who is a member of the professional class. Question this person about the relation between professional identity and personal identity, job security, and any other issue that you think of based on your reading of this selection. Then do the same thing with someone who is a blue-collar worker. Write a paper presenting your findings.

Stephanie Coontz

A Nation of Welfare Families

Born in Seattle, Washington in 1944, Coontz is a college professor and writer who studies the changing American family. Her works include *The Social Origins of Private Life: A History of American Families* (1988), *The Way We Never Were: American Families and the Nostalgia Trap* (1992) , and *The Way We Really Are: Ending the War over America's Changing Families* (1997). In this 1992 essay for *Harper's,* she explores the historical role of the U.S. government in providing welfare for its citizens.

———— ★ ————

The current political debate over family values, personal responsibility, and welfare takes for granted the entrenched American belief that dependence on government assistance is a recent and destructive phenomenon. Conservatives tend to blame this dependence on personal irresponsibility aggravated by a swollen welfare apparatus that saps individual initiative. Liberals are more likely to blame it on personal misfortune magnified by the harsh lot that falls to losers in our competitive market economy. But both sides believe that "winners" in America make it on their own, that dependence reflects some kind of individual or family failure, and that the ideal family is the self-reliant unit of traditional lore—a family that takes care of its own, carves out a future for its children, and never asks for handouts. Politicians at both ends of the ideological spectrum have wrapped themselves in the mantle of these "family values," arguing over *why* the poor have not been able to make do without assistance, or whether aid has exacerbated their situation, but never questioning the assumption that American families traditionally achieve success by establishing their independence from the government.

The myth of family self-reliance is so compelling that our actual national and personal histories often buckle under its emotional weight. "We always stood on our own two feet," my grandfather used to say about his pioneer heritage, whenever he walked me to the top of the hill to survey the property in Washington State that his family had bought for next to nothing after it had been logged off in the early 1900s. Perhaps he didn't know that the land came so cheap because much of it was part of a federal subsidy originally allotted to the railroad companies, which had received 183 million acres of the public domain in the nineteenth century. These federal giveaways were the

1

2

233

original source of most major Western logging companies' land, and when some of these logging companies moved on to virgin stands of timber, federal lands trickled down to a few early settlers who were able to purchase them inexpensively.

3   Like my grandparents, few families in American history—whatever their "values"—have been able to rely solely on their own resources. Instead, they have depended on the legislative, judicial, and social-support structures set up by governing authorities, whether those authorities were the clan elders of Native American societies, the church courts and city officials of colonial America, or the judicial and legislative bodies established by the Constitution.

4   At America's inception, this was considered not a dirty little secret but the norm, one that confirmed our social and personal interdependence. The idea that the family should have the sole or even primary responsibility for educating and socializing its members, finding them suitable work, or keeping them from poverty and crime was not only ludicrous to colonial and revolutionary thinkers but dangerously parochial.

5   Historically, one way that government has played a role in the well-being of its citizens is by regulating the way that employers and civic bodies interact with families. In the early twentieth century, for example, as a response to rapid changes ushered in by a mass-production economy, the government promoted a "family wage system." This system was designed to strengthen the ability of the male breadwinner to support a family without having his wife or children work. This family wage system was not a natural outgrowth of the market. It was a *political* response to conditions that the market had produced: child labor, rampant employment insecurity, recurring economic downturns, an earnings structure in which 45 percent of industrial workers fell below the poverty level and another 40 percent hovered barely above it, and a system in which thousands of children had been placed in orphanages or other institutions simply because their parents could not afford their keep. The state policies involved in the establishment of the family wage system included abolition of child labor, government pressure on industrialists to negotiate with unions, federal arbitration, expansion of compulsory schooling—and legislation discriminating against women workers.

6   But even such extensive regulation of economic and social institutions has never been enough: government has always supported families with direct material aid as well. The two best examples of the government's history of material aid can be found in what many people consider the ideal models of self-reliant families: the Western pioneer family and the 1950s suburban family. In both cases, the ability of these families to establish and sustain themselves required massive underwriting by the government.

Pioneer families, such as my grandparents, could never have moved   7
west without government-funded military mobilizations against the
original Indian and Mexican inhabitants or state-sponsored economic investment in transportation systems. In addition, the Homestead Act of
1862 allowed settlers to buy 160 acres for $10—far below the govern-
ment's cost of acquiring the land—if the homesteader lived on and improved the land for five years. In the twentieth century, a new form of
public assistance became crucial to Western families: construction of
dams and other federally subsidized irrigation projects. During the
1930s, for example, government electrification projects brought pumps,
refrigeration, and household technology to millions of families.

The suburban family of the 1950s is another oft-cited example of   8
familial self-reliance. According to legend, after World War II a new,
family-oriented generation settled down, saved their pennies, worked
hard, and found well-paying jobs that allowed them to purchase
homes in the suburbs. In fact, however, the 1950s suburban family was
far more dependent on government assistance than any so-called underclass family of today. Federal GI benefit payments, available to 40
percent of the male population between the ages of twenty and twenty-
four, permitted a whole generation of men to expand their education
and improve their job prospects without forgoing marriage and children. The National Defense Education Act retooled science education
in America, subsidizing both American industry and the education of
individual scientists. Government-funded research developed the alu-
minum clapboards, prefabricated walls and ceilings, and plywood
paneling that comprised the technological basis of the postwar housing
revolution. Government spending was also largely responsible for the
new highways, sewer systems, utility services, and traffic-control programs that opened up suburbia.

In addition, suburban home ownership depended on an unprece-   9
dented expansion of federal regulation and financing. Before the war,
banks often required a 50 percent down payment on homes and normally issued mortgages for five to ten years. In the postwar period,
however, the Federal Housing Authority, supplemented by the GI Bill,
put the federal government in the business of insuring and regulating
private loans for single-home construction. FHA policy required down
payments of only 5 to 10 percent of the purchase price and guaranteed
mortgages of up to thirty years at interest rates of just 2 to 3 percent.
The Veterans Administration required a mere dollar down from veterans. Almost half the housing in suburbia in the 1950s depended on
such federal programs.

The drawback of these aid programs was that although they worked   10
well for recipients, nonrecipients—disproportionately poor and urban—
were left far behind. While the general public financed the roads that
suburbanites used to commute, the streetcars and trolleys that served

urban and poor families received almost no tax revenues, and our previously thriving rail system was allowed to decay. In addition, federal loan policies, which were a boon to upwardly mobile white families, tended to systematize the pervasive but informal racism that had previously characterized the housing market. FHA redlining practices, for example, took entire urban areas and declared them ineligible for loans, while the government's two new mortgage institutions, the Federal National Mortgage Association and the Government National Mortgage Association (Fannie Mae and Ginny Mae) made it possible for urban banks to transfer savings out of the cities and into new suburban developments in the South and West.

11   Despite the devastating effects on families and regions that did not receive such assistance, government aid to suburban residents during the 1950s and 1960s produced in its beneficiaries none of the demoralization usually presumed to afflict recipients of government handouts. Instead, federal subsidies to suburbia encouraged family formation, residential stability, upward occupational mobility, and rising educational aspirations among youth who could look forward to receiving such aid. Seen in this light, the idea that government subsidies intrinsically induce dependence, undermine self-esteem, or break down family ties is exposed as no more than a myth.

12   I am not suggesting that the way to solve the problems of poverty and urban decay in America is to quadruple our spending on welfare. Certainly there are major reforms needed in our current aid policies to the poor. But the debate over such reform should put welfare in the context of *all* federal assistance programs. As long as we pretend that only poor or single-parent families need outside assistance, while normal families "stand on their own two feet," we will shortchange poor families, overcompensate rich ones, and fail to come up with effective policies for helping out families in the middle. Current government housing policies are a case in point. The richest 20 percent of American households receives three times as much federal housing aid—mostly in tax subsidies—as the poorest 20 percent receives in expenditures for low-income housing.

13   Historically, the debate over government policies toward families has never been over *whether* to intervene but *how:* to rescue or to warehouse, to prevent or to punish, to moralize about values or mobilize resources for education and job creation. Today's debate, lacking such historical perspective, caricatures the real issues. Our attempt to sustain the myth of family self-reliance in the face of all the historical evidence to the contrary has led policymakers into theoretical contortions and practical miscalculations that are reminiscent of efforts by medieval philosophers to maintain that the earth and not the sun was the center of the planetary system. In the sixteenth century, leading European thinkers insisted that the planets and the sun all revolved around

the earth—much as American politicians today insist that our society revolves around family self-reliance. When evidence to the contrary mounted, defenders of the Ptolemaic universe postulated all sorts of elaborate planetary orbits in order to reconcile observed reality with their cherished theory. Similarly, rather than admit that all families need some kind of public support, we have constructed ideological orbits that explain away each instance of middle-class dependence as an "exception," an "abnormality," or even an illusion. We have distributed public aid to families through convoluted bureaucracies that have become impossible to track; in some cases the system has become so cumbersome that it threatens to collapse around our ears. It is time to break through the old paradigm of self-reliance and substitute a new one that recognizes that assisting families is, simply, what government does.

★ *Meaning and Understanding*

1. How does Coontz define the conservative and liberal views on government assistance?

2. What does Coontz mean in paragraph 1 when she refers to the "entrenched American belief that dependence on government assistance is a recent and destructive phenomenon"?

3. Why does she term the idea of family self-reliance a "myth"?

4. What connection does Coontz make between the Western pioneer family and the 1950s suburban family?

5. In what way, according to Coontz, does the debate over government assistance resemble the debates over the Ptolemaic system?

★ *Techniques and Strategies*

1. Why does Coontz quote her grandfather in paragraph 2?

2. What kind of evidence does Coontz provide to help support her argument?

3. Who is the intended audience for this selection? How do you know?

4. What is Coontz's thesis? Do you think that she has supported it adequately? Why or why not?

5. Analyze the last paragraph—the conclusion—of this essay. In what ways is it an effective closing to the piece? How is the last sentence a particularly powerful culmination to Coontz's argument?

★ Speaking of Values

1. What is "self-reliance"? What role does it play in the myth of American culture? How important is it to you, your family, friends, and associates?

2. Coontz calls into question "the idea that the family should have the sole or even primary responsibility for educating and socializing its members. Should the family have this responsibility? Why or why not? If not the family, who else should?

3. Coontz challenges the idea that government assistance programs "induce dependence, undermine self esteem, or break down family ties." What is your view on the matter? Do government programs have a negative effect or a positive effect? Support your views.

4. Coontz suggests that each of the government programs or policies she mentions is a kind of entitlement. Is it possible to look at some of these policies as compensatory instead? For instance, the GI benefits she mentions compensated the men and women who served in the armed forces for the time they had sacrificed. How does looking at these programs in this way affect Coontz's argument? Explain.

★ Values Conversation

Coontz points to the positive role of government "in regulating the way that employers and civic bodies interact with families." Should government play this role? Why or why not? Form groups to discuss these questions. Report back to the class on your findings.

★ Writing about Values

1. Coontz characterizes both the conservative and the liberal positions on dependence on government assistance. Choose a side and write a paper defending your position.

2. Do some library research on either the Homestead Act of 1862, the GI Bill of Rights, or the "family wage system." Write a paper explaining the reasons for the policy you select, the public response to it, and its benefits or consequences to society.

3. Write a letter to the editor of your local newspaper either supporting or challenging a government assistance program in your city or state.

Values in Review

1. Gary Soto, Don J. Snyder, and Henry David Thoreau each in his own manner treats work as an almost spiritual, rather than merely a practical, experience. Said another way, each of these writers views work as a kind of transcendent activity. Write a paper comparing and contrasting the views of each of these men toward work and life.

2. Frank McCourt, Stephanie Coontz, William Branigin, and Jonathan Kozol write about the devastating effects of unemployment and poverty on the family as well as on the individual. Write a paper in which you identify the particular point of view of each of these writers and then try to formulate a thesis that incorporates all their views. Finally, synthesize these views in your conclusion.

3. For many people, work and the workplace are simply elements in life that must be tolerated in order to survive. For Arlie Russell Hochschild and Jean Bethke Elshtain, however, work has a different significance. Identify the views of these two writers on work and the workplace and write a paper comparing and contrasting those views.

Chapter 4

Health and Health Care

Visiting day

Doctors and nurses

HMOs

Emergency room

Television doctor shows

AIDS

Staying young

Assisted suicide

Fred Hechinger

They Tortured My Mother

Offering an account of his terminally ill mother's final days, Fred Hechinger (1920–1997), a former education editor for the *New York Times*, portrays one individual in the grips of the medical establishment.

———— ★ ————

The hospital was a torture chamber. Doctors were the torturers. 1

My mother, age 94, entered the hospital on Dec. 10 after severe internal bleeding. A large, malignant tumor in the colon was found. Although we had serious reservations about an operation at her age, we were told that the alternative would be the horror of bleeding to death. 2

We had no choice. We did, however, sign papers requesting no resuscitation and impressed on the doctors my mother's and our wish that no heroic efforts be made to prolong her life. The doctors' description of the operation was insulting and patronizing. Within a week, they said, my mother would be back home as good as before. 3

The horror story began immediately after the operation. My mother had been put on a respirator during surgery. The device, placed in her mouth like the bit of an unruly horse, would never be removed. She would never again be able to speak. 4

On the first Sunday after the operation, with her own doctor out of town, I tried unsuccessfully for hours to reach the covering physician through his service. When I finally reached him in the late afternoon, he insisted that he had met with me at length earlier in the day. He had confused me with another patient's relative and had never seen my mother's chart. 5

Subsequently we were told my mother was being treated "aggressively" to build up her strength so the respirator might be removed. Even to a layman, this seemed likely only to prolong the suffering. Sedation was kept to a minimum in order not to distort readings of vital signs. 6

I visited my mother almost every day even though we could not communicate. On Christmas Day her eyes were open, reflecting fear and horror. Her hands, swollen to three times their normal size, were tied to the bed to prevent her from removing any tubes. Despite this, she constantly raised her hands, palms upward, as if to ask "Why are you doing this to me?" On the unlikely chance that she might hear me, I could only repeat the doctors' lie: "You'll be better soon." I will always feel guilty. 7

8   The residents assured us that my mother could feel no pain. I knew—I saw with my own eyes—that this was not true. Several days later the doctors called me for permission either to make an incision in my mother's stomach to insert a feeding tube or to insert a tube through her nose. I was never told of the alternative of *not* inserting any tube and letting nature take its benign course.

9   When my mother developed pneumonia, the fact was withheld from us for two days until a young resident inadvertently let it slip. By that time, treatment with antibiotics was already under way. The brutal extension of life continued.

10   At this point, malfunction of the kidneys had worsened. My mother's face was swollen beyond recognition. Her lips were raw from the respirator. I finally insisted on increased sedation.

11   I last saw my mother at 2:30 P.M. on Dec. 29. An understanding resident told me that the end was near. At approximately 5:30 a young doctor called to say that my mother had died. Momentary relief overshadowed anger. Now anger will linger for a long time:

12   Anger at a system that makes torture legal.

13   Anger at the medical profession that fights hard to protect its own prerogatives but has shown little courage in fighting inhumane legal restrictions which make doctors accomplices in torture.

14   Anger at doctors who are so wedded to charts and monitors that they seem oblivious of patients' pain.

15   At the funeral parlor I was told that I would be required to identify my mother. A few minutes later the men who were dealing with the body reversed that. They wanted to spare me a final look at the havoc modern medicine had wreaked on her.

★ Meaning and Understanding

1. What do you think is the main point of this selection?

2. Why is Hechinger's mother in the hospital?

3. The writer tells us that he and his family asked that the doctors perform "no heroic efforts" to sustain his mother's life. What does "heroic" mean in this case?

4. Hechinger says that the doctor's explanation was "insulting and patronizing." What does he mean by this?

5. In paragraph 7, after he tells his mother that she will be better soon, Hechinger remarks that he "will always feel guilty." Why will he always feel guilty?

6. Why does the writer refer in paragraph 9 to the doctors' attempts to prolong his mother's life as "brutal"?

★ Techniques and Strategies

1. The writer organizes the piece chronologically. Why does he choose this organizing strategy?

2. Look again at the opening and closing images of the selection. How are they different, and how do they contribute to your understanding of the writer's point?

3. Paragraphs 12, 13, and 14 all begin with the same word: "Anger." Why does the writer use this technique of repetition, and what effect does it have?

4. Look at the opening paragraph. How does it capture the reader's attention?

5. Who is the audience for this piece? What evidence is there in the selection to support your point of view?

6. What is the tone of the piece? What words help you determine the tone? What did you think this essay was going to be about when you first read the title?

★ Speaking of Values

1. The medical profession has an obligation and responsibility both to prolong life and to mitigate suffering. But which goal should prevail when the two are in conflict? Why?

2. What seems to be the attitude of the doctors toward the patient's family? Toward the patient herself? Why would physicians behave in the manner described by the writer?

3. In several places in the selection the writer suggests that he knows better than the doctors about what is happening to his mother. Does he? Explain why or why not. How can family members be more perceptive than the doctors? When can a family member's perceptions interfere with a patient's recovery?

4. Do you think some doctors are "oblivious of patients' pain"? Why or why not?

5. Why did the doctors not tell the writer that his mother had developed pneumonia? Do doctors have a right to withhold information if they deem it to be in the best interests of the patient? Why or why not?

★ Values Conversation

Almost everyone has had experiences with doctors and the medical profession. Form groups and discuss your best and your worst experiences. Be sure to analyze what made those experiences so good or so bad.

★ *Writing about Values*

1. Find a copy of the Hippocratic oath and study it. Then write a paper discussing the professional and personal values that it implies doctors should embrace.

2. Write about a good experience or a bad experience you have had with doctors. Be sure to explain the medical situation fully—that is, who was the patient and what was wrong—and what made the experience positive or negative.

3. The American Medical Association and individual hospital panels claim to serve as watchdogs for the judgments, actions, and behaviors of physicians and other medical workers. Do you think doctors and others in the field are subject to enough external regulation? Too much? Would regulation of any kind have helped Hechinger's mother? What would you propose as an appropriate method of oversight for medical workers? Write an essay in which you address these issues.

George Simpson

The War Room at Bellevue

Born in Virginia in 1950, George Simpson joined the staff of *Newsweek* in 1972 and was appointed *Newsweek's* director of public affairs in 1978. He has written for the *New York Times, Sport, Glamour, New York* magazine, and other major publications. In this piece he shows life in a busy hospital's Adult Emergency Service from 9 o'clock on a Friday night into the early hours of the next morning.

――――― ★ ―――――

Bellevue. The name conjures up images of an indoor war zone: the wounded and bleeding lining the halls, screaming for help while harried doctors in blood-stained smocks rush from stretcher to stretcher, fighting a losing battle against exhaustion and the crushing number of injured. "What's worse," says a long-time Bellevue nurse, "is that we have this image of being a hospital only for..." She pauses, then lowers her voice; "for crazy people."

Though neither battlefield nor Bedlam is a valid image, there is something extraordinary about the monstrous complex that spreads for five blocks along First Avenue in Manhattan. It is said best by the head nurse in Adult Emergency Service: "If you have any chance for survival, you have it here." Survival—that is why they come. Why do injured cops drive by a half-dozen other hospitals to be treated at Bellevue? They've seen the Bellevue emergency team in action.

9:00 P.M. It is a Friday night in the Bellevue emergency room. The after-work crush is over (those who've suffered through the day, only to come for help after the five-o'clock whistle has blown) and it is nearly silent except for the mutter of voices at the admitting desk, where administrative personnel discuss who will go for coffee. Across the spotless white-walled lobby, ten people sit quietly, passively, in pastel plastic chairs, waiting for word of relatives or to see doctors. In the past 24 hours, 300 people have come to the Bellevue Adult Emergency Service. Fewer than 10 percent were true emergencies. One man sleeps fitfully in the emergency ward while his heartbeat, respiration, and blood pressure are monitored by control consoles mounted over his bed. Each heartbeat trips a tiny bleep in the monitor, which attending nurses can hear across the ward. A half hour ago, doctors in the trauma room withdrew a six-inch stiletto blade from his back. When he is stabilized, the patient will be moved upstairs to the twelve-bed Surgical Intensive Care Unit.

245

4   9:05 P.M. An ambulance backs into the receiving bay, its red and yellow lights flashing in and out of the lobby. A split second later, the glass doors burst open as a nurse and an attendant roll a mobile stretcher into the lobby. When the nurse screams, "Emergent!" the lobby explodes with activity as the way is cleared to the trauma room. Doctors appear from nowhere and transfer the bloodied body of a black man to the treatment table. Within seconds his clothes are stripped away, revealing a tiny stab wound in his left side. Three doctors and three nurses rush around the victim, each performing a task necessary to begin treatment. Intravenous needles are inserted into his arms and groin. A doctor draws blood for the lab, in case surgery is necessary. A nurse begins inserting a catheter into the victim's penis and continues to feed in tubing until the catheter reaches the bladder. Urine flows through the tube into a plastic bag. Doctors are glad not to see blood in the urine. Another nurse records pulse and blood pressure.

5   The victim is in good shape. He shivers slightly, although the trauma room is exceedingly warm. His face is bloodied, but shows no major lacerations. A third nurse, her elbow propped on the treatment table, asks the man a series of questions, trying to quickly outline his medical history. He answers abruptly. He is drunk. His left side is swabbed with yellow disinfectant and a doctor injects a local anesthetic. After a few seconds another doctor inserts his finger into the wound. It sinks in all the way to the knuckle. He begins to rotate his finger like a child trying to get a marble out of a milk bottle. The patient screams bloody murder and tries to struggle free.

6   Meanwhile in the lobby, a security guard is ejecting a derelict who has begun to drink from a bottle hidden in his coat pocket. "He's a regular, was in here just two days ago," says a nurse. "We checked him pretty close then, so he's probably okay now. Can you believe those were clean clothes we gave him?" The old man, blackened by filth, leaves quietly.

7   9:15 P.M. A young Hispanic man interrupts, saying his pregnant girl friend, sitting outside in his car, is bleeding heavily from her vagina. She is rushed into an examination room, treated behind closed doors, and rolled into the observation ward, where, much later in the night, a gynecologist will treat her in a special room—the same one used to examine rape victims. Nearby, behind curtains, the neurologist examines an old white woman to determine if her headaches are due to head injury. They are not.

8   9:45 P.M. The trauma room has been cleared and cleaned mercilessly. The examination rooms are three-quarters full—another overdose, two asthmatics, a young woman with abdominal pains. In the hallway, a derelict who has been sleeping it off urinates all over the stretcher. He sleeps on while attendants change his clothes. An ambulance—one of four that patrol Manhattan for Bellevue from 42nd Street to Houston, river to

river—delivers a middle-aged white woman and two cops, the three of them soaking wet. The woman has escaped from the psychiatric floor of a nearby hospital and tried to drown herself in the East River. The cops fished her out. She lies on a stretcher shivering beneath white blankets. Her eyes stare at the ceiling. She speaks clearly when an administrative worker begins routine questioning. The cops are given hospital gowns and wait to receive tetanus shots and gamma globulin—a hedge against infection from the befouled river water. They will hang around the E.R. for another two hours, telling their story to as many as six other policemen who show up to hear it. The woman is rolled into an examination room, where a male nurse speaks gently: "They tell me you fell into the river." "No," says the woman, "I jumped. I have to commit suicide." "Why?" asks the nurse. "Because I'm insane and I can't help [it] . I have to die." The nurse gradually discovers the woman has a history of psychological problems. She is given dry bedclothes and placed under guard in the hallway. She lies on her side, staring at the wall.

The pace continues to increase. Several more overdose victims arrive by ambulance. One, a young black woman, had done a striptease on the street just before passing out. A second black woman is semiconscious and spends the better part of her time at Bellevue alternately cursing it and pleading with the doctors. Attendants find a plastic bottle coated with methadone in the pocket of a Hispanic O.D. The treatment is routinely the same, and sooner or later involves vomiting. Just after doctors begin to treat the O.D., he vomits great quantities of wine and methadone in all directions. "Lovely business, huh?" laments one of the doctors. A young nurse confides that if there were other true emergencies, the overdose victims would be given lower priority. "You can't help thinking they did it to themselves," she says, "while the others are accident victims." 9

10:30 P.M. A policeman who twisted his knee struggling with an "alleged perpetrator" is examined and released. By 10:30, the lobby is jammed with friends and relatives of patients in various stages of treatment and recovery. The attendant who also functions as a translator for Hispanic patients adds chairs to accommodate the overflow. The medical walk-in rate stays steady—between eight and ten patients waiting. A pair of derelicts, each with battered eyes, appear at the admitting desk. One has a dramatically swollen face laced with black stitches. 10

11:00 P.M. The husband of the attempted suicide arrives. He thanks the police for saving his wife's life, then talks at length with doctors about her condition. She continues to stare into the void and does not react when her husband approaches her stretcher. 11

Meanwhile, patients arrive in the lobby at a steady pace. A young G.I. on leave has lower-back pains; a Hispanic man complains of pain in his side; occasionally parents hurry through the adult E.R. carrying 12 children into the pediatric E.R. A white woman of about 50 marches into the lobby from the walk-in entrance. Dried blood covers her right eyebrow and upper lip. She begins to perform. "I was assaulted on 28th and Lexington, I was," she says grandly, "and I don't have to take it *anymore.* I was a bride 21 years ago, and, God, I was beautiful then." She has captured the attention of all present. "I was there when the boys came home—on Memorial Day—and I don't have to take this kind of treatment."

13   As midnight approaches, the nurses prepare for the shift change. They must brief the incoming staff and make sure all reports are up-to-date. One young brunet says, "Christ, I'm gonna go home and take a shower—I smell like vomit."

14   11:50 P.M. The triage nurse is questioning an old black man about chest pains, and a Hispanic woman is having an asthma attack, when an ambulance, its sirens screaming full tilt, roars into the receiving bay. There is a split-second pause as everyone drops what he or she is doing and looks up. Then all hell breaks loose. Doctors and nurses are suddenly sprinting full-out toward the trauma room. The glass doors burst open and the occupied stretcher is literally run past me. Cops follow. It is as if a comet has whooshed by. In the trauma room it all becomes clear. A half-dozen doctors and nurses surround the lifeless form of a Hispanic man with a shotgun hole in his neck the size of your fist. Blood pours from a second gaping wound in his chest. A respirator is slammed over his face, making his chest rise and fall as if he were breathing. "No pulse," reports one doctor. A nurse jumps on a stool and, leaning over the man, begins to pump his chest with her palms. "No blood pressure," screams another nurse. The ambulance driver appears shaken. "I never thought I'd get here in time," he stutters. More doctors from the trauma team upstairs arrive. Wrappings from syringes and gauze pads fly through the air. The victim's eyes are open yet devoid of life. His body takes on a yellow tinge. A male nurse winces at the gunshot wound. "This guy really pissed off somebody," he says. This is no ordinary shooting. It is an execution. IV's are jammed into the body in the groin and arms. One doctor has been plugging in an electrocardiograph and asks everyone to stop for a second so he can get a reading. "Forget it," shouts the doctor in charge. "No time." "Take it easy, Jimmy," someone yells at the head physician. It is apparent by now that the man is dead, but the doctors keep trying injections and finally they slit open the chest and reach inside almost up to their elbows. They feel the extent of the damage and suddenly it is all over. "I told 'em he was dead," says one nurse, withdrawing. "They didn't listen." The room is very still. The doctors are momentarily disgusted, then go on about their business. The room clears quickly. Finally there is only a male nurse and the still-warm body, now waxy-yellow, with huge ribs exposed on both sides of the chest and giant

holes in both sides of the neck. The nurse speculates that this is yet another murder in a Hispanic political struggle that has brought many such victims to Bellevue. He marvels at the extent of the wounds and repeats, "This guy was really blown away."

Midnight. A hysterical woman is hustled through the lobby into an examination room. It is the dead man's wife, and she is nearly delirious. "I know he's dead, I know he's dead," she screams over and over. Within moments the lobby is filled with anxious relatives of the victim, waiting for word on his condition. The police are everywhere asking questions, but most people say they saw nothing. One young woman says she heard six shots, two louder than the other four. At some point, word is passed that the man is, in fact, dead. Another woman breaks down in hysterics; everywhere young Hispanics are crying and comforting each other. Plainclothes detectives make a quick examination of the body, check on the time of pronouncement of death, and begin to ask questions, but the bereaved are too stunned to talk. The rest of the uninvolved people in the lobby stare dumbly, their injuries suddenly paling in light of a death.   15

12:30 A.M. A black man appears at the admission desk and says he drank poison by mistake. He is told to have a seat. The ambulance brings in a young white woman, her head wrapped in white gauze. She is wailing terribly. A girl friend stands over her, crying, and a boyfriend clutches the injured woman's hands, saying, "I'm here, don't worry, I'm here." The victim has fallen downstairs at a friend's house. Attendants park her stretcher against the wall to wait for an examination room to clear. There are eight examination rooms and only three doctors. Unless you are truly an emergency, you will wait. One doctor is stitching up the elbow of a drunk who's been punched out. The friends of the woman who fell down the stairs glance up at the doctors anxiously, wondering why their friend isn't being treated faster.   16

1:10 A.M. A car pulls into the bay and a young Hispanic asks if a shooting victim has been brought here. The security guard blurts out, "He's dead." The young man is stunned. He peels his tires leaving the bay.   17

1:20 A.M. The young woman of the stairs is getting stitches in a small gash over her left eye when the same ambulance driver who brought in the gunshot victim delivers a man who has been stabbed in the back on East 3rd Street. Once again the trauma room goes from 0 to 60 in five seconds. The patient is drunk, which helps him endure the pain of having the catheter inserted through his penis into his bladder. Still he yells, "That hurts like a bastard," then adds sheepishly, "Excuse me, ladies." But he is not prepared for what comes next. An X-ray reveals a collapsed right lung. After just a shot of local anesthetic, the doctor slices open his side and inserts a long plastic tube. Internal bleeding had kept the lung pressed down and prevented it from rein-   18 flating. The tube releases the pressure. The ambulance driver says the cops grabbed the guy who ran the eight-inch blade into the victim's back. "That's not the one," says the man. "They got the wrong guy." A nurse reports that there is not much of the victim's type blood available at the hospital. One of the doctors says that's okay, he won't need surgery. Meanwhile blood pours from the man's knife wound and the tube in his side. As the nurses work, they chat about personal matters, yet they respond immediately to orders from either doctor. "How ya doin'?" the doctor asks the patient. "Okay," he says. His blood spatters on the floor.

19   So it goes into the morning hours. A Valium overdose, a woman who fainted, a man who went through the windshield of his car. More overdoses. More drunks with split eyebrows and chins. The doctors and nurses work without complaint. "This is nothing, about normal, I'd say," concludes the head nurse. "No big deal.

★ Meaning and Understanding

1. What is a "war room"?

2. Who are the people who come to the emergency room after work? Why do they wait?

3. Why are the doctors "momentarily disgusted" during the incident in paragraph 14 with the dead man?

4. Why isn't the young girl who fell down the stairs treated more quickly?

5. What does "triage" mean? Why is the trauma room "cleaned mercilessly"?

6. How do you explain the action of the young man who peels his tires (paragraph 17)?

★ Techniques and Strategies

1. How does Simpson organize the essay? Is the organizational pattern effective? Why or why not?

2. Why does Simpson refer to Bellevue's emergency room as a war room? What other war references can you identify in the essay? What does "Bellevue" mean? Is the name in any way ironic? Do you think it was meant to be?

3. What do quotations from nurses at both the beginning and the end of the essay contribute to its structure? Why does the writer use this technique?

4. Who is the intended audience for this essay? The tone? What is the writer's purpose here?

5. How does the juxtaposition of the young Hispanic woman and the "old white woman" function in paragraph 7? What point do you think Simpson is trying to make here?

6. Simpson seems to punctuate his description with statements like "All hell broke loose" and "the trauma room goes from 0 to 60 in five seconds." How do these familiar, if not trite, statements help you understand the point he is trying to make?

★ *Speaking of Values*

1. Who are the most important people in this selection: doctors, nurses, or patients? Why has the writer emphasized the people he has? Give reasons for your answer.

2. What is the attitude of the doctors and nurses toward the patients? How do you know? Are their behaviors appropriate, do you think? Explain your point.

3. Bellevue is located in New York City. What picture of the city emerges from this essay?

4. The author states that "injured cops drive by a half-dozen other hospitals to be treated at Bellevue." What does this suggest about the quality of medical treatment offered at Bellevue? Explain.

5. Does Bellevue have a reputation as being a hospital "only for crazy people"? If so, why do you think it does? Does anything in the essay suggest that the description has some validity?

★ *Values Conversation*

Triage is an accepted manner of dealing with emergency patients. However, the practice raises many ethical issues. Form groups and identify some issues that might arise from triage. How does your group feel about the practice?

★ *Writing about Values*

1. The physicians and nurses represented here appear hard working and dedicated. Do they match your impressions of medical staff you have met? Write an essay to describe and explain your experiences (or a single experience) with physicians and nurses.

2. Visit the emergency room at a local hospital during both a slow and a busy time and observe the scene. Try to interview some of the hospital staff about how they feel about their jobs, the patients, each other, and so on. Then write a paper presenting your findings.

3. Write a descriptive essay about some busy, hectic place you know: a school cafeteria, a sports arena, a shopping mall. Use concrete sensory language to convey an accurate picture of the scene.

Paul R. McHugh

The Kevorkian Epidemic

Born in 1931, Paul R. McHugh is the Henry Phipps Professor and director
of the Department of Psychiatry and Behavioral Sciences at the Johns
Hopkins University School of Medicine. He is the author, with Phillip R.
Slavney, of *The Perspectives of Psychiatry* and *Psychiatric Polarities*.
McHugh writes here about the controversial issue of assisted suicide.

———— ★ ————

Dr. Jack Kevorkian of Detroit has been in the papers most days this past 1
summer and autumn helping sick people kill themselves. He is said to
receive hundreds of calls a week. Although his acts are illegal by statute and common law in Michigan, no one stops him. Many citizens, including members of three juries, believe he means well, perhaps
thinking: Who knows? Just maybe, we ourselves shall need his services
some day.

To me it looks like madness from every quarter. The patients are 2
mad by definition in that they are suicidally depressed and demoralized; Dr. Kevorkian is "certifiable" in that his passions render him, as
the state code specifies, "dangerous to others"; and the usually reliable
people of Michigan are confused and anxious to the point of incoher-
ence by terrors of choice that are everyday issues for doctors. These
three disordered parties have converged, provoking a local epidemic of
premature death.

Let me begin with the injured hosts of this epidemic, the patients 3
mad by definition. At this writing, more than forty, as best we know,
have submitted to Dr. Kevorkian's deadly charms. They came to him
with a variety of medical conditions: Alzheimer's disease, multiple
sclerosis, chronic pain, amyotrophic lateral sclerosis, cancer, drug addiction, and more. These are certainly disorders from which anyone
might seek relief. But what kind of relief do patients with these conditions usually seek when they do not have a Dr. Kevorkian to extinguish
their pain?

Both clinical experience and research on this question are extensive— 4
and telling. A search for death does not accompany most terminal or
progressive diseases. Pain-ridden patients customarily call doctors for
remedies, not for termination of life. Physical incapacity, as with advanced arthritis, does not generate suicide. Even amyotrophic lateral
sclerosis, or Lou Gehrig's disease, a harrowing condition I shall describe

presently, is not associated with increased suicide amongst its sufferers. Most doctors learn these facts as they help patients and their families burdened by these conditions.

5   But we don't have to rely solely upon the testimonies of experienced physicians. Recently cancer patients in New England were asked about their attitudes toward death. The investigators—apparently surprised to discover a will to live when they expected to find an urge to die—reported in the *Lancet* (vol. 347, pp. 1805–1810, 1996) two striking findings. First, that cancer patients enduring pain were not inclined to want euthanasia or physician-assisted suicide. In fact, "patients actually experiencing pain were more likely to find euthanasia or physician-assisted suicide unacceptable." Second, those patients inclined toward suicide—whether in pain or not—were suffering from depression. As the investigators noted: "These data indicate a conflict between attitudes and possible practices related to euthanasia and physician-assisted suicide. These *interventions* were approved of for terminally ill patients with unremitting pain, but these are not the patients most likely to request such *interventions*.... There is *some* concern that with legislation of euthanasia or physician-assisted suicide non-psychiatric physicians, who generally have a poor ability to detect and treat depression, may allow life-ending *interventions* when treatment of depression may be more appropriate." (Italics added to identify mealymouthed expressions: *interventions* means homicides, and *some* means that we investigators should stay cool in our concerns—after all, it's not we who are dying.)

6   None of this is news to psychiatrists who have studied suicides associated with medical illnesses. Depression, the driving force in most cases, comes in two varieties: symptomatic depression found as a feature of particular diseases—that is, as one of the several symptoms of that disease; and demoralization, the common state of mind of people in need of guidance but facing discouraging circumstances alone. Both forms of depression render patients vulnerable to feelings of hopelessness that, if not adequately confronted, may lead to suicide.

7   Let me first concentrate on the symptomatic depressions because an understanding of them illuminates much of the problem. By the term *symptomatic*, psychiatrists mean that with some physical diseases suicidal depression is one of the condition's characteristic features. Careful students of these diseases come to appreciate that this variety of depression is not to be accepted as a natural feeling of discouragement provoked by bad circumstances—that is, similar to the downhearted state of, say, a bankrupt man or a grief-stricken widow. Instead the depression we are talking about here, with its beclouding of judgment, sense of misery, and suicidal inclinations, is a symptom identical in nature to the fevers, pains, or loss of energy that are signs of the disease itself.

A good and early example of the recognition of symptomatic de-   8
pression is found in George Huntington's classical (1872) description
of the disorder eventually named after him: Huntington's disease.
Huntington had first seen the condition when he was a youth visiting
patients with his father, a family doctor on Long Island. He noted that
one of the characteristic features of the condition was "the tendency
to . . . that form of insanity which leads to suicide." Even now between
7 and 10 percent of non-hospitalized patients with Huntington's disease do succeed in killing themselves. Psychiatrists and neurologists
have perceived that Parkinson's disease, multiple sclerosis, Alzheimer's disease, AIDS dementia, and some cerebral-vascular strokes
all have this same tendency to provoke "that form of insanity which
leads to suicide."

That these patients are insane is certain. They are overcome with a   9
sense of hopelessness and despair, often with the delusional belief that
they are in some way useless, burdensome, or even corrupt perpetrators of evil. One of my patients with Huntington's disease felt that Sa-
tan was dwelling within her and that she acted in accordance with his
wishes. These patients lose their capacity to concentrate and reason,
they have a pervasive and unremitting feeling of gloom, and a constant, even eager willingness to accept death. These characteristics of
symptomatic depression recur in all the diseases mentioned above.
Multiple sclerosis (MS) patients are frequently afflicted by it. Some five
or six of Dr. Kevorkian's patients had MS.

The problematic nature of symptomatic depression goes beyond   10
the painful state of mind of the patient. Other observers—such as family members and physicians—may well take the depressive's disturbed, indeed insane, point of view as a proper assessment of his or
her situation. It was this point that Huntington, long before the time of
modern anti-depressant treatment, wished to emphasize by identifying
it as an insanity. He knew that failure to diagnose this feature will lead
to the neglect of efforts to treat the patient properly and to protect him
or her from suicide until the symptom remits.

Such neglect is a crucial blunder, because, whether the underlying   11
condition is Huntington's disease, Alzheimer's disease, MS, or something else, modern anti-depressant treatment is usually effective at re-
lieving the mood disorder and restoring the patient's emotional
equilibrium. In Michigan and in Holland, where physician-assisted
suicide also takes place, these actions to hasten death are the ultimate
neglect of patients with symptomatic depression; they are, really, a
form of collusion with insanity.

The diagnosis of symptomatic depression is not overly difficult if   12
its existence is remembered and its features systematically sought. But
many of its characteristics—such as its capacity to provoke bodily
pains—are not known to all physicians. The fact that such depression

occurs in dire conditions, such as Huntington's disease, may weigh against its prompt diagnosis and treatment. Again and again, kindly intended physicians presume that a depression "makes sense"—given the patient's situation—and overlook the stereotypic signs of the insanity. They presume justifiable demoralization and forget the pharmacologically treatable depressions.

13   Over the last decade, at least among psychiatrists, the reality of symptomatic depressions has become familiar and treatment readiness has become the rule. Yet not all sick patients with life-threatening depression have symptomatic depressions. Many physically ill patients are depressed for perfectly understandable reasons, given the grueling circumstances of their progressive and intractable disease. Just as any misfortune can provoke grief and anxiety, so can awareness of loss of health and of a closed future.

14   Well-titled *demoralization,* this depression, too, has a number of attributes. It waxes and wanes with experiences and events, comes in waves, and is worse at certain times—such as during the night, when contemplating future discomforts and burdens, and when the patient is alone or uninstructed about the benefits that modern treatments can bring him.

15   In contrast to the symptomatic depressions that run their own course almost independent of events, demoralization is sensitive to circumstances and especially to the conduct of doctors toward the patient. Companionship, especially that which provides understanding and clear explanations of the actions to be taken in opposing disease and disability, can be immensely helpful in overcoming this state and sustaining the patient in a hopeful frame of mind.

16   The obverse is also true. If faced by inattentive physicians—absentee physicians most commonly—patients can become more discouraged and utterly demoralized by what they assume is their physician's resignation from a hopeless battle. All patients afflicted with disease—curable or incurable—are susceptible to bleak assumptions about their future and their value. These susceptibilities can be magnified or diminished by the behavior of their physicians.

17   The therapeutic implication here is that despairing assumptions wither if directly combated and shown to be an inaccurate analysis of the situation. Demoralization is an eminently treatable mental condition. Hopeless doctors, however, ready to see patients as untreatable, produce hopeless patients. The combination of the the two produces a zeal for terminating effort. "What's the point?" becomes the cry of both patient and doctor.

18   *This is the point:* Depression, both in the form of a symptomatic mental state and in the form of demoralization, is the result of illness and circumstances combined and is treatable just as are other effects of illness. These treatments are the everyday skills of many physicians,

but particularly of those physicians who are specialists in these disorders and can advance the treatments most confidently.

Most suicidally depressed patients are not rational individuals who have weighed the balance sheet of their lives and discovered more red than black ink. They are victims of altered attitudes about themselves and their situation, which cause powerful feelings of hopelessness to abound. Doctors can protect them from these attitudes by providing information, guidance, and support all along the way. Dr. Kevorkian, however, trades upon the vulnerabilities and mental disorders of these patients and in so doing makes a mockery of medicine as a discipline of informed concern for patients.

Let us turn to Dr. Kevorkian, the agent of this epidemic in Michigan, and consider why I think that he is "certifiably" insane, by which I mean that he suffers from a mental condition rendering him dangerous to others.

Without question, Dr. Kevorkian has proven himself dangerous, having participated in killing more than forty people already, with no end in sight. Dr. Kevorkian, by the way, does not shy from the word *killing*. He prescribes it and even coined a term for his practice—*medicide,* that is: "the termination of life performed by...professional medical personnel (such as a doctor, nurse, paramedic, physician's assistant, or medical technologist)." [Kevorkian, J., *Prescription: Medicide,* Prometheus Books, Buffalo, New York, 1991, page 202.] (Note his sense of a whole industry of killing to come, with much of it to be carried out by technicians because the doctors are busy.)

The question is whether his behavior is a product of a mental disorder. Not everyone agrees on an answer. Indeed the *British Medical Journal (BMJ)* described Dr. Kevorkian as a "hero."

His champions see no discernible motive for Dr. Kevorkian other than that he believes his work is fitting. The *BMJ* notes that greed for money or fame or some sadistic urge does not motivate Dr. Kevorkian. They make much of the fact that he does not charge a fee for killing. Because of the absence of such motives, the editors presume that he is a hero among doctors since it is only a "personal code of honor that admits of no qualification" that leads him into action.

But let us look rather more closely at "personal codes that admit no qualification." We have seen a few of them before and not all were admirable. As Dr. Kevorkian motors around Michigan carrying cylinders of carbon monoxide or bottles of potassium chloride to dispatch the sick, his is the motivation of a person with an "overvalued idea," a diagnostic formulation first spelled out by the psychiatrist Carl Wernicke in 1906. Wernicke differentiated overvalued ideas from obsessions and delusions. Overvalued ideas are often at the motivational heart of "personal codes that admit no qualification" and certainly provide a drive as powerful as that of hunger for money, fame, or sexual gratification.

25   An individual with an overvalued idea is someone who has taken up an idea shared by others in his milieu or culture and transformed it into a ruling passion or "monomania" for himself. It becomes the goal of all his efforts and he is prepared to sacrifice everything—family, reputation, health, even life itself—for it. He presumes that what he does in its service is right regardless of any losses that he or others suffer for it. He sees all opposition as at best misguided and at worst malevolent.

26   For Dr. Kevorkian, people may die before their time and the fabric of their families may be torn apart, but it's all for the good if he can presume they were "suffering pain unnecessarily" and he has eliminated it. He scorns all opposition—in particular constitutional democratic opposition   as resting on bad faith or ignorance. Empowered by his idea, he feels free to disregard the law and any of its officers.

27   An overvalued idea has three characteristics: (1) it is a self-dominating but not idiosyncratic opinion, given great importance by (2) intense emotional feelings over its significance, and evoking (3) persistent behavior in its service. For Dr. Kevorkian, thinking about how to terminate the sick has become his exclusive concern. His belief in the justice of his ideas is intense enough for him to starve himself if thwarted by law.

28   Dr. Kevorkian thinks that all opposition to him is "bad faith" and thus worthy of contempt—a contempt he expresses with no reservation. He is fond of saying that the judicial system of our country is "corrupt," the religious members of our society are "irrational," the medical profession is "insane," the press is "meretricious."

29   He considers his own behavior "humanitarian." Dr. Kevorkian holds himself beyond reproach, even after killing one patient he believed had multiple sclerosis but whose autopsy revealed no evidence of that disease and another patient with the vague condition of "chronic fatigue syndrome" in whom no pathological process could be found at autopsy—only Kevorkian's poison. He acts without taking a careful medical history, trying alternative treatments, or reflecting on how his actions affect such people as surviving family members.

30   Dr. Kevorkian's is a confident business. As the news reports flow out of Michigan, it appears that his threshold for medicide is getting lower. Physician-assisted suicide that had previously demanded an incurable disease such as Alzheimer's is now practiced upon patients with such chronic complaints as pelvic pain and emphysema, whose life expectancy cannot be specified. He can justify the active termination of anyone with an ailment—which is just what might be expected once the boundary against active killing by doctors has been breached. What's to stop him now that juries have found his actions to be de facto legal in Michigan?

31   A crucial aspect of overvalued ideas is that, in contrast to delusions, they are not idiosyncratic. They are ideas that can be found in a

proportion of the public—often an influential proportion. It is from such reservoirs of opinion that the particular individual harnesses and amplifies an idea with the disproportionate zeal characteristic of a ruling passion. That Dr. Kevorkian can find people in the highest places—even within the medical profession—to support his ideas and say that they see heroism in his actions is not surprising, given the passion of the contemporary debate over euthanasia. In this way the person with the overvalued idea may be seen, by those who share his opinion but not his self-sacrificing zeal, as giving expression to their hopes—disregarding the slower processes of democracy, filled with prejudice against all who resist, and pumped up with a sense of a higher purpose and justice.

People such as Dr. Kevorkian have found a place in history. With 32 some, with the passage of time, we come to agree with the idea if not the method by which the idea was first expressed. Such was John Brown, the abolitionist, ready to hack five anonymous farmers to death in the Pottowatomi massacre to advance his cause. With others we may come to tolerate some aspect of the idea but see its expression in actual behavior as ludicrous. Such was Carry Nation, the scourge of Kansas barkeeps and boozers, who went to jail hundreds of times for chopping up saloons with a small hatchet in the cause of temperance. Finally, for some, we come to recognize the potential for horror in an overvalued idea held by a person in high authority. Such was Adolf Hitler.

But how is it that anxieties and confusions about medical practice 33 and death can so afflict the judicious people of Michigan as to paralyze them before the outrageous behavior of Dr. Kevorkian and thus generate an environment for this epidemic? In Michigan these states of mind derive from conflicting concerns over medical decisions. The citizens—like any inexpert group—are relatively uninformed about what doctors can do for patients, even in extreme situations. Conflicting goals and unfamiliar practices—common enough around medical decisions—produce anxiety and confusion every time.

No one thinks happily about dying, especially dying in pain. Death 34 is bad; dying can be worse. Anyone who says he does not fear dying—and all the pain and suffering tied to it—has probably not experienced much in life.

This concern, though, certainly has been exaggerated in our times, 35 even though now much can be done to relieve the heaviest burdens of terminally ill patients. Yet through a variety of sources—such as movies, newspapers, and essays—all the negative aspects of dying have been emphasized, the agonies embellished, and the loss of control represented by disease accentuated. Horror stories feed upon one another, and rumors of medical lack of interest grow into opinions that doctors both neglect the dying and hold back relief. Doctors are regularly accused of surrendering to professional taboos or to legal advice to avoid risk of malpractice or prosecution—and in this way are presumed ready to sacrifice their patients out of selfish fear for themselves.

36   On the contrary, most doctors try to collaborate with patients and do listen to their wishes, especially when treatments that carry painful burdens are contemplated. As Dr. Kevorkian can demonstrate—with videotapes, no less—the patients he killed asked him repeatedly for help in dying rather than for help in living. Do not they have some right to die at their own hands steadied by Dr. Kevorkian? Is not the matter of assisted suicide simply a matter of rights and wants to which any citizen of Michigan is entitled?

37   The idea of a right to suicide provokes most psychiatrists. Psychiatry has worked to teach everyone that suicide is not an uncomplicated, voluntary act to which rights attach. It has shown that suicide is an act provoked, indeed compelled, by mental disorder—such as a disorienting depression or a set of misdirected, even delusionary, ideas. In that sense psychiatry taught that suicidal people were not "responsible" for this behavior—no matter what they said or wrote in final letters or testaments—any more than they would be for epileptic seizures.

38   This idea—generated from the careful study of the clinical circumstances and past histories of suicidal patients—gradually prevailed in civil law and even in the canon law of churches. As a result, laws against suicide were repealed—not to make suicide a "right" but to remove it from the status of a crime.

39   We psychiatrists thought we had done a worthy thing for our society, for families of patients, and even for patients themselves. We were not saying, not for a moment, that we approved of suicide. Far from it. We knew such deaths to be ugly and misguided—misguided in particular because the disposition to die, the wish for suicide, was, on inspection, often a symptom of the very mental disorders that psychiatry treats. Suicide in almost all cases is as far from a rational choice based on a weighing of the balance books of life as is responding to hallucinated voices or succumbing to the paranoid ideas of a charismatic madman such as Jim Jones, who at Jonestown directed a gruesome exhibition of mass assisted suicide.

40   Psychiatrists were united in their views about suicide and shook their heads when contemplating past traditions when suicides were considered scandalous. We did not think too deeply into the consequences of our actions. For, after suicide ceased to be a crime, it soon became a fight and, conceivably under some circumstances, such as when costs of care grow onerous, an obligation. Psychiatrists, who had worked for decades demonstrating that suicides were insane acts, are now recruited in Holland to assure that requests for suicide made by patients offered "no hope of cure" by their doctors are "rational."

41   What had begun as an effort at explanation and understanding of the tragic act of suicide has developed into complicity in the seduction

of vulnerable people into that very behavior. The patients are seduced just as the victims in Jonestown were—by isolating them, sustaining their despair, revoking alternatives, stressing examples of others choosing to die, and sweetening the deadly poison by speaking of death with dignity. If even psychiatrists succumb to this complicity with death, what can be expected of the lay public in Michigan?

At the heart of the confusion lies the contention that if the aim of medicine is to eliminate suffering and if only the killing of the patient will relieve the suffering, then killing is justified. On this logic rests Dr. Kevorkian's repeatedly successful defense before the juries of Michigan. 42

Yet the aim of medicine cannot simply be to prevent suffering. Not only would that be an impossible task, given the nature of human life, but it would diminish the scope of human potential—almost all of which demands some travail. The elimination of suffering is a veterinary rather than a medical goal. But veterinarians eliminate their animal subjects for other reasons than suffering. This fact can occasionally startle us. 43

When the race horse Cavonnier, second in the 1996 Kentucky Derby, pulled up lame during the Belmont Stakes later in the year, everyone watching on television feared that he must have broken a bone in his leg, with the inevitable consequences. His trainer provided brief comfort when he came on television to describe what had turned out to be a ligamentous rather than a bony injury to the animal. "This will probably end his racing career," he noted, "but it is not a life-threatening injury." He then paused, before adding, "However, he *is* a gelding." An ominous comment for Cavonnier and one worth remembering when anyone says, in defense of killing infirm people, "They shoot horses, don't they?" They do, but for many reasons other than just to protect horses from suffering. Sometimes it's to save money. Are we ready for the Cavonnier test for ourselves? 44

The idea that diseases herald only mortality and death, to be hurried along if their burdens are overwhelming, is not only an ethical error but a fundamental misunderstanding of contemporary medical science. Contemporary physician/scientists do not think of diseases as "entities," "things," "maledictions," and, in this sense, signposts to the grave, but as processes in life for which the body has ways of compensating and resisting, even if only temporarily. Diseases, in this way, are construed as forms of life under altered circumstances rather than as modes of death. 45

Because diseases are processes rather than entities, efforts to sustain life, alleviate symptoms, and moderate impairments represent collaborations with nature itself. These efforts remain the essence of doctoring, the whole reason for investing in the study of diseases and the body's responses to them. Physician-assisted suicide and euthanasia attack the very premises on which medical science and practice are 46 progressing today and do so by denying the life that scientific conceptions of disease represent. Life with dignity—not death with dignity—is what doctors aim for in their practice and in their science.

47   Medicine is one of the practical arts—a fact old enough to be known to Aristotle—among which are included navigation, economics, and architecture and for which the goal is usually obvious and unquestioned. For medicine, actions to prevent, alleviate, and cure are aimed at the obvious goal of sustaining the life and health of patients. Technical progress through scientific discoveries assists these actions, rendering them more effective. But modern techniques can seem in some circumstances to forestall the inevitable, prolong suffering, deny reality with little or no gain to the patient. Dr. Kevorkian writes and disseminates stories on this theme to justify his actions and to bolster his support. Allow me to present a story in which the conflict between preserving life and surrendering to disease was resolved by doctors who recognized their limits while striving to facilitate and extend a person's best experiences.

48   Nelson Butters was one of America's most distinguished neuropsychologists of the last twenty-five years. He died in 1995 at age fifty-eight after suffering for just under three years from the nightmare known as Lou Gehrig's disease. This disease is a relentless and progressive wasting of the body because of an atrophic degeneration of the nerves that innervate the muscles. As the body wastes away over the course of months, the mind is customarily unaffected and witnesses these depredations. It anticipates further weakness and ultimate death from a loss of strength to breathe. Such an affliction you would not wish on your worst enemy. Dr. Jack Kevorkian lives to terminate—the earlier the better—any patient smitten by it.

49   My colleague and friend Nelson Butters saw it through to its natural end. In so doing—without making it his mission—he rebuked those who cannot (or will not) differentiate incurable diseases, of which there are many, from untreatable patients, of which there are few.

50   Nelson was a great scientist and an indomitable man. He took on all of life's challenges, personal and professional, with vigor and courage. But when he learned that he had Lou Gehrig's disease, he was shaken and responded with a most natural discouragement. "I'd rather die than be helpless," he said several times to his doctors. Yet he proved willing to try the assistance they offered him at each of the bad patches in his course, so that he could continue to enjoy what remained despite his illness. He had neurologists aiding him with his growing weakness, and he had psychiatrists and psychologists ready to assist him when he was tormented by his prospects.

51   He had bad times. They came mostly when some partial surrender to the disease was required—accepting a wheelchair, retreating to bed, undergoing a tracheostomy to facilitate breathing—but after each pro-

cedure, and despite its implicit indication that his condition was progressing, he recovered his cheer as he found himself more comfortable and able to continue his work with students and colleagues and his life with his family.

Like Stephen Hawking, Nelson toward the end made use of computers to communicate and work. This permitted him to edit a major journal in neuropsychology, even when he could move only one finger and then only one toe. With these small movements he used E-mail to write to colleagues everywhere—usually on professional matters, but also to transmit amusing academic gossip.

Eventually, Nelson lost all his strength. He was left with only eye-blinking signals, breathing with the help of a machine. Then he asked his doctors, with his family around him, that the ventilator cease breathing for him. This was done, and on a weekend he slipped into a coma and died—thirty-four months after his symptoms began.

Nelson, his family, and his doctors had achieved much together. They fought to enable him to sustain purposeful life as long as possible. They weathered distressing, powerfully painful portions of his clinical course. The doctors never suggested a poison to shorten his life. When there was still something to do, they encouraged him to try to do it and helped allay his reluctance at the prospect. And in the end they surrendered to the illness without betraying their mission or letting contemporary technology drag them along.

It was grim. Everyone who knew him was saddened to think that Nelson had to suffer so. But everyone also was struck by how he overcame the disease by staying purposeful, lively, and wittily intelligent right through to the end, teaching much to all of us.

I tell this story because many believe that permitting a progressive infirmity to continue right out to its natural end is cruel and pointless. It certainly is tough. Any gains need to be identified. In fact, the gains for Nelson Butters were several.

Most obvious among them was the continuation of Nelson's work as a scientist, an editor, and a teacher for many months, despite his illness. This was no trivial gain, for he was an inventive scientist with deep insight into his discipline. He continued to function effectively and to enjoy his work and the accomplishments of his students.

Another gain was an extended duration of Nelson's company to his family and his friends. Again, no trivial matter, for he was a lovable person. One of his daughters decided to help nurse him through his trials, and after his death, reflecting on all she had seen and done, she decided to take up a career in nursing incapacitated people.

Finally, there was the appreciation—to the point of amazement—on the part of his doctors of the value he fashioned from their efforts to help him. They told me how he had taken what they offered and made more of it—more than they expected and more in the form of continuing work and personal life—than they thought could be achieved. This was as true of the neurologists who offered means to offset his physical impairments as it was of the psychiatrists who at times of particular discouragement helped him keep going.

60   These gains were made easier because Nelson was such a good man and had such a good family to support him. Yet I sensed the awe felt by the doctors themselves for what had been accomplished in the end. Almost despite themselves and their own feelings about this awful disease, they had been partners with Nelson in a great achievement. They had carried out excellently the task set before doctors—help the patient encounter and resist the chaos of disease for as long as possible—and thus preserve the purposeful character of life to its end.

61   In Nelson's life a set of interwoven but distinct purposes—husband, father, teacher, scientist—were sustained by him with the help of several doctors. And this happened despite the depredations of a crushing disease and the recurrent waves of discouragement that naturally accompany the loss of vitality and the realization of impending death.

62   But there was something more in Nelson's story. For all that he was surrounded by devoted nurses, technicians, family, and physicians, death came to him alone just as it will to each of us. Its approach confronts us all with the challenge to decide what moves us, what matters most, what we love. Nelson loved life. He wanted as much of it as he could have. Through this love he won a victory over death—for himself, for his family, for all who knew him.

63   This is really what distinguishes him from Dr. Kevorkian, his sad victims, and those who support his cause. None of them love life the way Nelson did—not enough, certainly, to work hard and suffer much for it, not enough to appreciate it throughout its course, when it flickers just as much as when it glows. And certainly not enough to realize that sometimes we need help to protect it so that we don't throw it away.

64   To be on the side of life provides a source of sanity. Be on the side of life and your course is clear, your efforts concentrated, the rules coherent. Bad patches can then be overcome, and even bad luck such as befell my friend Nelson Butters can be turned into something good. Be on the side of death and things fall apart, chaos reigns, and the fearful passions evoked by conflicting aims make malice, misdirection, sentiment, and compassion all look the same.

65   One can think of ways to combat the deadly convergence of madnesses in Michigan and to deter the spread of this local epidemic to other regions of our country. The suicidal patients certainly should be treated for their depressive vulnerabilities by doctors able to assist them with their underlying illnesses. Dr. Kevorkian, the agent of their extinction, should be stopped by whatever means the state has at its disposal to stay dangerous men. And the people of Michigan should be

taught about the capacities of modern medicine. With this information, the hope is, they will emerge from their anxious confusions, accept mortality for what it is rather than for what they imagine, and, at last, end their support for this insanity.

★ Meaning and Understanding

1. Who is Dr. Jack Kevorkian? Why is McHugh writing about him?

2. The title of this selection suggests that the author believes there is an "epidemic" running rampant in American society. What is this "epidemic"? How is the use of this word particularly appropriate, given the subject matter of the essay?

3. The writer mentions Lou Gehrig's disease several times. Who was Lou Gehrig and why is the disease named after him? Who is Stephen Hawking?

4. What distinction does the writer make between "symptomatic depression" and "demoralization"? Between "overvalued ideas" and "delusions"?

5. What does McHugh propose as a treatment for mood disorder?

6. Why does the writer consider Kevorkian "certifiably insane"?

7. The writer describes medicine, along with navigation, architecture, and economics, as "one of the practical arts." What is a "practical art"? How, if at all, do you think medicine is essentially different from the other "practical arts"?

★ Techniques and Strategies

1. Who do you think is the intended audience for this piece? What evidence is there in the essay to support your choice?

2. Where do you think the writer comes closest to stating the thesis of the essay? What is the thesis?

3. In paragraph 44 McHugh recounts the story of the racehorse Cavonnier. What do you think is the point of the story? How does it help you understand his thesis?

4. How do the opening and closing paragraphs successfully frame the essay?

5. We are told in paragraph 48 that Nelson Butters "was one of America's most distinguished neuropsychologists of the last twenty-five years." Given his illness, how is this information useful to our understanding of McHugh' point? Does it in any way weaken his point? Explain.

★ *Speaking of Values*

1. The writer asserts that "anyone who says he does not fear dying—and all the pain and suffering tied to it—has probably not experienced much in life." Do you agree with this statement? Why or why not?

2. McHugh argues that the desire for suicide stems from a psychological disorder, not a physical one. That is, people who suffer from physical ailments do not necessarily look to suicide for relief, but rather suicide is a consequence of depression. What do you think about the interpretation? What evidence does McHugh provide to support his point?

3. What is a "right"? How is it conferred? How does it differ from an "obligation"?

4. The writer asserts that "the aim of medicine cannot simply be to prevent suffering." Do you agree? Why or why not?

5. McHugh seems to be arguing that disease, as a part of life, should not be construed as a signal to terminate life, even when the burdens of the disease seem overwhelming: "Life with dignity—not death with dignity—is what doctors aim for in their practice and in their science." But who is to decide when "life with dignity" is no longer possible? How does McHugh deal with this question? How would you deal with it? Explain.

6. Look at the "gains" for Nelson Butters that McHugh identifies (paragraphs 57–59). Are you persuaded that they were worth his sufferings? Why or why not? Support your point of view.

★ *Values Conversation*

Most of us understandably do not like to think about our own deaths or the deaths of dear ones. Yet as medicine becomes more and more capable of sustaining life, we may find it necessary to do so. In other words, we may have to decide under what circumstances we no longer wish to have life sustained by medical means. Form groups and discuss the circumstances under which you or a close relative or friend might want to die with no further medical intervention. Try to avoid simple generalities such as "I don't want to suffer" or "I don't want pain." Rather, make an attempt to construct a coherent rationale for your decision, one that is clear and could be understood even if you yourself were rendered incapable of communicating with your doctors or family.

★ *Writing about Values*

1. Do you think people have a "right" to take their own lives? To whom does one's "life" belong? Write a paper in which you argue for or

against the principle of a "right" to suicide. Be sure to address the question of who "owns" a person's life.

2. The question of whether doctors should prolong life even if the patient cannot be cured is a very controversial one today. What do you think? Write a paper discussing the pros and cons of the issue. Be sure to make clear your own point of view.

3. Many hospitals and medical facilities now employ "bioethics consultants," usually philosophers, as advisors on serious medical questions such as whether or not to sustain artificially the life of a terminally ill patient. What is your view on the use of a thoughtful committee of people to determine whether or not a person should live or die? Write an essay to address the issue.

Eudora Welty

A Visit of Charity

Eudora Welty was born in Jackson, Mississippi, in 1909, where she still lives. Welty, best known as a short story writer and novelist, has also earned acclaim for two critical studies, *Place in Fiction* (1958) and *Three Papers on Fiction* (1962). Her fiction includes *A Curtain of Green and Other Stories* (1941), *The Robber Bridegroom* (1942), *Delta Wedding* (1946), *The Golden Apples* (1949), and *The Optimist's Daughter* (1972). In this short story Welty shows a young girl performing a required act of charity.

———— ★ ————

1   It was mid-morning—a very cold, bright day. Holding a potted plant before her, a girl of fourteen jumped off the bus in front of the Old Ladies' Home, on the outskirts of town. She wore a red coat, and her straight yellow hair was hanging down loose from the pointed white cap all the little girls were wearing that year. She stopped for a moment beside one of the prickly dark shrubs with which the city had beautified the Home, and then proceeded slowly toward the building, which was of whitewashed brick and reflected the winter sunlight like a block of ice. As she walked vaguely up the steps she shifted the small pot from hand to hand; then she had to set it down and remove her mittens before she could open the heavy door.

2   "I'm a Campfire Girl. . . . I have to pay a visit to some old lady," she told the nurse at the desk. This was a woman in a white uniform who looked as if she were cold; she had close-cut hair which stood up on the very top of her head exactly like a sea wave. Marian, the little girl, did not tell her that this visit would give her a minimum of only three points in her score.

3   "Acquainted with any of our residents?" asked the nurse. She lifted one eyebrow and spoke like a man.

4   "With any old ladies? No—but—that is, any of them will do," Marian stammered. With her free hand she pushed her hair behind her ears, as she did when it was time to study Science.

5   The nurse shrugged and rose. "You have a nice *multiflora cineraria* there," she remarked as walked ahead down the hall of closed doors to pick out an old lady.

6   There was loose, bulging linoleum on the floor. Marian felt as if she were walking on the waves, but the nurse paid no attention to it. There was a smell in the hall like the interior of a clock. Everything was silent

until, behind one of the doors, an old lady of some kind cleared her throat like a sheep bleating. This decided the nurse. Stopping in her tracks, she first extended her arm, bent her elbow, and leaned forward from the hips—all to examine the watch strapped to her wrist; then she gave a loud double-rap on the door.

"There are two in each room," the nurse remarked over her shoulder. 7

"Two what?" asked Marian without thinking. The sound like a 8
sheep's bleating almost made her turn around and run back.

One old woman was pulling the door open in short, gradual jerks, 9
and when she saw the nurse a strange smile forced her old face danger-
ously awry. Marian, suddenly propelled by the strong, impatient arm of the nurse, saw next the sideface of another old woman, even older, who was lying flat in bed with a cap on and and a counterpane drawn up to her chin.

"Visitor," said the nurse, and after one more shove she was off up 10
the hall.

Marian stood tongue-tied; both hands held the potted plant. The 11
old woman, still with that terrible, square smile (which was a smile of welcome) stamped on her bony face, a waiting.... Perhaps she said something. The old woman in bed said nothing at all, and she did not look around.

Suddenly Marian saw a hand, quick as a bird claw, reach up in the 12
air and pluck the white cap off her head. At the same time, another claw to match drew her all the way into the room, and the next moment the door closed behind her.

"My, my, my," said the old lady at her side. 13

Marian stood enclosed by a bed, a washstand and a chair; the tiny 14
room had altogether too much furniture. Everything smelled wet— even the bare floor. She held onto the back of the chair, which was wicker and felt soft and damp. Her heart beat more and more slowly, her hands got colder and colder, and she could not hear whether the old women were saying anything or not. She could not see them very clearly. How dark it was! The window shade was down, and the only door was shut. Marian looked at the ceiling.... It was like being caught in a robbers' cave, just before one was murdered.

"Did you come to be our little girl for a while?" the first robber 15
asked.

Then something was snatched from Marian's hand—the little pot- 16
ted plant.

"Flowers!" screamed the old woman. She stood holding the pot in 17
an undecided way. "Pretty flowers," she added.

Then the old woman in bed cleared her throat and spoke. "They are 18
not pretty," she said, still without looking around, but very distinctly.

Marian suddenly pitched against the chair and sat down in it. 19

20   "Pretty flowers," the first old woman insisted. "Pretty—pretty...."

21   Marian wished she had the little pot back for just a moment—she had forgotten to look at the plant herself before giving it away. What did it look like?

22   "Stinkweeds," said the other old woman sharply. She had a bunchy white forehead and red eyes like a sheep. Now she turned them toward Marian. The fogginess seemed to rise in her throat again, and she bleated. "Who—are—you?"

23   To her surprise, Marian could not remember her name. "I'm a Campfire Girl," she said finally.

24   "Watch out for the germs," said the old woman like a sheep, not addressing anyone.

25   "One came out last month to see us," said the first old woman.

26   A sheep or a germ? wondered Marian dreamily, holding onto the chair.

27   "Did not!" cried the other old woman.

28   "Did so! Read to us out of the Bible, and we enjoyed it!" screamed the first.

29   "Who enjoyed it!" said the woman in bed. Her mouth was unexpectedly small and sorrowful, like a pet's.

30   "We enjoyed it," insisted the other. "You enjoyed it—I enjoyed it."

31   "We all enjoyed it," said Marian, without realizing that she had said a word.

32   The first old woman had just finished putting the potted plant high, high on the top of the wardrobe, where it could hardly be seen from below. Marian wondered how she had ever succeeded in placing it there, how she could ever have reached so high.

33   "You mustn't pay any attention to old Addie," she now said to the little girl. "She's ailing today."

34   "Will you shut your mouth?" said the woman in bed. "I am not."

35   "You're a story."

36   "I can't stay but a minute—really, I can't," said Marian suddenly. She looked down at the wet floor and thought that if she were sick in here they would have to let her go.

37   With much to-do the first old woman sat down in a rocking chair—still another piece of furniture!—and began to rock. With the fingers of one hand she touched a very dirty cameo pin on her chest. "What do you do at school?" she asked.

38   "I don't know..." said Marian. She tried to think but she could not.

39   "Oh, but the flowers are beautiful," the old woman whispered. She seemed to rock faster and faster; Marian did not see how anyone could rock so fast.

40   "Ugly," said the woman in bed.

41   "If we bring flowers—" Marian began, and then fell silent. She had almost said that if Campfire Girls brought flowers to the Old Ladies'

Home, the visit would count one extra point, and if they took a Bible with them on the bus and read it to the old ladies, it counted double. But the old woman had not listened, anyway; she was rocking and watching the other one, who watched back from the bed.

"Poor Addie is ailing. She has to take medicine—see?" she said, pointing a horny finger at a row of bottles on the table, and rocking so that her black comfort shoes lifted off the floor like a little child's.   42

"I am no more sick than you are," said the woman in bed.   43

"Oh, yes you are!"   44

"I just got more sense than you have, that's all," said the other old woman, nodding her head.   45

"That's only the contrary way she talks when *you all* come," said the first old lady with sudden intimacy. She stopped the rocker with a neat pat of her feet and leaned toward Marian. Her hand reached over—it felt like a petunia leaf, clinging and just a little sticky.   46

"Will you hush! Will you hush!" cried the other one.   47

Marian leaned back rigidly in her chair.   48

"When I was a little girl like you, I went to school and all," said the old woman in the same intimate, menacing voice. "Not here—another town...."   49

"Hush!"said the sick woman. "You never went to school. You never came and you never went. You never were anything—only here. You never were born! You don't know anything. Your head is empty, your heart and hands and your old black purse are all empty, even that little old box you brought with you you brought empty—you showed it to me. And yet you talk, talk, talk, talk, talk all the time until I think I'm losing my mind! Who are you? You're a stranger—a perfect stranger! Don't you know you're a stranger? Is it possible that they have actually done a thing like this to anyone—sent them in a stranger to talk, and rock and tell away her whole long rigmarole? Do they seriously suppose that I'll be able to keep it up, day in, day out, night in, night out, living in the same room with a terrible old woman—forever?"   50

Marian saw the old woman's eyes grow bright and turn toward her. This old woman was looking at her with despair and calculation in her face. Her small lips suddenly dropped apart, and exposed a half circle of false teeth with tan gums.   51

"Come here, I want to tell you something," she whispered. "Come here!"   52

Marian was trembling, and her heart nearly stopped beating altogether for a moment.   53

"Now, now Addie." said the first old woman. "That's not polite. Do you know what's really the matter with old Addie today?" She, too, looked at Marian; one of her eyelids drooped low.   54

"The matter?" the child repeated stupidly. "What's the matter with her?"   55

56　　"Why, she's mad because it's her birthday!" said the first old woman, beginning to rock again and giving a little crow as though she had answered her own riddle.

57　　"It is not, it is not!" screamed the old woman in bed. "It is not my birthday, no one knows when that is but myself, and will you please be quiet and say nothing more, or I'll go straight out of my mind!" She turned her eyes toward Marian again, and presently she said in the soft, foggy voice, "When the worst comes to the worst, I ring this bell, and the nurse comes." One of her hands was drawn out from under the patched counterpane—a thin little hand with enormous black freckles. With a finger which would not hold still she pointed at a little bell on the table among the bottles.

58　　"How old are you?" Marian breathed. Now she could see the old woman in bed very closely and plainly, and very abruptly, from all sides, as in dreams. She wondered about her—she wondered for a moment as though there was nothing else in the world to wonder about. It was the first time such things had happened to Marian.

59　　"I won't tell!"

60　　The old face on the pillow, where Marian was bending over it, slowly gathered and collapsed. Soft whimpers came out of the small open mouth. It was a sheep that she sounded like—a little lamb. Marian's face drew very close, the yellow hair hung forward.

61　　"She's crying!" She turned a bright, burning face up to the first old woman.

62　　"That's Addie for you," the old woman said spitefully.

63　　Marian jumped up and moved toward the door. For the second time, the claw almost touched her hair, but it was not quick enough. The little girl put her cap on.

64　　"Well, it was a real visit," said the old woman, following Marian through the doorway and all the way out into the hall. Then from behind she suddenly clutched the child with her sharp little fingers. In an affected, high-pitched whine she cried, "Oh, little girl, have you a penny to spare for a poor old woman that's not got anything of her own? We don't have a thing in the world—not a penny for candy—not a thing! Little girl, just a nickel—a penny—"

65　　Marian pulled violently against the old hands for a moment before she was free. Then she ran down the hall, without looking behind her and without looking at the nurse, who was reading *Field & Stream* at her desk. The nurse, after another triple motion to consult her wrist watch, asked automatically the question put to visitors in all institutions: "Won't you stay and have dinner with *us*?"

66　　Marian never replied. She pushed the heavy door open into the cold air and ran down the steps.

67　　Under the prickly shrub she stooped and quickly, without being seen, retrieved a red apple she had hidden there.

Her yellow hair under the white cap, her scarlet coat, her bare   68
knees all flashed in the sunlight as she ran to meet the big bus rocketing
through the street.

"Wait for me!" she shouted. As though at an imperial command,   69
the bus ground to a stop.

She jumped on and took a big bite out of the apple.   70

★ Meaning and Understanding

1. What is Marian's motive for visiting the Old Ladies' Home? What is the implication of her assertion that "I have to pay a visit to some old lady"?

2. What kind of person does Marian seem to be? The old ladies? How do you know?

3. How are the old ladies different? Explain the differences in their behaviors.

4. What is the main point of this story?

5. What does the old lady mean when she remarks to Marian about Addie's behavior: "That's only the contrary way she talks when *you all* come"?

6. Is it really Addie's birthday? If not, why does the other old woman say that it is?

★ Techniques and Strategies

1. Welty describes the Old Ladies' Home building as reflecting the "winter sunlight like a block of ice." Analyze this metaphor in terms of the action of the story. Why is it appropriate that the story takes place in the winter?

2. The writer describes the old women's hands as "bird claws" and uses other images of birds in the story. What does the bird imagery tell us about the characters?

3. How is Marian dressed for this visit? Is there anything about her ensemble which seems inappropriate to the occasion? Why or why not?

4. How does the nurse function in the story? Is there anything significant about her identifying the potted plant as "*multiflora cineraria*"? In reading *Field & Stream*? If so, what is it?

5. Comment on Marian's attitude as the story progresses? In what ways does she change?

6. What does the title mean? What elements of irony can you identify in the title? Where in the story do you find other examples of irony?

★ *Speaking of Values*

1. Is what Marian offers real charity or is it something else? What comment about the value of charity does Welty's story make?

2. What is the purpose behind organizations and groups requiring their members to make visits to hospitals and nursing homes? Do you think it is a good practice? Why or why not? What does Welty think? In what ways is required charity a linchpin of our culture's values? How does Marian demonstrate the failings of mandatory charity?

3. What commentary does the story seem to provide about "Old Ladies' Homes"? Do such places, or places like them, exist today? Where? What purpose do they serve?

4. Describe the relation between the two old women whom Marian visits. How do you explain this relation?

5. What does the relation between the two old women say about people living together under a heath care system's rules? About friendship and acquaintanceship?

★ *Values Conversation*

Form groups and identify the elements that you consider essential for true charity. The notion of charity lies deep in the American values system, starting, of course, with support for charity in the Bible and extending into many areas of our culture's mores. Like the Campfire Girls, many groups and organizations require charity of members; many schools now make students perform mandatory community service; and our tax code allows deductions for charitable gifts. What is your group's view of charity in American culture? Report your views to the whole class.

★ *Writing about Values*

1. Write a definition of *charity*. Include the advantages and disadvantages of the concept as a key element in American society.

2. What are your views on "required volunteerism"—a relatively new concept in American society, and, at the very least, a verbal paradox. Should people like Marion and millions of schoolchildren over the country be required to volunteer for charitable work? Why or why not?

3. Different societies may have different ways of dealing with old people. If you were designing a set of guidelines for how a civilized society should treat its old people, what would it be? Write an essay to address this issue.

Suzanne Gordon

What Nurses Stand For

Born in New York City in 1945 and educated at Cornell and Johns Hopkins, Suzanne Gordon has been a teacher, a reporter, and a writer. Among her books are *Black Mesa: The Angel of Death* (1973), *Lonely in America* (1975), and, most recently, *Life Support: Three Nurses on the Front Lines* (1997). In this essay she explains the role of the nurse in caring for the sick.

———— ★ ————

At four o'clock on a Friday afternoon the hematology-oncology clinic at Boston's Beth Israel Hospital is quiet. Paddy Connelly and Frances Kiel, two of the eleven nurses who work in the unit, sit at the nurses' station—an island consisting of two long desks equipped with phones, which ring constantly, and computers. They are encircled by thirteen blue-leather reclining chairs, in which patients may spend only a brief time, for a short chemotherapy infusion, or an entire afternoon, to receive more complicated chemotherapy or blood products. At one of the chairs Nancy Rumplik is starting to administer chemotherapy to a man in his mid-fifties who has colon cancer. 1

Rumplik is forty-two and has been a nurse on the unit for seven years. She stands next to the wan-looking man and begins to hang the intravenous drugs that will treat his cancer. As the solution drips through the tubing and into his vein, she sits by his side, watching to make sure that he has no adverse reaction. 2

Today she is acting as triage nurse–the person responsible for patients who walk in without an appointment, for patients who call with a problem but can't reach their primary nurse, for the smooth functioning of the unit, and, of course, for responding to any emergencies. Rumplik's eyes thus constantly sweep the room to check on the other patients. She focuses for a moment on a heavy-set African-American woman in her mid-forties, dressed in a pair of navy slacks and a brightly colored shirt, who is sitting in the opposite corner. Her sister, who is younger and heavier, is by her side. The patient seems fine, so Rumplik returns her attention to the man next to her. Several minutes later she looks up again, checks the woman, and stiffens. There is now a look of anxiety on the woman's face. Rumplik, leaning forward in her chair, stares at her. 3

"What's she getting?" she mouths to Kiel. 4

5   Looking at the patient's chart, Frances Kiel names a drug that has been known to cause severe allergic reactions. In that brief moment, as the two nurses confer, the woman suddenly clasps her chest. Her look of anxiety turns to terror. Her mouth opens and shuts in silent panic. Rumplik leaps up from her chair, as do Kiel and Connelly, and sprints across the room.

6   "I can't breathe," the woman sputters when Rumplik is at her side. Her eyes bulging, she grasps Rumplik's hand tightly; her eyes roll back as her head slips to the side. Realizing that the patient is having an anaphylactic reaction (her airway is swelling and closing), Rumplik immediately turns a small spigot on the IV tubing to shut off the drip. At the same instant Kiel calls a physician and the emergency-response team. By this time the woman is struggling for breath.

7   Kiel slips an oxygen mask over the woman's head and wraps a blood-pressure cuff around her arm. Connelly administers an antihistamine to stop the allergic reaction, and cortisone to decrease the inflammation blocking her airway. The physician, an oncology fellow, arrives within minutes. He assesses the situation and then notices the woman's sister standing paralyzed, watching the scene. "Get out of here!" he commands sharply. The woman moves away as if she had been slapped.

8   Just as the emergency team arrives, the woman's breathing returns to normal and the look of terror fades from her face. Taking Rumplik's hand again, she looks up and says, "I couldn't breathe. I just couldn't breathe." Rumplik gently explains that she has had an allergic reaction to a drug and reassures her that it has stopped.

9   After a few minutes, when the physician is certain that the patient is stable, he and the emergency-response team walk out of the treatment area, but the nurses continue to comfort the shaken woman. Rumplik then crosses the room to talk with her male patient, who is ashen-faced at this reminder of the potentially lethal effects of the medication that he and others are receiving. Responding to his unspoken fears, Rumplik says quietly, "It's frightening to see something like that. But it's under control."

10   He nods silently, closes his eyes, and leans his head back against the chair. Rumplik goes over to the desk where Connelly and Kiel are breathing a joint sigh of relief. One of the nurses comments on the physician's treatment of the patient's sister. "Did you hear him? He just told her to get out."

11   Wincing with distress, Rumplik looks around for the sister. She goes into the waiting room, where the woman is sitting in a corner, looking bereft and frightened. Rumplik sits down next to her, explains what happened, and suggests that the patient could probably benefit from some overnight company. Then she adds, "I'm sorry the doctor talked to you like that. You know, it's a very anxious time for all of us."

At this gesture of respect and recognition the woman, who has ev-   12
ery strike—race, class, and sex—against her when dealing with elite
white professionals in this downtown hospital, smiles solemnly. "I understand. Thank you."

Nancy Rumplik returns to her patient.   13

I Am Ready to Die

It is 6:00 P.M. Today Jeannie Chaisson, a clinical nurse specialist, arrived   14
at her general medical unit at seven in the morning and cared for patients until three-thirty in the afternoon. At home now, she makes herself a pot of coffee and sits down in the living room, cradling her cup.
Just as she is shedding the strain of the day, the phone rings.

It's the husband of one of Chaisson's patients—a sixty-three-year-   15
old woman suffering from terminal multiple myeloma, a cancer of the
bone marrow. When Chaisson left the hospital, she knew the family
was in crisis. Having endured the cancer for several years, the woman
is exhausted from the pain, from the effects of the disease and failed
treatments, and from the pain medication on which she has become increasingly dependent. Chaisson knows she is ready to let death take
her. But her husband and daughter are not.

Now the crisis that was brewing has exploded. Chaisson's caller is   16
breathless, frantic with anxiety, as he relays his wife's pleas. She wants
to die. She is prepared to die. She says the pain is too much. "You've
got to do something," he implores Chaisson. "Keep her going—stop
her from doing this."

Chaisson knows that it is indeed time for her to do something—but,   17
sadly, not what the anguished husband wishes. "Be calm," she tells him.
"Please hold on. We'll all talk together. I'm coming right in." Leaving a
note for her family, she gets into her car and drives back to the hospital.

When Chaisson walks into the patient's room, she is not surprised   18
by what she finds. Seated next to the bed is the visibly distraught husband. Behind him the patient's twenty-five-year-old daughter paces
in front of a picture window with a view across Boston. The patient
is lying in a state somewhere between consciousness and coma,
shrunken by pain and devoured by the cancer's progress. Chaisson
has seen scenes like this many times before in her fifteen-year career
as a nurse.

As she looks at the woman, she can understand why her husband   19
and her daughter are so resistant. They remember her as she first appeared to Chaisson, three years ago—a bright, feisty sixty-year-old
woman, her nails tapered and polished, her hair sleekly sculpted into a
perfect silver pouf. Chaisson remembers the day, during the first of
many admissions to the unit, when she asked the woman if she wanted
her hair washed.

20   The woman replied in astonishment, "I do not wash my hair. I have it done. Once a week."

21   Now her hair is unkempt, glued to her face with sweat. Her nails are no longer polished. Their main work these days is to dig into her flesh when the pain becomes too acute. The disease has slowly bored into her bones. Simply to stand is painful and could even be an invitation to a fracture. Her pelvis is disintegrating. The nurses have inserted an indwelling catheter, because having a bedpan slipped underneath her causes agony, but she has developed a urinary-tract infection. Because removing the catheter will make the infection easier to treat, doctors suggest this course of action. Yet if the catheter is removed, the pain will be intolerable each time she has to urinate.

22   When the residents and interns argued that failure to treat the infection could mean the patient would die, Chaisson responded, "She's dying anyway. It's her disease that is killing her, not a urinary-tract infection." They relented.

23   Now the family must confront this reality.

24   Chaisson goes to the woman's bed and gently wakes her. Smiling at her nurse, the woman tries to muster the energy to explain to her husband and her daughter that the pain is too great and she can no longer attain that delicate balance, so crucial to dying patients, between fighting off pain and remaining alert for at least some of the day. Only when she is practically comatose from drugs can she find relief.

25   "I am ready to die," she whispers weakly.

26   Her husband and daughter contradict her—there is still hope.

27   Jeannie Chaisson stands silent during this exchange and then intervenes, asking them to try to take in what their loved one is telling them. Then she repeats the basic facts about the disease and its course. "At this point there is no treatment for the disease," she explains, "but there is treatment for the pain, to make the patient comfortable and ease her suffering." Chaisson spends another hour sitting with them, answering their questions and allowing them to feel supported. Finally the family is able to heed the patient's wishes—leave the catheter in and do not resuscitate her if she suffers a cardiac arrest. Give her enough morphine to stop the pain. Let her go.

28   The woman visibly relaxes, lies back, and closes her eyes. Chaisson approaches the husband and the daughter, with whom she has worked for so long, and hugs them both. Then she goes out to talk to the medical team.

29   Before leaving for home, Chaisson again visits her patient. The husband and the daughter have gone for a cup of coffee. The woman is quiet. Chaisson sits down at the side of her bed and takes her hand. The woman opens her eyes. Too exhausted to say a word, she merely squeezes the nurse's hand in gratitude. For the past three years Chais-

son has helped her to fight her disease and live as long as possible. Now she is here to help her die.

The Endangered RN

When we hear the word "hospital," technology and scientific invention 30 spring to mind: mechanical ventilators, dialysis machines, intravenous pumps, biomedical research, surgery, medication. These, many believe, are the life supports in our health-care system. This technology keeps people alive, and helps to cure and heal them.

In fact there are other, equally important life supports in our 31 health-care system: the 2.2 million nurses who make up the largest profession in health care, the profession with the highest percentage of women, and the second largest profession after teaching. These women and men weave a tapestry of care, knowledge, and trust that is critical to patients' survival.

Nancy Rumplik and Jeannie Chaisson have between them more 32 than a quarter century's experience caring for the sick. They work in an acute-care hospital, one of Harvard Medical School's teaching hospitals. Beth Israel not only is known for the quality of its patient care but also is world-renowned for the quality of its nursing staff and its institutional commitment to nursing.

The for-profit, market-driven health care that is sweeping the na- 33 tion is threatening this valuable group of professionals. To gain an advantage in the competitive new health-care marketplace, hospitals all over the country are trying to cut their costs. One popular strategy is to lay off nurses and replace them with lower-paid, less-skilled workers.

American hospitals already use 20 percent fewer nurses than their 34 counterparts in other industrialized countries. Nursing does provide attractive middle-income salaries. In 1992 staff nurses earned, on average, $33,000 a year. Clinical nurse specialists, who have advanced education and specialize in a particular field, earned an average of $41,000, and nurse practitioners, who generally have a master's degree and provide primary-care services, earned just under $44,000. Yet RN salaries and benefits altogether represent only about 16 percent of total hospital costs.

Nevertheless, nurses are a major target of hospital "restructuring" 35 plans, which in some cases have called for a reduction of 20 to 50 percent in registered nursing staff.

The process of job elimination, deskilling, and downgrading seri- 36 ously erodes opportunities for stable middle-class employment in nursing as in other industries. However, as the late David Gordon documented in his book *Fat and Mean: The Corporate Squeeze of Working Americans and the Myth of Managerial "Downsizing,"* reduced "head counts" among production or service workers don't necessarily mean that higher-level jobs (and the pay and perquisites associated with them) are being chopped as well. In fact, Gordon argued, many headline-grabbing exercises in corporate cost-cutting leave executive compensation untouched, along with other forms of managerial "bloat."

37   Even in this era of managed-care limits on physicians' compensation, nurses' pay is relatively quite modest. And the managers of care themselves—particularly hospital administrators and health-maintenance-organization executives—are doing so well that even doctors look underpaid by comparison.

38   According to the business magazine *Modern Healthcare's* 1996 physician-compensation report, the average salary in family practice is $128,096, in internal medicine $135,755, in oncology $164,621, in anesthesiology $193,242, and in general surgery $199,342. Some specialists earn more than a million dollars a year.

39   A survey conducted in 1995 by *Hospitals & Health Networks*, the magazine of the American Hospital Association, found that the average total cash compensation for hospital CEOs was $188,500. In large hospitals the figure went up to $280,900, and in for-profit chains far higher. In 1995, at age forty-three, Richard Scott, the CEO of Columbia/Healthcare Corporation, received a salary of $2,093,844. He controlled shares in Columbia/HCA worth $359.5 million.

40   In 1994 compensation for the CEOs of the seven largest for-profit HMOs averaged $7 million. Even those in the not-for-profit sector of insurance earn startling sums: in 1995 John Burry Jr., the chairman and CEO of Ohio Blue Cross and Blue Shield, was paid $1.6 million. According to a report in *Modern Healthcare*, a proposed merger with the for-profit Columbia/HCA would have paid him $3 million "for a decade-long no-compete contract.... [and] up to $7 million for two consulting agreements."

41   At the other end of the new health-care salary spread are "unlicensed assistive personnel" (UAPs), who are now being used instead of nurses. They usually have little background in health care and only rudimentary training. Yet UAPs may insert catheters, read EKGs, suction tracheotomy tubes, change sterile dressings, and perform other traditional nursing functions. To keep patients from becoming unduly alarmed about—or even aware of—this development, some hospitals now prohibit nurses from wearing any badges that identify them as RNs. Thus everyone at the bedside is some kind of generic "patient-care technician"—regardless of how much or how little training and experience she or he has.

42   In some health-care facilities other nonprofessional staff—janitors, housekeepers, security guards, and aides—are also being "cross-trained" and transformed into "multi-skilled" workers who can be assigned to nursing duties. One such employee was so concerned about

the impact of this on patient care that he recently wrote a letter to Timothy McCall, M.D., a critic of multi-skilling, after reading a magazine article the latter had written on the subject.

> I am an employee of a 95-bed, long-term care facility. My position is that of a security guard. Ninety-five percent of my job consists of maintenance, housekeeping, admitting persons into clinical lab to pick-up & leave specimens. Now a class, 45 minutes, is being given so employees can feed, give bedpans & move patients. My expertise is in law enforcement & security, 25 years. I am not trained or licensed in patient care, maintenance, lab work, etc.... This scares me. Having untrained, unlicensed people performing jobs, in my opinion, is dangerous.

Training of RN replacements is indeed almost never regulated by 43 state licensing boards. There are no minimum requirements governing the amount of training that aides or cross-trained workers must have before they can be redeployed to do various types of nursing work. Training periods can range from a few hours to six weeks. One 1994 study cited in a 1996 report by the Institute of Medicine on nursing staffing found that

> 99 percent of the hospitals in California reported less than 120 hours of on-the-job training for newly hired ancillary nursing personnel. Only 20 percent of the hospitals required a high school diploma. The majority of hospitals (59 percent) provided less than 20 hours of classroom instruction and 88 percent provided 40 hours or less of instruction time.

Because the rapidly accelerating UAP trend is so new, its impact 44 on patient care has not yet been fully documented. However, in a series of major studies over the past twenty years researchers have directly linked higher numbers and greater qualifications of registered nurses on hospital units to lower mortality rates and decreased lengths of hospital stay. Reducing the number of expert nurses in the hospital, the community, and homes endangers patients' lives and wastes scarce resources. Choosing to save money by reducing nursing care aggravates the impersonality of a medical system that tends to turn human beings into their diseases and the doctors who care for them into sophisticated clinical machines. When they're sick, patients do not ask only what pills they should take or what operations they should have. They are preoccupied with questions such as Why me? Why now? Nurses are there through this day-by-day, minute-by-minute attack on the soul. They know that for the patient not only a sick or infirm body but also a life, a family, a community, a society, needs to heal.

Media Stereotypes

45   Although nurses help us to live and die, in the public depiction of
health care patients seem to emerge from hospitals without ever having benefited from their assistance. Whether patients are treated in an
emergency room in a few short hours or on a critical-care unit for
months on end, we seem to assume that physicians are responsible for
all the successes—and failures—in our medical system. In fact, we
seem to believe that they are responsible not only for all of the curing
but also for much of the caring.

46   Nurses remain shadowy figures moving mysteriously in the background. In television series they often appear as comic figures. On TV's
short-lived *Nightingales,* on the sitcom *Nurses,* and on the medical
drama *Chicago Hope* nurses are far too busy pining after doctors or racing off to aerobics classes to care for patients.

47   *ER* gives nurses more prominence than many other hospital
shows, but doctors on *ER* are constantly barking out commands to perform the simplest duties—get a blood pressure, call the OR—to experienced emergency-room nurses. In reality the nurses would have
thought of all this before the doctor arrived. In an emergency room as
busy and sophisticated as the one on *ER,* the first clinician a patient
sees is a triage nurse, who assesses the patient and dictates what he
needs, who will see him, and when. Experienced nurses will direct
less-experienced residents (and have sometimes done so on *ER*), suggesting a medication, a test, consultation with a specialist, or transfer to
the operating room. The great irony of *ER* is that Carol Hathaway, the
nurse in charge, is generally relegated to comforting a child or following a physician's orders rather than, as would occur in real life, helping
to direct the staff in saving lives.

48   Not only do doctors dominate on television but they are the focus
of most hard-news health-care coverage. Reporters rarely cover innovations in nursing, use nurses as sources, or report on nursing research.
The health-care experts whom reporters or politicians consult are invariably physicians, representatives of physician organizations, or policy specialists who tend to look at health care through the prism of
economics. "Who Counts in News Coverage of Health Care?," a 1990
study by the Women, Press & Politics Project, in Cambridge, Massachusetts, of health-care coverage in the *New York Times,* the *Los Angeles
Times,* and the *Washington Post,* found that out of 908 quotations that
appeared in three months' worth of health-care stories, nurses were the
sources for ten.

49   The revolution in health care has become big news. Occasionally
reporters will turn their attention to layoffs in nursing, but the story is
rarely framed as an important public-health issue. Rather, it is gener-

ally depicted as a labor-management conflict. Nursing unions are battling with management. Nurses say this; hospital administrators claim
that. Whom can you believe?

Worse still, this important issue may be couched in the stereotypes   50
of nursing or of women's work in general. A typical example appeared
on *NBC Nightly News* in September of 1994. The show ran a story that
involved a discussion of the serious problems, including deaths, resulting from replacing nurses with unlicensed aides. The anchor introduced it as "a new and controversial way of administering TLC."
Imagine how the issue would be characterized if 20 to 50 percent of
staff physicians were eliminated in thousands of American hospitals.
Would it not be front-page news, a major public-health catastrophe?
Patients all over the country would be terrified to enter hospitals. Yet
we learn about the equivalent in nursing with only a minimum of concern. If laying off thousands of nurses results only in the loss of a little
TLC, what difference does it make if an aide replaces a nurse?

Nursing is not simply a matter of TLC. It's a matter of life and   51
death. In hospitals, which employ 66 percent of America's nurses,
nurses monitor a patient's condition before, during, and after high-tech
medical procedures. They adjust medications, manage pain and the
side effects of treatment, and instantly intervene if a life-threatening
change occurs in a patient's condition.

In our high-tech medical system nurses care for the body and the   52
soul. No matter how sensitive, caring, and attentive physicians are,
nurses are often closer to the patient's needs and wishes. That's not because they are inherently more caring but because they spend far more
time with patients and are likely to know them better. This time and
knowledge allows them to save lives. Nurses also help people to adjust
to the lives they must live after they have recovered. And when death
can no longer be delayed, nurses help patients confront their own mortality with at least some measure of grace and dignity.

The Stigma of Sickness

There is another reason that nurses' work so often goes unrecognized.   53
Even some of the patients who have benefited the most from nurses'
critical care are unable to credit its importance publicly. Because nurses
observe and cushion what the physician and writer Oliver Sacks has
called human beings' falling "radically into sickness," they are a reminder of the pain, fear, vulnerability, and loss of control that adults
find difficult to tolerate and thus to discuss. A man who has had a successful heart bypass will boast of his surgeon's accomplishments to
friends at a dinner party. A woman who has survived a bone-marrow

transplant will extol her oncologist's triumph in the war against cancer to her friends and relatives. But what nurses did for those two patients will rarely be mentioned. It was a nurse who bathed the cardiac patient and comforted him while he struggled with the terror of possible death. It was a nurse who held the plastic dish under the cancer patient's lips as she was wracked with nausea, and who wiped a bottom raw from diarrhea. As Claire Fagin and Donna Diers have explained in an eloquent essay titled "Nursing as Metaphor," nurses stand for intimacy. They are our secret sharers. Even though they are lifelines during illness, when control is restored the residue of our anxiety and mortality clings to them like dust, and we flee the memory.

54   At one moment a nurse like Nancy Rumplik or Jeannie Chaisson may be involved in a sophisticated clinical procedure that demands expert judgment and advanced training in the latest technology. The next moment she may do what many people consider trivial or menial work, such as emptying a bedpan, giving a sponge bath, administering medication, or feeding or walking a patient.

55   The fact that nurses' work incorporates many so-called menial tasks that don't demand total attention is not a reason to replace nurses with less-skilled workers. This hands-on care allows nurses to explore patients' physical condition *and* to register their anxiety and fear. It allows them to save lives *and* to ascertain when it's appropriate to help patients die. It is only in watching nurses weave the tapestry of care that we grasp its integrity and its meaning for a society that too easily forgets the value of things that are beyond price.

★ Meaning and Understanding

1. What do you think is the main point of this selection?

2. How many nurses are there in this country? How, according to Gordon, are they threatened?

3. What points does the writer make about nurses' salaries? How much do chief executive officers (CEOs) of HMOs make?

4. What are "unlicensed assistive personnel" (UAPs)? How does the writer feel about them?

5. What do "deskilling" and "multiskilling" mean?

6. What does Gordon mean when she asserts that nurses "are our secret sharers?"

7. What reason does the writer give for nurses being "closer to the patient's needs and wishes"?

★ Techniques and Strategies

1. What is the purpose of the narrative that takes up the first eleven paragraphs? How does the story create a context for the rest of the essay?

2. Look at the sentences that conclude each of the first two sections. How are they similar? What effect is the writer trying to achieve?

3. Where do you think the writer comes closest to stating the thesis of the essay?

4. Why does Gordon concentrate on a discussion of money and salaries in the third section? How does that discussion alter the tone of the piece? Generally speaking, what is the overall tone of the essay?

5. What purpose is served by the writer's discussion of the ways in which the media portray nurses?

6. In the final paragraph the writer uses a tapestry metaphor. How does that metaphor help you understand her point?

★ Speaking of Values

1. How are doctors portrayed in this essay? Nurses? Do you think Gordon presents a balanced picture? Why or why not?

2. Nursing is a profession largely staffed by women. What does this fact contribute to the treatment nurses receive from the public? Do the relative incomes of doctors and nurses also play a role? Explain.

3. What is your view of "de-skilling"? Is it ethical? Why or why not? What does it imply about the perception of nursing as a profession?

4. Do you agree with the writer that we tend to associate doctors with healing and nurses with sickness? Why or why not?

5. The writer states that it is not at all unusual for nurses to "direct" doctors in regard to appropriate treatment? What is your reaction to this point? How does it affect your view of nurses? Of doctors?

★ Values Conversation

One of the key issues raised in this paper is the relation between appropriate health care and the financial support required to provide it. Form groups to discuss these issues. Should society bear the burden of treating its sick no matter what the cost? Should costs figure into medical decisions? Should we replace some health care professionals with lesser-skilled workers in order to spread financial resources? Why or why not?

★ *Writing about Values*

1. Write a paper about an experience, good or bad, that you may have had while in a hospital. You might have been a patient or just been visiting someone. In any case, be sure to explain why the experience was good or bad and what part doctors and nurses played in it.

2. Gordon makes much of the salaries of hospital administrators, doctors, and nurses in her essay. Do some research to find out how these salaries may have changed in relation to one another over the last 50 or so years. Also, find out what you can about "comparable worth" laws in various parts of the country. Then write a paper arguing whether or not you think nurses' salaries are "equitable." Be sure to consider the responsibilities of their jobs along with the responsibilities of doctors and administrators.

3. What are the ideal qualities of nurses, from your point of view? Write an essay in which you indicate the essential features of a nursing professional.

Burkhard Bilger

TV's Powerful Doctor Shows versus the HMO

Burkhard Bilger is a senior editor of *The Sciences* and a contributing editor of *Health* who writes on contemporary issues in medicine, health, and science. In this essay he explores the relations among popular television medical shows, health management organizations, and the medical establishment.

Tommy Wilmette slouches against a doorjamb with coiled reptilian calm, his hooded eyes searching for signs of weakness in his lumbering prey. A specialist in hostile takeovers, Wilmette has set his sights on a new victim: Chicago Hope Hospital. "You're too expensive; your surgeries aren't cost-effective," he tells one of the hospital's finest doctors, who also happens to be his ex-wife. "In fact, you're exactly the kind of doctor I'll be eliminating when we downsize."   1

Just across town and a couple of prime-time evenings later, para- 2
medics wheel a new patient into County General Hospital's emergency room, rattling off staccato symptoms: "Two-day-old male infant, full-term vaginal delivery, found cyanotic in his crib, resp 50, heart rate 160."

"When was he born?"   3
"Yesterday night."   4
"When did he come back from the hospital?"   5
"This morning."   6
"Somebody sent a mother and child home after one night?"   7
"Yup. Welcome to managed care."   8

Or, more precisely, welcome to managed care on television.   9

One show takes place in mood-lighted hallways and gleaming of- 10
fices, the other in a dumpy, hyperkinetic emergency room. One centers on smug superstar surgeons, the other on frazzled medical students and residents. One caters to patients who can afford the very best; the other is overrun by the health-care system's dispossessed: drug addicts, illegal immigrants, patients on Medicare or Medicaid or with no insurance at all. Yet for all their dissimilarities, *Chicago Hope* and *ER* share an affinity stronger than their Chicago setting and near-identical opening credits: both shows have a deep distrust, if not contempt, for the business of medicine.

11   As a doctor on *Chicago Hope* put it in an episode earlier this year: "When a bean counter tells me he has to pull up guidelines on a computer screen to see whether my wheezing patient qualifies for a tank of oxygen, I have a problem."

12   *ER*, Thursday nights at 10 on NBC, and *Chicago Hope*, Monday nights at 10 on CBS, have found rich pickings in the scorched landscape of health care reform. And the popularity of these two medical dramas gives them great power to shape public debate on the subject. Their characters battle health maintenance organizations and debate politicians over budget cuts. They show viewers, in graphic style, just what's at stake. "I would love to think that we have some kind of political impact," said John Tinker, executive producer of "Chicago Hope." "In fact, if Hillary is reading this, perhaps she can pick up a pen and write us an episode."

13   Chances are, Mr. Tinker would be disappointed with the First Lady's efforts. Both shows are often very good at portraying personal ethical conundrums—whether, for instance, a nurse should risk losing her job by telling her employers that she is HIV positive. But they do less well by health policy. Having scratched at a few inflamed issues— malpractice, the cost and danger of exotic treatments, and rationing limited health care dollars—the writers apply a balm of stubbornly old-fashioned family values: doctors are noble despite their failings; the more sophisticated the treatment the better, and a human life, however tenuous its hold, is worth saving at any cost.

14   Medical dramas have long held up a warped mirror to the country's health care system. In the 1960's, when shows like *Ben Casey* and *Dr. Kildare* flashed the American Medical Association's seal of approval during their credits, the A.M.A. was allowed to censor scripts. As a result, doctors were rarely shown making mistakes or driving fancy cars, much less cursing or having sex. "In a way it came back to bite them," said Joseph Turow, a professor of communication at the Annenberg School for Communications at the University of Pennsylvania and author of the book *Playing Doctor: Television, Storytelling and Medical Power.* "People would say, 'Gee, how come my physician isn't like Dr. Kildare?'"

15   These days, television's doctors make mistakes all the time, and sex is a weekly plot point. But to keep a flattering light on their souls, medical dramas keep the doctors poorer than ever. On *ER* they live in shabby flats, eat at greasy diners and ride motorcycles or the subway. They have been transformed, improbably, into antiheroes.

16   All of which gives a lopsided spin to any talk of health care costs. Greedy HMOs and greedy insurance companies are frequent whipping boys, but greedy doctors are rarely mentioned. For all their foibles, doctors are the people's saviors, not their extortionists. "I think that viewers get what they want from medicine on television," said Arthur Caplan, director of the Center for Bioethics at the University of Penn-

sylvania. "And there is a sort of schizophrenia about medicine. People will say that they are angry about health care, but doctors are still the modern priesthood."

The hospitals, by the same token, are like embattled fortresses,   17
their patients like villagers fleeing from rapacious invaders. Chicago Hope is under siege from entrepreneurs; County General was nearly shut down by a strapped county government, then had to cope with overflow from another hospital that got the ax instead. Although the writers usually get the details right, the bigger picture can be lost or misrepresented. At County General, there was no policy wonk on hand to mention that American hospitals, on average, are filled to only 60 percent capacity. There was no convenient chart showing that HMOs have helped bring the growth of health care spending in the private sector below the rate of inflation for the first time in decades.

On *ER* doctors fight to give their patients basic care; on *Chicago*   18
Hope they fight to give them baboon heart transplants. But the underlying philosophy is the same: where health care is concerned, cost should be no object. "You talk about saving Medicare from bankruptcy, but your real intent is to slash its costs to balance your state and Federal budgets," the in-house lawyer at Chicago Hope declared at a State Senate hearing in one episode. "Well, I'm going to tell you something: more people die with your plan, Senator."

HMOs are the preferred targets for such slings and arrows. "The   19
kinds of managed care we tend to see in these shows is the money-grubbing, profit-grabbing, bottom-line-obsessed version," Mr. Caplan said. "They play the same role that Russians and Arabs used to play in movies: dark forces against which the forces of light must battle."

Last year on *Chicago Hope,* an HMO ended a doctor's contract be-   20
cause he ordered too many tests. When the doctor took the HMO to court, he explained its strategy to the judge: "They told me I could treat patients like usual, and at first I could. Then six months later, with 80 percent of my practice HMO patients, they knew they had me. Then they start with the squeeze: no X-ray, no consults, no ultrasound." Turning to the HMO's lawyer, he concluded, "You forced me to give less treatment, inferior treatment, and it stinks!"

An impassioned performance but ultimately futile. The lawyer   21
made some cracks about fat country-club doctors, the judge declared that "greed is wonderful, greed works," and the doctor lost his suit.

"We try to present both sides of the story, but I do think that HMOs   22
come out as the bad guys," Mr. Tinker of *Chicago Hope* said. "It's going to be hard to write a positive portrayal of an HMO because I'm terrified of getting sick in this country."

As more people run up against the barriers of managed care, fear   23
of HMOs is becoming a common affliction. Medical dramas are better at diagnosing that fear than prescribing cures for it, said Gail Wilensky,

who ran the Medicaid and Medicare programs in the Bush Administration. "But they're less offensive than some of the documentary shows," she adds. "It's when '60 Minutes' goes after health care that I end up shouting at the TV."

24   The bias in *ER* and *Chicago Hope* is partly unavoidable, a byproduct of dramatic writing and of seeing medicine through doctors' eyes. Chicago Hope Hospital is so real to Mr. Tinker that he audibly winces when describing its fictional financial woes.

25   At *ER*, the writers identify more with their characters than with their hospital. Health care issues are only convenient devices, like truth serums, that the writers inject into characters' lives to force some revelation from them.

26   "We don't really scan the headlines for hot issues because we don't want the show to feel like that," said Neal Baer, a writer and co-producer of the show. "We want it to be a show where doctors are confronted by ordinary patients, and it just so happens that they reflect debate."

27   As a result, perhaps, *ER* has found its dramatic voice faster than *Chicago Hope,* where the writers tend to read the headlines assiduously and characters are more likely to become mouthpieces for health care diatribes. "At *ER* if you're alive at the end of the day, you're ahead of the game," Mr. Tinker said. "At our hospital, we have to turn the tide, not just stem it. We have to make a difference in medicine."

28   It's a far riskier enterprise. But at its best, *Chicago Hope* peers unwaveringly at the troubled heart of health care. The same episode that cast the HMO lawyer as the Prince of Darkness, for instance, had another story line that threw a subtle light on the costs and risks of modern medicine. In it, a man with a brain aneurysm was told he had only a year to live—unless he consented to two simultaneous experimental surgeries. The show's two star surgeons persuaded him to do it.

29   In the end, the surgeries were "successful," but the patient died. While the doctor and the HMO lawyer were haggling over a few dollars wasted on tests, tens of thousands were being thrown away on a grand but dubious gesture. "We killed him," one of the surgeons admitted. "He had maybe a year to live, to be with his grandkids, and we took that year."

30   A few more moments like that, and medical dramas may do justice to the Devil's bargains facing health care. But then viewers may just switch back to *Monday Night Football.*

★ Meaning and Understanding

1. Who are Ben Casey and Dr. Kildare?

2. What are Medicaid and Medicare?

3. What do you think is the main point of this essay?

4. The writer mentions a "policy wonk" in paragraph 17. What is a "policy wonk," and why should one have been on hand?

5. In paragraph 10 we are told that one of the shows mentioned takes place in "a dumpy, hyperkinetic emergency room." What does "hyperkinetic" mean?

6. What bias does the writer report in *ER* and *Chicago Hope*?

★ Techniques and Strategies

1. What is the thesis of the essay? How do you know?

2. The selection begins with a strong metaphor describing Tommy Wilmette. What is the metaphor and how does it contribute to your understanding of the essay? What other metaphors and figurative expressions help you envision the writer's point?

3. Who is the intended audience for this selection? What evidence in the piece leads you to your belief?

4. What effect does the dialogue beginning in paragraph 2 have on your understanding of the writer's point?

5. What is your reaction to the last paragraph? How successful is it as the conclusion of the essay?

★ Speaking of Values

1. Bilger remarks that doctors on TV "have been transformed, improbably, into antiheroes." What is an antihero? Do you agree with his assessment? Why or why not? In what way have doctors been portrayed as heroes in the past?

2. Do these shows seem to "have a deep distrust, if not contempt, for the business of medicine," as the writer puts it? Why do you think shows like the ones mentioned are so hostile to the financial realities of medical treatment?

3. Compare and contrast the pictures presented here of the medical community offered on both *Chicago Hope* and *ER*. What picture of the medical profession do they present? What picture of managed care organizations do they present?

4. If, as one observer notes, people are angry about health care, why do we consider doctors to be the "modern priesthood"? What are the implications of that analogy? Do you agree with it? Why or why not?

5. Look at the "old-fashioned values" listed at the end of paragraph 13. Do you agree with them? Why or why not?

★ Values Conversation

Doctors and medicine are familiar and popular subjects of successful television programs. How do you account for their popularity? Form groups and discuss. What element of American values does the medical show phenomenon reflect?

★ Writing about Values

1. Choose two or three "lawyer shows" on television over the years. Then write a paper comparing and contrasting the portraits of lawyers and the law that they present.

2. Television is obviously a very powerful medium in terms of influencing public opinion. However, the writer seems to imply in the conclusion to his essay that no matter how important a point a television show tries to make, if it does not entertain, the audience will simply change the channel. Do you agree with his point? Why or why not? Why should what is presented on television even concern us?

   Write a paper analyzing the balance between entertainment and serious discussion on television. Remember to consider the possible consequences of the balance tipping too far to either side and whether or not it is possible to maintain an even balance.

3. Write a paper on HMOs. What is your opinion about the central role that they now play in this country's medical care system?

Ann Louise Bardach

The Stealth Virus: AIDS and Latinos

Ann Louise Bardach writes about contemporary culture for *Vanity Fair,* the *New Republic,* and other magazines. In this essay she examines the impact of AIDS on the Latino community.

———— ★ ————

Freddie Rodriguez is discouraged. He has just come from his after-   1
noon's activity of trying to stop men from having unprotected sex in Miami's Alice Wainwright Park, a popular gay cruising spot. Rodriguez, 29, is a slim, handsome Cuban-American with a pale, worried face who works for Health Crisis Network. "I take a bag of condoms to the park with me and I try talking to people before they duck in the bushes and have sex," he explains. "I tell them how dangerous it is. Sometimes I beg them to use a condom. Sometimes they listen to me. Today, no one was interested." Most of the men, he says, are Latinos and range in age from 16 to 60. Many are married and would never describe themselves as gay. "Discrimination is not really the issue here. Most Latinos do not identify themselves as gay, so they're not discriminated against," he says, his voice drifting off. "Ours is a culture of denial."

To understand why the second wave of AIDS is hitting Latinos par-   2
ticularly hard, one would do well to start in Miami. Once a mecca for retirees, South Beach today is a frenzy of dance and sex clubs, for hetero- and homosexual alike. "We have the highest rate of heterosexual transmission in the country, the second-highest number of babies born with AIDS and we are number one nationwide for teen HIV cases," says Randi Jenson, reeling off a litany that clearly exhausts him. Jenson supervises the Miami Beach HIV/AIDS Project and sits on the board of the Gay, Lesbian and Bisexual Community Center. "And we have the highest rate of bisexuality in the country." When I ask how he knows this, he says, "Trust me on this one, *we know*...The numbers to watch for in the future will be Hispanic women—the wives and girlfriends."

Already, AIDS is the leading cause of death in Miami and Fort Lau-   3
derdale for women ages 25 to 44, four times greater than the national average. According to the Centers for Disease Control and Prevention (CDC), AIDS cases among Hispanics have been steadily rising. But any foray into the Latino subculture shows that the numbers do not tell the

whole story, and may not even tell half. CDC literature notes that "it is believed that AIDS-related cases and deaths for Latinos are understated by at least 30 percent. Many Hispanics do not and cannot access HIV testing and health care." Abetted by widespread shame about homosexuality, a fear of governmental and medical institutions (particularly among undocumented immigrants) and cultural denial as deep as Havana Harbor, AIDS is moving silently and insistently through Hispanic America. It is the stealth virus.

4   "No one knows how many Latino HIV cases are out there," Damian Pardo, an affable Cuban-American, who is president of the board of Health Crisis Network, tells me over lunch in Coral Gables. "All we know is that the numbers are not accurate—that the actual cases are far higher. Everyone in the community lies about HIV." Everyone, according to Pardo, means the families, the lovers, the priests, the doctors and the patients. "The Hispanic community in South Florida is far more affluent than blacks. More often than not, people see their own family doctor who simply signs a falsified death certificate. It's a conspiracy of silence and everyone is complicitous."

5   Freddie Rodriguez—smart, affluent, urbane—didn't learn that Luis, his Nicaraguan lover, was HIV-positive until it was too late to do anything about it. "He was my first boyfriend. He would get sick at times but he refused to take a blood test. He said that it was impossible for him to be HIV-positive. I believed him. One day, he disappeared. Didn't come home, didn't go to work—just disappeared." Frantic, Rodriguez called the police and started phoning hospitals. Finally, Luis turned up at Jackson Memorial Hospital. He had been discovered unconscious and rushed to intensive care. When Rodriguez arrived at the hospital, he learned that his lover was in the AIDS wing. Even then, Luis insisted it was a mistake. Two weeks later, he was dead. "I had to tell Luis's family that he was gay," Rodriguez says, "that I was his boyfriend and that he had died of AIDS. They knew nothing. He lived a completely secret life."

6   Although Rodriguez was enraged by his lover's cowardice, he understood his dilemma all too well. He remembered how hard it was to tell his own family. "When I was 22, I finally told my parents that I was gay. My mother screamed and ran out of the room. My father raised his hands in front of his eyes and told me, 'Freddie do you see what's in front of me? It's a big, white cloud. I do not hear anything, see anything and I cannot remember anything because it is all in this big white cloud.' And then he left the room." One of Rodriguez's later boyfriends, this one Peruvian, was also HIV-positive, but far more duplicitous. "He flat out lied to me when I asked him. He knew, but he only told me after we broke up, *after* we had unsafe sex," says Rodriguez, who remains HIV-negative. "Part of the *machismo* ethic," Rodriguez explains, "is not wearing a condom."

Miami's Body Positive, which provides psychological and non-   7
clinical services to AIDS patients, is housed in a pink concrete bubble
off Miami's Biscayne Boulevard. The building and much of its fund-
ing are provided by founder Doris Feinberg, who lost both her sons
to AIDS during the late 1980s. The gay Cuban-American star of
MTV's "The Real World," Pedro Zamora, worked here for the last
five years of his life and started its P.O.P. program—Peer Outreach
for Persons Who Are Positive. Ernie Lopez, a 26-year-old Nicaraguan
who has been Body Positive's director for the last five years, estimates that 40 percent of the center's clients are Latino, in a Miami
population that is 70 percent Hispanic. On the day I visit, I see mostly
black men at the facility. Lopez warns me not to be fooled. "The Latino numbers are as high as the blacks, but they are not registered," he
says. "Latinos want anonymity. They come in very late—when they
are desperate and their disease is very progressed. Often it's too late
to help them."

"Soy completo," is what they often say in Cuba, meaning, "I'm a to-   8
tal human being." It is the preferred euphemism for bisexuality and in
the *machista* politics of Latino culture, bisexuality is a huge step up
from being gay. It is this cultural construct that prevents many Latin
men from acknowledging that they could be vulnerable to HIV, because it is this cultural construct that tells them they are not gay. Why
worry about AIDS if only gay men get AIDS? "To be bisexual is a
code," says Ernesto Pujol, a pioneer in Latino AIDS education. "It
means, 'I sleep with men but I still have power.' I think there is a legitimate group of bisexuals, but for many bisexuality is a codified and covered homosexuality." Self-definitions can get even more complex. "I'm
not gay," a well-known intellectual told me in Havana last year. "How
could I be gay? My boyfriend is married and has a family."

Without putting too fine a point on it, what defines a gay man in   9
some segments of the Latino world is whether he's on the top or the
bottom during intercourse. "The salient property of the *maricon*," my
Cuban friend adds, "is his passivity. If you're a 'top,'—*el bugaron*—
you're not a faggot." Moreover, there are also many heterosexual Latino men who do not regard sex with another man as a homosexual act.
"A lot of heterosexual Latinos—say, after a few drinks—will fuck a
transvestite as a surrogate woman," says Pujol, 'and that is culturally
acceptable—absolutely acceptable." Hence the potential for HIV transmission is far greater than in the mainstream Anglo world.

According to Pujol, "only Latinos in the States are interested in   10
other gay men. They have borrowed the American liberated gay
model. In Latin America, the hunt is for 'straight' men. Look at the
transvestites on Cristina's (the Spanish-language equivalent of
"Oprah") talk show. Their boyfriends are always some macho hunk
from the *bodega*." Chino, a Cuban gay now living in Montreal, typifies

the cultural divide. "I don't understand it here," he says scornfully. "It's like girls going out with girls."

11   "If you come out," says Jorge B., a Cuban artist in Miami Beach, "you lose your sex appeal to 'straight' men" (straight in this context meaning married men who have sex with other men). The Hispanic preference for "straight men" is so popular that bathhouses such as Club Bodycenter in Coral Gables are said to cater to a clientele of older married men who often pick up young lovers after work before joining their families for dinner. Some men will not risk going to a gay bar, says Freddie Rodriguez. "They go to public restrooms where they can't be identified." While many gay Hispanics do eventually "come out," they do so at a huge price—a shattering loss of esteem within their family and community. "The priest who did Mass at my grandfather's funeral denied communion to me and my brother," recalls Pardo. "He knew from my mother's confession that we were gay."

12   Latino attitudes here are, of course, largely imported, their cultural fingerprints lifted straight out of Havana, Lima or Guatemala City. Consider Chiapas, Mexico, where gay men were routinely arrested throughout the 1980s; many of their bodies were later found dumped in a mass grave. Or Ecuador, where it is against the law to be a homosexual, and effeminate behavior or dress can be grounds for arrest. Or Peru, where the Shining Path has targeted gays for assassination. Or Colombia, where death squads do the same, characteristically mutilating their victims' genitals.

13   While Latino hostility to homosexuals in the United States tends to be less dramatic, it can also be virulent, particularly when cradled in reactionary politics. In Miami, right-wing Spanish-language stations daily blast their enemies as "communists, traitors and Castro puppets." But the epithet reserved for the most despised is "homosexual" or "*maricon*." When Nelson Mandela visited Miami in 1990, he was denounced daily as a "*marijuanero maricon*"—a pot-smoking faggot—for having supported Fidel Castro.

★ Meaning and Understanding

1. How does Freddie Rodriguez try to address the AIDS health crisis? Why is he discouraged? How long do you think he has performed his current activity?

2. Why does Bardach single out the South Beach area in Miami Beach? What data does Randi Jensen provide about the area? Who is he?

3. Why do many Hispanics avoid HIV testing? Why does Bardach refer to AIDS as the "stealth virus"?

4. What is Body Positive? Why was it founded?

5. According to the writer, what is the relation between homosexuality and bisexuality in the Latino culture? What do some Latino men mean when they assert *"Soy completo"*?

★ Techniques and Strategies

1. What do you understand the title of the selection to denote?

2. Bardach uses narrative strategies in this selection. Why? Why does she quote from the spoken remarks of so many different people?

3. Who is the intended audience? What evidence in the essay helps support your choice?

4. What is the thesis of this essay?

5. Why does the author use so many Spanish words?

6. Bardach is often very frank in dealing with Latino homosexuality. Is her frankness warranted? Explain.

★ Speaking of Values

1. What does Freddie Rodriguez mean when he says, "Ours is a culture of denial"? What has produced this cultural defense mechanism? What problems do you think it engenders?

2. What is the "conspiracy of silence" the writer refers to? Who is conspiring? Why? What dangers do you see in this conspiracy?

3. How do the values of the homeland culture—values in "Havana, Lima, or Guatemala City," to quote the writer—affect the values of North American Latinos? Is this a special condition of Spanish cultures, or would you say that other cultures exercise similar values on their transplanted citizens? Explain your response.

4. Many films, plays, and television programs focus on the AIDS dilemma. Which have you found most illuminating? Which have treated the Latino side of the AIDS epidemic? Explain.

★ Values Conversation

In the context of the AIDS struggle among Latino men, this piece raises many questions about privacy and public life. Should one's sexuality be open for scrutiny? Should one, in fact, disclose one's private life and behaviors to family and friends—or have it disclosed by others? Remember that many people do approve of such openness, feeling that "outing" and "coming out of the closet" are accepted cultural actions; others disapprove of what they call a culture of therapy where personal confessions and bared souls seem needlessly revelatory and burdensome to others with their own problems.

★ *Writing about Values*

1. Choose a group or civic organization dedicated to fighting AIDS. Interview some of the people who work there to ascertain what specific populations they deal with and what problems they may have with that population. Then write a paper reporting on your findings.

2. Do library research on the history of AIDS—how it began, how the public learned about it, what new medical procedures are available. Write an essay about the disease's progress and treatment.

3. Write a paper in which you define the term *machismo*. How does the larger culture see the word? How do Latinos see it? What similarities and differences do you note? What values inhere in the approaches to the concept of *machismo*?

Jeffrey Kluger

Can We Stay Young?

Born in 1954, Jeffrey Kluger writes about science and health issues. Here, in a piece for *Time* magazine, he discusses some scientific theories of the human aging process and the possibility for longer life.

The rules for aging are quietly being broken. Armed with a growing knowledge of biology, a new breed of longevity specialists is teasing out answers to longer life. 1

History shows it's possible. In 1900 the life expectancy for a person born in the United States was 47.3 years. According to U.S. figures, the average life expectancy is now nearly 76, with many Americans living well beyond. Says James Vaupel, a Duke University demographer, "There is no evidence that human life expectancy is anywhere close to its ultimate limit." 2

The modern era of aging research began in 1961 when cell biologist Leonard Hayflick made a significant discovery. Troubled by the question of where aging begins, Hayflick, now a professor at the University of California San Francisco School of Medicine and author of the book *How and Why We Age*, wondered: Did the cells themselves falter, dragging down the whole human organism? Or could cells live on indefinitely were it not for age-related deterioration in the tissues they make up? 3

To find out, Hayflick placed fetal cells in a petri dish. Freed from the responsibility of keeping a larger organism alive, they did the only other thing they knew how to do: divide. They doubled their number, and then doubled the doubling. After repeating itself about 50 times, the cycle suddenly stopped. Then the cells did something a lot like aging: they consumed less food, and their membranes deteriorated. 4

Hayflick repeated the experiment, using cells from a 70-year-old. This time the cellular aging began a lot earlier, after 20 or 30 doublings. 5

For gerontologists this was monumental; it meant that somewhere in each cell was an hourglass that gave it only so much time to live and no more. Could this cellular timekeeper be found—and reset? 6

Energy for Life

Scientists who study aging have taken two approaches to achieving this goal. The first is the cellular-damage model of aging. 7

8   Like all organisms, cells produce waste as they metabolize energy. One of the most troublesome byproducts of this process is a free radical, an ordinary oxygen molecule with an extra electron. The molecule seeks to rectify this electrical imbalance by careening about, trying to bond with other molecules. A lifetime of this can damage cells, leading to a range of disorders from cancer to more general symptoms of aging such as wrinkles and arthritis.

9   In recent years some nutritionists have advocated diets high in fruits and vegetables containing antioxidants—substances that are believed to sop up free radicals and carry them out of the body. But antioxidants have an uneven record. In some studies they seem to be associated with a dramatic reduction in cancer or other diseases; in other studies, an increase. In either case, few contemporary aging researchers think self-medicating at a salad bar can significantly extend the human life-span.

10   Far more promising might be new research into another byproduct of cellular metabolism: glycosylation—or what cooks call browning. When foods such as turkey, bread and caramel are heated, proteins bind with sugars, causing the surface to darken and turn soft and sticky. In the 1970s biochemists hypothesized that the same reaction might occur in people suffering from diabetes. When sugars and proteins bond, they attract other proteins, which form a sticky, weblike network that could stiffen joints, block arteries and cloud clear tissues such as the lens of the eye, leading to cataracts. Diabetics suffer from all these ailments.

11   But so do the aged. Was it possible that as the cells of nondiabetics metabolize sugars, the same glycosylation might take place, only much slower? Studies seemed to say yes.

12   The gooey glycosylation residue has been given an appropriate acronym: AGE, for advanced glycosylation end products. Investigators at the Picower Institute for Medical Research in Manhasset, New York, are working on a drug, pimagedine, that acts as an AGE solvent by dissolving the connection between AGE and the proteins around it. Essentially it helps unstick what AGE gums up.

No-Fat Centenarians

13   An alternative to changing the way cells process nutrients is to give them less to process in the first place. Studies have shown that rats whose caloric intake is 30 to 40 percent lower than that of a control group tend to live up to 40 percent longer. For a man, that would translate to a spartan diet of just about 1500 calories a day—in exchange for 30 extra years of life.

14   Just how this business of swapping food for time works is not entirely clear, but George Roth, molecular physiologist with the National

Institute on Aging in Bethesda, Maryland, has some ideas. When calories are restricted, Roth explains, body temperature drops about 1.8 degrees Fahrenheit. Lower temperature means a less vigorous metabolism, which means less food is processed. "The animals switch from a growth mode to a survival mode," Roth says. "They get fewer calories, so they burn fewer. I think caloric restriction could take us well beyond a life-span of 80," he adds. "After all, you rarely see a fat centenarian."

In a nation of consumers for whom caloric belt-tightening can   15
mean merely a smaller serving of french fries with their bacon cheese-burgers, it may be more realistic to imitate caloric restriction pharmaco-logically. "Essentially," explains Roth, "we'd use a pill to trick a cell into thinking less food is coming in."

But caloric reduction is essentially maintenance work: little more   16
than patching holes in a sinking ship. What some researchers really want is to get down into the body's engine room—the genes themselves—and rebuild things from the boilers up. Remarkably, it appears there may be a way.

Tip of the Shoelace

Hayflick left a question unanswered: why do cells die? In the years fol-   17
lowing his work, biologists looked for a gene that enforced cellular mortality, but found nothing. One thing that did catch their eyes, how-ever, was a small area at the tip of chromosomes that had no discernible purpose. Dubbed a telomere, it resembled nothing so much as the plas-tic cuff at the end of a shoelace.

Each time a cell divided, the daughter cells it produced had a little   18
less telomere. Finally, when the cell reached its Hayflick's limit of 50 or so replications, the telomere was reduced to a mere nub. Only a few cells were spared telomere loss. Among them were sperm and cancer cells—-the cells characterized by their ability to divide not just 50 times but thousands.

Working with a single-cell pond organism, molecular biologists   19
Carol Greider and Elizabeth Blackburn, then with the University of California at Berkeley, discovered in 1984 a telomere-preserving en-zyme they dubbed telomerase. Five years later, Gregg Morin at Yale University identified the same substance in cancer cells, In the petri dish the agent of eternal life had been found.

At Geron Corporation, a biopharmaceutical firm based in Menlo   20
Park, Calif., biologist Calvin Harley is working to find the genes that direct telomerase production, believing he might be able to manipulate them so the regulator for the enzyme can be turned on and off at will.

"With a pill or with cell therapy, I think we may be able to treat ag-   21
ing in very specific areas," Harley says.

Superworms

22   Other genes implicated in aging have already been flushed out of hiding. Nematodes in Siegfried Hekimi's genetics lab at McGill University in Montreal have been known to survive up to 75 days. Outside the lab, the tiny, transparent worms barely last nine.

23   Hekimi created his little Überworms by breeding long-lived individuals, extending the life-spans of the next generation. He then searched the animals' chromosomes until he found the mutated gene responsible, a gene he dubbed Clock-1.

24   When Hekimi went looking for similar clock genes in people, he found one so similar, he says, "that it's possible the whole clock system works the same way. If we find all of the human clock genes, we can perhaps slow them down just a little, so we can extend life expectancy just a little."

25   The problem is the sheer number of genes involved. Geneticist George Martin at the University of Washington in Seattle believes that even if only a few master-clock genes directly guide aging in humans, up to 7000 more might be peripherally involved. Re-engineering even one is an exquisitely complex process. Re-engineering all 7000 would be impossible.

26   While the genes involved in the aging process can't yet be manipulated, many researchers are using what they've learned about them to attack disease.

27   Researchers at Geron recently used telomerase RNA to block an enzyme in a cancer culture. Elsewhere investigators are looking into using the AGE drug pimagedine to help clear arteries and improve cardiac health, adding 13.9 years to average national life expectancy.

28   Researchers believe there's no reason many adults won't one day live to see 120. For people dreaming of immortality, that prospect may fall a little short. But four or five additional decades sounds like a splendid first step.

★ *Meaning and Understanding*

1. In the opening sentence Kluger asserts, "The rules for aging are quietly being broken." What are the "rules" he is referring to? And why are they "quietly" being broken?

2. What does Kluger mean in the opening paragraph when he says that scientists are "teasing out" answers to the question of aging?

3. What contribution did Leonard Hayflick make in our understanding of aging?

4. What are the two approaches to dealing with the aging process that scientists have studied?

5. What are George Roth's ideas on caloric restriction and aging?

6. What does the writer suggest is the main problem involved in "slowing down" human clock genes?

★ Techniques and Strategies

1. What is the thesis of this essay?

2. Who is the intended audience? What evidence in the essay helps support your choice?

3. What is the tone of the essay? How do you know? Is it consistent throughout? If not, where does it shift?

4. The writer draws on figurative language—the metaphor in paragraph 16 and the analogy in paragraph 14, for example. Are the figures effective in helping you understand the writer's point? Why or why not?

5. The writer uses a variety of transitions to help produce a coherent essay. Which transitions do you find most effective? Why?

6. What expectations does the writer set for the reader by the title of the selection? Why does he state the title as a question?

7. What is your reaction to the last paragraph as the essay's conclusion?

★ Speaking of Values

1. We generally think of the traditional human life span as "three score and ten"—that is, seventy years. Should there be a limit to human life expectancy? Why or why not?

2. The writer apparently believes that extending human life by slowing down the aging process is a positive goal. What do you think?

3. In more than one place Kluger comments on the eating habits of Americans. In what way do these habits connect to his theme? Does he imply that Americans seem to be more concerned about aging than other cultures? Explain.

4. Suppose more people in America lived to be 120. What would our society be like under such conditions?

5. American culture has long had a fascination with youth. Our models, television stars, and political leaders (to name a few) go out of their way to appear and act youthful. Why do we stress youthfulness so much? How do we compare in this attitude to other cultures—European and Asian? Is ours a healthy or unhealthy attitude? Explain.

★ *Values Conversation*

Extending the life expectancy of human beings seems to be a desirable objective. However, doing so may have consequences as well, consequences that are personal, social, and even global. Form groups and list and discuss as many potential problems or obstacles with extending human life expectancy as you can.

★ *Writing about Values*

1. Choose one or two of the problems identified by your group in the Values Conversation activity exercise and write a paper in which you discuss some possible solutions. Remember that your solutions may not be easy ones; you may well have to choose among competing values, all of which have a degree of legitimacy and validity. Try to make as persuasive a case as possible.

2. Statistics about aging and life expectancy can sometimes be misleading. Do some library research to find out about human life expectancy over the last five hundred years. Then write a paper about what the data tell us about the issue of human life expectancy.

3. How long would you like to live? Wait—don't answer too quickly! Think carefully about the question and write a paper explaining why you would like to live to a certain age. Be sure to discuss what you would do, how you would live, and what you see as potential pleasures and problems.

Values in Review

1. Fred Hechinger, Suzanne Gordon, and George Simpson comment on the quality of the health care available to us. Write an essay in which you examine the picture of our health care system that emerges from these three essays. Which aspects do you find most appealing? Which do you find most disturbing? What does a society's programs for caring for its sick and dying say about the society's values?

2. The images of physicians and nurses that emerge from the selections in this chapter are varied and often contradictory. Drawing on what you have read here, write an essay in which you consider the health care giver in American culture. How do the writers confirm or challenge your own contact with caregivers? What qualities should we look for in the people who serve the sick?

3. Many of these selections deal with profound issues relative to patients—their rights, their treatment, their self image. Write a paper about patients' rights, drawing on selections like Hechinger's, Bardach's, Welty's, and McHugh's.

AMERICAN VALUES

Focus on *Life*

As you consider the various selections in Part I—chapters on family, education, health, and health care—what do you see as the fundamental values Americans hold in regard to *life*, the first inalienable right guaranteed in the Declaration of Independence? Write an essay in which you identify American society's key life values as you have gleaned them from your readings. Be sure to analyze the appropriateness of these values in terms of your own view of American society and to imagine how Thomas Jefferson and his peers would have responded to the way our current values reflect the right to *life* as secured in the Declaration.

Part II

Liberty

Liberty—perhaps no word better expresses the sentiment fueling the intellectual and social revolutions that transformed modern thought and life in the century of the founding of the United States as a nation. The writers of the Declaration of Independence declared "liberty" an inalienable right, and the claims of monarchy a tyranny from whose chains humanity must break free. American life in the last two centuries has challenged liberty as a living concept, as slavery has given way to freedom, political subjugation to suffrage, and, for many, exclusion to inclusion.

In the days of the revolutionary era on the North American continent and abroad, liberty was an extremely radical notion. At its heart, to the revolutionaries liberty meant human rights. Kingships of the era insisted on regulating the beliefs and writings of all citizens, and this idea of people control and supervision rankled free thinkers who took up the revolutionary cause. Give us the right to worship as we please, they said, not as the king demands. Liberate us from capricious rules and inbred judiciaries corrupted by monarchy. Terminate censorship and its patronizing, paternalistic essence. Let us write what we please and speak what we wish in public and private. What the citizens of the eighteenth century demanded as liberty would challenge many governments, even enlightened governments, today. Hear the kind of liberty vouchsafed by the French Revolution's Declaration of the Rights of

Man, issued in the early days of France's upheaval: "Liberty consists in being able to do anything that does not harm another person." *Anything?* Which nations of the world would endorse so sweeping a proclamation? The firebrands in France demanded a country free of limits except those that assure the same rights to all citizens. Any call for such unbridled freedom of individual growth and potential challenged the controlling monarchy and aristocracy at its very core. This was undeniable sedition.

In fact, to our republic's forebears liberty meant not only individual human rights; it also meant innovative government, founded in the sovereignty of citizens. That is, only the people had the power and right to limit individual action and define the structures of dominion. All people had political equality, this notion of liberty proclaimed. Self-determination, ethnic freedom, humane justice, equality of opportunity, constitutional limits on executive authority—for these radical Enlightenment notions of liberty Americans sacrificed much in the revolution that ravaged our country. France, too, experienced the ravages of sacrifice: by the end of the century, well over a hundred thousand people had died in violence attributable to the 1789 Revolution—shocking numbers indeed. Yet the cause seemed so right and worth the great loss there and in America. George Gordon, Lord Byron, the flamboyant British poet, summed up the feelings of a new age: "Revolution," he wrote, "Alone can save the earth from hell's pollution." Indeed, modern life flowers from the ideas, reforms, and inspirations seeded in the eighteenth century's battlegrounds.

The writers in this section called *Liberty*, the second part in our effort to explore American values, consider the idea from many perspectives—linguistic, legal, political, and religious, each in his or her way measuring old principles against realities.

From the earliest days of the republic, American patriots linked language and liberty, viewing free speech as an essential to democracy's growth. In Chapter 5, Language and Speech, we present lively investigations of the state of language in U.S. society as an indicator of economic, gender, social, ethnic, and racial relations. Some writers look to legal realities, arguing for or against old practices or new initiatives. Against the backdrop of the First Amendment on one hand and the miserable history of racial hatred and violence on the other, Charles Lawrence III argues for limiting free speech through legislation. Considering the English-only movement that would establish English as our "official language," Robert D. King considers America's legacy of tolerance in linguistic terms. The connections between language and color get rich examination in this section, too. In "From Outside, In," Barbara Mellix reflects on her own struggle between "black English" and academic English, the pressures and pulls as she constructs a clear personal voice. That class and gender shape language and habits of speech is also presented articulately here. In "Women's Conversations," Deborah Tannen suggests a difference in male and female styles of communication. And Stephen Birmingham in "Telling Them Apart" demonstrates what he regards as the semantic signs of class in America. In "Body in Trouble," and "Under My Skin," respectively, Nancy Mairs and Sunil Garg identify ways in which our words convey our prejudices. Taken together, the selections in this chapter examine American speech as an American value, tracing its role in the play of liberty, both individual and communal. Are we, in fact, what we say and how we say it? Language undergirds the liberty assured us by the Declaration.

In Chapter 6, Law and Politics, we turn to the Declaration of Independence itself, both as a grievance against a particular king and a general statement of political principle, dazzling in both its ideas and its reach. And against the backdrop of Jefferson's words, we present other declarations on subjects as diverse as women's rights, majority rule, death penalty, civil disobedience, and drug laws. Echoing Jefferson's phrasing, Elizabeth Cady Stanton discusses the "natural" and "inalienable" rights of women denied equal rights under the law almost a hundred years after the nation's founding. And a hundred years after Stanton's articulate complaint, Martin Luther King, Jr., writes from Birmingham jail to explain the ethics in breaking laws that defy the "law of God" and what King sees as the sense and spirit of the Declaration of Independence and Constitution. In our time, Supreme Court Justice William J. Brennan challenges the death penalty's morality and legality in depriving citizens of the natural right to dignity—and an outspoken politician, Edward I. Koch, former mayor of New York City, argues powerfully for the death penalty. The two essays by these writers frame the either–or argument of capital punishment in our country. Acknowledging the often different and sometimes differing communities in American life, Lani Guinier in her provocatively titled piece, "The Tyranny of the Majority," questions the fairness of winner-take-all majority rule. Also in this chapter, we look at an early argument for public responsibility in the scandal that rocked the Clinton presidency in 1998. The moral chords of the Declaration and Constitution resonate in all pieces as writers assess contemporary realities against the principles of the democracy and republic.

In Chapter 7, Rights and Beliefs, writers look at faith and convictions in American life—in both large religions and private contemplation. Founded, in part, to secure religious rights, the American colonies and the ensuing nation have served as the arena for protracted debate on the practice and place of belief in American life. For three centuries, American leaders have reflected—and often conflicted—on issues of religion. Thomas Paine's "Profession of Faith" articulates the argument that faith is, above all, fidelity to one's beliefs, the most private of arrangements.

As if in response, Theodore Roosevelt's "Going to Church" urges Americans toward traditional churchgoing. And decades later, another President, Jimmy Carter, recounts how he carried his faith and his oath of office in his White House years, balancing the laws of his church with the laws of the land. For all its religion—and sometimes because of religion—America has known violence and combat; war and weapons, sometimes in God's name, have provided a creed for many. This chapter examines the violent legacy and its claims on the human spirit. In "An Episode of War" Stephen Crane reveals the very ordinary yet shocking details of battle when a lieutenant receives a wound, at once routine and serious—and ultimately, just another sacrifice to the war effort. Richard Wright in "Almos' a Man" explores, through poignant narrative, the lure a gun provides to young men. The writers in the chapter consider other beliefs, too—that America is a dream worth dying for, that difference means danger, that America is in spiritual despair—each writer taking his or her part in a conversation about the state of spirit and belief in our nation.

Defining liberty, then, through American voices, we turn to language, law, individual and group rights, speech, politics, and deeply held beliefs—all part of the American values landscape and vital in our efforts to understand the world we inhabit today.

Chapter 5
Language and Speech

Proud words

Upper-class English

Racist speech

"People of color"

Official English

Black English

Language as metaphor

Women's language

The First Amendment

Stephen Birmingham

Telling Them Apart

Stephen Birmingham, born in 1932, worked for many years as an adver-
tising copywriter. The author of twenty-two books, he now teaches Jour-
nalism at the University of Cincinnati. In this essay he looks at the
language of upper-class Americans.

———— ★ ————

1   Whenever you hear an American speak of a *terrace* rather than a *patio*,
of a *house* rather than a *home* or an *apartment*, of a *sofa* rather than a *dav-
enport* or *couch*, of *curtains* rather than *drapes*, of *guests for dinner* rather
than *company*, of a *long dress* rather than a *formal*, of a *dinner jacket* rather
than a *tuxedo*, and of *underwear* rather than *lingerie*, chances are you are
in the presence of a member of the American upper class. Upper-class
Americans use the toilet, not the lavatory or the commode or the facilities or the loo or the little boys' room. Upper-class Americans go to
boarding schools, not prep schools, where they earn grades, not marks.
Upper-class Americans are either rich (not wealthy) or poor (not less
well-off), and the prices they pay for things are either high (not expensive) or cheap (not inexpensive). Upper-class Americans say "Hello,"
not "Pleased to meet you,"and "What?" not "Pardon me?" Upper-class
American women do not have bosoms. They have breasts, or even tits
when they are among their own kind, when other vulgarisms frequently emerge. The familiar four-letter word for sexual intercourse is
a perfectly acceptable upper-class expression.

2   Brevity, simplicity, and the avoidance of euphemism are the chief
hallmarks of the upper-class American vocabulary. When an upper-
class American feels sick, he says just that, and never "I feel ill" or "I
feel nauseous." Cuteness is anathema. Thus in an upper-class American house you would never find a den or a rumpus room or a family
room, though you might find a library or a playroom. Upper-class
Americans do not own bedroom suites or dining room suites or any
other kind of suites, or "suits." They own furniture, and if it is particularly good furniture, it is often simply called wood. Pretentiousness is
similarly shunned. Thus to an upper-class American a tomato is a
tom*ay*to, not a tom*ah*to. Upper-class Americans write "R.S.V.P." on the
corners of their invitations, never "The favor of a reply is requested."
Upper-class Americans give and go to parties, never to affairs, and if

the affair being talked about is of the romantic variety, it is always, specifically, a love affair.

But, most important, the American upper class never talks about   3
the upper class, or about any other sort of class, for that matter. Partly
this is a question of delicacy and taste. It is simply not upper class to talk
about class. Also, in a constitutionally classless society where an upper
class has managed to emerge anyway, there is a feeling among members
of the upper class that they are a somewhat illicit entity, a possibly endangered species. If one were to go about boasting of being upper class,
who knows what sort of angry mob from below might rise up and challenge the precious barricades? So you will never hear a member of the
upper class talk of "the right people," or "nice people," or even "the
people we know." Instead it will be "our friends," or, more often, "our
family and friends." This way, the polite illusion is created that the
American aristocracy is a private, even secret, club, whose members all
know each other and whose rules are observed without ever having to
be written down or otherwise made public. Most frequently, when the
American aristocracy speaks of itself in a general sense, it is in terms of
"people," as in, "What will people say?" And if a member of the upper
class behaves—as can happen—in a non-upper-class way, the reaction is
"People just don't *do* that!"

In an upwardly mobile society, in which nearly everybody dreams   4
of elevating himself to a higher social or economic stratum, there are
some rules of upper-class behavior that are easy to learn. For example,
when upper-class women swim, they do the Australian crawl, never the
breaststroke or backstroke. It is easy to remember that the finger bowl
has no function whatsoever—certainly not to dabble one's fingers in—
and is to be removed, with the doily, and set at the upper left of one's
plate, after which the dessert spoon and fork are to be removed from
the service plate and placed on either side of it. It is easy to remember
that it is acceptable to eat asparagus with one's fingers (if no tongs have
been provided), while it is not acceptable to pick up the chop or the
chicken leg in the same manner, unless one is dining *en famille*. It is
never proper to squeeze the juice from a grapefruit half into a spoon.

But there are other more subtle, arcane codes by which members of   5
the American aristocracy recognize each other and send signals to each
other and that are more difficult to learn—which, it might be added, is the
whole unwritten point of there being such codes. In addition to language
and vocabulary, recognition is by name and by the association of name
with place. Thus one should be able to remember that Ingersolls and Cad-
waladers and Chews and *some* Morrises are from Philadelphia, while
other Morrises are from New York and New Jersey, and so when meeting
a Morris it is important to find out which family he or she represents.
Livingstons, Jays, Bownes, Lawrences, Schieffelins, Iselins, Schuylers,

and Fishes are from New York, while Otises, Saltonstalls, and Gardners are from Boston. Gardiners are from New York. Hoppins and Browns are from Providence, Pringles and Pinckneys are from Charleston, Des Loges are from St. Louis, Stumpfs are pre-oil Texas, and Chandlers are Los Angeles.

6   Over the past generation, America's upper-class boarding schools and colleges have become thoroughly democratized, but members of the upper class can still send signals to one another by the way they designate their schools. An upper-class Yale alumnus, for example, would never say that he had graduated "from Yale." He would say that he had studied "at New Haven." Following is a list of other upper-class schools and colleges, with their special upper-class designations:

Actual Name	Upper-class Designation
The Taft School	Watertown
The Hotchkiss School	Lakeville
St. Mark's School	Southborough
St. Paul's School	Concord
Miss Porter's School	Farmington
The Foxcroft School	Virginia
The Ethel Walker School	Simsbury
Choate-Rosemary Hall School	Wallingford
Smith College	Northampton
Vassar College	Poughkeepsie

7   But even more important and difficult than remembering names and their ancient associations with cities is mastering the American upper-class accent. Just as in England, where class is defined by ac-cent, the American aristocracy has developed an accent peculiar to it-self. It is a curious hybrid derived, in part, from the flat vowel sounds of New England, as well as from the New York accent that is some-times described as "Brooklynese," with random borrowings from the drawl of the antebellum South. From the South comes a tendency to drop final consonants—as in "somethin'" or "anythin'"—or to elide initial letters in words such as "them," which makes a statement such as "I can't think of anything to give them" sound very much like "I cahnt think o' anythin' to give 'em." Final r's are also dropped, whereby *paper* comes out "papuh," and *rear* is "reah." Interior r's are elided as well, so that *apart* becomes "apaht," and *church* becomes "chuhch." Final s's are almost, but not quite, lisped, so that the word *birds* is pronounced something like "budzh." Perhaps most difficult to master are the vowel sounds in simple words like *were*, where the audi-ble vowel sound of the *e* almost sounds like the *i* in *prism*. On top of this, particularly among men, there has long been something called the boarding school stammer, a speech pattern whose origins are unclear

but which may descend from the British public school stammer: "I—uh—oh, I say—wha-what would you say to—uh—," et cetera.

In perfecting an American upper-class accent, one rule to remem- 8
ber is the upper-class injunction to keep a stiff upper lip. The upper lip
moves very little in American upper-class speech. But of course members of the American upper class do not have to be taught how to speak
this way. They learn it from the cradle.

★ Meaning and Understanding

1. What is the main point of the selection?

2. Why does the American upper class never talk about class? What is
   the "delicacy of taste"?

3. Why does the upper class give new or different names to the schools
   they and their children attend?

4. The people of this group use a specific accent. How do you explain its
   origins?

5. What is the "public school stammer"? Where does it come from and
   how do you explain its presence in the speech of the American upper
   class?

★ Techniques and Strategies

1. In what ways does Birmingham use comparison and contrast to advance his point?

2. What do these sentences mean: "Cuteness is anathema," and "Pretentiousness is similarly shunned"? What is their effect?

3. What are some examples of effective images in the essay?

4. How do the examples in paragraph 1 contribute to the writer's thesis?

5. Who is the *them* in the title? Why did the writer use a pronoun here instead of nouns—*upper class*, for example?

★ Speaking of Values

1. How does the essay actually give you the skills for "Telling Them
   Apart"? Are you more or better able to tell "them" apart now that you
   have read the essay? Why or why not?

2. What does the piece express about class structure in America? About
   American values in general?

3. A *euphemism* is an indirect reference, a substituted, usually less blunt expression or name. To refer to the House and Senate of the U.S. government as "Capitol Hill" or to refer to New York City as "the Big Apple" are both examples of euphemism. According to Birmingham, the upper-class avoids euphemisms, yet euphemistic names for colleges and schools seem to be very common to the group. How do you explain this phenomenon? Why are some euphemisms good and others not, do you think?

4. What is the tone of the piece? What impression is the writer trying to give of the upper class? Is he being fair? Why do you think so?

5. If the writer is correct, it seems that the upper class spends considerable time trying not to be so obviously upper class—trying to hide or be ambiguous or indirect about it. Why would members of the upper class have this goal? What does this attitude indicate about upper-class values?

★ *Values Conversation*

What is the relation between language and class in American society—even though many argue that ours is a classless society? Form groups to discuss how language does or does not betray one's social, economic, ethnic, or cultural roots? Is this good or bad? Why? Report your group's findings to the class at large.

★ *Writing about Values*

1. Write an essay called "Telling _____ Apart" in which you identify special language use or speech patterns that characterize an individual or a group of people whom you know and that set that group off from another group. Your title might be "Telling San Franciscans Apart," "Telling High School Students Apart," or "Telling Farm Children Apart." Remember, the purpose is to use examples of speech, accent, and language to make your point.

2. Write an essay about euphemisms in our society. What do they tell you about American values?

3. Write a narrative essay in which you show how a particular language pattern or word use influenced the outcome of an event.

Robert D. King

Should English Be the Law?

Born in 1936, Robert D. King is a linguist and mathematician teaching at the University of Texas at Austin. He is the author of *Historical Linguistics and Generative Grammar* (1969), and most recently of *Nehru and the Language Politics of India* (1997). In this essay he assesses the value of making English the official language of the United States.

———————— ★ ————————

We have known race riots, draft riots, labor violence, secession, antiwar protests, and a whiskey rebellion, but one kind of trouble we've never had: a language riot. Language riot? It sounds like a joke. The very idea of language as a political force—as something that might threaten to split a country wide apart—is alien to our way of thinking and to our cultural traditions.

This may be changing. On August 1 of last year the U.S. House of Representatives approved a bill that would make English the official language of the United States. The vote was 259 to 169, with 223 Republicans and thirty-six Democrats voting in favor and eight Republicans, 160 Democrats, and one independent voting against. The debate was intense, acrid, and partisan. On March 25 of last year the Supreme Court agreed to review a case involving an Arizona law that would require public employees to conduct government business only in English. Arizona is one of several states that have passed "Official English" or "English Only" laws. The appeal to the Supreme Court followed a 6-to-5 ruling, in October of 1995, by a federal appeals court striking down the Arizona law. These events suggest how divisive a public issue language could become in America—even if it has until now scarcely been taken seriously.

Traditionally, the American way has been to make English the national language—but to do so quietly, locally, without fuss. The Constitution is silent on language: the Founding Fathers had no need to legislate that English be the official language of the country. It has always been taken for granted that English *is* the national language, and that one must learn English in order to make it in America.

To say that language has never been a major force in American history or politics, however, is not to say that politicians have always resisted linguistic jingoism. In 1753 Benjamin Franklin voiced his concern that German immigrants were not learning English: "Those [Germans] who come hither are generally the most ignorant Stupid Sort of their own Nation.... they will soon so out number us, that all the advantages we have will not, in My Opinion, be able to preserve our language, and even our government will become precarious." Theodore Roosevelt articulated the unspoken American linguistic-melting-pot theory when he boomed, "We have room for but one language here, and that is the English language, for we intend to see that the crucible turns our people out as Americans, of American nationality, and not as dwellers in a polyglot boarding house." And: "We must have but one flag. We must also have but one language. That must be the language of the Declaration of Independence, of Washington's Farewell address, of Lincoln's Gettysburg speech and second inaugural."

Official English

5   TR's linguistic tub-thumping long typified the tradition of American politics. That tradition began to change in the wake of the anything-goes attitudes and the celebration of cultural differences arising in the 1960s. A 1975 amendment to the Voting Rights Act of 1965 mandated the "bilingual ballot" under certain circumstances, notably when the voters of selected language groups reached five percent or more in a voting district. Bilingual education became a byword of educational thinking during the 1960s. By the 1970s linguists had demonstrated convincingly—at least to other academics—that black English (today called African-American vernacular English or Ebonics) was not "bad" English but a different kind of authentic English with its own rules. Predictably, there have been scattered demands that black English be included in bilingual-education programs.

6   It was against this background that the movement to make English the official language of the country arose. In 1981 Senator S. I. Hayakawa, long a leading critic of bilingual education and bilingual ballots, introduced in the U.S. Senate a constitutional amendment that not only would have made English the official language but would have prohibited federal and state laws and regulations requiring the use of other languages. His English Language Amendment died in the Ninety-seventh Congress.

7   In 1983 the organization called U.S. English was founded by Hayakawa and John Tanton, a Michigan ophthalmologist. The primary purpose of the organization was to promote English as the official language of the United States. (The best background readings on America's "neolinguisticism" are the books *Hold Your Tongue*, by James Crawford, and *Language Loyalties*, edited by Crawford, both published in 1992.) Official English initiatives were passed by California in 1986, by Arkansas, Mississippi, North Carolina, North Dakota, and South Carolina in 1987, by Colorado, Florida, and Arizona in 1988, and by

Alabama in 1990. The majorities voting for these initiatives were generally not insubstantial: California's, for example, passed by 73 percent.

It was probably inevitable that the Official English (or English Only—the two names are used almost interchangeably) movement would acquire a conservative, almost reactionary undertone in the 1990s. Official English is politically very incorrect. But its cofounder John Tanton brought with him strong liberal credentials. He had been active in the Sierra Club and Planned Parenthood, and in the 1970s served as the national president of Zero Population Growth. Early advisers of U.S. English resist ideological pigeonholing: they included Walter Annenberg, Jacques Barzun, Bruno Bettelheim, Alistair Cooke, Denton Cooley, Walter Cronkite, Angier Biddle Duke, George Gilder, Sidney Hook, Norman Podhoretz, Arnold Schwarzenegger, and Karl Shapiro. In 1987 U.S. English installed as its president Linda Chávez, a Hispanic who had been prominent in the Reagan Administration. A year later she resigned her position, citing "repugnant" and "anti-Hispanic" overtones in an internal memorandum written by Tanton. Tanton, too, resigned, and Walter Cronkite, describing the affair as "embarrassing," left the advisory board. One board member, Norman Cousins, defected in 1986, alluding to the "negative symbolic significance" of California's Official English initiative, Proposition 63. The current chairman of the board and CEO of U.S. English is Mauro E. Mujica, who claims that the organization has 550,000 members.

8

The popular wisdom is that conservatives are pro and liberals con. True, conservatives such as George Will and William F. Buckley Jr. have written columns supporting Official English. But would anyone characterize as conservatives the present and past U.S. English board members Alistair Cooke, Walter Cronkite, and Norman Cousins? One of the strongest opponents of bilingual education is the Mexican-American writer Richard Rodríguez, best known for his eloquent autobiography, *Hunger of Memory*, (1982). There is a strain of American liberalism that defines itself in nostalgic devotion to the melting pot.

9

For several years relevant bills awaited consideration in the U.S. House of Representatives. The Emerson Bill (H.R. 123), passed by the House last August, specifies English as the official language of government, and requires that the government "preserve and enhance" the official status of English. Exceptions are made for the teaching of foreign languages; for actions necessary for public health, international relations, foreign trade, and the protection of the rights of criminal defendants; and for the use of "terms of art" from languages other than English. It would, for example, stop the Internal Revenue Service from sending out income-tax forms and instructions in languages other than English, but it would not ban the use of foreign languages in census materials or documents dealing with national security. *"E Pluribus*

10

Unum" can still appear on American money. U.S. English supports the bill.

11   What are the chances that some version of Official English will become federal law? Any language bill will face tough odds in the Senate, because some western senators have opposed English Only measures in the past for various reasons, among them a desire by Republicans not to alienate the growing number of Hispanic Republicans, most of whom are uncomfortable with mandated monolingualism. Texas Governor George W. Bush, too, has forthrightly said that he would oppose any English Only proposals in his state. Several of the Republican candidates for President in 1996 (an interesting exception is Phil Gramm) endorsed versions of Official English, as has Newt Gingrich. While governor of Arkansas, Bill Clinton signed into law an English Only bill. As President, he has described his earlier action as a mistake.

12   Many issues intersect in the controversy over Official English: immigration (above all), the rights of minorities (Spanish-speaking minorities in particular), the pros and cons of bilingual education, tolerance, how best to educate the children of immigrants, and the place of cultural diversity in school curricula and in American society in general. The question that lies at the root of most of the uneasiness is this: Is America threatened by the preservation of languages other than English? Will America, if it continues on its traditional path of benign linguistic neglect, go the way of Belgium, Canada, and Sri Lanka— three countries among many whose unity is gravely imperiled by language and ethnic conflicts?

Language and Nationality

13   Language and nationalism were not always so intimately intertwined. Never in the heyday of rule by sovereign was it a condition of employment that the King be able to speak the language of his subjects. George I spoke no English and spent much of his time away from England, attempting to use the power of his kingship to shore up his German possessions. In the Middle Ages nationalism was not even part of the picture: one owed loyalty to a lord, a prince, a ruler, a family, a tribe, a church, a piece of land, but not to a nation and least of all to a nation as a language unit. The capital city of the Austrian Hapsburg empire was Vienna, its ruler a monarch with effective control of peoples of the most varied and incompatible ethnicitites, and languages, throughout Central and Eastern Europe. The official language, and the lingua franca as well, was German. While it stood—and it stood for hundreds of years—the empire was an anachronistic relic of what for most of human history had been the normal relationship between country and language: none.

The marriage of language and nationalism goes back at least to Ro-   14
manticism and specifically to Rousseau, who argued in his *Essay on the
Origin of Languages* that language must develop before politics is possible and that language originally distinguished nations from one another. A little-remembered aim of the French Revolution—itself the
legacy of Rousseau—was to impose a national language on France,
where regional languages such as Provençal, Breton, and Basque were
still strong competitors against standard French, the French of the Ile
de France. As late as 1789, when the Revolution began, half the population of the south of France, which spoke Provençal, did not understand
French. A century earlier the playwright Racine said that he had had to
resort to Spanish and Italian to make himself understood in the southern French town of Uzès. After the Revolution nationhood itself became aligned with language.

In 1846 Jacob Grimm, one of the Brothers Grimm of fairy-tale   15
fame but better known in the linguistic establishment as a forerunner
of modern comparative and historical linguists, said that "a nation is
the totality of people who speak the same language." After midcen-
tury, language was invoked more than any other single criterion to
define nationality. Language as a political force helped to bring about
the unification of Italy and of Germany and the secession of Norway
from its union with Sweden in 1905. Arnold Toynbee observed—
unhappily—soon after the First World War that "the growing consciousness of Nationality had attached itself neither to traditional
frontiers nor to new geographical associations but almost exclusively
to mother tongues."

The crowning triumph of the new desideratum was the Treaty of   16
Versailles, in 1919, when the allied victors of the First World War began
redrawing the map of Central and Eastern Europe according to nationality as best they could. The magic word was "self-determination," and
none of Woodrow Wilson's Fourteen Points mentioned the word "language" at all. Self-determination was thought of as being related to
"nationality," which today we would be more likely to call "ethnicity";
but language was simpler to identify than nationality or ethnicity.
When it came to drawing the boundary lines of various countries—
Czechoslovakia, Yugoslavia, Romania, Hungary, Albania, Bulgaria,
Poland—it was principally language that guided the draftsman's hand.
(The main exceptions were Alsace-Lorraine, South Tyrol, and the
German-speaking parts of Bohemia and Moravia.) Almost by default
language became the defining characteristic of nationality.

And so it remains today. In much of the world, ethnic unity and   17
cultural identification are routinely defined by language. To be Arab is
to speak Arabic. Bengali identity is based on language in spite of the division of Bengali-speakers between Hindu India and Muslim Bangladesh. When eastern Pakistan seceded from greater Pakistan in 1971, it

named itself Bangladesh: *desa* means "country"; *bangla* means not the Bengali people or the Bengali territory but the Bengali language.

18   Scratch most nationalist movements and you find a linguistic grievance. The demands for independence of the Baltic states (Latvia, Lithuania, and Estonia) were intimately bound up with fears for the loss of their respective languages and cultures in sea of Russianness. In Belgium the war between French and Flemish threatens an already weakly fused country. The present atmosphere of Belgium is dark and anxious, costive; the metaphor of divorce is a staple of private and public discourse. The lines of terrorism in Sri Lanka are drawn between Tamil Hindus and Sinhalese Buddhists—and also between the Tamil and Sinhalese languages. Worship of the French language fortifies the movement for an independent Quebec. Whether a united Canada will survive into the twenty-first century is a question too close to call. Much of the anxiety about language in the United States is probably fueled by the "Quebec problem": unlike Belgium, which is a small European country, or Sri Lanka, which is halfway around the world, Canada is our close neighbor.

19   Language is a convenient surrogate for nonlinguistic claims that are often awkward to articulate, for they amount to a demand for more political and economic power. Militant Sikhs in India call for a state of their own: Khalistan ("Land of the Pure" in Punjabi). They frequently couch this as a demand for a linguistic state, which has a certain simplicity about it, a clarity of motive—justice, even, because states in India are normally linguistic states. But the Sikh demands blend religion, economics, language, and retribution for sins both punished and unpunished in a country where old sins cast long shadows.

20   Language is an explosive issue in the countries of the former Soviet Union. The language conflict in Estonia has been especially bitter. Ethnic Russians make up almost a third of Estonia's population, and most of them do not speak or read Estonian, although Russians have lived in Estonia for more than a generation. Estonia has passed legislation requiring knowledge of the Estonian language as a condition of citizenship. Nationalist groups in independent Lithuania sought restrictions on the use of Polish—again, old sins, long shadows.

21   In 1995 protests erupted in Moldova, formerly the Moldavian Soviet Socialist Republic, over language and the teaching of Moldovan history. Was Moldovan history a part of Romanian history or of Soviet history? Was Moldova's language Romanian? Moldovan—earlier called Moldavian—*is* Romanian, just as American English and British English are both English. But in the days of the Moldavian SSR, Moscow insisted that the two languages were different, and in a piece of linguistic nonsense required Moldavian to be written in the Cyrillic alphabet to strengthen the case that it was not Romanian.

22   The official language of Yugoslavia was Serbo-Croatian, which was never so much a language as a political accommodation. The Serbian

and Croatian languages are mutually intelligible. Serbian is written in the Cyrillic alphabet, is identified with the Eastern Orthodox branch of the Catholic Church, and borrows its high-culture words from the east—from Russian and Old Church Slavic. Croatian is written in the Roman alphabet, is identified with Roman Catholicism, and borrows its high-culture words from the west—from German, for example, and Latin. One of the first things the newly autonomous Republic of Serbia did, in 1991, was to pass a law decreeing Serbian in the Cyrillic alphabet the official language of the country. With Croatia divorced from Serbia, the Croatian and Serbian languages are diverging more and more. Serbo-Croatian has now passed into history, a language-museum relic from the brief period when Serbs and Croats called themselves Yugoslavs and pretended to like each other.

Slovakia, relieved now of the need to accommodate to Czech cosmopolitan sensibilities, has passed a law making Slovak its official language. (Czech is to Slovak pretty much as Croatian is to Serbian.) Doctors in state hospitals must speak to patients in Slovak, even if another language would aid diagnosis and treatment. Some 600,000 Slovaks—more than 10 percent of the population—are ethnically Hungarian. Even staff meetings in Hungarian-language schools must be in Slovak. (The government dropped a stipulation that church weddings be conducted in Slovak after heavy opposition from the Roman Catholic Church.) Language inspectors are told to weed out "all sins perpetrated on the regular Slovak language." Tensions between Slovaks and Hungarians, who had been getting along, have begun to arise.   23

The twentieth century is ending as it began—with trouble in the Balkans and with nationalist tensions flaring up in other parts of the globe. (Toward the end of his life Bismarck predicted that "some damn fool thing in the Balkans" would ignite the next war.) Language isn't always part of the problem. But it usually is.   24

Unique Otherness

Is there no hope for language tolerance? Some countries manage to maintain their unity in the face of multilingualism. Examples are Finland, with a Swedish minority, and a number of African and Southeast Asian countries. Two others could not be more unlike as countries go: Switzerland and India.   25

German, French, Italian, and Romansh are the languages of Switzerland. The first three can be and are used for official purposes; all four are designated "national" languages. Switzerland is politically almost hyperstable. It has language problems (Romansh is losing ground), but they are not major, and they are never allowed to threaten national unity.   26

27   Contrary to public perception, India gets along pretty well with a host of different languages. The Indian constitution officially recognizes nineteen languages, English among them. Hindi is specified in the constitution as the national language of India, but that is a pious postcolonial fiction: outside the Hindi-speaking northern heartland of India, people don't want to learn it. English functions more nearly than Hindi as India's lingua franca.

28   From 1947, when India obtained its independence from the British, until the 1960s blood ran in the streets and people died because of language. Hindi absolutists wanted to force Hindi on the entire country, which would have split India between north and south and opened up other fracture lines as well. For as long as possible Jawaharlal Nehru, independent India's first Prime Minister, resisted nationalist demands to redraw the capricious state boundaries of British India according to language. By the time he capitulated, the country had gained a precious decade to prove its viability as a union.

29   Why is it that India preserves its unity with not just two languages to contend with, as Belgium, Canada, and Sri Lanka have, but nineteen? The answer is that India, like Switzerland, has a strong national identity. The two countries share something big and almost mystical that holds each together in a union transcending language. That something I call "unique otherness."

30   The Swiss have what the political scientist Karl Deutsch called "learned habits, preferences, symbols, memories, and patterns of landholding": customs, cultural traditions, and political institutions that bind them closer to one another than to people of France, Germany, or Italy living just across the border and speaking the same language. There is Switzerland's traditional neutrality, its system of universal military training (the "citizen army"), its consensual allegiance to a strong Swiss franc—and fondue, yodeling, skiing, and mountains. Set against all this, the fact that Switzerland has four languages doesn't even approach the threshold of becoming a threat.

31   As for India, what Vincent Smith, in the *Oxford History of India,* calls its "deep underlying fundamental unity" resides in institutions and beliefs such as caste, cow worship, sacred places, and much more. Consider *dharma, karma,* and *maya,* the three root convictions of Hinduism; India's historical epics; Gandhi; *ahimsa* (nonviolence); vegetarianism; a distinctive cuisine and way of eating; marriage customs; a shared past; and what the Indologist Ainslie Embree calls "Brahmanical ideology." In other words, "We are Indian; we are different."

32   Belgium and Canada have never managed to forge a stable national identity; Czechoslovakia and Yugoslavia never did either. Unique otherness immunizes countries against linguistic destabilization. Even Switzerland and especially India have problems; in any country with as many different languages as India has, language will never *not* be a

problem. However, it is one thing to have a major illness with a bleak prognosis; it is another to have a condition that is irritating and occasionally painful but not life-threatening.

History teaches a plain lesson about language and governments: there is almost nothing the government of a free country can do to change language usage and practice significantly, to force its citizens to use certain languages in preference to others, and to discourage people from speaking a language they wish to continue to speak. (The rebirth of Hebrew in Palestine and Israel's successful mandate that Hebrew be spoken and written by Israelis is a unique event in the annals of language history.) Quebec has since the 1970s passed an array of laws giving French a virtual monopoly in the province. One consequence—unintended, one wishes to believe—of these laws is that last year kosher products imported for Passover were kept off the shelves, because the packages were not labeled in French. Wise governments keep their hands off language to the extent that it is politically possible to do so.

We like to believe that to pass a law is to change behavior; but passing laws about language, in a free society, almost never changes attitudes or behavior. Gaelic (Irish) is living out a slow, inexorable decline in Ireland despite enormous government support of every possible kind since Ireland gained its independence from Britain. The Welsh language, in contrast, is alive today in Wales in spite of heavy discrimination during its history. Three out of four people in the northern and western counties of Gwynedd and Dyfed speak Welsh.

I said earlier that language is a convenient surrogate for other national problems. Official English obviously has a lot to do with concern about immigration, perhaps especially Hispanic immigration. America may be threatened by immigration; I don't know. But America is not threatened by language.

The usual arguments made by academics against Official English are commonsensical. Who needs a law when, according to the 1990 census, 94 percent of American residents speak English anyway? (Mauro E. Mujica, the chairman of U.S. English, cites a higher figure: 97 percent.) Not many of today's immigrants will see their first language survive into the second generation. This is in fact the common lament of first-generation immigrants: their children are not learning their language and are losing the culture of their parents. Spanish is hardly a threat to English, in spite of isolated (and easily visible) cases such as Miami, New York City, and pockets of the Southwest and southern California. The everyday language of south Texas is Spanish, and yet south Texas is not about to secede from America.

But empirical, calm arguments don't engage the real issue: language is a symbol, an icon. Nobody who favors a constitutional ban against flag burning will ever be persuaded by the argument that the flag is, after all, just a "piece of cloth." A draft card in the 1960s was never merely a piece of paper. Neither is a marriage license.

38   Language, as one linguist has said, is "not primarily a means of communication but a means of communion." Romanticism exalted language, made it mystical, sublime—a bond of national identity. At the same time, Romanticism created a monster: it made of language a means for destroying a country.

39   America has that unique otherness of which I spoke. In spite of all our racial divisions and economic unfairness, we have the frontier tradition, respect for the individual, and opportunity; we have our love affair with the automobile; we have in our history a civil war that freed the slaves and was fought with valor; and we have sports, hot dogs, hamburgers, and milk shakes—things big and small, noble and petty, important and trifling. "We are Americans; we are different."

40   If I'm wrong, then the great American experiment will fail—not because of language but because it is no longer means anything to be an American; because we have forfeited that "willingness of the heart" that F. Scott Fitzgerald wrote was America; because we are no longer joined by Lincoln's "mystic chords of memory."

41   We are not even close to the danger point. I suggest that we relax and luxuriate in our linguistic richness and our traditional tolerance of language differences. Language does not threaten American unity. Benign neglect is a good policy for any country when it comes to language, and it's a good policy for America.

★ Meaning and Understanding

1. What is the main point of the selection?

2. What does King see as the Democrats' and Republicans' attitudes toward English only? What kind of "political force" does King think that language can be? What does he think language can do?

3. How far back does the writer trace the "one language, one nation" paradigm? Who are the two individuals he notes in this regard?

4. Does the writer think that the variety of languages in the United States threatens this country's unity? Why or why not?

5. What is "unique otherness"?

6. What, according to King, does history teach us about language and governments?

★ Techniques and Strategies

1. What is your reaction to the first sentence of the essay? How does it engage your attention?

2. Why does King provide a history of long-ago attitudes toward language in other countries? What does this strategy accomplish for the essay's purpose?

3. Writers use *rhetorical questions* to produce an effect or make an assertion, not engender a reply. The writer asks several rhetorical questions over the course of the essay, not the least of which is the title. What other examples of rhetorical questions can you find?

4. How does the writer use the two court proceedings he cites at the end of paragraph 2? What do these events suggest?

5. What is your view of the last paragraph of the essay? How does it bring an appropriate close to the piece?

★ Speaking of Values

1. How does a "nostalgic devotion to the melting pot" affect some liberals, according to King? What does he mean by this point? Why might you agree or disagree with his point here?

2. King mentions the Emerson bill, which would make English the official language of the government. He notes that the bill provides for several exceptions. What are these exceptions? Do you agree with them? Why or why not?

3. The writer raises the question of a national language in many different countries. How do the problems of Romania, Belgium, or Canada compare to the relative equilibrium of Switzerland and India? How do the problems in both of these groups compare to problems in the United States? What do some of these controversies tell you of the values placed on language by some nations?

4. How is "language a convenient surrogate for nonlinguistic claims"? What does that mean? Do you agree? Why or why not? What is wrong or right about this tendency?

5. What do you think Canada's proximity to the United States has to do with U.S. anxiety over a national language? What other national anxiety does the writer cite as possibly contributing to the prevailing English-only attitude? How does this aspect of the discussion affect your opinion?

★ Values Conversation

Form groups and discuss the issue of English as the official language of the country. What advantages does your group see in an English-only rule? What problems do you see?

★ *Writing about Values*

1. Write an essay to answer the question of the title from your own perspective. Support any assertions with concrete details. Should English be the law? Why or why not? What consequences do you foresee for your position?

2. Write an essay called "Language Tolerance" in which you explain how people living in the same geographical area but speaking different languages can respect each other's language use and live harmoniously.

3. Respond in a well-reasoned argumentative essay to this statement by King. "America may be threatened by immigration. I don't know. But America is not threatened by language."

Chang-rae Lee

Mute in an English-Only World

Author of the book *Native Speaker* (1995), Chang-rae Lee was born in 1965. He received his MFA from the University of Oregon, where he teaches creative writing. In this selection he shows the effects of the English language on his Korean-born mother in America.

———————— ★ ————————

When I read of the troubles in Palisades Park, New Jersey, over the proliferation of Korean-language signs along its main commercial strip, I unexpectedly sympathized with the frustrations, resentments and fears of the longtime residents. They clearly felt alienated and even unwelcome in a vital part of their community. The town, like seven others in New Jersey, has passed laws requiring that half of any commercial sign in a foreign language be in English. 1

Now I certainly would never tolerate any exclusionary ideas about who could rightfully settle and belong in the town. But having been raised in a Korean immigrant family, I saw every day the exacting price and power of language, especially with my mother, who was an outsider in an English-only world. 2

In the first years we lived in America, my mother could speak only the most basic English, and she often encountered great difficulty whenever she went out. 3

We lived in New Rochelle, New York, in the early 1970s, and most of the local businesses were run by the descendants of immigrants who, generations ago, had come to the suburbs from New York City. Proudly dotting Main Street and North Avenue were Italian pastry and cheese shops, Jewish tailors and cleaners and Polish and German butchers and bakers. If my mother's marketing couldn't wait until the weekend, when my father had free time, she would often hold off until I came home from school to buy the groceries. 4

Though I was only 6 or 7 years old, she insisted that I go out shopping with her and my younger sister. I mostly loathed the task, partly because it meant I couldn't spend the afternoon playing catch with my friends but also because I knew our errands would inevitably lead to an awkward scene, and that I would have to speak up to help my mother. 5

6   I was just learning the language myself, but I was a quick study, as children are with new tongues. I had spent kindergarten in almost complete silence, hearing only the high nasality of my teacher and comprehending little but the cranky wails and cries of my classmates. But soon, seemingly mere months later, I had already become a terrible ham and mimic, and I would crack up my father with impressions of teachers, his friends and even himself. My mother scolded me for aping his speech, and the one time I attempted to make light of hers I rated a roundhouse smack on my bottom.

7   For her, the English language was not very funny. It usually meant trouble and a good dose of shame, and sometimes real hurt. Although she had a good reading knowledge of the language from university classes in South Korea, she had never practiced actual conversation. So in America, she used English flashcards and phrase books and watched television with us kids. And she faithfully carried a pocket workbook illustrated with stick-figure people and compound sentences to be filled in.

8   But none of it seemed to do her much good. Staying mostly at home to care for us, she didn't have many chances to try out sundry words and phrases. When she did, say, at the window of the post office, her readied speech would stall, freeze, sometimes altogether collapse.

9   One day was unusually harrowing. We ventured downtown in the new Ford Country Squire my father had bought her, an enormous station wagon that seemed as long—and deft—as an ocean liner. We were shopping for a special meal for guests visiting that weekend, and my mother had heard that a particular butcher carried fresh oxtails, which she needed for a traditional soup.

10   We'd never been inside the shop, but my mother would pause before its window, which was always lined with whole hams, crown roasts and ropes of plump handmade sausages. She greatly esteemed the bounty with her eyes, and my sister and I did also, but despite our desirous cries she'd turn us away and instead buy the packaged links at the Finast supermarket, where she felt comfortable looking them over and could easily spot the price. And, of course, not have to talk.

11   But that day she was resolved. The butcher store was crowded, and as we stepped inside the door jingled a welcome. No one seemed to notice. We waited for some time, and people who entered after us were now being served. Finally, an old woman nudged my mother and waved a little ticket, which we hadn't taken. We patiently waited again, until one of the beefy men behind the glass display hollered our number.

12   My mother pulled us forward and began searching the cases, but the oxtails were nowhere to be found. The man, his big arms crossed, sharply said, "Come on, lady, whaddya want?" This unnerved her, and she somehow blurted the Korean word for oxtail, soggori.

The butcher looked as if my mother had put something sour in his 13
mouth, and he glanced back at the lighted board and called the next
number.

Before I knew it, she had rushed us outside and back in the wagon, 14
which she had double-parked because of the crowd. She was furious, almost vibrating with fear and grief, and I could see she was about to cry.

She wanted to go back inside, but now the driver of the car we 15
were blocking wanted to pull out. She was shooing us away. My
mother, who had just earned her driver's license, started furiously
working the pedals. But in her haste she must have flooded the engine,
for it wouldn't turn over. The driver started honking and then another
car began honking as well, and soon it seemed the entire street was
shrieking at us.

In the following years, my mother grew steadily more comfortable 16
with English. In Korean, she could be fiery, stern, deeply funny and
ironic; in English, just slightly less so. If she was never quite fluent, she
gained enough confidence to make herself clearly known to anyone,
and particularly to me.

Five years ago, she died of cancer, and some months after we bur- 17
ied her I found myself in the driveway of my father's house, washing
her sedan. I liked taking care of her things; it made me feel close to her.
While I was cleaning out the glove compartment, I found her pocket
English workbook, the one with the silly illustrations. I hadn't seen it in
nearly 20 years. The yellowed pages were brittle and dog-eared. She
had fashioned a plain-paper wrapping for it, and I wondered whether
she meant to protect the book or hide it.

I don't doubt that she would have appreciated doing the family 18
shopping on the new Broad Avenue of Palisades Park. But I like to
think, too, that she would have understood those who now complain
about the Korean-only signs.

I wonder what these same people would have done if they had 19
seen my mother studying her English workbook—or lost in a store.
Would they have nodded gently at her? Would they have lent a kind
word?

★ Meaning and Understanding

1. What is the main point of the essay?

2. The writer is Korean yet sympathizes with "longtime residents" who
   feel alienated by commercial signs, which are not printed—at least
   partially—in English. What, exactly, is the writer for or against?

3. Why did the writer loathe the task of going shopping with his mother?
   How do you explain the tension both people felt? Was it the same?

4. Why did the writer's mother not see anything funny in the English language? How did she try to build her English skills? Did her efforts help? Why or why not?

5. Why did the family usually skip the butcher shop for the Finast super-market? What prompted the mother's resolve to visit the butcher? How was she treated there?

6. What is the significance of the "pocket English workbook" Chang-rae Lee's mother left in the glove compartment of the sedan?

★ *Techniques and Strategies*

1. What successful elements of narrative do you find this essay?

2. What is the intended audience for the piece? How can you tell?

3. The writer's mother had problems with the English language. Why, then, does the writer say that he sympathizes with English speakers who object to Korean language signs in a New Jersey commercial strip? Is he sincere, do you think? Ironic? Using reverse psychology? How effective is his approach and why?

4. How does the fact that the writer is Korean affect the main point of the essay?

5. How has Chang-rae Lee brought to life the moment in the butcher shop and, afterwards, in the automobile? What sensory details make you respond to the setting? What do the spoken words of the butcher contribute to the scene?

★ *Speaking of Values*

1. The essay chronicles the kinds of problems speakers of other lan-guages have when they come up against American language and cul-ture. What ways can you suggest for easing the language burden on nonnative speakers? Or do you think that the issue of language in this case is insurmountable? Explain why you hold the ideas that you do.

2. The writer refers to mimicking his own father and the resulting laughter. However, when the writer mimics his mother, a reprimand follows. How do you explain such different reactions to the same kind of situation?

3. The writer portrays the butcher shop as a very busy place and the butcher who dealt with the Korean family as a busy man. Does the ac-tivity of the place justify his behavior? Why or why not? What does his response to the mother tell you about his sense of values regarding speakers of other languages?

4. Nationalizing English would necessitate a change in individual citizen's identities and behaviors, but how and why would that resulting change be different from the multilingualism prevalent in so many countries of the world?

5. Chang-rae Lee implies that his mother "would have understood those who now complain about the Korean-only signs." What is he trying to suggest about the values his mother holds about people and language? Do you agree that his mother might understand? Why?

★ Values Conversation

Form groups to discuss whether—and how—American society should ease the burden of speakers of other languages who come to live and work here. Report your group's findings to the rest of the class.

★ Writing about Values

1. Write an essay about a time you or someone you know helped someone communicate an idea to someone who didn't understand it.

2. Write an essay that examines the pros and cons of being either monolingual or multilingual.

3. Write an essay examining the relation between language and identity.

Nancy Mairs

Body in Trouble

Nancy Mairs was born in 1943. She has taught at the University of California and the University of Arizona and has written a number of works including collections of poems, *In All the Rooms of the Yellow House* (1984), and essays, *Remembering the Bone House* (1989). In this essay from *Waist-High in the World* (1996), she describes how physical disability affects one's perspective on the world.

———— ★ ————

1   In biblical times, physical and mental disorders were thought to signify possession by demons. In fact, Jesus's proficiency at casting these out accounted for much of his popularity among the common folk (though probably not among swine). People who were stooped or blind or subject to seizures were clearly not okay as they were but required fixing, and divine intervention was the only remedy powerful enough to cleanse them of their baleful residents.

2   Theologically as well as medically, this interpretation of the body in trouble now seems primitive, and yet we perpetuate the association underlying it. A brief examination of "dead" metaphors (those which have been so thoroughly integrated into language that we generally overlook their analogical origins) demonstrates the extent to which physical vigor equates with positive moral qualities. "Keep your chin up," we say (signifying courage), "and your eyes open" (alertness); "stand on your own two feet" (independence) "and tall" (pride); "look straight in the eye" (honesty) or "see eye to eye" (accord); "run rings around" (superiority). By contrast, physical debility connotes vice, as in "sit on your ass" (laziness), "take it lying down" (weakness), "listen with half an ear" (inattention), and get left "without a leg to stand on" (unsound argument). The way in which the body occupies space and the quality of the space it occupies correlate with the condition of the soul: it is better to be admired as "high-minded" than "looked down on" for one's "low morals," to be "in the know" than "out of it," to be "up front" than "back-handed," to be "free as a bird" than "confined to a wheelchair."

3   Now, the truth is that, unless you are squatting or six years old, I can never look you straight in the eye, and I spend all my time sitting on my ass except when I'm taking it lying down. These are the realities of life in a wheelchair (though in view of the alternatives—bed, chair,

or floor—"confinement" is the very opposite of my condition). And the fact that the soundness of the body so often serves as a metaphor for its moral health, its deterioration thus implying moral degeneracy, puts me and my kind in a quandary. How can I possibly be "good"? Let's face it, wicked witches are not just ugly (as sin); they're also bent and misshapen (crooked). I am bent and misshapen, therefore ugly, therefore wicked. And I have no way to atone.

It is a bind many women, not just the ones with disabilities, have   4
historically found themselves in by virtue of their incarnation in a sociolinguistic system over which they have had relatively little power. (Notice how virile the virtues encoded in the examples above.) Female bodies, even handsome and wholesome ones, have tended to give moralists fits of one sort or another (lust, disgust, but seldom trust). As everyone who has read the *Malleus Maleficarum* knows, "All witchcraft comes from carnal Lust which is in Women insatiable." If a good man is hard to find, a good woman is harder, unless she's (1) prepubescent, (2) senile, or (3) dead; and even then, some will have their doubts about her. It is tricky enough, then, trying to be a good woman at all, but a crippled woman experiences a kind of double jeopardy. How can she construct a world that will accommodate her realities, including her experience of her own goodness, while it remains comprehensible to those whose world-views are founded on premises alien or even inimical to her sense of self?

Disability is at once a metaphorical and a material state, evocative   5
of other conditions in time and space—childhood and imprisonment come to mind—yet "like" nothing but itself. I can't live it or write about it except by conflating the figurative and the substantial, the "as if" with the relentlessly "what is." Let me illustrate with an experience from a couple of years ago, when George and I went to a luncheon honoring the Dalai Lama, held at a large resort northwest of Tucson. Although we were not enrolled in the five-day workshop he had come here to lead, we found ourselves in the hallway when the meeting room disgorged the workshop participants—all fourteen hundred of them—into a narrow area further constricted by tables laden with bells, beads, and brochures. And let me tell you, no matter how persuaded they were of the beauty and sacredness of all life, not one of them seemed to think that any life was going on below the level of her or his own gaze. "Down here!" I kept whimpering at the hips and buttocks and bellies pressing my wheelchair on all sides. "Down here! There's a person down here!" My only recourse was to roll to one side and hug a wall.

Postmodern criticism, feminist and otherwise, makes a good deal   6
of the concept of wall-hugging, or marginality, which is meant to suggest that some segment of the population—black, brown, yellow, or

red, poor, female, lesbian, what have you—is shouldered to the side, heedlessly or not, by some perhaps more numerous and certainly more powerful segment, most frequently wealthy, well-educated Euro-American males. Regardless of the way marginality is conceived, it is never taken to mean that those on the margin occupy a physical space literally outside the field of vision of those in the center, so that the latter trip unawares and fall into the laps of those they have banished from consciousness unless these scoot safely out of the way. "Marginality" thus means something altogether different to me from what it means to social theorists. It is no metaphor for the power relations between one group of human beings and another but a literal description of where I stand (figuratively speaking): over here, on the edge, out of bounds, beneath your notice. I embody the metaphors. Only whether or not I like doing so is immaterial.

7   It may be this radical materiality of my circumstances, together with the sense I mentioned earlier that defect and deformity bar me from the ranks of "good" women, which have spurred me in the past, as they no doubt will go on doing, to put the body at the center of all my meditations, my "corpus," if you will. Not that I always write *about* the body, though I often do, but that I always write, consciously, *as* a body. (This quality more than any other, I think, exiles my work from conventional academic discourse. The guys may be writing with the pen/penis, but they pretend at all times to keep it in their pants.) And it is this—my—crippled female body that my work struggles to redeem through that most figurative of human tools: language. Because language substitutes a no-thing for a thing, whereas a body is pure thing through and through, this task must fail. But inevitable disappointment does not deprive labor of its authenticity.

8   And so I use inscription to insert my embodied self into a world with which, over time, I have less and less in common. Part of my effort entails reshaping both that self and that world in order to reconcile the two. We bear certain responsibilities toward each other, the world and I, and I must neither remove myself from it nor permit it to exclude me if we are to carry these out. I can't become a "hopeless cripple" without risking moral paralysis; nor can the world, except to its own diminishment, refuse my moral participation.

9   But is a woman for whom any action at all is nearly impossible capable of right action, or am I just being morally cocky here? After all, if I claim to be a good woman, I leave myself open to the question: Good for what? The most straightforward answer is the most tempting: Good for nothing. I mean really. I can stand with assistance but I can't take a step; I can't even spread my own legs for sex anymore. My left arm doesn't work at all, and my right one grows weaker almost by the day. I am having more and more trouble raising a fork or a cup to my lips. (It is possible, I've discovered, though decidedly odd, to drink even

coffee and beer through a straw.) I can no longer drive. I lack the stamina to go out to work. If I live to see them, I will never hold my own grandchildren. These incapacities constitute a stigma that, according to social scientist Erving Goffman, removes me from normal life into a "discredited" position in relation to society.

From the point of view of the Catholic Church, to which I belong, 10 however, mine must be just about the ideal state: too helpless even for the sins other flesh is heir to. After all, parties aren't much fun now that I meet the other revelers eye to navel, and getting drunk is risky since I can hardly see straight cold sober. No matter how insatiable my carnal Lust, nobody's likely to succumb to my charms and sully my reputation. But I am, by sympathy at least, a Catholic *Worker*, part of a community that wastes precious little time fretting about the seven deadlies, assuming instead that the moral core of being in the world lies in the care of others, in *doing* rather than *being* good. How can a woman identify herself as a Catholic Worker if she can't even cut up carrots for the soup or ladle it out for the hungry people queued up outside the kitchen door? Physical incapacity certainly appears to rob such a woman of moral efficacy.

Well, maybe moral demands should no longer be placed on her. 11 Perhaps she ought simply to be "excused" from the moral life on the most generous of grounds: that she suffers enough already, that she has plenty to do just to take care of herself. This dismissive attitude tends to be reinforced when the woman lives at the height of your waist. Because she "stands" no higher than a six-year-old, you may unconsciously ascribe to her the moral development of a child (which, in view of Robert Coles's findings, you will probably underestimate) and demand little of her beyond obedience and enough self-restraint so that she doesn't filch candy bars at the checkout counter while you're busy writing a check. (God, I can't tell you how tempting those brightly wrapped chunks are when they're smack up against your nose.) "Stature" is an intrinsic attribute of moral life, and the woman who lacks the one may be judged incapable of the other.

I am exaggerating here, of course, but only a little. Beyond cheer- 12 fulness and patience, people don't generally expect much of a cripple's character. And certainly they presume that care, which I have placed at the heart of moral experience, flows in one direction, "downward": as from adult to child, so from well to ill, from whole to maimed. This condescension contributes to what Goffman calls "spoiled identity," though he does not deal satisfactorily with the damage it inflicts: without reciprocity, the foundation of any mature moral relationship, the person with a defect cannot grow "up" and move "out" into the world but remains constricted in ways that make being "confined to a wheelchair" look trivial. And so I would say that while it is all right to excuse me from making the soup (for the sake of the soup, probably more than "all right"), you must never—even with the best intentions, even with my own complicity—either enable or require me to withdraw from moral life altogether.

13   So much for carrot-cutting, then, or any other act involving sharp instruments. But wait! One sharp instrument is left me: my tongue. (Here's where metaphor comes in handy.) And my computer keyboard is ... just waist high. With these I ought to be able to concoct another order of soup altogether (in which I'll no doubt find myself up to my ears). In other words, what I can still *do*—so far—is write books. Catholic Workers being extraordinarily tolerant of multiplicity, on the theory that it takes all kinds of parts to form a body, this activity will probably be counted good enough.

14   The world to which I am a material witness is a difficult one to love. But I am not alone in it now; and as the population ages, more and more people—a significant majority of them women—may join me in it, learning to negotiate a chill and rubble-strewn landscape with impaired eyesight and hearing and mobility, searching out some kind of home there. Maps render foreign territory, however dark and wide, fathomable. I mean to make a map. My infinitely harder task, then, is to conceptualize not merely a habitable body but a habitable world: a world that wants me in it.

★ Meaning and Understanding

1. What is the main point of the selection?

2. Why does Mairs note "dead" metaphors or the euphemisms associating behavior with physical reality and vigor?

3. The writer refers to a "sociolinguistic system" (paragraph 4) that seems to be controlled by some and to exert power over others. What is she referring to? What examples does she note? Can you think of any more?

4. How or why must the writer conflate "the figurative and the substantial, the 'as if' with the relentlessly 'what is'"? What does she mean? What example does she give and how does it apply here?

5. How is the writer a Catholic Worker?

6. How is "stature an intrinsic attribute of moral life" (paragraph 11)?

7. What is the writer's point about morality?

★ Techniques and Strategies

1. How does Mairs first try to make it clear that language is tricky or difficult, something that we should all be more thoughtful about?

2. What is Mairs's purpose in this piece? Who is her audience?

3. Mairs makes a number of statements in parentheses. Identify some of them. What purpose do the parenthetical comments serve?

4. How does the writer use the *Malleus Maleficarum* and references to witches and witchcraft?

5. Where does Mairs use definition as a rhetorical strategy? Why does she use it?

★ Speaking of Values

1. How does language force us to communicate in certain ways that can be unfair at times? Can language prevent us from really communicating? Whether you feel the answer is yes or no, explain how you reached your conclusion.

2. Mairs notes that disability is "at once a metaphorical and a material state." She also mentions other, similar states: "childhood and imprisonment come to mind." How is being disabled similar to these conditions?

3. How do language and grammar reflect aspects of gender? Does the language system imply a set of values when we use it to refer to people as *he*? Or do you see the use of *he* as a linguistic convenience developed over time and not meant to imply gender in every usage? Explain your point.

4. Mairs says in paragraph 3 that "the soundness of the body so often serves as a metaphor for its moral health." What does she mean? Why might you agree or disagree with her? What values does she imply about our language?

★ Values Conversation

Form groups and discuss the incident Mairs presents about the luncheon for the Dalai Lama. What point is she trying to make? What is the relation between the avowed values of the crowd and how they treated two people in wheelchairs? Why might you agree or disagree with Mairs's point?

★ Writing about Values

1. Write an essay in which you define the word *marginality*. Give examples to support your view.

2. Write an essay about how society should accommodate people with disabilities. Do you think society does a good job here? Or are disabled people unfairly treated despite society's best intentions to the contrary?

3. Imagine yourself with a disability. What elements in American society would concern you most? What language uses would you wish to change or advance?

Sunil Garg

Under My Skin

Born in 1963, Sunil Garg is a policy analyst in Chicago. In this essay that originally appeared in the *New York Times,* Garg considers the phrase "person of color" and how it has affected his life.

——————— ★ ———————

1   I am a person of color—or at least that is how people often categorize me. Yet what do they mean by that?

2   Certainly, I am brown. My parents emigrated from India in the early 1960's, and I have always thought of myself as Indian-American. But I have never seriously thought of myself as a brown man or as a person of color.

3   I was first confronted with the term when I was accepted to the John F. Kennedy School of Government at Harvard University a few years ago. I received an invitation from the school to attend a special orientation for "students of color." Suddenly, the color of my skin qualified me for special attention.

4   What was the purpose of separating the student body into two groups, whites and those with "color"? Students had not even had the opportunity to introduce themselves on their own terms. By allowing a separate orientation in addition to the general one, the school sent a message to students that color was the one way it had chosen to define the student body.

5   Other students at the Kennedy School explained to me that the term "people of color" includes those who have historically been alienated or oppressed by the Western white world and whose perspectives and cultures have not been properly heard or appreciated.

6   Yet this explanation creates a false relationship between color and culture. Having color does not give anyone a particular culture, nor does having color mean that one's culture or perspective differs from that of whites. I, for instance, identify almost exclusively with Western culture.

7   People can also become disaffected from American culture because of their religious beliefs, their class, sex or even their weight. Yet the term "people of color" implies that only skin color separates and alienates individuals from society.

8   The term also lumps together the different experiences and challenges facing racial and ethnic groups in the United States. Many times, "people of color" will be used when discussing discrimination, when

in fact different groups feel different degrees of discrimination. For instance, a black youth in Harlem has a different experience with racism than does a middle-class Indian-American like myself.

By creating this false union among most of the world's population, the term "people of color" also promotes the idea that Western culture and whites are the exercisers of all power and the perpetrators of all evil. One need not be a student of history, however, to understand that racism and oppression are known in almost every nation and that factors beyond color lead men and women to oppress their brethren. 9

I am not denying the existence of racism in America or the importance of skin color in our society. But my fear is that the term "people of color" creates an environment not where cultural diversity is increased, but where alternative perspectives are reduced to tales of racism and victimization. 10

As the ethnic and racial composition of our nation changes substantially, we need to understand and relate to one another, regardless of the color of our skin. 11

We need to find ways to appreciate our country's true diverse perspectives, cultures, knowledge and experiences. This is a far greater challenge, but a necessary one. 12

★ Meaning and Understanding

1. What circumstances first placed Garg into the "of color" category?

2. What message does Garg believe his special orientation sent to students?

3. What ways, other than through skin color, does Garg feel can people become disaffected from American culture?

4. According to the writer, what does the label "people of color" say about power and evil?

5. Why does Garg feel that the "of color" label does not increase cultural diversity?

★ Techniques and Strategies

1. How does the title serve the essay? In what ways does the title have more than one meaning?

2. What is the thesis of the essay?

3. How does the first paragraph—the introduction—serve the essay? How did it engage your attention as a reader?

4. What supporting details has Garg used to back up his argument? Where do you think he might have provided more details? Why?

5. How has Garg achieved unity in the essay? In what ways do the ideas here focus on a single, essential idea?

★ Speaking of Values

1. What is your reaction to the term "people of color"? Why? What arguments advanced by Garg would you support? Challenge? What values do users of the phrase reveal?

2. In what ways can people's "religious beliefs, their class, sex or even their weight" make them disaffected from American culture? What evidence can you provide to support or challenge Garg's point here?

3. What false relation does the writer see between color and culture? Why might you agree or disagree with him?

4. What, in Garg's view, are the differences between himself and "a black youth in Harlem"? What other differences can you suggest? According to the writer, what effect will these differences have? Why might you agree or disagree with his assertion here?

5. Garg believes that "racism and oppression are known to almost every nation" and that "factors beyond color" are responsible. Why might you agree or disagree with this point?

★ Values Conversation

Form groups to discuss the pros and cons of labeling and categorizing people. Discuss whether having no such labels would be possible and whether any labels can avoid stereotypes. Devise alternatives—and propose ways to promote identity awareness without creating divisive separations between groups. Then consider the viability of your proposed alternatives. Report your group's findings to the class at large.

★ Writing about Values

1. Write an essay examining the pros and cons of your relation to a specific racial, ethnic, or national group. How is membership in this group a part of your identity, and how are the behaviors or affinities that you have a result of belonging to the group?

2. Write your own essay called "Under My Skin" in which you show how your skin color or other physical characteristics influenced the way people viewed or labeled you.

3. Garg argues that "we need to understand and relate to one another regardless of the color of our skin." Write an essay either to propose how to achieve that goal or to challenge it.

Charles R. Lawrence III

On Racist Speech

Born in 1943, Charles R. Lawrence III was educated at Haverford College. He is a law professor who has taught at San Francisco University and Stanford and the author of *The Bakke Case* and many articles. In this selection he examines the relation between the right of free speech and the offensive speech that right sometimes protects.

——————— ★ ———————

I have spent the better part of my life as a dissenter. As a high school   1
student, I was threatened with suspension for my refusal to participate
in a civil defense drill, and I have been a conspicuous consumer of my
First Amendment liberties ever since. There are very strong reasons for
protecting even racist speech. Perhaps the most important of these is
that such protection reinforces our society's commitment to tolerance
as a value, and that by protecting bad speech from government regulation, we will be forced to combat it as a community.

But I also have a deeply felt apprehension about the resurgence of   2
racial violence and the corresponding rise in the incidence of verbal
and symbolic assault and harassment to which blacks and other traditionally subjugated and excluded groups are subjected. I am troubled
by the way the debate has been framed in response to the recent surge
of racist incidents on college and university campuses and in response
to some universities' attempts to regulate harassing speech. The problem has been framed as one in which the liberty of free speech is in conflict with the elimination of racism. I believe this has placed the bigot
on the moral high ground and fanned the rising flames of racism.

Above all, I am troubled that we have not listened to the real vic-   3
tims, that we have shown so little understanding of their injury, and
that we have abandoned those whose race, gender, or sexual preference
continues to make them second-class citizens. It seems to me a very sad
irony that the first instinct of civil libertarians has been to challenge
even the smallest, most narrowly framed efforts by universities to provide black and other minority students with the protection the Constitution guarantees them.

The landmark case of *Brown v. Board of Education* is not a case that   4
we normally think of as a case about speech. But *Brown* can be
broadly read as articulating the principle of equal citizenship. *Brown*
held that segregated schools were inherently unequal because of the

message that segregation conveyed—that black children were an untouchable caste, unfit to go to school with white children. If we understand the necessity of eliminating the system of signs and symbols that signal the inferiority of blacks, then we should hesitate before proclaiming that all racist speech that stops short of physical violence must be defended.

5   University officials who have formulated policies to respond to incidents of racial harassment have been characterized in the press as "thought police," but such policies generally do nothing more than impose sanctions against intentional face-to-face insults. When racist speech takes the form of face-to-face insults, catcalls, or other assaultive speech aimed at an individual or small group of persons, it falls directly within the "fighting words" exception to First Amendment protection. The Supreme Court has held that words which "by their very utterance inflict injury or tend to incite an immediate breach of the peace" are not protected by the First Amendment.

6   If the purpose of the First Amendment is to foster the greatest amount of speech, racial insults disserve that purpose. Assaultive racist speech functions as as a preemptive strike. The invective is experienced as a blow, not as a proffered idea, and once the blow is struck, it is unlikely that a dialogue will follow. Racial insults are particularly undeserving of First Amendment protection because the perpetrator's intention is not to discover truth or initiate dialogue but to injure the victim. In most situations, members of minority groups realize that they are likely to lose if they respond to epithets by fighting and are forced to remain silent and submissive.

7   Courts have held that offensive speech may not be regulated in public forums such as streets where the listener may avoid the speech by moving on, but the regulation of otherwise protected speech has been permitted when the speech invades the privacy of the unwilling listener's home or when the unwilling listener cannot avoid the speech. Racist posters, fliers, and graffiti in dormitories, bathrooms, and other common living spaces would seem to clearly fall within the reasoning of these cases. Minority students should not be required to remain in their rooms in order to avoid racial assault. Minimally, they should find a safe haven in their dorms and in all other common rooms that are a part of their daily routine.

8   I would also argue that the university's responsibility for ensuring that these students receive an equal educational opportunity provides a compelling justification for regulations that ensure them safe passage in all common areas. A minority student should not have to risk becoming the target of racially assaulting speech every time he or she chooses to walk across campus. Regulating vilifying speech that cannot be anticipated or avoided would not preclude announced speeches and rallies—situations that would give minority-group members and their

allies the chance to organize counterdemonstrations or avoid the speech altogether.

The most commonly advanced argument against the regulation of racist speech proceeds something like this: We recognize that minority groups suffer pain and injury as the result of racist speech, but we must allow this hate mongering for the benefit of society as a whole. Freedom of speech is the lifeblood of our democratic system. It is especially important for minorities because often it is their only vehicle for rallying support for the redress of their grievances. It will be impossible to formulate a prohibition so precise that it will prevent the racist speech you want to suppress without catching in the same net all kinds of speech that it would be unconscionable for a democratic society to suppress.   9

Whenever we make such arguments, we are striking a balance on the one hand between our concern for the continued free flow of ideas and the democratic process dependent on that flow, and, on the other, our desire to further the cause of equality. There can be no meaningful discussion of how we should reconcile our commitment to equality and our commitment to free speech until it is acknowledged that there is real harm inflicted by racist speech and that this harm is far from trivial.   10

To engage in a debate about the First Amendment and racist speech without a full understanding of the nature and extent of that harm is to risk making the First Amendment an instrument of domination rather than a vehicle of liberation. We have not known the experience of victimization by racist, misogynist, and homophobic speech, nor do we equally share the burden of the societal harm it inflicts. We are often quick to say that we have heard the cry of the victims when we have not.   11

The *Brown* case is again instructive because it speaks directly to the psychic injury inflicted by racist speech by noting that the symbolic message of segregation affected "the hearts and minds" of Negro children "in a way unlikely ever to be undone." Racial epithets and harassment often cause deep emotional scarring and feelings of anxiety and fear that pervade every aspect of a victim's life.   12

Brown also recognized that black children did not have an equal opportunity to learn and participate in the school community if they bore the additional burden of being subjected to the humiliation and psychic assault contained in the message of segregation. University students bear an analogous burden when they are forced to live and work in an environment where at any moment they may be subjected to denigrating verbal harassment and assault. The same injury was addressed by the Supreme Court when it held that sexual harassment that creates a hostile or abusive work environment violates the ban on sex discrimination in employment of Title VII of the Civil Rights Act of 1964.   13

Carefully drafted university regulations would bar the use of words as assault weapons and leave unregulated even the most heinous of   14 ideas when those ideas are presented at times and places and in manners that provide an opportunity for reasoned rebuttal or escape from immediate injury. The history of the development of the right to free speech has been one of carefully evaluating the importance of free expression and its effects on other important societal interests. We have drawn the line between protected and unprotected speech before without dire results. (Courts have, for example, exempted from the protection of the First Amendment obscene speech and speech that disseminates official secrets, that defames or libels another person, or that is used to form a conspiracy or monopoly.)

15   Blacks and other people of color are skeptical about the argument that even the most injurious speech must remain unregulated because, in an unregulated marketplace of ideas, the best ones will rise to the top and gain acceptance. Our experience tells us quite the opposite. We have seen too many good liberal politicians shy away from the issues that might brand them as being too closely allied with us.

16   Whenever we decide that racist speech must be tolerated because of the importance of maintaining societal tolerance for all unpopular speech, we are asking blacks and other subordinated groups to bear the burden for the good of all. We must be careful that the ease with which we strike the balance against the regulation of racist speech is in no way influenced by the fact that the cost will be borne by others. We must be certain that those who will pay that price are fairly represented in our deliberations and that they are heard.

17   At the core of the argument that we should resist all government regulation of speech is the ideal that the best cure for bad speech is good, that ideas that affirm equality and the worth of all individuals will ultimately prevail. This is an empty ideal unless those of us who would fight racism are vigilant and unequivocal in that fight. We must look for ways to offer assistance and support to students whose speech and political participation are chilled in a climate of racial harassment.

18   Civil rights lawyers might consider suing on behalf of blacks whose right to an equal education is denied by a university's failure to ensure a nondiscriminatory educational climate or conditions of employment. We must embark upon the development of a First Amendment jurisprudence grounded in the reality of our history and our contemporary experience. We must think hard about how best to launch legal attacks against the most indefensible forms of hate speech. Good lawyers can create exceptions and narrow interpretations that limit the harm of hate speech without opening the floodgates of censorship.

19   Everyone concerned with these issues must find ways to engage actively in actions that resist and counter the racist ideas that we would have the First Amendment protect. If we fail in this, the victims of hate speech must rightly assume that we are on the oppressors' side.

★ Meaning and Understanding

1. What is Lawrence's main point about the First Amendment?

2. What is the structure of the current regulation of free speech in terms of the invasion of privacy?

3. The writer presents an important desegregation case, *Brown* v. *Board of Education,* to establish legal precedents for his opinions and to establish alternative limitations to racist speech. How does he propose using the case?

4. What is the "fighting words" exception to First Amendment protection?

5. How do racial insults "disserve" the First Amendment?

6. Why does Lawrence feel nonregulation of the First Amendment is the "ideal"? The writer states that this ideal can become "empty." What does he mean?

★ Techniques and Strategies

1. What is the thesis of the essay?

2. How does the writer's first sentence help establish his argument? The first paragraph?

3. In what ways is the essay an argument against regulating free speech? How is it an argument supporting limits on free speech? What is your reaction to this seeming paradox? Is the writer merely fencesitting? Or do you find merit in the opposing philosophies?

4. Where does Lawrence use narration and exemplification in the essay? How do these strategies contribute to the argument?

5. Where does the writer use definition and comparison? How do these strategies contribute to the argument?

★ Speaking of Values

1. The writer proposes both limiting and not limiting racist speech. Can we have it both ways? How?

2. What is our "society's commitment to tolerance as a value," do you think? Why or how is this tolerance important?

3. How have recent attempts by universities to regulate harassing speech framed this conflict? The writer proposes that these actions actually place bigots on "moral high ground." Why might you agree or disagree?

4. What are "thought police"? How can they actually limit free speech? What do you think of this notion?

5. The writer notes that certain types of speech—obscene speech, speech that disseminates official secrets, speech that defames or libels a person, or speech that is used to form a conspiracy or monopoly—may suffer legal repercussions even under the First Amendment. Do you find this consequence acceptable? Why or why not?

6. What does the writer mean when he suggests in the final paragraph that those who do not counter racist ideas protected by the First Amendment might be accused of being on the oppressor's side?

★ Values Conversation

The writer claims that racist speech limits a student's opportunity to get an education and that universities should be responsible for ensuring equal educational opportunity. Do you agree or disagree with either aspect of this premise? Form groups and discuss your views on these matters.

★ Writing about Values

1. Write an essay in which you narrate an incident involving racist speech and its effects in order to reveal your point of view on the topic. Be sure to examine whether some manner of regulation of racist speech may have produced a different outcome to the situation.

2. What are your views on government regulation, in general? Choose one or two familiar areas—economics, law, taxes, health care, smoking—and analyze the effects of government oversights as you present your point of view.

3. A known racist arrives to speak to an assembled group of students on your campus. Write a letter to the editor of your school newspaper to argue for or against the Institution's sponsorship of this event and what it says about the Institution's values.

Carl Sandburg

Primer Lesson

Carl Sandburg (1878–1967) was reared in poverty in Illinois as the son of
Swedish immigrants and went on to become a "poet of the people." His
Chicago Poems in 1916 established his reputation, which grew considerably in his lifetime. In "Primer Lesson" he examines in a very brief poem
the impulse of pride and its manifestation in language.

———— ★ ————

Look out how you use proud words.
When you let proud words go, it is
   not easy to call them back.
They wear long boots, hard boots; they
   walk off proud; they can't hear you   5
   calling—
Look out how you use proud words.

★ Meaning and Understanding

1. What is Sandburg's point in this brief poem?

2. What is a primer lesson?

3. Why does the poet imply that someone might want to call the proud
   words back?

★ Techniques and Strategies

1. What is the significance of the title? If the poem is about "proud
   words," why didn't Sandburg use that phrase as the title of the poem?

2. Identify the metaphor in the poem. What is your reaction to it? What
   does it make you see?

3. What is the effect of the repetition of the first and last lines of the
   poem? Where else do you note repetition? In such a short poem, why
   do you think Sandburg repeats words and phrases as he does?

★ *Speaking of Values*

1. How do you think Sandburg would define "proud words"? How would you define it?

2. In what sense do proud words "wear long, hard boots"? Do you agree with the point that the poet is expressing here?

3. What does Sandburg seem to be saying about the power of spoken language? What relation does he imply between language and emotion?

★ *Values Conversation*

In groups of four or five students, identify some examples of proud words and how they can make people feel. Draw on your own experience or on books you've read or films you've seen.

★ *Writing about Values*

1. Write an essay about a time that you or someone you know used proud words to a loved one. What were the effects of the words used?

2. Write an essay about a time that you tried to call back proud words. Were you successful? Why or why not?

3. Write an essay about pride as an element in human values.

Deborah Tannen

Women's Conversations

Born in 1945, Deborah Tannen is University Professor and professor of linguistics at Georgetown University. She writes about gender issues and language and is the author of *You Just Don't Understand: Women and Men in Conversation* (1990) and *Gender and Discourse* (1994). In this piece she focuses on the characteristics of men's and women's conversations.

---- ★ ----

Elizabeth Aries, a professor of psychology at Amherst College, set out   1
to show that highly intelligent, highly educated young women are no longer submissive in conversations with male peers. And indeed she found that the college women did talk more than the college men in small groups she set up. But what they said was different. The men tended to set the agenda by offering opinions, suggestions, and information. The women tended to react, offering agreement or disagreement. Furthermore, she found that body language was as different as ever: The men sat with their legs stretched out, while the women gathered themselves in. Noting that research has found that speakers using the open-bodied position are more likely to persuade their listeners, Aries points out that talking more may not ensure that women will be heard.

In another study, Aries found that men in all-male discussion   2
groups spent a lot of time at the beginning finding out "who was best informed about movies, books, current events, politics, and travel" as a means of "sizing up the competition" and negotiating "where they stood in relation to each other." This glimpse of how men talk when there are no women present gives an inkling of why displaying knowledge and expertise is something that men find more worth doing than women. What the women in Aries's study spent time doing was "gaining a closeness through more intimate self-revelation."

It is crucial to bear in mind that both the women and the men in   3
these studies were establishing camaraderie, and both were concerned with their relationships to each other. But different aspects of their relationships were of primary concern: their place in a hierarchical order for the men, and their place in a network of intimate connections for the women. The consequence of these disparate concerns was very different ways of speaking.

4   Thomas Fox is an English professor who was intrigued by the differences between women and men in his freshman writing classes. What he observed corresponds almost precisely to the experimental findings of Aries and Leet-Pellegrini. Fox's method of teaching writing included having all the students read their essays to each other in class and talk to each other in small groups. He also had them write papers reflecting on the essays and the discussion groups. He alone, as the teacher, read these analytical papers.

5   To exemplify the two styles he found typical of women and men, Fox chose a woman, Ms. M, and a man, Mr. H. In her speaking as well as her writing, Ms. M. held back what she knew, appearing uninformed and uninterested, because she feared offending her classmates. Mr. H spoke and wrote with authority and apparent confidence because he was eager to persuade his peers. She did not worry about persuading; he did not worry about offending.

6   In his analytical paper, the young man described his own behavior in the mixed-gender group discussions as if he were describing the young men in Leet-Pellegrini's and Aries's studies:

> In my sub-group I am the leader. I begin every discussion by stating my opinions as facts. The other two members of the sub-group tend to sit back and agree with me. . . . I need people to agree with me.

Fox comments that Mr. H reveals "a sense of self, one that acts to change himself and other people, that seems entirely distinct from Ms. M's sense of self, dependent on and related to others."

7   Calling Ms. M's sense of self "dependent" suggests a negative view of her way of being in the world—and, I think, a view more typical of men. This view reflects the assumption that the alternative to independence is dependence. If this is indeed a male view, it may explain why so many men are cautious about becoming intimately involved with others: It makes sense to avoid humiliating dependence by insisting on independence. But there is another alternative: *inter*dependence.

8   The main difference between these alternatives is symmetry. Dependence is an asymmetrical involvement: One person needs the other, but not vice versa, so the needy person is one-down. Interdependence is symmetrical: Both parties rely on each other, so neither is one-up or one-down. Moreover, Mr. H's sense of self is also dependent on others. He requires others to listen, agree, and allow him to take the lead by stating his opinions first.

9   Looked at this way, the woman and man in this group are both dependent on each other. Their differing goals are complementary, although neither understands the reasons for the other's behavior. This would be a fine arrangement, except that their differing goals result in alignments that enhance his authority and undercut hers.

Fox also describes differences in the way male and female students   10
in his classes interpreted a story they read. These differences also reflect assumptions about the interdependence or independence of individuals. Fox's students wrote their responses to "The Birthmark" by
Nathaniel Hawthorne. In the story, a woman's husband becomes obsessed with a birthmark on her face. Suffering from her husband's re-
vulsion at the sight of her, the wife becomes obsessed with it too and, in
a reversal of her initial impulse, agrees to undergo a treatment he has
devised to remove the birthmark—a treatment that succeeds in removing the mark, but kills her in the process.

Ms. M interpreted the wife's complicity as a natural response to   11
the demand of a loved one: The woman went along with her husband's lethal schemes to remove the birthmark because she wanted to
please and be appealing to him. Mr. H blamed the woman's insecurity and vanity for her fate, and he blamed her for voluntarily submitting to her husband's authority. Fox points out that he saw her as
individually responsible for her actions, just as he saw himself as individually responsible for his own actions. To him, the issue was independence: The weak wife voluntarily took a submissive role. To
Ms. M, the issue was interdependence: The woman was inextricably
bound up with her husband, so her behavior could not be separated
from his.

Fox observes that Mr. H saw the writing of the women in the class   12
as spontaneous—they wrote whatever popped into their heads. Nothing could be farther from Ms. M's experience as she described it: When
she knew her peers would see her writing, she censored everything
that popped into her head. In contrast, when she was writing something that only her professor would read, she expressed firm and articulate opinions.

There is a striking but paradoxical complementarity to Ms. M's and   13
Mr. H's styles, when they are taken together. He needs someone to listen and agree. She listens and agrees. But in another sense, their dove-
tailing purposes are at cross-purposes. He misinterprets her
agreement, intended in a spirit of connection, as a reflection of status
and power: He thinks she is "indecisive" and "insecure." Her reasons
for refraining from behaving as he does—firmly stating opinions as
facts—have nothing to do with her attitudes toward her knowledge, as
he thinks they do, but rather result from her attitudes toward her relationships with her peers.

These experimental studies by Leet-Pellegrini and Aries, and the   14
observations by Fox, all indicate that, typically, men are more comfortable than women in giving information and opinions and speaking in
an authoritative way to a group, whereas women are more comfortable
than men in supporting others.

★ Meaning and Understanding

1. What major findings does Elizabeth Aries report about women's conversations?

2. In what ways do women and men perceive the differences between the ways they converse? Do they perceive these differences in the same ways? What, according to the writer, is the differences?

3. What are the results of Fox's study?

4. How are Aries's and Fox's findings similar? Are they mutually exclusive, or do they complement each other? How?

5. Do Ms. M and Mr. H have a mutually beneficial relationship in terms of conversation? Why or why not?

★ Techniques and Strategies

1. What is the thesis of this selection?

2. How does Tannen use comparison and contrast strategies?

3. What does the reference to body language contribute to the piece?

4. What is the effect of including the excerpt from Mr. H's essay? Why do you suppose a parallel excerpt from Ms. M's essay does not exist? Is there any reference to Ms. M's essay? What kind of reference is it?

5. What is the effect of the extended explanation of the varying responses to Nathaniel Hawthorne's story "The Birthmark?" (You can read Hawthorne's story on pages 563–576 of this book.) What do these varying responses do for the piece?

★ Speaking of Values

1. Based on your own experience, how do men and women relate to each other in conversations? How do they reflect the points made in this piece? How do your experiences challenge the assertions here?

2. What values do women reflect when they carry on a conversation? Men?

3. How are the differences between men and women's communication strategies related to social or biological norms? What values of the society do these differing approaches reveal?

4. Tannen names and defines the term *interdependence*. What is the meaning of the term? What values does it imply?

5. Aries's study implies that men find displaying knowledge and expertise more worthwhile than women do. How does your experience support or challenge that assumption?

★ Values Conversation

If Tannen is right that men and women communicate differently, what does this fact imply about the ongoing debate over equal rights for both sexes? Form groups and discuss.

★ Writing about Values

1. Write an essay to characterize and explain other differences between men and women. Avoid the obvious and stereotypical. Draw on comparison and contrast strategies.

2. Write an analytic essay called "Men's Conversations" in which you explain the characteristics of and values implicit in men's speech and how men relate to each other through language.

3. Choose a book or a film you know and enjoy and explain how men and women might interpret it differently.

Barbara Mellix

From Outside, In

Barbara Mellix is a writer and teacher currently at the University of Pittsburgh in the Arts and Sciences program. In this selection, she looks at the role of both standard and black English in her own life and the life of her family.

──────── ★ ────────

1   Two years ago, when I started writing this paper, trying to bring order out of chaos, my ten-year-old daughter was suffering from an acute attack of boredom. She drifted in and out of the room complaining that she had nothing to do, no one to "be with" because none of her friends were at home. Patiently I explained that I was working on something special and needed peace and quiet, and I suggested that she paint, read, or work with her computer. None of these interested her. Finally, she pulled up a chair to my desk and watched me, now and then heaving long, loud sighs. After two or three minutes (nine or ten sighs), I lost my patience. "Looka here, Allie," I said, "you too old for this kinda carryin' on. I done told you this is important. You wronger than dirt to be in here haggin' me like this and you know it. Now git on outta here and leave me off before I put my foot all the way down."

2   I was at home, alone with my family, and my daughter understood that this way of speaking was appropriate in that context. She knew, as a matter of fact, that it was almost inevitable; when I get angry at home, I speak some of my finest, most cherished black English. Had I been speaking to my daughter in this manner in certain other environments, she would have been shocked and probably worried that I had taken leave of my sense of propriety.

3   Like my children, I grew up speaking what I considered two distinctly different languages—black English and standard English (or as I thought of them then, the ordinary everyday speech of "country" coloreds and "proper" English)—and in the process of acquiring these languages, I developed an understanding of when, where, and how to use them. But unlike my children, I grew up in a world that was primarily black. My friends, neighbors, minister, teachers—almost everybody I associated with every day—were black. And we spoke to one another in our own special language: *That sho is a pretty dress you got on. If she don' soon leave me off I'm gon tell her head a mess. I was so mad I could'a pissed a blue nail. He all the time trying to low-rate somebody. Ain't that just about the nastiest thing you ever set ears on?*

Then there were the "others," the "proper" blacks, transplanted   4
relatives and one-time friends who came home from the city for weddings, funerals, and vacations. And the whites. To these we spoke standard English. "Ain't?" my mother would yell at me when I used the
term in the presence of "others." "You *know* better than that." And I
would hang my head in shame and say the "proper" word.

I remember one summer sitting in my grandmother's house in   5
Greeleyville, South Carolina, when it was full of the chatter of city relatives who were home on vacation. My parents sat quietly, only now
and then volunteering a comment or answering a question. My
mother's face took on a strained expression when she spoke. I could
see that she was being careful to say just the right words in just the
right way. Her voice sounded thick, muffled. And when she finished
speaking, she would lapse into silence, her proper smile on her face.
My father was more articulate, more aggressive. He spoke quickly, his
words sharp and clear. But he held his proud head higher, a signal that
he, too, was uncomfortable. My sisters and brothers and I stared at our
aunts, uncles, and cousins, speaking only when prompted. Even then,
we hesitated, formed our sentences in our minds, then spoke softly,
shyly.

My parents looked small and anxious during those occasions, and   6
I waited impatiently for our leave-taking when we would mock our
relatives the moment we were out of their hearing. "Reeely," we would
say to one another, flexing our wrists and rolling our eyes, "how dooo
you stan' this heat? Chile, it just too hy*ooo*-mid for words." Our relatives had made us feel "country," and this was our way of regaining
pride in ourselves while getting a little revenge in the bargain. The
words bubbled in our throats and rolled across our tongues, a balming.

As a child I felt this same doubleness in uptown Greeleyville where   7
the whites lived. "Ain't that a pretty dress you're wearing!" Toby, the
town policeman, said to me one day when I was fifteen. "Thank you
very much," I replied, my voice barely audible in my own ears. The
words felt wrong in my mouth, rigid, foreign. It was not that I had
never spoken that phrase before—it was common in black English,
too—but I was extremely conscious that this was an occasion for
proper English. I had taken out my English and put it on as I did my
church clothes, and I felt as if I were wearing my Sunday best in the
middle of the week. It did not matter that Toby had not spoken gram-
matically correct English. He was white and could speak as he wished.
I had something to prove. Toby did not.

Speaking standard English to whites was our way of demonstrating   8
that we knew their language and could use it. Speaking it to standard-
English-speaking blacks was our way of showing them that we, as well
as they, could "put on airs." But when we spoke standard English, we

acknowledged (to ourselves and to others—but primarily to ourselves) that our customary way of speaking was inferior. We felt foolish, embarrassed, somehow diminished because we were ashamed to be our real selves. We were reserved, shy in the presence of those who owned and/or spoke *the* language.

9   My parents never set aside time to drill us in standard English. Their forms of instruction were less formal. When my father was feeling particularly expansive, he would regale us with tales of his exploits in the outside world. In almost flawless English, complete with dialogue and flavored with gestures and embellishment, he told us about his attempt to get a haircut at a white barbershop; his refusal to acknowledge one of the town merchants until the man addressed him as "Mister"; the time he refused to step off the sidewalk uptown to let some whites pass; his airplane trip to New York City (to visit a sick relative) during which the stewardesses and porters—recognizing that he was a "gentleman"—addressed him as "Sir." I did not realize then—nor, I think, did my father—that he was teaching us, among other things, standard English and the relationship between language and power.

10   My mother's approach was different. Often, when one of us said "I'm gon wash off my feet," she would say, "And what will you walk on if you wash them off?" Everyone would laugh at the victim of my mother's "proper" mood. But it was different when one of us children was in a proper mood. "You think you are so superior," I said to my oldest sister one day when we were arguing and she was winning. "Superior!" my sister mocked. "You mean I'm acting 'biggidy'?" My sisters and brothers sniggered, then joined in teasing me. Finally, my mother said, "Leave your sister alone. There's nothing wrong with using proper English." There was a half-smile on her face. I had gotten "uppity," had "put on airs" for no good reason. I was at home, alone with the family, and I hadn't been prompted by one of my mother's proper moods. But there was also a proud light in my mother's eyes; her children were learning English very well.

11   Not until years later, as a college student, did I begin to understand our ambivalence toward English, our scorn of it, our need to master it, to own and be owned by it—an ambivalence that extended to the public-school classroom. In our school, where there were no whites, my teachers taught standard English but used black English to do it. When my grammar-school teachers wanted us to write, for example, they usually said something like, "I want y'all to write five sentences that make a statement. Anybody git done before the rest can color." It was probably almost those exact words that led me to write these sentences in 1953 when I was in the second grade:

The white clouds are pretty.
There are only 15 people in our room.

We will go to gym.
We have a new poster.
We may go out doors.

Second grade came after "Little First" and "Big First," so by then I knew the implied rules that accompanied all writing assignments. Writing was an occasion for proper English. I was not to write in the way we spoke to one another: The white clouds pretty; There ain't but 15 people in our room; We going to gym; We got a new poster; We can go out in the yard. Rather I was to use the language of "other": clouds *are,* there *are,* we *will,* we *have,* we *may.*

My sentences were short, rigid, perfunctory, like the letters my mother wrote to relatives: 12

> Dear Papa,
>
> How are you? How is Mattie? Fine I hope. We are fine. We will come to see you Sunday. Cousin Ned will give us a ride.
>
> Love,
> Daughter

The language was not ours. It was something from outside us, something we used for special occasions.

But my coloring on the other side of that second-grade paper is different. I drew three hearts and a sun. The sun has a smiling face that radiates and envelops everything it touches. And although the sun and its world are enclosed in a circle, the colors I used—red, blue, green, purple, orange, yellow, black—indicate that I was less restricted with drawing and coloring than I was with writing standard English. My valentines were not just red. My sun was not just a yellow ball in the sky.   13

By the time I reached the twelfth grade, speaking and writing standard English had taken on new importance. Each year, about half of the newly graduated seniors of our school moved to large cities—particularly in the North—to live with relatives and find work. Our English teacher constantly corrected our grammar: "Not 'ain't,' but 'isn't.'" We seldom wrote papers, and even those few were usually plot summaries of short stories. When our teacher returned the papers, she usually lectured on the importance of using standard English: "I *am;* you *are;* he, she, or it *is,*" she would say, writing on the chalkboard as she spoke. "How you gon git a job talking about 'I is,' or 'I isn't' or 'I ain't'?"   14

In Pittsburgh, where I moved after graduation, I watched my aunt and uncle—who had always spoken standard English when in Greeleyville—switch from black English to standard English to a mixture of the two, according to where they were or who they were with. At home and with certain close relatives, friends, and neighbors, they   15 spoke black English. With those less close, they spoke a mixture. In public and with strangers, they generally spoke standard English.

16   In time, I learned to speak standard English with ease and to switch smoothly from black to standard or a mixture, and back again. But no matter where I was, no matter what the situation or occasion, I continued to write as I had in school:

> Dear Mommie,
>
> How are you? How is everybody else? Fine I hope. I am fine. So are Aunt and Uncle. Tell everyone I said hello. I will write again soon.
>
>   Love,
>   Barbara

At work, at a health insurance company, I learned to write letters to customers. I studied form letters and letters written by co-workers, memorizing the phrases and the ways in which they were used. I dictated:

> Thank you for your letter of January 5. We have made the changes in your coverage you requested. Your new premium will be $150 every three months. We are pleased to have been of service to you.

In a sense, I was proud of the letters I wrote for the company: they were proof of my ability to survive in the city, the outside world—an indication of my growing mastery of English. But they also indicate that writing was still mechanical for me, something that didn't require much thought.

17   Reading also became a more significant part of my life during those early years in Pittsburgh. I had always liked reading, but now I devoted more and more of my spare time to it. I read romances, mysteries, popular novels. Looking back, I realize that the books I liked best were simple, unambiguous: good versus bad and right versus wrong with right rewarded and wrong punished, mysteries unraveled and all set right in the end. It was how I remembered life in Greeleyville.

18   Of course I was romanticizing. Life in Greeleyville had not been so very uncomplicated. Back there I had been—first as a child, then as a young woman with limited experience in the outside world—living in a relatively closed-in society. But there were implicit and explicit principles that guided our way of life and shaped our relationships with one another and the people outside—principles that a newcomer would find elusive and baffling. In Pittsburgh, I had matured, become more experienced: I had worked at three different jobs, associated with a wider range of people, married, had children. This new environment with different prescripts for living required that I speak standard English much of the time, and slowly, imperceptibly, I had ceased seeing a

sharp distinction between myself and "others." Reading romances and mysteries, characterized by dichotomy, was a way of shying away from change, from the person I was becoming.

But that other part of me—that part which took great pride in my ability to hold a job writing business letters—was increasingly drawn to the new developments in my life and the attending possibilities, opportunities for even greater change. If I could write letters for a nationally known business, could I not also do something better, more challenging, more important? Could I not, perhaps, go to college and become a school teacher? For years, afraid and a little embarrassed, I did no more than imagine this different me, this possible me. But sixteen years after coming north, when my youngest daughter entered kindergarten, I found myself unable—or unwilling—to resist the lure of possibility. I enrolled in my first college course: Basic Writing, at the University of Pittsburgh.   19

For the first time in my life, I was required to write extensively about myself. Using the most formal English at my command, I wrote these sentences near the beginning of the term: 20

> One of my duties as a homemaker is simply picking up after others. A day seldom passes that I don't search for a mislaid toy, book, or gym shoe, etc. I change the Ty-D-Bol, fight "ring around the collar," and keep our laundry smelling "April fresh." Occasionally, I settle arguments between my children and suggest things to do when they're bored. Taking telephone messages for my oldest daughter is my newest (and sometimes most aggravating) chore. Hanging the toilet paper roll is my most insignificant.

My concern was to use "appropriate" language, to sound as if I belonged in a college classroom. But I felt separate from the language—as if it did not and could not belong to me. I couldn't think and feel genuinely in that language, couldn't make it express what I thought and felt about being a housewife. A part of me resented, among other things, being judged by such things as the appearance of my family's laundry and toilet bowl, but in that language I could only imagine and write about a conventional housewife.

For the most part, the remainder of the term was a period of adjustment, a time of trying to find my bearings as a student in a college composition class, to learn to shut out my black English whenever I composed, and to prevent it from creeping into my formulations; a time for trying to grasp the language of the classroom and reproduce it in my prose; for trying to talk about myself in that language, reach others through it. Each experience of writing was like standing naked and revealing my imperfection, my "otherness." And each new assignment was another chance to make myself over in language, reshape myself,   21 make myself "better" in my rapidly changing image of a student in a college composition class.

22   But writing became increasingly unmanageable as the term progressed, and by the end of the semester, my sentences sounded like this:

> My excitement was soon dampened, however, by what seemed like a small voice in the back of my head saying that I should be careful with my long awaited opportunity. I felt frustrated and this seemed to make it difficult to concentrate.

There is a poverty of language in these sentences. By this point, I knew that the clichéd language of my Housewife essay was unacceptable, and I generally recognized trite expressions. At the same time, I hadn't yet mastered the language of the classroom, hadn't yet come to see it as belonging to me. Most notable is the lifelessness of the prose, the apparent absence of a person behind the words. I wanted those sentences—and the rest of the essay—to convey the anguish of yearning to, at once, become something more and yet remain the same. I had the sensation of being split in two, part of me going into a future the other part didn't believe possible. As that person, the student writer at that moment, I was essentially mute. I could not—in the process of composing—use the language of the old me, yet I couldn't imagine myself in the language of "others."

23   I found this particularly discouraging because at midsemester I had been writing in a much different way. Note the language of this introduction to an essay I had written then, near the middle of the term:

> Pain is a constant companion to the people in "Footwork." Their jobs are physically damaging. Employers are insensitive to their feelings and in many cases add to their problems. The general public wounds them further by treating them with disgrace because of what they do for a living. Although the workers are as diverse as they are similar, there is a definite link between them. They suffer a great deal of abuse.

The voice here is stronger, more confident, appropriating terms like "physically damaging," "wounds them further," "insensitive," "diverse"—terms I couldn't have imagined using when writing about my own experience—and shaping them into sentences like, "Although the workers are as diverse as they are similar, there is a definite link between them." And there is the sense of a personality behind the prose, someone who sympathizes with the workers: "The general public wounds them further by treating them with disgrace because of what they do for a living."

24   What caused these differences? I was, I believed, explaining other people's thoughts and feelings, and I was free to move about in the lan-

guage of "others" so long as I was speaking *of* others. I was unaware that I was transforming into my best classroom language my own thoughts and feelings about people whose experiences and ways of speaking were in many ways similar to mine.

The following year, unable to turn back or to let go of what had be-   25
come something of an obsession with language (and hoping to catch and hold the sense of control that had eluded me in Basic Writing), I enrolled in a research writing course. I spent most of the term learning how to prepare for and write a research paper. I chose sex education as my subject and spent hours in libraries, searching for information, reading, taking notes. Then (not without messiness and often-demoralizing frustration) I organized my information into categories, wrote a thesis statement, and composed my paper—a series of paraphrases and quotations spaced between carefully constructed transitions. The process and results felt artificial, but as I would later come to realize I was passing through a necessary stage. My sentences sounded like this:

> This reserve becomes understandable with examination of who the abusers are. In an overwhelming number of cases, they are people the victims know and trust. Family members, relatives, neighbors and close family friends commit seventy-five percent of all reported sex crimes against children, and parents, parent substitutes and relatives are the offenders in thirty to eighty percent of all reported cases. While assault by strangers does occur, it is less common, and is usually a single episode. But abuse by family members, relatives and acquaintances may continue for an extended period of time. In cases of incest, for example, children are abused repeatedly for an average of eight years. In such cases, "the use of physical force is rarely necessary because of the child's trusting, dependent relationship with the offender. The child's cooperation is often facilitated by the adult's position of dominance, an offer of material goods, a threat of physical violence, or a misrepresentation of moral standards."

The completed paper gave me a sense of profound satisfaction, and I   26
read it often after my professor returned it. I know now that what I was pleased with was the language I used and the professional voice it helped me maintain. "Use better words," my teacher had snapped at me one day after reading the notes I'd begun accumulating from my research, and slowly I began taking on the language of my sources. In my next set of notes, I used the word "vacillating"; my professor applauded. And by the time I composed the final draft, I felt at ease with terms like "overwhelming number of cases," "single episode," and "reserve," and I shaped them into sentences similar to those of my "expert" sources.

If I were writing the paper today, I would of course do some   27
things differently. Rather than open with an anecdote—as my teacher suggested—I would begin simply with a quotation that caught my

interest as I was researching my paper (and which I scribbled, without its source, in the margin of my notebook): "Truth does not do so much good in the world as the semblance of truth does evil." The quotation felt right because it captured what was for me the central idea of my essay— an idea that emerged gradually during the making of my paper—and expressed it in a way I would like to have said it. The anecdote, a hypothetical situation I invented to conform to the information in the paper, felt forced and insincere because it represented—to a great degree—my teacher's understanding of the essay, *her* idea of what in it was most significant. Improving upon my previous experiences with writing, I was beginning to think and feel in the language I used, to find my own voices in it, to sense that how one speaks influences how one means. But I was not yet secure enough, comfortable enough with the language to trust my intuition.

28   Now that I know that to seek knowledge, freedom, and autonomy means always to be in the concentrated process of becoming—always to be venturing into new territory, feeling one's way at first, then getting one's balance, negotiating, accommodating, discovering one's self in ways that previously defined "others"—I sometimes get tired. And I ask myself why I keep on participating in this highbrow form of violence, this slamming against perplexity. But there is no real futility in the question, no hint of that part of the old me who stood outside standard English, hugging to herself a disabling mistrust of a language she thought could not represent a person with her history and experience. Rather, the question represents a person who feels the consequence of her education, the weight of her possibilities as a teacher and writer and human being, a voice in society. And I would not change that person, would not give back the good burden that accompanies my growing expertise, my increasing power to shape myself in language and share that self with "others."

29   "To speak," says Frantz Fanon, "means to be in a position to use a certain syntax, to grasp the morphology of this or that language, but it means above all to assume a culture, to support the weight of a civilization."* To write means to do the same, but in a more profound sense. However, Fanon also says that to achieve mastery means to "get" in a position of power, to "grasp," to "assume." This, I have learned—both as a student and subsequently as a teacher—can involve tremendous emotional and psychological conflict for those attempting to master academic discourse. Although as a beginning student writer I had a fairly good grasp of ordinary spoken English and was proficient at what Labov calls "code-switching" (and what John Baugh in *Black Street Speech* terms "style shifting"), when I came face to face with the demands of

Black Skin, White Masks (1952; rpt. New York: Grove Press, 1967), pp. 17–18.

academic writing, I grew increasingly self-conscious, constantly aware of my status as a black and a speaker of one of the many black English vernaculars—a traditional outsider. For the first time, I experienced my sense of doubleness as something menacing, a built-in enemy. Whenever I turned inward for salvation, the balm so available during my childhood, I found instead this new fragmentation which spoke to me in many voices. It was the voice of my desire to prosper, but at the same time it spoke of what I had relinquished and could not regain: a safe way of being, a state of powerlessness which exempted me from responsibility for who I was and might be. And it accused me of betrayal, of turning away from blackness. To recover balance, I had to take on the language of the academy, the language of "others." And to do that, I had to learn to imagine myself a part of the culture of that language, and therefore someone free to manage that language, to take liberties with it. Writing and rewriting, practicing, experimenting, I came to comprehend more fully the generative power of language. I discovered—with the help of some especially sensitive teachers—that through writing one can continually bring new selves into being, each with new responsibilities and difficulties, but also with new possibilities. Remarkable power, indeed. I write and continually give birth to myself.

★ *Meaning and Understanding*

1. What "two languages" did Mellix grew up speaking?

2. What do the anecdote of the first paragraph and the explanation of the second tell you about how the writer feels toward speech and its appropriate use? How and why was Mellix's use of black English "inevitable" in her exchange with her daughter?

3. Why are Mellix's family members, particularly her parents, so careful about their speech that summer day at the grandmother's house? What do this nervousness and care indicate?

4. How is it possible that the teachers in the writer's school used black English to teach "proper" English?

5. What does Mellix do for an insurance company? Why does she enjoy her job?

6. Does the writer use the "right" English when she begins doing college writing assignments? Why or why not? By which assignment does the writer feel she has "learned" to use the language well?

7. Why is it necessary for the writer to imagine herself "in the language of 'others'"? What does she mean by this point?

★ *Techniques and Strategies*

1. What is the thesis of the essay? What is the significance of the title?

2. At one point, the writer and her family make fun of the speech of "city relatives." What does this scene contribute to the essay?

3. Mellix recounts an argument between herself and her eldest sister in which the former calls the latter "superior." What effect does the writer achieve by including this exchange and its aftermath in the essay?

4. Reread the quote that the writer uses to begin her concluding paragraph. What is the effect of quoting at all and of using this quote in particular?

5. What do the final sentences of the essay indicate about the writer's ability to use language? Would you call these final sentences, particularly the final three, especially powerful or useful? Why or why not?

★ *Speaking of Values*

1. What does Mellix mean when she notes that she grew up surrounded by blacks ("friends, neighbors, ministers, teachers") and that her own children will apparently not? Will Mellix's daughter be somehow "missing out?" How and on what? Why might you agree or disagree with the point here?

2. At one point in paragraph 8 the writer notes that "we were reserved, shy in the presence of those who owned and/or spoke *the* language." Can a language be owned, do you think? What does the writer mean by language ownership? Has the writer become an "owner" of the language? What makes you think so?

3. When Toby, the policeman, uses the word *ain't*, what goes through the writer's mind? How accurate is Mellix in pointing out the differing rules of language behavior?

4. What is your view on shifting language use and style in order to achieve particular goals? How is this shifting of styles practical, appropriate, reasonable? How is it contrived, artificial, dishonest?

5. How is it possible that "through writing one can continually bring new selves into being" (paragraph 29)? Is this the most valuable aspect of writing? Why or why not?

★ *Values Conversation*

In paragraph 22, Mellix asserts that she "hadn't yet mastered the language of the classroom." What does she mean? What is the language of your college classroom? Form groups to discuss the issue. Do members of your group agree on the characteristics of classroom language? Have you mastered it? Should you? Gather the group's reasons for its opinions and report to the class at large.

★ *Writing about Values*

1. Write an essay in which you show how you or someone you know served as a translator or go-between in order to facilitate communication between two other people. Pay particular attention to the moments when you felt conflicted or unsure of how to relay information in either direction.

2. Write a paper in which you discuss the ways that you changed your speech patterns in order to get or keep a certain job or to achieve and maintain a certain level or grade.

3. Mellix says at the very end of the essay that "through writing one can continually bring new selves into being, each with new responsibilities and difficulties, but also with new possibilities. Remarkable power, indeed. I write and continually give birth to myself." Write an essay to analyze that comment and to argue about its validity or lack of validity.

Values in Review

1. Nancy Mairs, Sunil Garg, Charles Lawrence III, and Carl Sandburg deal with the way language can hurt, whether deliberately or inadvertently. Write an essay about how some of these writers see the effects of language use in our culture. What values do the pieces imply about language?

2. Robert D. King and Chang-rae Lee consider the powerful role of English in the lives of Americans. How do these two essays relate to each other? "English-only" issues lie at the heart of both pieces, yet the writers explore their topics in very different ways. Write an essay to consider the similarities and differences in topic, approach, and conclusions in these two pieces.

3. Deborah Tannen and Barbara Mellix make a claim for special language codes related to racial and (or) gender identity. What resonances do you find in the essays by these two writers? What differences? Write a paper analyzing the essays as reflections on language for unique groups.

Chapter 6

Law and Politics

Democracy

The death penalty

Public and private morality

Minority rights

Passive resistance

Washington politics

Women's rights

Majority rules

Thomas Jefferson

The Declaration of Independence

Thomas Jefferson (1743–1826) was the third president of the United States. A member of the Second Continental Congress, Jefferson drafted the Declaration of Independence, which emerged in draft form on June 28, 1776 from a Congressional committee of five. Contributions by Benjamin Franklin and John Adams are apparent; yet the precision and lucidity of expression signal Jefferson as the author.

———— ★ ————

In CONGRESS, July 4, 1776.

THE UNANIMOUS DECLARATION of the thirteen united STATES OF AMERICA.

1   When in the Course of human events, it becomes necessary for one people to dissolve the political bands which have connected them with another, and to assume among the powers of the earth, the separate and equal station to which the Laws of Nature and of Nature's God entitle them, a decent respect to the opinions of mankind requires that they should declare the causes which impel them to the separation.——— We hold these truths to be self-evident, that all men are created equal, that they are endowed by their Creator with certain unalienable Rights, that among these are Life, Liberty and the pursuit of Happiness.— That to secure these rights, Governments are instituted among Men, deriving their just powers from the consent of the governed,—That whenever any Form of Government becomes destructive of these ends, it is the Right of the People to alter or to abolish it, and to institute new Government, laying its foundation on such principles and organizing its powers in such form, as to them shall seem most likely to effect their Safety and Happiness. Prudence, indeed, will dictate that Governments long established should not be changed for light and transient causes; and accordingly all experience hath shewn, that mankind are more disposed to suffer, while evils are sufferable, than to right themselves by abolishing the forms to which they are accustomed. But when a long train of abuses and usurpations, pursuing invariably the same Object, evinces a design to reduce them under absolute Despotism, it is their right, it is their duty, to throw off such Government, and to provide new Guards for their future security.—Such has been the pa-

tient sufferance of these Colonies; and such is now the necessity which constrains them to alter their former Systems of Government. The history of the present King of Great Britain is a history of repeated injuries and usurpations, all having in direct object the establishment of an absolute Tyranny over these States. To prove this, let Facts be submitted to a candid world.——He has refused his Assent to Laws, the most wholesome and necessary for the public good.——He has forbidden his Governors to pass Laws of immediate and pressing importance, unless suspended in their operation till his Assent should be obtained; and when so suspended, he has utterly neglected to attend to them.——He has refused to pass other Laws for the accommodation of large districts of people, unless those people would relinquish the right of Representation in the Legislature, a right inestimable to them and formidable to tyrants only.——He has called together legislative bodies at places unusual, uncomfortable, and distant from the depository of their public Records, for the sole purpose of fatiguing them into compliance with his measures.——He has dissolved Representative Houses repeatedly, for opposing with manly firmness his invasions on the rights of the people.——He has refused for a long time, after such dissolutions, to cause others to be elected; whereby the Legislative powers, incapable of Annihilation, have returned to the People at large for their exercise; the State remaining in the mean time exposed to all the dangers of invasion from without, and convulsions within.——He has endeavoured to prevent the population of these States; for that purpose obstructing the Laws for Naturalization of Foreigners; refusing to pass others to encourage their migrations hither, and raising the conditions of new Appropriations of Lands.——He has obstructed the Administration of Justice, by refusing his Assent to Laws for establishing Judiciary powers.——He has made Judges dependent on his Will alone, for the tenure of their offices, and the amount and payment of their salaries.— He has erected a multitude of New Offices, and sent hither swarms of Officers to harass our people, and eat out their substance.——He has kept among us, in times of peace, Standing Armies without the Consent of our legislatures.——He has affected to render the Military independent of and superior to the Civil power.——He has combined with others to subject us to a jurisdiction foreign to our constitution, and unacknowledged by our laws; giving his Assent to their Acts of pretended Legislation:—For Quartering large bodies of armed troops among us:—For protecting them, by a mock Trial, from punishment for any Murders which they should commit on the Inhabitants of these States:—For cutting off our Trade with all parts of the world:—For imposing Taxes on us without our Consent:—For depriving us in many cases, of the benefits of Trial by Jury:—For transporting us beyond Seas to be tried for pretended offences:—For abolishing the free System of

English Laws in a neighbouring Province, establishing therein an Arbitrary government, and enlarging its Boundaries so as to render it at once an example and fit instrument for introducing the same absolute rule into these Colonies:—For taking away our Charters, abolishing our most valuable Laws, and altering fundamentally the Forms of our Governments:—For suspending our own Legislatures, and declaring themselves invested with power to legislate for us in all cases whatsoever.—He has abdicated Government here, by declaring us out of his Protection and waging War against us:—He has plundered our seas, ravaged our Coasts, burnt our towns, and destroyed the lives of our people.—He is at this time transporting large Armies of foreign Mercenaries to compleat the works of death, desolation and tyranny, already begun with circumstances of Cruelty & perfidy scarcely paralleled in the most barbarous ages, and totally unworthy the Head of a civilized nation.—He has constrained our fellow Citizens taken Captive on the high Seas to bear Arms against their Country, to become the executioners of their friends and Brethren, or to fall themselves by their Hands.— He has excited domestic insurrections amongst us, and has endeavoured to bring on the inhabitants of our frontiers, the merciless Indian Savages, whose known rule of warfare, is an undistinguished destruction of all ages, sexes and conditions. In every stage of these Oppressions We have Petitioned for Redress in the most humble terms: Our repeated Petitions have been answered only by repeated injury. A Prince, whose character is thus marked by every act which may define a Tyrant, is unfit to be the ruler of a free people. Nor have We been wanting in attentions to our British brethren. We have warned them from time to time of attempts by their legislature to extend an unwarrantable jurisdiction over us. We have reminded them of the circumstances of our emigration and settlement here. We have appealed to their native justice and magnanimity, and we have conjured them by the ties of our common kindred to disavow these usurpations, which, would inevitably interrupt our connections and correspondence. They too have been deaf to the voice of justice and of consanguinity. We must, therefore, acquiesce in the necessity, which denounces our Separation, and hold them, as we hold the rest of mankind, Enemies in War, in Peace Friends.

2   WE, THEREFORE, the Representatives of the UNITED STATES OF AMERICA, in General Congress Assembled, appealing to the Supreme Judge of the world for the rectitude of our intentions, do, in the Name, and by Authority of the good People of these Colonies, solemnly publish and declare, That these United Colonies are, and of Right ought to be FREE AND INDEPENDENT STATES; that they are Absolved from all Allegiance to the British Crown, and that all political connection between them and the State of Great Britain, is and ought to be totally dissolved; and that as Free and Independent States, they have full Power to levy War, con-

clude Peace, contract Alliances, establish Commerce, and to do all other Acts and Things which Independent States may of right do.— And for the support of this Declaration, with a firm reliance on the protection of divine Providence, we mutually pledge to each other our Lives, our Fortunes and our sacred Honor.

★ Meaning and Understanding

1. Why does Jefferson enumerate the causes that impel the new nation to separate from England?

2. What are the self-evident truths detailed here? Why does the writer call them "self-evident"? Under what circumstances does Jefferson say that people can abolish government?

3. Jefferson identifies a "train of abuses" that he lays at the feet of the king of Great Britain, George III, who ruled from 1760 to 1820. Which abuses do you find most significant? Why?

4. Why did the writer create a document of this sort, containing a long list of grievances, as opposed to a short, clear declaration of war? How is a declaration of independence inherently different from a declaration of war?

★ Techniques and Strategies

1. Why does the writer use lists to make his point? What is your response to this strategy?

2. The Declaration of Independence is two paragraphs long—a first very long paragraph and a second short one. The sentences themselves are lengthy. Why has Jefferson used such a stylistic approach, do you think? How does the frequent use of dashes affect the presentation?

3. Where does the writer use figurative language—hyperbole or overstatement, for example? How does this use affect the argument?

4. Scholars point to the Declaration as one of the most brilliant examples of argument in recorded history. How did the document achieve such status? Is it the writing itself, or simply the events that the writing precedes, that give it its importance? Explain your answer.

5. Comment on the quality of the final paragraph as a suitable (or unsuitable) conclusion to the piece.

★ Speaking of Values

1. "When…it becomes necessary for one people to dissolve the political bands which have connected them with another…a decent respect to the

opinions of mankind requires that they should declare the causes which impel them to the separation." What exactly does this sentence mean? Do you agree with it? Why is "declaring the causes" so important?

2. Examine the grievances listed in the document and then think about and discuss whether any of these conditions exist currently in our society. In other words, might a group like Jefferson's have cause to declare a separation from the current government? Or do you think that the U.S. government today has by and large avoided cause for most of the grievances raised in the Declaration? Explain your position.

3. Jefferson accuses King George of being a tyrant. Do you agree, based on the evidence presented here? What examples of tyrannical government can you identify in today's world?

★ Values Conversation

Form groups and discuss the right of people to break away from unjust government. Under what circumstances should people today "dissolve the political bands which have connected them with another"?

★ Writing about Values

1. Think of a relationship that you have with another individual and that you once felt or now feel is unfair and must change. In an open letter to this acquaintance, offer a list of grievances and state what you plan to do about them.

2. Represent England and write an open letter as a reply to the Colonies' Declaration. Explain why you believe the issues that the Declaration cites are within the rights of a "mother-nation."

3. The ringing phrase "Life, Liberty, and the Pursuit of Happiness" is one of the most memorable in the English language. Write an essay explaining why you believe that the phrase has captured the imagination of men and women from the eighteenth century to our present day.

Lani Guinier

The Tyranny of the Majority

Lani Guinier is a law professor. Born in 1950, she received her B.A. from Radcliffe College in 1971 and a J.D. from Yale. She has written extensively on constitutional law, voting rights, race, and gender theory. In this piece she explores the relation between majority rule and minority rights.

———— ★ ————

I have always wanted to be a civil rights lawyer. This lifelong ambition is based on a deep-seated commitment to democratic fair play—to playing by the rules as long as the rules are fair. When the rules seem unfair, I have worked to change them, not subvert them. When I was eight years old, I was a Brownie. I was especially proud of my uniform, which represented a commitment to good citizenship and good deeds. But one day, when my Brownie group staged a hatmaking contest, I realized that uniforms are only as honorable as the people who wear them. The contest was rigged. The winner was assisted by her milliner mother, who actually made the winning entry in full view of all the participants. At the time, I was too young to be able to change the rules, but I was old enough to resign, which I promptly did.

To me, fair play means that the rules encourage everyone to play. They should reward those who win, but they must be acceptable to those who lose. The central theme of my academic writing is that not all rules lead to elemental fair play. Some even commonplace rules work against it.

The professional milliner competing with amateur Brownies stands as an example of rules that are patently rigged or patently subverted. Yet, sometimes, even when rules are perfectly fair in form, they serve in practice to exclude particular groups from meaningful participation. When they do not encourage everyone to play, or when, over the long haul, they do not make the losers feel as good about the outcomes as the winners, they can seem as unfair as the milliner who makes the winning hat for her daughter.

Sometimes, too, we construct rules that force us to be divided into winners and losers when we might have otherwise joined together. This idea was cogently expressed by my son, Nikolas, when he was four years old, far exceeding the thoughtfulness of his mother when she was an eight-year-old Brownie. While I was writing one of my law journal articles, Nikolas and I had a conversation about voting prompted by a

1

2

3

4

Sesame Street Magazine exercise. The magazine pictured six children: four children had raised their hands because they wanted to play tag; two had their hands down because they wanted to play hide-and-seek. The magazine asked its readers to count the number of children whose hands were raised and then decide what game the children would play.

5   Nikolas quite realistically replied, "They will play both. First they will play tag. Then they will play hide-and-seek." Despite the magazine's "rules," he was right. To children, it is natural to take turns. The winner may get to play first or more often, but even the "loser" gets something. His was a positive-sum solution that many adult rule-makers ignore.

6   The traditional answer to the magazine's problem would have been a zero-sum solution: "The children—all the children—will play tag, and only tag." As a zero-sum solution, everything is seen in terms of "I win; you lose." The conventional answer relies on winner-take-all majority rule, in which the tag players, as the majority, win the right to decide for all the children what game to play. The hide-and-seek preference becomes irrelevant. The numerically more powerful majority choice simply subsumes minority preferences.

7   In the conventional case, the majority that rules gains all the power and the minority that loses gets none. For example, two years ago Brother Rice High School in Chicago held two senior proms. It was not planned that way. The prom committee at Brother Rice, a boys' Catholic high school, expected just one prom when it hired a disc jockey, picked a rock band, and selected music for the prom by consulting student preferences. Each senior was asked to list his three favorite songs, and the band would play the songs that appeared most frequently on the lists.

8   Seems attractively democratic. But Brother Rice is predominantly white, and the prom committee was all white. That's how they got two proms. The black seniors at Brother Rice felt so shut out by the "democratic process" that they organized their own prom. As one black student put it "For every vote we had, there were eight votes for what they wanted. . . . [W]ith us being in the minority we're always outvoted. It's as if we don't count."

9   Some embittered white seniors saw things differently. They complained that the black students should have gone along with the majority: "The majority makes a decision. That's the way it works."

10   In a way, both groups were right. From the white students' perspective, this was ordinary decisionmaking. To the black students, majority rule sent the message: "we don't count" is the "way it works" for minorities. In a racially divided society, majority rule may be perceived as majority tyranny.

11   That is a large claim, and I do not rest my case for it solely on the actions of the prom committee in one Chicago high school. To expand the range of the argument, I first consider the ideal of majority rule itself, particularly as reflected in the writings of James Madison and

other founding members of our Republic. These early democrats explored the relationship between majority rule and democracy. James Madison warned, "If a majority be united by a common interest, the rights of the minority will be insecure." The tyranny of the majority, according to Madison, requires safeguards to protect "one part of the society against the injustice of the other part."

For Madison, majority tyranny represented the great danger to our   12
early constitutional democracy. Although the American revolution was fought against the tyranny of the British monarch, it soon became clear that there was another tyranny to be avoided. The accumulations of all powers in the same hands, Madison warned, "whether of one, a few, or many, and whether hereditary, self-appointed, or elective, may justly be pronounced the very definition of tyranny."

As another colonist suggested in papers published in Philadelphia,   13
"We have been so long habituated to a jealousy of tyranny from monarchy and aristocracy, that we have yet to learn the dangers of it from democracy." Despotism had to be opposed "whether it came from Kings, Lords or the people."

The debate about majority tyranny reflected Madison's concern that   14
the majority may not represent the whole. In a homogeneous society, the interest of the majority would likely be that of the minority also. But in a heterogeneous community, the majority may not represent all competing interests. The majority is likely to be self-interested and ignorant or indifferent to the concerns of the minority. In such case, Madison observed, the assumption that the majority represents the minority is "altogether fictitious."

Yet even a self-interested majority can govern fairly if it cooper-   15
ates with the minority. One reason for such cooperation is that the self-interested majority values the principle of reciprocity. The self-interested majority worries that the minority may attract defectors from the majority and become the next governing majority. The Golden Rule principle of reciprocity functions to check the tendency of a self-interested majority to act tyrannically.

So the argument for the majority principle connects it with the   16
value of reciprocity: You cooperate when you lose in part because members of the current majority will cooperate when they lose. The conventional case for the fairness of majority rule is that it is not really the rule of a fixed group—The Majority—on all issues; instead it is the rule of shifting majorities, as the losers at one time or on one issue join with others and become part of the governing coalition at another time or on another issue. The result will be a fair system of mutually beneficial cooperation. I call a majority that rules but does not dominate a Madisonian Majority.

The problem of majority tyranny arises, however, when the self-   17
interested majority does not need to worry about defectors. When the

majority is fixed and permanent, there are no checks on its ability to be overbearing. A majority that does not worry about defectors is a majority with total power.

18   In such a case, Madison's concern about majority tyranny arises. In a heterogeneous community, any faction with total power might subject "the minority to the caprice and arbitrary decisions of the majority, who instead of consulting the interest of the whole community collectively, attend sometimes to partial and local advantages."

19   "What remedy can be found in a republican Government, where the majority must ultimately decide," argued Madison, but to ensure "that no one common interest or passion will be likely to unite a majority of the whole number in an unjust pursuit." The answer was to disaggregate the majority to ensure checks and balances or fluid, rotating interests. The minority needed protection against an overbearing majority, so that "a common sentiment is less likely to be felt, and the requisite concert less likely to be formed, by a majority of the whole."

20   Political struggles would not be simply a contest between rulers and people; the political struggles would be among the people themselves. The work of government was not to transcend different interests but to reconcile them. In an ideal democracy, the people would rule, but the minorities would also be protected against the power of majorities. Again, where the rules of decisionmaking protect the minority, the Madisonian Majority rules without dominating.

21   But if a group is unfairly treated, for example, when it forms a racial minority, *and* if the problems of unfairness are not cured by conventional assumptions about majority rule, then what is to be done? The answer is that we may need an *alternative* to winner-take-all majoritarianism. With Nikolas's help, I now call the alternative the "principle of taking turns." In a racially divided society, this principle does better than simple majority rule if it accommodates the values of self-government, fairness, deliberation, compromise, and consensus that lie at the heart of the democratic ideal.

22   In my legal writing, I follow the caveat of James Madison and other early American democrats. I explore decisionmaking rules that might work in a multi-racial society to ensure that majority rule does not become majority tyranny. I pursue voting systems that might disaggregate The Majority so that it does not exercise power unfairly or tyrannically. I aspire to a more cooperative political style of decisionmaking to enable all of the students at Brother Rice to feel comfortable attending the same prom. In looking to create Madisonian Majorities, I pursue a positive-sum, taking-turns solution.

23   Structuring decisionmaking to allow the minority "a turn" may be necessary to restore the reciprocity ideal when a fixed majority refuses to cooperate with the minority. If the fixed majority loses its incentive to follow the Golden Rule principle of shifting majorities, the minority

never gets to take a turn. Giving the minority a turn does not mean the minority gets to rule; what it does mean is that the minority gets to influence decisionmaking and the majority rules more legitimately.

Instead of automatically rewarding the preferences of the monolithic majority, a taking-turns approach anticipates that the majority rules, but is not overbearing. Because those with 51 percent of the votes are not assured 100 percent of the power, the majority cooperates with, or at least does not tyrannize, the minority.

The sports analogy of "I win; you lose" competition within a political hierarchy makes sense when only one team can win; Nikolas's intuition that it is often possible to take turns suggests an alternative approach. Take family decisionmaking, for example. It utilizes a taking-turns approach. When parents sit around the kitchen table deciding on a vacation destination or activities for a rainy day, often they do not simply rely on a show of hands, especially if that means that the older children always prevail or if affinity groups among the children (those who prefer movies to video games, or those who prefer baseball to playing cards) never get to play their activity of choice. Instead of allowing the majority simply to rule, the parents may propose that everyone take turns, going to the movies one night and playing video games the next. Or as Nikolas proposes, they might do both on a given night.

Taking turns attempts to build consensus while recognizing political or social differences, and it encourages everyone to play. The taking-turns approach gives those with the most support more turns, but it also legitimates the outcome from each individual's perspective, including those whose views are shared only by a minority.

In the end, I do not believe that democracy should encourage rule by the powerful—even a powerful majority. Instead, the ideal of democracy promises a fair discussion among self-defined equals about how to achieve our common aspirations. To redeem that promise, we need to put the idea of taking turns and disaggregating the majority at the center of our conception of representation. Particularly as we move into the twenty-first century as a more highly diversified citizenry, it is essential that we consider the ways in which voting and representational systems succeed or fail at encouraging Madisonian Majorities.

To use Nikolas's terminology, "it is no fair" if a fixed, tyrannical majority excludes or alienates the minority. It is no fair if a fixed, tyrannical majority monopolizes all the power all the time. It is no fair if we engage in the periodic ritual of elections, but only the permanent majority gets to choose who is elected. Where we have tyranny by The Majority, we do not have genuine democracy.

My life's work, with the essential assistance of people like Nikolas, has been to try to find the rules that can best bring us together as a democratic society. Some of my ideas about democratic fair play were grossly mischaracterized in the controversy over my nomination to be

Assistant Attorney General for Civil Rights. Trying to find rules to encourage fundamental fairness inevitably raises the question posed by Harvard Professor Randall Kennedy in a summary of this controversy: "What is required to create political institutions that address the needs and aspirations of all Americans, not simply whites, who have long enjoyed racial privilege, but people of color who have long suffered racial exclusion from policymaking forums?" My answer, as Professor Kennedy suggests, varies by situation. But I have a predisposition, reflected in my son's yearning for a positive-sum solution, to seek an integrated body politic in which all perspectives are represented and in which all people work together to find common ground. I advocate empowering voters and their representatives in ways that give even minority voters a chance to influence legislative outcomes.

30   But those in the majority do not lose; they simply learn to take turns. This is a positive-sum solution that allows all voters to feel that they participate meaningfully in the decisionmaking process. This is a positive-sum solution that makes legislative outcomes more legitimate.

31   I have been roundly, and falsely, criticized for focusing on outcomes. Outcomes are indeed relevant, but *not* because I seek to advance particular ends, such as whether the children play tag or hide-and-seek, or whether the band at Brother Rice plays rock music or rap. Rather, I look to outcomes as *evidence* of whether all the children—or all the high school seniors—feel that their choice is represented and considered. The purpose is not to guarantee "equal legislative outcomes"; equal opportunity to *influence* legislative outcomes regardless of race is more like it.

32   For these reasons, I sometimes explore alternatives to simple, winner-take-all majority rule. I do not advocate any one procedural rule as a universal panacea for unfairness. Nor do I propose these remedies primarily as judicial solutions. They can be adopted only in the context of litigation after the court first finds a legal violation.

33   Outside of litigation, I propose these approaches as political solutions if, depending on the local context, they better approximate the goals of democratic fair play. One such decisionmaking alternative is called cumulative voting, which could give all the students at Brother Rice multiple votes and allow them to distribute their votes in any combination of their choice. If each student could vote for ten songs, the students could plump or aggregate their votes to reflect the intensity of their preferences. They could put ten votes on one song; they could put five votes on two songs. If a tenth of the students opted to "cumulate" or plump all their votes for one song, they would be able to select one of every ten or so songs played at the prom. The black seniors could have done this if they chose to, but so could any other cohesive group of sufficient size. In this way, the songs preferred by a

majority would be played most often, but the songs the minority enjoyed would also show up on the play list.

Under cumulative voting, voters get the same number of votes as   34
there are seats or options to vote for, and they can then distribute their votes in any combination to reflect their preferences. Like-minded voters can vote as a solid bloc or, instead, form strategic, cross-racial coalitions to gain mutual benefits. This system is emphatically not racially based; it allows voters to organize themselves on whatever basis they wish.

Corporations use this system to ensure representation of minority   35
shareholders on corporate boards of directors. Similarly, some local municipal and county governments have adopted cumulative voting to ensure representation of minority voters. Instead of awarding political power to geographic units called districts, cumulative voting allows voters to cast ballots based on what they think rather than where they live.

Cumulative voting is based on the principle of one person–one vote   36
because each voter gets the same total number of votes. Everyone's preferences are counted equally. It is not a particularly radical idea; thirty states either require or permit corporations to use this election system. Cumulative voting is certainly not antidemocratic because it emphasizes the importance of voter choice in selecting public or social policy. And it is neither liberal nor conservative. Both the Reagan and Bush administrations approved cumulative voting schemes pursuant to the Voting Rights Act to protect the rights of racial- and language-minority voters.

But, as in Chilton County, Alabama, which now uses cumulative   37
voting to elect both the school board and the county commission, any politically cohesive group can vote strategically to win representation. Groups of voters win representation depending on the exclusion threshold, meaning the percentage of votes needed to win one seat or have the band play one song. That threshold can be set case by case, jurisdiction by jurisdiction, based on the size of minority groups that make compelling claims for representation.

Normally the exclusion threshold in a head-to-head contest is 50   38
percent, which means that only groups that can organize a majority can get elected. But if multiple seats (or multiple songs) are considered simultaneously, the exclusion threshold is considerably reduced. For example, in Chilton County, with seven seats elected simultaneously on each governing body, the threshold of exclusion is now one-eighth. Any group with the solid support of one-eighth the voting population cannot be denied representation. This is because any self-identified minority can plump or cumulate all its votes for one candidate. Again, minorities are not defined solely in racial terms.

As it turned out in Chilton County, both blacks and Republicans   39
benefited from this new system. The school board and commission

now each have three white Democrats, three white Republicans, and one black Democrat. Previously, when each seat was decided in a head-to-head contest, the majority not only ruled but monopolized. Only white Democrats were elected at every prior election during this century.

40   Similarly, if the black and white students at Brother Rice have very different musical taste, cumulative voting permits a positive-sum solution to enable both groups to enjoy one prom. The majority's preferences would be respected in that their songs would be played most often, but the black students could express the intensity of their preferences too. If the black students chose to plump all their votes on a few songs, their minority preferences would be recognized and played. Essentially, cumulative voting structures the band's repertoire to enable the students to take turns.

41   As a solution that permits voters to self-select their identities, cumulative voting also encourages cross-racial coalition building. No one is locked into a minority identity. Nor is anyone necessarily isolated by the identity they choose. Voters can strengthen their influence by forming coalitions to elect more than one representative or to select a range of music more compatible with the entire student body's preferences.

42   Women too can use cumulative voting to gain greater representation. Indeed, in other countries with similar, alternative voting systems, women are more likely to be represented in the national legislature. For example, in some Western European democracies, the national legislatures have as many as 37 percent female members compared to a little more than 5 percent in our Congress.

43   There is a final benefit from cumulative voting. It eliminates gerrymandering. By denying protected incumbents safe seats in gerrymandered districts, cumulative voting might encourage more voter participation. With greater interest-based electoral competition, cumulative voting could promote the political turnover sought by advocates of term limits. In this way, cumulative voting serves many of the same ends as periodic elections or rotation in office, a solution that Madison and others advocated as a means of protecting against permanent majority factions.

44   A different remedial voting tool, one that I have explored more cautiously, is supermajority voting. It modifies winner-take-all majority rule to require that something more than a bare majority of voters must approve or concur before action is taken. As a uniform decisional rule, a supermajority empowers any numerically small but cohesive group of voters. Like cumulative voting, it is race-neutral. Depending on the issue, different members of the voting body can "veto" impending action.

45   Supermajority remedies give bargaining power to all numerically inferior or less powerful groups, be they black, female, or Republican. Supermajority rules empower the minority Republicans in the Senate

who used the Senate filibuster procedure in the spring of 1993 to "veto" the president's proposed economic stimulus package. The same concept of a minority veto yielded the Great Compromise in which small-population states are equally represented in the Senate.

I have never advocated (or imagined) giving an individual member of a legislative body a personal veto. Moreover, I have discussed these kinds of exceptional remedies as the subject of court-imposed solutions only when there has been a violation of the statute and only when they make sense in the context of a particular case. I discuss supermajority rules as a judicial remedy only in cases where the court finds proof of consistent and deeply engrained polarization. It was never my intent that supermajority requirements should be the norm for all legislative bodies, or that simple majority voting would ever in itself constitute a statutory or constitutional violation.   46

Both the Reagan and Bush administrations took a similar remedial approach to enforcement of the Voting Rights Act. In fact, it was the Reagan administration that *approved* the use of supermajority rules as a remedial measure in places like Mobile, Alabama, where the special five-out-of-seven supermajority threshold is still in place today and is credited with increasing racial harmony in that community.   47

But—and here I come directly to the claims of my critics—some apparently fear that remedies for extreme voting abuses, remedies like cumulative voting or the Mobile supermajority, constitute "quotas"—racial preferences to ensure minority rule. While cumulative voting, or a supermajority, is quite conventional in many cases and race neutral, to order it as a remedy apparently opens up possibilities of nonmajoritarianism that many seem to find quite threatening.   48

Indeed, while my nomination was pending, I was called "antidemocratic" for suggesting that majority voting rules may not fairly resolve conflict when the majority and minority are permanently divided. But alternatives to majority voting rules in a racially polarized environment are too easily dismissed by this label. As Chief Justice [Warren] Burger wrote for the Supreme Court, "There is nothing in the language of the Constitution, our history, or our cases that requires that a majority always prevail on every issue." In other words, there is *nothing inherent in democracy that requires majority rule*. It is simply a custom that works efficiently when the majority and minority are fluid, are not monolithic, and are not permanent.   49

Other democracies frequently employ alternatives to winner-take-all majority voting. Indeed, only five Western democracies, including Britain and the United States, still use single-member-district, winner-take-all systems of representation. Germany, Spain, the Netherlands, and Sweden, among other countries, elect their legislatures under some alternative to winner-take-all majority voting. As the *New Yorker*, in a comment on my nomination, observed, President Clinton was   50 right in calling some of my ideas "difficult to defend," but only because "Americans, by and large, are ignorant of the existence, let alone the details, of electoral systems other than their own."

51   No one who had done their homework seriously questioned the fundamentally democratic nature of my ideas. Indeed, columnists who attacked my ideas during my nomination ordeal have praised ideas, in a different context, that are remarkably similar to my own. Lally Weymouth wrote, "There can't be democracy in South Africa without a measure of formal protection for minorities." George Will has opined, "The Framers also understood that stable, tyrannical majorities can best be prevented by the multiplication of minority interests, so the majority at any moment will be just a transitory coalition of minorities." In my law journal articles, I expressed exactly the same reservations about unfettered majority rule and about the need sometimes to disaggregate the majority to ensure fair and effective representation for all substantial interests.

52   The difference is that the minority I used to illustrate my academic point was not, as it was for Lally Weymouth, the white minority in South Africa. Nor, did I write, as George Will did, about the minority of well-to-do landlords in New York City. I wrote instead about the political exclusion of the black minority in many local county and municipal governing bodies in America.

53   Yet these same two journalists and many others condemned me as antidemocratic. Apparently, it is not controversial to provide special protections for affluent landlords or minorities in South Africa but it is "divisive," "radical," and "out of the mainstream" to provide similar remedies to black Americans who, after centuries of racial oppression, are still excluded.

54   Talking about racial bias at home has, for many, become synonymous with advocating revolution. Talking about racial divisions, in itself, has become a violation of the rules of polite society.

55   We seem to have forgotten that dialogue and intergroup communication are critical to forging consensus. In my case, genuine debate was shut down by techniques of stereotyping and silencing. As Professor Randall Kennedy observes, I was "punished" as the messenger reporting the bad news about our racial situation. I dared to speak when I should have been silent.

56   My nomination became an unfortunate metaphor for the state of race relations in America. My nomination suggested that as a country, we are in a state of denial about issues of race and racism. The censorship imposed against me points to a denial of serious public debate or discussion about racial fairness and justice in a true democracy. For many politicians and policymakers, the remedy for racism is simply to stop talking about race.

57   Sentences, words, even phrases separated by paragraphs in my law review articles were served up to demonstrate that I was violating

the rules. Because I talked openly about existing racial divisions, I was branded "race obsessed." Because I explored innovative ways to remedy racism, I was branded "antidemocratic." It did not matter that I had suggested race-neutral election rules, such as cumulative voting, as an alternative to remedy racial discrimination. It did not matter that I never advocated quotas. I became the Quota Queen.

The vision behind my by-now-notorious law review articles and my less-well-known professional commitments has always been that of a fair and just society, a society in which even adversely affected parties believe in the system because they believe the process is fair and the process is inclusive. My vision of fairness and justice imagines a full and effective voice for all citizens. I may have failed to locate some of my ideas in the specific factual contexts from which they are derived. But always I have tried to show that democracy in a heterogeneous society is incompatible with rule by a racial monopoly of any color. 58

I hope that we can learn three positive lessons from my experience. The first lesson is that those who stand for principles may lose in the short run, but they cannot be suppressed in the long run. The second lesson is that public dialogue is critical to represent all perspectives; no one viewpoint should be permitted to monopolize, distort, caricature, or shape public debate. The tyranny of The Majority is just as much a problem of silencing minority viewpoints as it is of excluding minority representatives or preferences. We cannot all talk at once, but that does not mean only one group should get to speak. We can take turns. Third, we need consensus and positive-sum solutions. We need a broad public conversation about issues of racial justice in which we seek win-win solutions to real-life problems. If we include blacks and whites, and women and men, and Republicans and Democrats, and even people with new ideas, we will all be better off. 59

Most of all, I hope we begin to consider the principle of taking turns as a means to bring us closer to the ideal of democratic fair play. [Supreme Court] Justice Potter Stewart wrote in 1964 that our form of representative self-government reflects "the strongly felt American tradition that the public interest is composed of many diverse interests, [which]...in the long run...can better be expressed by a medley of component voices than by the majority's monolithic command." In that "strongly felt American tradition," I hope more of us aspire to govern like Madisonian Majorities through "a medley of component voices." In that "strongly felt American tradition," I hope more of us come to reject the "monolithic command" of The fixed Majority. 60

After all, government is a public experiment. Let us not forget [Supreme Court] Justice Louis Brandeis's advice at the beginning of this century: "If we guide by the light of reason, we must let our minds be bold." At the close of the same century, I hope we rediscover the bold 61 solution to the tyranny of The Majority, which has always been more democracy, not less.

★ Meaning and Understanding

1. What is Guinier's main point about fairness?

2. What is the "Tyranny of the Majority"? What attributes characterize a majority that has the power—and perhaps the inclination—to tyrannize?

3. In the writer's view, what role do race or minority rights play in changing the strategy and structure of the government?

4. What is a Madisonian Majority?

5. The writer cites several writers who oppose her position; in what way do they find Guinier's point of view "antidemocratic"?

6. What three lessons does Guinier hope we can learn from her experience?

★ Techniques and Strategies

1. What is Guinier's thesis? How successful is she in supporting it with detail?

2. How does the writer's short narrative of her experience as a Brownie influence the essay?

3. How do the exercise in *Sesame Street Magazine* and the subsequent conversation with her son Nikolas influence the essay?

4. Why does Guinier introduce the proms at the Brother Rice High School in Chicago? What point does the situation there help her make?

5. What is the utility of relying so heavily upon the words and ideas of James Madison in this essay?

6. Toward the end of the essay, the writer quotes several Supreme Court justices. What is the effect of this strategy? How do the quotations help her argument?

★ Speaking of Values

1. How does Guinier define fair play? Do you agree or disagree with her definition? In what ways is our society focused on an "I win; you lose" philosophy? In what ways is it focused on a "positive-sum" philosophy of taking turns? Which have you experienced more? Why, do you think?

2. The writer asserts in paragraph 10 that "in a racially divided society, majority rule may be perceived as majority tyranny." Why might you agree or disagree with her in terms of U.S. society today?

3. What is your reaction to James Madison's statement that "if a majority be united by a common interest, the rights of the minority will be insecure"? What instances can you provide to support Madison's assertion? To challenge it?

4. Professor Randall Kennedy noted that the furor over Guinier's nomination by President Clinton in fact amounted to "punishing" her "as the messenger reporting the bad news." What was the "bad news"? Why was it bad at all? Was the punishment appropriate? Why or why not? How, in general, does American society react to messengers who deliver bad news? Give examples to support your position.

5. How has talking about racial bias "become synonymous with advocating revolution" (paragraph 5)? How has talking about racial divisions "become a violation of the rules of polite society"? What evidence can you provide either to support or challenge Guinier's assertion here?

★ Values Conversation

Form groups and discuss the following statement by Chief Justice Warren Burger: "There is nothing in the language of the Constitution, our history, or our cases that requires that a majority always prevail on an issue." What values does the statement reflect? How accurate is it in portraying the views held by most Americans? How does Burger's statement support or challenge the Bill of Rights?

★ Writing about Values

1. Write an essay that reflects your views on the relation between majority rule and minority rights. Are the two compatible? Why or why not?

2. Write an essay called "The Tyranny of the Minority."

3. Write an essay on what you see as "the rules that can best bring us together as a democracy."

Walt Whitman

For You O Democracy

Walt Whitman (1819–1892), whose *Leaves of Grass* changed the landscape
of American poetry through its unconventional use of meter and rhyme,
wrote about the greatness of democracy, which he celebrates in this poem.

——————— ★ ———————

Come, I will make the continent indissoluble,
I will make the most splendid race the sun ever shone upon,
I will make divine magnetic lands,
    With the love of comrades,
5   With the life-long love of comrades.

I will plant companionship thick as trees
    along all the rivers of America, and along the
    shores of the great lakes, and all over the prairies,
I will make inseparable cities with their arms about each
10   other's necks.
    By the love of comrades,
    By the manly love of comrades.

For you these from me, O Democracy, to serve you ma femme!
For you, for you I am trilling these songs.

★ *Meaning and Understanding*

1. What does the poet say he will plant along the rivers of America?
   What is the significance of the image?

2. What does the poet mean by "inseparable cities"?

3. What does "ma femme" mean? Who does it refer to? What is the significance of the phrase?

★ *Techniques and Strategies*

1. Whitman worked as a nurse in the Civil War to the sick and wounded
   of both the North and South and wrote extensively on the war. What
   references, subtle or otherwise, do you find to the Civil War? How, for
   example, may we read "continent indissoluble" as such a reference?

2. The poem comes from a collection called *Calamus*. The calamus is a water reed used in mythology as a symbol of comradeship among men. How does Whitman draw on the symbolic implications of the word in this brief poem?

3. What are "divine magnetic lands"? What does the image make you see or think of?

4. How does the poet use repetition in the poem? What is the effect of the inconsistent length of the lines? Of the stanzas?

5. What erotic imagery does Whitman use? Why does he use such imagery? How does it help establish his point?

6. Identify the metaphors in the poem. How effective are they in creating visual snapshots?

★ Speaking of Values

1. What is your view of the power of comradeship? How is it related to loyalty? What values do comradeship and loyalty suggest?

2. What is the relation between democracy and comradeship as established in the poem?

3. What role does the poet play in democracy? Look at the last line of the poem. How does it establish the poet's place in the scheme Whitman is describing? What does the poet give to democracy in Whitman's poem? What is the poet's role in today's society? The twentieth-century poet Ezra Pound called poets "the antennae of the race." What do you think he meant? How does Whitman fulfill that classification in this poem?

★ Values Conversation

What part does comradeship play in American society? How does comradeship relate to democracy as we now experience it? Is Whitman's point valid even now or is it an old-fashioned concept, good for the nineteenth century but not for us as we move into the twenty-first? How has comradeship—or lack of it—influenced the course of history in our day? Form groups to discuss these questions and report your group's findings to the class at large.

★ Writing about Values

1. Write a definition of comradeship. Draw upon your own experiences or on what you have read or observed.

2. What do you think Whitman would think of the kind of democracy we have today? Write an essay to identify some features of our democratic society and explain how Whitman might respond to it.

3. Write your own brief poem called "For You O Democracy."

Elizabeth Cady Stanton

Speech to the New York State Legislature, February 18, 1860

Elizabeth Cady Stanton (1815–1902) helped organize the first women's rights convention in 1848 in Seneca Falls, New York. A feminist and social reformer, she calls attention in this speech to what she sees as inequities in the treatment of women.

———— ★ ————

Gentlemen of the Judiciary:—There are certain natural rights as inalienable to civilization as are the rights of air and motion to the savage in the wilderness. The natural rights of the civilized man and woman are government, property, the harmonious development of all their powers, and the gratification of their desires. There are a few people we now and then meet who, like Jeremy Bentham,[1] scout the idea of natural rights in civilization, and pronounce them mere metaphors, declaring that there are no rights aside from those the law confers. If the law made man too, that might do, for then he could be made to order to fit the particular niche he was designed to fill. But inasmuch as God made man in His own image, with capacities and powers as boundless as the universe, whose exigencies no mere human law can meet, it is evident that the man must ever stand first; the law but the creature of his wants; the law giver but the mouthpiece of humanity. If, then, the nature of a being decides its rights, every individual comes into this world with rights that are not transferable. He does not bring them like a pack on his back, that may be stolen from him, but they are a component part of himself, the laws which ensure his growth and development. The individual may be put in the stocks, body and soul, may be dwarfed, crippled, killed, but his rights no man can get; they live and die with him.

Though the atmosphere is forty miles deep all round the globe, no man can do more than fill his own lungs. No man can see, hear, or smell but just so far; and though hundreds are deprived of these senses, his are not the more acute. Though rights have been abundantly

[1]Jeremy Bentham was a British philosopher who opposed the idea of natural rights.

supplied by the good Father, no man can appropriate to himself those that belong to another. A citizen can have but one vote, fill but one office, though thousands are not permitted to do either. These axioms prove that woman's poverty does not add to man's wealth, and if, in the plenitude of his power, he should secure to her the exercise of all her God-given rights, her wealth could not bring poverty to him. There is a kind of nervous unrest always manifested by those in power, whenever new claims are started by those out of their own immediate class. The philosophy of this is very plain. They imagine that if the rights of this new class be granted, they must, of necessity, sacrifice something of what they already possess. They can not divest themselves of the idea that rights are very much like lands, stocks, bonds, and mortgages, and that if every new claimant be satisfied, the supply of human rights must in time run low. You might as well carp at the birth of every child, lest there should not be enough air left to inflate your lungs; at the success of every scholar, for fear that your draughts at the fountain of knowledge could not be so long and deep; at the glory of every hero, lest there be no glory left for you. . . .

3   If the object of government is to protect the weak against the strong, how unwise to place the power wholly in the hands of the strong. Yet that is the history of all governments, even the model republic of these United States. You who have read the history of nations, from Moses down to our last election, where have you ever seen one class looking after the interests of another? Any of you can readily see the defects in other governments, and pronounce sentence against those who have sacrificed the masses to themselves; but when we come to our own case, we are blinded by custom and self-interest. Some of you who have no capital can see the injustice which the laborer suffers; some of you who have no slaves, can see the cruelty of his oppression; but who of you appreciate the galling humiliation, the refinements of degradation, to which women (the mothers, wives, sisters, and daughters of freemen) are subject, in this the last half of the nineteenth century? How many of you have ever read even the laws concerning them that now disgrace your statute-books? In cruelty and tyranny, they are not surpassed by any slaveholding code in the Southern States; in fact they are worse, by just so far as woman, from her social position, refinement, and education, is on a more equal ground with the oppressor.

4   Allow me just here to call the attention of that party[2] now so much interested in the slave of the Carolinas, to the similarity in his condition and that of the mothers, wives, and daughters of the Empire State. The negro has no name. He is Cuff Douglas or Cuffy Brooks, just whose Cuffy he may chance to be. The woman has no name. She is Mrs. Rich-

[2]The Republican party.

ard Roe or Mrs. John Doe, just whose Mrs. she may chance to be. Cuffy has no right to his earnings; he can not buy or sell, or lay up anything that he can call his own. Mrs. Roe has no right to her earnings; she can neither buy nor sell, make contracts, nor lay up anything that she can call her own. Cuffy has no right to his children; they can be sold from him at any time. Mrs. Roe has no right to her children; they may be bound out to cancel a father's debts of honor. The unborn child, even by the last will of the father, may be placed under the guardianship of a stranger and a foreigner. Cuffy has no legal existence; he is subject to restraint and moderate chastisement. Mrs. Roe has no legal existence; she has not the best right to her own person. The husband has the power to restrain, and administer moderate chastisement.

Blackstone[3] declares that the husband and wife are one, and   5
learned commentators have decided that that one is the husband. In all civil codes, you will find them classified as one. Certain rights and immunities, such and such privileges are to be secured to white male citizens. What have women and negroes to do with rights? What know they of government, war, or glory?

The prejudice against color, of which we hear so much, is no stron-   6
ger than that against sex. It is produced by the same cause, and manifested very much in the same way. The negro's skin and the woman's sex are both *prima facie* evidence that they were intended to be in subjection to the white Saxon man. The few social privileges which the man gives the woman, he makes up to the negro in civil rights. The woman may sit at the same table and eat with the white man; the free negro may hold property and vote. The woman may sit in the same pew with the white man in church; the free negro may enter the pulpit and preach. Now, with the black man's right to suffrage, the right unquestioned, even by Paul,[4] to minister at the altar, it is evident that the prejudice against sex is more deeply rooted and more unreasonably maintained than that against color. As citizens of a republic, which should we most highly prize, social privileges or civil right? The latter, most certainly.

To those who do not feel the injustice and degradation of the condi-   7
tion, there is something inexpressibly comical in man's "citizen woman." It reminds me of those monsters I used to see in the old world, head and shoulders woman, and the rest of the body sometimes fish and sometimes beast. I used to think, What a strange conceit! but now I see how perfectly it represents man's idea! Look over all his laws concerning us, and you will see just enough of woman to tell of her existence;

---

[3]His *Commentaries on the Laws of England* (1765–1769) stated that a woman submerged her identity in that of her husband when she married.

[4]Paul said that women should not speak in church (I Corinthians 14:34–36).

all the rest is submerged, or made to crawl upon the earth. Just imagine an inhabitant of another planet entertaining himself some pleasant evening in searching over our great national compact, our Declaration of Independence, our Constitutions, or some of our statute-books; what would he think of those "women and negroes" that must be so fenced in, so guarded against? Why, he would certainly suppose we were monsters, like those fabulous giants or Brobdignagians of olden times, so dangerous to civilized man, from our size, ferocity, and power. Then let him take up our poets, from Pope down to Dana;[5] let him listen to our Fourth of July toasts, and some of the sentimental adulations of social life, and no logic could convince him that this creature of the law, and this angel of the family altar, could be one and the same being. Man is in such a labyrinth of contradictions with his marital and property rights; he is so befogged on the whole question of maidens, wives, and mothers, that from pure benevolence we should relieve him from this troublesome branch of legislation. We should vote, and make laws for ourselves. Do not be alarmed, dear ladies! You need spend no time reading Grotius, Coke, Puffendorf, Blackstone, Bentham, Kent, and Story,[6] to find out what you need. We may safely trust the shrewd selfishness of the white man, and consent to live under the same broad code where he has so comfortably ensconced himself. Any legislation that will do for man, we may abide by most cheerfully....

8   But, say you, we would not have women exposed to the grossness and vulgarity of public life, or encounter what she must at the polls. When you talk, gentlemen, of sheltering woman from the rough winds and revolting scenes of real life, you must be either talking for effect, or wholly ignorant of what the facts of life are. The man, whatever he is, is known to the woman. She is the companion, not only of the accomplished statesman, the orator, and the scholar; but the vile, vulgar, brutal man has his mother, his wife, his sister, his daughter. Yes, delicate, refined, educated women are in daily life with the drunkard, the gambler, the licentious man, the rogue, and the villain; and if man shows out what he is anywhere, it is at his own hearthstone. There are over forty thousand drunkards in this State. All of these are bound by the ties of family to some woman. Allow but a mother and a wife to each, and you have over eighty thousand women. All these have seen their fathers, brothers, husbands, sons, in the lowest and most debased stages of obscenity and degradation. In your own circle of friends, do you not know refined women whose whole lives are darkened and saddened by gross and brutal associations? Now, gentlemen, do you

---

[5]Alexander Pope was an eighteenth-century English poet, and Richard Henry Dana, Sr. was a nineteenth-century poet and essayist.

[6]Legal philosophers from the seventeenth to nineteenth centuries.

talk to woman of a rude jest or jostle at the polls, where noble, virtuous men stand ready to protect her person and her rights, when, alone in the darkness and solitude and gloom of night, she has trembled on her own threshold, awaiting the return of a husband from his midnight revels?—when, stepping from her chamber, she has beheld her royal monarch, her lord and master—her legal representative—the protector of her property, her home, her children, and her person, down on his hands and knees slowly crawling up the stairs? Behold him in her chamber—in her bed! The fairy tale of "Beauty and the Beast" is far too often realized in life. Gentlemen, such scenes as woman has witnessed at her own fireside, where no eye save Omnipotence could pity, no strong arm could help, can never be realized at the polls, never equaled elsewhere, this side the bottomless pit. No, woman has not hitherto lived in the clouds, surrounded by an atmosphere of purity and peace—but she has been the companion of man in health, in sickness, and in death, in his highest and in his lowest moments. She has worshipped him as a saint and an orator, and pitied him as madman or a fool. In Paradise, man and woman were placed together, and so they must ever be. They must sink or rise together. If man is low and wretched and vile, woman can not escape the contagion, and any atmosphere that is unfit for woman to breathe is not fit for man. Verily, the sins of the fathers shall be visited upon the children to the third and fourth generation. You, by your unwise legislation, have crippled and dwarfed womanhood, by closing to her all honorable and lucrative means of employment, have driven her into the garrets and dens of our cities, where she now revenges herself on your innocent sons, sapping the very foundations of national virtue and strength. Alas! for the young men just coming on the stage of action, who soon shall fill your vacant places—our future Senators, our Presidents, the expounders of our constitutional law! Terrible are the penalties we are now suffering for the ages of injustice done to woman.

Again, it is said that the majority of women do not ask for any change in the laws; that it is time enough to give them the elective franchise when they, as a class, demand it. 9

Wise statesmen legislate for the best interests of the nation; the State, for the highest good of its citizens; the Christian, for the conversion of the world. Where would have been our railroads, our telegraphs, our ocean steamers, our canals and harbors, our arts and sciences, if government had withheld the means from the far-seeing minority? This State established our present system of common schools, fully believing that educated men and women would make better citizens than ignorant ones. In making this provision for the education of its children, had they waited for a majority of the urchins of this State to petition for schools, how many, think you, would have asked to be transplanted from the street to the schoolhouse? Does the State wait for the criminal to ask for 10 his prison-house? the insane, the idiot, the deaf and dumb for his asylum? Does the Christian, in his love to all mankind, wait for the majority of the benighted heathen to ask him for the gospel? No; unasked and unwelcomed, he crosses the trackless ocean, rolls off the mountain of superstition that oppresses the human mind, proclaims the immortality of the soul, the dignity of manhood, the right of all to be free and happy.

11   No, gentlemen, if there is but one woman in this State who feels the injustice of her position, she should not be denied her inalienable rights, because the common household drudge and the silly butterfly of fashion are ignorant of all laws, both human and Divine. Because they know nothing of governments, or rights, and therefore ask nothing, shall my petitions be unheard? I stand before you the rightful representative of woman, claiming a share in the halo of glory that has gathered round her in the ages, and by the wisdom of her past words and works, her peerless heroism and self-sacrifice, I challenge your admiration; and moreover claiming, as I do, a share in all her outrages and sufferings, in the cruel injustice, contempt, and ridicule now heaped upon her, in her deep degradation, hopeless wretchedness, by all that is helpless in her present condition, that is false in law and public sentiment, I urge your generous consideration; for as my heart swells with pride to behold woman in the highest walks of literature and art, it grows big enough to take in those who are bleeding in the dust.

12   Now do not think, gentlemen, we wish you to do a great many troublesome things for us. We do not ask our legislators to spend a whole session in fixing up a code of laws to satisfy a class of most unreasonable women. We ask no more than the poor devils in the Scripture asked, "Let us alone."[7] In mercy, let us take care of ourselves, our property, our children, and our homes. True, we are not so strong, so wise, so crafty as you are, but if any kind friend leaves us a little money, or we can by great industry earn fifty cents a day, we would rather buy bread and clothes for our children than cigars and champagne for our legal protectors. There has been a great deal written and said about protection. We, as a class, are tired of one kind of protection, that which leaves us everything to do, to dare, and to suffer, and strips us of all means for its accomplishment. We would not tax man to take care of us. No, the Great Father has endowed all his creatures with the necessary powers for self-support, self-defense, and protection. We do not ask man to represent us; it is hard enough in times like these for man to carry backbone enough to represent himself. So long as the mass of men spend most of their time on the fence, not knowing which way to jump, they are surely in no condition to tell us where we had better

[7]Mark 1:24.

stand. In pity for man, we would no longer hang like a millstone round his neck. Undo what man did for us in the dark ages, and strike out all special legislation for us; strike the words "white male" from all our constitutions, and then, with fair sailing, let us sink or swim, live or die, survive or perish together.

At Athens, an ancient apologue tells us, on the completion of the temple of Minerva, a statue of the goddess was wanted to occupy the crowning point of the edifice. Two of the greatest artists produced what each deemed his masterpiece. One of these figures was the size of life, admirably designed, exquisitely finished, softly rounded, and beautifully refined. The other was of Amazonian stature, and so boldly chiselled that it looked more like masonry than sculpture. The eyes of all were attracted by the first, and turned away in contempt from the second. That, therefore, was adopted, and the other rejected, almost with resentment, as though an insult had been offered to a discerning public. The favored statue was accordingly borne in triumph to the place for which it was designed, in the presence of applauding thousands, but as it receded from their upturned eyes, all, all at once agaze upon it, the thunders of applause unaccountably died away—a general misgiving ran through every bosom—the mob themselves stood like statues, as silent and as petrified, for as it slowly went up, and up, the soft expression of those chiseled features, the delicate curves and outlines of the limbs and figure, became gradually fainter and fainter, and when at last it reached the place for which it was intended, it was a shapeless ball, enveloped in mist. Of course, the idol of the hour was now clamored down as rationally as it had been cried up, and its dishonored rival, with no good will and no good looks on the part of the chagrined populace, was reared in its stead. As it ascended, the sharp angles faded away, the rough points became smooth, the features full of expression, the whole figure radiant with majesty and beauty. The rude hewn mass, that before had scarcely appeared to bear even the human form, assumed at once the divinity which it represented, being so perfectly proportioned to the dimensions of the building, and to the elevation on which it stood, that it seemed as though Pallas herself had alighted upon the pinnacle of the temple in person, to receive the homage of her worshipers.

The woman of the nineteenth century is the shapeless ball in the lofty position which she was designed fully and nobly to fill. The place is not too high, too large, too sacred for woman, but the type that you have chosen is far too small for it. The woman we declare unto you is the rude, misshapen, unpolished object of the successful artist. From your standpoint, you are absorbed with the defects alone. The true artist sees the harmony between the object and its destination. Man, the sculptor, has carved out his ideal, and applauding thousands welcome his success. He has made a woman that from his low standpoint looks fair and beautiful, a being without rights, or hopes, or fears but in him—neither noble, virtuous, nor independent. Where do we see, in Church or State, in schoolhouse or at the fireside, the much talked-of moral power of woman? Like those Athenians, we have bowed down and worshiped in woman, beauty, grace, the exquisite proportions, the soft and beautifully rounded outline, her delicacy, refinement, and silent helplessness—all well when she is viewed simply as an object of sight, never to rise one foot above the dust from which she sprung. But if she is to be raised up to adorn a temple, or represent a divinity—if she is to fill the niche of wife and counsellor to true and noble men, if she is to be the mother, the educator of a race of heroes or martyrs, of a Napoleon, or a Jesus—then must the type of womanhood be on a larger scale than that yet carved by man.

15   In vain would the rejected artist have reasoned with the Athenians as to the superiority of his production; nothing short of the experiment they made could have satisfied them. And what of your experiment, what of your wives, your homes? Alas! for the folly and vacancy that meet you there! But for your clubhouses and newspapers, what would social life be to you? Where are your beautiful women? your frail ones, taught to lean lovingly and confidingly on man? Where are the crowds of educated dependents—where the long line of pensioners on man's bounty? Where all the young girls, taught to believe that marriage is the only legitimate object of a woman's pursuit—they who stand listlessly on life's shores, waiting, year after year, like the sick man at the pool of Bethesda,[8] for someone to come and put them in? These are they who by their ignorance and folly curse almost every fireside with some human specimen of deformity or imbecility. These are they who fill the gloomy abodes of poverty and vice in our vast metropolis. These are they who patrol the streets of our cities, to give our sons their first lessons in infamy. These are they who fill our asylums, and make night hideous with their cries and groans.

16   The women who are called masculine, who are brave, courageous, self-reliant and independent, are they who in the face of adverse winds have kept one steady course upward and onward in the paths of virtue and peace—they who have taken their gauge of womanhood from their own native strength and dignity—they who have learned for themselves the will of God concerning them. This is our type of womanhood. Will you help us raise it up, that you too may see its beautiful proportions—that you may behold the outline of the goddess who is yet to adorn your temple of Freedom? We are building a model republic; our edifice will one day need a crowning glory. Let the artists be wisely chosen. Let them begin their work. Here is a temple to Liberty, to human rights, on whose portals behold the glorious declaration,

[8]John 5:5–7.

"All men are created equal." The sun has never yet shone upon any of man's creations that can compare with this.

★ Meaning and Understanding

1. What is the main idea of the reading? What does Stanton want the state legislature to do?

2. What does the writer believe are the "natural rights of the civilized man and woman" (paragraph 1)?

3. How are rights like or not like "lands, stocks, bonds, and mortgages" (paragraph 2)? Can the supply of human rights run low?

4. Why is man in "such a labyrinth of contradictions with his marital and property rights"? Why is he "befogged on the question of maidens, wives, and mothers" (paragraph 7)? What does the writer suggest will alleviate this situation, and why does she think it will work?

5. What is the writer calling for in paragraph 12 when she writes: "strike out all special legislation for us; strike the words 'white male' from all our constitutions, and then, with fair sailing, let us sink or swim, live or die, survive or perish together"?

★ Techniques and Strategies

1. Stanton's purpose is to persuade her audience through logical argument to accept her point of view. What argumentative strategies does she use? What techniques of persuasion does she draw on?

2. Comment on the first two sentences after the salutation, "Gentlemen of the Judiciary." How do they serve as the opening to a speech before the legislature? What is your reaction? Do they make you pay attention? Do they make you angry? Annoyed? Proud? Why?

3. Why does Stanton use an extended comparison between slaves and women? Is it an accurate comparison, do you think? Or is it merely a rhetorical flourish? Does it make slavery seem not so bad or the treatment of women worse than it might have been? Or are the two conditions alive with similarities as Stanton has painted them?

4. How does the writer use an extended metaphor concerning the Old World views of half woman–half beast or half woman–half fish? How does the metaphor relate to her argument?

5. Stanton uses a number of analogies. What do they contribute to her argument? Identify one or two analogies and analyze them.

6. What does the extended example about the temple of Minerva contribute to the essay?

★ Speaking of Values

1. "Any of you can readily see the defects in other governments, and pronounce sentence against those who have sacrificed the masses to
   themselves; but when we come to our own case, we are blinded by
   custom and self interest." What does Stanton mean by this statement
   in paragraph 3? What cultural values does it imply? Why night you
   agree or disagree with it?

2. Stanton argues that as citizens of a republic we should value civil
   rights over social privileges. Why might you agree or disagree with
   her? How would most people in American society today feel about
   this point? Why?

3. The writer states that unwise legislation has "crippled and dwarfed
   womanhood, by closing to her all honorable and lucrative means of
   employment." How could legislating whether women have the right
   to work or what fields they can enter cripple and dwarf womanhood?
   Do such laws exist today? What are they?

4. What point is the writer making when she notes that urchins did not
   ask for schools, nor criminals for prisons, nor missionaries for the right
   to attempt to spread their faith? Examine the similarities and differences among these examples. Do they all work in the same way? Why
   or why not?

5. How does Stanton's list of inalienable rights compare and contrast
   with those spelled out by Jefferson in the Declaration of Independence? Explain your point of view.

★ Values Conversation

Form groups and discuss the state of women's rights in our country today.
Are women equal to men in most areas of U.S. society? Where do women
not share equally? What would you do to improve the situations?

★ Writing about Values

1. Write an essay on the rights of women in today's society.

2. Think of a group of people who oppose an idea you maintain—lowering
   the drinking age, granting citizenship to illegal immigrants, making
   abortion completely illegal (or completely legal), or ending the death
   penalty, for example. Write a speech to persuade your opponents to
   side with you.

3. Write a paper to respond to this quote from Stanton's speech: "Then must
   the type of womanhood be on a larger scale than that yet carved by man."

Edward I. Koch

Death and Justice

Edward I. Koch was born in New York City in 1924. He served in Congress and was mayor of that city for twelve years. He is a writer, recently of a play *Murder on 34th Street,* and is a radio and television commentator. In this essay he writes in favor of the death penalty.

———— ★ ————

Last December a man named Robert Lee Willie, who had been convicted of raping and murdering an 18-year-old woman, was executed in the Louisiana state prison. In a statement issued several minutes before his death, Mr. Willie said: "Killing people is wrong. . . . It makes no difference whether it's citizens, countries, or governments. Killing is wrong." Two weeks later in South Carolina, an admitted killer named Joseph Carl Shaw was put to death for murdering two teenagers. In an appeal to the governor for clemency, Mr. Shaw wrote: "Killing is wrong when I did it. Killing is wrong when you do it. I hope you have the courage and moral strength to stop the killing."

It is a curiosity of modern life that we find ourselves being lectured on morality by cold-blooded killers. Mr. Willie previously had been convicted of aggravated rape, aggravated kidnapping, and the murders of a Louisiana deputy and a man from Missouri. Mr. Shaw committed another murder a week before the two for which he was executed, and admitted mutilating the body of the 14-year-old girl he killed. I can't help wondering what prompted these murderers to speak out against killing as they entered the death-house door. Did their new-found reverence for life stem from the realization that they were about to lose their own?

Life is indeed precious, and I believe the death penalty helps to affirm this fact. Had the death penalty been a real possibility in the minds of these murderers, they might well have stayed their hand. They might have shown moral awareness before their victims died, and not after. Consider the tragic death of Rosa Velez, who happened to be home when a man named Luis Vera burglarized her apartment in Brooklyn. "Yeah, I shot her," Vera admitted. "She knew me, and I knew I wouldn't go to the chair."

During my 22 years in public service, I have heard the pros and cons of capital punishment expressed with special intensity. As a district leader, councilman, congressman, and mayor, I have represented constituencies generally thought of as liberal. Because I support the death penalty for heinous crimes of murder, I have sometimes been the subject of emotional and outraged attacks by voters who find my position reprehensible or worse. I have listened to their ideas. I have weighed their objections carefully. I still support the death penalty. The reasons I maintain my position can be best understood by examining the arguments most frequently heard in opposition.

5   1. *The death penalty is "barbaric."* Sometimes opponents of capital punishment horrify with tales of lingering death on the gallows, of faulty electric chairs, or of agony in the gas chamber. Partly in response to such protests, several states such as North Carolina and Texas switched to execution by lethal injection. The condemned person is put to death painlessly, without ropes, voltage, bullets, or gas. Did this answer the objections of death penalty opponents? Of course not. On June 22, 1984, the *New York Times* published an editorial that sarcastically attacked the new "hygienic" method of death by injection, and stated that "execution can never be made humane through science." So it's not the method that really troubles opponents. It's the death itself they consider barbaric.

6   Admittedly, capital punishment is not a pleasant topic. However, one does not have to like the death penalty in order to support it any more than one must like radical surgery, radiation, or chemotherapy in order to find necessary these attempts at curing cancer. Ultimately we may learn how to cure cancer with a simple pill. Unfortunately, that day has not yet arrived. Today we are faced with the choice of letting the cancer spread or trying to cure it with the methods available, methods that one day will almost certainly be considered barbaric. But to give up and do nothing would be far more barbaric and would certainly delay the discovery of an eventual cure. The analogy between cancer and murder is imperfect, because murder is not the "disease" we are trying to cure. The disease is injustice. We may not like the death penalty, but it must be available to punish crimes of cold-blooded murder, cases in which any other form of punishment would be inadequate and, therefore, unjust. If we create a society in which injustice is not tolerated, incidents of murder—the most flagrant form of injustice—will diminish.

7   2. *No other major democracy uses the death penalty.* No other major democracy—in fact, few other countries of any description—are plagued by a murder rate such as that in the United States. Fewer and fewer Americans can remember the days when unlocked doors were the norm and murder was a rare and terrible offense. In America the murder rate climbed 122 percent between 1963 and 1980. During that same period, the murder rate in New York City increased by almost 400 percent, and the statistics are even worse in many other cities. A study at M.I.T. showed that based on 1970 homicide rates a person who lived

in a large American city ran a greater risk of being murdered than an American soldier in World War II ran of being killed in combat. It is not surprising that the laws of each country differ according to differing conditions and traditions. If other countries had our murder problem, the cry for capital punishment would be just as loud as it is here. And I daresay that any other major democracy where 75 percent of the people supported the death penalty would soon enact it into law.

3. *An innocent person might be executed by mistake.* Consider the 8 work of Adam Bedau, one of the most implacable foes of capital punishment in this country. According to Mr. Bedau, it is "false sentimentality to argue that the death penalty should be abolished because of the abstract possibility that an innocent person might be executed." He cites a study of the 7,000 executions in this country from 1893 to 1971, and concludes that the record fails to show that such cases occur. The main point, however, is this. If government functioned only when the possibility of error didn't exist, government wouldn't function at all. Human life deserves special protection, and one of the best ways to guarantee that protection is to assure that convicted murderers do not kill again. Only the death penalty can accomplish this end. In a recent case in New Jersey, a man named Richard Biegenwald was freed from prison after serving 18 years for murder; since his release he has been convicted of committing four murders. A prisoner named Lemuel Smith, who, while serving four life sentences for murder (plus two life sentences for kidnapping and robbery) in New York's Green Haven Prison, lured a woman corrections officer into the chaplain's office and strangled her. He then mutilated and dismembered her body. An additional life sentence for Smith is meaningless. Because New York has no death penalty statute, Smith has effectively been given a license to kill.

But the problem of multiple murder is not confined to the nation's 9 penitentiaries. In 1981, 91 police officers were killed in the line of duty in this country. Seven percent of those arrested in the cases that have been solved had a previous arrest for murder. In New York City in 1976 and 1977, 85 persons arrested for homicide had a previous arrest for murder. Six of these individuals had two previous arrests for murder, and one had four previous murder arrests. During those two years the New York police were arresting for murder persons with a previous arrest for murder on the average of one every 8.5 days. This is not surprising when we learn that in 1975, for example, the median time served in Massachusetts for homicide was less than two-and-a-half years. In 1976 a study sponsored by the Twentieth Century Fund found that the average time served in the United States for first-degree murder is ten years. The median time served may be considerably lower.

4. *Capital punishment cheapens the value of human life.* On the con- 10 trary, it can be easily demonstrated that the death penalty strengthens the value of human life. If the penalty for rape were lowered, clearly it

would signal a lessened regard for the victims' suffering, humiliation, and personal integrity. It would cheapen their horrible experience, and expose them to an increased danger of recurrence. When we lower the penalty for murder, it signals a lessened regard for the value of the victim's life. Some critics of capital punishment, such as columnist Jimmy Breslin, have suggested that a life sentence is actually a harsher penalty for murder than death. This is sophistic nonsense. A few killers may decide not to appeal a death sentence, but the overwhelming majority make every effort to stay alive. It is by exacting the highest penalty for the taking of human life that we affirm the highest value of human life.

11   5. *The death penalty is applied in a discriminatory manner.* This factor no longer seems to be the problem it once was. The appeals process for a condemned prisoner is lengthy and painstaking. Every effort is made to see that the verdict and sentence were fairly arrived at. However, assertions of discrimination are not an argument for ending the death penalty but for extending it. It is not justice to exclude everyone from the penalty of the law if a few are found to be so favored. Justice requires that the law be applied equally to all.

12   6. *Thou Shalt Not Kill.* The Bible is our greatest source of moral inspiration. Opponents of the death penalty frequently cite the sixth of the Ten Commandments in an attempt to prove that capital punishment is divinely proscribed. In the original Hebrew, however, the Sixth Commandment reads, "Thou Shalt Not Commit Murder," and the Torah specifies capital punishment for a variety of offenses. The biblical viewpoint has been upheld by philosophers throughout history. The greatest thinkers of the 19th century—Kant, Locke, Hobbes, Rousseau, Montesquieu, and Mill—agreed that natural law properly authorizes the sovereign to take life in order to vindicate justice. Only Jeremy Bentham was ambivalent. Washington, Jefferson, and Franklin endorsed it. Abraham Lincoln authorized executions for deserters in war-time. Alexis de Tocqueville, who expressed profound respect for American institutions, believed that the death penalty was indispensable to the support of social order. The United States Constitution, widely admired as one of the seminal achievements in the history of humanity, condemns cruel and inhuman punishment, but does not condemn capital punishment.

13   7. *The death penalty is state-sanctioned murder.* This is the defense with which Messrs. Willie and Shaw hoped to soften the resolve of those who sentenced them to death. By saying in effect, "You're no better than I am," the murderer seeks to bring his accusers down to his own level. It is also a popular argument among opponents of capital punishment, but a transparently false one. Simply put, the state has rights that the private individual does not. In a democracy, those rights are given to the state by the electorate. The execution of a lawfully con-

demned killer is no more an act of murder than is legal imprisonment an act of kidnapping. If an individual forces a neighbor to pay him money under threat of punishment, it's called extortion. If the state does it, it's called taxation. Rights and responsibilities surrendered by the individual are what give the state its power to govern. This contract is the foundation of civilization itself.

Everyone wants his or her rights, and will defend them jealously. Not everyone, however, wants responsibilities, especially the painful responsibilities that come with law enforcement. Twenty-one years ago a woman named Kitty Genovese was assaulted and murdered on a street in New York. Dozens of neighbors heard her cries for help but did nothing to assist her. They didn't even call the police. In such a climate the criminal understandably grows bolder. In the presence of moral cowardice, he lectures us on our supposed failings and tries to equate his crimes with our quest for justice.   14

The death of anyone—even a convicted killer—diminishes us all. But we are diminished even more by a justice system that fails to function. It is an illusion to let ourselves believe that doing away with capital punishment removes the murderer's deed from our conscience. The rights of society are paramount. When we protect guilty lives, we give up innocent lives in exchange. When opponents of capital punishment say to the state: "I will not let you kill in my name," they are also saying to murderers: "You can kill in your *own* name as long as I have an excuse for not getting involved."   15

It is hard to imagine anything worse than being murdered while neighbors do nothing. But something worse exists. When those same neighbors shrink back from justly punishing the murderer, the victim dies twice.   16

★ Meaning and Understanding

1. Who are Robert Lee Willie and Joseph Carl Shaw?

2. What is Koch's stand on the death penalty? How, according to the writer, have many people responded to his position?

3. What seven points does Koch raise by way of explaining "the arguments most frequently heard in opposition" to the death penalty? How does Koch answer the objections?

4. Who was Kitty Genovese and why does Koch raise her name in paragraph 14?

5. What two issues, according to Koch, diminish humanity? Which of the two does he find more diminishing? Why?

★ Techniques and Strategies

1. What is Koch's thesis in this essay?

2. Why does Koch provide names of various criminals and victims? What do they add to the essay? What does Koch's use of statistics contribute to the argument?

3. Why has the writer chosen the cancer analogy for his argument against critics who call the death penalty barbaric? How does he then challenge the analogy?

4. What value do you find in Koch's inclusion of arguments raised against his own position? In fact, he structures the essay around opposing arguments. What advantages do you see in that strategy? What disadvantages?

5. What is your reaction the last sentence of the essay? How does it interact with the title?

★ Speaking of Values

1. Koch implies that the sudden reverence for life shown by two known killers is a result of "the realization that they were about to lose their own." Do you think that the death penalty can influence killers and would-be killers in this way? Why or why not? What support can you offer for your position?

2. The writer dismisses with citations and expert testimony the argument advanced by many who oppose the death penalty: "an innocent person might be executed by mistake." What is your position on this point? How has Koch convinced you—or not convinced you—that this element of the argument is invalid?

3. Koch states that capital punishment strengthens the value of human life. What is your reaction to this argument?

4. How effective is Koch in his use of Christian scripture to make his point? Does he convince you with these citations? What would those who oppose the death penalty argue in response, do you think?

5. "When we protect guilty lives," Koch argues, "we give up innocent lives in exchange." Why might you agree or disagree with this point? How would death penalty opponents respond to Koch?

★ Values Conversation

Form groups to discuss each of the opposing arguments Koch raises and the responses he makes to them. Where has he convinced members of the group that his point is the valid one? Where do members of the group feel that he has not made his point successfully? Has Koch managed to change any minds of people in your group? Report your group's findings to the rest of the class.

★ *Writing about Values*

1. Write a letter to Edward Koch in which you refute the seven arguments he makes in favor of capital punishment. In other words, argue against the death penalty.

2. Apparently Koch and other like-minded people have convinced legislators across the country about capital punishment: many states, including New York State, now allow the death penalty. Write an essay about the issue of capital punishment as "state-sanctioned murder" or "state-sanctioned justice."

3. Research one or more of the philosophers Koch names in paragraph 12 for their stated positions on capital punishment. Then write an essay about your findings.

William Joseph Brennan, Jr.

What the Constitution Requires

William Joseph Brennan, Jr., born in 1906, served as an associate justice of
the Supreme Court from 1956 to 1990. Here he writes against the death
penalty.

———— ★ ————

1   In 1956, Dwight D. Eisenhower appointed me to the Supreme Court.
Now, at 90, I am frequently asked to identify the Court's greatest
achievements in my 34-year tenure. High on my list is the protection of
individual rights and human dignity.

2   Our Constituion is a charter of human rights, dignity and self-
determination. I approached my responsibility of interpreting it as a
20th-century American, for the genius of the Constitution rests not in
any static meaning it may have had in a world dead and gone but in its
evolving character. Only from this perspective has the Court been able
to erect some of liberty's most enduring monuments, such as the decision (in 1954) that a public school cannot slam its doors on pupils because of their color.

3   In my time, it was the living Constitution that required the police
to inform the accused of their fundamental rights of defense (in 1966).
Only the freedom to reinterpret constitutional language enabled us to
conclude (in 1962 and 1964) that each American should have an equal
vote and (in 1970) that the Government may not cut a welfare recipient's lifeline without holding a hearing.

4   But we do not yet have justice for all who do not partake in the
abundance of American life. One area of law more than any other be-
smirches the constitutional vision of human dignity. My old friend Justice Harry Blackmun called it the "machinery of death." It is the death
penalty.

5   The statistics paint a chilling portrait of racial discrimination on
death row. Yet the ultimate problem is more fundamental. The barbaric
death penalty violates our Constitution. Even the most vile murderer
does not release the state from its obligation to respect dignity, for the
state does not honor the victim by emulating his murderer. Capital
punishment's fatal flaw is that it treats people as objects to be toyed
with and discarded. But I refuse to despair. One day the Court will out-
law the death penalty. Permanently.

The task of nurturing the constitutional ideal of dignity does not   6
rest solely with the nine Justices, or even the cadre of Federal and state
judges. We all share the burden.

If I have drawn one lesson in 90 years, it is this: To strike a blow for   7
freedom allows a man to walk a little taller and raise his head a little
higher. While he can, he must.

★ Meaning and Understanding

1. What is the main point of the essay?

2. What does Brennan list as the Court's greatest achievement? What are
   some of "liberty's enduring monuments"?

3. According to the writer, what is capital punishment's "fatal flaw"?

4. How would abolishing the death penalty "strike a blow for freedom"?

5. What does Justice Blackmun mean by "the machinery of death"?

★ Techniques and Strategies

1. Why has Brennan chosen the title he has for the essay? In what way is
   it an accurate title for the piece? In what way does it engage the
   reader? Is opposition to the death penalty, in fact, *required* by the U.S.
   Constitution?

2. Why does Brennan reflect on his past service to the country and his
   current age in the first paragraph? What do these strategies contribute
   to the argument?

3. Brennan includes parenthetical dates in four places in the essay. Why
   does he do this? What historical issues do these dates refer to?

4. This is a very short essay for a very weighty topic, written as a guest
   editorial for the *New York Times*, a nationally syndicated newspaper.
   What do you think of the essay's length? Does it make its point force-
   fully in just a few words—a model of brevity and intelligence? Or is it
   insubstantial and, because of its length, not rich enough in supporting
   detail?

5. How does the last paragraph serve the essay? What is the value of the
   two familiar metaphors?

★ Speaking of Values

1. Brennan asserts that the state will "honor the victim by emulating his
   murderer." Why might you agree or disagree with his position?

2. What is your reaction to the term "the machinery of death"? Is it appropriate or inappropriate, fair or unfair? Does it portray the situation accurately or overload the issue with emotion? Explain your response.

3. What should the society do about those who violate the human rights, dignity, and self-determination of others—through murder or kidnapping, let us say? What is the relation of capital punishment to the assertion that the "Constitution is a charter of human rights, dignity and self-determination" (paragraph 2)?

4. Brennan says that striking a blow for freedom is one of humanity's highest goals. Why might you agree or disagree with this point? What blows for freedom can people today strike?

★ *Values Conversation*

Form groups and discuss the issue of capital punishment. Do you agree with Brennan that "it treats people as objects to be toyed with and discarded"? What does your group think of this decade's dramatic increase in state-supported executions under capital punishment statutes? Report your group's conclusions to the rest of the class.

★ *Writing about Values*

1. Think of yourself as a representative of the state or government. Write an essay in support of or against capital punishment. Why is your point of view the best choice for the nation?

2. Go to the library and research some of the statistics the writer cites on racial discrimination or the death penalty—for example, on the latter's deterrence of crime. How does this information affect your point of view? Write an essay discussing your views and referring to the research.

3. Write an essay called "To Strike a Blow for Freedom."

Martin Luther King, Jr.

Letter from Birmingham Jail[1]

Martin Luther King, Jr. (1929–1968) was an American religious leader and political spokesman who helped form the civil rights movement of the 1950s and 1960s. In 1964 he won the Nobel Peace Prize. King was assassinated in Memphis, Tennessee, four years later. In this letter he lays out some of the principles of civil disobedience that motivated his leadership.

★

MY DEAR FELLOW CLERGYMEN:

While confined here in the Birmingham city jail, I came across your recent statement calling my present activities "unwise and untimely." Seldom do I pause to answer criticism of my work and ideas. If I sought to answer all the criticisms that cross my desk, my secretaries would have little time for anything other than such correspondence in the course of the day, and I would have no time for constructive work. But since I feel that you are men of genuine good will and that your criticisms are sincerely set forth, I want to try to answer your statement in what I hope will be patient and reasonable terms. [1]

I think I should indicate why I am here in Birmingham, since you have been influenced by the view which argues against "outsiders coming in." I have the honor of serving as president of the Southern Christian Leadership Conference, an organization operating in every southern state, with headquarters in Atlanta, Georgia. We have some eighty-five affiliated organizations across the South, and one of them is the Alabama Christian Movement for Human Rights. Frequently we share staff, educational, and financial resources with our affiliates. Several months ago the affiliate here in Birmingham asked us to be on call to engage in a nonviolent direct-action program if such were deemed necessary. We readily consented, and when the hour came we lived up [2]

---

[1]This response to a published statement by eight fellow clergymen from Alabama (Bishop C. C. J. Carpenter, Bishop Joseph A. Durick, Rabbi Milton L. Grafman, Bishop Paul Hardin, Bishop Holan B. Harmon, the Reverend George M. Murray, the Reverend Edward V. Ramage and the Reverend Earl Stallings) was composed under somewhat constricting circumstances. Begun on the margins of the newspaper in which the statement appeared while I was in jail, the letter was continued on scraps of writing paper supplied by a friendly Negro trusty, and concluded on a pad my attorneys were eventually permitted to leave me. Although the text remains in substance unaltered, I have indulged in the author's prerogative of polishing it for publication. [King's note].

to our promise. So I, along with several members of my staff, am here because I was invited here. I am here because I have organizational ties here.

3   But more basically, I am in Birmingham because injustice is here. Just as the prophets of the eighth century B.C. left their villages and carried their "thus saith the Lord" far beyond the boundaries of their home towns, and just as the Apostle Paul left his village of Tarsus and carried the gospel of Jesus Christ to the far corners of the Greco-Roman world, so am I compelled to carry the gospel of freedom beyond my own home town. Like Paul, I must constantly respond to the Macedonian call for aid.

4   Moreover, I am cognizant of the interrelatedness of all communities and states. I cannot sit idly by in Atlanta and not be concerned about what happens in Birmingham. Injustice anywhere is a threat to justice everywhere. We are caught in an inescapable network of mutuality, tied in a single garment of destiny. Whatever affects one directly, affects all indirectly. Never again can we afford to live with the narrow, provincial "outside agitator" idea. Anyone who lives inside the United States can never be considered an outsider anywhere within its bounds.

5   You deplore the demonstrations taking place in Birmingham. But your statement, I am sorry to say, fails to express a similar concern for the conditions that brought about the demonstrations. I am sure that none of you would want to rest content with the superficial kind of social analysis that deals merely with effects and does not grapple with underlying causes. It is unfortunate that demonstrations are taking place in Birmingham, but it is even more unfortunate that the city's white power structure left the Negro community with no alternative.

6   In any nonviolent campaign there are four basic steps: collection of the facts to determine whether injustices exist; negotiation; self-purification; and direct action. We have gone through an these steps in Birmingham. There can be no gainsaying the fact that racial injustice engulfs this community. Birmingham is probably the most thoroughly segregated city in the United States. Its ugly record of brutality is widely known. Negroes have experienced grossly unjust treatment in the courts. There have been more unsolved bombings of Negro homes and churches in Birmingham than in any other city in the nation. These are the hard, brutal facts of the case. On the basis of these conditions, Negro leaders sought to negotiate with the city fathers. But the latter consistently refused to engage in good-faith negotiation.

7   Then, last September, came the opportunity to talk with leaders of Birmingham's economic community. In the course of the negotiations, certain promises were made by the merchants—for example, to remove the stores' humiliating racial signs. On the basis of these promises, the Reverend Fred Shuttlesworth and the leaders of the Alabama Christian

Movement for Human Rights agreed to a moratorium on all demonstrations. As the weeks and months went by, we realized that we were the victims of a broken promise. A few signs, briefly removed, returned; the others remained.

As in so many past experiences, our hopes had been blasted, and the shadow of deep disappointment settled upon us. We had no alternative except to prepare for direct action, whereby we would present our very bodies as a means of laying our case before the conscience of the local and the national community. Mindful of the difficulties involved, we decided to undertake a process of self-purification. We began a series of workshops on nonviolence, and we repeatedly asked ourselves: "Are you able to accept blows without retaliating?" "Are you able to endure the ordeal of jail?" We decided to schedule our direct-action program for the Easter season, realizing that except for Christmas, this is the main shopping period of the year. Knowing that a strong economic-withdrawal program would be the by-product of direct action, we felt that this would be the best time to bring pressure to bear on the merchants for the needed change.   8

Then it occurred to us that Birmingham's mayoral election was coming up in March, and we speedily decided to postpone action until after election day. When we discovered that the Commissioner of Public Safety, Eugene "Bull" Connor, had piled up enough votes to be in the run-off, we decided again to postpone action until the day after the run-off so that the demonstrations could not be used to cloud the issues. Like many others, we waited to see Mr. Connor defeated, and to this end we endured postponement after postponement. Having aided in this community need, we felt that our direct-action program could be delayed no longer.   9

You may well ask, "Why direct action? Why sit-ins, marches, and so forth? Isn't negotiation a better path?" You are quite right in calling for negotiation. Indeed, this is the very purpose of direct action. Nonviolent direct action seeks to create such a crisis and foster such a tension that a community which has constantly refused to negotiate is forced to confront the issue. It seeks so to dramatize the issue that it can no longer be ignored. My citing the creation of tension as part of the work of the nonviolent-resister may sound rather shocking. But I must confess that I am not afraid of the word "tension." I have earnestly opposed violent tension, but there is a type of constructive, nonviolent tension which is necessary for growth. Just as Socrates felt that it was necessary to create a tension in the mind so that individuals could rise from the bondage of myths and half-truths to the unfettered realm of creative analysis and objective appraisal, so must we see the need for nonviolent gadflies to create the kind of tension in society that will help men rise from the dark depths of prejudice and racism to the majestic heights of understanding and brotherhood.   10

11   The purpose of our direct-action program is to create a situation so crisis-packed that it will inevitably open the door to negotiation. I therefore concur with you in your call for negotiation. Too long has our beloved Southland been bogged down in a tragic effort to live in monologue rather than dialogue.

12   One of the basic points in your statement is that the action that I and my associates have taken in Birmingham is untimely. Some have asked: "Why didn't you give the new city administration time to act?" The only answer that I can give to this query is that the new Birmingham administration must be prodded about as much as the outgoing one, before it will act. We are sadly mistaken if we feel that the election of Albert Boutwell as mayor will bring the millennium to Birmingham. While Mr. Boutwell is a much more gentle person than Mr. Connor, they are both segregationists, dedicated to maintenance of the status quo. I have hope that Mr. Boutwell will be reasonable enough to see the futility of massive resistance to desegregation. But he will not see this without pressure from devotees of civil rights. My friends, I must say to you that we have not made a single gain in civil rights without determined legal and nonviolent pressure. Lamentably, it is an historical fact that privileged groups seldom give up their privileges voluntarily. Individuals may see the moral light and voluntarily give up their unjust posture; but, as Reinhold Niebuhr[2] has reminded us, groups tend to be more immoral than individuals.

13   We know through painful experience that freedom is never voluntarily given by the oppressor; it must be demanded by the oppressed. Frankly, I have yet to engage in a direct-action campaign that was "well timed" in the view of those who have not suffered unduly from the disease of segregation. For years now I have heard the word "Wait!" It rings in the ear of every Negro with piercing familiarity. This "Wait" has almost always meant "Never." We must come to see, with one of our distinguished jurists, that "justice too long delayed is justice denied."

14   We have waited for more than 340 years for our constitutional and God-given rights. The nations of Asia and Africa are moving with jet-like speed toward gaining political independence, but we still creep at horse-and-buggy pace toward gaining a cup of coffee at a lunch counter. Perhaps it is easy for those who have never felt the stinging darts of segregation to say, "Wait." But when you have seen vicious mobs lynch your mothers and fathers at will and drown your sisters and brothers at whim; when you have seen hate-filled policemen curse, kick, and even kill your black brothers and sisters; when you see the vast majority of your twenty million Negro brothers smothering in an airtight cage of poverty in the midst of an affluent society; when you

[2]A Protestant religious leader (1892–1971).

suddenly find your tongue twisted and your speech stammering as you seek to explain to your six-year-old daughter why she can't go to the public amusement park that has just been advertised on television, and see tears welling up in her eyes when she is told that Funtown is closed to colored children, and see ominous clouds of inferiority beginning to form in her little mental sky, and see her beginning to distort her personality by developing an unconscious bitterness toward white people; when you have to concoct an answer for a five-year-old son who is asking: "Daddy, why do white people treat colored people so mean?"; when you take a cross-country drive and find it necessary to sleep night after night in the uncomfortable corners of your automobile because no motel will accept you; when you are humiliated day in and day out by nagging signs reading "white" and "colored"; when your first name becomes "nigger," your middle name becomes "boy" (however old you are) and your last name becomes "John," and your wife and mother are never given the respected title "Mrs."; when you are harried by day and haunted by night by the fact that you are a Negro, living constantly at tiptoe stance, never quite knowing what to expect next, and are plagued with inner fears and outer resentments; when you are forever fighting a degenerating sense of "nobodiness"—then you will understand why we find it difficult to wait. There comes a time when the cup of endurance runs over, and men are no longer willing to be plunged into the abyss of despair. I hope, sirs, you can understand our legitimate and unavoidable impatience.

You express a great deal of anxiety over our willingness to break   15
laws. This is certainly a legitimate concern. Since we so diligently urge people to obey the Supreme Court's decision of 1954 outlawing segregation in the public schools, at first glance it may seem rather paradoxical for us consciously to break laws. One may well ask: "How can you advocate breaking some laws and obeying others?" The answer lies in the fact that there are two types of laws: just and unjust. I would be the first to advocate obeying just laws. One has not only a legal but a moral responsibility to obey just laws. Conversely, one has a moral responsibility to disobey unjust laws. I would agree with St. Augustine[3] that "an unjust law is no law at all."

Now, what is the difference between the two? How does one deter-   16
mine whether a law is just or unjust? A just law is a man-made code that squares with the moral law or the law of God. An unjust law is a code that is out of harmony with the moral law. To put it in the terms of St. Thomas Aquinas:[4] An unjust law is a human law that is not rooted in eternal law and natural law. Any law that uplifts human personality

[3]Early Christian church father (354–430).
[4]A renowned philosopher and Christian leader (1225–1274).

is just. Any law that degrades human personality is unjust. All segregation statutes are unjust because segregation distorts the soul and damages the personality. It gives the segregator a false sense of superiority and the segregated a false sense of inferiority. Segregation, to use the terminology of the Jewish philosopher Martin Buber,[5] substitutes an "I-it" relationship for an "I-thou" relationship and ends up relegating persons to the status of things. Hence segregation is not only politically, economically and sociologically unsound, it is morally wrong and sinful. Paul Tillich[6] said that sin is separation. Is not segregation an existential expression of man's tragic separation, his awful estrangement, his terrible sinfulness? Thus it is that I can urge men to obey the 1954 decision of the Supreme Court, for it is morally right; and I can urge them to disobey segregation ordinances, for they are morally wrong.

17   Let us consider a more concrete example of just and unjust laws. An unjust law is a code that a numerical or power majority group compels a minority group to obey but does not make binding on itself. This is *difference* made legal. By the same token, a just law is a code that a majority compels a minority to follow and that it is willing to follow itself. This is *sameness* made legal.

18   Let me give another explanation. A law is unjust if it is inflicted on a minority that, as a result of being denied the right to vote, had no part in enacting or devising the law. Who can say that the legislature of Alabama which set up that state's segregation laws was democratically elected? Throughout Alabama all sorts of devious methods are used to prevent Negroes from becoming registered voters, and there are some counties in which, even though Negroes constitute a majority of the population, not a single Negro is registered. Can any law enacted under such circumstances be considered democratically structured?

19   Sometimes a law is just on its face and unjust in its application. For instance, I have been arrested on a charge of parading without a permit. Now, there is nothing wrong in having an ordinance which requires a permit for a parade. But such an ordinance becomes unjust when it is used to maintain segregation and to deny citizens the First-Amendment privilege of peaceful assembly and protest.

20   I hope you are able to see the distinction I am trying to point out. In no sense do I advocate evading or defying the law, as would the rabid segregationist. That would lead to anarchy. One who breaks an unjust law must do so openly, lovingly, and with a willingness to accept the penalty. I submit that an individual who breaks a law that conscience tells him is unjust and who willingly accepts the penalty of imprison-

[5](1878–1965).
[6]Another American Protestant, who was a theologian (1886–1965).

ment in order to arouse the conscience of the community over its injustice, is in reality expressing the highest respect for law.

Of course, there is nothing new about this kind of civil disobedience. It was evidenced sublimely in the refusal of Shadrach, Meshach, and Abednego to obey the laws of Nebuchadnezzar,[7] on the ground that a higher moral law was at stake. It was practiced superbly by the early Christians, who were willing to face hungry lions and the excruciating pain of chopping blocks rather than submit to certain unjust laws of the Roman Empire. To a degree, academic freedom is a reality today because Socrates practiced civil disobedience.[8] In our own nation, the Boston Tea Party represented a massive act of civil disobedience.

We should never forget that everything Adolf Hitler did in Germany was "legal" and everything the Hungarian freedom fighters did in Hungary was "illegal." It was "illegal" to aid and comfort a Jew in Hitler's Germany. Even so, I am sure that, had I lived in Germany at the time, I would have aided and comforted my Jewish brothers. If today I lived in a Communist country where certain principles dear to the Christian faith are suppressed, I would openly advocate disobeying that country's antireligious laws.

I must make two honest confessions to you, my Christian and Jewish brothers. First, I must confess that over the past few years I have been gravely disappointed with the white moderate. I have almost reached the regrettable conclusion that the Negro's great stumbling block in his stride toward freedom is not the White Citizen's Counciler or the Ku Klux Klanner, but the white moderate, who is more devoted to "order" than to justice; who prefers a negative peace which is the absence of tension to a positive peace which is the presence of justice; who constantly says, "I agree with you in the goal you seek, but I cannot agree with your methods of direct action"; who paternalistically believes he can set the timetable for another man's freedom; who lives by a mythical concept of time and who constantly advises the Negro to wait for a "more convenient season." Shallow understanding from people of good will is more frustrating than absolute misunderstanding from people of ill will. Lukewarm acceptance is much more bewildering than outright rejection.

I had hoped that the white moderate would understand that law and order exist for the purpose of establishing justice and that where they fail in this purpose they become the dangerously structured dams that block the flow of social progress. I had hoped that the white moderate would understand that the present tension in the South is a necessary

[7]See Daniel 3.

[8]The Athenians tried the Greek philosopher Socrates for corrupting youth by his teaching methods. He was put to death.

phase of the transition from an obnoxious negative peace, in which the Negro passively accepted his unjust plight, to a substantive and positive peace, in which all men will respect the dignity and worth of human personality. Actually, we who engage in nonviolent direct action are not the creators of tension. We merely bring to the surface the hidden tension that is already alive. We bring it out in the open, where it can be seen and dealt with. Like a boil that can never be cured so long as it is covered up but must be opened with all its ugliness to the natural medicines of air and light, injustice must be exposed, with all the tension its exposure creates, to the light of human conscience and the air of national opinion, before it can be cured.

25   In your statement you assert that our actions, even though peaceful, must be condemned because they precipitate violence. But is this a logical assertion? Isn't this like condemning a robbed man because his possession of money precipitated the evil act of robbery? Isn't this like condemning Socrates because his unswerving commitment to truth and his philosophical inquiries precipitated the act by the misguided populace in which they made him drink hemlock? Isn't this like condemning Jesus because his unique God-consciousness and never-ceasing devotion to God's will precipitated the evil act of crucifixion? We must come to see that, as the federal courts have consistently affirmed, it is wrong to urge an individual to cease his efforts to gain his basic constitutional rights because the quest may precipitate violence. Society must protect the robbed and punish the robber.

26   I had also hoped that the white moderate would reject the myth concerning time in relation to the struggle for freedom. I have just received a letter from a white brother in Texas. He writes: "All Christians know that the colored people will receive equal rights eventually, but it is possible that you are in too great a religious hurry. It has taken Christianity almost two thousand years to accomplish what it has. The teachings of Christ take time to come to earth." Such an attitude stems from a tragic misconception of time, from the strangely irrational notion that there is something in the very flow of time that will inevitably cure all ills. Actually, time itself is neutral; it can be used either destructively or constructively. More and more I feel that the people of ill will have used time much more effectively than have the people of good will. We will have to repent in this generation not merely for the hateful words and actions of the bad people, but for the appalling silence of the good people. Human progress never rolls in on wheels of inevitability; it comes through the tireless efforts of men willing to be co-workers with God, and without this hard work, time itself becomes an ally of the forces of social stagnation. We must use time creatively, in the knowledge that the time is always ripe to do right. Now is the time to make real the promise of democracy and transform our pending national elegy into a creative psalm of brotherhood. Now is the time to lift our na-

tional policy from the quicksand of racial injustice to the solid rock of human dignity.

You speak of our activity in Birmingham as extreme. At first I was rather disappointed that fellow clergymen would see my nonviolent efforts as those of an extremist. I began thinking about the fact that I stand in the middle of two opposing forces in the Negro community. One is a force of complacency, made up in part of Negroes who, as a result of long years of oppression, are so drained of self-respect and a sense of "somebodiness" that they have adjusted to segregation; and in part of a few middle-class Negroes who, because of a degree of academic and economic security and because in some ways they profit by segregation, have become insensitive to the problems of the masses. The other force is one of bitterness and hatred, and it comes perilously close to advocating violence. It is expressed in the various black nationalist groups that are springing up across the nation, the largest and best-known being Elijah Muhammad's Muslim movement.[9] Nourished by the Negro's frustration over the continued existence of racial discrimination, this movement is made up of people who have lost faith in America, who have absolutely repudiated Christianity, and who have concluded that the white man is an incorrigible "devil." 27

I have tried to stand between these two forces, saying that we need emulate neither the "do-nothingism" of the complacent nor the hatred and despair of the black nationalist. For there is the more excellent way of love and nonviolent protest. I am grateful to God that, through the influence of the Negro church, the way of nonviolence became an integral part of our struggle. 28

If this philosophy had not emerged, by now many streets of the South would, I am convinced, be flowing with blood. And I am further convinced that if our white brothers dismiss as "rabblerousers" and "outside agitators" those of us who employ nonviolent direct action, and if they refuse to support our nonviolent efforts, millions of Negroes will, out of frustration and despair, seek solace and security in black-nationalist ideologies—a development that would inevitably lead to a frightening racial nightmare. 29

Oppressed people cannot remain oppressed forever. The yearning for freedom eventually manifests itself, and that is what has happened to the American Negro. Something within has reminded him of his birthright of freedom, and something without has reminded him that it can be gained. Consciously or unconsciously, he has been caught up by the *Zeitgeist*, and with his black brothers of Africa and his brown and yellow brothers of Asia, South America and the Caribbean, the United States Negro is moving with a sense of great urgency toward the promised 30

[9]Elijah Muhammed (1897–1975), became the leader of the Nation of Islam in 1934.

land of racial justice. If one recognizes this vital urge that has engulfed the Negro community, one should readily understand why public demonstrations are taking place. The Negro has many pent-up resentments and latent frustrations, and he must release them. So let him march; let him make prayer pilgrimages to the city hall; let him go on freedom rides—and try to understand why he must do so. If his repressed emotions are not released in nonviolent ways, they will seek expression through violence; this is not a threat but a fact of history. So I have not said to my people, "Get rid of your discontent." Rather, I have tried to say that this normal and healthy discontent can be channeled into the creative outlet of nonviolent direct action. And now this approach is being termed extremist.

31   But though I was initially disappointed at being categorized as an extremist, as I continued to think about the matter I gradually gained a measure of satisfaction from the label. Was not Jesus an extremist for love: "Love your enemies, bless them that curse you, do good to them that hate you, and pray for them which despitefully use you, and persecute you." Was not Amos an extremist for justice: "Let justice roll down like waters and righteousness like an ever-flowing stream." Was not Paul an extremist for the Christian gospel: "I bear in my body the marks of the Lord Jesus." Was not Martin Luther an extremist: "Here I stand; I cannot do otherwise, so help me God." And John Bunyan:[10] "I will stay in jail to the end of my days before I make a butchery of my conscience." And Abraham Lincoln: "This nation cannot survive half slave and half free." And Thomas Jefferson: "We hold these truths to be self-evident, that all men are created equal. . . ." So the question is not whether we will be extremists, but what kind of extremists we will be. Will we be extremists for hate or for love? Will we be extremists for the preservation of injustice or for the extension of justice? In that dramatic scene on Calvary's hill three men were crucified. We must never forget that all three were crucified for the same crime—the crime of extremism. Two were extremists for immorality, and thus fell below their environment. The other, Jesus Christ, was an extremist for love, truth, and goodness, and thereby rose above his environment. Perhaps the South, the nation, and the world are in dire need of creative extremists.

32   I had hoped that the white moderate would see this need. Perhaps I was too optimistic; perhaps I expected too much. I suppose I should have realized that few members of the oppressor race can understand the deep groans and passionate yearnings of the oppressed race, and still fewer have the vision to see that injustice must be rooted out by strong, persistent, and determined action. I am thankful, however, that

[10]British author and preacher (1628–1688). Amos was a prophet of the Old Testament. Paul was a New Testament apostle; Martin Luther (1483–1546) was a reformer for the Protestants in Germany.

some of our white brothers in the South have grasped the meaning of this social revolution and committed themselves to it. They are still too few in quantity, but they are big in quality. Some—such as Ralph McGill, Lillian Smith, Harry Golden, James McBride Dabbs, Ann Braden, and Sarah Patton Boyle—have written about our struggle in eloquent and prophetic terms. Others have marched with us down nameless streets of the South. They have languished in filthy, roach-infested jails, suffering the abuse and brutality of policemen who view them as "dirty nigger lovers." Unlike so many of their moderate brothers and sisters, they have recognized the urgency of the moment and sensed the need for powerful "action" antidotes to combat the disease of segregation.

Let me take note of my other major disappointment. I have been so greatly disappointed with the white church and its leadership. Of course, there are some notable exceptions. I am not unmindful of the fact that each of you has taken some significant stands on this issue. I commend you, Reverend Stallings, for your Christian stand on this past Sunday, in welcoming Negroes to your worship service on a non-segregated basis. I commend the Catholic leaders of this state for integrating Spring Hill College several years ago. 33

But despite these notable exceptions, I must honestly reiterate that I have been disappointed with the church. I do not say this as one of those negative critics who can always find something wrong with the church. I say this as a minister of the gospel, who loves the church; who was nurtured in its bosom; who has been sustained by its spiritual blessings and who will remain true to it as long as the cord of life shall lengthen. 34

When I was suddenly catapulted into the leadership of the bus protest in Montgomery, Alabama, a few years ago,[11] I felt we would be supported by the white church. I felt that the white ministers, priests, and rabbis of the South would be among our strongest allies. Instead, some have been outright opponents, refusing to understand the freedom movement and misrepresenting its leaders; all too many others have been more cautious than courageous and have remained silent behind the anesthetizing security of stainedglass windows. 35

In spite of my shattered dreams, I came to Birmingham with the hope that the white religious leadership of this community would see the justice of our cause and, with deep moral concern, would serve as the channel through which our just grievances could reach the power structure. I had hoped that each of you would understand. But again I have been disappointed. 36

---

[11]Rosa Parks refused to move to the part of the bus reserved for Negroes, and in December 1955 the bus protest began.

37   I have heard numerous southern religious leaders admonish their worshipers to comply with a desegregation decision because it is the law, but I have longed to hear white ministers declare: "Follow this decree because integration is morally right and because the Negro is your brother." In the midst of blatant injustices inflicted upon the Negro, I have watched white churchmen stand on the sideline and mouth pious irrelevancies and sanctimonious trivialities. In the midst of a mighty struggle to rid our nation of racial and economic injustice, I have heard many ministers say: "Those are social issues, with which the gospel has no real concern." And I have watched many churches commit themselves to a completely otherworldly religion which makes a strange, un-Biblical distinction between body and soul, between the sacred and the secular.

38   I have traveled the length and breadth of Alabama, Mississippi, and all the other southern states. On sweltering summer days and crisp autumn mornings I have looked at the South's beautiful churches with their lofty spires pointing heavenward. I have beheld the impressive outlines of her massive religious-education buildings. Over and over I have found myself asking: "What kind of people worship here? Who is their God? Where were their voices when the lips of Governor Barnett dripped with words of interposition and nullification? Where were they when Governor Wallace gave a clarion call for defiance and hatred?[12] Where were their voices of support when bruised and weary Negro men and women decided to rise from the dark dungeons of complacency to the bright hills of creative protest?"

39   Yes, these questions are still in my mind. In deep disappointment I have wept over the laxity of the church. But be assured that my tears have been tears of love. There can be no deep disappointment where there is not deep love. Yes, I love the church. How could I do otherwise? I am in the rather unique position of being the son, the grandson, and the great-grandson of preachers. Yes, I see the church as the body of Christ. But, oh! How we have blemished and scarred that body through social neglect and through fear of being nonconformists.

40   There was a time when the church was very powerful—in the time when the early Christians rejoiced at being deemed worthy to suffer for what they believed. In those days the church was not merely a thermometer that recorded the ideas and principles of popular opinion; it was a thermostat that transformed the mores of society. Whenever the early Christians entered a town, the people in power became disturbed and immediately sought to convict the Christians for being "disturbers of the peace" and "outside agitators." But the Christians pressed on, in

[12]George Wallace (1919–1998) was governor of Alabama and fought to exclude black students from the University of Alabama. Governor of Mississippi Ross Barnett (1898–1988), fought James Meredith's admission to the University of Mississippi.

the conviction that they were "a colony of heaven," called to obey God rather than man. Small in number, they were big in commitment. They were too God-intoxicated to be "astronomically intimidated." By their effort and example they brought an end to such ancient evils as infanticide and gladiatorial contests.

Things are different now. So often the contemporary church is a   41
weak, ineffectual voice with an uncertain sound. So often it is an arch-defender of the status quo. Far from being disturbed by the presence of the church, the power structure of the average community is consoled by the church's silent—and often even vocal—sanction of things as they are.

But the judgment of God is upon the church as never before. If to-   42
day's church does not recapture the sacrificial spirit of the early church, it will lose its authenticity, forfeit the loyalty of millions, and be dismissed as an irrelevant social club with no meaning for the twentieth century. Every day I meet young people whose disappointment with the church has turned into outright disgust.

Perhaps I have once again been too optimistic. Is organized reli-   43
gion too inextricably bound to the status quo to save our nation and the world? Perhaps I must turn my faith to the inner spiritual church, the church within the church, as the true *ekklesia*[13] and the hope of the world. But again I am thankful to God that some noble souls from the ranks of organized religion have broken loose from the paralyzing chains of conformity and joined us as active partners in the struggle for freedom. They have left their secure congregations and walked the streets of Albany, Georgia, with us. They have gone down the highways of the South on tortuous rides for freedom. Yes, they have gone to jail with us. Some have been dismissed from their churches, have lost the support of their bishops and fellow ministers. But they have acted in the faith that right defeated is stronger than evil triumphant. Their witness has been the spiritual salt that has preserved the true meaning of the gospel in these troubled times. They have carved a tunnel of hope through the dark mountain of disappointment.

I hope the church as a whole will meet the challenge of this decisive   44
hour. But even if the church does not come to the aid of justice, I have no despair about the future. I have no fear about the outcome of our struggle in Birmingham, even if our motives are at present misunderstood. We will reach the goal of freedom in Birmingham and all over the nation, because the goal of America is freedom. Abused and scorned though we may be, our destiny is tied up with America's destiny. Before the pilgrims landed at Plymouth, we were here. Before the pen of Jefferson etched the majestic words of the Declaration of Independence

---

[13]In the Greek New Testament, the word for the early Christian church.

across the pages of history, we were here. For more than two centuries our forebears labored in this country without wages; they made cotton king; they built the homes of their masters while suffering gross injustice and shameful humiliation—and yet out of a bottomless vitality they continued to thrive and develop. If the inexpressible cruelties of slavery could not stop us, the opposition we now face will surely fail. We will win our freedom because the sacred heritage of our nation and the eternal will of God are embodied in our echoing demands.

45   Before closing I feel impelled to mention one other point in your statement that has troubled me profoundly. You warmly commended the Birmingham police force for keeping "order" and "preventing violence." I doubt that you would have so warmly commended the police force if you had seen its dogs sinking their teeth into unarmed, nonviolent Negroes. I doubt that you would so quickly commend the policemen if you were to observe their ugly and inhumane treatment of Negroes here in the city jail; if you were to watch them push and curse old Negro women and young Negro girls; if you were to see them slap and kick old Negro men and young boys; if you were to observe them, as they did on two occasions, refuse to give us food because we wanted to sing our grace together. I cannot join you in your praise of the Birmingham police department.

46   It is true that the police have exercised a degree of discipline in handling the demonstrators. In this sense they have conducted themselves rather "nonviolently" in public. But for what purpose? To preserve the evil system of segregation. Over the past few years I have consistently preached that nonviolence demands that the means we use must be as pure as the ends we seek. I have tried to make clear that it is wrong to use immoral means to attain moral ends. But now I must affirm that it is just as wrong, or perhaps even more so, to use moral means to preserve immoral ends. Perhaps Mr. Connor and his policemen have been rather nonviolent in public, as was Chief Pritchett in Albany, Georgia, but they have used the moral means of nonviolence to maintain the immoral end of racial injustice. As T. S. Eliot has said, "The last temptation is the greatest treason: To do the right deed for the wrong reason."

47   I wish you had commended the Negro sit-inners and demonstrators of Birmingham for their sublime courage, their willingness to suffer, and their amazing discipline in the midst of great provocation. One day the South will recognize its real heroes. They will be the James Merediths, with the noble sense of purpose that enables them to face jeering and hostile mobs, and with the agonizing loneliness that characterizes the life of the pioneer. They will be old, oppressed, battered Negro women, symbolized in a seventy-two-year-old woman in Montgomery, Alabama, who rose up with a sense of dignity and with her people decided not to ride segregated buses, and who responded with

ungrammatical profundity to one who inquired about her weariness: "My feets is tired, but my soul is at rest." They will be the young high school and college students, the young ministers of the gospel and a host of their elders, courageously and nonviolently sitting in at lunch counters and willingly going to jail for conscience' sake. One day the South will know that when these disinherited children of God sat down at lunch counters, they were in reality standing up for what is best in the American dream and for the most sacred values in our Judeo-Christian heritage, thereby bringing our nation back to those great wells of democracy which were dug deep by the founding fathers in their formulation of the Constitution and the Declaration of Independence.

Never before have I written so long a letter. I'm afraid it is much too long to take your precious time. I can assure you that it would have been much shorter if I had been writing from a comfortable desk, but what else can one do when he is alone in a narrow jail cell, other than write long letters, think long thoughts, and pray long prayers? 48

If I have said anything in this letter that overstates the truth and indicates an unreasonable impatience, I beg you to forgive me. If I have said anything that understates the truth and indicates my having a patience that allows me to settle for anything less than brotherhood, I beg God to forgive me. 49

I hope this letter finds you strong in the faith. I also hope that circumstances will soon make it possible for me to meet each of you, not as an integrationist or a civil rights leader but as a fellow clergyman and a Christian brother. Let us all hope that the dark clouds of racial prejudice will soon pass away and the deep fog of misunderstanding will be lifted from our fear-drenched communities, and in some not too distant tomorrow the radiant stars of love and brotherhood will shine over our great nation with all their scintillating beauty. 50

> Yours for the cause of Peace and Brotherhood,
> Martin Luther King, Jr.

★ Meaning and Understanding

1. What is the main point of the reading?

2. What are the two reasons the writer notes for writing this letter?

3. What are the four basic steps in any nonviolent campaign? Which of these steps has resulted in the jailing of the writer?

4. How is the "tension" the writer notes good? How is nonviolent tension constructive and necessary? What does he mean when he states: "We merely bring to the surface the hidden tension which is already alive"?

5. What does King mean by "justice too long delayed is justice denied"?

6. For the writer, what is wrong with the "paternalistic" behavior of moderate whites?

★ *Techniques and Strategies*

1. The writer cites many examples of what African-Americans have endured over the years. How do the examples affect your reaction to the argument?

2. The writer further supports his argument by citing many individuals, either by noting the statements they made or the things they did. Why does King use this strategy, do you think?

3. Why does the writer make references to biblical events? How do they enhance his argument?

4. In paragraph 14—and other places as well—King uses richly figurative language. Examine some of the images in the selection—"horse and buggy pace toward gaining a cup of coffee at a lunch counter," "ominous clouds of inferiority beginning to form in her little mental sky," for example. What do the figurative statements contribute to the selection?

5. Read the last two paragraphs with an eye to their quality as the conclusion of an argument. Are they effective? Why or why not? How do they serve the purpose of the letter?

★ *Speaking of Values*

1. King indicates a number of disappointments with white moderates about the treatment of blacks in American society. Was he right to be disappointed? Why or why not? How would King feel about whites today if he could examine the current scene in America's black-white relations?

2. King lodges a great deal of criticism against the church and organized religion. Why does he make those points? How do you react to them? What do you make of his idea that his disappointment comes from deep love?

3. What are King's views on extremism? Why was he at first disappointed at being categorized as an extremist, then satisfied by the label? How would you feel if someone applied the label to you or someone you knew?

4. Do you agree that "groups tend to be more immoral than individuals"? Why or why not? What immoral groups do you know of that might support King's conclusion?

5. King believes that "there is something in the very flow of time that will inevitably cure all ills." Is this true, do you think? How so? How does protest against the status quo affect the passage of time? What does this imply about protest, especially nonviolent protest?

6. King says "I submit that an individual who breaks a law that conscience tells him is unjust, and who willingly accepts the penalty of imprisonment in order to arouse the conscience of the community over its injustice, is in reality expressing the highest respect for the law." How is this true or not true? Can one respect the law by disobeying it?

★ *Values Conversation*

Divide into groups and discuss the issue of nonviolent resistance. How does it contribute to a just society? What are its consequences both for the society and the people resisting the law? Contrast nonviolent, direct action resistance as advocated by Martin Luther King, Jr., with violent resistance. What does each accomplish? How should a just society deal with these two forms of behavior?

★ *Writing about Values*

1. Using King's views on extremism as a starting point, write an essay in which you define the term.

2. Write a well-reasoned, argumentative essay about something you have seen at school or work or home or in your surrounding community that strikes you as unfair and improper.

3. Write a letter to your local newspaper to argue for or against nonviolent resistance as a principle of opposing laws that individuals believe are unjust. Use as examples the nonviolent resistance you have noted around contemporary issues and events—efforts regarding abortion, police brutality, or labor unrest, for example.

Gertrude Himmelfarb

Private Lives,
Public Morality

Gertrude Himmelfarb was born in New York City in 1922 and received her Ph.D. from the University of Chicago. For many years she was a Distinguished Professor at the City University of New York. Dr. Himmelfarb served on the President's Advisory Commission on the Economic Role of Women. She is also the author of many works, including *Darwin and the Darwinian Revolution* (1959) and *Marriage and Morals among the Victorians* (1986). Writing in response to early stages of the sexual impropriety scandal in the 1998 Clinton presidency, Himmelfarb explores the territory of public morality.

1   The defining moment in every historic trial—the Dreyfus case, most notably, or the O.J. Simpson case—comes when it is no longer the defendant who is on trial, but the public. We have now reached that point in the investigation of President Clinton. Although he has not been formally charged with wrongdoing, the President is on trial—in the court of public opinion. By the same token, the public too is on trial, relentlessly analyzed by scores of pollsters.

2   At first the public was discreet, professing to defer judgment until all the evidence was in. But with each revelation, more and more people have come to believe that the President is indeed guilty of sexual impropriety of some kind with "that woman," as he has referred to Monica Lewinsky.

3   At the same time, many insist that this judgment is not only premature, but also irrelevant. Such alleged affairs, they say, are private and have no bearing on the President's conduct as President—whereupon they proceed to bestow on him the highest approval ratings of his career.

4   In the United States—not France or Sweden, where people pride themselves on their "sophistication"—this verdict needs explaining. One explanation is simple: the economy is booming, the people are content, and this is all that matters.

5   The difficulty is that other polls suggest people are more concerned about their moral condition than their material well-being; 75 percent say that the most important issue confronting us is "moral decay."

6   Or there is the political explanation, which applies particularly to women, who are among the President's most loyal defenders. They

have been quick to pass judgment on other public men accused of sexual improprieties, but in this case they are tolerant of a President they consider a political ally—all the more because they are intolerant of a woman, like Paula Jones, whom they find socially uncongenial.

Another explanation is that people are so distressed by the recent accusations against Mr. Clinton that they are in denial and so condemn the messenger—the media or the independent counsel, Kenneth Starr—to divert attention from the accusations.   7

Still another explanation derives from polls showing that many Americans believe that all consensual sexual relations are private, therefore exempt from moral judgment. This is the classic "Who is to say?" argument. Who is to say what is right or wrong, moral or immoral? Morality is a "personal affair," we are told—for everyone, including the President.   8

In such a state of moral relativism, the only certitude left is the law. What is important, people say, is not whether the President had an affair, but whether he lied about it under oath. This alone makes him subject to public sanction and legal penalty.   9

Thus we confront the spectacle of one legislator after another refusing to answer the question, "If the President is proved to have had an affair with Monica Lewinsky, would you regard this as improper?" ("Improper" is the current euphemism for "immoral.") The question, they protest, is hypothetical. They then retreat to the equally hypothetical but comfortable legal proposition that if Mr. Clinton is proved to have lied under oath, then the law should take its course.   10

But the law is a feeble surrogate for manners and morals. If the President is an ambiguous "role model" for young people, so are parents who pronounce morality to be a "personal affair," who pride themselves on being "nonjudgmental," who think it sophisticated and broad-minded to give the President a moral latitude that, one hopes (and surveys confirm), they themselves do not exercise.   11

President Clinton has a good deal to answer for, not only for his behavior, if the accusations are substantiated, but in making the public his accomplice—putting it on trial and exposing its moral equivocations. The President's legacy, some now say, will be the memory of a scandal-ridden Administration. The public's legacy will be a further vulgarization and demoralization of society.   12

★ Meaning and Understanding

1. What was the Dreyfus case? What did its "defining moment" reveal?

2. What does Himmelfarb mean by "the court of public opinion" (paragraph 1)? Whom has it tried in the Clinton investigation?

3. Himmelfarb writes: "At first the public was discreet." What does this mean? Whose judgment is this?

4. Himmelfarb compares attitudes toward sexuality the United States to the "sophistication" of France and Sweden. What does she mean by this?

5. What does the author mean by "condemn the messenger" (paragraph 7) in relation to the Clinton investigation?

6. What does Himmelfarb mean by "moral relativism" (paragraph 9)?

★ *Techniques and Strategies*

1. What is Himmelfarb's thesis in this essay?

2. The essay begins with a consideration of President Clinton and ends with a judgment of the public. Where in the essay does Himmelfarb link these two topics? How convincing is this linkage? Why?

3. The essay reviews different public responses to the 1998 investigation of President Bill Clinton before his public confession of an "improper relationship" with Monica Lewinsky, a White House intern. Identify the responses that Himmelfarb considers most revealing. To which responses, if any, is she most sympathetic? Where and how does she convey this sympathy?

4. Look at the body paragraphs and identify transitional phrases. How effective are these? Why?

5. What is the author's tone toward her subject? What do the introduction and conclusion add to the tone? What language choices add to the tone?

★ *Speaking of Values*

1. What is Himmelfarb's attitude toward the pollsters who report public opinion? Does she find them reliable, trivial, or reflective? How can you tell? What is *your* opinion of the quality and uses of media polls? Why? How do polls, if at all, contribute to how and what we think and value?

2. In dealing with public figures, the essay relates private actions, including sex, to public respect. What in this issue do you find most important as a moral principle—privacy, public trust, or something else that you value?

3. Himmelfarb distinguishes between "moral condition and material well-being." What different analyses does she present about Americans and their financial and ethical states? What is your sense of the relation be-

tween economics and ethics? Do you believe most people put morality before economic self-interest? On what evidence do you base this judgment? What examples of extremely ethical or extremely material-istic responses most interest you?

4. Himmelfarb wrote this essay in the early days of the Clinton scandal, before all relevant information came to light. Now that you have a more complete picture through the news, how valid is Himmelfarb's argu-ment? Have events that succeeded the writing of "Private Lives, Public Morality" contributed anything to how we should view this essay?

★ Values Conversation

Divide into groups and identify a scandal that you believe displayed a sig-nificant moral dilemma. Chose a scandal in history or in the life of your community or school. As a group present the values at play in the public or press response.

★ Writing about Values

1. Write an essay about the president—or political leader—whom you find most impressive as a moral, or immoral, figure.

2. Write an essay about a time when you or someone you know experi-enced public scrutiny for a matter you thought private.

3. Define moral relativism—and discuss it as a principle or practice, or both.

Patricia J. Williams

An Ear for an Ear

Born in 1951, Patricia J. Williams is a professor of law at Columbia University. She is also the author of *Alchemy of Race and Rights* (1991) and most recently of *The Rooster's Egg* (1995). In this piece for *The Nation* she looks at the "eye-for-an-eye" philosophy that undergirds legal systems.

———— ★ ————

1 During the Middle Ages, there were a number of recorded instances in which animals—mad dogs, rampaging bulls and swarming locusts—were prosecuted for various crimes and misdemeanors. In 1474 in the city of Bâle, a raucously deep-throated hen, apparently suffering from "hydropic malformation of the oviduct," was mistaken for a cock and burned at the stake for laying an egg. As anyone knows, real cocks' eggs are rich in the lipids, proteins and amino acids so necessary for authentic witch's brew. And, when left to incubate in the heat of the noonday sun, they're known for hatching baby basilisks, those evil-eyed gargoyle-ish things with the deadly breath. So no doubt about it, better safe than sorry.

2 Thanks to the vigilance of our methodical forebears, roosters who lay eggs are a thing of the distant past. Yet given a postmodern world still beset by unnatural creation, there are times when I wonder what lessons might be gleaned from those trials by fire in which poor Chanticleer was purified into wispy, crispy medieval McNuggets. It's intriguing: The authorities didn't just kill the offending bird but rather executed it with full magisterial process, pomp, piety, colorful headgear and legal formality. We humans have always needed rituals to draw like curtains over the unknown. As scholar Nicholas Humphrey put it, animal trials flourished in a world "at the edge of explanatory darkness."

3 My head is in the Middle Ages these days because I've been trying to make sense of a rash of cases the politics of whose prosecution seem as unlikely to achieve traditional criminological goals as hanging a wayward hog. I'm thinking of cases against adolescent girls in which life imprisonment or the death penalty has been urged despite evidence of significant emotional turmoil. In particular, I'm thinking of Melissa Drexler, the New Jersey teenager who, in a trance of pre-partum denial and post-partum shock, gave birth at her prom, allegedly strangled the newborn in the bathroom and then, leaving an extremely

bloody trail, went back to the party for the salad course and one last dance.

Quickly, now, I'm not arguing that what she did wasn't heinous, or   4
shouldn't be sanctioned. But I do want to focus on those significant numbers of voices who argue that charging first-degree murder is an appropriate response. I have heard this argued in almost all the so-called trashcan baby cases—situations where the adolescent defendants run the gamut from victims of incest, to retarded girls, to runaways who are terrified of assaultive parents, to children whose rigid sense of religious orthodoxy drives them over the edge and, most troubling of all: the seemingly well-heeled, well-balanced kids who have everything and, panicked to death, still toss their quick and their dead into the toilets and trashcans of suburban America.

Many seem to think that such tragedy is inspired by some mon-   5
strous moral force that is both inhuman and unrelated to social influence. Again, bearing in mind that I want neither to forget the victims nor to forgive intentional violence, is it nonetheless possible to make some connection between the sudden prevalence of such cases and some of our recent social policies? After all, here it is Anno Domini 1997, the second decade of the AIDS plague and, *mirabile dictu,* we are actually defunding sex education in schools. The entire field of social work, including family therapy and guidance counseling, is under attack by powerful conservative think tanks like the Heritage Foundation and the Manhattan Institute. Our most popular forms of infotainment teach that violence holds the answer to all life's obstacles—but that complaining about being on the receiving end is "political correctness" or "victimology." Incidents of rape and incest are underreported and disbelieved. Birth control or prenatal care for minors—to say nothing of abortion—is overshadowed by "squeal laws" requiring parental permission for any number of medical procedures. Welfare "reforms" have insured that life-on-one's-own for young single mothers has been made not only shameful but despicable, not only undesirable but materially unsustainable.

Those who thought all this social pressure would send young peo-   6
ple flocking toward abstinence or adoption seem positively flapdoodled: Exorcise the demons. Send them all to jail for life—no, death! Burn them at the stake on prime-time TV! And so we prosecute our foolish children, at younger and younger ages, we incarcerate them as adults and for longer and longer periods. We craft drastic policies based on nostalgia—nostalgia being the sugar-plumped addiction of amnesiacs. From Ronald Reagan to Promise Keepers, the rush to return us to the Victorian era has brought with it many of the forgotten ills of the past. Moreover, the political disingenuity of this moment has us sailing backward in time to the draconian stance of "an eye for an eye" (or, as I

suppose we shall learn to say in the "iconic" aftermath of our Tyson-tinged millennium, "an ear for an ear"). Such a shift signals, as Stanford Law School professor Lawrence Friedman once put it, the criminal justice system's having become, "relatively speaking, *offense-minded* . . . [focusing] more on the acts themselves, less on the actor." Discussions of intentionality and mitigation degenerate into free-for-all disparagement of "excuses"—as though to allow nuance into our judgments were to abandon reason for relativism.

7   But there are degrees of culpability in even the most awful tragedies. In a culture where so many have been touched by violent crime, it is hard, this most basic tenet of human rights: to accord defendants their humanity. But when we dehumanize even our pariahs, when "free agency" bears little reference either to individual state of mind or social constraint, we turn real—albeit awful—people into demons and devils, basilisks and behemoths. In so doing, we condemn them and ourselves to repetition.

8   If the physical sciences rescued us from some of the excesses of the Middle Ages, is it possible that we humans are still in the Dark Ages as to the social sciences? Is it conceivable that we have entered a time when religious fundamentalism coupled with the amorality of extreme forms of economic libertarianism threaten to wipe out our Alexandrian libraries of humanist enterprise?

★ Meaning and Understanding

1. For what crime was a hen prosecuted in 1474 in Bâle?

2. What distinction does Williams draw between killing and executing the offending animal?

3. What legal cases today does Williams liken to prosecuting animals? Why does she make the comparison? What particular observation does the writer make about Melissa Drexler in paragraph 3?

4. What connection does Williams make between the terrible tragedies of murder she notes and "some of our recent social policies"? Which social policies does the writer state as influencing "the sudden prevalence" of the murder cases referred to in the essay?

5. What, according to Williams in paragraph 7, is wrong with dehumanizing "real—albeit awful—people into demons and devils"?

★ Techniques and Strategies

1. What is the effect of opening the essay with a discussion of animal prosecutions in the Middle Ages? How does Williams return to that

period in the last paragraph? In what ways does this strategy help unify the essay?

2. What is Williams's thesis here? Why does she repeat her desire not to forget the victims? How does this assertion strengthen her argument?

3. Williams presents many allusions in this piece. Comb the essay for these allusions and explain as many of them as you can. For example, what do these allusions mean: "a raucously deep-throated hen" (paragraph 1); "Chanticleer" and "medieval McNuggets" (paragraph 2); "infotainment" (paragraph 5); "from Ronald Reagan to Promise Keepers" and "our Tyson-tinged millennium" (paragraph 6)? Why does she make these allusions?

4. The essay has a colloquial, humorous, yet ironic cast. Find examples of these elements in the essay. What do these stylistic techniques tell you about Williams's intended audience?

5. What is the effect of the exclamatory sentences in paragraph 6? Of the final paragraph composed only of two long questions? What is Williams aiming for in each case, do you think? Has she accomplished her goals?

★ Speaking of Values

1. Williams raises questions about a legal system founded—as ours is, to some degree—on the "eye-for-an-eye" philosophy. Why might you agree or disagree with her point?

2. In what ways do social policies affect people's behavior, do you think? Or consider the question the other way around: In what ways does people's behavior affect social policies? Explain your response.

3. Why might you agree or disagree with Williams's assertion that our society teaches "that violence holds the answer to all life's obstacles"?

4. What is your reaction to the quotation from Lawrence Friedman in paragraph 6? Do we in fact as a society focus "more on the acts themselves, less on the actor"? And if we do, what do you find right or wrong with that approach?

5. How would you respond to the questions posed in the last paragraph?

★ Values Conversation

The issue of violent adolescent offenders, particularly in cases of young girls, sometimes with the assistance of their boyfriends, who murder their newborn children, has galvanized public opinion over the last few years.

What, in your estimation, should be the appropriate response to "the so-called trashcan baby cases" or similar acts? On what elements of American values should we act in dealing with these youthful offenders? Form groups to discuss your responses. Consider the points Williams raises as well as other relevant issues. Then report to the class at large the findings of your group.

★ Writing about Values

1. Do research on some case of violent death brought about by a youthful offender, looking especially at the verdict in the case. Write a letter to the judge or jury members explaining why you agree or disagree with their findings.

2. Write an essay about the relation between social policy and human behavior.

3. Write an essay called "An Ear for an Ear" in which you argue for or against the tendency noted by Lawrence Friedman to concentrate in our criminal justice system "more on the acts themselves, less on the actor."

Values in Review

1. Edward I. Koch, William J. Brennan, and Patricia Williams address the issue of punishment in American society. Using their essays as starting points, write a paper on the values implicit in our justice system today.

2. Although they write about very different issues, Lani Guinier and Martin Luther King, Jr., bring an African-American perspective to the discussion of law and politics. Write an essay in which you try to define that perspective. What similarities do you note in the two writers' beliefs? What differences? How can their thinking inform our legal and political systems?

3. What support for and challenges to the laudable goals of the Declaration of Independence do the selections in this chapter offer? Write an essay that shows the interrelations between Jefferson's values and the values stated or implied in at least two of the pieces in Chapter 6.

Chapter 7

Rights and Beliefs

War

Escape from oppression

Church going

Colliding religious values

America's spiritual despair

Professions of faith

Communism

Michael Norman

The Hollow Man

Michael Norman was born in Illinois in 1947. He worked in newspapers and radio before becoming a professor at the University of Iowa. His books include *Haunted Heartland* (1991) and *Haunted America* (1994) written with his partner Beth Scott. In this piece, which he first delivered as a talk in the Bemis Free Lectures series in Lincoln, Massachusetts, he draws on his experiences in Vietnam to explain what war means to him.

———— ★ ————

I am going to level with you: I hate the war. I have hated the war since   1
the day I walked off the battlefield. I hate it now even as it works its way up my throat and slips across my tongue—to you.

I hate the war so much I can no longer think of it in any terms other   2
than personal. I no longer give a damn about its political legacy, about its cultural vicissitudes, its historical aftershocks, its literary revisionism, its misapplied lessons, its frauds and fakes and Johnny-come-latelies. My hate, my unbridled passion, sweeps all that away. For me Vietnam now is the first person singular.

I am, I always will be, what I was—a boy pulled from his time, a   3
man who left something essential behind him. You ask, where am I now? I answer, still in the killing zone.

I am fire and I am smoke. I am a dark red spot on a dusty road. I am   4
corpses stacked like cordwood on the fender of a tank. I am a little girl crying before my burning house.

Most of all, I am afraid. I am crouched atop this ridge at the head of   5
a column and something is moving in front of me—there, across the divide. A tree is moving, turning, now half tree and half man, a tree-man holding a rifle, a rifle pointed at me. I am reaching for my weapon, I am pulling back the slide to put a round in the chamber. I must kill this man before he kills me. I must take his life away from him. My hand shakes. I will ask God to steady my hand. I will ask God to help me kill this man killing me.

And now I am rifling his body, picking in his pockets, pulling his   6
wallet from his pants. Here is Dong. And here is Dong's wife. And here is Dong's child. Mine was the bullet that left them alone.

I, too, of course, am dead. The bullet that killed Dong killed me.   7
One shot, two souls. I now am a hollow man, empty and alone. My psyche has a cicatrix.

8   I am at home now, sitting in church. The bishop is in fine voice this Christmas Eve, telling the congregation that God is on our side, that the war is just, the enemy evil. I am getting up now, in full view of all these people and my parents, getting right up without so much as an excuse me and walking out into the cold air and swearing never to go back, never again. I hope Dong can see all this. Semper fidelis, Dong.

9   I am chasing a career, sitting at the rewrite desk of my newspaper, and a colleague is complaining about all these mewling, crying Vietnam veterans demanding everyone's attention, these scruffy men marching in the street. And I say, tell me, my friend, what bad battles left you so bitter? And he says, actually, you see, actually he did not wear a uniform. He could have served, you see, but he really didn't believe in the war, you see, and damn if he was going to be cannon fodder for someone else's cause. And I say, yes, I see. I really do see.

10   And now I have written a book about the war, a five-years-in-the-making book, a book meant to exorcise all the ghosts, exorcise me, the ghost I've become. I am sitting in a San Francisco radio station and the host of the program is saying to me, Mike, may I call you Mike? Yes? Good. Mike, I bet this book was great therapy, wasn't it. Don't you feel, well, healed? And I am stumped, right there in front of hundreds of thousands of listeners. I want to say, Well, Mr. Host, I am healed. As a matter of fact we're all healed, every man jack one of us, even my friend Squeaky, who lost an eye, and my friend Belknap, who had his hip and hand blown off, and my friend Charles, who has a metal plate in his skull. We're all feeling a whole lot better. Healed? You want me healed? Should I invoke Eliot? *Time is no healer because the patient is no longer here.*

11   The truth is I'm not really playing it straight with you here. I gave Dong a name he didn't have and put him in a place where he wasn't. I found the body and saw the pictures and that was truth enough for me. As for the rest, most of it happened, not exactly as I have delivered it here, but then, when it comes to the war, I don't know anymore where my memory ends and where my dreams take over. With the war there is no telling what is true. The truth always turns on the meaning of life and I have been talking about death.

12   So I have no truth. My grandfather was gassed in the trenches of Argonne, my father narrowly escaped the beaches of Normandy. War makes men like me, hollow men, men weighed down by memory, out of time and out of place, men who spend their lives trying to recover what has been lost, men haunted by the awful mystery that spared them, that left them alone, walking in the empty spaces.

★ Meaning and Understanding

1. What is Norman's principal assertion about the war?

2. Who is Dong? What is Norman's relation to him?

3. What happens on Christmas Eve in Norman's church?

4. What does the radio host ask Norman? How does he respond?

5. What wartime experiences did the writer's father and grandfather have? What do "the trenches of Argonne" and "the beaches of Normandy" refer to?

★ Techniques and Strategies

1. What is the significance of the title of this essay? How does Norman explain its meaning in the last paragraph?

2. What is your reaction to the first sentence in the essay? The second? The third? How do those three sentences engage the reader?

3. What is Norman's purpose in the essay? Who do you think his audience is? How can you tell?

4. What is the significance of the graphic descriptions of Dong?

5. Many sentences here begin with the pronoun "I." What is the effect of this stylistic technique? How does it interact with the content of the essay (look particularly at the last sentence of paragraph 1)?

6. Where do you find examples of irony? Why does the writer use irony? How is it appropriate (or inappropriate) for the essay's content?

★ Speaking of Values

1. What values is the writer trying to establish about the experience of war? In what ways is war a first person singular to anyone who has participated in it? How is it not a first person singular?

2. One cannot help but notice the tension here between the person who experiences war and the person who observes it from afar. Is it possible for people who do not live through war to understand all its horrors, terrors, and complexities? If your answer is yes, explain why you think so. What would Norman respond to that question? If you think he would say no, explain why you think he wrote this essay.

3. What significance should we attach to the statements made by the bishop and the writer's reaction to it? How might Norman have reacted if he had heard the comments in a classroom, say, or at a bar with friends? Why does he walk out of the church ceremony and swear never to go back? Do you find this response appropriate? Why or why not?

4. The Vietnam War was a particularly contentious and unpopular event in American history. Why? How has Norman captured the conflict in his essay?

5. What is the meaning of the quotation from T. S. Eliot, the influential twentieth-century poet? How does it capture the essence of Norman's point? In what ways does the statement reflect responses to any traumatic event? In what ways is it accurate only for war experiences?

★ *Values Conversation*

Norman writes that he was "a boy pulled from his time, a man who left something essential behind." Form groups and discuss that statement as a kind of emblem for the human element in war. What is your reaction to drawing teenagers into battle to defend their country? What does it mean to be pulled from time? What does it mean to leave something essential behind? How do you think you would react if called to battle?

★ *Writing about Values*

1. Write an essay about hate and show how it affects the person experiencing that emotion. You might choose to define the word, or to narrate a moment that you saw hate in action, or to classify different kinds of hatred.

2. Do some research about the Vietnam conflict. Write an essay about some aspect of the war. Why was the public attitude toward the Vietnam War so ambivalent?

3. Write about a traumatic event that you or someone you know experienced and explain how it affected your life well after the event took place.

Stephen Crane

An Episode of War

Stephen Crane (1871–1900) was the youngest child in a family of fourteen siblings and made his mark on American letters as a journalist, novelist, poet, and writer of short stories. He is best known for the novels *Maggie: A Girl of the Streets* (1893) and *The Red Badge of Courage* (1895). In "An Episode of War" he tells the story of a young lieutenant newly wounded at war.

———— ★ ————

The lieutenant's rubber blanket lay on the ground, and upon it he had poured the company's supply of coffee. Corporals and other representatives of the grimy and hot-throated men who lined the breast-work had come for each squad's portion.   1

The lieutenant was frowning and serious at this task of division. His lips pursed as he drew with his sword various crevices in the heap, until brown squares of coffee, astoundingly equal in size, appeared on the blanket. He was on the verge of a great triumph in mathematics, and the corporals were thronging forward, each to reap a little square, when suddenly the lieutenant cried out and looked quickly at a man near him as if he suspected it was a case of personal assault. The others cried out also when they saw blood upon the lieutenant's sleeve.   2

He had winced like a man stung, swayed dangerously, and then straightened. The sound of his hoarse breathing was plainly audible. He looked sadly, mystically, over the breast-work at the green face of a wood, where now were many little puffs of white smoke. During this moment the men about him gazed statuelike and silent, astonished and awed by this catastrophe which happened when catastrophes were not expected—when they had leisure to observe it.   3

As the lieutenant stared at the wood, they too swung their heads, so that for another instant all hands, still silent, contemplated the distant forest as if their minds were fixed upon the mystery of a bullet's journey.   4

The officer had, of course, been compelled to take his sword into his left hand. He did not hold it by the hilt. He gripped it at the middle of the blade, awkwardly. Turning his eyes from the hostile wood, he looked at the sword as he held it there, and seemed puzzled as to what to do with it, where to put it. In short, this weapon had of a sudden become a strange thing to him. He looked at it in a kind of stupefaction, as if he had been endowed with a trident, a sceptre, or a spade.   5

6   Finally he tried to sheath it. To sheath a sword held by the left hand, at the middle of the blade, in a scabbard hung at the left hip, is a feat worthy of a sawdust ring. This wounded officer engaged in a desperate struggle with the sword and the wobbling scabbard, and during the time of it he breathed like a wrestler.

7   But at this instant the men, the spectators, awoke from their stone-like poses and crowded forward sympathetically. The orderly-sergeant took the sword and tenderly placed it in the scabbard. At the time, he leaned nervously backward, and did not allow even his finger to brush the body of the lieutenant. A wound gives strange dignity to him who bears it. Well men shy from his new and terrible majesty. It is as if the wounded man's hand is upon the curtain which hangs before the revelations of all existence—the meaning of ants, potentates, wars, cities, sunshine, snow, a feather dropped from a bird's wing; and the power of it sheds radiance upon a bloody form, and makes the other men understand sometimes that they are little. His comrades look at him with large eyes thoughtfully. Moreover, they fear vaguely that the weight of a finger upon him might send him headlong, precipitate the tragedy, hurl him at once into the dim, gray unknown. And so the orderly-sergeant, while sheathing the sword, leaned nervously backward.

8   There were others who proffered assistance. One timidly presented his shoulder and asked the lieutenant if he cared to lean upon it, but the latter waved him away mournfully. He wore the look of one who knows he is the victim of a terrible disease and understands his helplessness. He again stared over the breast-work at the forest, and then, turning, went slowly rearward. He held his right wrist tenderly in his left hand as if the wounded arm was made of very brittle glass.

9   And the men in silence stared at the wood, then at the departing lieutenant; then at the wood, then at the lieutenant.

10   As the wounded officer passed from the line of battle, he was enabled to see many things which as a participant in the fight were unknown to him. He saw a general on a black horse gazing over the lines of blue infantry at the green woods which veiled his problems. An aide galloped furiously, dragged his horse suddenly to a halt, saluted, and presented a paper. It was, for a wonder, precisely like a historical painting.

11   To the rear of the general and his staff a group, composed of a bugler, two or three orderlies, and the bearer of the corps standard, all upon maniacal horses, were working like slaves to hold their ground, preserve their respectful interval, while the shells boomed in the air about them, and caused their chargers to make furious quivering leaps.

12   A battery, a tumultuous and shining mass, was swirling toward the right. The wild thud of hoofs, the cries of the riders shouting blame and praise, menace and encouragement, and, last, the roar of the wheels, the slant of the glistening guns, brought the lieutenant to an intent pause. The battery swept in curves that stirred the heart; it made halts

as dramatic as the crash of a wave on the rocks, and when it fled onward this aggregation of wheels, levers, motors had a beautiful unity,
as if it were a missile. The sound of it was a war-chorus that reached
into the depths of man's emotion.

The lieutenant, still holding his arm as if it were of glass, stood   13
watching this battery until all detail of it was lost, save the figures of
the riders, which rose and fell and waved lashes over the black mass.

Later, he turned his eyes toward the battle, where the shooting   14
sometimes crackled like bush fires, sometimes sputtered with exasperating irregularity, and sometimes reverberated like the thunder. He
saw the smoke rolling upward and saw crowds of men who ran and
cheered, or stood and blazed away at the inscrutable distance.

He came upon some stragglers, and they told him how to find the   15
field hospital. They described its exact location. In fact, these men, no
longer having part in the battle, knew more of it than others. They told
the performance of every corps, every division, the opinion of every
general. The lieutenant, carrying his wounded arm rearward, looked
upon them with wonder.

At the roadside a brigade was making coffee and buzzing with talk   16
like a girls' boarding school. Several officers came out to him and inquired concerning things of which he knew nothing. One, seeing his
arm, began to scold. "Why, man, that's no way to do. You want to fix
that thing." He appropriated the lieutenant and the lieutenant's
wound. He cut the sleeve and laid bare the arm, every nerve of which
softly fluttered under his touch. He bound his handkerchief over the
wound, scolding away in the meantime. His tone allowed one to think
that he was in the habit of being wounded every day. The lieutenant
hung his head, feeling, in this presence, that he did not know how to be
correctly wounded.

The low white tents of the hospital were grouped around an old   17
schoolhouse. There was here a singular commotion. In the foreground
two ambulances interlocked wheels in the deep mud. The drivers were
tossing the blame of it back and forth, gesticulating and berating, while
from the ambulances, both crammed with wounded, there came an occasional groan. An interminable crowd of bandaged men were coming
and going. Great numbers sat under the trees nursing heads or arms or
legs. There was a dispute of some kind raging on the steps of the
schoolhouse. Sitting with his back against a tree a man with a face as
grey as a new army blanket was serenely smoking a corncob pipe. The
lieutenant wished to rush forward and inform him that he was dying.

A busy surgeon was passing near the lieutenant. "Good morning,"   18
he said, with a friendly smile. Then he caught sight of the lieutenant's
arm, and his face at once changed. "Well, let's have a look at it." He
seemed possessed suddenly of a great contempt for the lieutenant. This
wound evidently placed the latter on a very low social plane. The doctor

cried out impatiently: "What mutton-head tied it up that way any-how?" The lieutenant answered, "Oh, a man."

19   When the wound was disclosed the doctor fingered it disdainfully. "Humph," he said, "You come along with me and I'll tend to you." His voice contained the same scorn as if he were saying, "You will have to go to jail."

20   The lieutenant had been very meek, but now his face flushed, and he looked into the doctor's eyes. "I guess I won't have it amputated," he said.

21   "Nonsense, man! Nonsense! Nonsense!" cried the doctor. "Come along, now. I won't amputate it. Come along. Don't be a baby."

22   "Let go of me," said the lieutenant, holding back wrathfully, his glance fixed upon the door of the old schoolhouse, as sinister to him as the portals of death.

23   And this is the story of how the lieutenant lost his arm. When he reached home, his sisters, his mother, his wife, sobbed for a long time at the sight of the flat sleeve. "Oh, well," he said, standing shamefaced amid these tears, "I don't suppose it matters so much as all that."

★ Meaning and Understanding

1. What is the subject of the story?

2. As the lieutenant divides up the coffee, what happens and how do he and the other soldiers react initially? What does Crane say about this?

3. How do the men show their sympathy for the lieutenant?

4. Why does the lieutenant want to rush forward and inform the man smoking the corncob pipe that he is dying?

5. As the lieutenant walks behind the lines to have his wound tended to, he sees images and scenes in stark relief. What does he see? What effect do they have on him?

★ Techniques and Strategies

1. The story tracks the lieutenant's shifting feelings about his injury and circumstances. Identify the lieutenant's sequence of emotions. How does the trajectory of his feelings influence the story's meaning?

2. After the lieutenant is wounded and tries to sheathe his sword, the orderly sergeant helps him in his effort. What is the nature of this help? What does the long passage describing the assistance (paragraph 7) contribute to the story?

3. Identify other descriptions in the story that seem particularly effective. Why do you find them effective?

4. Consider the first sentence of the final paragraph. What is remarkable about it? How do you respond to it? What does it add to your sense of the story's meaning?

5. How do you feel about the title? How does it capture Crane's purpose, do you think?

★ Speaking of Values

1. What is the writer saying about war? Why might you agree or disagree with his point of view?

2. Crane takes pains to describe how the lieutenant deals with his sword after he is wounded? Why? How does the sword take on more meaning than just an implement that a wounded soldier must contend with?

3. During the long walk behind the front line, what is the lieutenant experiencing and how does it affect his perceptions once he gets to his destination? What does being wounded do for the way a person sees the world, do you think?

4. Why doesn't the lieutenant want to go into the schoolhouse? What does he associate with the schoolhouse? What values do you think his actions here assert?

5. How and why did the lieutenant's eventual apathy about his wound develop? What do you think Crane is saying here about war?

★ Values Conversation

Form groups and discuss the lengths to which each person in the group would go in the face of great fear. Examine and discuss the relations among fear, irrationality, and belief. What place does fear occupy in the framework of American values and how we should deal with it? How do the culture's expectations match your group's beliefs?

★ Writing about Values

1. Write an essay about experiencing or witnessing an accident and the various ways people responded to it.

2. Do some research about the psychological reactions of soldiers in battle. Apply this knowledge to Crane's story by advancing a thesis about the hero.

3. Write an essay that presents and analyzes Crane's view of war as you understand it from "An Episode of War." In what ways does the story challenge conventional notions of war's romanticism and valorous action?

Andre Dubus

Imperiled Men

Andre Dubus was born in 1936 and served as a marine from 1958 to 1964, when he resigned his commission as a captain to pursue an MFA at the University of Iowa. He is the author of many works, including *The Lieutenant* (1967) and a number of short stories. In this selection he looks at the issue of gays in the military by examining the fate of a navy pilot in World War II and Korea.

———— ★ ————

1   He was a navy pilot in World War II and in Korea, and when I knew him in 1961 for a few months before he killed himself he was the Commander of the Air Group aboard the USS *Ranger*, an aircraft carrier, and we called him by the acronym CAG. He shot himself with his .38 revolver because two investigators from the Office of Naval Intelligence came aboard ship while we were anchored off Iwakuni in Japan and gave the ship's captain a written report of their investigation of CAG's erotic life. CAG was a much-decorated combat pilot, and his duty as a commander was one of great responsibility. The ship's executive officer, also a commander, summoned CAG to his office, where the two investigators were, and told him that his choices were to face a general court-martial or to resign from the navy. Less than half an hour later CAG was dead in his stateroom. His body was flown to the United States; we were told that he did not have a family, and I do not know where he was buried. There was a memorial service aboard ship, but I do not remember it; I only remember a general sadness like mist in the passageways.

2   I did not really know him. I was a first lieutenant then, a career marine; two years later I would resign and become a teacher. On the *Ranger* I was with the marine detachment; we guarded the planes' nuclear weapons stored below decks, ran the brig, and manned one of the antiaircraft gun mounts. We were fifty or so enlisted men and two officers among a ship's crew of about 3,000 officers and men. The Air Group was not included in the ship's company. They came aboard with their planes for our seven-month deployment in the western Pacific. I do not remember the number of pilots and bombardier-navigators, mechanics and flight controllers, and men who worked on the flight deck, but there were plenty of all, and day and night you could hear planes catapulting off the front of the deck and landing on its rear.

The flight deck was 1,052 feet long, the ship weighed 81,000 tons   3
fully loaded, and I rarely felt its motion. I came aboard in May for a
year of duty, and in August we left our port in San Francisco Bay and
headed for Japan. I had driven my wife and three young children home
to Louisiana, where they would stay during the seven months I was at
sea, and every day I longed for them. One night on the voyage across
the Pacific I sat in the wardroom drinking coffee with a lieutenant commander at one of the long tables covered with white linen. The wardroom was open all night because men were always working. The
lieutenant commander told me that Soviet submarines tracked us, they
recorded the sound of our propellers and could not be fooled by the
sound of a decoy ship's propellers, and that they even came into San
Francisco Bay to do this; our submarines did the same with Soviet carriers. He said that every time we tried in training exercises to evade
even our own submarines we could not do it, and our destroyers could
not track and stop them. He said, "So if the whistle blows we'll get a
nuclear fish up our ass in the first thirty minutes. Our job is to get the
birds in the air before that. They're going to Moscow."
    "Where will they land afterward?"   4
    "They won't. They know that."   5
    The voyage to Japan was five or six weeks long because we did not   6
go directly to Japan; the pilots flew air operations. Combat units are always training for war, but these men who flew planes, and the men in
orange suits and ear protectors who worked on the flight deck during
landings and takeoffs, were engaging in something not at all as playful
as marine field exercises generally were. They were imperiled. One pilot told me that from his fighter-bomber in the sky the flight deck
looked like an aspirin tablet. On the passage to Japan I became friendly
with some pilots, drinking coffee in the wardroom, and I knew what
CAG looked like because he was CAG. He had dark skin and alert
eyes, and he walked proudly. Then in Japan I sometimes drank with
young pilots. I was a robust twenty-five-year-old, one of two marine
officers aboard ship, and I did not want to be outdone at anything by
anyone. But I could not stay with the pilots; I had to leave them in the
bar, drinking and talking and laughing, and make my way back to the
ship to sleep and wake with a hangover. Next day the pilots flew; if we
did not go to sea, they flew from a base on land. Once I asked one of
them how he did it.
    "The pure oxygen. Soon as you put on the mask, your head clears."   7
    It was not simply the oxygen, and I did not understand any of   8
these wild, brave, and very efficient men until years later when I read
Tom Wolfe's *The Right Stuff*.
    It was on that same tour that I saw another pilot die. I worked be-   9
low decks with the marine detachment, but that warm gray afternoon

the entire ship was in a simulated condition of war, and my part was to stand four hours of watch in a small turret high above the ship. I could move the turret in a circular way by pressing a button, and I looked through binoculars for planes or ships in the 180-degree arc of our port side. On the flight deck planes were taking off; four could do this in quick sequence. Two catapults launched planes straight off the front of the ship, and quickly they rose and climbed. The third and fourth catapults were on the port side where the flight deck angled sharply out to the left, short of the bow. From my turret I looked down at the ship's bridge and the flight deck. A helicopter flew low near the ship, and planes were taking off. On the deck were men in orange suits and ear protectors; on both sides of the ship, just beneath the flight deck, were nets for these men to jump into, to save themselves from being killed by a landing plane that veered or skidded or crashed. One night I'd inspected a marine guarding a plane on the flight deck; we had a sentry there because the plane carried a nuclear bomb. I stepped from a hatch into the absolute darkness of a night at sea and into a strong wind that lifted my body with each step. I was afraid it would lift me off the deck and hurl me into the sea, where I would tread water in that great expanse and depth while the ship went on its way; tomorrow they would learn that I was missing. I found the plane and the marine; he stood with one arm around the cable that held the wing to the deck.

10   In the turret I was facing aft when it happened: Men in orange were at the rear of the flight deck, then they sprinted forward, and I rotated my turret toward the bow and saw a plane in the gray sea and an orange-suited pilot lying facedown in the water, his parachute floating beyond his head, moving toward the rear of the ship. The plane had dropped off the port deck and now water covered its wing, then its cockpit, and it sank. The pilot was behind the ship; his limbs did not move, his face was in the sea, and his parachute was filling with water and starting to sink. The helicopter hovered low and a sailor on a rope descended from it; he wore orange, and I watched him coming down and the pilot floating and the parachute sinking beneath the waves. There was still some length of parachute line remaining when the sailor reached the pilot; he grabbed him; then the parachute lines tightened their pull and drew the pilot down. There was only the sea now beneath the sailor on the rope. Then he ascended.

11   I shared a stateroom with a navy lieutenant, an officer of medical administration, a very tall and strong man from Oklahoma. He had been an enlisted man, had once been a corpsman aboard a submarine operating off the coast of the Soviet Union, and one night their periscope was spotted, destroyers came after them, and they dived and sat at the bottom and listened by sonar to the destroyers' sonar trying to find them. He told me about the sailor who had tried to save the pilot.

In the dispensary they gave him brandy, and the sailor wept and said he was trained to do that job, and this was his first time, and he had failed. Of course he had not failed. No man could lift another man attached to a parachute filled with water. Some people said the helicopter had not stayed close enough to the ship while the planes were taking off. Some said the pilot was probably already dead; his plane dropped from the ship, and he ejected himself high into the air, but not high enough for his parachute to ease his fall. This was all talk about the mathematics of violent death; the pilot was killed because he flew airplanes from a ship at sea.

He was a lieutenant commander, and I knew his face and name. As he was being catapulted, his landing gear on the left side broke off and his plane skidded into the sea. He was married; his widow had been married before, also to a pilot who was killed in a crash. I wondered if it were her bad luck to meet only men who flew; years later I believed that whatever in their spirits made these men fly also drew her to them.   12

I first spoke to CAG at the officers' club at the Navy base in Yokosuka. The officers of the Air Group hosted a party for the officers of the ship's company. We wore civilian suits and ties, and gathered at the club to drink. There were no women. The party was a matter of protocol, probably a tradition among pilots and the officers of carriers; for us young officers it meant getting happily drunk. I was doing this with pilots at the bar when one of them said, "Let's throw CAG into the pond."   13

He grinned at me, as I looked to my left at the small shallow pond with pretty fish in it; then I looked past the pond at CAG, sitting on a soft leather chair, a drink in his hand, talking quietly with two or three other commanders sitting in soft leather chairs. All the pilots with me were grinning and saying yes, and the image of us lifting CAG from his chair and dropping him into the water gave me joy, and I put my drink on the bar and said, "Let's *go.*"   14

I ran across the room to CAG, grabbed the lapels of his coat, jerked him up from his chair, and saw his drink spill onto his suit; then I fell backward to the floor, still holding his lapels, and pulled him down on top of me. There was no one else with me. He was not angry yet, but I was a frightened fool. I released his lapels and turned my head and looked back at the laughing pilots. Out of my vision the party was loud, hundreds of drinking officers who had not seen this, and CAG sounded only puzzled when he said, "What's going on?"   15

He stood and brushed at the drink on his suit, watching me get up from the floor. I stood not quite at attention but not at ease either. I said, "Sir, I'm Marine Lieutenant Dubus. Your pilots fooled me." I nodded toward them at the bar, and CAG smiled. "They said, 'Let's throw CAG into the pond.' But, sir, the joke was on me."   16

17   He was still smiling.

18   "I'm very sorry, sir."

19   "That's all right, Lieutenant."

20   "Can I get the Commander another drink, sir?"

21   "Sure," he said, and told me what he was drinking, and I got it from the bar, where the pilots were red-faced and happy, and brought it to CAG, who was sitting in his chair again with the other commanders. He smiled and thanked me, and the commanders smiled; then I returned to the young pilots and we all laughed.

22   Until a few months later, on the day he killed himself, the only words I spoke to CAG after the party were greetings. One night I saw him sitting with a woman in the officers' club, and I wished him good evening. A few times I saw him in the ship's passageways; I recognized him seconds before the features of his face were clear: he had a graceful, athletic stride that dipped his shoulders. I saluted and said, "Good morning, sir" or "Good afternoon, sir." He smiled as he returned my salute and greeting, his eyes and voice mirthful, and I knew that he was seeing me again pulling him out of his chair and down to the floor, then standing to explain myself and apologize. I liked being a memory that gave him sudden and passing amusement.

23   On a warm sunlit day we were anchored off Iwakuni, and I planned to go with other crew members on a bus to Hiroshima. I put on civilian clothes and went down the ladder to the boat that would take us ashore. I was not happily going to Hiroshima; I was going because I was an American, and I felt that I should look at it and be in it. I found a seat on the rocking boat, then saw CAG in civilian clothes coming down the ladder. There were a few seats remaining, and he chose the one next to me. He asked me where I was going, then said he was going to Hiroshima, too. I was relieved and grateful; while CAG was flying planes in World War II, I was a boy buying savings stamps and bringing scrap metal to school. On the bus he would talk to me about war, and in Hiroshima I would walk with him and look with him, and his seasoned steps and eyes would steady mine. Then from the ship above us the officer of the deck called down, "CAG?"

24   CAG turned and looked up at him, a lieutenant junior grade in white cap and short-sleeved shirt and trousers.

25   "Sir, the executive officer would like to see you."

26   I do not remember what CAG said to me. I only remember my disappointment when he told the boat's officer to go ashore without him. All I saw in CAG's face was the look of a man called from rest back to his job. He climbed the ladder, and soon the boat pulled away.

27   Perhaps when I reached Hiroshima CAG was already dead; I do not remember the ruins at ground zero or what I saw in the museum. I walked and looked, and stood for a long time at a low arch with an

open space at the ground, and in that space was a stone box that held
the names of all who died on the day of the bombing and all who had
died since because of the bomb. That night I ate dinner ashore, then
rode the boat to the ship, went to my empty room, climbed to my upper bunk, and slept for only a while, till the quiet voice of my roommate woke me: "The body will be flown to Okinawa."

I looked at him standing at his desk and speaking into the tele-   28
phone.

"Yes. A .38 in the temple. Yes."   29

I turned on my reading lamp and watched him put the phone   30
down. He was sad, and he looked at me. I said, "Did someone commit
suicide?"

"CAG."   31

"CAG?"   32

I sat up.   33

"The ONI investigated him."   34

Then I knew what I had not known I knew, and I said, "Was he a   35
homosexual?"

"Yes."   36

My roommate told me the executive officer had summoned CAG   37
to his office, shown him the report, and told him that he could either resign or face a general court-martial. Then CAG went to his room. Fifteen minutes later the executive officer phoned him; when he did not
answer, the executive officer and the investigators ran to his room. He
was on his bunk, shot in the right temple, his pilot's .38 revolver in his
hand. His eyelids fluttered; he was unconscious but still alive, and he
died from bleeding.

"They *ran*?" I said. "They *ran* to his room?"   38

Ten years later one of my shipmates came to visit me in Massachu-   39
setts; we had been civilians for a long time. In my kitchen we were
drinking beer, and he said, "I couldn't tell you this aboard ship, because I worked in the legal office. They called CAG back from that boat
you were on because he knew the ONI was aboard. His plane was on
the ground at the base in Iwakuni. They were afraid he was going to fly
it and crash into the sea and they'd lose the plane."

All 3,000 of the ship's crew did not mourn. Not every one of the   40
hundreds of men in the Air Group mourned. But the shock was general
and hundreds of men did mourn, and each morning we woke to it, and
it was in our talk in the wardroom and in the passageways. In the
closed air of the ship it touched us, and it lived above us on the flight
deck and in the sky. One night at sea a young pilot came to my room;
his face was sunburned and sad. We sat in desk chairs, and he said,
"The morale is very bad now. The whole Group. It's just shot."

"Did y'all know about him?"   41

42   "We all knew. We didn't care. We would have followed him into hell."

43   Yes, they would have followed him; they were ready every day and every night to fly with him from a doomed ship and follow him to Moscow, to perish in their brilliant passion.

★ Meaning and Understanding

1. Why did "CAG" shoot himself?

2. How many stories of pilots dying does the essay recount? Why do you think Dubus includes the story of the pilot who falls into the sea?

3. What does the episode with the writer at the officers' club reveal about CAG's character?

4. Why was the writer going to Hiroshima? How did he feel about CAG going with him?

5. What does the young pilot mean when he says to the writer, "We didn't care. We would have followed him into hell" (paragraph 42)?

★ Techniques and Strategies

1. Besides the writer, only CAG is named in the essay. What effect does this have on the essay? Why doesn't Dubus name CAG or the other men?

2. The essay makes much use of dialogue. Identify dialogue that you consider particularly effective. What does it contribute to character and the meanings of the piece?

3. What do you think of the essay's title? Who are the "imperiled men"?

4. The writer uses figurative language and imagery sparely, yet to great effect. What, for example, is your reaction to the simile at the end of paragraph 1? What other images contribute visual meaning to the piece?

5. What is the effect on the essay of the last few paragraphs, set ten years after the major event in the essay? What does the writer gain by leaping so many years forward to resume the story and bring the essay to a close?

★ Speaking of Values

1. The essay considers the fate of a homosexual military hero. What is the legal status of homosexuals in the military today? What do you think the policy should be?

2. Dubus sets his essay against military conflicts and conflagrations—Russia versus America, America versus Japan, nuclear missiles, atomic bombs, and so on. From reading the essay, what do you think Dubus thinks about war? On what particulars in the essay do you base this judgment? What do *you* think about war?

3. The essay explores what the author perceived as pilot culture—including heavy drinking. Do you think there is a relation between the pilots' job and drinking—as it's presented in the essay? What is the nature of the connection? Consider any group of workers and an entrenched habit or behavior that you've noticed in them or one that's often associated with them (truck drivers, teachers, firefighters, and so on). Do you see a linkage between work and character or between work and behavior? How do our jobs and their pressures or joys contribute to who we are or how we act? What do you think Dubus would say?

4. Hiroshima was a particularly terrible episode in modern history that still haunts the world. Dubus writes: "I was not happily going to Hiroshima; I was going because I was an American, and I felt that I should look at it and be in it." Check a history text on the issues regarding Hiroshima during the time portrayed in the essay. What do you think Dubus means in his comment about going there? How does Dubus's essay capture the legacy of Hiroshima?

5. Secrecy has a strong presence in the essay—military secrecy and secret missions, secrecy among friends and colleagues. What value does the essay assign to the different secrets? Are they related in some way? What is your view of secrets and their role in personal life and public life?

★ *Values Conversation*

Form groups to discuss the role of homosexual men and women in American society today. Compared with fifty or so years ago, many would argue that gays have made considerable progress in their quest for rights, acceptance, and recognition. Others would argue that the society has a long way to go in wiping out prejudice against homosexuals. What do members of your group think?

★ *Writing about Values*

1. Write an essay in which you define the word "manly" or "manliness."

2. Do research on attitudes toward homosexuality in another culture or time. Write an essay in which you explain this attitude and show ways the culture or period expressed the attitude.

3. The essay ends with the sentence: "Yes, they would have followed him; they were ready every day and every night to fly with him from a doomed ship and follow him to Moscow, to perish in their brilliant passion." Write an essay on what you think that final sentence asserts about men, war, loyalty, human connections, or all of these.

Thomas Paine

Profession of Faith

Thomas Paine (1737–1809) was one of the leaders in the American Revolution and a contributor to the nation's political philosophy. Born in Britain, he came to America in 1774 and soon thereafter published one of the seminal works of the period, *Common Sense* (1776), which examined the source and purpose of government and helped rally American citizens to freedom's cause. Paine also wrote *The Rights of Man* (1791–1792) and *The Age of Reason* (1794–1795). In this excerpt from *The Age of Reason* he offers his thoughts on religion.

——————— ★ ———————

It has been my intention for several years past to publish my thoughts 1
upon Religion. I am well aware of the difficulties that attend the subject; and from that consideration had reserved it to a more advanced period of life. I intended it to be the last offering I should make to my fellow-citizens of all nations, and that at a time when the purity of the motive that induced me to it could not admit of a question, even by those who might disapprove the work.

The circumstance that has now taken place in France[1] of the total 2
abolition of the whole national order of priesthood and of everything appertaining to compulsive systems of religion and compulsive articles of faith, has not only precipitated my intention, but rendered a work of this kind exceedingly necessary; lest, in the general wreck of superstition, of false systems of government, and false theology, we lose sight of morality, of humanity, and of the theology that is true.

As several of my colleagues, and others of my fellow-citizens of 3
France, have given me the example of making their voluntary and individual profession of faith, I also will make mine; and I do this with all that sincerity and frankness with which the mind of man communicates with itself.

I believe in one God, and no more; and I hope for happiness be- 4
yond this life.

I believe in the equality of man, and I believe that religious duties 5
consist in doing justice, loving mercy, and endeavoring to make our fellow-creatures happy.

[1]French revolutionaries after 1792 attacked the clergy, closing churches, abolishing sabbath and the Christian calendar, and promoting paganism.

6   But lest it should be supposed that I believe many other things in addition to these, I shall, in the progress of this work, declare the things I do not believe and my reasons for not believing them.

7   I do not believe in the creed professed by the Jewish church, by the Roman church, by the Greek church, by the Turkish church, by the Protestant church, nor by any church that I know of. My own mind is my own church.

8   All national institutions of churches—whether Jewish, Christian, or Turkish—appear to me no other than human inventions set up to terrify and enslave mankind and monopolize power and profit.

9   I do not mean by this declaration to condemn those who believe otherwise. They have the same right to their belief as I have to mine. But it is necessary to the happiness of man that he be mentally faithful to himself. Infidelity does not consist in believing or in disbelieving; it consists in professing to believe what he does not believe.

10   It is impossible to calculate the moral mischief, if I may so express it, that mental lying has produced in society. When a man has so far corrupted and prostituted the chastity of his mind as to subscribe his professional belief to things he does not believe, he has prepared himself for the commission of every other crime. He takes up the trade of a priest for the sake of gain, and, in order to *qualify* himself for that trade, he begins with a perjury. Can we conceive anything more destructive to morality than this?

11   Soon after I had published the pamphlet, COMMON SENSE in America, I saw the exceeding probability that a revolution in the system of government would be followed by a revolution in the system of religion. The adulterous connection of church and state, wherever it had taken place, whether Jewish, Christian, or Turkish, had so effectually prohibited, by pains and penalties, every discussion upon established creeds and upon first principles of religion, that until the system of government should be changed those subjects could not be brought fairly and openly before the world; but that whenever this should be done, a revolution in the system of religion would follow. Human inventions and priestcraft would be detected, and man would return to the pure, unmixed, and unadulterated belief of one God, and no more.

★ Meaning and Understanding

1. Restate in your own words the phrase "compulsive systems of religion and compulsive articles of faith" (paragraph 2).

2. What is Paine's faith?

3. Does Paine approve of people who practice faiths different than his own? How do you know?

4. What does Paine mean by "the chastity of his mind"?

5. What does Paine think about the separation of church and state?

★ Techniques and Strategies

1. What is the thesis of this piece?

2. Characterize the writer's style. Is it embellished, ambiguous, straight-forward? How does this style help to advance the piece's meaning?

3. What do the first three paragraphs—before the actual "profession"—add to the piece?

4. Paine's "profession" builds on assertions of both what he believes and what he does not believe. Does the inclusion of both beliefs and nonbeliefs together seem effective to you? Why?

5. What is the purpose of the rhetorical question at the end of paragraph 10?

★ Speaking of Values

1. Does the writer seem tolerant or intolerant, or both? Why do you think so? What values does the piece present about religion?

2. Paine writes, "My own mind is my own church." What does he mean by this remark? Why might you agree or disagree with him? In what ways is his notion part of American values? In what ways not?

3. Explain the writer's ideas about infidelity. What do you think he means by the word? What does the word infidelity usually refer to in our society?

4. What is Paine's attitude toward truth and being true to oneself?

5. Paine calls for "a revolution in the system of religion." Why? Has such a revolution taken place in America? Anywhere else you can think of?

6. The writer asserts as a key principle "the unadulterated belief of one God, and no more" (paragraph 11). Why does he make this assertion? Do not major world religions follow this precept? In what ways? Why, then, is Paine raising this point with such passion?

★ Values Conversation

Paine writes, "I believe that religious duties consist in doing justice, loving mercy, and endeavoring to make our fellow-creatures happy." Form groups and discuss the elements of religion Paine enumerates in that statement.

How does your group feel about them as essential notions? In what ways do organized religions today practice those notions? In what way do they not? What other elements would your group add to a list of religious fundamentals?

★ *Writing about Values*

1. Write an essay in which you profess your faith about something important to you. Make the essay a letter to a friend who has asked you what you believe and why.

2. Write a paper in which you discuss an incident of religious persecution that you might have experienced, witnessed, or read or heard about. Examine not only what happened but also why it happened.

3. Some people see religion as the highest form of humanity's intellectual and emotional aspirations. Others assert that religion is the "opiate of the people"—meaning that it lulls them into accepting their misery, dulling them to painful social realities. What value do you think religion serves in people's lives? Use examples from history, current events, or your personal experience to support your belief.

Theodore Roosevelt

Going to Church

Theodore Roosevelt (1858–1919), the twenty-sixth president of the
United States, was a Spanish–American war hero. He served as governor
of New York State, and, as vice president, became president on the assassination of President William McKinley (1901). *The Winning of the West* (4
vols, 1889–1896) tells of his adventures. In this essay Roosevelt examines
what he sees as the role of the church in people's lives.

──────── ★ ────────

1. In this actual world a churchless community, a community where
men have abandoned and scoffed at or ignored their religious needs, is
a community on the rapid downgrade. It is perfectly true that occasional individuals or families may have nothing to do with church or
with religious practices and observances and yet maintain the highest
standard of spirituality and of ethical obligation. But this does not affect the case in the world as it now is, any more than that exceptional
men and women under exceptional conditions have disregarded the
marriage tie without moral harm to themselves interferes with the
larger fact that such disregard if at all common means the complete
moral disintegration of the body politic.

2. Church work and church attendance mean the cultivation of the
habit of feeling some responsibility for others and the sense of braced
moral strength which prevents a relaxation of one's own moral fiber.

3. There are enough holidays for most of us which can quite properly be devoted to pure holiday making. . . . Sundays differ from other
holidays—among other ways—in the fact that there are fifty-two of
them every year. . . . On Sunday, go to church.

4. Yes, I know all the excuses. I know that one can worship the Creator and dedicate oneself to good living in a grove of trees, or by a running brook, or in one's own house, just as well as in church. But I also
know as a matter of cold fact the average man does *not* thus worship or
thus dedicate himself. If he stays away from church he does not spend
his time in good works or in lofty meditation. He looks over the colored
supplement of the newspaper.

5. He may not hear a good sermon at church. But unless he is very
unfortunate he will hear a sermon by a good man who, with his good
wife, is engaged all the week long in a series of wearing and humdrum
and important tasks for making hard lives a little easier.

6   6. He will listen to and take part in reading some beautiful passages from the Bible. And if he is not familiar with the Bible, he has suffered a loss. . . .

7   7. He will probably take part in singing some good hymns.

8   8. He will meet and nod to, or speak to, good, quiet neighbors. . . . He will come away feeling a little more charitably toward all the world, even toward those excessively foolish young men who regard church-going as rather a soft performance.

9   9. I advocate a man's joining in church works for the sake of showing his faith by his works.

10   10. The man who does not in some way, active or not, connect himself with some active, working church misses many opportunities for helping his neighbors, and therefore, incidentally, for helping himself.

★ Meaning and Understanding

1. According to Roosevelt, can a person be good if he doesn't go to church? Why?

2. What important values does going to church instill in people?

3. What is the writer's attitude toward the Bible?

4. According to the writer, is helping one's neighbors a good thing? Why?

5. What excuses does Roosevelt name for not going to church?

★ Techniques and Strategies

1. The writer asserts ten reasons for going to church. How do the points relate to one another?

2. How would you describe Roosevelt's style? Academic, stern, folksy? Does the style contribute to the piece's effectiveness? How?

3. The writer notes that Sundays differ from other holidays and says that "there are fifty-two of them every year. On Sunday, go to church." How does this direct imperative strike you? Does it make you want to "obey"? Why or why not?

4. Roosevelt states his reasons tersely. What is the effect of this brevity on the reader? What effect do the extreme brevity and simplicity of reasons 7 and 8 have on the reader?

5. What value for the reader does the numbering of reasons have? Would the piece be as effective were no numbers included? Why or why not?

★ *Speaking of Values*

1. The writer says that he knows "as a matter of cold fact the average man" does not worship in his own house and on his own terms— though he's familiar with these "excuses." Do you agree that people generally do not live spiritual lives without frequenting houses of worship? Explain your views.

2. Roosevelt advocates a man "showing his faith by his works." Do you agree that actions and deeds tell us about a person's faith? Why or why not?

3. Roosevelt discusses the disregard of marriage, believing that the practice, if widespread, would lead to the "complete moral disintegration of the body politic." Do you agree? Why or why not?

4. How do you account for the drop in attendance at churches, temples, and synagogues in America today? How would Roosevelt react to America's current churchgoing practices?

5. Roosevelt says that a churchless community is a community "on the rapid downgrade." Why might you agree or disagree with that observation?

★ *Values Conversation*

Form groups and discuss the ways in which a decrease in churchgoing does or does not affect American culture and why.

★ *Writing about Values*

1. Write an essay in which you identify reasons for or against formal worship.

2. Write an essay in which you identify and analyze some spiritual experience—whether from formal religion or not—that has affected the kind of person you are.

3. Develop a definition of "moral fiber."

Jimmy Carter

Prayer and the Civic Religion

Born in 1924, Jimmy Carter was the thirty-ninth president of the United States. Since leaving office in 1980, he has contributed to Habitat for Humanity, election reform in Latin America, and many other causes. In this selection he explores the wisdom of the American doctrine of the separation of church and state.

1 I grew up in a conservative Baptist family in which we honored some basic premises that had defined Baptists for more than three and a half centuries. One of the most fundamental was the separation of church and state, based on Jesus' admonition to "render to Caesar the things that are Caesar's and to God the things that are God's."

2 We considered it proper for citizens to influence public policy but not for a religious group to attempt to control the processes of a democratic government or for public officials to interfere in religious affairs.

3 During the last two decades, these principles have been challenged, often successfully, by Christian fundamentalists. Under the banner of the Christian Coalition, they have merged with the conservative wing of the Republican Party, becoming an active force in politics and enjoying a series of election successes.

4 They had their first serious setback this year when Bill Clinton was re-elected, and "only" 62 percent of born-again Christians voted against him. In a New York Times interview, Pat Robertson, the Christian Coalition's president, condemned Republican campaign leaders as "incompetent," and vowed to play a more active role in upcoming elections.

5 As a Presidential candidate in 1976, I tried to avoid any religious subject, but when questioned one April night at the home of a North Carolina supporter, I said I was a "born-again Christian." From then until the end of the campaign, national reporters made a big deal of what seemed natural to me and my hosts, making clear to me that injecting religion into politics was a mistake.

6 This and other incidents made me extra careful to separate my official status as President from the private worship habits of my family. I never permitted religious services to be held in the White House. With as little publicity as possible, we worshiped at the nearest Baptist church when we were in Washington, and at Camp David the chaplain

from a nearby Army base conducted private services for us and a few of the Navy families stationed there.

Yet I prayed more during those four years than at any other time in my life, primarily for patience, courage and the wisdom to make good decisions. I also prayed for peace—for ourselves and others. When Iran was holding our hostages, I asked for their safe return to freedom. 7

Since publication of my new book, "Living Faith," I have been asked whether my Christian beliefs ever differed from my duties as President. There were a few such conflicts but I always honored my oath to "preserve, protect and defend the Constitution of the United States." For instance, I have never believed that Jesus Christ would agree with Supreme Court decisions approving abortion or the death penalty, but I honored such rulings to the best of my ability, at the same time attempting to minimize what I considered to be their adverse impact. 8

Jesus proclaimed that his ministry was to "bring good news to the poor, to proclaim freedom for the prisoners, recovery of sight for the blind, and to release the oppressed." But I believe that it is usually government officeholders and not religious leaders who are in the forefront of this struggle to alleviate suffering, provide homes for the homeless, eliminate the stigma of poverty or racial discrimination, preserve peace and rehabilitate prisoners. 9

There is little doubt that many church members are more self-satisfied, committed to the status quo and exclusive of dissimilar people than most political officeholders are because officeholders face internal competition from challengers dealing successfully with human problems. 10

There is a subtle but important difference between the highest commitments of religious faith and public office. Most great religions espouse the golden rule, based on agape—love or self-sacrifice, for the benefit of others. A government's ultimate goals are to preserve security and to insure justice, to treat people fairly, to guarantee their rights, to alleviate suffering, and to try to resolve disputes peacefully. Both are worthy ideas, but neither is easy to reach. 11

★ Meaning and Understanding

1. What issue is the writer discussing?

2. How was Carter reared, and what does he believe about the separation of church and state?

3. Considering Carter's religious views, how do you feel about his position on the separation of church and state?

4. How does the writer feel about Supreme Court decisions? When he was president, did he uphold them? Why or why not?

5. The writer is religious and quotes Jesus regarding his own desire to help the poor and the oppressed. Does he believe most religious leaders are concerned about these issues? Why?

6. What lesson did the writer learn from the incident in which he told reporters he was a "born-again Christian"?

★ *Techniques and Strategies*

1. What is Carter's thesis?

2. What, in your opinion, is the single most effective moment of the essay? Why?

3. What specific reasoning does Carter follow for maintaining the separation of church and state? How does this line of reasoning affect the essay?

4. Characterize the style of the essay. Is it argumentative? Intimate? Preachy? Something else? How does the style contribute to the essay and its points?

5. Who is Carter's audience in this essay? How can you tell?

★ *Speaking of Values*

1. Carter asserts that most church members are more "committed to the status quo" than most elected officials. Do you agree? What experiences or observations inform your opinion? Do you believe this is the "right" way for each group to be? Why?

2. What is your reaction to the writer's respect for the separation of church and state? Can you see any value in a greater relationship between the two? If so, why and how? If not, what problems do you foresee?

3. Carter specifies certain Supreme Court decisions that conflict with Christian thinking. What other Supreme Court decisions might counter religious doctrine, Christian or otherwise? Where do you stand in the dilemma?

4. The writer discusses the paradox of believing one thing and doing another. How would you describe the morality of this predicament? Do you think it is possible as well as ethical? Why? Have you ever found yourself, or observed someone else, in a situation like this? How do you feel about your or that person's actions?

5. Carter sees the government as on the cutting edge of the struggle to follow Jesus' teaching regarding the poor, the imprisoned, the blind,

and the oppressed. Why might you agree or disagree? If these are governmental functions, where does religion fit in?

★ *Values Conversation*

Form groups and discuss the separation of church and state in America today. Is the separation still useful as a principle? Why? What sort of America do you imagine we would have without this separation?

★ *Writing about Values*

1. Write an essay in which you advance your opinion on the separation of church and state. You may want to draw on your own experiences, perhaps in school, to support your point.

2. Write an essay called "Religion and Power."

3. The writer states that government and religion have different goals. Write an essay in which you compare the goals of each institution, suggesting their common or contrasting concerns.

William J. Bennett

Revolt against God: America's Spiritual Despair

William J. Bennett was born in Brooklyn, New York in 1943. He has a
Ph.D. from the University of Texas and degrees from Williams College
and Harvard Law School. He served as Secretary of Education under
Ronald Reagan and director of national drug control policy under
George Bush. In this address to the Heritage Foundation on its twentieth
anniversary in 1994, he describes what he perceives as the consequences
of America's lack of religious faith.

———— ★ ————

1   We gather in a spirit of celebration. But tonight I speak out of a spirit of
concern—for this evening my task is to provide an assessment of the
social and cultural condition of modern American society. And while
many people agree that there is much to be concerned about these
days, I don't think that people fully appreciate the depth, or even the
nature, of what threatens us—and, therefore, we do not yet have a firm
hold on what it will take to better us. We need to have an honest conversation about these issues.

2   A few months ago I had lunch with a friend of mine, a man who has
written for a number of political journals and who now lives in Asia.
During our conversation the topic turned to America—specifically,
America as seen through the eyes of foreigners.

3   During our conversation, he told me what he had observed during
his travels: that while the world still regards the United States as the
leading economic and military power on earth, this same world no
longer beholds us with the moral respect it once did. When the rest of
the world looks at America, he said, they see no longer a "shining city
on a hill." Instead, they see a society in decline, with exploding rates of
crime and social pathologies. We all know that foreigners often come
here in fear—and once they are here, they travel in fear. It is our shame
to realize that they have good reason to fear; a record number of them
get killed here.

4   Today, many who come to America believe they are visiting a de-
graded society. Yes, America still offers plenty of jobs, enormous opportunity, and unmatched material and physical comforts. But there is
a growing sense among many foreigners that when they come here,

they are slumming. I have, like many of us, an instinctive aversion to foreigners harshly judging my nation; yet I must concede that much of what they think is true.

"You're Becoming American"

I recently had a conversation with a D.C. cab driver who is doing grad-   5
uate work at American University. He told me that once he receives his masters degree he is going back to Africa. His reason? His children. He doesn't think they are safe in Washington. He told me that he didn't want them to grow up in a country where young men will paw his daughter and expect her to be an "easy target," and where his son might be a different kind of target—the target of violence from the hands of other young males. "It is more civilized where I come from," said this man from Africa. I urged him to move outside of Washington; things should improve.

But it is not only violence and urban terror that signal decay. We   6
see it in many forms. *Newsweek* columnist Joe Klein recently wrote about Berenice Belizaire, a young Haitian girl who arrived in New York in 1987. When she arrived in America she spoke no English and her family lived in a cramped Brooklyn apartment. Eventually Berenice en-rolled at James Madison High School, where she excelled. According to Judith Khan, a math teacher at James Madison, "[The immigrants are] why I love teaching in Brooklyn. They have a drive in them that we no longer seem to have." And far from New York City, in the beautiful Berkshire mountains where I went to school, Philip Kasinitz, an assis-tant professor of sociology at Williams College, has observed that Americans have become the object of ridicule among immigrant stu-dents on campus. "There's an interesting phenomenon. When immi-grant kids criticize each other for getting lazy or loose, they say, 'You're becoming American,'" Kasinitz says. "Those who work hardest to keep American culture at bay have the best chance of becoming Amer-ican success stories."

Last year an article was published in the *Washington Post* which   7
pointed out how students from other countries adapt to the lifestyle of most American teens. Paulina, a Polish high school student studying in the United States, said that when she first came here she was amazed by the way teens spent their time. According to Paulina:

> In Warsaw, we would talk to friends after school, go home and eat with our parents and then do four or five hours of homework. When I first came here, it was like going into a crazy world, but now I am get-ting used to it. I'm going to Pizza Hut and watching TV and doing less work in school. I can tell it is not a good thing to get used to.

8   Think long and hard about these words, spoken by a young Polish girl about America: "When I first came here it was like going into a crazy world, but now I am getting used to it." And, "I can tell it is not a good thing to get used to."

9   Something has gone wrong with us.

Social Regression

10   This is a conclusion which I come to with great reluctance. During the late 1960s and 1970s, I was one of those who reacted strongly to criticisms of America that swept across university campuses. I believe that many of those criticisms—"Amerika" as an inherently repressive, imperialist, and racist society—were wrong then, and they are wrong now. But intellectual honesty demands that we accept facts that we would sometimes like to wish away. Hard truths are truths nonetheless. And the hard truth is that something has gone wrong with us.

11   America is not in danger of becoming a third world country; we are too rich, too proud and too strong to allow that to happen. It is not that we live in a society completely devoid of virtue. Many people live well, decently, even honorably. There are families, schools, churches and neighborhoods that work. There are places where virtue is taught and learned. But there is a lot less of this than there ought to be. And we know it. John Updike put it this way: "The fact that . . . we still live well cannot ease the pain of feeling that we no longer live nobly."

12   Let me briefly outline some of the empirical evidence that points to cultural decline, evidence that while we live well materially, we don't live nobly. Earlier this year I released, through the auspices of the Heritage Foundation, *The Index of Leading Cultural Indicators,* the most comprehensive statistical portrait available of behavioral trends over the last thirty years. Among the findings: since 1960, the population has increased 41 percent; the Gross Domestic Product has nearly tripled; and total social spending, by all levels of government (measured in constant 1990 dollars) has risen from $142.7 billion to $787 billion—more than a five-fold increase.

13   But during the same thirty-year period, there has been a 560 percent increase in violent crime; more than a 400 percent increase in illegitimate births; a quadrupling in divorces; a tripling of the percentage of children living in single-parent homes; more than a 200 percent increase in the teenage suicide rate; and a drop of 75 points in the average S.A.T. scores of high-school students.

14   These are not good things to get used to.

15   Today 30 percent of all births and 68 percent of black births are illegitimate. By the end of the decade, according to the most reliable pro-

jections, 40 percent of all American births and 80 percent of minority births will occur out of wedlock.

These are not good things to get used to.   16

And then there are the results of an ongoing teacher survey. Over the   17
years teachers have been asked to identify the top problems in America's schools. In 1940 teachers identified them as talking out of turn; chewing gum; making noise; running in the hall; cutting in line; dress code infractions; and littering. When asked the same question in 1990, teachers identified drug use; alcohol abuse; pregnancy; suicide; rape; robbery; and assault. These are not good things to get used to, either.

Consider, too, where the United States ranks in comparison with   18
the rest of the industrialized world. We are at or near the top in rates of abortions, divorces, and unwed births. We lead the industrialized world in murder, rape and violent crime. And in elementary and secondary education, we are at or near the bottom in achievement scores.

These facts alone are evidence of substantial social regression. But   19
there are other signs of decay, ones that do not so easily lend themselves to quantitative analyses (some of which I have already suggested in my opening anecdotes). What I am talking about is the moral, spiritual and aesthetic character and habits of a society—what the ancient Greeks referred to as its *ethos*. And here, too, we are facing serious problems. For there is a coarseness, a callousness, a cynicism, a banality, and a vulgarity to our time. There are just too many signs of de-civilization—that is, civilization gone rotten. And the worst of it has to do with our children. Apart from the numbers and the specific facts, there is the ongoing, chronic crime against children: the crime of making them old before their time. We live in a culture which at times seems almost dedicated to the corruption of the young, to assuring the loss of their innocence before their time.

This may sound overly pessimistic or even alarmist, but I think this   20
is the way it is. And my worry is that people are not unsettled enough; I don't think we are angry enough. We have become inured to the cultural rot that is setting in. Like Paulina, we are getting used to it, even though it is not a good thing to get used to. People are experiencing atrocity overload, losing their capacity for shock, disgust, and outrage. A few weeks ago eleven people were murdered in New York City within ten hours—and as far as I can tell, it barely caused a stir.

Two weeks ago a violent criminal, who mugged and almost killed   21
a 72-year-old man and was shot by a police officer while fleeing the scene of the crime, was awarded $4.3 million. Virtual silence.

And during last year's Los Angeles riots, Damian Williams and   22
Henry Watson were filmed pulling an innocent man out of a truck, crushing his skull with a brick, and doing a victory dance over his fallen body. Their lawyers then built a successful legal defense on the proposition that people cannot be held accountable for getting caught

up in mob violence. ("They just got caught up in the riot," one juror told the *New York Times*. "I guess maybe they were in the wrong place at the wrong time.") When the trial was over and these men were found not guilty on most counts, the sound you heard throughout the land was relief. We are "defining deviancy down," in Senator Moynihan's memorable phrase. And in the process we are losing a once-reliable sense of civic and moral outrage.

Urban Surrender

23   Listen to this story from former New York City Police Commissioner Raymond Kelly:

> A number of years ago there began to appear, in the windows of auto-mobiles parked on the streets of American cities, signs which read: "No radio." Rather than express outrage, or even annoyance at the possibility of a car break-in, people tried to communicate with the po-tential thief in conciliatory terms. The translation of "no radio" is: "Please break into someone else's car, there's nothing in mine." These "no radio" signs are flags of urban surrender. They are hand-written capitulations. Instead of "no radio," we need new signs that say "no surrender."

24   And what is so striking today is not simply the increased *number* of violent crimes, but the *nature* of those crimes. It is no longer "just" mur-der we see, but murders with a prologue, murders accompanied by acts of unspeakable cruelty and inhumanity.

25   From pop culture, with our own ears, we have heard the terrible debasement of music. Music, harmony and rhythm find their way into the soul and fasten mightily upon it, Plato's *Republic* teaches us. Because music has the capacity to lift us up or to bring us down, we need to pay more careful attention to it. It is a steep moral slide from Bach, and even Buddy Holly, to Guns 'n Roses and 2 Live Crew. This week an indicted murderer, Snoop Doggy Dogg, saw his rap album, *Doggystyle*, debut at number one. It may be useful for you to read, as I have, some of his lyrics and other lyrics from heavy metal and rap music, and then ask yourself: how much worse could it possibly get? And then ask yourself: what will happen when young boys who grow up on mean streets, without fathers in their lives, are con-stantly exposed to music which celebrates the torture and abuse of women?

26   There is a lot of criticism directed at television these days—the ca-sual cruelty, the rampant promiscuity, the mindlessness of sit-coms and soap operas. Most of the criticisms are justified. But this is not the worst of it. The worst of television is the daytime television talk shows, where indecent exposure is celebrated as a virtue. It is hard to remember now,

but there was once a time when personal failures, subliminal desires, and perverse taste were accompanied by guilt or embarrassment, at least by silence.

Today these are a ticket to appear as a guest on the *Sally Jessy*   27 *Raphael Show,* or one of the dozens or so shows like it. I asked my staff to provide me with a list of some of the daytime talk-show topics from only the last two weeks. They include: cross-dressing couples; a three-way love affair; a man whose chief aim in life is to sleep with women and fool them into thinking that he is using a condom during sex; women who can't say no to cheating; prostitutes who love their jobs; a former drug dealer; and an interview with a young girl caught in the middle of a bitter custody battle. These shows present a two-edged problem to society: the first edge is that some people want to appear on these shows in order to expose themselves. The second edge is that lots of people are tuning in to watch them expose themselves. This is not a good thing to get used to.

Who's to blame? Here I would caution conservatives against the   28 tendency to blame liberals for our social disorders. Contemporary liberalism does have a lot for which to answer; many of its doctrines have wrought a lot of damage. Universities, intellectuals, think tanks, and government departments have put a lot of poison into the reservoirs of national discourse. But to simply point the finger of blame at liberals and elites is wrong. The hard fact of the matter is that this was not something done to us; it is also something we have done to ourselves. Liberals may have been peddling from an empty wagon, but we were buying.

Much of what I have said is familiar to many of you. Why is this   29 happening? What is behind all this? Intelligent arguments have been advanced as to why these things have come to pass. Thoughtful people have pointed to materialism and consumerism; an overly permissive society; the writings of Rousseau, Marx, Freud, Nietzsche; the legacy of the 1960s; and so on. There is truth in almost all of these accounts. Let me give you mine.

Spiritual Acedia

I submit to you that the real crisis of our time is spiritual. Specifically,   30 our problem is what the ancients called *acedia*. *Acedia* is the sin of sloth. But *acedia,* as understood by the saints of old, is *not* laziness about life's affairs (which is what we normally think sloth to be). *Acedia* is something else; properly understood, *acedia* is an aversion to and a negation of *spiritual* things. *Acedia* reveals itself as an undue concern for external affairs and worldly things. *Acedia* is spiritual torpor; an absence of zeal for divine things. And it brings with it, according to the ancients, "a sadness, a sorrow of the world."

31   *Acedia* manifests itself in man's "joyless, ill-tempered, and self-seeking rejection of the nobility of the children of God." The slothful man *hates* the spiritual, and he wants to be free of its demands. The old theologians taught that *acedia* arises from a heart steeped in the worldly and carnal, and from a *low esteem* of divine things. It eventually leads to a hatred of the good altogether. With hatred comes more rejection, more ill-temper, more sadness, and sorrow.

32   Spiritual *acedia* is not a new condition, of course. It is the seventh capital sin. But today it is in ascendance. In coming to this conclusion, I have relied on two literary giants—men born on vastly different continents, the product of two completely different worlds, and shaped by wholly different experiences—yet writers who possess strikingly similar views, and who have had a profound impact on my own thinking. It was an unusual and surprising moment to find their views coincident.

33   When the late novelist Walker Percy was asked what concerned him most about the future of America, he answered:

> Probably the fear of seeing America, with all its great strength and beauty and freedom...gradually subside into decay through default and be defeated, not by the Communist movement...but from within by weariness, boredom, cynicism, greed and in the end helplessness before its great problems.

34   And here are the words of the prophetic Aleksandr Solzhenitsyn (echoing his 1978 Harvard commencement address in which he warned of the West's "spiritual exhaustion"):

> In the United States the difficulties are not a Minotaur or a dragon—not imprisonment, hard labor, death, government harassment and censorship—but cupidity, boredom, sloppiness, indifference. Not the acts of a mighty all-pervading repressive government but the failure of a listless public to make use of the freedom that is its birthright.

35   What afflicts us, then, is a corruption of the heart, a turning away in the soul. Our aspirations, our affections and our desires are turned toward the wrong things. And only when we turn them toward the right things—toward enduring, noble, spiritual things—will things get better.

36   Lest I leave the impression of bad news on all fronts, I do want to be clear about the areas where I think we have made enormous gains: material comforts, economic prosperity and the spread of democracy around the world. The American people have achieved a standard of living unimagined 50 years ago. We have seen extraordinary advances in medicine, science and technology. Life expectancy has increased more than 20 years during the last six decades. Opportunity and equal-

ity have been extended to those who were once denied them. And of course America prevailed in our "long, twilight struggle" against communism. Impressive achievements, all.

Yet even with all of this, the conventional analysis is still that this   37
nation's major challenges have to do with getting more of the same: achieving greater economic growth, job creation, increased trade, health care, or more federal programs. Some of these things are desirable, such as greater economic growth and increased trade; some of them are not, such as more federal programs. But to look to any or all of them as the solution to what ails us is akin to assigning names to images and shadows, it so widely misses the mark.

If we have full employment and greater economic growth—if we   38
have cities of gold and alabaster—but our children have not learned how to walk in goodness, justice, and mercy, then the American experiment, no matter how gilded, will have failed.

I realize I have laid down strong charges, a tough indictment. Some   39
may question them. But if I am wrong, if my diagnosis is not right, then someone must explain to me this: why do Americans feel so bad when things are economically, militarily and materially so good? Why amidst this prosperity and security are enormous numbers of people—almost 70 percent of the public—saying, that we are off track? This paradox is described in the Scottish author John Buchan's work. Writing a half-century ago, he described the "coming of a too garish age, when life would be lived in the glare of neon lamps and the spirit would have no solitude." Here is what Buchan wrote about his nightmare world:

> In such a [nightmare] world everyone would have leisure. But everyone would be restless, for there would be no spiritual discipline in life.... It would be a feverish, bustling world, self-satisfied and yet malcontent, and under the mask of a riotous life there would be death at the heart. In the perpetual hurry of life there would be no chance of quiet for the soul.... In such a bagman's paradise, where life would be rationalised and padded with every material comfort, there would be little satisfaction for the immortal part of man.

During the last decade of the twentieth century, many have   40
achieved this bagman's paradise. And this is not a good thing to get used to.

In identifying spiritual exhaustion as the central problem, I part   41
company with many. There *is* a disturbing reluctance in our time to talk seriously about matters spiritual and religious. Why? Perhaps it has to do with the modern sensibility's profound discomfort with the language and the commandments of God. Along with other bad habits, we have gotten used to not talking about the things which matter most—and so, we don't.

42   One will often hear that religious faith is a private matter that does not belong in the public arena. But this analysis does not hold—at least on some important points. Whatever your faith—or even if you have none at all—it is a fact that when millions of people stop believing in God, or when their belief is so attenuated as to be belief in name only, enormous public consequences follow. And when this is accompanied by an aversion to spiritual language by the political and intellectual class, the public consequences are even greater. How could it be otherwise? In modernity, *nothing* has been more consequential, or more public in its consequences, than large segments of American society privately turning away from God, or considering Him irrelevant, or declaring Him dead. Dostoyevsky reminded us in *Brothers Karamazov* that "if God does not exist, everything is permissible." We are now seeing "everything." And much of it is not good to get used to.

Social Regeneration

43   What can be done? First, here are the short answers: do not surrender; get mad; and get in the fight. Now, let me offer a few, somewhat longer, prescriptions.

44   1. At the risk of committing heresy before a Washington audience, let me suggest that our first task is to recognize that, in general, we place too much hope in politics. I am certainly not denying the impact (for good and for ill) of public policies. I would not have devoted the past decade of my life to public service—and I could not work at the Heritage Foundation—if I believed that the work with which I was engaged amounted to nothing more than striving after wind and ashes. But it is foolish, and futile, to rely primarily on politics to solve moral, cultural, and spiritual afflictions.

45   The last quarter-century has taught politicians a hard and humbling lesson: there are intrinsic limits to what the state can do, particularly when it comes to imparting virtue, and forming and forging character, and providing peace to souls. Samuel Johnson expressed this (deeply conservative and true) sentiment when he wrote, "How small, of all that human hearts endure, That part which laws or kings can cause or cure!"

46   King Lear was a great king—sufficient to all his political responsibilities and obligations. He did well as king, but as a father and a man, he messed up terribly. The great king was reduced to the mud and ignominy of the heath, cursing his daughters, his life, his gods. Politics *is* a great adventure; it is greatly important; but its proper place in our lives has been greatly exaggerated. Politics—especially inside the Beltway politics—has too often become the graven image of our time.

47   2. We must have public policies that once again make the connection between our deepest beliefs and our legislative agenda. Do we Americans, for example, believe that man is a spiritual being with a potential for

individual nobility and moral responsibility? Or do we believe that his ultimate fate is to be merely a soulless cog in the machine of state? When we
teach sex-education courses to teenagers, do we treat them as if they are
young animals in heat? Or, do we treat them as children of God?

In terms of public policy, the failure is not so much intellectual; it is   48
a failure of will and courage. Right now we are playing a rhetorical
game: we say one thing, and we do another. Consider the following:

- We say that we desire from our children more civility and responsibility, but in many of our schools we steadfastly refuse to
  teach right and wrong.
- We say that we want law and order in the streets, but we allow
  criminals, including violent criminals, to return to those same
  streets.
- We say that we want to stop illegitimacy, but we continue to
  subsidize the kind of behavior that virtually guarantees high
  rates of illegitimacy.
- We say that we want to discourage teenage sexual activity, but
  in classrooms all across America educators are more eager to
  dispense condoms than moral guidance.
- We say that we want more families to stay together, but we liber-
  alize divorce laws and make divorce easier to attain.
- We say that we want to achieve a color-blind society and judge
  people by the content of their character, but we continue to
  count by race, skin and pigment.
- We say that we want to encourage virtue and honor among the
  young, but it has become a mark of sophistication to shun the
  language of morality.

3. We desperately need to recover a sense of the fundamental pur-   49
pose of education, which is to provide for the intellectual *and* moral education of the young. From the ancient Greeks to the founding fathers,
moral instruction was *the* central task of education. "If you ask what is
the good of education," Plato said, "the answer is easy—that education
makes good men, and that good men act nobly." Jefferson believed that
education should aim at improving one's "morals" and "faculties."
And of education, John Locke said this: "'Tis virtue that we aim at, hard
virtue, and not the subtle arts of shifting." Until a quarter-century or so
ago, this consensus was so deep as to go virtually unchallenged. Having departed from this time-honored belief, we are now reaping the
whirlwind. And so we talk not about education as the architecture of
souls, but about "skills facilitation" and "self-esteem" and about being
"comfortable with ourselves."

4. As individuals and as a society, we need to return religion to its   50
proper place. Religion, after all, provides us with moral bearings. And

if I am right and the chief problem we face is spiritual impoverishment, then the solution depends, finally, on spiritual renewal. I am not speaking here about coerced spiritual renewal—in fact, there is no such thing—but about renewal freely taken.

51   The enervation of strong religious beliefs—*in both our private lives as well as our public conversations*—has de-moralized society. We ignore religion and its lessons at our peril. But instead of according religion its proper place, much of society ridicules and disdains it, and mocks those who are serious about their faith. In America today, the only respectable form of bigotry is bigotry directed against religious people. This antipathy toward religion cannot be explained by the well-publicized moral failures and financial excesses of a few leaders or charlatans, or by the censoriousness of some of their followers. No, the reason for hatred of religion is because it forces modern man to confront matters he would prefer to ignore.

52   Every serious student of American history, familiar with the writings of the founders, knows the civic case for religion. It provides society with a moral anchor—and nothing else has yet been found to substitute for it. Religion tames our baser appetites, passions, and impulses. And it helps us to thoughtfully sort through the "ordo amoris," the order of the loves.

53   But remember, too, that for those who believe, it is a mistake to treat religion merely as a useful means to worldly ends. Religion rightly demands that we take seriously not only the commandments of the faith, but that we also take seriously the object of the faith. Those who believe know that although we are pilgrims and sojourners and wanderers in this earthly kingdom, ultimately we are citizens of the City of God—a City which man did not build and cannot destroy, a City where there is no sadness, where the sorrows of the world find no haven, and where there is peace the world cannot give.

Pushing Back

54   Let me conclude. In his 1950 Nobel Prize acceptance speech, William Faulkner declared, "I decline to accept the end of man." Man will not merely endure but prevail because, as Faulkner said, he alone among creatures "has a soul, a spirit capable of compassion and sacrifice and endurance."

55   Today we must in the same way decline to accept the end of moral man. We must carry on the struggle, for our children. We will push back hard against an age that is pushing hard against us. When we do, we will emerge victorious against the trials of our time. When we do, we will save our children from the decadence of our time.

56   We have a lot of work to do. Let's get to it.

★ *Meaning and Understanding*

1. What is this essay saying about the United States? What does the writer feel has happened to international awareness of this country, and why?

2. What differences does the Polish student Paulina notice between the schooling she received in Poland and what she has received in the United States?

3. What has "gone wrong with us"?

4. How are we "defining deviancy down"?

5. "I submit to you that the real crisis of our time is spiritual," the writer says in paragraph 30, and he goes on to identify *acedia*. What is he referring to? How does the reference help him make his point?

6. How has politics "too often become the graven image of our time"? According to the writer, how are we citizens of the City of God?

★ *Techniques and Strategies*

1. Does the structure of the piece, which was originally a speech, seem to work as an essay? In what ways is the selection a good (or poor) speech? A good (or poor) essay?

2. Bennett provides a number of literary references here. What do they contribute to the essay?

3. How does the writer use rhetorical questions? Identify some of the more interesting ones.

4. Identify some of Bennett's references to pop culture and particularly to pop music. What do they contribute to the essay? How do they help the writer make his point?

5. Is the writer's evidence of "cultural decline" convincing? Why or why not?

6. How do the writer's repeated references to Greek culture and words affect his argument?

★ *Speaking of Values*

1. Why does Bennett believe American students have become the objects of ridicule among immigrant students on some campuses? How is this observation true or untrue for the campuses you know personally? Why or how is it true that "those who work hardest to keep American culture at bay have the best chance of becoming American success stories"? Does this statement make sense, and do you agree?

2. In your opinion, do the statistics the writer cites on illegitimate births indicate "cultural decline"? Why or why not? Is it possible that the institution of marriage is experiencing a decline but the institution of parenting is not? On what evidence do you base your opinion? Are parenting and marriage permanently linked in terms of American values? Why or why not?

3. What does the rising rate of divorce have to do with values? The rising number of children being reared in single-parent homes? Are these changes dramatic challenges to American ideals, or do they represent the growth and development of new values that in turn will become fundamental to America's value system? Explain your views.

4. "We live in a culture which at times seems almost dedicated to the corruption of the young, to assuring the loss of their innocence before their time." Why might you agree or disagree? What have you observed that could confirm or challenge this point of view? How long, in fact, do you think we should preserve the innocence of youth? Does the writer sound "overly pessimistic or even alarmist"? Why or why not?

5. Why might you agree that "people [are] experiencing atrocity overload, losing their capacity for shock, disgust, and outrage"? Why might you disagree?

6. What are Bennett's four facets of "social regeneration"? In what ways are these accurate and realistic observations and suggestions? In what ways do you find them off base? How do your observations and experiences confirm or deny his proposals?

★ *Values Conversation*

Form groups and discuss the statement from John Updike that Bennett cites: "The fact that . . . we still live well cannot ease the pain of feeling that we no longer live nobly." First of all, ask each member of the group to establish a personal opinion as to whether "we still live well." Now discuss and define noble acts. What exactly is *noble*? Who decides when an action is noble? Now discuss the latter part of the quote: "we no longer live nobly." How do you react to this sentiment now? Why do you react this way? Now deal with Updike's statement again. Do you agree with him? Why or why not?

★ *Writing about Values*

1. Consider the New York police commissioner's reference to "urban surrender" regarding the "no radio" signs in the windows of cars (paragraph 23). Write an essay in which you discuss one or more examples of urban surrender.

2. Carefully choose a daytime talk show to watch and write about. Interview others who have watched the show and write an essay discussing the impact the show seems to have had upon them and the studio audience. You may want to look into the talk show scandals of the early 1990s.

3. Interview several immigrant students and ask them questions that you determine after having read this essay. Use their responses as the basis of an essay in which you support or challenge Bennett's basic premises about how immigrant students view the United States and their American fellow students.

Peggy Fletcher Stack

Temple Wars: When Values Collide

Born in 1951, Peggy Fletcher Stack is a staff writer for the *Salt Lake City Tribune,* where this article originally appeared. In this selection she describes attempts to build Mormon churches in Massachusetts and Montana and raises the issue of "property rights versus religious freedom."

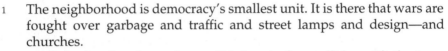

1   The neighborhood is democracy's smallest unit. It is there that wars are fought over garbage and traffic and street lamps and design—and churches.

2   It is also the place where self-interest often collides with the transcendent—or property rights versus religious freedom.

3   These powerful American values nearly always clash when The Church of Jesus Christ of Latter-day Saints chooses an upscale neighborhood for one of its enormous temples.

4   While new temples have been welcomed in Utah in recent years, and property values nearby have soared, that is not always the case outside the heart of Mormondom.

5   From Denver to Orlando to Seattle to Chicago to Dallas, neighborhoods have fought strenuously against the building of a temple in their midst.

6   The lights will overpower us, the traffic will ensnare us, the view will overwhelm us, critics argue. Stung by the criticism, Mormons, with their history of persecution, routinely sense bigotry.

7   That pattern is apparent once again as today's battles are being fought in Belmont, Mass., near Boston, and Billings, Mont.

8   While the Boston temple plan was approved this week by the local zoning board, the proposed temple site in Billings has been rejected once and is awaiting a second hearing in February.

9   "Though we got approval, we have really emerged hurt and wounded," said Clayton Christensen, a Belmont Mormon who was part of the local organizing committee. "We'd do it a lot differently if we had another shot at the process."

10   Boston Mormons had the responsibility to get approval for the temple plans but only LDS Church officials in Salt Lake City had the

authority to make changes, said Christensen, who teaches at Harvard Business School. "That made the process far more confrontational than it really needed to be."

In May 1995, LDS President Gordon B. Hinckley strolled around 11 the 8.9 acres the church owned in Belmont, Mass., and six months later, he announced it as the site for a new temple to serve 38,000 New England Mormons.

From that fall until the following May, the church developed plans 12 for the site, which included a temple resembling the one in Salt Lake City.

But neighbors, accustomed to their tree-lined streets dotted with 13 mansions old and new, had trouble imagining a massive church building towering above them on Belmont Hill, the most visible rise west of Boston.

About that time, Belmont-area Mormons began an intensive series 14 of meetings with the neighborhood to try to explain what a temple is, how it differs from a local chapel, and what its impact on the neighborhood would be. Church members even went door to door to try to reach any neighbors who had not attended the meetings.

Property owners closest to the new temple asked for studies of the 15 traffic patterns, impact of headlights, noise, lighting and particularly the blasting involved in construction. They also worried that real estate values would plummet and the building's shadow would cast them in darkness.

Letters flew back and forth in local newspapers. Cartoonists lampooned both sides while opponents and proponents traded accusations of misrepresentation. 16

In response to complaints, the LDS Church scaled back parking 17 lots, increased the density of plantings, and revised the lighting plan to make it softer.

Then opponents focused on the height of the spires. In the original 18 plan, developed by a Boston architect working with the Salt Lake City church offices, the tallest spire was to be 156 feet high, much taller than Belmont's 72-foot limit on the height of structures.

After complaints, the church reduced the height of the tallest spire 19 to 139 feet and asked for a zoning variance.

Hundreds of residents turned out for public hearings to discuss the 20 spires. The church prepared comparative studies of the height of other local church spires and so did the opponents. Local Mormon representatives argued that the spires had religious significance and were essential to the design.

Another issue was that the temple is closed to all but a small per- 21 centage of Mormons who have temple recommends, which attest to their adherence to the faith's tenets and allow them to enter the temple for sacred ordinances.

22   "It will serve only a small number of local Mormons, not the entire community," said John Forster, an opponent of the temple.

23   Boiling beneath it all was the issue of religious tolerance.

24   Though most of Belmont's residents, the regional chapter of the American Jewish Congress, and a group of Protestant clergy came out in favor of the temple proposal, Mormons felt battered and misunderstood.

25   "We have worked so hard to build a reputation as warm, caring and supportive people in the community," Christensen said. "Now much of that is lost."

26   Opponents swore that their opposition was to the structure, not the religion.

27   "Every time anyone opposes the Mormons, they yell about 'anti-Mormon discrimination'," Forster said.

28   Another opponent Joyce Jones, whose property is across the street from the proposed temple, said: "If it were my very own church and they wanted to build a building of this size, I would oppose it."

29   But this week *Boston Globe* editorial writer Eileen McNamara put it this way: "The battle of Belmont Hill is not about zoning; it's about fear of the unknown."

30   She described opposition to construction of the Catholic Cathedral of the Holy Cross in Boston's south end 121 years ago. The cathedral was designed to serve a "suspect immigrant Irish population" who faced fierce discrimination, McNamara wrote.

31   "Mormons, as suspect in modern-day Belmont as Catholics were in 19th-century Boston, are entitled to do what generations of believers have done before them: give expression to their faith in stone and steel."

32   In August, the LDS Church announced that it had purchased land for a temple in Billings' West End area known as "the Rims," which features a view of the city's magnificent rimrock formations.

33   Once again the church chose an upscale, elite neighborhood, and once again the neighbors resisted.

34   A group of residents quickly organized the Billings Rims Preservation Society (BRPS) "to protect the integrity of the Rims from inappropriate development," said Deborah Anspach, one of the group's leaders.

35   BRPS, made up of about 200 residents, raised all the same issues—traffic, property values, lighting, and so on. Anspach and her husband, John Hanson, set out on a tour of other LDS temples throughout the West and came back convinced that their neighborhood was the wrong place for such a large structure.

36   "Imagine this huge edifice at night, brightly lighted by search-lights," wrote Anspach and Hanson in a *Billings Gazette* guest editorial.

37   "Imagine a sky washed out by artificial lighting to the point the stars are dimmed. Imagine the size of the parking lot required to service such a building. . . . It would be akin to placing a high-rise directly in front of Mount Rushmore."

In order to move forward on building plans for a temple to serve   38
60,000 Mormons in a four-state region including Montana, the LDS
Church asked Billings to annex the 33.9 acres of church-owned land.
Annexation was needed so that the temple could have city services, including water and sewer lines and police and fire protection.

The annexation request was denied at an emotion-packed meeting in   39
late October. The church is planning to resubmit its request on Monday.

After the rejection, the town of Lovell, Wyo., 90 miles south of Bill-   40
ings, offered the church 160 acres complete with utility hookups. But
the LDS Church continued to focus its efforts on Billings.

Recently the Temple Task Force Committee invited neighbors to a   41
meeting to explain all about the temple and hear the neighbors' concerns.

"We came out after three hours without knowing much," Anspach   42
said. "The most concrete information we got was that they were thinking of modeling it after the one in St. Louis."

When opponents asked about height, they were given a range of   43
heights. They were told nothing about lighting, she said.

The problem is the design cannot be completed without annex-   44
ation, said Richard Larsen, chair of the temple committee and former
mayor of Billings.

"There isn't anyone who would like more information than Dick   45
Larsen," he said. But the church uses the process of getting site approval "to help custom design a temple for a specific area."

As the architects design the temple, they "will want to respond to   46
every neighborhood issue that is raised," Larsen said.

Opponents again have been labeled "anti-Mormon," a charge Ans-   47
pach vehemently denies.

"It is disheartening to us when those accusations are leveled at us,"   48
Anspach said. "This is not a religious issue at all. It is strictly a land-use
issue—a question of location, location, location."

Yet, she said, Mormons seem unwilling to take her statements at   49
face value.

Anspach and her husband keep a file marked, "Unacceptable," in   50
which she tosses all correspondence that attacks her character or the
LDS faith.

She acknowledged that the temple discussions have "ripped the   51
community apart."

"I knew there would be debate," she said, "but I honestly never ex-   52
pected the kind of hostility that has been generated."

★ Meaning and Understanding

1. Explain the author's assertion about neighborhoods and democracy in
   paragraph 1.

2. Why was the height of the spire such a hotly contested issue in Belmont?

3. "Every time anyone opposes the Mormons, they yell about 'anti-Mormon discrimination,'" one temple opponent states (paragraph 27). What evidence do you find in the article to support the Mormon charge of discrimination?

4. Why does the Mormon church want to move forward on plans for a temple in Billings?

5. What kinds of neighborhoods are Billings and Belmont? Is this important? Why do you think?

★ *Techniques and Strategies*

1. What is the writer's thesis? How does the title of the essay contribute to it?

2. When the writer states, "Boiling beneath it all was the issue of religious tolerance" (paragraph 23), what is your response to the metaphor? Does it help convince you of the point? Why?

3. What contribution to the article does the quote from Anspach and Hanson's *Billings Gazette* editorial make?

4. What does the writer's reference to Eileen McNamara's pro-LDS editorial contribute the argument?

5. The article appeared first in the *Salt Lake City Tribune*; Salt Lake City, as you know, has a large Mormon population. How does Stack reflect an understanding of her audience in the essay?

★ *Speaking of Values*

1. What do you think is the principle cause of conflict in Billings and Belmont? Why? Have you ever seen a neighborhood ripped apart by opposing views? What was at the bottom of the issue, in your opinion?

2. Can you imagine other situations in which issues of property rights and beliefs might clash in a similar way? What are they?

3. Eileen McNamara of the *Boston Globe* equates the treatment of the Mormons in Belmont to the contested construction of a nineteenth-century Catholic cathedral in Boston. Are these issues comparable? Why or why not?

4. What values are colliding here? What does the "collision" tell you about American religious values?

5. Anspach asserts that the issue is not a religious one: "It is strictly a land-use issue—a question of location, location, location." Why might you agree or disagree with this position?

★ *Values Conversation*

One critic of the Billings temple states that the conflict "ripped the community apart." Form groups and together come up with a list of suggestions for constructive community action in a comparable conflict. What values do your suggestions advance?

★ *Writing about Values*

1. Write an essay in which you describe an experience of religious discrimination that you observed, experienced, or learned about.

2. Write an essay that uses personal experience in which you examine the idea that "the neighborhood is democracy's smallest unit."

3. Write an essay in which you take up the issue that the essay discusses. Imagine that this incident is happening in your own neighborhood. Write a letter to the editor of your local paper in which you express your views and why you have them.

Richard Wright

Almos' a Man

Richard Wright (1908–1960) was a novelist and political activist. Largely
self-educated, he became one of America's most important writers, creating such works as *Native Son* (1940) and the autobiographical *Black Boy*
(1945). In this story he explores the consequences of a young man's decision to get a gun.

———— ★ ————

1   Dave struck out across the fields, looking homeward through paling
light. Whut's the usa talkin wid em niggers in the field? Anyhow, his
mother was putting supper on the table. Them niggers can't understan
nothing. One of these days he was going to get a gun and practice shooting, then they can't talk to him as though he were a little boy. He slowed,
looking at the ground. Shucks, Ah ain scareda them even ef they are big-
gern me! Aw, Ah know whut Ahma do.... Ahm going by ol Joe's sto n
git that Sears Roebuck catlog n look at them guns. Mabbe Ma will lemme
buy one when she gits mah pay from ol man Hawkins. Ahma beg her t
gimme some money. Ahm ol ernough to hava gun. Ahm seventeen. Almos a man. He strode, feeling his long, loose-jointed limbs. Shucks, a
man oughta hava little gun aftah he done worked hard all day....

2   He came in sight of Joe's store. A yellow lantern glowed on the
front porch. He mounted steps and went through the screen door, hearing it bang behind him. There was a strong smell of coal oil and mackerel fish. He felt very confident until he saw fat Joe walk in through the
rear door, then his courage began to ooze.

3   "Howdy, Dave! Whutcha want?"

4   "How yuh, Mistah Joe? Aw, Ah don wanna buy nothing. Ah jus
wanted t see ef yuhd lemme look at tha ol catlog erwhile."

5   "Sure! You wanna see it here?"

6   "Nawsuh. Ah wans t take it home wid me. Ahll bring it back termorrow when Ah come in from the fiels."

7   "You plannin on buyin something?"

8   "Yessuh."

9   "Your ma letting you have your own money now?"

10   "Shucks. Mistah Joe, Ahm gittin t be a man like anybody else!"

11   Joe laughed and wiped his greasy white face with a red bandanna.

12   "Whut you plannin on buyin?"

Dave looked at the floor, scratched his head, scratched his thigh, 13
and smiled. Then he looked up shyly.

"Ahll tell yuh, Mistah Joe, ef yuh promise yuh won't tell." 14

"I promise." 15

"Waal, Ahma buy a gun." 16

"A gun? Whut you want with a gun?" 17

"Ah wanna keep it." 18

"You ain't nothing but a boy. You don't need a gun." 19

"Aw, lemme have the catlog, Mistah Joe. Ahll bring it back." 20

Joe walked through the rear door. Dave was elated. He looked 21
around at barrels of sugar and flour. He heard Joe coming back. He
craned his neck to see if he were bringing the book. Yeah, he's got it!
Gawddog, he's got it!

"Here, but be sure you bring it back. It's the only one I got." 22

"Sho, Mistah Joe." 23

"Say, if you wanna buy a gun, why don't you buy one from me? I 24
gotta gun to sell."

"Will it shoot?" 25

"Sure it'll shoot." 26

"Whut kind is it?" 27

"Oh, it's kinda old.... A lefthand Wheeler. A pistol. A big one." 28

"Is it got bullets in it?" 29

"It's loaded." 30

"Kin Ah see it?" 31

"Where's your money?" 32

"Whut yuh wan fer it?" 33

"I'll let you have it for two dollars." 34

"Just two dollahs? Shucks, Ah could buy tha when Ah git mah pay." 35

"I'll have it here when you want it." 36

"Awright, suh. Ah be in fer it." 37

He went through the door, hearing it slam again behind him. 38
Ahma git some money from Ma n buy me a gun! Only two dollahs! He
tucked the thick catalogue under his arm and hurried.

"Where yuh been, boy?" His mother held a steaming dish of black- 39
eyed peas.

"Aw, Ma, Ah jus stopped down the road t talk wid th boys." 40

"Yuh know bettah than t keep suppah waitin." 41

He sat down, resting the catalogue on the edge of the table. 42

"Yuh git up from there and git to the well n wash yosef! Ah ain fee- 43
din no hogs in mah house!"

She grabbed his shoulder and pushed him. He stumbled out of the 44
room, then came back to get the catalogue.

"Whut this?" 45

"Aw, Ma, it's jusa catlog." 46

47   "Who yuh git it from?"

48   "From Joe, down at the sto."

49   "Waal, thas good. We kin use it around the house."

50   "Naw, Ma." He grabbed for it. "Gimme mah catlog, Ma."

51   She held onto it and glared at him.

52   "Quit hollerin at me! Whut's wrong wid yuh? Yuh crazy?"

53   "But Ma, please. It ain mine! It's Joe's! He tol me t bring it back t im termorrow."

54   She gave up the book. He stumbled down the back steps, hugging the thick book under his arm. When he had splashed water on his face and hands, he groped back to the kitchen and fumbled in a corner for the towel. He bumped into a chair; it clattered to the floor. The catalogue sprawled at his feet. When he had dried his eyes he snatched up the book and held it again under his arm. His mother stood watching him.

55   "Now, ef yuh gonna acka fool over that ol book, Ahll take it n burn it up."

56   "Naw, Ma, please."

57   "Waal, set down n be still!"

58   He sat down and drew the oil lamp close. He thumbed page after page, unaware of the food his mother set on the table. His father came in. Then his small brother.

59   "Whutcha got there, Dave?" his father asked.

60   "Jusa catlog," he answered, not looking up.

61   "Yawh, here they is!" His eyes glowed at blue and black revolvers. He glanced up, feeling sudden guilt. His father was watching him. He eased the book under the table and rested it on his knees. After the blessing was asked, he ate. He scooped up peas and swallowed fat meat without chewing. Buttermilk helped to wash it down. He did not want to mention money before his father. He would do much better by cornering his mother when she was alone. He looked at his father uneasily out of the edge of his eye.

62   "Boy, how come yuh don quit foolin wid tha book n eat yo suppah?"

63   "Yessuh."

64   "How yuh n ol man Hawkins gittin erlong?"

65   "Suh?"

66   "Can't yuh hear? Why don yuh lissen? Ah ast yu how wuz yuh n ol man Hawkins gittin erlong?"

67   "Oh, swell, Pa. Ah plows mo lan than anybody over there."

68   "Waal, yuh oughta keep yo min on whut yuh doin."

69   "Yessuh."

70   He poured his plate full of molasses and sopped at it slowly with a chunk of cornbread. When all but his mother had left the kitchen, he still sat and looked again at the guns in the catalogue. Lawd, ef Ah only had the pretty one! He could almost feel the slickness of the weapon with his fingers. If he had a gun like that he would polish it and keep it shining so it would never rust. N Ahd keep it loaded, by Gawd!

"Ma?"   71

"Hunh?"   72

"Ol man Hawkins give yuh mah money yit?"   73

"Yeah, but ain no usa yuh thinkin bout thowin nona it erway. Ahm   74
keepin tha money sos yuh kin have cloes t go to school this winter."

He rose and went to her side with the open catalogue in his palms.   75
She was washing dishes, her head bent low over a pan. Shyly he raised
the open book. When he spoke his voice was husky, faint.

"Ma, Gawd knows Ah wans one of these."   76

"One of whut?" she asked, not raising her eyes.   77

"One of these," he said again, not daring even to point. She glanced   78
up at the page, then at him with wide eyes.

"Nigger, is yuh gone plum crazy?"   79

"Aw, Ma—"   80

"Git outta here! Don yuh talk t me bout no gun! Yuh a fool!"   81

"Ma, Ah kin buy one fer two dollahs."   82

"Not ef Ah knows it yuh ain!"   83

"But yuh promised one more—"   84

"Ah don care whut Ah promised! Yuh ain nothing but a boy yit!"   85

"Ma, ef yuh lemme buy one Ahll never ast yuh fer nothing no mo."   86

"Ah tol yuh t git outta here! Yuh ain gonna toucha penny of tha   87
money fer no gun! Thas how come Ah has Mistah Hawkins t pay yo
wages t me, cause Ah knows yuh ain got no sense."

"But Ma, we needa gun. Pa ain got no gun. We needa gun in the   88
house. Yuh kin never tell whut might happen."

"Now don yuh try to maka fool outta me, boy! Ef we did hava gun   89
yuh wouldn't have it!"

He laid the catalogue down and slipped his arm around her waist.   90
"Aw, Ma, Ah done worked hard alls summer n ain ast yuh fer nothin, is
Ah, now?"

"Thas whut yuh spose t do!"   91

"But Ma, Ah wants a gun. Yuh kin lemme have two dollahs outta mah   92
money. Please Ma. I kin give it to Pa. . . . Please, Ma! Ah loves yuh, Ma."

When she spoke her voice came soft and low.   93

"Whut yuh wan wida gun, Dave? Yuh don need no gun. Yuhll git   94
in trouble. N ef yo Pa jus thought Ah let yuh have money t buy a gun
he'd hava fit."

"Ahll hide it, Ma. It ain but two dollahs."   95

"Lawd, chil, whuts wrong wid yuh?"   96

"Ain nothing wrong, Ma. Ahm almos a man now. Ah wans a gun."   97

"Who gonna sell yuh a gun?"   98

"Ol Joe at the sto."   99

"N it don cos but two dollahs?"   100

"Thas all, Ma. Just two dollahs. Please, Ma."   101

She was stacking the plates away; her hands moved slowly, reflec-   102
tively. Dave kept an anxious silence. Finally, she turned to him.

103   "Ahll let yuh git tha gun ef yuh promise me one thing."

104   "Whuts tha, Ma?"

105   "Yuh bring it straight back t me, yuh hear? It'll be fer Pa."

106   "Yessum! Lemme go now, Ma."

107   She stooped, turned slightly to one side, raised the hem of her dress, rolled down the top of her stocking, and came up with a slender wad of bills.

108   "Here," she said. "Lawd knows yuh don need no gun. But yer Pa does. Yuh bring it right back t me, yuh hear? Ahma put it up. Now ef yuh don, Ahma have yuh Pa lick yuh so hard yuh won ferget it."

109   "Yessum."

110   He took the money, ran down the steps, and across the yard.

111   "Dave! Yuuuuuuh Daaaaaave!"

112   He heard, but he was not going to stop now. "Naw, Lawd!"

113   The first movement he made the following morning was to reach under his pillow for the gun. In the gray light of dawn he held it loosely, feeling a sense of power. Could killa man wida gun like this. Kill anybody, black or white. And if he were holding this gun in his hand nobody could run over him; they would have to respect him. It was a big gun, with a long barrel and a heavy handle. He raised and lowered it in his hand, marveling at its weight.

114   He had not come straight home with it as his mother had asked; instead he had stayed out in the fields, holding the weapon in his hand, aiming it now and then at some imaginary foe. But he had not fired it; he had been afraid that his father might hear. Also he was not sure he knew how to fire it.

115   To avoid surrendering the pistol he had not come into the house until he knew that all were asleep. When his mother had tiptoed to his bedside late that night and demanded the gun, he had first played 'possum; then he had told her that the gun was hidden outdoors, that he would bring it to her in the morning. Now he lay turning it slowly in his hands. He broke it, took out the cartridges, felt them, and then put them back.

116   He slid out of bed, got a long strip of old flannel from a trunk, wrapped the gun in it, and tied it to his naked thigh while it was still loaded. He did not go in to breakfast. Even though it was not yet daylight, he started for Jim Hawkins' plantation. Just as the sun was rising he reached the barns where the mules and plows were kept.

117   "Hey! That you, Dave?"

118   He turned. Jim Hawkins stood eying him suspiciously.

119   "What're yuh doing here so early?"

120   "Ah didn't know Ah wuz gittin up so early, Mistah Hawkins. Ah wuz fixin t hitch up ol Jenny n take her t the fiels."

121   "Good. Since you're here so early, how about plowing that stretch down by the woods?"

"Suits me, Mistah Hawkins." 122

"O.K. Go to it!" 123

He hitched Jenny to a plow and started across the fields. Hot dog! 124
This was just what he wanted. If he could get down by the woods, he
could shoot his gun and nobody would hear. He walked behind the
plow, hearing the traces creaking, feeling the gun tied tight to his thigh.

When he reached the woods, he plowed two whole rows before he 125
decided to take out the gun. Finally he stopped, looked in all directions, then untied the gun and held it in his hand. He turned to the
mule and smiled.

"Know whut this is, Jenny? Naw, yuh wouldn't know! Yuhs just ol 126
mule! Anyhow, this is a gun, n it kin shoot, by Gawd!"

He held the gun at arm's length. Whut t hell, Ahma shoot this 127
thing! He looked at Jenny again.

"Lissen here, Jenny! When Ah pull this ol trigger Ah don wan yuh 128
t run n acka fool now."

Jenny stood with head down, her short ears pricked straight. Dave 129
walked off about twenty feet, held the gun far out from him, at arm's
length, and turned his head. Hell, he told himself, Ah ain afraid. The
gun felt loose in his fingers; he waved it wildly for a moment. Then
he shut his eyes and tightened his forefinger. Bloom! The report half-
deafened him and he thought his right hand was torn from his arm. He
heard Jenny whinnying and galloping over the field, and he found
himself on his knees squeezing his fingers hard between his legs. His
hand was numb; he jammed it into his mouth, trying to warm it, trying
to stop the pain. The gun lay at his feet. He did not quite know what
had happened. He stood up and stared at the gun as though it were a
live thing. He gritted his teeth and kicked the gun. Yuh almos broke
mah arm! He turned to look for Jenny; she was far over the fields, tossing her head and kicking wildly.

"Hol on there, ol mule!" 130

When he caught up with her she stood trembling, walling her big 131
white eyes at him. The plow was far away; the traces had broken. Then
Dave stopped short, looking, not believing. Jenny was bleeding. Her
left side was red and wet with blood. He went closer. Lawd have
mercy! Wondah did Ah shoot this mule? He grabbed for Jenny's mane.
She flinched, snorted, whirled, tossing her head.

"Hol on now! Hol on." 132

Then he saw the hole in Jenny's side, right between the ribs. It was 133
round, wet, red. A crimson stream streaked down the front leg, flowing
fast. Good Gawd! Ah wuznt shootin at tha mule. He felt panic. He
knew he had to stop that blood, or Jenny would bleed to death. He had
never seen so much blood in all his life. He chased the mule for half a
mile, trying to catch her. Finally she stopped, breathing hard, stumpy
tail half arched. He caught her mane and led her back to where the

plow and gun lay. Then he stopped and grabbed handfuls of damp black earth and tried to plug the bullet hole. Jenny shuddered, whinnied, and broke from him.

134   "Hol on! Hol on now!"

135   He tried to plug it again, but blood came anyhow. His fingers were hot and sticky. He rubbed dirt hard into his palms, trying to dry them. Then again he attempted to plug the bullet hole, but Jenny shied away, kicking her heels high. He stood helpless. He had to do something. He ran at Jenny; she dodged him. He watched a red stream of blood flow down Jenny's leg and form a bright pool at her feet.

136   "Jenny... Jenny..." he called weakly.

137   His lips trembled. She's bleeding t death! He looked in the direction of home, wanting to go back, wanting to get help. But he saw the pistol lying in the damp black clay. He had a queer feeling that if he only did something, this would not be; Jenny would not be there bleeding to death.

138   When he went to her this time, she did not move. She stood with sleepy, dreamy eyes; and when he touched her she gave a low-pitched whinny and knelt to the ground, her front knees slopping in blood.

139   "Jenny... Jenny..." he whispered.

140   For a long time she held her neck erect; then her head sank, slowly. Her ribs swelled with a mighty heave and she went over.

141   Dave's stomach felt empty, very empty. He picked up the gun and held it gingerly between his thumb and forefinger. He buried it at the foot of a tree. He took a stick and tried to cover the pool of blood with dirt—but what was the use? There was Jenny lying with her mouth open and her eyes walled and glassy. He could not tell Jim Hawkins he had shot his mule. But he had to tell something. Yeah, Ahll tell em Jenny started gittin wil n fell on the joint of the plow.... But that would hardly happen to a mule. He walked across the field slowly, head down.

142   It was sunset. Two of Jim Hawkins' men were over near the edge of the woods digging a hole in which to bury Jenny. Dave was surrounded by a knot of people; all of them were looking down at the dead mule.

143   "I don't see how in the world it happened," said Jim Hawkins for the tenth time.

144   The crowd parted and Dave's mother, father, and small brother pushed into the center.

145   "Where Dave?" his mother called.

146   "There he is," said Jim Hawkins.

147   His mother grabbed him.

148   "Whut happened, Dave? Whut yuh done?"

149   "Nothing."

150   "C'mon, boy, talk," his father said.

151   Dave took a deep breath and told the story he knew nobody believed.

"Waal," he drawled. "Ah brung ol Jenny down here sos Ah could do   152
mah plowin. Ah plowed bout two rows, just like yuh see." He stopped
and pointed at the long rows of upturned earth. "Then something musta
been wrong wid ol Jenny. She wouldn't ack right a-tall. She started snor-
tin n kickin her heels. Ah tried to hol her, but she pulled erway, rearin n
goin on. Then when the point of the plow was stickin up in the air, she
swung erroun n twisted herself back on it. . . . She stuck hersef n started t
bleed. N fo Ah could do anything, she wuz dead."

"Did you ever hear of anything like that in all your life?" asked Jim   153
Hawkins.

There were white and black standing in the crowd. They mur-   154
mured. Dave's mother came close to him and looked hard into his face.

"Tell the truth, Dave," she said.   155

"Looks like a bullet hole ter me," said one man.   156

"Dave, whut yuh do wid tha gun?" his mother asked.   157

The crowd surged in, looking at him. He jammed his hands into his   158
pockets, shook his head slowly from left to right, and backed away. His
eyes were wide and painful.

"Did he hava gun?" asked Jim Hawkins.   159

"By Gawd, Oh tol yuh tha wuz a gunwound," said a man, slapping   160
his thigh.

His father caught his shoulders and shook him till his teeth rattled.   161

"Tell whut happened, yuh rascal! Tell whut. . . ."   162

Dave looked at Jenny's stiff legs and began to cry.   163

"Whut yuh do wid tha gun?" his mother asked.   164

"Come on and tell the truth," said Hawkins. "Ain't nobody going   165
to hurt you. . . ."

His mother crowded close to him.   166

"Did yuh shoot tha mule, Dave?"   167

Dave cried, seeing blurred white and black faces.   168

"Ahh ddinnt gggo tt sshoooot hher. . . . Ah sssswear off Gawd Ahh   169
ddint. . . . Ah wuz a-tryin t sssee ef the ol gggun would sshoot—"

"Where yuh git the gun from?" his father asked.   170

"Ah got it from Joe, at the sto."   171

"Where yuh git the money?"   172

"Ma give it t me."   173

"He kept worryin me, Bob. . . . Ah had t. . . . Ah tol im t bring the   174
gun right back t me. . . . It was fer yuh, the gun."

"But how yuh happen to shoot that mule?" asked Jim Hawkins.   175

"Ah wuznt shootin at the mule, Mistah Hawkins. The gun jumped   176
when Ah pulled the trigger. . . N for Ah knowed anything Jenny was
there a-bleedin."

Somebody in the crowd laughed. Jim Hawkins walked close to   177
Dave and looked into his face.

"Well, looks like you have bought you a mule, Dave."   178

179   "Ah swear fo Gawd, Ah didn't go t kill the mule, Mistah Hawkins!"

180   "But you killed her!"

181   All the crowd was laughing now. They stood on tiptoe and poked heads over one another's shoulders.

182   "Well, boy, looks like yuh done bought a dead mule! Hahaha!"

183   "Ain tha ershame."

184   "Hohohohoho."

185   Dave stood, head down, twisting his feet in the dirt.

186   "Well, you needn't worry about it, Bob," said Jim Hawkins to Dave's father. "Just let the boy keep on working and pay me two dollars a month."

187   "Whut yuh wan fer yo mule, Mistah Hawkins?"

188   Jim Hawkins screwed up his eyes.

189   "Fifty dollars."

190   "Whut yuh do wid tha gun?" Dave's father demanded.

191   Dave said nothing.

192   "Yuh wan me t take a tree lim n beat yuh till yuh talk!"

193   "Nawsuh!"

194   "Whut yuh do wid it?"

195   "Ah thowed it erway."

196   "Where?"

197   "Ah . . . Ah thowed it in the creek."

198   "Waal, c mon home. N firs thing in the mawnin git to tha creek n fin tha gun."

199   "Yessuh."

200   "Whut yuh pay fer it?"

201   "Two dollahs."

202   "Take tha gun n git yo money back n carry it t Mistah Hawkins, yuh hear? N don fergit Ahma lam you black bottom good fer this! Now march yosef on home, suh!"

203   Dave turned and walked slowly. He heard people laughing. Dave glared, his eyes welling with tears. Hot anger bubbled in him. Then he swallowed and stumbled on.

204   That night Dave did not sleep. He was glad that he had gotten out of killing the mule so easily, but he was hurt. Something hot seemed to turn over inside him each time he remembered how they had laughed. He tossed on his bed, feeling his hard pillow. N Pa says he's gonna beat me. . . . He remembered other beatings, and his back quivered. Naw, naw, Ah sho don wan im t beat me tha way no mo. . . . Dam em all! Nobody ever gave him anything. All he did was work. They treat me like a mule. . . . N then they beat me. . . . He gritted his teeth. N Ma had t tell on me.

205   Well, if he had to, he would take old man Hawkins that two dollars. But that meant selling the gun. And he wanted to keep that gun. Fifty dollahs fer a dead mule.

He turned over, thinking how he had fired the gun. He had an itch
to fire it again. Ef other men kin shoota gun, by Gawd, Ah kin! He was
still listening. Mebbe they all sleepin now.... The house was still. He
heard the soft breathing of his brother. Yes, now! He would go down
and get that gun and see if he could fire it! He eased out of bed and
slipped into overalls.

The moon was bright. He ran almost all the way to the edge of the
woods. He stumbled over the ground, looking for the spot where he
had buried the gun. Yeah, here it is. Like a hungry dog scratching for a
bone he pawed it up. He puffed his black cheeks and blew dirt from the
trigger and barrel. He broke it and found four cartridges unshot. He
looked around; the fields were filled with silence and moonlight. He
clutched the gun stiff and hard in his fingers. But as soon as he wanted
to pull the trigger, he shut his eyes and turned his head. Naw, Ah can't
shoot wid mah eyes closed n mah head turned. With effort he held his
eyes open; then he squeezed. Blooooom! He was stiff, not breathing.
The gun was still in his hands. Dammit, he'd done it! He fired again.
Blooooom! He smiled. Blooooom! Blooooom! Click, click. There! It was
empty. If anybody could shoot a gun, he could. He put the gun into his
hip pocket and started across the fields.

When he reached the top of a ridge he stood straight and proud in
the moonlight, looking at Jim Hawkins's big white house, feeling the
gun sagging in his pocket. Lawd, ef Ah had jus one mo bullet Ahd taka
shot at tha house. Ahd like t scare ol man Hawkins jussa little.... jussa
enough to let im know Dave Sanders is a man.

To his left the road curved, running to the tracks of the Illinois Central. He jerked his head, listening. From far off came a faint hoooof-
hoooof; hoooof-hoooof; hoooof-hoooof.... That's number eight. He
took a swift look at Jim Hawkins's white house; he thought of Pa, of
Ma, of his little brother, and the boys. He thought of the dead mule
and heard hoooof-hoooof; hoooof-hoooof; hoooof-hoooof.... He stood
rigid. Two dollahs a mont. Les see now.... Tha means itll take bout
two years. Shucks! Ahll be dam! He started down the road, toward the
tracks. Yeah, here she comes! He stood beside the track and held himself stiffly. Here she comes, erroun the ben.... C mon, yuh slow poke!
C mon! He had his hand on his gun; something quivered in his stomach. Then the train thundered past, the gray and brown boxcars rum-
bling and clinking. He gripped the gun tightly; then he jerked his hand
out of his pocket. Ah betcha Bill wouldn't do it! Ah betcha.... The cars
slid past, steel grinding upon steel. Ahm riding yuh ternight so hep
me Gawd! He was hot all over. He hesitated just a moment; then he
grabbed, pulled atop of a car, and lay flat. He felt his pocket; the gun
was still there. Ahead the long rails went glinting in moonlight,
stretching away, away to somewhere, somewhere where he could be a
man....

★ Meaning and Understanding

1. Characterize Dave. In what way or ways is he "almos'" a man?

2. What is the writer's main idea in the piece?

3. What does Dave do to Jenny? What is his initial response to his own action?

4. What does Dave's father tell him to do? What does Dave do? Why?

5. Who is black and who is white in the story? Are these facts important? Why or why not?

★ Techniques and Strategies

1. Consider the dialogue used in the story. What does it contribute to the story's meaning?

2. What effect does the use of dialect have on the story?

3. Locate places where the writing takes you close to Dave's consciousness. How effective are these renderings of thought? Wright integrates a standard third-person narrative with Dave's innermost thoughts and feelings. What effect does this technique have on the quality of the story? Why didn't Wright relate the narrative in first person?

4. What is the relation between the title of the story and its theme? How does irony come into play?

5. What imagery adds particular visual quality to this story, in your opinion?

★ Speaking of Values

1. What idea of manhood does the story consider? How prevalent is such an idea now in America? In your life?

2. Dave thinks, "Them niggers can'understan nothing." What is the story's attitude to this "racial" reference? What is your attitude toward such language—in art and in life?

3. In what ways is the story about the rites of passage through adolescence to adulthood? How do some of the thoughts and feelings characterize men and women alike? In what ways is this story only about men, do you think?

4. Of all the events in the story, which do you think leads Dave to run off at the end? How is his behavior typical of youths trying to become adults? How is it atypical?

5. What insights, if any, does Wright's story provide about random violence? How does it help you understand the reckless, senseless violence we hear about regularly in American society?

★ *Values Conversation*

Form groups and identify reasons for youth violence. Is it caused by a crisis in values? What else do you think contributes to the lure of violence? Why don't the apparent consequences of violence deter adolescents?

★ *Writing about Values*

1. Write an essay in which you discuss the pros and cons of the right to bear arms—or the wisdom of the regulation of guns in American society.

2. Write an essay in which you discuss a time when you made or witnessed someone making a poor decision because of immaturity.

3. Consider the ways in which a symbol or symbols attach to an abstraction—such as the gun to "manhood." Write an essay in which you explore the causes or the effects of the linkage.

Erica Manfred

I Was a Red-Diaper Baby

Erica Manfred is a journalist who has published in *Parenting Magazine* and the *New York Times Magazine*. In this essay she describes life with her American communist parents in the 1960s.

———— ★ ————

1   I never thought I would feel nostalgic about Communism. As a 60's activist and child of lefty parents, I once took as gospel beliefs that now seem quaint: human beings are basically good; if people, not capitalists, owned the means of production, poverty would disappear; economic equality could cure all social ills. Misguided and dangerous though Communism was, the passion for social justice and compassion for working people that it represented is gone from the planet, and I, for one, miss it.

2   Although to their deaths they never admitted it to me, my parents were both card-carrying Communists. How do I know? I can't tell you. I was brought up never to reveal such information. When friends visited my parents, instead of telling me to put out the cheese and crackers, I was instructed to hide The National Guardian, a genuinely mind-numbing lefty publication. In addition to being told never to get into a car with a stranger, I was instructed never to answer a stranger's questions—the questioner might be F.B.I.

3   As a teen-ager, I was secretly disdainful of my peers because they were oblivious to the suffering of others. My family and I were part of a morally superior secret society that cared more about the fate of the world than did our bourgeois, materialistic neighbors. We—whose showplace home could have been in House and Garden—worried about poverty, racism and injustice, while they worried about how to keep up with the Joneses. Pursued by the evil forces of anti-Communism, we did not name names. As it happened, no one asked my parents to name anyone, but they swore they wouldn't have anyway.

4   My grandparents were socialists who escaped the ghettos of Russia to fight for the right to unionize in America. My parents were Communists who fought for social justice in the 1930s. As the third generation of this proud leftist family, I wanted to make good.

5   As an activist in the 60's, however, I lacked oomph. I missed out on the freedom rides—too obsessed with a guy in my math class. I overslept for the big civil rights demonstration. I did climb over the wall to

the Pentagon in 1967 but was too chicken (and too cold) to stick around for the tear gas. I joined a women's consiousness-raising group but was so intimidated by all those fierce women that I dropped out.

In 1968, I went to Cuba and signed up for the Venceremos Brigade, American leftists who were invited to help with the sugar cane harvest. That experience was my reality check.   6

I'd spent my life on the ideological left in self-styled anarchist groups with utopian dreams of participatory democracy. I discovered that an actual Communist dictatorship bore no resemblance to my fantasy. While the Cubans mechanically spewed forth the party line, the notorious Weathermen, who had joined the brigade to recruit new members, used Maoist brainwashing techniques, like all-night criticism and self-criticism sessions, to induce us to sign up. I realized I'd rather be ruled by Richard Nixon than by the kids in the Weather tent. At least you could vote him out.   7

When I got back, I traded in my politics and went into therapy. But I feared disgracing my family. I felt disloyal about being more concerned with my own turmoil than the world's. My mother wanted to know who was supposed to carry the torch of radicalism into the next century. But what torch?   8

The Weatherpeople were clearly delusional as well as dangerous. My parents passionately believed that the Soviet Union was the promised land, another treacherous fantasy. I recognized that anarchism was a utopian crock. What was left? Did political passion, no matter how idealistic, inevitably lead to fanaticism? I became a cynic, disbelieving any group's claims to a corner on the truth.   9

What remains of the left in today's me-first political climate leaves no room for grand social visions The younger generation of leftists has splintered into interest groups—each defending its turf with more arrogant political correctness than my die-hard Stalinist parents—without any unifying vision of a just and compassionate society.   10

Though I long ago dropped the torch, my upbringing has had certain long-term effects. I cannot cross a picket line. I am constitutionally averse to Republicans. I feel guilty every time I miss a demonstration for a good cause. (Lucky for me there aren't too many of those these days.) As with other wishy-washy liberals, my political life consists of voting for the least objectionable candidate.   11

I still long, though, for a political movement I could wholeheartedly embrace. In my fantasy party we would support the interests of the poor and working classes, not the rich; we would fight for the rights of animals and the environment; we would combat discrimination wherever we found it, and, most important, we would not only tolerate but encourage dissent.   12

Maybe the next generation.   13

★ *Meaning and Understanding*

1. What does the writer mean by the term "red diaper"?

2. What details of family background—parents, grandparents—does Manfred provide? Why do you think she includes those details?

3. What does "Venceremos" mean? What was the Venceremos Brigade? Summarize Manfred's experience with the brigade.

4. Who were the "notorious Weathermen"? What does the writer say about them?

5. What is Manfred's attitude toward leftist causes? Is it simple or complex? How do you know?

★ *Techniques and Strategies*

1. In paragraph 1 the writer talks of the "gospel beliefs" she once held and now finds "quaint." What is the effect of her rendition of these beliefs? Do they sound like full-bodied ideas? Simple-minded notions? Nonsense? What in the phrasing contributes to the effect? What historical or social realities might work against these beliefs in the reader's mind?

2. The writer offers a description of her own character. Where do you find this? How effective is the passage? How does it make use of description and illustration? How does character or personality seem to contribute to the writer's political activity?

3. Does the writer state a thesis directly? If so, where? What is the thesis?

4. The essay explores several contradictions. Identify a few that you find interesting. Where are they? What is the central contradiction? Do you find it believable? Why or why not? How do the essay's contradictions relate to the essay's thesis?

5. How effective is the conclusion of the essay? What impact does the next to last paragraph have? The last sentence? What ideas do they convey? How does the tone of the ending seem to you? Heartfelt? Wise-guyish? Urgent? Explain your views.

★ *Speaking of Values*

1. What values is the writer suggesting in her essay? Are the different values related to each other? If so, how?

2. There is a tension in the piece between cynicism and sincere belief. How possible is it for the two mental modes to coexist? How do cyni-

cism and hopefulness interact in people? What value does each—and the two together—have in people's lives?

3. Leftist values and movements have significantly influenced and shaped thinking and events in the last two centuries. In what ways? Does the essay convey your sense of communist and left-of-liberal realities and ideas? How?

4. The writer says she "recognized that anarchism was a utopian crock." What is anarchism? What in it is utopian? What other ideas or movements do you consider utopian? What do you think about utopian ideas? What value, if any, can they have in our lives?

5. Manfred links her ambitions with her family's past philosophy and actions (paragraphs 3–4). In what ways do the beliefs of our families influence our goals and ambitions? How do your family's political, social, or economic attitudes influence your goals? Is this for good or bad, in your view? Why?

★ Values Conversation

Manfred writes, "Maybe the next generation," as she identifies the social longings that live in her still. Form groups and identify the social dreams members of your group hold. For example, do you wish for equality for all people? The end to poverty? Uniform health care? Is there a commonality of dreams among group members? Do the social dreams have substance or are they platitudes? Do the dreams seem realizable? How? When? Report your group's work to the class at large.

★ Writing about Values

1. Write an essay in which you define nostalgia—and illustrate it through personal experiences or observations.

2. Do some research on a social movement in America—socialism, anarchism, communism, utopianism, or some other movement you're interested in. Write an essay on some aspect of the movement—its core beliefs, strategies, appeal, excesses, enemies, key moment, or whatever your research suggests is an interesting area of the subject.

3. Write about a belief that you once embraced but have come to distance yourself from. What was the belief? What happened to disenchant you? What do you think about the idea now? Do some affection and hope still linger? Develop a strong thesis about the nature of your connection to the belief—and support the thesis with concrete details and examples.

Values in Review

1. Dubus, Crane, Wright, and Norman all consider the subject of war, violence, and identity. Choose at least two selections and identify a central perception that the writings share. How do the selections relate to one another?

2. Carter, Paine, and Roosevelt present three public leaders' views about religion. How do their positions differ? Where do you stand among the three?

3. Erica Manfred looks to particular secular beliefs as a spiritual source. What does the central figure in each essay believe? How do the ideas relate to one another?

4. How would William J. Bennett react to Erica Manfred's essay? Would he consider her an example of "America's spiritual despair"? Why or why not? Write a letter from Bennett to Manfred about the issues she raises.

AMERICAN VALUES

Focus on *Liberty*

The Declaration of Independence asserts *Liberty* as the second inalienable right of American citizens. The essays, stories, and poems you have read in the three chapters of Part II have looked at liberty from a variety of viewpoints. What is your view of *Liberty* now, from the American values perspective? Write an essay to address the notion of liberty informed by your reading here and supported by your experience. You may choose to develop a definition of liberty, or to classify the various kinds of liberty you see, or to argue for or against the essence of liberty as you observe it. You might choose to compare and (or) contrast the concept of liberty today with the concept of liberty advanced and practiced by our forebears.

Part III

The Pursuit of Happiness

What Jefferson meant by "the pursuit of happiness" is a question that historians have debated vigorously, almost as if it were the meaning of happiness itself. Perhaps Jefferson meant to distinguish himself, and his new nation, from the rights that John Locke declared essential "life, liberty, and property." Perhaps replacing the word "property" with the phrase "pursuit of happiness" reflects Jefferson's mistrust of entrenched wealth and ownership. Historian Gary Wills has suggested that "pursuit of happiness" was a common enough contemporary phrase for Jefferson to use comfortably and without confusion. If so, what did the term mean to eighteenth-century minds? That natural laws rule humans just as physical laws rule objects? That it is natural for humans to move away from pain and toward happiness—just as it is natural for an apple to fall to earth? And, finally, what is the nature of that happiness? Did Jefferson have a particular moral meaning here—the greatest happiness for the greatest numbers of people? Private rights to engender public well-being and happiness?

For centuries, against old texts and new realities, scholars have reflected on the curious phrase "pursuit of happiness." Meanwhile, citizens have reflected on what gives us happiness—as individuals and communities and as a nation. And immigrants have sought, and still seek, in our nation a new life promising happiness, or even just the chance of it if one pursues the dream.

Few would deny that love is essential to happiness. This last part, then, begins with Chapter 8, Love. Here writers explore love as a value from youth through the advancing stages of life and within varying lifestyles. Poe's poem "Annabel Lee" shows a relation extending from childhood to adulthood, even beyond the grave. Through either personal reflection, political polemic, or both, several selections consider love's relation to marriage. And here we get to see many different definitions of marriage—monogamous, heterosexual, homosexual, polygamous. Elizabeth Joseph, for example, calmly and rationally supports a connubial relation that makes her one of many wives for the same husband, all living happily together (she says) as a single family unit. Andrew Sullivan and Lisa Schiffren seem to debate each other about the distinctly twenty-first century issue of same-sex marriages, a volatile concept to governments and religions alike. Selections also consider sexuality and eroticism in our culture—from the place of sex in children's lives to the role of economics in the creation of the modern man. Barbara Ehrenreich sees the advent of *Playboy* magazine and its incredible success as a phenomenon of the 1950s that boldly challenged family life and traditional family responsibility. With tongue in cheek, John Collier in his story "The Chaser" imagines a drug-induced love so powerful and overwhelming that it requires an antidote. Love—the selections seem to ask—what is that entity and what have we made of it? And, perhaps most important for the context of this book, how does love play its role in the pursuit of happiness, and what does the practice of love say about American values?

In Chapter 9, Wealth and Leisure, we find reflections on the American dream as myth and reality. The New World promised for centuries a new life with new wealth, if one exerted effort and will to accomplish. In "The Way to Wealth," Benjamin Franklin, the voice of practical industriousness, warns us from the eighteenth century to work hard and avoid idleness. Keep your nose to the grindstone, he says to his readers. Yet what is the true meaning of the promised good life? Even Franklin knew that few readers would heed his advice to the letter. Has America brought new freedom and new leisure in its inalienable right to the pursuit of happiness? Many essays in this chapter explore our pastimes as measures of our sensibilities; in sports, travel, and movies, for example, writers see American values at play and at risk. William Zinsser reveals the joys of travel to exotic lands and rejoices in leisure explorations, Charles McGrath calls for a more relaxed attitude about children's television programming—and both of these writers stand in opposition to Franklin's admonitions not to squander time. For our national pastime, Hank Aaron, a baseball legend, bristles as he watches the sport change from a moral proving ground to a commercial trap. Marcus Mabry looks at the "two worlds" of America—privilege and poverty—to show the psychological burdens of leaving one for the other. For the leisure activity of hunting, David Stout reminds us of the lives at stake. Dorothy Parker and Mari Evans in separate pieces look at moments in which rich meets poor, humorously revealing the basic misunderstanding between the classes in our "classless" society.

No student of modern society can overstate the real or imagined role of scientific and technological advance in the realization of the American dream. In Chapter 10, Science and Technology, we examine America's imaginings in these areas alongside attendant realities. Again we turn to Benjamin Franklin, this time for his voice as an enthusiast of science in the spirit of England's Francis Bacon, looking to a future of "man over matter." In Franklin's imagination, science would improve the quality of life dramatically, and he wished that it also could improve human character. In the next century, Edgar Allen Poe in his poem "To Science" chastises science, "Who alterest all things with thy peering eyes": the poetic imagination and scientific methodology, he believed, conflicted with each other. How could such enmity produce happiness? Nathaniel Hawthorne, perhaps the country's most famous moralist, shows the dangers of the "altering" scientific impulse in his famous short story "The Birthmark." Other selections here show writers positioned between these extremes of love for, and antipathy toward, science's ways. We see the routes facing women whose passion for science leads them to careers that meet roadblocks and demand unreasonable compromise. Harold Herzog's "Human Morality and Animal Research" explores the complexities of ethics and scientific advancement. Some writers consider the brave new world of computer technology and the power and pollution of electronic and industrial proliferation. And finally we see the values at work among the men and women who actually "do" science. All in all, this chapter asks us to examine science and technology as part of American values—as conduits to imagined dreams, future happiness, and unexpected nightmares.

Finally, we consider in Chapter 11, Individual and Community, a theme that defines America in its most human complexity. One's view of self and society and their successful balance certainly are major factors in the happiness equation. Writers have made much of the "rugged individualism" that supported American expansion. But equally potent, others have suggested, is an American community spirit—from Native American "nations," to abolitionist "undergrounds," to today's "communitarianism." The last chapter in Part III amounts to a lively examination of this tension. Emerson advances "Self-Reliance" and adherence to a personal truth; Whitman in "Song of Myself' celebrates his own human spirit and life force. Jules Feiffer shows how a cartoonist created Superman, one of America's enduring myths—"the ultimate assimilationist fantasy" in Feiffer's words. James Madison, one of the nation's founders, considers the dangers of factions in a burgeoning democracy. But what are we to make of these beliefs? Do they oppose community? Do they praise self as an instance of abundant existence and our best bet to profound connection with others and the Other? Or are they simply the romantic assertions of the self-absorbed? When we turn to Bret Harte in "The Outcasts of Poker Flat," we see an oddly defined community that began in self-absorption and culminated in mutual support and dependency. Lucie Prinz inveighs against an adult society that will not take responsibility for the behavior of its youth. Factions and outcasts, immigrants and aliens—the writings in Chapter 11 examine these contradictory yet related themes as concrete realities and conceptual challenges to the legacy of a democratic republic and its defining values.

To what lengths, then, do we go to pursue happiness? What in fact is happiness? Why should a new government concern itself with the joy of its people and posterity's assurance of it? Finally, what values does our search for happiness reveal about us and the world we inhabit?

Chapter 8
Love

Marriage breakup

Falling in love

Wedding ceremonies

Same-sex marriage

Childhood sweethearts

Monogamy and polygamy

Sex is for adults

Walter Kirn

My Parents' Bust-Up, and Mine

Born in 1962, Walter Kirn is the American cultural correspondent for the British Broadcasting Company (BBC) and the author of two books, *My Hard Bargain* (1990) and *She Needed Me* (1992). In this essay Kirn describes the effects of his parents' divorce in his life.

———— ★ ————

1   My parents stayed together for the sake of the children. When the children were grown and settled, my parents divorced—for their own sake. My brother was 25 and single, studying for a graduate degree; I was 27 and newly married, about to publish my first book of stories. Because Mom and Dad had decided to tough it out (29 years in all), we faced their breakup not as vulnerable kids but as self-sufficient adults. You'd think it would have been easier that way: no custody battle, no child-support brouhaha, no change of schools, no teen-age identity crisis.

2   You'd think I'd *thank* my parents for their decision.

3   Here is what I learned though: when the rug is pulled out from under you emotionally, it isn't necessarily an advantage to be standing on your own two feet. Nothing is quite so shocking, somehow, as news you have been half-expecting all your life.

4   I got the word on a pay phone, in a Salt Lake City Dairy Queen. My wife and I had been camping in the Rockies and were ready to fly home to New York. My parents, who'd been camping with us, had already driven back to Minnesota, the state where I grew up. The trip had been tense, my parents grumpy and distant, but I felt I had to phone them. I had read something wild in the local paper: a dead school friend of mine whose funeral had been a month ago (his overturned raft was found floating in Puget Sound) had turned up alive in a tiny western jail.

5   "Karl faked his own death!" I told my mother. "Can you believe it?"

6   "Walt, I'm leaving your father. I'm moving out tonight. Our marriage is over. I'm sorry. We're really finished."

7   I stood there. All around me families licked ice-cream cones. Big happy Mormon families, by the looks of them.

8   "I'm sorry," my mother said. Her voice was gravelly. "Maybe you could call your brother and give him the telephone number where I'll be staying."

When I hung up, my wife asked what was wrong. We'd been mar- 9
ried less than two years, and I knew in an instant that we would not
have wed if what had just happened had happened years earlier. I
wouldn't have had the faith, the optimism. Indeed, I was already losing it.

"They're getting divorced," I said. 10

My wife just sighed. Her own parents had split up when she was 11
tiny. "It's probably for the best," she said. "After seeing them together,
I'm not surprised."

"Well, I am!" I shouted. "*I'm* surprised!" 12

I was and I wasn't; I just needed to shout. I shouted a lot that year. 13
Shouted so much, in fact, and so crazily (often while drunk and often in
my sleep) that by year's end I'd be divorced myself.

Let's take the bust-ups in order, though. 14

Let's follow the long, branching crack from the beginning. 15

Some people grew up during the Depression, some during World 16
War II or Vietnam. That's how they place themselves historically; as
children of some great, defining calamity.

I grew up during Divorce. 17

Though it took two more decades to infect me personally, the plague 18
broke out around 1973—at least in the sheltered Middle West. We were
living, our buttoned-down family of four, in a Minnesota village whose
men commuted to dentist-accountant-type jobs in Minneapolis-St. Paul.
The town had a white clapboard general store, a hilltop elementary
school. Our horizon was ringed by soft, round human hills, the streets
shaded by towering vase-shaped elms.

Two evils struck at once; the elms started dying, felled by a Dutch 19
beetle, and my friends' parents started splitting up, victims of a more
mysterious bug. (I sensed at the time that it came from our television
sets, bred during episodes of "Love American Style" and the swanky
"cocktail party" sketches of "Laugh-In.") The sounds of that summer
still come to me; chain saws outside, bickering inside.

To an 11-year-old, it felt like doomsday. Kids started disappearing 20
from school, whisked away by feuding parents. For Sale signs sprouted
in weed-infested yards. One Sunday morning, while selling Cub Scout
candy, I rang the doorbell of a neighbor's house where I had recently
attended a friend's birthday party. The husband answered, gray and
unshaven, holding a gin-filled novelty glass whose pinup girl stripped
naked when ice was added. Behind him, the house was scarily empty.
Stark.

"Sorry, out of cash," the man said, slurring. "I'd find some loose 21
change in the couch, except she took the couch."

The plague spread so quickly and widely that, two years later, kids 22
like me who still lived with both parents were feeling a little out of it

socially. The gangs of divorced kids had an edgy glamour, while I felt like a blob of normalcy. Divorced kids smoked, both cigarettes and pot—often right at the kitchen table with their exhausted-looking single moms. Many divorced boys could strike matches one-handed, handle a knife or a kung fu throwing star.

23   But I was happy my parents were staying together. When Mom and Dad fought—which was happening more often—I prayed on my knees for the roars and shrieks to cease. When mealtime silences grew strained, I burst into upbeat accounts of my day. When I found a parent weeping in the garage or raving about suicide in the bathroom (not uncommon events by the time I was 13), I tried to change the subject to sports or television.

24   Finally, to save ourselves, we moved. We left our blighted village for sunny Phoenix. There, Dad found God, and we joined the Mormon Church. Family unity was the Mormons' true gospel, and many of the converts were like us: middle-class households about to snap, desperate for old-time religion's sturdy clamp.

25   For us, the clamp held. My parents' marriage stabilized. We moved back to Minnesota, to a farm. And from this parched foundation, I took off, achieving everything they could have wanted for me, degrees from Princeton and Oxford, a lovely wife, a successful career as a writer in New York. I felt lucky, grateful—and I still do. I know full well that if my parents had split, these wonderful things might never have happened to me. The problem is that when my parents *did* split, if felt as if none of them ever had.

26   At first, I reacted well to the divorce, I thought. The issue was infidelity, but I was a grown-up: affairs were part of life. I agreed with my wife: my parents' marriage had been on life support for years. Pulling the plug would be painful, but necessary, and in time they'd both be better off. "It's not as if anyone's died," my wife reminded me, "or fallen gravely ill." My wife's mother was a paraplegic suffering from multiple sclerosis, so these words had force. I decided my minor family trauma didn't warrant a big emotional breakdown, so I resolved not to have one.

27   It didn't work. Having an independent life, I was disappointed to learn, didn't prevent me from being absorbed into my parents' crisis. The all-consuming childhood desire to keep the family whole came roaring back. I may have moved out of my parents' house, but I'd never truly left home.

28   I became exceedingly odd. I stopped being able to enter stores and banks. I'd freeze at the threshold and send my wife in, convinced that the clerk or teller was angry at me. I got funny about money too. My wife and I had an income and plenty of savings, yet I nearly bit off her hand one day for misplacing a $5 bill. "I *earned* that money!" I raged about it for hours, convinced that bankruptcy was truly near. Then I

fled our apartment and rode the subway all night. I fantasized I was homeless, and I enjoyed this thought.

Back home, the bust-up was growing uglier. (Home was still the   29
Middle West, I'd discovered, despite my years in New York.) My work, strangely enough, was going well. I wrote a weekly magazine column that readers seemed to like, but I needed to chain-smoke and drink to get the words out. The hacking cough I developed appealed to me much as the homeless fantasy had, but my wife was worried. She suggested I talk to a therapist.

Instead, I talked to my dissolving family. That Dairy Queen call   30
was just the first of hundreds. With me in New York, my parents in Minnesota and my brother in Illinois, the long-distance carriers had us where they wanted us: thousands of miles apart and in crisis.

The Kirn family built its own Internet of grief that year. We surfed   31
the Web of dysfunction. The calls flew in all directions. Two by two, in every combination, family members shared secrets, swore pacts, rehearsed deceptions and blurted confessions. The breakup was painful enough by itself, but the electronic filters made it maddening. If the divorce had happened in my youth, while I still lived at home, I probably would have witnessed tearful pleas, thunderous accusations, rattling door slams. Emotions would have been attached to scenes. The images might have been wounding, but at least they would have been something to hold on to.

Instead, I underwent cyber-split. An electronic, disembodied trauma.   32
With no one to look in the eyes, I grew untrustworthy. I stopped listening to everyone. The divorce had made my world seem unreliable, but the phone calls had rendered it unreal. Only the calling patterns themselves held meaning for me. By interpreting busy signals, call-waiting beeps and the behavior of answering machines, I could figure out who was speaking to whom and who was whose enemy.

Back in the physical realm, things were bad. My wife was staying   33
with friends. My money tantrums, boozy workathons and grocery-store terrors had finally got to her. Plus, I was feeling jealous all the time. And not bathing. And bawling at breakfast.

The solution, I decided, was to move. Now that my childhood   34
home was gone, the dream of buying my own house consumed me. When my wife returned, we discussed the idea. She seemed agreeable, but wanted to wait. That week, I flew to Montana to cover a doomsday cult and stayed in a sweet little town full of bars and low-priced, tree-shaded houses. I drank steadily for two weeks, then bought one. My wife was shocked.

I moved out West alone, carrying my computer and gym bag. My   35
wife considered following me, but I had an affair and we divorced instead. Our split was quick and fairly amicable, which allowed me to feel superior to my parents, who were still in court. I phoned each of

them from my echoey, empty new house to announce my own divorce, and when they didn't show sufficient pity, I went drinking downtown and passed out on some railroad tracks.

36   I woke up hung over, but thrilled. I was a divorced kid, too, now a sexy, wild outcast. I'd been abandoned and wronged, but also freed. I embraced chaos that summer. Just hours after seeing my father face to face for the first time in a year, I fell into a trance of recrimination and drove a Jeep off a cliff. It rolled four times, falling hundreds of feet, and landed on its roof in a stream. Upside down and bleeding from the head, I looked at my bashed-up girlfriend in the passenger seat. "This is it," she said. "We're breaking up." It was the funniest remark I'd ever heard. Dead men can't be threatened, and I was dead inside. Soon, I might even be dead on the outside.

37   Therapy, sobriety, exercise, meditation, friends and anti-depressants. Everything helps. But such comeback stories are boring. In fact, six years afterward, my parents' breakup still gnaws at me. No more holiday feasts. A host of lingering legal squabbles, a brain that seems irreparably torn between Mom's side and Dad's side. And the question of whether I'm thankful they held on long enough to undermine me as a man rather than wound me as a boy seems insoluble. Still, I sometimes wonder, *What if?* A lot of those teen-age divorced kids I once knew sank and never resurfaced, but the ones who survived seem enviably vibrant to me. They're dynamic, open, unafraid. They play in the best new rock bands, write visionary computer software. The road less taken is where they're most at home. Me, I'm halting, ironic, a stricken traditionalist. Institutions others dismiss, I'm still hopeful about.

38   Like marriage. As I write this, my second wedding is days away. Her name is Maggie, and I'll be her first husband. The ceremony will take place in a church. Maggie seems confident we'll grow old together, despite the fact her mother and father have each been married three times. She might be right. To me, our prospects seem cloudier. But what the hell.

39   Love may be fated to sour and spread suffering, but what am I supposed to do about it? Crying for doomed humanity is God's job.

40   Me, I'm off to marry my sweetheart.

★ *Meaning and Understanding*

1. What does the writer refer to when he says, "Nothing is quite so shocking, somehow, as news you've been half expecting all your life" (paragraph 3)?

2. When the writer first hangs up the phone after learning about his parents' divorce, he says of his own relationship, "I knew in an instant that we would not have wed if what just happened had happened years earlier." What does he mean?

3. "Some people grew up during the Great Depression, some during World War II.... They place themselves historically.... I grew up during Divorce." What does this statement in paragraphs 16 and 17 mean?

4. What happens to the writer and to his own marriage when he learns of his parents' plans?

5. What event seems to have prompted the writer to turn his life around?

★ Techniques and Strategies

1. The writer recalls "a parent weeping in the garage or raving about suicide," during his childhood. What other powerful images does the essay offer? What senses do they stimulate—sight, sound, and so on? What effect do they have on your thinking about keeping families together?

2. Find instances of the writer's using humor. How effective do you find these?

3. A newspaper article spurred the phone call in which the writer first heard of his parents' divorce. How do this detail and its placement influence the essay? Why do you think the writer includes it?

4. Into how many principle sections does Kirn divide his essay? How do these divisions help him organize his material? How is the material within the sections organized? Comment overall on the effectiveness of the essay's organization and development.

5. The essay ends with the statement, "Me, I'm off to marry my sweetheart." What do the essay's final paragraphs suggest to you about the evolution of the writer's thinking and feeling? Does the end of the essay satisfy you? Why or why not?

★ Speaking of Values

1. Where was the writer when he first learned about the divorce? Why is this ironic? What is the essay's central irony about divorce and families? Do you agree with the point Kirn is making here? Why?

2. The writer discusses an "Internet of grief," a "Web of dysfunction," a "cyber-split," an "electronic, disembodied trauma." What is he referring to and what kinds of things is he suggesting about the "Information superhighway" and our human connections?

3. After his parents announce and then initiate their divorce, the writer begins a series of odd behaviors that reveals how he was actually quite disturbed despite his age and maturity. What does this suggest about the relation between childhood and adulthood? How convincing is this central perception of the essay?

4. Kirn describes his parents' marriage but does not lay blame. Do the details he includes tell you some things about the marriage and his parents that he does not dwell on? What are these? What do they influence you to think about the parents' character and values?

5. "Love may be fated to sour and spread suffering, but what am I supposed to do about it?" Kirn asks in the next-to-last paragraph of the essay. What does he mean? Why might you agree or disagree with the sentiment expressed here? What values does the remark imply?

★ Values Conversation

Form groups and discuss the writer's idea that sometimes young children whose parents divorce may well be able psychologically to deal with the situation better than an adult child. Assuming this is true, why might it be so? If you do not agree, explain your reasoning. Is there is any systematic way to help children deal with divorce? What might this be?

★ Writing about Values

1. Do some research to determine statistics surrounding marriage, divorce, and children in your state or in the country at large and then write an essay in which you advance a thesis about the effect of divorce on children. (See Wallerstein's essay "The Children of Divorce" on page 76.)

2. Write an essay about parental sacrifice. You may want to look at the causes or the effects on parents, children, or both. Draw on personal experience, observation, reading, film, or TV.

3. Write about a conflict in a family that finally ended in a breach. Identify the underlying problems, the immediate battle that caused the rift, and the nature of relations subsequently. Make your people and their story come alive.

Elizabeth Joseph

My Husband's Nine Wives

Elizabeth Joseph is a lawyer in Utah who wrote this essay for the *New York Times* as a guest editorial in 1991. Joseph explores the nature of "plural marriage," which, she believes, for "compelling social reasons makes the life style attractive to the modern career woman."

I married a married man. 1

In fact, he had six wives when I married him 17 years ago. Today, 2
he has nine.

In March, the Utah Supreme Court struck down a trial court's rul- 3
ing that a polygamist couple could not adopt a child because of their
marital style. Last month, the national board of the American Civil Liberties Union, in response to a request from its Utah chapter, adopted a
new policy calling for the legalization of polygamy.

Polygamy, or plural marriage, as practiced by my family is a para- 4
dox. At first blush, it sounds like the ideal situation for the man and an
oppressive one for the women. For me, the opposite is true. While polygamists believe that the Old Testament mandates the practice of plural marriage, compelling social reasons make the life style attractive to
the modern career woman.

Pick up any women's magazine and you will find article after arti- 5
cle about the problems of successfully juggling career, motherhood and
marriage. It is a complex act that many women struggle to manage
daily; their frustrations fill up the pages of those magazines and consume the hours of afternoon talk shows.

In a monogamous context, the only solutions are compromises. 6
The kids need to learn to fix their own breakfast, your husband needs
to get used to occasional microwave dinners, you need to divert more
of your income to insure that your pre-schooler is in a good day care
environment.

I am sure that in the challenge of working through these compro- 7
mises, satisfaction and success can be realized. But why must women
only embrace a marital arrangement that requires so many trade-offs?

When I leave for the 60-mile commute to court at 7 A.M., my 2-year- 8
old daughter, London, is happily asleep in the bed of my husband's
wife, Diane. London adores Diane. When London awakes, about the

time I'm arriving at the courthouse, she is surrounded by family members who are as familiar to her as the toys in her nursery.

9   My husband Alex, who writes at night, gets up much later. While most of his wives are already at work, pursuing their careers, he can almost always find one who's willing to chat over coffee.

10   I share a home with Delinda, another wife, who works in town government. Most nights, we agree we'll just have a simple dinner with our three kids. We'd rather relax and commiserate over the pressures of our work day than chew up our energy cooking and doing a ton of dishes.

11   Mondays, however, are different. That's the night Alex eats with us. The kids, excited that their father is coming to dinner, are on their best behavior. We often invite another wife or one of his children. It's a special event because it only happens once a week.

12   Tuesday night, it's back to simplicity for us. But for Alex and the household he's dining with that night, it's their special time.

13   The same system with some variation governs our private time with him. While spontaneity is by no means ruled out, we basically use an appointment system. If I want to spend Friday evening at his house, I make an appointment. If he's already "booked," I either request another night or if my schedule is inflexible, I talk to the other wife and we work out an arrangement. One thing we've all learned is that there's always another night.

14   Most evenings, with the demands of career and the literal chasing after the needs of a toddler, all I want to do is collapse into bed and sleep. But there is also the longing for intimacy and comfort that only he can provide, and when those feelings surface, I ask to be with him.

15   Plural marriage is not for everyone. But it is the life style for me. It offers men the chance to escape from the traditional, confining roles that often isolate them from the surrounding world. More important, it enables women, who live in a society full of obstacles, to fully meet their career, mothering and marriage obligations. Polygamy provides a whole solution. I believe American women would have invented it if it didn't already exist.

★ Meaning and Understanding

1. What is the essay's topic?

2. Why does the writer say plural marriage is a "paradox"?

3. What are some of the freedoms that the writer says her marital status provides her?

4. Why are Monday nights "special"?

5. What does the writer do for a living?

★ Techniques and Strategies

1. How does the writer develop her argument? What use does she make of examples? How do the examples relate to the questions and concerns that the essay raises? How effective are the examples?

2. What effect do the narrative details in paragraphs 8–12 have on the essay?

3. What is Joseph's tone in the essay—preachy, homey, matter-of-fact, polemical? How does this tone affect you and your response to the essay's position?

4. The essay is carefully worded and written because the topic is so volatile. But it includes some striking phrases. Which phrases seem most striking? Why?

5. What is the effect on the audience of the one-sentence paragraph opening? Of the two-sentence paragraph immediately following? Why do you think Joseph has chosen such short paragraphs to launch her argument?

★ Speaking of Values

1. Clearly the writer is in favor of polygamy. Does the writer explain polygamy and how it works well enough to dispel *some* of the negative beliefs that individuals may have about the topic? Why and how? How has she influenced your view of the practice of polygamy?

2. The writer is a lawyer and the practice she discusses, polygamy, is illegal in many states. How do these facts affect your reading of the essay? Can lawyers, who work to defend the legal system, morally disobey laws they do not agree with—and still serve the law appropriately? Why or why not?

3. "Most evenings, with the demands of career and the literal chasing after the needs of a toddler, all I want to do is collapse into bed and sleep." How does this statement in paragraph 4 bear upon the argument? How does it affect your opinion of the writer's position?

4. The writer, the seventh of nine wives, says that this form of marriage "offers men the chance to escape from the traditional, confining roles that often isolate them from the surrounding world." What does she

mean? How do you react to this statement? What do you see as traditional, confining elements that require escape from marriage?

5. Consider the essay's final statement. Do you agree that polygamy "provides a whole solution"? Why or why not?

★ *Values Conversation*

Joseph refers to some of the difficulties many modern women experience in terms of "juggling career, motherhood and marriage." Form groups and consider solutions to the problem. As a group, identify your own social solutions. How does your group feel about Joseph's solution?

★ *Writing about Values*

1. Assume that you could have the "ideal" marriage, either someday or evolving from your current marital situation. What characteristics would that marriage have? Write an essay that identifies and explains the elements of an ideal marriage.

2. Write an essay about your experience or observation of multiple love relations. What effect did this have on you or the parties you're writing about?

3. Write an essay in which you compare men's and women's needs in marriage.

Edgar Allan Poe

Annabel Lee

Edgar Allan Poe (1809–1849) is one of America's major writers and one of the founders of such genres as mystery, horror, and science fiction. His most renowned works include "The Raven" and stories such as "The Fall of the House of Usher" and "The Masque of the Red Death." In this lyrical ballad, published after Poe's death, the poet writes about the loss of a beautiful love.

———— ★ ————

It was many and many a year ago,
 In a kingdom by the sea,
That a maiden there lived whom you may know
 By the name of Annabel Lee;—
And this maiden she lived with no other thought   5
 Than to love and be loved by me.

She was a child and *I* was a child,
 In this kingdom by the sea,
But we loved with a love that was more than love—
 I and my Annabel Lee—   10
With a love that the winged seraphs of Heaven
 Coveted her and me.

And this was the reason that, long ago,
 In this kingdom by the sea,
A wind blew out of a cloud by night   15
 Chilling my Annabel Lee;
So that her highborn kinsmen came
 And bore her away from me,
To shut her up in a sepulchre
 In this kingdom by the sea.   20

The angels, not half so happy in Heaven,
 Went envying her and me:—
Yes! that was the reason (as all men know,
 In this kingdom by the sea)
That the wind came out of the cloud, chilling   25
 And killing my Annabel Lee.

But our love it was stronger by far than the love
    Of those who were older than we—
    Of many far wiser than we—
30   And neither the angels in Heaven above
    Nor the demons down under the sea,
Can ever dissever my soul from the soul
    Of the beautiful Annabel Lee:—

For the moon never beams without bringing me dreams
35   Of the beautiful Annabel Lee;

And the stars never rise but I see the bright eyes
    Of the beautiful Annabel Lee;
And so, all the night-tide, I lie down by the side
Of my darling, my darling, my life and my bride,
40   In her sepulchre there by the sea—
    In her tomb by the side of the sea.

★ Meaning and Understanding

1. What is the relation between the speaker in the poem and Annabel Lee?

2. What happened to Annabel Lee, and how does the speaker feel about her fate?

3. Who has come to take Annabel Lee away, and where have they taken her?

4. Where does the speaker sleep?

★ Techniques and Strategies

1. How does Poe use rhyme in the poem? How does the rhyme affect you and add to the poem's meaning?

2. Identify what you consider to be the poem's strongest images. Which are the most effective? Why?

3. What is the effect of the reference to envious angels in heaven? Does the poem strike you as real or fantastical? Why?

4. The poem contains some grim and spooky lines. Which are the most chilling to you? Do you consider them effective? Why or why not?

5. Poe repeats a number of words and phrases in the poem. Identify some of them. What is the effect of all these repetitions?

★ Speaking of Values

1. What value is the speaker trying to establish about the experience of love? Do you agree with his point of view? Does love generally last beyond the grave? Why or why not? If so, how? If you believe not, why not?

2. What is the "acceptable" period of time that must pass before a widow or widower can remarry, do you think? What would you think about a husband or wife who claimed such devotion that he or she planned never to remarry after the death of a mate? Why?

3. The love in this poem, a psychiatrist might argue, is obsessive. Identify a love situation—from personal experience, observation, or reading—that strikes you as obsessive. What elements give it its obsessive quality? What advice are you inclined to give one or both of the parties involved? Why?

4. The speaker in "Annabel Lee" pits children's love against adult love, declaring the former stronger. Do you agree that adults don't love as strongly as children? On what do you base your opinion? What other values—besides love—show differences in young and adult moral or emotional habits? Which "world"—young or adult—do you feel you belong to? How does this identification play out in terms of your love feelings or values generally?

★ Values Conversation

Divide into groups and discuss whether the level of devotion that the speaker feels for Annabel Lee seems extraordinary. How? Is it appealing or repulsive? How so? How would you characterize this love? Can a person realize when he or she is close to this kind of state? Are there any ways to identify this type of behavior in oneself or others? What advice would you give someone in this intense state? How does this intense devotion affect one's whole being and the play of other values in one's life?

★ Writing about Values

1. Write an essay that considers a defining emotional experience—love or something else—in your life or the life of someone you know. What happened? Why? What moral lessons are to be learned?

2. Do some research into the life of Poe and his marriage. Write an essay in which you discuss the relation you see between his life and the poem.

3. Write an essay about "young love." You may wish to define the phenomenon, show its causes or effects or both, explore an interesting example—or some combination of these.

Ellen Hopkins

Sex Is for Adults

Ellen Hopkins is a journalist and a contributing editor to *Rolling Stone*. In
this 1992 essay she approaches the issue of teenage sex and an educational program that promotes abstinence as a valid response.

— ★ —

1   Remember how drunken driving used to be kind of funny? Or if not
funny, inevitable, especially for the young. When I was in high school
(I'm thirty-five), only losers worried about the alcoholic consumption
of the person behind the wheel. Fourteen years later, when my sister
made her way through the same suburban high school, designated
drivers had become the norm and only losers swerved off into the
night.

2   I was reminded of this remarkable evolution in attitude when I began to explore the idea that teaching abstinence to teenagers need not
be the province of right-wing crazies. Could it be that teenage sex is no
more inevitable than we once thought teenage drunken driving? Is it
possible to make a liberal, feminist argument for pushing abstinence in
the schools? I believe it is.

3   The argument goes like this:

Sex education doesn't work.

4   There are lots of nice things to be said for sex education. It makes kids
more knowledgeable, more tolerant, and maybe even more skillful lovers. But it does not do the one thing we all wish it would: make them
more responsible.

5   In a landmark study of ten exemplary programs published by the
Centers for Disease Control in 1984, no evidence was found that
knowledge influenced teenagers' behavior significantly. Supporters of
sex education point to studies that show that educated teenagers are
slightly more likely to use birth control. Opponents point to studies
that show they are slightly more likely to have sex at a younger age. No
one points to the many studies that compare the pregnancy rates of the
educated and the ignorant: depressingly similar.

Even if sex education worked, birth control doesn't.

6   At least it doesn't work often enough. The Alan Guttmacher Institute, a
research organization that specializes in reproductive health, estimates

526

that up to 36 percent of women in their early twenties will get pregnant while relying on male use of condoms in the first year; and with the supposedly foolproof pill, up to 18 percent of teenage girls get pregnant in the first year. (The more effective and more expensive contraceptive Norplant is not widely available to young women.) If you project these failure rates a few years ahead, unintended pregnancy begins to look uncomfortably close to an inevitability.

So let's follow one sexually active teenager who does just what she's statistically likely to do. Her options are bleak.

If she wants an abortion, good luck to her if she's poor, under eighteen, or doesn't live near a big city. The simplest abortion costs about $300. Only twelve states have no laws requiring parental consent or notification for minors seeking an abortion. And 83 percent of America's counties don't even have an abortion provider.

What if our teenager chose to have the baby and give it up for adoption? While there's a dearth of solid follow-up research on birth mothers, surrendering the flesh of your flesh is obviously wrenching. Suppose our teenager keeps the baby. She may be ruining her life. Only 50 percent of women who have their first child at seventeen or younger will have graduated from high school by the age of thirty. And many of those who do have merely gotten a General Education Development degree, which is of such dubious worth that the army no longer accepts recruits with it.

Even a ruined life may be better than a life cut short by AIDS.

If condoms—or young condom users—are so unreliable that up to 36 percent of young women get pregnant in a single year of use, what does that say about our teenager's chances of being exposed to HIV as she "protects" herself with a latex sheath?

Our teenager, though, leads a charmed life. Or so she thinks. Even if she doesn't get pregnant and none of her boyfriends is HIV positive, she still puts herself at substantial risk for later infertility.

More than 12 million episodes of sexually transmitted diseases occur each year in the United States, and two-thirds of those afflicted are under twenty-five. Most such diseases can damage the female and male reproductive systems. Infectious-disease experts estimate that after just one episode of pelvic inflammatory disease (a common result of contracting sexually transmitted disease), 35 percent of women become infertile. After three episodes, the odds of becoming infertile soar to more than 75 percent. Many infertility specialists believe that one of the prime causes of today's high infertility rate is that so many baby boomers had sex early and with multiple partners.

Current recommendations for "safer" sex are unrealistic.

11   Our teenager knows that before going to bed with someone, she and the guy are supposed to exchange detailed sexual histories. Tandem AIDS tests are next, and if both can forge a monogamy pact, they will use condoms (and a more reliable form of birth control like the pill) for six months and then get tested again.

12   Does our teenager hammer out these elaborate social contracts every time Cupid calls? Of course not.

13   I had always assumed that abstinence lessons were synonymous with Sex Respect, the religious right's curriculum that uses fear to pressure kids to avoid all sexual activity—including necking—until marriage. While supporters claim success, their evaluation techniques are problematic. Plus, imagine those poor kids having to chant silly Sex Respect slogans ("Control your urgin', be a virgin" is my favorite).

14   But studies of a program in Atlanta's public schools suggest that promoting abstinence can be done intelligently and effectively. Eighth graders are taught by peer counselors (popular, reasonably chaste kids from the upper grades—kids who look like they *could* have sex if they wanted it). Their message is simple: Sex is for grown-ups. Weirdly, it works. By the end of the eighth grade, girls who weren't in the program were as much as fifteen times more likely to have begun having sex as those who were.

15   While the program in Atlanta is backed up by contraceptive counseling, kids who choose to have sex are erratic birth-control users and just as likely to get pregnant as sexually active kids who aren't in the program.

16   In other words, sex is for grown-ups. I feel strange writing this. Then I remember my first heady experimentations (at a relatively geriatric age) and contrast them with those of a sixteen-year-old girl who recently visited Planned Parenthood in Westchester county. Three boys were with her, their relationship to her unclear. On the admittance form, the girl wrote that she wasn't in a relationship and had been sexually active for some time. An exam proved her pregnant. Her entire being was joyless.

17   I once thought I'd tell my young son that anything goes—so long as he used condoms. Now I'm not so sure. Not only do I want my son to live, I don't want him to miss out on longing—longing for what he isn't yet ready to have.

★ Meaning and Understanding

1. What is the topic of the essay?

2. What is the main point the writer advances?

3. What is the writer's reason for mentioning the current teenage practice of "designated drivers"?

4. Where does the writer see herself politically—right, radical, liberal?

5. What advice does Hopkins think she will give her son?

★ Techniques and Strategies

1. What is the function of the italicized section headings? How effective are they in advancing the writer's thesis?

2. What do you think is the writer's purpose in the essay? Who do you think her audience is? What tells you this?

3. Identify several examples used in the essay. Which do you find most effective? Why?

4. Where does the essay refer to studies and statistics? How useful are these?

5. Where do you find examples of humor? Why do you think Hopkins uses humor? How appropriate is it for the topic? Why?

★ Speaking of Values

1. What is the main value that Hopkins advances about sex?

2. The author writes for *Rolling Stone*—a "hip" monthly magazine. Do you see a contradiction between being hip and advocating sexual abstinence for the young? Why or why not?

3. Fear of AIDS and teenage pregnancy echoes through the essay. Yet Hopkins says she is opposed to the religious right's fear tactics. How does her own approach differ?

4. The writer suggests promoting abstinence "intelligently and effectively." What do you see as the relation between sex and intelligence?

5. Hopkins focuses on the physical dangers of sex—in disease and pregnancy. What other kinds of risks do you see in teenage sex? How serious a threat do these present in your opinion?

★ Values Conversation

Hopkins concludes that "sex is for grown-ups." Form groups to discuss how a similar statement can be made about other activities. What else that children may participate in is best left to adults? Why? What makes adults better able to face the experience(s)?

★ *Writing about Values*

1. Write an essay about the emotional repercussions of young people having sex. Identify and explain some nonphysical repercussions.

2. Do some research on AIDS or another sexually transmitted disease. Write an essay about some aspect of the disease.

3. Write an essay comparing safe sex with abstinence. Which do you favor and why?

Barbara Ehrenreich

Playboy *Joins the Battle of the Sexes*

Barbara Ehrenreich was born in Butte, Montana in 1941. She is a Guggenheim Fellow who received a Ph.D. from Rockefeller University and is the author of many works, including *The Hearts of Men* (1986) and *The Worst Years of Our Lives* (1990). In this selection she examines the rise in popularity of *Playboy* magazine and its relation to male culture.

———— ★ ————

I don't want my editors marrying anyone and getting a lot of foolish notions in their heads about "togetherness," home, family, and all that jazz.

—Hugh Hefner

The first issue of *Playboy* hit the stands in December 1953. The first centerfold—the famous nude calendar shot of Marilyn Monroe—is already legendary. Less memorable, but no less prophetic of things to come, was the first feature article in the issue. It was a no-holds-barred attack on "the whole concept of alimony," and secondarily, on money-hungry women in general, entitled "Miss Gold-Digger of 1953." From the beginning, *Playboy* loved women—large-breasted, long-legged young women, anyway—and hated wives.

The "Miss Gold-Digger" article made its author a millionaire—not because Hugh Hefner paid him so much but because Hefner could not, at first, afford to pay him at all, at least not in cash. The writer, Burt Zollo (he signed the article "Bob Norman"; even Hefner didn't risk putting his own name in the first issue), had to accept stock in the new magazine in lieu of a fee. The first print run of 70,000 nearly sold out and the magazine passed the one-million mark in 1956, making Hefner and his initial associates millionaires before the end of the decade.

But *Playboy* was more than a publishing phenomenon, it was like the party organ of a diffuse and swelling movement. Writer Myron Brenton called it the "Bible of the beleaguered male."[1] *Playboy* readers taped the centerfolds up in their basements, affixed the rabbit-head insignia to the rear window of their cars, joined Playboy clubs if they

[1]Quoted in Joe L. Dubbert, *A Man's Place: Masculinity in Transition* (Englewood Cliffs, N.J.: Prentice-Hall, Inc., 1979), p. 269.

531

could afford to and, even if they lived more like Babbits than Bunnies, imagined they were "playboys" at heart. The magazine encouraged the sense of membership in a fraternity of male rebels. After its first reader survey, *Playboy* reported on the marital status of its constituency in the following words: "Approximately half of PLAYBOY'S readers (46.8%) are free men and the other half are free in spirit only."[2]

4   In the ongoing battle of the sexes, the *Playboy* offices in Chicago quickly became the male side's headquarters for war-time propaganda. Unlike the general-audience magazines the dominated fifties' news-stands—*Life, Time,* the *Saturday Evening Post, Look,* etc.—*Playboy* didn't worry about pleasing women readers. The first editorial, penned by Hefner himself, warned:

> We want to make clear from the very start, we aren't a "family maga-zine." If you're somebody's sister, wife or mother-in-law and picked us up by mistake, please pass us along to the man in your life and get back to your *Ladies' Home Companion.*

When a Memphis woman wrote in to the second issue protesting the "Miss Gold-Digger" article, she was quickly put in her place. The arti-cle, she wrote, was "the most biased piece of tripe I've ever read," and she went on to deliver the classic anti-male rejoinder:

> Most men are out for just one thing. If they can't get it any other way, sometimes they consent to marry the girl. Then they think they can brush her off in a few months and move on to new pickings. They *ought* to pay, and pay, and pay.

The editors' printed response was, "Ah, shaddup!"

5   Hefner laid out the new male strategic initiative in the first issue. Recall that in their losing battle against "female domination," men had been driven from their living rooms, dens and even their basement tool shops. Escape seemed to lie only in the great outdoors—the golf courses, the fishing hole or the fantasy world of Westerns. Now Hefner announced his intention to reclaim *the indoors for men.* "Most of today's 'magazines for men' spend all their time out-of-doors—thrashing through thorny thickets or splashing about in fast flowing streams," he observed in the magazine's first editorial. "But we don't mind telling you in advance—we plan spending most of our time inside. WE like our apartment." For therein awaited a new kind of good life for men:

> We enjoy mixing up cocktails and an *hors d'oeuvre* or two, putting a lit-tle mood music on the phonograph and inviting in a female acquain-tance for a quiet discussion on Picasso, Nietzsche, jazz, sex.

[2]"Meet the *Playboy* Reader," *Playboy,* April 1958, p. 63.

Women would be welcome after men had reconquered the indoors, but only as guests—maybe overnight guests—but not as wives.

In 1953, the notion that the good life consisted of an apartment with mood music rather than a ranch house with a barbecue pit was almost subversive. Looking back, Hefner later characterized himself as a pioneer rebel against the gray miasma of conformity that gripped other men. At the time the magazine began, he wrote in 1963, Americans had become "increasingly concerned with security, the safe and the sure, the certain and the known ... it was unwise to voice an unpopular opinion ... for it could cost a man his job and his good name."[3] Hefner himself was not a political dissident in any conventional sense; the major intellectual influence in his early life was the Kinsey report, and he risked his good name only for the right to publish bare white bosoms. What upset him was the "conformity, togetherness, anonymity and slow death" men were supposed to endure when the good life, the life which he himself came to represent, was so close at hand.[4]

In fact, it was close at hand, and, at the macroeconomic level, nothing could have been more in conformity with the drift of American culture than to advocate a life of pleasurable consumption. The economy, as Riesman, Galbraith and their colleagues noted, had gotten over the hump of heavy capital accumulation to the happy plateau of the "consumer society." After the privations of the Depression and the war, Americans were supposed to enjoy themselves—held back from total abandon only by the need for Cold War vigilance. Motivational researcher Dr. Ernest Dichter told businessmen:

> We are now confronted with the problem of permitting the average American to feel moral ... even when he is spending, even when he is not saving, even when he is taking two vacations a year and buying a second or third car. One of the basic problems of prosperity, then, is to demonstrate that the hedonistic approach to his life is a moral, not an immoral one.[5]

This was the new consumer ethic, the "fun morality" described by sociologist Martha Wolfenstein, and *Playboy* could not have been better designed to bring the good news to men.

If Hefner was a rebel, it was only because he took the new fun morality seriously. As a guide to life, the new imperative to enjoy was a contradiction with the prescribed discipline of "conformity" and *Playboy*'s daring lay in facing the contradiction head-on. Conformity, or

---

[3]Hugh Hefner, "The Playboy Philosophy," *Playboy*, January 1963, p. 41.
[4]Frank Brady, *Hefner* (New York: Macmillan Pub. Co., 1974), p. 98.
[5]Quoted in Douglas T. Miller and Marion Nowak, *The Fifties: The Way We Really Were* (Garden City, N.Y.: Doubleday & Company, Inc., 1977) 119.

"maturity," as it was more affirmatively labeled by the psychologists, required unstinting effort: developmental "tasks" had to be performed, marriages had to be "worked on," individual whims had to be subordinated to the emotional and financial needs of the family. This was true of both sexes, of course. No one pretended that the adult sex roles—wife/mother and male breadwinner—were "fun." They were presented in popular culture as achievements, proofs of the informed acquiescence praised as "maturity" or, more rarely, lamented as "slow death." Women would not get public license to have fun on a mass scale for more than a decade, when Helen Gurley Brown took over *Cosmopolitan* and began promoting a tamer, feminine version of sexual and material consumerism. But *Playboy* shed the burdensome aspects of the adult male role at a time when businessmen were still refining the "fun morality" for mass consumption, and the gray flannel rebels were still fumbling for responsible alternatives like Riesman's "autonomy." Even the magazine's name defied the convention of hard-won maturity—*Playboy*.

9   *Playboy*'s attack on the conventional male role did not, however, extend to the requirement of earning a living. There were two parts to adult masculinity: One was maintaining a monogamous marriage. The other was working at a socially acceptable job; and *Playboy* had nothing against work. The early issues barely recognized the white-collar blues so fashionable in popular sociology. Instead, there were articles on accoutrements for the rising executive, suggesting that work, too, could be a site of pleasurable consumption. Writing in his "*Playboy* Philosophy" series in 1963, Hefner even credited the magazine with inspiring men to work harder than they might: "...*Playboy* exists, in part, as a motivation for men to expend greater effort on their work, develop their capabilities further and climb higher on the ladder of success." This kind of motivation, he went on, "is obviously desirable in our competitive, free enterprise system," apparently unaware that the average reader was more likely to be a white-collar "organization man" or blue-collar employee rather than a free entrepreneur like himself. Men should throw themselves into their work with "questing impatience and rebel derring-do." They should overcome their vague, ingrained populism and recognize wealth as an achievement and a means to personal pleasure. Only in one respect did Hefner's philosophy depart from the conventional, Dale Carnegie-style credos of male success: *Playboy* believed that men should make money; it did not suggest that they share it.

10   *Playboy* charged into the battle of the sexes with a dollar sign on its banner. The issue was money: Men made it; women wanted it. In *Playboy*'s favorite cartoon situation an elderly roué was being taken for a ride by a buxom bubblebrain, and the joke was on him. The message, squeezed between luscious full-color photos and punctuated with fe-

male nipples, was simple: You can buy sex on a fee-for-service basis, so don't get caught up in a long-term contract. Phil Silvers quipped in the January 1957 issue:

> A tip to my fellow men who might be on the brink of disaster: when the little doll says she'll live on your income, she means it all right. But just be sure to get another one for yourself.[6]

Burt Zollo warned in the June 1953 issue:

> It is often suggested that woman is more romantic than man. If you'll excuse the ecclesiastical expression—*phooey!*... All woman wants is security. And she's perfectly willing to crush man's adventurous, freedom-loving spirit to get it.[7]

To stay free, a man had to stay single.

The competition, meanwhile, was still fighting a rearguard battle   11
for patriarchal authority within marriage. In 1956, the editorial director of *True* attributed his magazine's success to the fact that it "stimulates the masculine ego at a time when man wants to fight back against women's efforts to usurp his traditional role as head of the family."[8] The playboy did not want his "traditional role" back; he just wanted out. Hefner's friend Burt Zollo wrote in one of the early issues:

> Take a good look at the sorry, regimented husbands trudging down every woman-dominated street in this woman-dominated land. Check what they're doing when you're out on the town with a different dish every night...Don't bother asking their advice. Almost to a man, they'll tell you marriage is the greatest. *Naturally.* Do you expect them to admit they made the biggest mistake of their lives?[9]

This was strong stuff for the mid-fifties. The suburban migration   12
was in full swing and *Look* had just coined the new noun "togetherness" to bless the isolated, exurban family. Yet here was *Playboy* exhorting its readers to resist marriage and "enjoy the pleasures the female has to offer without becoming emotionally involved"—or, of course, financially involved. Women wrote in with the predictable attacks on immaturity: "It is...the weak-minded little idiot boys, not yet grown up, who are afraid of getting 'hooked.'" But the men loved it. One alliterative genius wrote in to thank *Playboy* for exposing those "cunning

---

[6]Phil Silvers, "Resolution: Never Get Married," *Playboy,* January 1957, p. 77.

[7]Burt Zollo, "Open Season on Bachelors," *Playboy,* June 1953, p. 37.

[8]Quoted in Myron Brenton, *The American Male* (New York: Coward, McCann, 1966), p. 30.

[9]Zollo, loc. cit.

cuties" with their "suave schemes" for landing a man. And, of course, it was *Playboy*, with its images of cozy concupiscence and extra-marital consumerism, that triumphed while *True* was still "thrashing through the thorny thickets" in the great, womanless outdoors.

13   One of the most eloquent manifestos of the early male rebellion was a *Playboy* article entitled "Love, Death and the Hubby Image," published in 1963. It led off with a mock want ad:

> TIRED OF THE RAT RACE?
> FED UP WITH JOB ROUTINE?
> Well, then... how would you like to make $8,000, $20,000—*as much as $50,000 and More* working at Home In Your Spare Time? No selling! No commuting! No time clocks to punch!
> BE YOUR OWN BOSS!!!
> Yes, an Assured Lifetime Income can be yours *now*, in an easy, low-pressure, part-time job that will permit you to spend most of each and every day as *you please!*—relaxing, watching TV, playing cards, socializing with friends!...

"Incredible though it may seem," the article began, "the above offer is completely legitimate. More than 40,000,000 Americans are already so employed..." They were, of course, wives.

14   According to the writer, William Iversen, husbands were self-sacrificing romantics, toiling ceaselessly to provide their families with "bread, bacon, clothes, furniture, cars, appliances, entertainment, vacations and country-club memberships." Nor was it enough to meet their daily needs; the heroic male must provide for them even after his own death by building up his savings and life insurance. "Day after day, and week after week the American hubby is thus invited to attend his own funeral." Iversen acknowledged that there were some mutterings of discontent from the distaff side, but he saw no chance of a feminist revival: The role of housewife "has become much too cushy to be abandoned, even in the teeth of the most crushing boredom." Men, however, had had it with the breadwinner role, and the final paragraph was a stirring incitement to revolt:

> The last straw has already been served, and a mere tendency to hemophilia cannot be counted upon to ensure that men will continue to bleed for the plight of the American woman. Neither double eyelashes nor the blindness of night or day can obscure the glaring fact that American marriage can no longer be accepted as an estate in which the sexes shall live half-slave and half-free.[10]

[10]William Iversen, "Love, Death and the Hubby Image," *Playboy*, September 1963, p. 92.

Playboy had much more to offer the "enslaved" sex than rhetoric: It   15
also proposed an alternative way of life that became ever more concrete
and vivid as the years went on. At first there were only the Playmates
in the centerfold to suggest what awaited the liberated male, but a
wealth of other consumer items soon followed. Throughout the late fifties, the magazine fattened on advertisements for imported liquor, ste-
reo sets, men's colognes, luxury cars and fine clothes. Manufacturers
were beginning to address themselves to the adult male as a consumer
in his own right, and they were able to do so, in part, because magazines like *Playboy* (a category which came to include imitators like *Penthouse, Gent* and *Chic*) allowed them to effectively "target" the potential
sybarites among the great mass of men. New products for men, like toi-
letries and sports clothes, appeared in the fifties, and familiar products,
like liquor, were presented in *Playboy* as accessories to private male
pleasures. The new male-centered ensemble of commodities presented
in *Playboy* meant that a man could display his status or simply flaunt
his earnings without possessing either a house or a wife—and this was,
in its own small way, a revolutionary possibility.

Domesticated men had their own commodity ensemble, centered   16
on home appliances and hobby hardware, and for a long time there
had seemed to be no alternative. A man expressed his status through
the size of his car, the location of his house, and the social and sartorial
graces of his wife. The wife and home might be a financial drag on a
man, but it was paraphernalia of family life that established his position in the occupational hierarchy. *Playboy*'s visionary contribution—
visionary because it would still be years before a significant mass of
men availed themselves of it—was to give the means of status to the
single man: not the power lawn mower, but the hi-fi set in mahogony
console; not the sedate, four-door Buick, but the racy little Triumph; not
the well-groomed wife, but the classy companion who could be rented
(for the price of drinks and dinner) one night at a time.

So through its articles, its graphics and its advertisements *Playboy*   17
presented, by the beginning of the sixties, something approaching a coherent program for the male rebellion: a critique of marriage, a strategy
for liberation (reclaiming the indoors as a realm for masculine pleasure)
and a utopian vision (defined by its unique commodity ensemble). It
may not have been a revolutionary program, but it was most certainly a
disruptive one. If even a fraction of *Playboy* readers had acted on it in the
late fifties, the "breakdown of the family" would have occurred a full fifteen years before it was eventually announced. Hundreds of thousands
of women would have been left without breadwinners or stranded in
court fighting for alimony settlements. Yet, for all its potential disrup-
tiveness, *Playboy* was immune to the standard charges leveled against
male deviants. You couldn't call it anti-capitalist or un-American, because it was all about making money and spending it. Hefner even told

his readers in 1963 that the *Playboy* spirit of acquisitiveness could help "put the United States back in the position of unquestioned world leadership." You *could* call it "immature," but it already called itself that, because maturity was about mortgages and life insurance and *Playboy* was about fun. Finally, it was impervious to the ultimate sanction against male rebellion—the charge of homosexuality. The playboy didn't avoid marriage because he was a little bit "queer," but, on the contrary, because he was so ebulliently, even compulsively heterosexual.

18   Later in the sixties critics would come up with what seemed to be the ultimately sophisticated charge against *Playboy*: It wasn't really "sexy." There was nothing erotic, *Time* wrote, about the pink-cheeked young Playmates whose every pore and perspiration drop had been air-brushed out of existence. Hefner was "puritanical" after all, and the whole thing was no more mischievous than "a Midwestern Methodist's vision of sin."[11] But the critics misunderstood *Playboy*'s historical role. *Playboy* was not the voice of the sexual revolution, which began, at least overtly, in the sixties, but the male rebellion, which had begun in the fifties. The real message was not eroticism, but escape—literal escape, from the bondage of breadwinning. For that, the breasts and bottoms were necessary not just to sell the magazine, but to protect it. When, in the first issue, Hefner talked about staying in his apartment, listening to music and discussing Picasso, there was the Marilyn Monroe centerfold to let you know there was nothing queer about these urbane and indoor pleasures. And when the articles railed against the responsibilities of marriage, there were the nude torsos to reassure you that the alternative was still within the bounds of heterosexuality. Sex—or Hefner's Pepsi-clean version of it—was there to legitimize what was truly subversive about *Playboy*. In every issue, every month, there was a Playmate to prove that a playboy didn't have to be a husband to be a man.

★ Meaning and Understanding

1. What does the essay say about how *Playboy* initially dealt with women and, particularly, wives?

2. Who and what was "Miss Gold-Digger of 1953"?

3. What was *Playboy*'s "new male strategic initiative"?

4. How did *Playboy* tap into the new "consumer society"?

5. As far as the writer is concerned, what was *Playboy*'s primary interest?

[11]"Think Clean," *Time*, March 3, 1967, p. 76.

★ *Techniques and Strategies*

1. The writer frequently quotes from the source she discusses. Does including all this material "from the opposition" weaken or strengthen her argument? Why?

2. Where does the writer make use of hyperbole or overstatement to advance her thesis? How effective are these strategies? Which of her statements seem shocking? Why?

3. The essay begins with a mention of the first *Playboy* centerfold. What do you think starting the essay in this way adds to the presentation? Where in the rest of the essay does Ehrenreich mention nudes? What is the effect of this treatment on her meaning?

4. How does the essay express the "battle" image—from the title onward? Cite examples and evaluate their effectiveness.

5. Why does Ehrenreich present a quote from Hugh Hefner before the first paragraph of her essay? Who is Hefner? What does Hefner's quote add to the text?

★ *Speaking of Values*

1. What do you think the writer believes about family life as a value? How is *Playboy* anti-family, according to the writer? Why might you agree or disagree with her position?

2. What kinds of values, particularly in the sense of monogamous relations, was an article entitled "Love, Death and the Hubby Image" espousing? What do you think Ehrenreich thinks about monogamy and maturity? What do you think about it?

3. What was *Playboy*'s "visionary contribution" to U.S. social structure? Do you agree? Why or why not?

4. Many believe that the "battle of the sexes" rages still. Why? Are there lessons in Ehrenreich's essay for today? What are they?

5. "The issue was money: Men made it; women wanted it." Ehrenreich sums up Playboy's charge "into the battle of the sexes" with that comment in paragraph 10. How would a magazine of today fare with such a philosophy at its core? Explain your answer.

★ *Values Conversation*

The writer states: "This was strong stuff for the mid-fifties. The suburban migration was in full swing. And *Look* had just coined the new noun 'togetherness' to bless the isolated, exurban family. Yet here was *Playboy* exhorting its readers to resist marriage and 'enjoy the pleasures the female has to offer without becoming emotionally involved'—or, of course, financially involved." Form groups and discuss how the set of male values *Playboy* espoused might have affected people of the time and how these influences are or are not still a part of our culture. For instance, consider the increase in fatherlessness and the attached issues of single-parent homes and so-called "deadbeat dads" and when these conditions began and developed to their current state. Could these things be related? How? Are there other issues to discuss as well?

★ *Writing about Values*

1. Choose a magazine targeted toward a certain gender. Write an essay defining the central gender messages you find there.

2. Write an essay that compares love and lust. Are the values different? Similar? In what ways?

3. Write an essay about responsibility and love. You may wish to define each of the terms or to narrate a story showing the two parting ways or coming together in a human event that you experienced or witnessed.

John Collier

The Chaser

Known for his macabre whimsical tales, John Collier (1901–1980) was a
playwright, novelist, screenwriter, poet, and short story writer. His most
popular works include *His Monkey Wife; or, Married to a Chimp* (1969).
Born in 1901 and educated in England, Collier died in Pacific Palisades,
California. In this story he puts a humorous twist on a young man's efforts to win the girl he loves.

———— ★ ————

Alan Austen, as nervous as a kitten, went up certain dark and creaky   1
stairs in the neighborhood of Pell Street, and peered about for a long
time on the dim landing before he found the name he wanted written
obscurely on one of the doors.

He pushed open this door, as he had been told to do, and found   2
himself in a tiny room, which contained no furniture but a plain kitchen
table, a rocking-chair, and an ordinary chair. On one of the dirty buff-
coloured walls were a couple of shelves, containing in all perhaps a
dozen bottles and jars.

An old man sat in the rocking-chair, reading a newspaper. Alan,   3
without a word, handed him the card he had been given. "Sit down,
Mr. Austen," said the old man very politely. "I am glad to make your
acquaintance."

"Is it true," asked Alan, "that you have a certain mixture that has—   4
er—quite extraordinary effects?"

"My dear sir," replied the old man, "my stock in trade is not very   5
large—I don't deal in laxatives and teething mixtures—but such as it is,
it is varied. I think nothing I sell has effects which could be precisely
described as ordinary."

"Well, the fact is . . ." began Alan.   6

"Here, for example," interrupted the old man, reaching for a bottle   7
from the shelf. "Here is a liquid as colourless as water, almost tasteless,
quite imperceptible in coffee, wine, or any other beverage. It is also
quite imperceptible to any known method of autopsy."

"Do you mean it is a poison?" cried Alan, very much horrified.   8

"Call it a glove-cleaner if you like," said the old man indifferently. 9
"Maybe it will clean gloves. I have never tried. One might call it a life-
cleaner. Lives need cleaning sometimes."

"I want nothing of that sort," said Alan.   10

11   "Probably it is just as well," said the old man. "Do you know the price of this? For one teaspoonful, which is sufficient, I ask five thousand dollars. Never less. Not a penny less."

12   "I hope all your mixtures are not as expensive," said Alan apprehensively.

13   "Oh dear, no," said the old man. "It would be no good charging that sort of price for a love potion, for example. Young people who need a love potion very seldom have five thousand dollars. Otherwise they would not need a love potion."

14   "I am glad to hear that," said Alan.

15   "I look at it like this," said the old man. "Please a customer with one article, and he will come back when he needs another. Even if it *is* more costly. He will save up for it, if necessary."

16   "So," said Alan, "you really do sell love potions?"

17   "If I did not sell love potions," said the old man, reaching for another bottle, "I should not have mentioned the other matter to you. It is only when one is in a position to oblige that one can afford to be so confidential."

18   "And these potions," said Alan. "They are not just—just—er—"

19   "Oh, no," said the old man. "Their effects are permanent, and extend far beyond the mere casual impulse. But they include it. Oh, yes, they include it. Bountifully, insistently. Everlastingly."

20   "Dear me!" said Alan, attempting a look of scientific detachment. "How very interesting!"

21   "But consider the spiritual side," said the old man.

22   "I do, indeed," said Alan.

23   "For indifference," said the old man, "they substitute devotion. For scorn, adoration. Give one tiny measure of this to the young lady—its flavour is imperceptible in orange juice, soup, or cocktails—and however gay and giddy she is, she will change altogether. She will want nothing but solitude and you."

24   "I can hardly believe it," said Alan. "She is so fond of parties."

25   "She will not like them any more," said the old man. "She will be afraid of the pretty girls you may meet."

26   "She will actually be jealous?" cried Alan in a rapture. "Of me?"

27   "Yes, she will want to be everything to you."

28   "She is, already. Only she doesn't care about it."

29   "She will, when she has taken this. She will care intensely. You will be her sole interest in life."

30   "Wonderful!" cried Alan.

31   "She will want to know all you do," said the old man. "All that has happened to you during the day. Every word of it. She will want to know what you are thinking about, why you smile suddenly, why you are looking sad."

32   "That is love!" cried Alan.

"Yes." said the old man. "How carefully she will look after you! She will never allow you to be tired, to sit in a draught, to neglect your food. If you are an hour late, she will be terrified. She will think you are killed, or that some siren has caught you." 33

"I can hardly imagine Diana like that!" cried Alan, overwhelmed with joy. 34

"You will not have to use your imagination," said the old man. "And, by the way, since there are always sirens, if by any chance you *should,* later on, slip a little, you need not worry. She will forgive you, in the end. She will be terribly hurt, of course, but she will forgive you—in the end." 35

"That will not happen," said Alan fervently. 36

"Of course not," said the old man. "But, if it did, you need not worry. She would never divorce you. Oh, no! And, of course, she will never give you the least, the very least, grounds for—uneasiness." 37

"And how much," said Alan, "is this wonderful mixture?" 38

"It is not as dear," said the old man, "as the glove-cleaner, or life-cleaner, as I sometimes call it. No. That is five thousand dollars, never a penny less. One has to be older than you are, to indulge in that sort of thing. One has to save up for it." 39

"But the love potion?" said Alan. 40

"Oh, that," said the old man, opening the drawer in the kitchen table, and taking out a tiny, rather dirty-looking phial. "That is just a dollar." 41

"I can't tell you how grateful I am," said Alan, watching him fill it. 42

"I like to oblige," said the old man. "Then customers come back, later in life, when they are better off, and want more expensive things. Here you are. You will find it very effective." 43

"Thank you again," said Alan. "Good-bye." 44

"Au revoir," said the old man. 45

★ Meaning and Understanding

1. What is the story's theme?

2. Why does the old man even discuss the "glove cleaner" if he knows Alan is neither interested nor "old enough"?

3. Does the old man make the relationship Alan will soon have with Diana sound good? What in the story supports your opinion?

4. Do you suppose Diana knows Alan is purchasing the potion? Would she approve?

★ Techniques and Strategies

1. Where does the author describe the building and room? How do these contribute to the atmosphere?

2. Discuss the use of dialogue in the story. What does it accomplish?

3. Where does the story convey the old man's opinion of love? What is this opinion? Is it idealized or realistic? How do you know?

★ Speaking of Values

1. "It is only when one is in a position to oblige that one can be so confidential." What does this sentence from paragraph 17 mean and how does it apply to the story?

2. The old man says, "Consider the spiritual side" and discusses how Diana's indifference toward Alan will change to devotion. But the old man also discusses some other behaviors Diana will develop which may well become problematic. What do you think the author is suggesting about marriage? Do you agree?

3. What is a "life cleaner" in the story? Why is it more expensive than a love potion? Why do people need life cleaners? What is the author saying about our wishes coming true? What values does the comment imply?

★ Values Conversation

Form groups and discuss relationships that you or people you know have tried to alter. How much have they been able to change a relationship? Why?

★ Writing about Values

1. Write an essay in which you discuss a specific romantic relationship or relationships in general in terms of this cliché: "Be careful what you wish for—you may get it."

2. Write an essay in which you discuss an instance in which you did not take some "good" advice about love and romance. What did you ultimately learn from the experience?

3. Write an essay, in the form of a letter to a friend, in which you suggest a big change in the friend's behavior and identify the benefits of this change.

Lisa Schiffren

Gay Marriage, an Oxymoron

Lisa Schiffren is a journalist who was educated at Bryn Mawr College.
She has published extensively in many magazines, including the *National
Review* and *The Wall Street Journal.* During the Bush administration, she
served as a speech writer for Vice President Dan Quayle.

------ ★ ------

As study after study and victim after victim testify to the social devasta- 1
tion of the sexual revolution, easy divorce and out-of-wedlock motherhood, marriage is fashionable again. And parenthood has transformed
many baby boomers into advocates of bourgeois norms.

Indeed, we have come so far that the surprise issue of the political 2
season is whether homosexual "marriage" should be legalized. The
Hawaii courts will likely rule that gay marriage is legal, and other
states will be required to accept those marriages as valid.

Considering what a momentous change this would be—a radical 3
redefinition of society's most fundamental institution—there has been
almost no real debate. This is because the premise is unimaginable to
many, and the forces of political correctness have descended on the discussion, raising the cost of opposition. But one may feel the same affection for one's homosexual friends and relatives as for any other, and be
genuinely pleased for the happiness they derive from relationships,
while opposing gay marriage for principled reasons.

"Same-sex marriage" is inherently incompatible with our culture's 4
understanding of the institution. Marriage is essentially a lifelong compact between a man and woman committed to sexual exclusivity and
the creation and nurture of offspring. For most Americans, the marital
union—as distinguished from other sexual relationships and legal and
economic partnerships—is imbued with an aspect of holiness. Though
many of us are uncomfortable using religious language to discuss social and political issues, Judeo-Christian morality informs our view of
family life.

Though it is not polite to mention it, what the Judeo-Christian tra- 5
dition has to say about homosexual unions could not be clearer. In a diverse, open society such as ours, tolerance of homosexuality is a
necessity. But for many, its practice depends on a trick of cognitive dis-
sonance that allows people to believe in the Judeo-Christian moral order while accepting, often with genuine regard, the different lives of

homosexual acquaintances. That is why, though homosexuals may believe that they are merely seeking a small expansion of the definition of
marriage, the majority of Americans perceive this change as a radical
deconstruction of the institution.

6   Some make the conservative argument that making marriage a
civil right will bring stability, an end to promiscuity and a sense of fairness to gay men and women. But they miss the point. Society cares
about stability in heterosexual unions because it is critical for raising
healthy children and transmitting the values that are the basis of our
culture.

7   Whether homosexual relationships endure is of little concern to society. That is also true of most childless marriages, harsh as it is to say.
Society has wisely chosen not to differentiate between marriages, because it would require meddling into the motives and desires of everyone who applies for a license.

8   In traditional marriage, the tie that really binds for life is shared responsibility for the children. (A small fraction of gay couples may
choose to raise children together, but such children are offspring of one
partner and an outside contributor.) What will keep gay marriages together when individuals tire of each other?

9   Similarly, the argument that legal marriage will check promiscuity
by gay males raises the question of how a "piece of paper" will do what
the threat of AIDS has not. Lesbians seem to have little problem with
monogamy, or the rest of what constitutes "domestication," despite the
absence of official status.

10   Finally, there is the so-called fairness argument. The Government
gives tax benefits, inheritance rights and employee benefits only to the
married. Again, these financial benefits exist to help couples raise children. Tax reform is an effective way to remove distinctions among
earners.

11   If the American people are interested in a radical experiment with
same-sex marriages, then subjecting it to the political process is the
right route. For a court in Hawaii to assume that it has the power to
radically redefine marriage is a stunning abuse of power. To present
homosexual marriage as a fait accompli, without national debate, is a
serious political error. A society struggling to recover from 30 years of
weakened norms and broken families is not likely to respond gently to
having an institution central to most people's lives altered.

★ Meaning and Understanding

1. What situation in Hawaii prompted the article?

2. What does the writer think about being friends with homosexuals?
   Why?

3. What does Schiffren see as the main purpose of marriage?

4. What claims does the writer make about Judeo-Christian tradition and homosexual unions?

5. What distinctions does the writer make between gay males and lesbians? Is the distinction valid, do you think? Why or why not?

★ Techniques and Strategies

1. What is the significance of the essay's title? How does it anticipate the essay's principle argument? What is an oxymoron?

2. What are the essay's supporting points? Which of these seems best expressed?

3. The writer admits to making a "harsh" statement about childless couples and their importance in society. Which other statements in the essay seem harsh? How do you think the harshness helps to sway or dissuade?

4. Study the introduction and conclusion. How well do they respectively set and reset the discussion?

5. Who is Schiffren's audience here? How can you tell?

★ Speaking of Values

1. What value does the writer place on children in society? Where do you find this value expressed? Why might you agree or disagree with her position here?

2. The essay opens its discussion by pointing a finger at the "the devastation of the sexual revolution." What does she mean by the sexual revolution? Do you agree with the writer's evaluation of the sexual revolution? Why or why not?

3. Schiffren makes the argument for open debate on the topic of gay marriage. Do you believe that our society has sufficiently explored the issue of gay marriage? Why or why not? What might we gain as a society from open discussion? What might we lose? What might we gain as individuals? What related issues do you think need debate?

4. Do you see any difference in the kind of life and relations the writer favors for one group of committed couples over another? Why? What are your thoughts about this difference in terms of the value of equality?

5. The writer states: "Tolerance of homosexuality is a necessity." How do most Americans today react to this idea, do you think? How do you

think Schiffren would define tolerance? How do you define it? Do you think her position on gay marriage reflects tolerance? Why or why not?

★ *Values Conversation*

Schiffren writes: "Marriage is essentially a lifelong compact between a man and woman committed to sexual exclusivity and the creation and nurture of offspring." Form groups and discuss that statement. What do you see marriage as, essentially? Report to the class your group's views on marriage in this context.

★ *Writing about Values*

1. Write an essay defining marriage.

2. Do some research on gay marriage or childless marriages. Write an essay about some aspect of such unions that interests you.

3. Write about a marriage or relation that a larger community challenges. How has the community response affected the relation and people involved? Draw on your personal experience or observations of people you know or characters in books, TV shows, or movies.

Andrew Sullivan

Let Gays Marry

Born in 1963, Andrew Sullivan was educated at Oxford and Harvard. He writes for the magazine *New Republic* and has written two books, *Bushisms* (1992) and *Virtually Normal* (1996). In this *Newsweek* editorial, Sullivan weighs the benefits of gay marriage.

---- ★ ----

A state cannot deem a class of persons a stranger to its laws," declared 1 the Supreme Court last week. It was a monumental statement. Gay men and lesbians, the conservative court said, are no longer strangers in America. They are citizens, entitled, like everyone else, to equal protection—no special rights, but simple equality.

For the first time in Supreme Court history, gay men and women 2 were seen not as some powerful lobby trying to subvert America, but as the people we truly are—the sons and daughters of countless mothers and fathers, with all the weaknesses and strengths and hopes of everybody else. And what we seek is not some special place in America but merely to be a full and equal part of America, to give back to our society without being forced to lie or hide or live as second-class citizens.

That is why marriage is so central to our hopes. People ask us why 3 we want the right to marry, but the answer is obvious. It's the same reason anyone wants the right to marry. At some point in our lives, some of us are lucky enough to meet the person we truly love. And we want to commit to that person in front of our family and country for the rest of our lives. It's the most simple, the most natural, the most human instinct in the world. How could anyone seek to oppose that?

Yes, at first blush, it seems like a radical proposal, but, when you 4 think about it some more, it's actually the opposite. Throughout American history, to be sure, marriage has been between a man and a woman, and in many ways our society is built upon that institution. But none of that need change in the slightest. After all, no one is seeking to take away anybody's right to marry, and no one is seeking to force any church to change any doctrine in any way. Particular religious arguments against same-sex marriage are rightly debated within the churches and faiths themselves. That is not the issue here: there is a separation between church and state in this country. We are only asking that when the government gives out *civil* marriage licenses, those of us who are gay should be treated like anybody else.

5   Of course, some argue that marriage is *by definition* between a man and a woman. But for centuries, marriage was *by definition* a contract in which the wife was her husband's legal property. And we changed that. For centuries, marriage was *by definition* between two people of the same race. And we changed that. We changed these things because we recognized that human dignity is the same whether you are a man or a woman, black or white. And no one has any more of a choice to be gay than to be black or white or male or female.

6   Some say that marriage is only about raising children, but we let childless heterosexual couples be married (Bob and Elizabeth Dole, Pat and Shelley Buchanan, for instance). Why should gay couples be treated differently? Others fear that there is no logical difference between allowing same-sex marriage and sanctioning polygamy and other horrors. But the issue of whether to sanction multiple spouses (gay or straight) is completely separate from whether, in the existing institution between two unrelated adults, the government should discriminate between its citizens.

7   This is, in fact, if only Bill Bennett[1] could see it, a deeply conservative cause. It seeks to change no one else's rights or marriages in any way. It seeks merely to promote monogamy, fidelity and the disciplines of family life among people who have long been cast to the margins of society. And what could be a *more* conservative project than that? Why indeed would any conservative seek to oppose those very family values for gay people that he or she supports for everybody else? Except, of course, to make gay men and lesbians strangers in their own country, to forbid them ever to come home.

★ *Meaning and Understanding*

1. What are Sullivan's reasons for wanting to legalize gay marriage?

2. What is the significance of the Supreme Court's opinion that "a state cannot deem a class of persons a stranger to its laws"?

3. According to the writer, why does the proposal to legalize gay marriage only "seem" radical?

4. How does Sullivan address the issue of religious arguments against same-sex marriages?

5. What issue does Sullivan raise about polygamy? Why does he raise it, do you think?

---

[1]Former Secretary of Education, William Bennett is a conservative spokesmen for American values. His essay, "Revolt against God: America's Spiritual Disaster," appears in Chapter 7 of this book.

★ *Techniques and Strategies*

1. The writer notes several reasons why gay marriage should be legalized. Which argument or arguments do you find most convincing? Why? Which argument or arguments do you find most questionable. Why?

2. What effect does the quotation from the Supreme Court opinion have on the reader? Where else in the essay does the writer consider specific people's opinions? To what end? How effective is the strategy?

3. How does the title reflect the thesis of this essay? How does Sullivan elaborate on the thesis?

4. Who is the audience for this piece? Why has the writer targeted this audience, do you think?

5. What is the effect of the writer's use of the first person plural ("we") instead of the first person singular ("I")?

6. Sullivan presents a number of arguments that oppose his. What are they? Why does he use them in his essay? How do they help convince you of his point?

★ *Speaking of Values*

1. The concept of equality, as stated in the first paragraph, seems clear and simple enough. Why, then, have gay rights in general met such resistance in the past? What is your feeling about gay rights and the degree of protection afforded gays under the Constitution?

2. Why do people want the right to marry? Is it, in fact, "the most simple, the most natural, the most human instinct in the world"? If so, how do you account for the opposition to gay marriage or other kinds of marriage that seem atypical—a young and old partner, partners from different religions or races?

3. Sullivan radically reverses prevalent notions by saying that gay marriage is "actually a conservative issue." Why might you agree or disagree with his view here?

4. Sullivan advances the argument that "marriage is by definition between a man and a woman" in an effort to refute it. What is your reaction to the argument here? The refutation?

5. Monogamy, fidelity, and the disciplines of family life: these are values dear to Americans. Why would people resist, then, the argument for gay marriage?

★ *Values Conversation*

Form groups and discuss the pros and cons for legalizing gay marriage. Consider the other groups' opinions and, if there are differences, have a class debate on the issue.

★ *Writing about Values*

1. Write an argumentative essay in which you express an opinion about gay marriage and substantiate it.

2. Do research to determine whether any states have completely legalized gay marriage or have created some sort of legal designation for unmarried couples, such as California's "domestic partners" status. Write an "update" on some of these legal decisions. How have they influenced attitudes locally?

3. Write an essay about monogamy as an ideal and a reality.

Phillip Lopate

Revisionist Nuptials

Phillip Lopate is a teacher in the New York City Public Schools system. He was born in 1943 and educated at Columbia University. He writes poetry, novels, and nonfiction, including *The Daily Round* (1976) and *Being with Children* (1989). Here he reviews the idea of traditional and untraditional marriage vows.

————— ★ —————

Nothing arouses my ire more than the practice of brides and grooms re-   1
writing the traditional wedding ceremony and making speeches of their vows. There is something unseemly about this intervention by the supposed recipient of grace, like Napoleon seizing the coronet and crowning himself.

Marriage I take to be a submission to the social and religious laws   2
of the community, and the charm of the traditional ceremony was that the participants were properly submissive. Often you could not even hear the responses, they were delivered in such a murmur. The silence of the listening couple, broken only at one point by shy monosyllabic avowals, made a nice contrast to the confident, expounding voice of the clergyman or officiating party. And the familiarity of the words had a lulling effect, allowing the audience's attention to stray to phys-ical details of dress and architecture. Traditionally, the couple were seen either in quarter-profile or with their backs fully turned. Now, as "backs to the audience" is considered a cardinal sin for stage perform-ers, such a posture emphasized that *this* man and woman were not be-fore us as entertainers, they were engaged in their own special drama, the importance of which permitted them the breaking of this old stage rule. Their backs provided also, I think, a screen of delicacy, to protect the feelings of those in the crowd who were less amorously blessed. It is bad enough to have to witness people in love vowing devotion for-ever, but to have them turn around and face us and boast is really too much.

The non-traditional newlyweds become orators instead of orants,   3
and, in doing so, encourage us to judge them by the stricter critical standards of rhetoric. "I liked your speech," one says afterward to the groom, as to a politician—rather than "I'm so happy for you!"

I went to a revisionist wedding recently. First the clergywoman,   4
dressed as an Indian princess, disdaining any prepared texts, improvised

a poem on the spot, chanting phrases about love and work and accompanying them with mime gestures of a Hopi-like nature, such as the pounding of maize and the tumbling of a waterfall. This took place in a crowded loft in Manhattan. Then friends and relatives delivered testimonials to the fine characters of the lovers. A young man, stocky and bearded, who—rumor circulated—still carried a torch for the bride, read one of Whitman's short sensual poems. It seemed an odd choice, in light of the fact that the clasped bosoms Whitman was referring to belonged to two hairy men. Was this a jinx on the newlyweds? Then the mother of the bride, a notoriously critical parent, expressed pride and pleasure in her daughter's recent professional successes and praised the gentleness of the groom. A sigh of relief went through the room that she had not been more patronizing. She was followed by the groom's nine-year-old daughter, who made a little speech about how much she was expecting to like her new mommy.

5   All these remarks were capped by the bride's and groom's prepared statements. Each several pages long, the speeches were models of nonsexist sentiment, with pledges to share the domestic work and respect the other's space. True, they were not all jargon: they had certain moments of attractive candor. The bride, for instance, stated that she was glad she would be gaining a daughter along with a husband, since she was forty and had no intention of bearing children now. The groom said he expected to retain feelings of solitude for the rest of his life. They came across in these statements as decent, warm people, yet whenever they spoke about their love, it was uncomfortable to listen in. Their language seemed more suited for a wedding anniversary than the start of a new adventure. The fact—known to all present but never mentioned—that they had been living together for six years crept into the tone of every sentence, lending both their vows an air of weary apologia.

6   Perhaps it would be hypocritical nowadays to pretend the bride and groom are virgins. But to present oneself as already staidly uxorious seems a step too far in the opposite extreme, and an insult to the drama of matrimony.

7   Not that there aren't some good arguments for revisionist wedding ceremonies. Many modern couples come from different faiths, and, given the difficulty of finding a liturgy of such neutrality that it does not mention Christ, the Torah, Buddha, or even God, one is naturally tempted to write one's own. The understandable objections of feminists to the phrase "man and wife" and to other patriarchal insinuations also make the traditional script problematic. There is also the creative urge to surpass the old form and devise something better, more contemporary. But in trying to update liturgy, one immediately runs into the danger of sounding both trendy and anachronistic: in

short, silly. The truth is that few of us have the theological gravity to pull off the revision of a religious rite.

I take exception in any case to the notion that modern life is bereft of rituals, and that we need self-consciously to re-sacralize the world. There are enough natural rites of passage of the deepest nature in any person's life span, from the discovery of sex to the death of a parent. Moreover, customs cannot be new-minted by composing personalized, disposable ceremonies for every occasion. A one-time-only tradition is no tradition at all.

For a while, there were weddings publicized because of their unusual locations: people married on home plate, or at the lettuce counter of the supermarket where they first met, or in a bowling alley. But the style of the eighties seems to be domestic. The couple is married at home, ensuring them maximum supervisory control over every detail. Perhaps because many are marrying for the second or third time, they may remember back with shame to the first youthful wedding, when they were steered about by parents and clergy. This time they will give *themselves* away.

Ah, hubris. The truth is that one way or another, the newlyweds-to-be remain sacrificial lambs led to the altar. Traditionally, this symbolism of sacrifice was expressed in the pair's cramped speech and handcuffed gestural constraint. Change that, allow them a chance to babble on, and you distort the true pathos of the situation.

If there is to be any reformation in the wedding ritual, I as an old Bachelor would propose that it be made more somber. Marriage is a serious, not to say tragic, business. Were I ever to marry again, I would like both bride and groom to be dressed in black, with sackcloth and ashes, and maybe a costumed Grim Reaper with scythe standing to the side, to remind the gathered assembly that here is the death of freedom and pleasure's variety.

★ Meaning and Understanding

1. What are revisionist nuptials?

2. For the writer, what gives the traditional wedding ceremony charm?

3. Why does the revisionist wedding, which the writer recounts, have "an air of weary apologia" (paragraph 5)?

4. Does the writer think there are any good reasons to revise the traditional wedding script? What, for instance?

5. What is *hubris* and why does the writer feel that individuals who revise traditions may be guilty of it?

★ Techniques and Strategies

1. What is Lopate's thesis? Where does he state it? What effect does this placement of thesis have on the reader?

2. In paragraph 1, the writer uses a simile, likening marrying couples to something else. What is the simile? How effective is it? Why? Where else does Lopate heighten his language figuratively? Can you find metaphor and overstatement? Where? What is the effect of these devices on the essay's meaning?

3. The writer praises traditional ceremonies for allowing "the audience's attention to stray to physical details of dress and architecture" (paragraph 2). What does this statement tell you about the writer's interests and attitudes?

4. Consider the descriptions in the essay—of the positions of the traditional bride and groom, for example, and of the recently seen revisionist wedding. What makes these descriptions effective?

5. What is your view of the last paragraph? How effective is it as a conclusion for the essay? Why do you think so? How might Lopate's attitude toward marriage in general have colored his approach and tone throughout the essay?

★ Speaking of Values

1. Why do nontraditional newlyweds become orators instead of orants? What would Lopate prefer? How do you feel about brides and grooms taking rhetorical control of their ceremonies? Do you think this control suggests that the marriages that follow are less traditional as well? Why or why not?

2. At the revisionist wedding he recently attended, the writer found certain of the newlyweds' sentiments to have an "attractive candor" (paragraph 5). What did they say to prompt his comment? How do you feel about their statements?

3. Lopate writes in paragraph 8: "There are enough natural rites of passage of the deepest nature in any person's life span." What do you think he is stating here about modern life and the opportunities for ritual? Do you agree? Why or why not?

4. The essay states a belief that marriage is a "submission to the social and religious laws of the community" (paragraph 2). Why might you agree or disagree with his point here? How do the married people you know submit to community's laws? How do they not?

5. In paragraph 11 Lopate calls marriage "the death of freedom and plea-sure's variety." What do you think he means? Is he serious? Why or why not? What do you think of this observation?

★ *Values Conversation*

"Customs cannot be new-minted by composing personalized, disposable ceremonies for every occasion. A one-time-only tradition is no tradition at all." Form groups and discuss this point. Use the traditional marriage cere-mony as your primary topic, but if the group would like to examine a different ceremony, do so. Are customs and traditions, by definition, some-thing that happen both systematically and repeatedly? Are the similarities between a revisionist wedding and a traditional wedding enough that the former is still a wedding?

★ *Writing about Values*

1. Write an essay in which you present a theory of marriage (à la Lopate's "submission theory"). Identify what you see as the crucial elements of a wedding ceremony in the spirit of that definition.

2. Classify the kinds of married love you have observed. Your essay can be playful or serious. It can argue a thesis—that one kind is the best, that they all have a core of something in common, or whatever you wish to express. Use examples from your life, celebrity lives, TV, books, or movies to substantiate your depiction and claims.

3. How would you summarize Lopate's marriage values from this piece? Write an essay that explores the values he asserts and compare them to your own.

Values in Review

1. Poe and Hopkins both consider love among children. How do their essays relate to each other? Write an essay that considers the similarities and differences in topic, approach, and conclusions in these two selections.

2. Consider the position of tradition in the essays by Schiffren and Lopate. Write an essay on what you see as the relation between marriage and tradition, reflecting on the assertions of these two writers.

3. The images of love in Chapter 8 are varied. What does love mean most essentially to you? Reflect on your position in relation to at least three readings in the chapter.

Chapter 9

Science and Technology

The Internet

Animal research

Global warming

Women in science

Media

Technology and the library

Scientific misconduct

Benjamin Franklin

Letter to Joseph Priestley

Benjamin Franklin (1706–1790) was a statesman for the emerging American republic, but he was also fascinated by the advance of eighteenth-century science. He was deeply committed to experimental observation, and his *Experiments and Observations on Electricity* (1751–1753) attracted readers from all over the world. He wrote to British scientists regularly; in this letter to Joseph Priestly, the discoverer of oxygen, Franklin considers the potential effects of science on humanity.

———— ★ ————

Passy, Feb. 8, 1780.

Dear Sir,

1   Your kind letter of September 27 came to hand but very lately, the bearer having stayed long in Holland. I always rejoice to hear of your being still employed in experimental researches into nature, and of the Success you meet with. The rapid Progress *true* Science now makes, occasions my regretting sometimes that I was born so soon. It is impossible to imagine the height to which may be carried, in a thousand years, the power of man over matter. We may perhaps learn to deprive large masses of their gravity, and give them absolute levity, for the sake of easy transport. Agriculture may diminish its labour and double its produce; all diseases may by sure means be prevented or cured, not excepting even that of old age, and our lives lengthened at pleasure even beyond the antediluvian standard. O that moral science were in as fair a way of improvement, that men would cease to be wolves to one another, and that human beings would at length learn what they now improperly call humanity!

2   I am glad my little paper on the *Aurora Borealis* pleased. If it should occasion further enquiry, and so produce a better hypothesis, it will not be wholly useless. I am ever, with the greatest and most sincere esteem, dear sir, yours very affectionately

B. Franklin.

★ *Meaning and Understanding*

1. Why does Franklin write to Priestly?

2. Why does Franklin sometimes regret that he was born too soon?

3. What does the writer believe that science might accomplish for objects with large masses?

4. What does Franklin believe possible in the realm of curing diseases?

5. What does he hope that "moral science" might accomplish? What does Franklin mean by the phrase "moral science"?

★ Techniques and Strategies

1. What would you say is the thesis of the letter—that is, what is Franklin trying to say to his correspondent?

2. What is the tone of the letter? What does the tone tell you of Franklin's relationship with Priestly, one of the most noted scientists of his age?

3. What does Franklin mean by the figurative expression "men would cease to be wolves to one another" (paragraph 1)? How does the metaphor help him make his point to Priestly?

★ Speaking of Values

1. In his complaint that he might have been born too soon, Franklin reflects an unabashed enthusiasm for the potential of science to influence our lives for the better. Now, more than 200 years later, what would Franklin say about the progress of science in general?

2. In what ways was Franklin right about the role he saw for science in affecting our health? In what ways was he wrong?

3. In his support for moral growth and progress for humanity, Franklin echoes the beliefs of his time, the period of the Enlightenment. Why might you agree or disagree that people are "wolves to each other" and that learning humanity toward each other is as important as scientific progress? Do Americans today value "moral science"? In what ways?

★ Values Conversation

Form groups and consider your views of the role of science in our lives. What scientific advances have helped humanity immeasurably over the years? How has science contributed to some of the problems we face as a nation? What is the most appropriate attitude to take toward supporting scientific advancement, do you think? What ethical issues should enter the conversation? Report your group's findings to the rest of the class.

★ Writing about Values

1. Write an essay in which you discuss the most technologically or scientifically advanced part of your everyday life and how it influences

your existence. For example, you might want to discuss the Internet, the automobile, video games, food processors, the movies, television, or hospital technology.

2. Write a letter to Franklin from the 1990s, telling him how his view of science was either fulfilled or off base.

3. Write an essay in which you explain how people could "cease to be wolves to one another" and learn "what they now improperly call humanity."

Nathaniel Hawthorne

The Birthmark

Nathaniel Hawthorne (1804–1864) wrote many novels and short stories in which he often focused on Puritan New England to explore the interactions between "the Actual and the Imaginary." Among his most famous novels are *The Scarlet Letter* (1850) and *The House of the Seven Gables* (1851). In "The Birthmark" he looks at the consequences when science tampers with nature.

———— ★ ————

In the latter part of the last century there lived a man of science, an eminent proficient in every branch of natural philosophy, who not long before our story opens had made experience of a spiritual affinity more attractive than any chemical one. He had left his laboratory to the care of an assistant, cleared his fine countenance from the furnace smoke, washed the stain of acids from his fingers, and persuaded a beautiful woman to become his wife. In those days when the comparatively recent discovery of electricity and other kindred mysteries of Nature seemed to open paths into the region of miracle, it was not unusual for the love of science to rival the love of woman in its depth and absorbing energy. The higher intellect, the imagination, the spirit, and even the heart might all find their congenial ailment in pursuits which, as some of their ardent votaries believed, would ascend from one step of powerful intelligence to another, until the philosopher should lay his hand on the secret of creative force and perhaps make new worlds for himself. We know not whether Aylmer possessed this degree of faith in man's ultimate control over Nature. He had devoted himself, however, too unreservedly to scientific studies ever to be weaned from them by any second passion. His love for his young wife might prove the stronger of the two; but it could only be by intertwining itself with his love of science, and uniting the strength of the latter to his own. 1

Such a union accordingly took place, and was attended with truly remarkable consequences and a deeply impressive moral. One day, very soon after their marriage, Aylmer sat gazing at his wife with a trouble in his countenance that grew stronger until he spoke. 2

"Georgiana," said he, "has it never occurred to you that the mark upon your cheek might be removed?" 3

"No, indeed," said she, smiling; but perceiving the seriousness of his manner, she blushed deeply. "To tell you the truth it has been so often called a charm that I was simple enough to imagine it might be so." 4

5   "Ah, upon another face perhaps it might," replied her husband; "but never on yours. No, dearest Georgiana, you came so nearly perfect from the hand of Nature that this slightest possible defect, which we hesitate whether to term a defect or a beauty, shocks me, as being the visible mark of earthly imperfection."

6   "Shocks you, my husband!" cried Georgiana, deeply hurt; at first reddening with momentary anger, but then bursting into tears. "Then why did you take me from my mother's side? You cannot love what shocks you!"

7   To explain this conversation it must be mentioned that in the centre of Georgiana's left cheek there was a singular mark, deeply interwoven, as it were, with the texture and substance of her face. In the usual state of her complexion—a healthy though delicate bloom—the mark wore a tint of deeper crimson, which imperfectly defined its shape amid the surrounding rosiness. When she blushed it gradually became more indistinct, and finally vanished amid the triumphant rush of blood that bathed the whole cheek with its brilliant glow. But if any shifting motion caused her to turn pale there was the mark again, a crimson stain upon the snow, in what Aylmer sometimes deemed an almost fearful distinctness. Its shape bore not a little similarity to the human hand, though of the smallest pygmy size. Georgiana's lovers were wont to say that some fairy at her birth hour had laid her tiny hand upon the infant's cheek, and left this impress there in token of the magic endowments that were to give her such sway over all hearts. Many a desperate swain would have risked life for the privilege of pressing his lips to the mysterious hand. It must not be concealed, however, that the impression wrought by this fairy sign manual varied exceedingly, according to the difference of temperament in the beholders. Some fastidious persons—but they were exclusively of her own sex—affirmed that the bloody hand, as they chose to call it, quite destroyed the effect of Georgiana's beauty, and rendered her countenance even hideous. But it would be as reasonable to say that one of those small blue stains which sometimes occur in the purest statuary marble would convert the Eve of Powers[1] to a monster. Masculine observers, if the birthmark did not heighten their admiration, contented themselves with wishing it away, that the world might possess one living specimen of ideal loveliness without the semblance of a flaw. After his marriage,—for he thought little or nothing about the matter before,—Aylmer discovered that this was the case with himself.

8   Had she been less beautiful,—if Envy's self could have found aught else to sneer at,—he might have felt his affection heightened by the prettiness of this mimic hand, now vaguely portrayed, now lost,

---

[1]A reference to the sculpture *Eve before the Fall*, by Hiram Powers, a nineteenth-century artist.

now stealing forth again and glimmering to and fro with every pulse of emotion that throbbed within her heart; but seeing her otherwise so perfect, he found this one defect grow more and more intolerable with every moment of their united lives. It was the fatal flaw of humanity which Nature, in one shape or another, stamps ineffaceably on all her productions, either to imply that they are temporary and finite, or that their perfection must be wrought by toil and pain. The crimson hand expressed the ineludible gripe in which mortality clutches the highest and purest of earthly mold, degrading them into kindred with the lowest, and even with the very brutes, like whom their visible frames return to dust. In this manner, selecting it as the symbol of his wife's liability to sin, sorrow, decay, and death, Aylmer's sombre imagination was not long in rendering the birthmark a frightful object, causing him more trouble and horror than ever Georgiana's beauty, whether of soul or sense, had given him delight.

At all the seasons which should have been their happiest, he invariably and without intending it, nay, in spite of a purpose to the contrary, reverted to this one disastrous topic. Trifling as it at first appeared, it so connected itself with innumerable trains of thought and modes of feeling that it became the central point of all. With the morning twilight Aylmer opened his eyes upon his wife's face and recognized the symbol of imperfection; and when they sat together at the evening hearth his eyes wandered stealthily to her cheek, and beheld, flickering with the blaze of the wood fire, the spectral hand that wrote mortality where he would fain have worshipped. Georgiana soon learned to shudder at his gaze. It needed but a glance with the peculiar expression that his face often wore to change the roses of her cheek into a deathlike paleness, amid which the crimson hand was brought strongly out, like a bas-relief of ruby on the whitest marble.

Late one night when the lights were growing dim, so as hardly to betray the stain on the poor wife's cheek, she herself, for the first time, voluntarily took up the subject.

"Do you remember, my dear Aylmer," said she, with a feeble attempt at a smile, "have you any recollection of a dream last night about this odious hand?"

"None! none whatever!" replied Aylmer, starting; but then he added, in a dry, cold tone, affected for the sake of concealing the real depth of his emotion, "I might well dream of it; for before I fell asleep it had taken a pretty firm hold of my fancy."

"And you did dream of it?" continued Georgiana, hastily; for she dreaded lest a gush of tears should interrupt what she had to say. "A terrible dream! I wonder that you can forget it. Is it possible to forget this one expression?—'It is in her heart now; we must have it out!' Reflect, my husband; for by all means I would have you recall that dream."

14   The mind is in a sad state when Sleep, the all-involving, cannot confine her spectres within the dim region of her sway, but suffers them to break forth, affrighting this actual life with secrets that perchance belong to a deeper one. Aylmer now remembered his dream. He had fancied himself with his servant Aminadab, attempting an operation for the removal of the birthmark; but the deeper went the knife, the deeper sank the hand, until at length its tiny grasp appeared to have caught hold of Georgiana's heart; whence, however, her husband was inexorably resolved to cut or wrench it away.

15   When the dream had shaped itself perfectly in his memory, Aylmer sat in his wife's presence with a guilty feeling. Truth often finds its way to the mind close muffled in robes of sleep, and then speaks with uncompromising directness of matters in regard to which we practise an unconscious self-deception during our waking moments. Until now he had not been aware of the tyrannizing influence acquired by one idea over his mind, and of the lengths which he might find in his heart to go for the sake of giving himself peace.

16   "Aylmer," resumed Georgiana, solemnly, "I know not what may be the cost to both of us to rid me of this fatal birthmark. Perhaps its removal may cause cureless deformity; or it may be the stain goes as deep as life itself. Again: do we know that there is a possibility, on any terms, of unclasping the firm gripe of this little hand which was laid upon me before I came into the world?"

17   "Dearest Georgiana, I have spent much thought upon the subject," hastily interrupted Aylmer. "I am convinced of the perfect practicability of its removal."

18   "If there be the remotest possibility of it," continued Georgiana, "let the attempt be made at whatever risk. Danger is nothing to me; for life, while this hateful mark makes me the object of your horror and disgust,—life is a burden which I would fling down with joy. Either remove this dreadful hand, or take my wretched life! You have deep science. All the world bears witness of it. You have achieved great wonders. Cannot you remove this little, little mark, which I cover with the tips of two small fingers? Is this beyond your power, for the sake of your own peace, and to save your poor wife from madness?"

19   "Noblest, dearest, tenderest wife," cried Aylmer, rapturously, "doubt not my power. I have already given this matter the deepest thought—thought which might almost have enlightened me to create a being less perfect than yourself. Georgiana, you have led me deeper than ever into the heart of science. I feel myself fully competent to render this dear cheek as faultless as its fellow; and then, most beloved, what will be my triumph when I shall have corrected what Nature left imperfect in her fairest work! Even Pygmalion, when his sculptured woman assumed life, felt not greater ecstasy than mine will be."

"It is resolved, then," said Georgiana, faintly smiling. "And, Aylmer, 20
spare me not, though you should find the birthmark take refuge in my
heart at last."

Her husband tenderly kissed her cheek—her right cheek—not that 21
which bore the impress of the crimson hand.

The next day Aylmer apprised his wife of a plan that he had 22
formed whereby he might have opportunity for the intense thought
and constant watchfulness which the proposed operation would require; while Georgiana, likewise, would enjoy the perfect repose essential to its success. They were to seclude themselves in the extensive
apartments occupied by Aylmer as a laboratory, and where, during his
toilsome youth, he had made discoveries in the elemental powers of
Nature that had roused the admiration of all the learned societies in
Europe. Seated calmly in this laboratory, the pale philosopher had investigated the secrets of the highest cloud region and of the profound-
est mines; he had satisfied himself of the causes that kindled and kept
alive the fires of the volcano; and had explained the mystery of foun-
tains, and how it is that they gush forth, some so bright and pure, and
others with such rich medicinal virtues, from the dark bosom of the
earth. Here, too, at an earlier period, he had studied the wonders of the
human frame, and attempted to fathom the very process by which Nature assimilates all her precious influences from earth and air, and from
the spiritual world, to create and foster man, her masterpiece. The latter pursuit, however, Aylmer had long laid aside in unwilling recognition of the truth—against which all seekers sooner or later stumble—
that our great creative Mother, while she amuses us with apparently
working in the broadest sunshine, is yet severely careful to keep her
own secrets, and, in spite of her pretended openness, shows us nothing
but results. She permits us, indeed, to mar, but seldom to mend, and,
like a jealous patentee, on no account to make. Now, however, Aylmer
resumed these half-forgotten investigations; not, of course, with such
hopes or wishes as first suggested them; but because they involved
much physiological truth and lay in the path of his proposed scheme
for the treatment of Georgiana.

As he led her over the threshold of the laboratory, Georgiana was 23
cold and tremulous. Aylmer looked cheerfully into her face, with intent
to reassure her, but was so startled with the intense glow of the birthmark upon the whiteness of her cheek that he could not restrain a
strong convulsive shudder. His wife fainted.

"Aminadab! Aminadab!" shouted Aylmer, stamping violently on 24
the floor.

Forthwith there issued from an inner apartment a man of low stat- 25
ure, but bulky frame, with shaggy hair hanging about his visage,
which was grimed with the vapors of the furnace. This personage had
been Aylmer's underworker during his whole scientific career, and was

admirably fitted for that office by his great mechanical readiness, and the skill with which, while incapable of comprehending a single principle, he executed all the details of his master's experiments. With his vast strength, his shaggy hair, his smoky aspect, and the indescribable earthiness that incrusted him, he seemed to represent man's physical nature; while Aylmer's slender figure, and pale, intellectual face, were no less apt a type of the spiritual element.

26   "Throw open the door of the boudoir, Aminadab," said Aylmer, "and burn a pastil."

27   "Yes, master," answered Aminadab, looking intently at the lifeless form of Georgiana; and then he muttered to himself, "If she were my wife, I'd never part with that birthmark."

28   When Georgiana recovered consciousness she found herself breathing an atmosphere of penetrating fragrance, the gentle potency of which had recalled her from her deathlike faintness. The scene around her looked like enchantment. Aylmer had converted those smoky, dingy, sombre rooms, where be had spent his brightest years in recondite pursuits, into a series of beautiful apartments not unfit to be the secluded abode of a lovely woman. The walls were hung with gorgeous curtains, which imparted the combination of grandeur and grace that no other species of adornment can achieve; and as they fell from the ceiling to the floor, their rich and ponderous folds, concealing all angles and straight lines, appeared to shut in the scene from infinite space. For aught Georgiana knew, it might be a pavilion among the clouds. And Aylmer, excluding the sunshine, which would have interfered with his chemical processes, had supplied its place with perfumed lamps, emitting flames of various hue, but all uniting in a soft, impurpled radiance. He now knelt by his wife's side, watching her earnestly, but without alarm; for he was confident in his science, and felt that he could draw a magic circle round her within which no evil might intrude.

29   "Where am I? Ah, I remember," said Georgiana, faintly; and she placed her hand over her cheek to hide the terrible mark from her husband's eyes.

30   "Fear not, dearest!" exclaimed he. "Do not shrink from me! Believe me, Georgiana, I even rejoice in this single imperfection, since it will be such a rapture to remove it."

31   "Oh, spare me!" sadly replied his wife. "Pray do not look at it again. I never can forget that convulsive shudder."

32   In order to soothe Georgiana, and, as it were, to release her mind from the burden of actual things, Aylmer now put in practice some of the light and playful secrets which science had taught him among its profounder lore. Airy figures, absolutely bodiless ideas, and forms of unsubstantial beauty came and danced before her, imprinting their momentary footsteps on beams of light. Though she had some indistinct

idea of the method of these optical phenomena, still the illusion was almost perfect enough to warrant the belief that her husband possessed sway over the spiritual world. Then again, when she felt a wish to look forth from her seclusion, immediately, as if her thoughts were answered, the procession of external existence flitted across a screen. The scenery and the figures of actual life were perfectly represented, but with that bewitching, yet indescribable difference which always makes a picture, an image, or a shadow so much more attractive than the original. When wearied of this, Aylmer bade her cast her eyes upon a vessel containing a quantity of earth. She did so, with little interest at first; but was soon startled to perceive the germ of a plant shooting upward from the soil. Then came the slender stalk; the leaves gradually unfolded themselves; and amid them was a perfect and lovely flower.

"It is magical!" cried Georgiana. "I dare not touch it." 33

"Nay, pluck it," answered Aylmer,—"pluck it, and inhale its brief 34 perfume while you may. The flower will wither in a few moments and leave nothing save its brown seed vessels; but thence may be perpetuated a race as ephemeral as itself."

But Georgiana had no sooner touched the flower than the whole 35 plant suffered a blight, its leaves turning coal-black as if by the agency of fire.

"There was too powerful a stimulus," said Aylmer, thoughtfully. 36

To make up for this abortive experiment, he proposed to take her 37 portrait by a scientific process of his own invention. It was to be effected by rays of light striking upon a polished plate of metal. Georgiana assented; but, on looking at the result, was affrighted to find the features of the portrait blurred and indefinable; while the minute figure of a hand appeared where the cheek should have been. Aylmer snatched the metallic plate and threw it into a jar of corrosive acid.

Soon, however, he forgot these mortifying failures. In the intervals 38 of study and chemical experiment he came to her flushed and exhausted, but seemed invigorated by her presence, and spoke in glowing language of the resources of his art. He gave a history of the long dynasty of the alchemists, who spent so many ages in quest of the universal solvent by which the golden principle might be elicited from all things vile and base. Aylmer appeared to believe that, by the plainest scientific logic, it was altogether within the limits of possibility to discover this long-sought medium; "but," he added, "a philosopher who should go deep enough to acquire the power would attain too lofty a wisdom to stoop to the exercise of it." Not less singular were his opinions in regard to the elixir vitae. He more than intimated that it was at his option to concoct a liquid that should prolong life for years, perhaps interminably; but that it would produce a discord in Nature which all the world, and chiefly the quaffer of the immortal nostrum, would find cause to curse.

39   "Aylmer, are you in earnest?" asked Georgiana, looking at him with amazement and fear. "It is terrible to possess such power, or even to dream of possessing it."

40   "Oh, do not tremble, my love," said her husband. "I would not wrong either you or myself by working such inharmonious effects upon our lives; but I would have you consider how trifling, in comparison, is the skill requisite to remove this little hand."

41   At the mention of the birthmark, Georgiana, as usual, shrank as if a redhot iron had touched her cheek.

42   Again Aylmer applied himself to his labors. She could hear his voice in the distant furnace room giving directions to Aminadab, whose harsh, uncouth, misshapen tones were audible in response, more like the grunt or growl of a brute than human speech. After hours of absence, Aylmer reappeared and proposed that she should now examine his cabinet of chemical products and natural treasures of the earth. Among the former he showed her a small vial, in which, he remarked, was contained a gentle yet most powerful fragrance, capable of impregnating all the breezes that blow across the kingdom. They were of inestimable value, the contents of that little vial; and, as he said so, he threw some of the perfume into the air and filled the room with piercing and invigorating delight.

43   "And what is this?" asked Georgiana, pointing to a small crystal globe containing a gold-colored liquid. "It is so beautiful to the eye that I could imagine it the elixir of life."

44   "In one sense it is," replied Aylmer; "or, rather, the elixir of immortality. It is the most precious poison that ever was concocted in this world. By its aid I could apportion the lifetime of any mortal at whom you might point your finger. The strength of the dose would determine whether he were to linger out years, or drop dead in the midst of a breath. No king on his guarded throne could keep his life if I, in my private station, should deem that the welfare of millions justified me in depriving him of it."

45   "Why do you keep such a terrific drug?" inquired Georgiana in horror.

46   "Do not mistrust me, dearest," said her husband, smiling; "its virtuous potency is yet greater than its harmful one. But see! here is a powerful cosmetic. With a few drops of this in a vase of water, freckles may be washed away as easily as the hands are cleansed. A stronger infusion would take the blood out of the cheek, and leave the rosiest beauty a pale ghost."

47   "Is it with this lotion that you intend to bathe my cheek?" asked Georgiana, anxiously.

48   "Oh, no," hastily replied her husband; "this is merely superficial. Your case demands a remedy that shall go deeper."

In his interviews with Georgiana, Aylmer generally made minute   49
inquiries as to her sensations and whether the confinement of the
rooms and the temperature of the atmosphere agreed with her. These
questions had such a particular drift that Georgiana began to conjecture that she was already subjected to certain physical influences, either breathed in with the fragrant air or taken with her food. She
fancied likewise, but it might be altogether fancy, that there was a stirring up of her system—a strange, indefinite sensation creeping through
her veins, and tingling, half painfully, half pleasurably, at her heart.
Still, whenever she dared to look into the mirror, there she beheld herself pale as a white rose and with the crimson birthmark stamped upon
her cheek. Not even Aylmer now hated it so much as she.

To dispel the tedium of the hours which her husband found it nec-   50
essary to devote to the processes of combination and analysis, Georgiana turned over the volumes of his scientific library. In many dark old
tomes she met with chapters full of romance and poetry. They were the
works of the philosophers of the middle ages, such as Albertus Mag-
nus, Cornelius Agrippa, Paracelsus, and the famous friar who created
the prophetic Brazen Head.[2] All these antique naturalists stood in advance of their centuries, yet were imbued with some of their credulity,
and therefore were believed, and perhaps imagined themselves to have
acquired from the investigation of Nature a power above Nature, and
from physics a sway over the spiritual world. Hardly less curious and
imaginative were the early volumes of the Transactions of the Royal Society, in which the members, knowing little of the limits of natural possibility, were continually recording wonders or proposing methods
whereby wonders might be wrought.

But to Georgiana the most engrossing volume was a large folio   51
from her husband's own hand, in which he had recorded every experiment of his scientific career, its original aim, the methods adopted for
its development, and its final success or failure, with the circumstances
to which either event was attributable. The book, in truth, was both the
history and emblem of his ardent, ambitious, imaginative, yet practical
and laborious life. He handled physical details as if there were nothing
beyond them; yet spiritualized them all, and redeemed himself from
materialism by his strong and eager aspiration towards the infinite. In
his grasp the veriest clod of earth assumed a soul. Georgiana, as she
read, reverenced Aylmer and loved him more profoundly than ever,
but with a less entire dependence on his judgment than heretofore.
Much as he had accomplished, she could not but observe that his most
splendid successes were almost invariably failures, if compared with

[2]Famous scientists through history. The "famous friar" is thirteenth-century scholar and
Franciscan Roger Bacon who supported inductive scientific reasoning.

the ideal at which he aimed. His brightest diamonds were the merest pebbles, and felt to be so by himself, in comparison with the inestimable gems which lay hidden beyond his reach. The volume, rich with achievements that had won renown for its author, was yet as melancholy a record as ever mortal hand had penned. It was the sad confession and continual exemplification of the shortcomings of the composite man, the spirit burdened with clay and working in matter, and of the despair that assails the higher nature at finding itself so miserably thwarted by the earthly part. Perhaps every man of genius in whatever sphere might recognize the image of his own experience in Aylmer's journal.

52   So deeply did these reflections affect Georgiana that she laid her face upon the open volume and burst into tears. In this situation she was found by her husband.

53   "It is dangerous to read in a sorcerer's books," said he with a smile, though his countenance was uneasy and displeased. "Georgiana, there are pages in that volume which I can scarcely glance over and keep my senses. Take heed lest it prove as detrimental to you."

54   "It has made me worship you more than ever," said she.

55   "Ah, wait for this one success," rejoined he, "then worship me if you will. I shall deem myself hardly unworthy of it. But come, I have sought you for the luxury of your voice. Sing to me, dearest."

56   So she poured out the liquid music of her voice to quench the thirst of his spirit. He then took his leave with a boyish exuberance of gaiety, assuring her that her seclusion would endure but a little longer, and that the result was already certain. Scarcely had he departed when Georgiana felt irresistibly impelled to follow him. She had forgotten to inform Aylmer of a symptom which for two or three hours past had begun to excite her attention. It was a sensation in the fatal birthmark, not painful, but which induced a restlessness throughout her system. Hastening after her husband, she intruded for the first time into the laboratory.

57   The first thing that struck her eye was the furnace, that hot and feverish worker, with the intense glow of its fire, which by the quantities of soot clustered above it seemed to have been burning for ages. There was a distilling apparatus in full operation. Around the room were retorts, tubes, cylinders, crucibles, and other apparatus of chemical research. An electrical machine stood ready for immediate use. The atmosphere felt oppressively close; and was tainted with gaseous odors which had been tormented forth by the processes of science. The severe and homely simplicity of the apartment with its naked walls and brick pavement, looked strange, accustomed as Georgiana had become to the fantastic elegance of her boudoir. But what chiefly, indeed almost solely, drew her attention, was the aspect of Aylmer himself.

58   He was pale as death, anxious and absorbed, and hung over the furnace as if it depended upon his utmost watchfulness whether the

liquid which it was distilling should be the draught of immortal happiness or misery. How different from the sanguine and joyous mien that he had assumed for Georgiana's encouragement!

"Carefully now, Aminadab; carefully, thou human machine; carefully, thou man of clay!" muttered Aylmer, more to himself than his assistant. "Now, if there be a thought too much or too little, it is all over." 59

"Ho! ho!" mumbled Aminadab. "Look, master! look!" 60

Aylmer raised his eyes hastily, and at first reddened, then grew paler than ever, on beholding Georgiana. He rushed towards her and seized her arm with a gripe that left the print of his fingers upon it. 61

"Why do you come hither? Have you no trust in your husband?" cried he, impetuously. "Would you throw the blight of that fatal birthmark over my labors? It is not well done. Go, prying woman, go!" 62

"Nay, Aylmer," said Georgiana with the firmness of which she possessed no stinted endowment, "it is not you that have a right to complain. You mistrust your wife; you have concealed the anxiety with which you watch the development of this experiment. Think not so unworthily of me, my husband. Tell me all the risk we run, and fear not that I shall shrink; for my share in it is far less than your own." 63

"No, no, Georgiana!" said Aylmer, impatiently; "it must not be." 64

"I submit," replied she calmly. "And, Aylmer, I shall quaff whatever draught you bring me; but it will be on the same principle that would induce me to take a dose of poison if offered by your hand." 65

"My noble wife," said Aylmer, deeply moved; "I knew not the height and depth of your nature until now. Nothing shall be concealed. Know, then, that this crimson hand, superficial as it seems, has clutched its grasp into your being with a strength of which I had no previous conception. I have already administered agents powerful enough to do aught except to change your entire physical system. Only one thing remains to be tried. If that fail us we are ruined." 66

"Why did you hesitate to tell me this?" asked she. 67

"Because, Georgiana," said Aylmer, in a low voice, "there is danger." 68

"Danger? There is but one danger—that this horrible stigma shall be left upon my cheek!" cried Georgiana. "Remove it, remove it, whatever be the cost, or we shall both go mad!" 69

"Heaven knows your words are too true," said Aylmer, sadly. "And now, dearest, return to your boudoir. In a little while all will be tested." 70

He conducted her back and took leave of her with a solemn tenderness which spoke far more than his words how much was now at stake. After his departure Georgiana became rapt in musings. She considered the character of Aylmer, and did it completer justice than at any previous moment. Her heart exulted, while it trembled, at his honorable love—so pure and lofty that it would accept nothing less than perfection nor miserably make itself contented with an earthlier nature than 71

he had dreamed of. She felt how much more precious was such a sentiment than that meaner kind which would have borne with the imperfection for her sake, and have been guilty of treason to holy love by
degrading its perfect idea to the level of the actual; and with her whole
spirit she prayed that, for a single moment, she might satisfy his highest
and deepest conception. Longer than one moment she well knew it could
not be; for his spirit was ever on the march, ever ascending, and each instant required something that was beyond the scope of the instant before.

72   The sound of her husband's footsteps aroused her. He bore a crystal goblet containing a liquor colorless as water, but bright enough to be
the draught of immortality. Aylmer was pale; but it seemed rather the
consequence of a highly-wrought state of mind and tension of spirit
than of fear or doubt.

73   "The concoction of the draught has been perfect," said he, in answer to Georgiana's look. "Unless all my science have deceived me, it
cannot fail."

74   "Save on your account, my dearest Aylmer," observed his wife, "I
might wish to put off this birthmark of mortality by relinquishing mortality itself in preference to any other mode. Life is but a sad possession
to those who have attained precisely the degree of moral advancement
at which I stand. Were I weaker and blinder it might be happiness.
Were I stronger, it might be endured hopefully. But, being what I find
myself, me thinks I am of all mortals the most fit to die."

75   "You are fit for heaven without tasting death!" replied her husband. "But why do we speak of dying? The draught cannot fail. Behold
its effect upon this plant."

76   On the window seat there stood a geranium diseased with yellow
blotches, which had overspread all its leaves. Aylmer poured a small
quantity of the liquid upon the soil in which it grew. In a little time,
when the roots of the plant had taken up the moisture, the unsightly
blotches began to be extinguished in a living verdure.

77   "There needed no proof," said Georgiana, quietly. "Give me the
goblet. I joyfully stake all upon your word."

78   "Drink, then, thou lofty creature!" exclaimed Aylmer, with fervid
admiration. "There is no taint of imperfection on thy spirit. Thy sensible frame, too, shall soon be all perfect."

79   She quaffed the liquid and returned the goblet to his hand.

80   "It is grateful," said she with a placid smile. "Methinks it is like water from a heavenly fountain; for it contains I know not what of unob-
trusive fragrance and deliciousness. It allays a feverish thirst that had
parched me for many days. Now, dearest, let me sleep. My earthly
senses are closing over my spirit like the leaves around the heart of a
rose at sunset."

81   She spoke the last words with a gentle reluctance, as if it required
almost more energy than she could command to pronounce the faint

and lingering syllables. Scarcely had they loitered through her lips ere she was lost in slumber. Aylmer sat by her side, watching her aspect with the emotions proper to a man the whole value of whose existence was involved in the process now to be tested. Mingled with this mood, however, was the philosophic investigation characteristic of the man of science. Not the minutest symptom escaped him. A heightened flush of the cheek, a slight irregularity of breath, a quiver of the eyelid, a hardly perceptible tremor through the frame,—such were the details which, as the moments passed, he wrote down in his folio volume. Intense thought had set its stamp upon every previous page of that volume, but the thoughts of years were all concentrated upon the last.

While thus employed, he failed not to gaze often at the fatal hand, 82 and not without a shudder. Yet once, by a strange and unaccountable impulse, he pressed it with his lips. His spirit recoiled, however, in the very act; and Georgiana, out of the midst of her deep sleep, moved uneasily and murmured as if in remonstrance. Again Aylmer resumed his watch. Nor was it without avail. The crimson hand, which at first had been strongly visible upon the marble paleness of Georgiana's cheek, now grew more faintly outlined. She remained not less pale than ever; but the birthmark, with every breath that came and went, lost somewhat of its former distinctness. Its presence had been awful; its departure was more awful still. Watch the stain of the rainbow fading out of the sky, and you will know how that mysterious symbol passed away.

"By Heaven! it is well-nigh gone!" said Aylmer to himself, in al- 83 most irrepressible ecstasy. "I can scarcely trace it now. Success! success! And now it is like the faintest rose color. The lightest flush of blood across her cheek would overcome it. But she is so pale!"

He drew aside the window curtain and suffered the light of natural 84 day to fall into the room and rest upon her cheek. At the same time he heard a gross, hoarse chuckle, which he had long known as his servant Aminadab's expression of delight.

"Ah, clod! ah, earthly mass!" cried Aylmer, laughing a sort of 85 frenzy, "you have served me well! Matter and spirit—earth and heaven—have both done their part in this! Laugh, thing of the senses! You have earned the right to laugh."

These exclamations broke Georgiana's sleep. She slowly unclosed 86 her eyes and gazed into the mirror which her husband had arranged for that purpose. A faint smile flitted over her lips when she recognized how barely perceptible was now that crimson hand which had once blazed forth with such disastrous brilliancy as to scare away all their happiness. But then her eyes sought Aylmer's face with a trouble and anxiety that he could by no means account for.

"My poor Aylmer!" murmured she. 87

"Poor? Nay, richest, happiest, most favored" exclaimed he. "My 88 peerless bride, it is successful! You are perfect!"

89   "My poor Aylmer," she repeated, with a more than human tenderness, "you have aimed loftily; you have done nobly. Do not repent that with so high and pure a feeling, you have rejected the best the earth could offer. Aylmer, dearest Aylmer, I am dying!"

90   Alas! it was too true! The fatal hand had grappled with the mystery of life, and was the bond by which an angelic spirit kept itself in union with a mortal frame. As the last crimson tint of the birthmark—that sole token of human imperfection—faded from her cheek, the parting breath of the now perfect woman passed into the atmosphere, and her soul, lingering a moment near her husband, took its heavenward flight. Then a hoarse, chuckling laugh was heard again! Thus ever does the gross fatality of earth exult in its invariable triumph over the immortal essence which, in this dim sphere of half development, demands the completeness of a higher state. Yet, had Aylmer reached a profounder wisdom, he need not thus have flung away the happiness which would have woven his mortal life of the selfsame texture with the celestial. The momentary circumstance was too strong for him; he failed to look beyond the shadowy scope of time, and living once for all in eternity, to find the perfect future in the present.

★ Meaning and Understanding

1. Describe the birthmark of the story's title.

2. Why is Aylmer disturbed by his wife's appearance? What does he propose? How does Georgiana react initially?

3. What was Aylmer's dream? What influence does it have on Georgiana?

4. What happens when Georgiana first enters Aylmer's laboratory?

5. What is the result of Aylmer's experiment on his wife's birthmark?

★ Techniques and Strategies

1. What is the theme of the story?

2. What is your reaction to the dialogue Hawthorne writes for his characters? Do you find it natural, religious, stilted, moralistic, old-fashioned? What does the type of dialogue tell you of Hawthorne's audience for the story?

3. What is Aminadab's function in the story? How does he serve as a counterpoint to Aylmer? What does he represent in symbolic terms?

4. The writer uses foreshadowing, a literary technique that predicts certain outcomes before they occur. How does Georgiana's fainting serve

as foreshadowing? Aminadab's comment, "If she were my wife, I'd never part with that birthmark"?

5. How does Hawthorne's use of imagery make the birthmark itself so memorable in readers' minds? How does the writer infuse it with both sensory concreteness and spirituality?

★ *Speaking of Values*

1. What values does Aylmer convey when he asks his wife about removing the birthmark? In what ways does he seem obsessed with it? How do obsessions work against people? How can obsessions be positive experiences?

2. Hawthorne raises the question in paragraph 1 about the "degree of faith in man's ultimate control over Nature." What is the degree of your faith in humanity's ultimate control over nature? Is this a goal our society should aim for? Why or why not?

3. About the birthmark itself, Hawthorne says in paragraph 8 that it was "the fatal flaw of humanity which Nature . . . stamps ineffaceably on all her productions." What does this comment tell you about Hawthorne's view of human imperfection? Why might you agree or disagree with his point of view?

4. What essential point do you think Hawthorne is making about science and humanity's use of it? Do you agree with him? Why or why not?

5. Regarding the *elixir vitae,* the potion that prolonged life, Georgiana says, "It is terrible to possess such a power, or even to dream of possessing it." Why is this power so "terrible to possess"? Do you think it terrible? Why or why not?

★ *Values Conversation*

Through gene splicing and other chromosomal manipulations, modem science allows us to come closer to achieving perfection in species than ever before. What is your view about the goal of physical perfection in animals, including humans? What moral or ethical issues do you see in using science to the end of producing "perfect" specimens? Form groups to discuss the matter. What would Hawthorne's reaction be?

★ *Writing about Values*

1. Write an essay on what you think should be the limits—if any—on scientific research.

2. Write an essay to explain the last sentence of the story: "The momentary circumstance was too strong for him; he failed to look beyond the shadowy scope of time, and living once for all in eternity, to find the perfect future in the present."

3. Write an essay in which you discuss the symbolism of the story.

Stephen Jay Gould

Dolly's Fashion and Louis's Passion

Stephen Jay Gould was born in New York City in 1941 and received his Ph.D. from Columbia. A Harvard professor of paleontology, Gould is known both for his work in evolutionary theory and for his popular writing on natural history and science in society. He is a regular contributor to *Natural History* magazine. Among his award-winning books are *The Panda's Thumb* (1980), *The Mismeasure of Man* (1981), and *Wonderful Life* (1989). Here he offers some thoughts on the issue of cloning and its implications for society.

———— ★ ————

Nothing can be more fleeting or capricious than fashion. What, then, can a scientist, committed to objective description and analysis, do with such a haphazardly moving target? In a classic approach, analogous to standard advice for preventing the spread of an evil agent ("kill it before it multiplies"), a scientist might say, "quantify before it disappears."

Francis Galton, Charles Darwin's charmingly eccentric and brilliant cousin, and a founder of the science of statistics, surely took this prescription to heart. He once decided to measure the geographic patterning of female beauty. He attached a piece of paper to a small wooden cross that he could carry, unobserved, in his pocket. He held the cross at one end in the palm of his hand and, with a needle secured between thumb and forefinger, made pinpricks on the three remaining projections (the two ends of the crossbar and the top).

He would rank every young woman he passed on the street into one of three categories—as beautiful, average, or substandard (by his admittedly subjective preferences)—and he would then place a pinprick for each woman into the designated domain of his cross. After a hard day's work, he tabulated the relative percentages by counting pinpricks. He concluded, to the dismay of Scotland, that beauty followed a simple trend from north to south, with the highest proportion of uglies in Aberdeen and the greatest frequency of lovelies in London.

Some fashions (tongue piercings, perhaps?) flower once and then disappear, hopefully forever. Others swing in and out of style, as if fastened to the end of a pendulum. Two foibles of human life strongly promote this oscillatory mode. First, our need to create order in a complex

579

world begets our worst mental habit: dichotomy, or our tendency to reduce an intricate set of subtle shadings to a choice between two diametrically opposed alternatives (each with moral weight and therefore ripe for
bombast and pontification, if not outright warfare): religion versus science, liberal versus conservative, plain versus fancy, *Roll Over Beethoven*
versus the *Moonlight Sonata*. Second, many deep questions about our
livelihoods, and the fates of nations, truly have no answers—so we cycle
the presumed alternatives of our dichotomies, one after the other, always hoping that, this time, we will find the nonexistent key.

5   Among oscillating fashions governed primarily by the swing of
our social pendulum, no issue could be more prominent for an evolutionary biologist, or more central to a broad range of political questions, than genetic versus environmental sources of human abilities
and behaviors. This issue has been falsely dichotomized for so many
centuries that English even features a mellifluous linguistic contrast for
the supposed alternatives: nature versus nurture.

6   As any thoughtful person understands, the framing of this question as an either-or dichotomy verges on the nonsensical. Both inheritance and upbringing matter in crucial ways. Moreover, an adult human
being, built by interaction of these (and other) factors, cannot be disag-
gregated into separate components with attached percentages. It be-
hooves us all to grasp why such common claims as "intelligence is 30
percent genetic and 70 percent environmental" have no sensible meaning at all and represent the same kind of error as the contention that all
overt properties of water may be revealed by noting an underlying
construction from two parts of one gas mixed with one part of another.

7   Nonetheless, a preference for either nature or nurture swings back
and forth into fashion as political winds blow and as scientific break-
throughs grant transient prominence to one or another feature in a
spectrum of vital influences. For example, a combination of political
and scientific factors favored an emphasis upon environment in the
years just following World War II: an understanding that Hitlerian horrors had been rationalized by claptrap genetic theories about inferior
races; the domination of psychology by behaviorist theories. Today, genetic explanations are all the rage, fostered by a similar mixture of social and scientific influences: for example, the rightward shift of the
political pendulum (and the cynical availability of "you can't change
them, they're made that way" as a bogus argument for reducing expenditures on social programs) and an overextension to all behavioral variation of genuinely exciting results in identifying the genetic basis of
specific diseases, both physical and mental.

8   Unfortunately, in the heat of immediate enthusiasm, we often mistake transient fashion for permanent enlightenment. Thus, many people
assume that the current popularity of genetic explanation represents a
final truth wrested from the clutches of benighted environmental de-

terminists of previous generations. But the lessons of history suggest that the worm will soon turn again. Since both nature and nurture can teach us so much—and since the fullness of our behavior and mentality represents such a complex and unbreakable combination of these and other factors—a current emphasis on nature will no doubt yield to a future fascination with nurture as we move toward better understanding by lurching upward from one side to another in our quest to fulfill the Socratic injunction: know thyself.

In my Galtonian desire to measure the extent of current fascination   9
with genetic explanations (before the pendulum swings once again and my opportunity evaporates), I hasten to invoke two highly newsworthy items of recent months. The subjects may seem quite unrelated—Dolly, the cloned sheep, and Frank Sulloway's book on the effects of birth order upon human behavior—but both stories share a common feature offering striking insight into the current extent of genetic preferences. In short, both stories have been reported almost entirely in genetic terms, but both cry out (at least to me) for a reading as proof of strong environmental influences. Yet no one seems to be drawing (or even mentioning) this glaringly obvious inference. I cannot imagine that anything beyond current fashion for genetic arguments can explain this puzzling silence. I am convinced that exactly the same information, if presented twenty years ago in a climate favoring explanations based on nurture, would have been read primarily in this opposite light. Our world, beset by ignorance and human nastiness, contains quite enough background darkness. Should we not let both beacons shine all the time?

Dolly must be the most famous sheep since John the Baptist desig-   10
nated Jesus in metaphor as "Lamb of God, which taketh away the sin of the world" (John: 1:29). She has certainly edged past the pope, the president, Madonna, and Michael Jordan as the best-known mammal of the moment. And all this for a carbon copy, a Xerox! I don't intend to drip cold water on this little lamb, cloned from a mammary cell of her mother, but I remain unsure that she's worth all the fuss and fear generated by her unconventional birth.

When one reads the technical article describing Dolly's manufac-   11
ture ("Viable Offspring Derived from Fetal and Adult Mammalian Cells," by I. Wilmut, A. E. Schnieke, J. McWhir, A. J. Kind, and K. H. S. Campbell, *Nature*, February 27, 1997), rather than the fumings and hyperbole of so much public commentary, one can't help feeling a bit underwhelmed and left wondering whether Dolly's story tells less than meets the eye.

I don't mean to discount or underplay the ethical issues raised by   12
Dolly's birth (and I shall return to this subject in a moment), but we are not about to face an army of Hitlers or even a Kentucky Derby run entirely by genetically identical contestants (a true test for the skills of jockeys and trainers). First, Dolly breaks no theoretical ground in biology, for

we have known how to clone in principle for at least two decades, but had developed no techniques for reviving the full genetic potential of differentiated adult cells. (Still, I admit that a technological solution can pack as much practical and ethical punch as a theoretical breakthrough. I suppose one could argue that the first atomic bomb only realized a known possibility.)

13   Second, my colleagues have been able to clone animals from embryonic cell-lines for several years, so Dolly is not the first mammalian clone, but only the first clone from an adult cell. Wilmut and colleagues also cloned sheep from cells of a nine-day embryo and a twenty-six-day fetus—and had much greater success. They achieved fifteen pregnancies (although not all proceeded to term) in thirty two recipients (that is, surrogate mothers for transported cells) of the embryonic cell-line, five pregnancies in sixteen recipients of the fetal cell-line, but only Dolly (one pregnancy in thirteen tries) for the adult cell-line. This experiment cries out for confirming repetition. (Still, I allow that current difficulties will surely be overcome, and cloning from adult cells, if doable at all, will no doubt be achieved more routinely as techniques and familiarity improve.)

14   Third, and more seriously, I remain unconvinced that we should regard Dolly's starting cell as adult in the usual sense of the term. Dolly grew from a cell taken from the "mammary gland of a six-year-old ewe in the last trimester of pregnancy" (to quote the technical article of Wilmut, et al.). Since the breasts of pregnant mammals enlarge substantially in late stages of pregnancy, some mammary cells, although technically adult, may remain unusually labile or even "embryolike" and thus able to proliferate rapidly to produce new breast tissue at an appropriate stage of pregnancy. Consequently, we may be able to clone only from unusual adult cells with effectively embryonic potential, and not from any stray cheek cell, hair follicle, or drop of blood that happens to fall into the clutches of a mad Xeroxer. Wilmut and colleagues admit this possibility in a sentence written with all the obtuseness of conventional scientific prose, and therefore almost universally missed by journalists: "We cannot exclude the possibility that there is a small proportion of relatively undifferentiated stem cells able to support regeneration of the mammary gland during pregnancy."

15   But if I remain relatively unimpressed by achievements thus far, I do not discount the monumental ethical issues raised by the possibility of cloning from adult cells. Yes, we have cloned fruit trees for decades by the ordinary process of grafting—and without raising any moral alarms. Yes, we may not face the evolutionary dangers of genetic uniformity in crop plants and livestock, for I trust that plant and animal breeders will not be stupid enough to eliminate all but one genotype from a species and will always maintain (as plant breeders do now) an active pool of genetic diversity in reserve. (But then, I suppose we

should never underestimate the potential extent of human stupidity—and agricultural seed banks could be destroyed by local catastrophes, while genetic diversity spread throughout a species guarantees maximal evolutionary robustness.)

Nonetheless, while I regard many widely expressed fears as exaggerated, I do worry deeply about potential abuses of human cloning, and I do urge a most open and thorough debate on these issues. Each of us can devise a personal worst-case scenario. Somehow, I do not focus upon the specter of a future Hitler making an army of ten million identical robotic killers, for if our society ever reaches a state in which such an outcome might be realized, we are probably already lost. My thoughts run to localized moral quagmires that we might actually have to face in the next few years (for example, the biotech equivalent of ambulance-chasing slimeballs among lawyers—a hustling little firm that scans the obits for reports of dead children and then goes to grieving parents with the following offer: "So sorry for your loss, but did you save a hair sample? We can make you another for a mere fifty thou"). 16

However, and still on the subject of ethical conundrums, but now moving to my main point about current underplaying of environmental sources for human behaviors, I do think that the most potent scenarios of fear, and the most fretful ethical discussions on late-night television, have focused on a nonexistent problem that all human societies solved millennia ago. We ask: Is a clone an individual? Would a clone have a soul? Would a clone made from my cell negate my unique personhood? 17

May I suggest that these endless questions—all variations on the theme that clones threaten our traditional concept of individuality—have already been answered empirically, even though public discussion of Dolly seems blithely oblivious to this evident fact. We have known human clones from the dawn of our consciousness. We call them identical twins—and they are far better clones than Dolly and her mother. Dolly shares only nuclear DNA with her mother's mammary cell, for the nucleus of this cell was inserted into an embryonic stem cell (whose own nucleus had been removed) of a surrogate female. Dolly then grew in the womb of this surrogate. 18

Identical twins share at least four additional (and important) properties that differ between Dolly and her mother. First, identical twins also house the same mitochondrial genes. (Mitochondria, the "energy factories" of cells, contain a small number of genes. We get our mitochondria from the cytoplasm of the egg cell that made us, not from the nucleus formed by the union of sperm and egg. Dolly received her nucleus from her mother, but her egg cytoplasm, and hence her mitochondria, from her surrogate.) Second, identical twins share the same set of maternal gene products in the egg. Genes don't grow embryos all by themselves. Egg cells contain protein products of maternal genes that 19 play a major role in directing the early development of the embryo. Dolly has her mother's nuclear genes, but her surrogate's gene products in the cytoplasm of her founding cell.

20   Third—and now we come to explicitly environmental factors— identical twins share the same womb. Dolly and her mother gestated in different places. Fourth, identical twins share the same time and culture (even if they fall into the rare category, so cherished by researchers, of siblings separated at birth and raised, unbeknownst to each other, in distant families of different social classes). The clone of an adult cell matures in a different world. Does anyone seriously believe that a clone of Beethoven would sit down one day to write a Tenth Symphony in the style of his early-nineteenth-century forebear?

21   So identical twins are truly eerie clones—ever so much more alike on all counts than Dolly and her mother. We do know that identical twins share massive similarities not only of appearance but also in broad propensities and detailed quirks of personality. Nonetheless, have we ever doubted the personhood of each member in a pair of identical twins? Of course not. We know that identical twins are distinct individuals, albeit with peculiar and extensive similarities. We give them different names. They encounter divergent experiences and fates. Their lives wander along disparate paths of the world's complex vagaries. They grow up as distinctive and undoubted individuals, yet they stand forth as far better clones than Dolly and her mother.

22   Why have we overlooked this central principle in our fears about Dolly? Identical twins provide sturdy proof that inevitable differences of nurture guarantee the individuality and personhood of each human clone. And since any future human Dolly must differ far more from her progenitor (in both the nature of mitochondria and maternal gene products and the nurture of different wombs and surrounding cultures) than any identical twin diverges from her sibling clone, why ask if Dolly has a soul or an independent life when we have never doubted the personhood or individuality of much more similar identical twins?

23   Literature has always recognized this principle. The Nazi loyalists who cloned Hitler in The Boys from Brazil also understood that they had to maximize similarities of nurture as well. So they fostered their little Hitler babies in families maximally like Adolf's own dysfunctional clan—and not one of them grew up anything like history's quintessential monster. Life, too, has always verified this principle. Eng and Chang, the original Siamese twins and the closest clones of all, developed distinct and divergent personalities. One became a morose alcoholic, the other remained a benign and cheerful man. We may not think much of the individuality of sheep in general (for they do set our icon of blind following and identical form as they jump over fences in mental schemes of insomniacs), but Dolly will grow up to be as unique and as ornery as any sheep can be.

A recent book by my friend Frank Sulloway also focuses on themes   24
of nature and nurture. He fretted over, massaged, and lovingly shep-
herded it toward publication for more than two decades. *Born to Rebel*
documents a crucial effect of birth order in shaping human personalities and styles of thinking. Firstborns, as sole recipients of parental attention until the arrival of later children, and as more powerful (by
virtue of age and size) than their subsequent siblings, tend to cast their
lot with parental authority and with the advantages of incumbent
strength. They tend to grow up competent and confident, but also conservative and unlikely to favor quirkiness or innovation. Why threaten
an existing structure that has always offered you clear advantages over
siblings? Later children, however, are (as Sulloway's title proclaims)
born to rebel. They must compete against odds for parental attention
long focused primarily elsewhere. They must scrap and struggle and
learn to make do for themselves. Laterborns therefore tend to be flexible, innovative, and open to change. The business and political leaders
of stable nations may be overwhelmingly firstborns, but the revolutionaries who have discombobulated our cultures and restructured our
scientific knowledge tend to be laterborns. Frank and I have been discussing his thesis ever since he began his studies. I thought (and suggested) that he should have published his results twenty years ago. I
still hold this opinion, for while I greatly admire his book and do recognize that such a long gestation allowed Frank to strengthen his case by
gathering and refining his data, I also believe that he became too committed to his central thesis and tried to extend his explanatory umbrella
over too wide a range, with arguments that sometimes smack of special
pleading and tortured logic.

Sulloway defends his thesis with statistical data on the relationship   25
of birth order and professional achievement in modern societies—and
by interpreting historical patterns as strongly influenced by characteristic differences in behavior of firstborns and laterborns. I found some
of his historical arguments fascinating and persuasive when applied to
large samples but often uncomfortably overinterpreted in attempts to
explain the intricate details of individual lives (for example, the effect
of birth order on the differential success of Henry VIII's various wives
in overcoming his capricious cruelties).

In a fascinating case, Sulloway chronicles a consistent shift in rela-   26
tive percentages of firstborns among successive groups in power during the French Revolution. The moderates initially in charge tended to
be firstborns. As the revolution became more radical, but still idealistic
and open to innovation and free discussion, laterborns strongly pre-
dominated. But when control then passed to the uncompromising
hardliners who promulgated the Reign of Terror, firstborns again ruled
the roost. In a brilliant stroke, Sulloway tabulates the birth orders for
several hundred delegates who decided the fate of Louis XVI in the

National Convention. Among hardliners who voted for the guillotine, 73 percent were firstborns; but of those who opted for the compromise of conviction with pardon, 62 percent were laterborns. Since Louis lost his head by a margin of one vote, an ever so slightly different mix of birth orders among delegates might have altered the course of history.

27   Since Frank is a good friend and since I have been at least a minor midwife to this project over two decades (although I don't accept all details of his thesis), I took an unusually strong interest in the delayed birth of *Born to Rebel*. I read the text and all the prominent reviews that appeared in many newspapers and journals. And I have been puzzled—stunned would not be too strong a word—by the total absence from all commentary of the simplest and most evident inference from Frank's data, the one glaringly obvious point that everyone should have stressed, given the long history of issues raised by such information.

28   Sulloway focuses nearly all his interpretation on an extended analogy (broadly valid in my judgment, but overextended as an exclusive device) between birth order in families and ecological status in a world of Darwinian competition. Children vie for limited parental resources, just as individuals struggle for existence (and ultimately for reproductive success) in nature. Birth orders place children in different "niches," requiring disparate modes of competition for maximal success. While firstborns shore up incumbent advantages, laterborns must grope and grub by all clever means at their disposal—leading to the divergent personalities of stalwart and rebel. Alan Wolfe, in my favorite negative review of Sulloway's book from the *New Republic* (December 23, 1996) writes: "Since firstborns already occupy their own niches, laterborns, if they are to be noticed, have to find unoccupied niches. If they do so successfully, they will be rewarded with parental investment." (Jared Diamond stresses the same theme in my favorite positive review from the *New York Review of Books*, November 14, 1996.)

29   As I said, I am willing to go with this program up to a point. But I must also note that the restriction of commentary to this Darwinian metaphor has diverted attention from the foremost conclusion revealed by a large effect of birth order upon human behavior. The Darwinian metaphor smacks of biology; we also erroneously think of biological explanations as intrinsically genetic (an analysis of this common fallacy could fill an essay or an entire book). I suppose that this chain of argument leads us to stress whatever we think that Sulloway's thesis might be teaching us about "nature" (our preference, in any case, during this age of transient fashion for genetic causes) under our erroneous tendency to treat the explanation of human behavior as a debate between nature and nurture.

30   But consider the meaning of birth-order effects for environmental influences, however unfashionable at the moment. Siblings differ genetically of course, but no aspect of this genetic variation correlates in

any systematic way with birth order. Firstborns and laterborns receive the same genetic shake within a family. Systematic differences in behavior between firstborns and laterborns cannot be ascribed to genetics. (Other biological effects may correlate with birth order—if, for example, the environment of the womb changes systematically with numbers of pregnancies—but such putative influences have no basis in genetic differences among siblings.) Sulloway's substantial birth-order effects therefore provide our best and ultimate documentation of nurture's power. If birth order looms so large in setting the paths of history and the allocation of people to professions, then nurture cannot be denied a powerfully formative role in our intellectual and behavioral variation. To be sure, we often fail to see what stares us in the face, but how can the winds of fashion blow away such an obvious point, one so relevant to our deepest and most persistent questions about ourselves?

In this case, I am especially struck by the irony of fashion's veil. As noted before, I urged Sulloway to publish this data twenty years ago, when (in my judgment) he could have presented an even better case because he had already documented the strong and general influence of birth order upon personality, but had not yet ventured upon the slippery path of trying to explain too many details with forced arguments that sometimes lapse into self-parody. If Sulloway had published in the mid-1970s, when nurture rode the pendulum of fashion in a politically more liberal age (probably dominated by laterborns!), I am confident that this obvious point about birth-order effects as proof of nurture's power would have won primary attention, rather than consignment to a limbo of invisibility. [31]

Hardly anything in intellectual life can be more salutatory than the separation of fashion from fact. Always suspect fashion (especially when the moment's custom matches your personal predilection); always cherish fact (while remembering than an apparent "fact" may only record a transient fashion). I have discussed two subjects that couldn't be "hotter," but cannot be adequately understood because a veil of genetic fashion now conceals the richness of full explanation by relegating a preeminent environmental theme to invisibility. Thus, we worry whether the first cloned sheep represents a genuine individual at all, while we forget that we have never doubted the distinct personhood guaranteed by differences in nurture to clones far more similar by nature than Dolly and her mother—identical twins. And we try to explain the strong effects of birth order only by invoking a Darwinian analogy between family place and ecological niche, while forgetting that these systematic effects cannot have a genetic basis and therefore prove the predictable power of nurture. [32]

So, sorry, Louis. You lost your head to the power of family environments upon head children. And hello, Dolly. May we forever restrict your mode of manufacture, at least for humans. But may genetic custom [33] never stale the infinite variety guaranteed by a lifetime of nurture in the intricate complexity of nature—this vale of tears, joy, and endless wonder.

★ Meaning and Understanding

1. Who was Francis Galton and what did he do, according to Gould?

2. In what way is Gould's method in the essay "Galtonian"?

3. What does Gould mean by "fashion" in the title and throughout the essay? What sort of "fashion" does he focus on most?

4. The essay calls "dichotomy" our "worst mental habit." How does Gould define "dichotomy"?

5. What kinds of cells was Dolly cloned from? What does Gould make of this fact?

6. Who were Eng and Chang?

7. What thesis does Frank Sulloway advance in his book?

8. Who is the Louis referred to in the title and essay? What happened to him?

★ Techniques and Strategies

1. What is the essay's thesis? Where does it first appear?

2. What do the opening few paragraphs contribute to the essay? Do you think the essay would be more persuasive without these paragraphs? Why?

3. The essay builds through two extended examples of intellectual fashion. How effective are these as examples? What common point about nature versus nurture does Gould make through them?

4. What rhetorical devices does Gould use in the final paragraph? What particular phrases do you find most effective? Why?

5. Gould challenges "dichotomy" as a mental habit. In what way does the essay escape "diametrically opposed alternatives" for the sake of "subtle shadings" (paragraph 4)? Which of Gould's details seem most subtle and interesting to you?

★ Speaking of Values

1. What is Gould's attitude toward the nature versus nurture debate? What is your present thinking about genetics versus environment as contrasting ideas? Why?

2. What is the "worst case scenario" that Gould imagines for human cloning? What is *your* "worst case scenario" for human cloning?

3. What sort of cloning nightmare does Gould consider unlikely? Do you agree? Why?

4. What do you think of Sulloway's assertion about birth order? Does your experience or observation suggest that the order of people's birth contributes significantly to their character or behavior? Why?

★ *Values Conversation*

Form groups and discuss instances in which environment played a forceful role in your life or the life of someone you know.

★ *Writing about Values*

1. Write an essay in which you discuss the pros and cons of genetic cloning.

2. Write an essay in which you discuss a time that environment seemed to play a forceful role in your or someone else's life.

3. Select a popular dichotomy besides nature versus nurture—mind versus matter, thought versus feelings, right versus wrong, and so on—and consider the ways in which the bold contrast does or does not make sense to you.

Clifford Stoll

The Internet? Bah!

Born in 1950, Clifford Stoll pays close attention to the claims and realities of our electronic world and is the author of the provocatively titled *Silicon Snake Oil: Second Thoughts on the Information Highway* (1995). In this essay for *Newsweek* he considers the role of the Internet and other computer-driven products in our lives.

———— ★ ————

1   After two decades online I'm perplexed. It's not that I haven't had a gas of the good time on the Internet. I've met great people and even caught a hacker or two. But today I'm uneasy about this most trendy and oversold community. Visionaries see a future of telecommuting workers, interactive libraries and multimedia classrooms. They speak of electronic town meetings and virtual communities. Commerce and business will shift from offices and malls to networks and modems. And the freedom of digital networks will make government more democratic.

2   Baloney. Do our computer pundits lack all common sense? The truth is no online database will replace your daily newspaper, no CD-ROM can take the place of a competent teacher and no computer network will change the way government works.

3   Consider today's online world. The Usenet, a worldwide bulletin board, allows anyone to post messages across the nation. Your word gets out, leapfrogging editors and publishers. Every voice can be heard cheaply and instantly. The result? Every voice is heard. The cacophony more closely resembles citizens band radio, complete with handles, harassment and anonymous threats. When most everyone shouts, few listen. How about electronic publishing? Try reading a book on disc. At best, it's an unpleasant chore: the myopic glow of a clunky computer replaces the friendly pages of a book. And you can't tote that laptop to the beach. Yet Nicholas Negroponte, director of the MIT Media Lab, predicts that we'll soon buy books and newspapers straight over the Internet. Uh, sure.

4   What the Internet hucksters won't tell you is that the Internet is an ocean of unedited data, without any pretense of completeness. Lacking editors, reviewers or critics, the Internet has become a wasteland of unfiltered data. You don't know what to ignore and what's worth reading. Logged onto the World Wide Web, I hunt for the date of the Battle of

Trafalgar. Hundreds of files show up, and it takes 15 minutes to un-ravel them—one's a biography written by an eighth grader, the second is a computer game that doesn't work and the third is an image of a London monument. None answers my question, and my search is peri-odically interrupted by messages like, "Too many connections, try again later."

Won't the Internet be useful in governing? Internet addicts clamor   5
for government reports. But when Andy Spano ran for county execu-tive in Westchester County, N.Y., he put every press release and posi-tion paper onto a bulletin board. In that affluent county, with plenty of computer companies, how many voters logged in? Fewer than 30. Not a good omen.

Then there are those pushing computers into schools. We're told   6
that multimedia will make schoolwork easy and fun. Students will happily learn from animated characters while taught by expertly tai-lored software. Who needs teachers when you've got computer-aided education? Bah. These expensive toys are difficult to use in classrooms and require extensive teacher training. Sure, kids love videogames—but think of your own experience: can you recall even one educational filmstrip of decades past? I'll bet you remember the two or three great teachers who made a difference in your life.

Then there's cyberbusiness. We're promised instant catalog   7
shopping—just point and click for great deals. We'll order airline tick-ets over the network, make restaurant reservations and negotiate sales contracts. Stores will become obsolete. So how come my local mall does more business in an afternoon than the entire Internet handles in a month? Even if there were a trustworthy way to send money over the Internet—which there isn't—the network is missing a most essential ingredient of capitalism: salespeople.

What's missing from this electronic wonderland? Human contact.   8
Discount the fawning techno-burble about virtual communities. Com-puters and networks isolate us from one another. A network chat line is a limp substitute for meeting friends over coffee. No interactive multi-media display comes close to the excitement of a live concert. And who'd prefer cybersex to the real thing? While the Internet beckons brightly, seductively flashing an icon of knowledge-as-power, this non-place lures us to surrender our time on earth. A poor substitute it is, this virtual reality where frustration is legion and where—in the holy names of Education and Progress—important aspects of human inter-actions are relentlessly devalued.

★ Meaning and Understanding

1. What, according to Stoll, do visionaries see in the future of technology?

2. Why is the writer uneasy about the Internet? What does Stoll think is the problem with Usenet, "a worldwide bulletin board" (paragraph 3)?

3. How does the case of Andy Spano support Stoll's contention that the Internet will not be useful in governing?

4. Why does Stoll not join the voices of approval for computers in the schools? For "cyberbusiness"?

5. What "important aspects of human interactions are relentlessly devalued" by the Internet?

★ Techniques and Strategies

1. What is Stoll's thesis? State it in your own words. How does the introduction lay the groundwork for the thesis?

2. Which examples do you find most effective in support of Stoll's argument? In general, how well does the writer use examples in the essay?

3. The writer uses a number of colorful colloquial words and expressions—*baloney; uh, sure; techno-burble;* and *nonplace,* for example. What is the effect of this stylistic strategy? What does it tell you of Stoll's intended audience?

4. What part of the argument do you find most convincing? Why? What weaknesses can you identify in the argument?

5. How does the title serve to engage readers? What does it tell you about the tone of the essay?

★ Speaking of Values

1. How do you account for the enthusiasm many people have for the Internet? What does this enthusiasm imply about our communication values?

2. In paragraph 2, Stoll says that technology will never replace newspapers, teachers, and government activities. Why might you agree or disagree with this observation? Do technological advances, in fact, seek to replace those entities? Explain your answer.

3. Stoll calls the Internet a "wasteland of unfiltered data." What does he mean? What is the problem with too much data, do you think?

4. Why might you agree or disagree that human contact is the essential ingredient for success and that its absence from the "electronic wonderland" is profound?

5. Stoll distinguishes in paragraph 6 between learning from technology (here, educational filmstrips) and learning from live teachers. Why might you agree or disagree with his position here? Is the comparison valid, do you think? Or is this an apples-and-oranges argument?

★ *Values Conversation*

Form groups and project the world of cyberspace fifty years from now. What role will computers play in our lives? Which of Stoll's admonitions will we heed? Which will we ignore? How will virtual reality stand up against reality itself? What levels of human interaction still will exist in the future?

★ *Writing about Values*

1. Does the Internet devalue human relationships? Write an argumentative essay in which you explain and substantiate your point of view. Use examples from your own experience.

2. Design the classroom of the future and write an essay about it. Deal with the role of technology and the role of the teacher.

3. Write an essay on the values implicit in a society that increasingly draws on electronic forms of communication and performance. What do we gain in such a world? What do we lose?

Jon Katz

Old Media, New Media and a Middle Way

Jon Katz is a New Yorker who was born in 1938 and educated at Antioch, the City University of New York, and the New School for Social Research. He is the author of *Gay American History: Lesbians and Gay Men in the U.S.* (1992). In this essay he considers the role of media in contemporary life.

————— ★ —————

1   The 1990s are the decade of the Mediaphobe.

2   The Mediaphobe is frightened and angry. His fear transcends traditional social, cultural and political boundaries. You almost have to admire the unity fear can generate: civil rights activists join forces with right-wing politicians; ex-hippies take up arms alongside Christian evangelists; a liberal boomer President stands shoulder to shoulder with his conservative challengers. A nation bitterly divided on an array of issues from gun control to Medicaid can unite on this: new media, popular culture, modern information technology—all of it endangers our young, corrodes our civic sphere, decivilizes us all.

3   The Mediaphobe defines media narrowly. News comes from a thick, sober daily newspaper, read front to back. Or from an evening newscast, with stories presented in order of descending importance. News does not come from *Inside Edition,* Larry King, Ricki Lake or Snoop Doggy Dogg. MTV News doesn't count. Nor does anything on a computer screen.

4   Yet for all the clucking by the traditional media, Americans both love and embrace the new cultural machinery. VCRs, computers and CD-ROMs are among the best-selling consumer products in American history, approaching portable phones and microwave ovens as ubiquitous fixtures of middle-class life. The computer culture has swiftly metamorphosed from a fringe countercultural movement little known outside its own techie borders to a mainstream information source used by millions of people, inhabited by the elderly, the pet-loving, the religious and the young, as well as nerds, Webheads and some of the world's largest corporations.

5   Notice the apparent contradiction.

6   Mediaphobia is exactly what it sounds like: not concern about real problems but an anxiety disorder, an increasingly irrational spiral of often unwarranted fears.

594

This cultural conflict, the endless nyaaah-nyaaahing about old ver-   7
sus new media, is pointless. Old and new media, perpetually at war,
have a kind of reflexive arrogance in common: each camp sees itself as
superior to the other. There is, of course, no good reason for us to have
to choose between old and new media. Both are valid and useful in
their way, and neither is going to go away. The emergence of new media and broader definitions of culture don't mean that newspapers,
book publishing and traditional television newscasts will or should
vanish. But we *are* groping for some sort of coherent response to all of
the confusing signals we are, sometimes literally, receiving.

The information world of the 1990s bears little relationship to that   8
of just several years ago, a time that feels as remote as ancient Babylon.
Remember those Nintendos and Segas that attached to television sets
and riveted your children? They were some of the first interactive (and
digital) tools we saw. Although typically denounced as hypnotic, violent and mind-numbing, many of the games were sophisticated and
challenging. They required young people to actively participate rather
than passively watch. Often played in groups rather than individually,
they involved social skills and strategizing. They required hand-eye co-
ordination. They could be intensely stimulating, sometimes even ad-
dictive. And children loved them; they took game playing to new
levels of engagement and imagination.

And channel switchers—"zappers"—may be the most subversive   9
political gadget ever invented. Along with VCRs, they were a network
mogul's worst nightmare. For decades, broadcasting was owned and
operated by three men: William Paley of CBS, David Sarnoff of NBC
and Leonard Goldenson of ABC. We saw only what they wanted us to
see, when they wanted to show it to us. Zappers and VCRs broke their
grip, giving far more control of the world's most powerful new medium to the people who use it.

Television viewers didn't have to watch ads anymore if they didn't   10
want to. They didn't have to watch boring programs anymore, either;
they could instantly shop around. They could go bowling and watch
Melrose Place on tape later, fast-forwarding through tiresome commercials and station breaks. Add the development of satellite technology,
which made CNN possible, and the unleashing of many-channel cable,
which brought real diversity to programming, and the transformation
of television was under way.

Television is our most underappreciated medium, mostly por-   11
trayed in terms of stupefying children and inciting violence, the proverbial vast wasteland. But it is a phenomenal thing. A television set is
easy to install and lasts for years. It brings the whole world into your
house, using little power. Lightning storms and freak accidents aside, it
turns on every time you want it to, producing clear color pictures and
good-quality sound. It costs one-fourth the price of a good computer. It

can occupy and amuse children, show the Oklahoma City Federal Building minutes after a bomb explodes, and go around the world to wars, cultural events and volcanic eruptions. It shows great old movies, history, drama and, yes, lots of trash too. Far more popular, enduring and important than most people acknowledge or realize, it is becoming one of our most interactive forms of communication.

12   As we've watched in wonder, the television has mutated into a full-blown information, amusement and communications center. The couch potato is an outdated myth. Television viewers are now entertainment producers and directors. They have options, controls, choices and machinery to run—even products to buy, surveys to vote in, questions to pose, numbers to call.

13   The notion that we have two distinct cultural choices has become widely accepted. If you are civilized and literate, you stand for thick biographies, sonatas, oil paintings. Otherwise, you watch "Ren and Stimpy," listen to degenerate hip-hop, zombie out on MTV videos or disconnect from the human race with your computer, gradually losing the art of coherent writing or speech.

14   From any distance, the construct of two such narrow choices seems pointless. Why should media and culture be defined by opportunistic politicians and out-of-touch journalists? Why can't we each make sensible choices that draw from different elements of media and culture, choices that challenge and educate our children, that fit into our lives?

15   We can, of course. Sanity begins by ignoring politicians and journalists and relying on individual common sense. Enlightened people will educate themselves about media and culture. They will figure out what they need, drawing from some old and some new sources of news, some old and some new culture, some nearly antiquated technology and some glitzy stuff. Bible-waving conservatives, hyperanxious boomer parents, Chicken Little reporters, censors and intellectuals do not have useful answers for us. Their definitions of decency and culture don't work anymore. Since they cannot guide us, we have to make our own way.

16   The Sensible Person will recognize that different media make sense at different stages of life. For the very young, for example, home entertainment systems incorporating computer games and CD-ROMs are perfect educational, creative and social tools. Parents have the right—the obligation—to screen this new medium early on and decide how their children can use it. Some games, for example, are racist, sexist and brutal; parents can make it clear from the outset that they won't buy them or allow them to be played in their homes. Other games—Myst, Civilization, the Sim City series—are extraordinarily educational. They require complex planning and reward patience and strategic thinking. They are best played cooperatively, in groups.

17   On-line computer services offer games, reference data bases and other opportunities for children to learn about the world. Some parents

ask their children to check the daily weather forecasts, since Government satellite maps of storm systems and other weather patterns are downloaded daily on accessible, easy-to-use systems like America Online's Weather Conference. Tasks like that not only familiarize young people with computers but also guide them toward the educational end of the digital culture. Parents can take their children on Web tours of the world's museums, whose best artworks are available via linked computer sites. They can steer them toward youth conferences, so that children can connect with their peers from all over the world.

Initially, sensible people will sit with their children, teaching them   18
not to give their phone numbers and addresses out, explaining that they should come to their parents if they encounter anything disturbing on line. The Sensible Person may even block services or conferences found to be inappropriate for young children. The Sensible Person knows that computer use requires and develops typing, language and reading skills. In fact, stories on CD-ROM are often easier and more fun for young people to read than books, because they are presented in interactive forms, so that the pace and imagery can be controlled.

As children get older, the Sensible Person can progressively with-   19
draw, understanding that adolescents will be drawn to rebellious, probably offensive, distinctly individualistic forms of culture on line, on cable, or in other new media forms. By this time the young people will also be researching school projects on line, critiquing movies and television shows on bulletin boards, connecting with like-minded pockets of culture.

At times, they may be exposed to pornographic imagery or lan-   20
guage. But perhaps it's time to start teaching children how to cope with sexually explicit imagery rather than persisting in the fiction that we can make it evaporate.

Young adults will access sophisticated cultural sites on the Internet.   21
Indeed, to browse the Web effectively, you almost have to be a college student or unemployed; nobody else has the time. As the young adults enter the work force, however, they will turn to other more specialized media: cable broadcasts, Web sites, on-line services, professional journals and trade magazines, books. But then, any Sensible Person continually alters his media choices as he moves through life. The sensible adult will no doubt continue to read books, which after all are portable, can sustain coffee stains, can be read over days or weeks, can be propped up on the reader's stomach in bed and make sense on wind-swept beaches.

The Sensible Person will also continue to go to movies, even   22
though films are available on PCTVs and other at-home media. Leaving the house and going to a movie theater isn't simply media consumption. But, of course, the sensible adult will also have a computer, modem and keyboard. He or she will use E-mail, a remarkably efficient, fast means of communication.

23   The sensible adult will subscribe to flexible news services: cable for breaking news, magazines for analysis and weekly summaries. If newspapers ever decide to respond creatively to the information revolution, people will continue to subscribe to them. But they will expect interactivity and be attracted to media that offer some.

24   The Sensible Person will increasingly turn to the Internet for specialized kinds of political information. American Indians have linked up all over the country, for example. "The Net is a tool that will allow us to forge bonds between the Indian nations," says one Indian leader. "The only thing we have now is the powwow circuit." Veterans have also used the Internet in this way, along with evangelists, gay teenagers, environmentalists and members of individual religious communities. The elderly are already pouring on line as a means of connecting with others who share their concerns about staying healthy and active, about forming communities when mobility is difficult, about dealing with approaching death.

25   On-line services offer new ways for political organizations to rally the like-minded, alert them to pending legislation, formulate strategy.

26   Through all the changes, his own and the world's, the Sensible Person will not buy Luddite notions that new technology is destroying civilization and turning us into ignorant zombies. Nor will he accept the idea, pervasive in the digital culture, that computer users represent some kind of master race. There is no reason to make such simple-minded and divisive choices. Each culture complements the other. Taken together, old and new media offer information, entertainment, community building, civilization.

★ Meaning and Understanding

1. What is a Mediaphobe?

2. What supporting details does Katz provide to support his notion in paragraph 4 that "Americans both love and embrace the new cultural machinery"?

3. What are "zappers"? Why does Katz consider them "the most subversive political gadget ever invented" (paragraph 9)?

4. Why does the writer consider television the most underappreciated medium?

5. What conclusions, according to Katz, will sensible people draw about media?

★ Techniques and Strategies

1. What is Katz's thesis? Where do you find the clearest statement of the thesis in the essay?

2. The writer builds his essay essentially around two terms, which he defines from a highly personal perspective. What are the terms? How well does he define them?

3. Who is the writer's audience? What is his purpose? How can you tell?

4. How does the long, elaborate list of what "the sensible person" will do affect the essay?

5. The writer is a journalist and yet he makes a point of saying that the public should not listen to journalists. Why does he make this assertion?

★ Speaking of Values

1. What is the "notion of two distinct cultural choices" (paragraph 13) that is widespread but opposed by Katz? Why does he oppose this notion? Why might you agree or disagree with him?

2. The writer sets forth strong arguments in favor of television and sees today's viewers as vastly different from yesterday's. Do you agree with his conclusions? His enthusiasm? Why or why not? What does the evolution of television in this way suggest about our values in the home?

3. Why do you suppose that interactive forms of entertainment are as popular as they are, particularly for children? Some people feel that reading a book allows a child's imagination to roam and develop freely whereas, they say, home interactive entertainment forms are more prescriptive and tell the child what to think. Do you agree? Why or why not?

4. Katz places great responsibility on parents for teaching their children how to shape their own media culture. Are parents up to the task, do you think? Why or why not? From your own experience and observation, what role do parents play in involving their children in media?

5. "Leaving the house and going to a movie theater isn't simply media consumption" (paragraph 22). What does the writer mean when he says this? Why might you agree or disagree?

★ Values Conversation

Katz has confidence that Americans will make sensible choices as the media and technology age advances. Do you share his confidence? Why or why not? Form groups to discuss your opinions; share the groups' conclusions with the rest of the class.

★ Writing about Values

1. Write an essay in which you describe people you know whom you would call Mediaphobes and explain why you place them in that category.

2. Do some research into the current state of the fight over the censorship of the Internet and write a paper discussing your point of view in relation to these matters.

3. Look into the future and write an essay about the influence of media in our lives fifty years from now. Explain both the positive and negative effects.

C. K. Gunsalus

Rethinking Unscientific Attitudes about Scientific Misconduct

C. K. Gunsalus was born in 1934 and received a Ph.D. from Boston University. She taught theology at Columbia Theological Seminary in Georgia and is currently the associate provost at the University of Illinois at Urbana. Gunsalus wrote *Liberation Preaching* (1980) and *In Accord: Let Us Worship* (1981) with Justo Luis Gonzalez. In this essay, adapted from a symposium paper she presented in 1997, Gunsalus discusses scientists who do not uphold the rules of their profession.

Many American scientists are fed up with press reports and questions 1
from Congress and the public about scientific misconduct. The concern
is drastically overblown, they say, and the government should spend
less time and money investigating the few bad apples and concentrate
on expanding appropriations for research. After all, some of the most
highly publicized charges of misconduct eventually have been dismissed, these scientists note. Relatively few scientists have been found
guilty of misconduct, so no elaborate investigative apparatus or intrusive federal rules are needed.

These feelings seem heartfelt and widely shared. What's worri- 2
some is how unscientific they appear.

What's unscientific? Well, it's unscientific to make repeated asser- 3
tions that scientific misconduct is an extremely small or non-existent
problem when we have few or no reliable data supporting those claims.
In an extreme example, a 1987 editorial in *Science* said: "99.9999% of all
published reports are truthful and accurate, often in rapidly advancing
frontiers where accurate data are difficult to collect."

There is no basis for this claim, despite the air of scientific precision 4
conferred by the four digits following the decimal point. Then (as now)
we had no direct data on the accuracy of the scientific literature. We
simply do not know whether a lot or just a little untruthful information
is published. In fact, many scientists vehemently objected a few years
ago to a proposed experiment to gather anonymous data on the prevalence of gross misconduct in biomedical research. In the absence of

such data, scientists are not exempt from the normal requirement that they be accurate in their public statements.

5   Moreover, think about the implications of the argument that because scientific misconduct is rare, government does not need regulations and an apparatus to respond. How would the public react to the thesis that because counterfeiting is rare, laws against it and facilities for testing suspect currency cannot be justified?

6   It's also unscientific to make repeated assertions about the causes of scientific misconduct. Here, too, we lack data. Yet the literature is awash with pronouncements. Typical is a report in *Chemical & Engineering News* of a session at the 1996 meeting of the American Chemical Society in which one panelist asserted: "But 'fraud in science' is not a real problem. That is because of the psychology of the perpetrators of fraud, and the self-checking nature of the system. The psychopathology of fraud is such that its perpetrators hardly ever contain themselves to manufacturing routine data. Instead, they doctor something important."

7   What are "routine data"? How does a chemist understand the psychological mindset of perpetrators of fraud without conducting research into the issue? Why are accomplished scientists speaking without evidence to support their assertions? The answer, I believe, is that some structural aspects of universities lead top scientists to minimize the existence of problems and to ignore the possibilities for misconduct that are inherent in research.

8   The first structural issue is what I call the paradox of the university: A good one is organized so that the active scientists are insulated from what it takes to run it, so that they can think creatively and do science. Productive scientists complain that they are plagued with administrative work and committees, but most of that work is focused on matters directly related to their professional lives—selecting their students and colleagues, and supervising research facilities. Very little is focused on the nitty-gritty of running a large enterprise: what it takes to turn the lights on every day, do the paperwork required by government agencies and foundations, pay the bills, dispose of hazardous wastes, or respond to the odd conduct of troubled individuals.

9   For the most part, this system operates as intended, so that working scientists can, in fact, remain naïve about the realities of day-to-day problems outside their labs. So it's natural that they fail to appreciate the need for rules and systems to deal with those problems. But it doesn't mean those rules and systems aren't necessary.

10   The second structural issue can be called the bias of the best. In their professional lives, the best people in an institution, particularly the best scientists with exemplary standards of conduct, typically associate only with other top scientists and outstanding students. They normally don't deal much with more-ordinary colleagues, including those whose work ethics or standards may be problematic.

They also have the power, when they do encounter misconduct, to   11
handle problems efficiently. Consider a recent, well-publicized case.
When Francis S. Collins, the highly respected director of the National
Center for Human Genome Research, found last year that a junior researcher had concocted data, he promptly retracted five published papers on leukemia. The length of the formal procedures to pin down the
fraud and respond to it can be measured in months in that case, compared to years in other cases.

The combined effect of the structural features I've noted is to shield   12
productive scientists—the sort who tend to become opinion leaders in
science—from encountering whole categories of problems. As a result,
many of them believe that problems are rare, that the few that occur
can be easily handled, and, thus, that no money need be spent to develop procedures and train people to deal with misconduct.

They are more concerned that rules about scientific conduct will be   13
(or have been) used to penalize creative and novel science. I have been
unable to find a single instance of that happening, though, and I have
been searching for some time, including directly querying those who
frequently voice this concern. In fact, with Drummond Rennie, deputy
editor of the *Journal of the American Medical Association,* I noted the lack
of examples in an article in the journal in 1993. Not one example has
been drawn to our attention since.

Some scientists also contend that government procedures for re-   14
sponding to misconduct are superfluous because science is "self cor-
recting." Indeed, the chemist quoted earlier in *Chemical & Engineering
News* on the "fact" that misconduct is not a problem also said: "And
there are extraordinarily efficient self-correcting features in the system
of science—the more interesting the discovery or creation, the more
likely it is to be repeated and tested."

Recall what Francis Collins encountered. He found that for two   15
years, one of his graduate students had published data that were systematically manufactured. The deception came to light, Collins said, when a
reviewer of the sixth manuscript in the series questioned whether the
data were fabricated. Note that it was two years before the misconduct
was discovered. Does fabrication that takes two years to discover in a
major project, headed by one of our preeminent scientists, demonstrate
the efficient operation of a "self-correcting" scientific system?

In short, I believe that the leaders of science need to be more realis-   16
tic about the nature of the enterprise that they supervise and defend.
This includes recognizing the changes wrought by the explosive
growth in the number of scientists and graduate students over the last
20 to 30 years. Too much of today's thinking about the internal workings of research is rooted in the mythology of the wise mentor standing
side-by-side with the apprentice, inculcating scientific standards and
traditions.

17   If this ever was an accurate depiction of science, it is not now. Today, faculty members run laboratories in major universities that routinely involve 20 or more people—students, postdoctoral students, and
technicians. How well are the traditions and ethical practices of science
being transmitted to students in such situations?

18   All institutions with research-training grants from the National Institutes of Health now must provide instruction in the responsible conduct of research. Some institutions have pioneered efforts such as the
"group mentoring" program run by Michael Zigmond and Beth Fischer
at the University of Pittsburgh. The best such programs, like theirs, offer
students guidance on a broad range of professional conduct, including
writing scientific papers, dealing ethically with human and animal subjects of research, and finding jobs. This information would (or should)
have been transmitted directly from mentor to apprentice in a smaller
system. Many institutions, however, do not offer comprehensive training; some simply arrange for one lecture on ethics each term.

19   Scientists need to realize that they are not accorded as much trust
as they once were. Our society is significantly more cynical and less
trusting than it was before the Vietnam War and Watergate. Universities, like almost every other sector of society, are much more heavily
regulated than in the past; many of those regulations were adopted after scandals broke. Rules for protecting human research subjects are a
perfect example, Congressional attention having been attracted by the
Tuskegee syphilis study and a 1966 *New England Journal of Medicine* article by Henry Beecher, a Harvard Medical School professor, describing
unethical treatment of humans in published research projects.

20   If scientists and their institutions do not develop the tools (either
internally or at the federal level) to deal effectively with misconduct, it
seems inevitable that scandal will follow, and that more external regulation will ensue. And rules imposed by outsiders are likely to be more
onerous than rules devised by scientists themselves.

21   Scientists also should realize that a startling number of legal claims
questioning internal decision making are filed against universities
these days. As a result, a conclusion among colleagues that serious scientific malfeasance has occurred may not hold up legally. The university's penalties against the malefactor may wind up being rescinded or
reduced.

22   What happens to the scientific environment when people violate
generally held concepts of right and wrong, and yet nothing happens
to them, either because their institution chooses not to act or because it
is powerless to act, as a result of inadequate rules and procedures?
What happens when allegations of misconduct are poorly handled or
white-washed, or when an innocent scientist is wrongly accused by a
malicious colleague and yet the investigation languishes for years, or
when a whistle blower is vindicated but still suffers retaliation?

Cynicism flourishes, morale erodes, and the cohesiveness of the   23
scientific enterprise suffers, all because of a failure to honor the scientific principle of an unbiased search for the truth. The effects are particularly devastating for students, who are supposed to be learning to act
according to the highest scientific and personal standards.

In light of all this, it becomes even more important for scientists to   24
base their opinions and actions upon factual understanding of how our
current system works—and doesn't. Right now, many scientists agree
that the system of dealing with misconduct charges desperately needs
overhauling, but they are resisting adoption of a revised federal definition that would clarify when serious misconduct has occurred and how
that should be determined.

The findings last year of the Congressionally mandated Commis-   25
sion on Research Integrity (on which I served) have been roundly criticized. The panel proposed expanding the current federal definition of
misconduct—fabrication, falsification, and plagiarism—to include intentional theft of, or damage to, research equipment or experiments. It
also would cover misconduct by scientists when they review the research proposals and manuscripts of other scientists. Finally, it would
add subdefinitions of each type of misconduct. For example, it would
define plagiarism as "the presentation of the documented words or
ideas of another as his or her own, without attribution appropriate for
the medium of presentation."

The recommendations were based on 15 months of public hearings   26
and on the examination of thousands of pages of material documenting
past cases of misconduct. Yet some scientists seem to fear that every
scientific dispute or disagreement would be transformed into the proverbial federal case if the definition of misconduct were changed. Some
object to the "legalistic" tone of the proposed definition or argue that
some acts, such as vandalism, already are covered by other regulations
or laws.

Scant attention is paid, however, to the fact that the legal shortcom-   27
ings of the *current* definition—its complete lack of specificity—have
subjected universities to unreasonable obstacles in administering it.
Nor is attention paid to the reality that state and local laws do not, in
practice, cover vandalism to research equipment and experiments.

I recently led a three-day workshop for university administrators   28
who investigate charges of research misconduct. Over and over, I heard
the current definition summed up this way: "It doesn't work. It just
doesn't work."

The current definition does not give enough guidance as to what   29
conduct is covered: Does plagiarism encompass only stolen words, or
ideas, too? How should investigators assess intent? How should they
attempt to prove that data have been fabricated, and how conclusive
must the proof be? What should be done in cases involving labs in

which the records are so poor that one really can't tell whether the published data were ever collected, or when?

30   Federal rules on misconduct are not going to disappear; Congress will see to that. So it is time for scientific leaders to respond realistically to efforts to improve the federal rules. Researchers must be willing to support the adoption of a workable federal definition of misconduct: one inclusive enough to cover the existing range of misconduct, treat all scientists involved fairly, and withstand legal challenges to investigators' conclusions.

31   Similarly, researchers must understand that finding the truth about charges of misconduct is a paramount obligation, and that charges must be investigated according to established procedures that are fair to the accuser and to the accused. Probes must rely upon facts—not personalities or reputations—as the basis for decisions.

32   We also must create environments in which questions about the responsible conduct of research are discussed freely. Students cannot become professionals entirely by osmosis or by taking a single ethics course. The gray areas that exist in the norms (and there are many) must be legitimate and common topics of conversation.

33   Institutions also should adopt and enforce higher standards of professional conduct than the bare minimum required under any federal definition of misconduct.

34   Together, all these actions can help produce the scholarly climate we need. Such changes clearly will require new leadership from within, however. The conservatism of academic senates has meant that little is done or has been done in the past to regulate the conduct of university scientists in the absence of an external requirement.

35   Scientists' current stand against a new definition of misconduct to replace the existing inadequate one is dangerous. Scandals happen. We do not have adequate tools to deal effectively with the next ones, which are sure to come.

★ Meaning and Understanding

1. What, according to Gunsalus, is unscientific about the way scientists generally portray scientific misconduct?

2. What assertion does the writer criticize from an American Chemical Society meeting?

3. What is "the paradox of the university" (paragraph 8)? What is the "bias of the best" (paragraph 10)?

4. Who is Francis Collins? What did he encounter? What questions does Gunsalus raise about Collins's findings?

5. What does the group mentoring program at the University of Pittsburgh provide?

6. Why are scientists not trusted as they once were, according to Gunsalus?

7. What proposals did the Congressional Commission on Research Integrity propose? How did members of the scientific community react to the proposals?

★ Techniques and Strategies

1. The first paragraph of the essay does not elaborate the writer's thesis; it elaborates the opposition's point of view. What in fact is the thesis here? Why has Gunsalus chosen the strategy she has to open the essay? How effective is it for you as a reader?

2. What analogy does the writer make about counterfeiting? How does it help her make her point?

3. What are the key elements in the writer's argument? Make a list of the main points Gunsalus makes to support her thesis. How does she develop her argument logically and systematically?

4. The writer asks and answers a number of questions throughout the essay. Which do you find most useful in supporting her argument? Why does she use this question and answer strategy?

5. How does Gunsalus' service on the congressionally mandated commission influence the essay? In what ways does the essay reflect a strong bias? How does the writer deal with her bias here?

★ Speaking of Values

1. "We simply do not know whether a lot or just a little untruthful information is published." What is your reaction to this statement? Should government set up and enforce regulations so that the science industry must validate its findings?

2. What are the concerns of the scientists who *do not* want any kind of regulation? What values do they represent in their points of view? What valid elements do you find in their concerns? Where do you think these concerns miss the mark? In your estimation, can science be "self-correcting" to an acceptable degree? Why or why not?

3. What is "the mythology of the wise mentor standing side-by-side with the apprentice, inculcating scientific standards and traditions" (paragraph 16)? Why does the writer feel it no longer applies to today's science industry? Why might you agree or disagree with her?

4. How does research-based malfeasance affect the students in the environment where it occurs, do you think? How does this relate to the notion of "learning" to be a scientist?

5. Gunsalus writes, "Scientists' current stand against a new definition of misconduct to replace the existing inadequate one is dangerous." Why might you agree or disagree with this comment?

★ *Values Conversation*

"What happens to the scientific environment when people violate generally held concepts of right and wrong, and yet nothing happens to them, either because their institution chooses not to act or because it is powerless to act, as a result of inadequate rules and procedures?" Form groups and attempt to answer this question. Report your conclusions to the rest of the class.

★ *Writing about Values*

1. You are a scientist who discovers that members of your team have falsified data. Write an essay about what you would do to address the situation. Explain the steps you would—or would not—take. What would result from your actions? Finally, indicate the values your actions would represent to the society.

2. Write an essay in which you discuss another "industry" in which creativity and isolation are common elements—the arts, the clergy, politics, or education, for example—in which you argue that self-monitoring in that arena either is or is not appropriate or inappropriate.

3. Write an argumentative essay in which you present the merits of either a self-imposed or a government-imposed regulatory system for the science industry.

Harold Herzog

Human Morality and Animal Research: Confessions and Quandaries

Harold Herzog was born in 1946. He teaches psychology at West Carolina University and is on the board of editors of the journal *Society and Animals*. In this essay from *The American Scholar* he explores the issues of animal rights and human responsibility, particularly the "moral consequences" of research.

———— ★ ————

The ethical complexities of scientific research using animals first hit me during my second year of graduate school. I had been assigned to work in the laboratory of a chemical ecologist who was studying the skin chemistry of animals. Part of my job was to make molecular extracts from earthworms. Live worms were immersed in distilled water that had been heated to 180 degrees. After two minutes, their bodies were removed and the remaining liquid centrifuged and frozen for later analysis. I had performed this procedure several times and had come to view it as another lab chore, one that I did not particularly enjoy, but that caused me no particular moral discomfort. The worms died almost instantly when dropped into the near-boiling water. And, after all, they were just worms.

One afternoon I was asked to do something different. A scientist at another university was undertaking similar studies on desert animals and had arranged for some of his chemical analysis to be done in our laboratory. Shortly thereafter a large cardboard box arrived air express from Utah containing a veritable menagerie: several kinds of insects, a pair of pale scorpions, a lizard about six inches long, a small snake, and a lovely gray mouse. The task of converting the animals to vials of clear liquid was delegated to me.

I had dumped more than a few live lobsters into boiling pots with nothing more than the slightest moral twinge, and I did not expect to be bothered by the procedures. For some reason, it made sense to start with the smallest and most primitive of the animals. I began with the crickets, which, like the worms, died almost immediately when I dropped them into the hot distilled water. No problem. Next, the arthropods. In the several days that they had been in the lab, I had come to like the scorpions. They had more body mass than the insects and took a little longer to die when I dropped them in the beaker. I began to wonder about what I was doing.

4   The lizard was the first vertebrate. My stomach turned queasy, I began to sweat, and my hands shook when I dropped it into the near-boiling water. The lizard did not die quickly. It thrashed about in the hot liquid for 10 or 15 seconds before becoming still.

5   The snake was an elegant racer probably about a year old. I have always been fascinated by snakes. I collected them as a kid, and I still deal with them as one of the handful of comparative psychologists who study ophidian behavior. I drank a slow cup of coffee between the lizard and the snake, putting off the inevitable as long as I could. More shaky hands, a sweaty brow, a queasy stomach. More thrashing reptile reduced to an inert carcass and molecules suspended in solution.

6   Something was clearly wrong. I was not upset by a logical pang of conscience telling me that I was doing something immoral; it was years later that I was drawn to philosophical treatises by animal advocates. No, my response was purely visceral, a physical nausea akin to the body's involuntary shudder in response to the odor of putrification.

7   Finally, the mouse. I weighed the mouse, poured the appropriate amount of distilled water into the beaker, and lighted the Bunsen burner. As the water approached the 180 degree mark, it dawned on me that I simply could not "do" the mouse. I turned off the flame and, with trepidation and relief, walked into the office of the laboratory manager, thinking that my career as a graduate student was over. I said that I had made almost all of the extracts, but that I would not do the mouse. Much to his credit, the supervisor did not ask me to continue. He wound up boiling the mouse.

8   I have thought about my predicament that day many times over the years. I am now struck by the similarity between my task that afternoon and the plight of the subjects in Stanley Milgram's infamous obedience experiments. The hapless participants in his studies were instructed to administer a series of electrical shocks of increasing intensity to other subjects in an adjacent room. As all introductory psychology students know, the majority of people in the experiment administered levels of shock that they thought would be extremely painful, if not lethal. Like Milgram's subjects, I was confronted with a series of escalating choice points, based on phylogenetic status rather than shock intensity. The difference between the Milgram experiment and my situation was that in his study the shocks were a ruse; the subjects were really confederates of the experimenter. In my laboratory, the animals really died.

9   I was not the only member of my graduate school cohort who struggled with the moral consequences of their research. My friend Ron Neibor had a bigger problem than I did. He worked with cats. The

focus of Neibor's dissertation was how the brain reorganizes itself after injury, a topic that was, unlike my explorations in chemical ecology, quite relevant to human health and well-being. Neibor did not choose cats because of any special curiosity about feline behavior. I suspect he would rather have worked with mice or rats. Cats, unfortunately, were the best model for the neural mechanisms that were his real interest. He employed a time-honored neuroscience technique; he surgically destroyed parts of the brains of his animals and observed the recovery of behavioral function over a period of months.

The problem was that Neibor liked his cats. His study lasted over a year, during which time he became quite attached to the two dozen animals in his control and experimental groups. Even on weekends and holidays he would drive to the lab, release his cats from their cages and play with them for hours. (This was long before federal regulations decreed that a few laboratory species be given the opportunity for daily exercise.) He thought of them as individuals. He talked about them, and he treated them more like pets than research animals.

His experimental protocol required that he confirm the location of the neurological lesions in animals in the experimental group through examination of their brain tissue. Part of this procedure, technically referred to as perfusion, is not pleasant under the best of circumstances. Each animal is injected with a lethal dose of anesthetic. Formalin is pumped through its veins via the heart, and the head is severed from the body. Heavy steel pliers are used to chip away the skull so that the hardened brain can be extracted and sliced into thin sections for microscopic analysis.

It took several weeks for Neibor to perfuse all of the cats in the experimental group. His personality changed. A naturally genuine and warm-hearted person, he became tense, withdrawn, shaky. Several graduate students working in his lab became concerned about his mental state, and they offered to perfuse his cats for him. Neibor refused, unwilling to dodge the moral consequences of his research. He did not talk very much during the weeks he was "sacrificing" his cats. Sometimes I noticed that his eyes were red, and he would look down as we passed in the halls.

These incidents provoked me to ask myself questions that I continue to struggle with two decades later. Is there really a difference between researchers who kill mice in the name of science and the legions of good people who smash their spines with snap traps or slowly poison them with D-Con because they prefer not to share their houses with small rodents? Why was it easy for me to plunge the crickets into hot water, hard for me to do the same with the lizard, and impossible for me to do it to the mouse? Was it a matter of size, phylogenetic status, nervous system development, or simply attractiveness (the mouse was really cute)? Would Neibor's plight have been any different if his experimental subjects had been rats? What were the relative roles of logic and sentimentality underlying the moral confusion that nagged Neibor and me?

14   The moral problems of animal researchers can be traced to Charles Darwin, who, incidentally, had personal qualms about vivisection. The Cartesian argument that humans and animals are fundamentally different was persuasive in the seventeenth century. To Descartes, animals were biological machines. Thus early physiologists interested in the mechanics of blood circulation had no more ethical qualms about nailing a live dog to a board prior to dissection than we might about ripping memory chips from a balky computer. Evolution, on the other hand, implies phyletic continuity—not just in anatomy and physiology, but also in behavior and mental experience. And, in the halls at the annual meeting of the Animal Behavior Society, there is serious talk these days of deception, intention, and consciousness among chickens and monkeys. (One of the ironies of the animal-research debate is that animal-rights activists often invoke recent discoveries about the mental capacities of animals when arguing against the very research that has uncovered these abilities.)

15   There are ethical implications to the notion of phylogenetic continuity of mental experience. An obvious paradox arises—the more a species is like us in its physiology, the more useful a model it is for human biomedical problems. But, precisely *because* a species resembles us biologically, the more likely it is that it experiences similar mental states. In short, the more justified the use of a species on scientific grounds, the less justified is its use on moral grounds.

16   There is a related problem that I struggle with as an animal researcher. I call my version "E. T.'s dilemma," though the central issue has been described under other labels by ethicists. At the end of Steven Spielberg's well-known film, E. T.'s mother returns to Earth to retrieve her errant son, a lovable alien who has spent several days running around southern California with his new friend, Elliot. There is a sentimental parting scene. Elliot pleads with E. T. "Stay?" he asks. E. T. wistfully shakes his head and croaks to Elliot, "Come?" But, both know that each must return to his own world. E. T. and his mother take off back to Zork, and Elliot returns to life in the suburbs.

17   Suppose for a minute that the film ends differently. Again, Elliot declines the invitation to join E. T. The extraterrestrial, however, does not take no for an answer. He grabs the boy by the arm and drags him kicking and screaming into the ship. The doors close, and they zoom off to Zork. An AIDS-like epidemic has struck the home planet, and humans are the best animal model. The question is: Does E. T. have the right to abduct Elliot to be used as the subject of research aimed at developing a vaccine to protect the Zorkians? Clearly, they are intellectually and spiritually advanced over humans. (E. T. fashioned a phone

out of junk to call home and made a dead flower blossom.) Research with animals is based on the premise that a "superior' species has the right to breed, kidnap, or kill members of "lesser" species for the advancement of knowledge. Though it violates my moral intuition, I see no way around the conclusion that E. T. has the right to abduct Elliot for his research. To do otherwise gives credence to the charge by animal-activist philosophers like Peter Singer and Tom Regan that our use of animals reflects self-serving speciesism, pure and simple.

The problem raised by E. T. is essentially that of ethical consistency.   18
But, we do not have to turn to hypothetical space aliens to find inconsistencies associated with animal research. Take, for example, the moral status of mice in research facilities. Several years ago I spent a sabbatical year working in the Laboratory of Reptile Ethology at the University of Tennessee. The laboratory is located on the third floor of the Walters Life Sciences Building, a state-of-the-art facility that houses about fifteen thousand mice each year along with a smattering of other research animals. The mice are housed in antiseptic rooms in the basement and are cared for by a fully certified staff. As is standard practice at universities receiving federal funds, each project involving animal subjects is reviewed by the University of Tennessee Institutional Animal Care and Use Committee, whose members are charged with weighing the potential benefits and costs of the experiments. All of the mice in the building belong to the same species, and they appear virtually identical. In terms of moral status, however, they belong to quite different categories.

The vast majority of the mice in Walters are good mice, the subjects   19
of the hundreds of biomedical and behavioral experiments conducted by faculty, postdoctoral researchers, and graduate students working in the building. I suspect that the bulk of this research is directly or indirectly related to the solution of biomedical problems that afflict our species. Though they do not have any voice in the matter, these animals live and die for our benefit. They are now covered under the federal Animal Welfare Act and are entitled to a certain legal status not granted the mice in your home or even to your dog. (A judge in Oklahoma once threw out a charge against a cock fighter, ruling that roosters were not covered under the state animal cruelty statutes because chickens were not animals. Lest we judge the judge too harshly, note that the Animal Welfare Act in essence also denies that mice and rats are animals, as they are excluded from coverage under the act. Recently a federal judge ruled that the exclusion of rodents under the law, while convenient for the research community, was arbitrary and illogical, although this matter is currently under appeal.)

There are also bad mice in Walters. The bad mice are pests, free-   20
ranging creatures that can occasionally be glimpsed scurrying down the gleaming fluorescent corridors. These animals are a potential threat

in an environment in which there is a premium on cleanliness and in which great care is taken to prevent cross contamination between rooms within the animal colony. These animals must be eliminated.

21   The staff of the animal facility has tried a number of different techniques to eradicate the bad mice. Household snap traps were found ineffective, and the staff was reluctant to use poison for fear of contaminating research animals. "Sticky traps" came to be the preferred method of rodent capture. Sticky traps are squares of cardboard coated with adhesive and imbued with a chemical mouse attractant, hence their alternate name, glue boards. The traps are placed in areas that pest mice frequent and are checked each morning. When a mouse steps on the trap, there is no escape; it only becomes more stuck as it struggles to free itself. Even though there is no poison embedded in the adhesive, over half of the mice found on the traps are dead, the result of struggle and stress. The rest are immediately killed by the staff.

22   Death by glue board is not humane, and I suspect that most animal-care committees would be reluctant to approve a study in which mice were glued to pieces of cardboard and left overnight. Thus there exists a peculiar situation in which treatment that is unacceptable for one category of animals is prescribed for animals of the same species that are of a different *moral* type. The irony of the situation is further compounded by the source of the bad mice. The building does not have a problem with wild mice invading the premises. The pests are virtually always good mice that have escaped, an inevitability in a facility housing many thousands of animals. As a staff member once said to me, "Once an animal hits the floor, it is a pest."

23   There is a third category of mice in the building, which is neither good nor bad. This category consists of mice that are food. The laboratory in which I worked specializes in the study of snake behavior. Most of the research animals were garter snakes, which thrive on a diet of worms and small fish. We did, however, keep some rat snakes and small boa constrictors, which need mammalian prey in order to thrive, and these mammals were mice ranging in size from newborns ("pinkies") to adults. Animal-care committees do not typically regulate the use of mice as snake food. After all, many reptiles will only eat live prey. Not providing them with an adequate diet of live rodents would ultimately result in their starvation, a clear violation of our ethical responsibilities.

24   In some experiments the role of a mouse as food or subject becomes clouded. Suppose Professor X wants to study the anti-predator strategies of mice. She plans to introduce live mice into a rattlesnake's cage and videotape the encounters between predator and prey. Now from the point of view of the mouse, there is little difference between being dropped into a rattler's cage for the purpose of being eaten or for the purpose of a study of its defensive responses. From a legal point of

view, however, these are quite different situations. If Professor X presents the mouse to the snake simply to provide her research animal with its weekly meal, she does not need to secure prior permission from the animal-care committee. If her motivation is to study how the mouse defends itself, she had best begin filling out the request forms. In this case, the moral and legal status of the animal hinges not on species, brain size, or even the amount of suffering it might be expected to experience, but on its label—pest, food, or research subject.

Animal-rights activists will no doubt take satisfaction in knowing that I am not alone in squirming when these issues come up over beers late at night at scientific conferences. But animal activists have their own problems with moral coherence. I suspect that it was my own unease with these issues that compelled me to venture out of ethology, my academic home territory, and foray into ethnology. I became interested in the lives and worldviews of animal activists—people who would like to put scientists like me out of business, people who change their lives because of an idea. For three years, I attended animal-rights demonstrations and meetings, accumulated philosophical treatises and political pamphlets, and, most important, interviewed several dozen activists in their homes.

This essay is not the place to describe the methods and results of these studies. Suffice it to say that the animal activists I interviewed rarely fit the stereotypes in which they are sometimes cast by scientists, and I was impressed by their intelligence, sincerity, and dedication. One aspect of my findings, though, is germane here. For many activists the effort at consistency between belief and behavior affected almost all aspects of their lives—what they wore and ate, who their friends and lovers were, their thoughts during the day and dreams at night. This effort took many forms. Several spoke of feeling guilty when they drove their cars down the street, knowing that the tires were made from animal products and that bugs would inexorably be squashed on their windshields. One man told me of his love of softball. But, while he had found an adequate plastic glove, there was no getting around the fact that good softballs are covered with the skin of cattle and horses. In describing her attempts at consistency, one activist told me, "I don't use toxic chemicals on my dog to get rid of fleas. Instead I try to pick them off and release them outside. I know they do not feel pain or anything, but I feel it is important to be consistent. If I draw the line somewhere between fish and mollusks, it isn't going to make sense."

But just like animal researchers, animal activists can rarely escape the moral ambiguities inherent in even seemingly benevolent relations with other species. Take pets. I was introduced to the moral problems of pet keeping in a curious manner. A friend of mine who is an animal activist told me that she had received a complaint about me from a fellow activist. She was told that I was procuring kittens from our local animal shelter and feeding them to Sam, my son's pet boa constrictor. My first response was laughter at a groundless charge. Sam was just a baby snake, much too small to swallow even the littlest kitten. The incident did, however, provoke me to consider the ethics of feeding the animals we keep in our homes as pets.

28   The person who made the charge against me has four cats that wander at will in her house and in the surrounding woods. Domestic cats, no less than their larger cousins, are carnivores. Unlike humans and even dogs, they need meat to live healthy and happy lives. My accuser was a vegetarian for whom, in the language of the movement, "meat stinks." Prisoners of their biological constitution, her cats did not share her personal aversion to flesh. Thus, while diligently avoiding the meat counter for herself, she was, nonetheless, obligated to ponder the relative merits of the flesh of cow, turkey, horse, and fish when selecting meals for her pets. Even bags of dried cat food are advertised as containing fresh meat. She was driven by love of her cats to become an unwitting participant in the factory farm system that she was fighting.

29   Feline dietary habits are related to another moral quagmire—the predation problem. Cats like to kill things. They are inveterate hunters even if amply supplied with the tastiest of commercial fare. Two ecologists recently asked a group of English cat owners to record as best they could the number of mammals and birds that their pets killed over a period of months. They concluded that the five million domestic cats in Britain kill at least seventy million small animals each year, an average of fourteen prey animals per cat. There are about sixty-five million pet cats in the United States, and I do not have to spell out the dangers these animals represent to the birds, chipmunks, and lizards of America. It is even possible that more furry and feathered creatures die in the claws of cats owned by animal activists than in all of the research laboratories in the United States. The predation problem is particularly acute for cat owners who, with all good intentions, offer handouts to wild birds. With sunflower seeds and beef suet, they inadvertently lure their avian friends to within a pounce of their coldly efficient pets.

30   Other moral complexities confront animal advocates who choose to enjoy the comfort of "companion animals." Like it or not, most pets are subservient creatures, ultimately maintained for the amusement and comfort they afford their owners. This fact has not escaped more sophisticated activists who struggle with the moral implications of *owning* a member of another species. This issue was addressed by one of the activists I interviewed.

31   QUESTION: Do you have pets now?

32   ANSWER: No.

33   QUESTION: For philosophical reasons?

ANSWER: Yes. Absolutely. I would love to have a pet. I grew up with   34
the companionship of a dog and a cat and know that it is a real special
thing. But I also think that it is wrong. Animals are not here for our
happiness. Up until recently I had a parrot. I would leave him free to
fly around my room. One day I just looked at him and said to myself,
This is wrong. It wants to be free. I just took it out in the backyard and
let it go—even though it was hand-fed and trained and I knew it
wouldn't survive in the wild. Since then I have thought that letting him
free was not the best thing for the bird—though I felt really good when
it flew up and into a tree for the first time it had ever been able to fly
really high. It was great, amazing. I was really happy to see that. I assume that he probably starved to death. It may have been more something that I was doing for myself than for the bird.

Enough said.   35

Animal activists use the phrase "the dreaded comparison" when   36
pointing out the similarity between the rhetoric used by nineteenth-
century advocates of slavery and twentieth-century defenders of animal
research. But the animal-rights movement may have its own "dreaded
comparison" in the issue of abortion. Several years ago I attended a
public lecture given by Ingrid Newkirk, co-founder of People for the
Ethical Treatment of Animals. Her formal presentation was followed by
the obligatory question-and-answer period that was dominated by hostile challenges from animal husbandry students from a local agriculture
college. Newkirk, as might be expected from one who spends considerable time in public forums, easily handled the questions and comments
from the more skeptical members of the audience. Predictably, the issue
of where one draws the proverbial line was thrown at the speaker ("Ms.
Newkirk...Do you think flies and mosquitoes have rights?"). Her answer was direct: "We are concerned with *all innocent life*."

I thought about her answer while returning home that night. At   37
some point during the long drive it occurred to me that there might be
a natural affinity between the two social movements in our society that
proclaim support for the rights of the innocent. I began to query my in-
terviewees about their attitudes toward abortion. Of the two dozen animal activists I interviewed, all but two supported "a woman's right to
choose." Some of the activists were completely comfortable with their
stance on abortion; in some cases they simply denied that there is any
association between the two issues. ("I simply fail to see the connection
between abortion and animal rights.") Others found their own pro-
choice views problematic ("Oh, please don't ask me about abortion. I
am so confused about it"). In only one case did a person tell me that he
had shifted from "pro-choice" to "pro-life" as a result of his beliefs
about the moral status of animals.

38   I should not have been surprised at this pattern. There have been a half-dozen or so sociological studies of the animal-rights movement. All have reported two salient demographic facts. Somewhere between two-thirds and three-fourths of animal activists are women, and, as a group, they tend to identify with the liberal side of the political spectrum. Liberal women rarely ally themselves with the right-to-life movement.

39   The divisiveness of the abortion issue among animal activists is illustrated by the following exchange between animal-rights activists, which recently arrived in my office through the miracle of electronic mail. It was posted on AR-TALK, an animal-rights computer bulletin board:

> *Message:* I'd be very surprised if there isn't a positive correlation between "in favor of animal rights and protection" and "pro-choice attitudes" for the simple reason that intelligent, reasonable, and humane people will tend to support both.
> *Response 1:* In other words, for intelligent, reasonable, and humane people, the unborn human child doesn't even count as much as an animal and thus deserves no protection?
> *Response 2:* I would like to put in my own two-cents' worth. I agree with those who want to keep the abortion issue out of AR-TALK. I am not against open discussion of the issue of abortion, but it is *not* the same question as whether animals have "rights," whether humans are or are not to have pets, eat meat, experiment with animals, etc.

40   Though a pro-choice advocate myself, I find the supposition that a person and a pigeon share more in terms of moral status than a person and a six-month-old fetus troubling, if not bizarre. Some of the major philosophical thinkers behind the animal-protection movement such as Peter Singer, Tom Regan, and Steven Sapontzis do a reasonable job of arguing that there is a moral distinction between the interests of animals and those of a fetus. But the intellectual shucking and jiving of the philosophers notwithstanding, I would not be surprised to find that pro-choice animal activists sometimes feel the same nagging discomfort I experience late at night when contemplating the fate of Elliot in the scaly hands of E. T.

41   I once heard Andrew Rowan, the author of *Of Mice, Models, and Men,* say, "The only thing consistent about human-animal relations is paradox." Twentieth-century history offers a splendid example of "Rowan's Principle"—the Nazi animal-protection movement. Though not generally known, Adolf Hitler came close to being an animal-rights activist. A strict vegetarian, he objected to vivisection and once stated that hunting and horse racing were the "last remnants of a dead feudal world." His views on the treatment of animals were apparently shared

by many of the Nazi ruling elite. Heinrich Himmler was "hysterical" in his opposition to hunting, and in one of history's great ironies, Hermann Göring wrote, "I will commit to concentration camps those who still think they can continue to treat animals as property."

This obscure historical footnote was brought to light in a remark- 42
able paper published recently in the journal *Anthrozoös* by Arnold Arluke and Boria Sax, respectively an anthropologist and a linguist. In methodical and chilling fashion, Arluke and Sax chronicle the rise of the animal-protection movement that flourished in Germany in the 1930s and 1940s under the leadership of the Nazi party. Strict laws governing animal research and the slaughter of animals for food were enacted. An endangered-species act was passed by the German legislature. The Nazis sponsored an early international conference on animal protection. The list goes on.

What are we to make of a culture in which government officials 43
were more concerned with the treatment of lobsters in restaurants than genocide, in which vivisection was abhorred, yet torturous medical "experimentation" on humans was condoned? Surely, Nazi animal protectionism is paradoxical. Not so for Professors Arluke and Sax. They argue that when one understands the cultural and intellectual milieu of pre-war Germany, the contradictions of Nazi animal advocacy become more apparent than real. They write, "Our analysis raises what is to most contemporaries a troubling and unsavory contradiction, namely, that Establishment concern for animals in Nazi Germany was combined with disregard for human life. This paradox vanishes, however, if we see that the treatment of animals under the Third Reich really tells us about the treatment of humans and the cultural rules and the problems of human society."

While I admire the elegance of their analysis, I beg to differ. We can 44
indeed follow the twisted logic that enabled the Nazis to construct a moral taxonomy in which some animals were endowed with higher moral status than some people. But does this really cause the paradox of a humane Hitler to vanish? Not for me. I suggest that Nazi animal protectionism is the ultimate paradox, one that we *should not* explain away for it may be the central metaphor haunting all of our relations with other species. Is a vegetarian Hitler any more paradoxical than the pain physiologist who administers electrical shocks to devocalized beagles in the quest for a better analgesia during the day but who is met at the door by his faithful cocker spaniel when he returns home from his laboratory? Or the animal-rights/vegetarian cat owner?

Neither animal researchers nor animal activists inhabit a tidy 45
moral universe. The different worldviews of animal-rights activists and scientists often make communication between scientists and activists about as productive as discussions between evolutionary biologists

and creationists. In words that apply all too aptly to the animal-research issue, Mary Midgely described the difficulty of discussion between moral vegetarians and meat-eaters: "The symbolism of meat-eating is never neutral. To himself, the meat-eater seems to be eating life. To the vegetarian, he seems to be eating death. There is a kind of gestalt-shift between the two positions which makes it hard to change and hard to raise questions on the matter at all without becoming embattled."

46   Animal-rights supporters are often portrayed by their opponents among scientists as hyper-emotional and anti-intellectual Luddites who value puppies and baby seals over healthy human children. Research with animals, says the scientist, is rarely more painful than the pervasive cruelty of nature. Besides, it is our only avenue for alleviating the disease and pestilence that afflicts our own and other species.

47   Not so, claims the activist. Scientists are cold and unfeeling, so blinded by years of socialization in laboratories and classrooms that they cannot see the suffering before their eyes or hear the cries of their innocent victims. For researchers, animals are Cartesian automata, objects to be used in the unending quest for fame, federal funds, and trivial knowledge. Biomedical research does not relieve suffering. It causes it. Further, animal research doesn't work—you cannot generalize from mice to men. And the scientific use of nonconsenting individuals, be it animals or humans, is an ill-gotten gain. Whether it works or not is irrelevant.

48   In reality, both are right—and wrong. True, most biomedical scientists I know aspire to tenure, full professorships, editorial boards, and a share of federal research funds. But they are drawn to animals from curiosity (not a trivial motive for scientists), a desire to make human life better, or a genuine reverence for the natural world.

49   True, too, many animal activists tend to empathize viscerally with the suffering that they see as the result of situations unfairly perpetrated on the innocent. It is also true that experiments on kittens and dogs are more likely to bring out the protesters than research on snakes. But in my view it is a mistake to dismiss the moral sensibilities of animal activists as "mere emotionalism." The philosophical underpinnings of the movement are rooted in cold, rigorous logic and are not as easy to refute as many scientists like to think. Contrary to stereotype, most activists do not scarf down cheeseburgers at McDonalds between demonstrations or wear leather shoes. Indeed, they labor under a particularly heavy personal moral burden.

50   Disagreements about the treatment of animals in research ultimately stem from our tendency to think simply about complex problems. Decisions about the use of other species are extraordinarily intricate, rooted more in the peculiarities of human psychology than in pure reason. Inevitably, the result is paradox and inconsistency. It is a complicated world for all but the true believers.

When asked where I stand on the animal-research issue, I have   51
taken to responding with Strachan Donnelley's phrase, "the troubled
middle." Granted, the troubled middle is not a comfortable place to be.
But, for most of us, neither are the alternatives.

★ Meaning and Understanding

1. What was the writer's reaction to killing a reptile for his graduate
   school study? How did he react to having to kill the mouse?

2. How does Ron Neibor's experiment bear upon the writer? How did
   Neibor's personality change? Why did it change?

3. What is "E. T.'s dilemma"?

4. What are ethology and ethnology? Why did Herzog choose one over
   the other?

5. What moral ambiguities do animal activists face? How does the example of the woman with four cats reflect the ambiguities? How do "predation problems" reflect the ambiguities?

6. How do animal activists interviewed by Herzog feel about abortion?
   How does he explain their reactions in political terms?

7. What is "Rowan's Principle" and what "splendid example" from
   twentieth-century history does the writer offer to explain it?

★ Techniques and Strategies

1. Why does Herzog begin the essay with a narration of his own experiences? What does the strategy contribute to the essay?

2. Why does Herzog use an image drawn from popular culture—the film
   E. T.—to identify an essential feature of his argument? What does the
   use of *E. T.* in this way tell you of the writer's intended audience?

3. What is the writer's thesis in the essay?

4. What is the purpose of the string of questions in paragraph 13? In what
   way are these rhetorical questions? How do they help the argument?

5. What is the effect on the argument of the point about Hitler and Nazi
   policy?

★ Speaking of Values

1. How is a researcher to deal with the "moral consequences of research"? What other jobs can you think of that have moral consequences? What are they?

2. "Disagreements about the treatment of animals in research ultimately stem from our tendency to think simply about complex problems" (paragraph 50). What does the writer mean when he says this? Why might you agree or disagree with his point?

3. Herzog writes, "One of the ironies of the animal research debate is that animal rights activists often invoke recent discoveries about the mental capacities of animals when arguing against the very research that has uncovered these abilities" (paragraph 14). How do you react to this dilemma?

4. Another moral dilemma the writer notes is that "phylogenetic continuity" (paragraph 15) dictates that the species that are more similar to us physiologically are more beneficial to study: through them we learn more about ourselves. And yet that similarity, that similar level of evolutionary development, necessarily extends to the species' mental states. These animals are like us in more ways than one. "In short, the more justified the use of a species on scientific grounds, the less justified is its use on moral grounds" (paragraph 15). How does this idea bear upon your sense of animal research as a practice? What resolutions, if any, can you pose for this dilemma?

5. What is the "troubled middle"? Do you agree that it's not a good place to be but better than the alternatives? Why or why not?

★ *Values Conversation*

Form groups and discuss the point that Herzog makes in paragraphs 48–51: that scientific researchers who use animal subjects and animal activists who oppose this use are both right and wrong. How are they right, from your group's point of view? How wrong? Do your group members choose the troubled middle or some other position?

★ *Writing about Values*

1. Write an essay in which you discuss your own moral position on animal rights.

2. Write an essay in which you point out how animal activists or scientists who use animals for research should or should not have pets. Explain your points carefully, paying close attention to the logic of your argument.

3. Write an essay to explain Andrew Rowan's point: "The only thing consistent about human-animal relations is paradox" (paragraph 41).

Edgar Allan Poe

To Science

Edgar Allan Poe (1809–1849) wrote only forty-eight poems in his short lifetime but made his mark as a writer of symbolic poetry that demonstrates great rhythmic control and a commitment to beauty. In this sonnet he directs himself to science and its effect on poetic imagination.

———— ★ ————

Science! true daughter of Old Time thou art!
    Who alterest all things with thy peering eyes.
Why preyest thou thus upon the poet's heart,
    Vulture, whose wings are dull realities?
How should he love thee? or how deem thee wise?   5
    Who wouldst not leave him in his wandering
To seek for treasure in the jewelled skies,
    Albeit he soared with an undaunted wing?
Hast thou not dragged Diana from her car?
    And driven the Hamadryad from the wood   10
To seek a shelter in some happier star?
    Hast thou not torn the Naiad from her flood,
The Elfin from the green grass, and from me
The summer dream beneath the tamarind tree?

1829, 1845

★ Meaning and Understanding

1. Why does Poe call Science "the true daughter of Old Time"?

2. Why does he address Science as "Vulture"? What does the poet mean when he says that Science preys "on the poet's heart"?

3. Diana was a Roman goddess whose "car" was the moon. What is Poe saying in line 9 of the poem? How did Science drag Diana out of her car?

4. Check a book of Greek mythology for the references to Hamadryad and Naiad. Who were these figures? What do you think Poe means them to symbolize in the poem?

5. How did Science snatch from the poet "The summer dream beneath the tamarind tree"?

★ Techniques and Strategies

1. Why has Poe alluded to so many classical figures? What does it add to the poem? How does this usage interact with the phrase "Old Time" in the first line?

2. A sonnet is a poem with a set rhyme scheme in fourteen lines. Why did Poe choose this form of poetry, so sharply defined by convention, to write his attack on science? What does the prescribed form add to the meaning of the poem?

3. Look at the poem's rhyme scheme. Which words rhyme with which others? How does the rhyming affect the poem?

4. Which images—particularly those making use of metaphor and personification (giving life to inanimate objects)—strike you as most impressive in the poem?

★ Speaking of Values

1. Poe clearly takes a negative view of science. How does science alter all things (line 2)? In what ways has science altered things in the twentieth century? What negative influences do you see in science? Positive?

2. The conflict Poe envisions is between science and the kind of creativity he identifies with poets and poetry. Why does Poe see these two practices—science and poetry—as antagonistic? Why might you agree or disagree with his observations? How does science influence other forms of artistic expression?

3. Examine some of the controversies surrounding science in world history. Look at the conflicts between Galileo and the Catholic Church; between Freud and fellow members of the medical establishment; between John Thomas Scopes, who violated Tennessee's laws by teaching evolution in the classroom, and religious leaders of America in 1925. What gave rise to these conflicts? How were they resolved?

4. In what ways does science deal with "dull realities" (line 4)? How is this a disadvantage to its methodology? An advantage? By calling science a vulture, what does Poe indicate about his own values? Do you think that he would prefer a world without scientific advance of any kind? Explain your point of view.

★ Values Conversation

Form groups to discuss the appropriate role of science in America today. How would you encourage science to expand its influence as part of our system of values? How would you limit its influence?

★ *Writing about Values*

1. Write an essay in which you identify and analyze a particular experience you had that helped you understand what you see as the appropriate role of science in our lives.

2. Write a letter to Poe from the point of view of a contemporary scientist, explaining to him why you think his sonnet is on or off the mark in its criticism of science.

3. In the library, read about men and women who have worked in both arenas—science and artistic creation—people like William Carlos Williams (a poet and physician) and Lewis Thomas (a biologist and essayist), for example. How do you account for their success in the two fields?

Bill McKibben

The Earth Does a Slow Burn

Bill McKibben is a science writer. He was born in 1960 in Palo Alto, California and received his education at Harvard. He is the author of many articles for newspapers and magazines and the book, *The End of Nature* (1989) and *Hope Human and Wild: True Stories of Living Lightly on Earth* (1997). In this essay he looks at what he sees as results of global warming.

———— ★ ————

1   We live on a new planet. That's what a string of recent scientific studies demonstrates. Because of global warming, caused by cars, factories and burning forests, the earth is shifting beneath us with stunning speed and unpredictability. Consider:

- The number of "extreme precipitation events" (rainfall of more than two inches in 24 hours) on this continent has jumped 20 percent since the turn of the century, according to a study by the National Oceanic and Atmospheric Administration.
- Spring comes a week earlier in the Northern Hemisphere, according to the Scripps Institution of Oceanography, which used carbon dioxide records to document its finding.
- Vegetation has increased 10 percent above the 45th parallel, which crosses Seattle and Milan, since 1980, according to Boston University scientists who analyzed satellite data to track solar radiation.
- The northern tundra may have warmed enough that in some years it adds carbon to the atmosphere instead of soaking it up, George Kling, a biologist at the University of Michigan, Ann Arbor, reported last winter.

2   Understand this about these changes: They are enormous. They do not represent small shifts at the margin, the slow evolution that has always occurred on earth. Spring a week earlier; 20 percent more storms, 10 percent more vegetation since 1980. These studies are like suddenly discovering that most Americans are 7 feet tall. If we were looking through a telescope and seeing the same things happen on some other planet, we would find it bizarre and fascinating. If someone's watching us, they're doubtlessly bewildered.

With this level of warming, the Antarctic ice sheet could fail more   3
quickly than previously believed. The most recent El Niño ocean
warming lasted five years, not the usual two, which researchers at the
National Center for Atmospheric Research think may result from the
extra global heating. *Lancet,* the British medical journal, reports that
yellow fever mosquitoes, previously unable to survive at altitudes
above 1,100 yards, now live in elevated parts of South America.

Even news that sounds good probably isn't; longer snow-free sea-   4
sons in the Northern Hemisphere mean that soils start to dry out that
much sooner. This and rising temperatures make drought much more
likely.

Compared with the magnitude of the situation, the response of our   5
politicians (and even most environmentalists) has been feeble. Although the United States promised at the 1992 Rio conference that we
wouldn't be emitting any more carbon dioxide in the year 2000 than we
did in 1990, we've done virtually nothing to meet our promise, and like
almost every other developed nation on earth we will miss the goal,
probably by more than 10 percent.

Now negotiators are trying for an agreement with more teeth—but   6
the deadlines are far away and the targets modest. Instead of locking
ourselves into a document that physics, biology and chemistry are rendering instantly outdated, it's probably better to convene the world's
leaders on the crumbling edge of the West Antarctic Ice Sheet. Maybe
then we'd get quick action.

Eight years ago, James Hansen, the NASA scientist who has used   7
his computer model of the climate to make the most prescient forecasts
about global warming, predicted that by the late 1990's the effects of
global warming would become apparent. For eight years, I've believed
this was true, and still this spring's flood of new data shocks and scares
me.

All those things that people said would happen if we didn't clean   8
up our act? They're happening. This is a new planet, not the earth we
were born on.

★ Meaning and Understanding

1. What changes in precipitation events does McKibben note?

2. What have satellite data revealed about vegetation above the 45th
   parallel?

3. What has resulted from the warming of the northern tundra, according
   to the writer?

4. What is El Niño? What is its significance in the essay?

5. Why does McKibben think the "response of our politicians" has been "feeble?"

★ Techniques and Strategies

1. What is McKibben's thesis?

2. How effective is the writer's argument in this brief essay? What information impresses you most and convinces you of McKibben's point? Where do you find his supporting information lacking? How does the brevity of the essay affect its success?

3. In paragraph 2, why does the writer repeat in summary form the same points he made in the previous paragraph? In what way does the technique contribute to the urgency implied in the essay?

4. How does the writer use expert testimony to advance his point? Which information from other sources do you find most impressive? Why?

5. McKibben gives away his own bias in paragraph 7. How does his long-standing belief in the earth's warming affect your view of his argument?

6. What is your reaction to the title? What is the metaphorical meaning of a "slow burn"? How does this meaning contribute to your appreciation of the title?

7. The writer apparently wants to alarm his readers. Which words or phrases sound the alarm?

★ Speaking of Values

1. Which of the specific developments the writer notes and attributes to global warming are most important, in your opinion? Why?

2. The writer says, "Even news that sounds good probably isn't." Why might you agree or disagree with his point of view in the context of global warming?

3. McKibben lays much of the blame for global warming at the feet of politicians and environmentalists. Why do you think so? Why has he not attacked the people who might have brought global warming about?

4. "This is a new planet," McKibben writes, "not the earth we were born on"—referring, of course, to the effects he sees of global warming. Do you agree with him? Why or why not?

5. What arguments do those who disagree with the threat of global warming advance? Why has the writer excluded any reference to opposing arguments?

★ *Values Conversation*

Form groups and lay out a strategy for a politician who opposes global warming and wants to implement policy changes that would affect the problem with some significance. How easy or difficult would a politician find this work?

★ *Writing about Values*

1. Write an essay in which you state and then justify your point of view regarding global warming. If you believe that people and nations should take steps to correct a serious international problem, explain why. If you believe no problem exists or that the problem is minimal or that it is a necessary consequence of a growing global economy, explain why.

2. Write an essay called "Earth: A New Planet" and argue that some issue (other than global warming) has made our planet "not the earth we were born on."

3. Cars, factories, burning forests: McKibben highlights these as the culprits of global warming. Write an essay on how to correct the problems implied by the writer for the three offenders.

Values in Review

1. Benjamin Franklin in "Letter to Joseph Priestly" and Edgar Allen Poe in "To Science" represent opposite poles in their attitudes toward science. Write an essay in which you compare and contrast the two positions, which were written nearly fifty years apart. If we consider each writer as a representative of his age, how do you account for the different values implicit in each selection?

2. Both Nathaniel Hawthorne in "The Birthmark" and Stephen Jay Gould in "Dolly's Fashion and Louis's Passion" explore science's potential to alter the composition of earth's creatures. What similarities and differences do you note in the writers' approaches to their topics? How is Gould's genetic engineering issue related to the "engineering" that Aylmer attempts on his beloved Georgiana? Again, how is each position a reflection of the values important to the age in which each writer lives?

3. Several essays in this section discuss both the promise and failures of modern science and technology: media, the Internet, and animal research, for example. How do these essays help establish a core of scientific values for our age? What are those values? How are they appropriate or inappropriate for the twenty-first century?

Chapter 10

Wealth and Leisure

Travel

Movieland

Standard of living

Getting rich

Affluence and poverty

Saturday morning television

Baseball

Hunting for sport

Benjamin Franklin

The Way to Wealth

Benjamin Franklin (1706–1790), statesman for the new Republic, signatory
to the Declaration of Independence, and inquisitive scientist, was perhaps
best known in his day for the homilies and advice he gave out in his *Poor
Richard's Almanac* (1733–58). "Poor Richard's" derives from "Poor
Robin's," the almanac in England dating to 1663. In this piece, Franklin
provides homespun views on how to secure wealth and keep busy.

————— ★ —————

Courteous Reader,

1   I have heard that nothing gives an author so great pleasure, as to
find his works respectfully quoted by other learned authors. This pleasure I have seldom enjoyed; for though I have been, if I may say it without vanity, an eminent author of almanacs annually now a full quarter
of a century, my brother authors in the same way, for what reason I
know not, have ever been very sparing in their applauses, and no other
author has taken the least notice of me, so that did not my writings produce me some solid pudding, the great deficiency of praise would have
quite discouraged me.

2   I concluded at length, that the people were the best judges of my
merit; for they buy my works; and besides, in my rambles, where I am
not personally known, I have frequently heard one or other of my ad-
ages repeated, with "as Poor Richard says" at the end on 't; this gave me
some satisfaction, as it showed not only that my instructions were regarded, but discovered likewise some respect for my authority; and I
own, that to encourage the practice of remembering and repeating those
wise sentences, I have sometimes quoted myself with great gravity.

3   Judge, then, how much I must have been gratified by an incident I
am going to relate to you. I stopped my horse lately where a great number of people were collected at a vendue[1] of merchant goods. The hour
of sale not being come, they were conversing on the badness of the
times and one of the company called to a plain clean old man, with
white locks, "Pray, Father Abraham, what think you of the times? Won't
these heavy taxes quite ruin the country? How shall we be ever able to
pay them? What would you advise us to?" Father Abraham stood up,
and replied, "If you'd have my advice, I'll give it you in short, for a *word*

[1]A sale.

to the wise is enough, and many words won't fill a bushel, as Poor Richard says." They joined in desiring him to speak his mind, and gathering round him, he proceeded as follows:

"Friends," says be, "and neighbors, the taxes are indeed very   4
heavy, and if those laid on by the government were the only ones we had to pay, we might more easily discharge them; but we have many others, and much more grievous to some of us. We are taxed twice as much by our idleness, three times as much by our pride, and four times as much by our folly; and from these taxes the commissioners cannot ease or deliver us by allowing an abatement. However, let us hearken to good advice, and something may be done for us; *God helps them that help themselves,* as Poor Richard says, in his Almanack of 1733.

"It would be thought a hard government that should tax its people   5
one-tenth part of their time, to be employed in its service. But idleness taxes many of us much more, if we reckon all that is spent in absolute sloth, or doing of nothing, with that which is spent in idle employments or amusements, that amount to nothing. Sloth, by bringing on diseases, absolutely shortens life. *Sloth, like rust, consumes faster than labor wears; while the used key is always bright,* as Poor Richard says. *But dost thou love life, then do not squander time, for that's the stuff life is made of,* as Poor Richard says. How much more than is necessary do we spend in sleep, forgetting that *the sleeping fox catches no poultry* and that *there will be sleeping enough in the grave,* as Poor Richard says.

"*If time be of all things the most precious, wasting time must be,* as Poor   6
Richard says, *the greatest prodigality;* since, as he elsewhere tells us, *lost time is never found again; and what we call time enough, always proves little enough:* let us then up and be doing, and doing to the purpose; so by diligence shall we do more with less perplexity. *Sloth makes all things difficult, but industry all easy,* as Poor Richard says; *and he that riseth late must trot all day, and shall scarce overtake his business at night;* while *laziness travels so slowly, that poverty soon overtakes him,* as we read in Poor Richard, who adds, *drive thy business, let not that drive thee,* and *early to bed, and early to rise, makes a man healthy, wealthy, and wise.*

"So what signifies wishing and hoping for better times. We may   7
make these times better, if we bestir ourselves. *Industry need not wish,* as Poor Richard says, *and he that lives upon hope will die fasting. There are no gains without pains; then help hands, for I have no lands,* or if I have, they are smartly taxed. And, as Poor Richard likewise observes, *he that hath a trade hath an estate; and he that hath a calling, hath an office of profit and honor;* but then the trade must be worked at, and the calling well followed, or neither the estate nor the office will enable us to pay our taxes. If we are industrious, we shall never starve, for, as Poor Richard says, *at the workingman's house hunger looks in, but dares not enter.* Nor will the bailiff or the constable enter, for *industry pays debts, while despair*

increases them, says Poor Richard. What though you have found no treasure, nor has any rich relation left you a legacy, *diligence is the mother of goodluck,* as Poor Richard says, and *God gives all things to industry. Then plow deep, while sluggards sleep, and you shall have corn to sell and to keep,* says Poor Dick. Work while it is called today, for you know not how much you may be hindered tomorrow, which makes Poor Richard say, *one today is worth two tomorrows,* and farther, *have you somewhat to do tomorrow, do it today.* If you were a servant, would you not be ashamed that a good master should catch you idle? Are you then your own master, *be ashamed to catch yourself idle,* as Poor Dick says. When there is so much to be done for yourself, your family, your country, and your gracious king, be up by peep of day; *let not the sun look down and say, inglorious here he lies.* Handle your tools without mittens; remember that *the cat in gloves catches no mice,* as Poor Richard says. 'Tis true there is much to be done, and perhaps you are weak-handed, but stick to it steadily; and you will see great effects, for *constant dropping wears away stones,* and *by diligence and patience the mouse ate in two the cable;* and *little strokes fell great oaks,* as Poor Richard says in his Almanack, the year I cannot just now remember.

8   "Methinks I hear some of you say, "must a man afford himself no leisure?" I will tell thee, my friend, what Poor Richard says, *employ thy time well, if thou meanest to gain leisure; and, since thou art not sure of a minute, throw not away an hour.* Leisure is time for doing something useful; this leisure the diligent man will obtain, but the lazy man never; so that, as Poor Richard says *a life of leisure and a life of laziness are two things.* Do you imagine that sloth will afford you more comfort than labor? No, for as Poor Richard says, *trouble springs from idleness, and grievous toil from needless ease. Many without labor, would live by their wits only, but they break for want of stock.* Whereas industry gives comfort, and plenty, and respect: *fly pleasures, and they'll follow you. The diligent spinner has a large shift,*[2] *and now I have a sheep and a cow, everybody bids me good morrow;* all which is well said by Poor Richard.

9   "But with our industry, we must likewise be steady, settled, and careful, and oversee our own affairs with our own eyes, and not trust too much to others, for, as Poor Richard says

> I never saw an oft-removed tree,
> Nor yet an oft-removed family,
> That throve so well as those that settled be.

And again, *three removes*[3] *is as bad a fire;* and again, *keep thy shop, and thy shop will keep thee;* and again, *if you would have your business done, go; if not, send.* And again,

[2]Wardrobe.
[3]Moves.

He that by the plough would thrive,
Himself must either hold or drive.

And again, *the eye of a master will do more work than both his hands*; and again, *want of care does us more damage than want of knowledge*; and again, *not to oversee workmen is to leave them your purse open.* Trusting too much to others' care is the ruin of many; for, as the Almanack says, *in the affairs of this world, men are saved, not by faith, but by the want of it;* but a man's own care is profitable; for, saith Poor Dick, *learning is to the studious,* and *riches to the careful,* as well as *power to the bold,* and *heaven to the virtuous,* and farther, *if you would have a faithful servant, and one that you like, serve yourself.* And again, he adviseth to circumspection and care, even in the smallest matters, because sometimes *a little neglect may breed great mischief;* adding, *for want of a nail the shoe was lost; for want of a shoe the horse was lost; and for want of a horse the rider was lost, being overtaken and slain by the enemy; all for want of care about a horseshoe nail.*

"So much for industry, my friends, and attention to one's own   10
business; but to these we must add frugality, if we would make our industry more certainly successful. A man may, if he knows not how to save as he gets, keep his nose all his life to the grindstone, and die not worth a groat[4] at last. A *fat kitten makes a lean will,* as Poor Richard says; and

Many estates are spent in the getting,
Since women for tea forsook spinning and knitting,
And men for punch forsook hewing and splitting.

If you would be wealthy, says he, in another Almanack, *think of saving as well as of getting: the Indies have not made Spain rich, because her outgoes are greater than her incomes.*

"Away then with your expensive follies, and you will not then   11
have so much cause to complain of hard times, heavy taxes, and chargeable families; for, as Poor Dick says,

Women and wine, game and deceit,
Make the wealth small and the wants great.

And farther, *what maintains one vice would bring up two children.* You   12
may think perhaps, that a little tea, or a little punch now and then, diet a little more costly, clothes a little finer, and a little entertainment now and then, can be no great matter; but remember what Poor Richard says, *many a little makes a mickle,*[5] and farther, *Beware of little expenses; a*

[4]A coin.
[5]Much.

small leak will sink a great ship; and again, *who dainties love shall beggars prove;* and moreover, *fools makes feasts, and wise men eat them.*

13   "Here you are all got together at this vendue of fineries and knick-nacks. You call them goods; but if you do not take care, they will prove evils to some of you. You expect they will be sold cheap, and perhaps they may for less than they cost; but if you have no occasion for them, they must be dear to you. Remember what Poor Richard says; *buy what thou hast no need of, and ere long thou shalt sell thy necessaries.* And again, *at a great pennyworth pause a while*: he means, that perhaps the cheapness is apparent only, and not real; or the bargain, by straightening thee in thy business, may do thee more harm than good. For in another place he says, *many have been ruined by buying good pennyworths.* Again, Poor Richard says, *'tis foolish to lay out money in a purchase of repentance;* and yet this folly is practiced every day at vendues, for want of minding the Almanack. *Wise men,* as Poor Dick says, *learn by others' harms, fools scarcely by their own;* but *felix quem faciunt aliena pericula cautum.*[6] Many a one, for the sake of finery on the back, have gone with a hungry belly, and half-starved their families. *Silks and satins, scarlet and velvets,* as Poor Richard says, *put out the kitchen fire.*

14   "These are not the necessaries of life; they can scarcely be called the conveniences; and yet only because they look pretty, how many want to have them! The artificial wants of mankind thus become more numerous than the natural; and, as Poor Dick says, *for one poor person, there are an hundred indigent.* By these, and other extravagancies, the genteel are reduced to poverty, and forced to borrow of those whom they formerly despised, but who through industry and frugality have maintained their standing; in which case it appears plainly, that *a plow-man on his legs is higher than a gentleman on his knees,* as Poor Richard says. Perhaps they have had a small estate left them, which they knew not the getting of; they think, "'Tis day, and will never be night"; that a little to be spent out of so much is not worth minding; *a child and a fool,* as Poor Richard says, *imagine twenty shillings and twenty years can never be spent* but, *always taking out of the meal-tub, and never putting in, soon comes to the bottom;* as Poor Dick says, *when the well's dry, they know the worth of water.* But this they might have known before, if they had taken his advice; *if you would know the value of money, go and try to borrow some;* *for, he that goes a-borrowing goes a-sorrowing;* and indeed so does he that lends to such people, when he goes to get it in again. Poor Dick farther advises, and says,

>   Fond pride of dress is sure a very curse;
>   E'er fancy you consult, consult your purse.

[6]Latin for "what comes before."

And again, *pride is as loud a beggar as want, and a great deal more saucy.* When you have bought one fine thing, you must buy ten more, that your appearance may be all of a piece; but Poor Dick says, *'tis easier to suppress the first desire, than to satisfy all that follow it.* And 'tis as truly folly for the poor to ape the rich, as for the frog to swell, in order to equal the ox.

> Great estates may venture more,
> But little boats should keep near shore.

'Tis, however, a folly soon punished; for *pride that dines on vanity sups on contempt,* as Poor Richard says. And in another place, *pride breakfasted with plenty, dined with poverty, and supped with infamy.* And after all, of what use is this pride of appearance, for which so much is risked so much is suffered? It cannot promote health, or ease pain; it makes no increase of merit in the person, it creates envy, it hastens misfortune.

> What is a butterfly? At best
> He's but a caterpillar dressed
> The gaudy fop's his picture just,

as Poor Richard says.

"But what madness must it be to run in debt for these superfluities!   15
We are offered, by the terms of this vendue, *six months' credit*; and that perhaps has induced some of us to attend it, because we cannot spare the ready money, and hope now to be fine without it. But, ah, think what you do when you run in debt: you give to another power over your liberty. If you cannot pay at the time, you will be ashamed to see your creditor; you will be in fear when you speak to him; you will make poor pitiful sneaking excuses, and by degrees come to lose your veracity, and sink into base downright lying; for, as Poor Richard says, *the second vice is lying, the first is running in debt.* And again, to the same purpose, *lying rides upon debt's back.* Whereas a free-born Englishman ought not to be ashamed or afraid to see or speak to any man living. But poverty often deprives a man of all spirit and virtue: *'tis hard for an empty bag to stand upright,* as Poor Richard truly says.

"What would you think of that prince, or that government, who   16
should issue an edict forbidding you to dress like a gentleman or a gentlewoman, on pain of imprisonment or servitude? Would you not say, that you were free, have a right to dress as you please, and that such an edict would be a breach of your privileges, and such a government tyrannical? And yet you are about to put yourself under that tyranny, when you run in debt for such dress! Your creditor has authority, at his pleasure to deprive you of your liberty, by confining you in gaol for life, or to sell you for a servant, if you should not be able to pay him!

When you have got your bargain, you may, perhaps, think little of payment; but *creditors,* Poor Richard tells us, *have better memories than debtors;* and in another place says, *creditors are a superstitious sect, great observers of set days and times.* The day comes round before you are aware, and the demand is made before you are prepared to satisfy it, or if you bear your debt in mind, the term which at first seemed so long, will, as it lessens, appear extremely short. Time will seem to have added wings to his heels as well as shoulders. *Those have a short Lent,* said Poor Richard, *who owe money to be paid at Easter.* Then since, as he says, *The borrower is a slave to the lender, and the debtor to the creditor,* disdain the chain, preserve your freedom; and maintain your independency. Be industrious and free; be frugal and free. At present, perhaps, you may think yourself in thriving circumstances, and that you can bear a little extravagance without injury; but,

> For age and want, save while you may;
> No morning sun lasts a whole day,

as Poor Richard says. Gain may be temporary and uncertain, but ever while you live, expense is constant and entire; and *'tis easier to build two chimneys than to keep one in fuel,* as Poor Richard says. So, *rather go to bed supperless than rise in debt.*

> Get what you can, and what you get hold;
> 'Tis the stone that will turn all your lead into gold,

as Poor Richard says. And when you have got the philosopher's stone, sure you will no longer complain of bad times, or the difficulty of paying taxes.

17   "This doctrine, my friends, is reason and wisdom; but after all, do not depend too much upon your own industry, and frugality, and prudence, though excellent things, for they may all be blasted without the blessing of heaven; and therefore, ask that blessing humbly, and be not uncharitable to those that at present seem to want it, but comfort and help them. Remember, Job suffered, and was afterwards prosperous.

18   "And now to conclude, *experience keeps a dear school, but fools will learn in no other, and scarce in that;* for it is true, *we may give advice, but we cannot give conduct,* as Poor Richard says: however, remember this, *they that won't be counseled, can't be helped,* as Poor Richard says: and farther, that, *if you will not hear reason, she'll surely rap your knuckles.*"

19   Thus the old gentleman ended his harangue. The people heard it, and approved the doctrine, and immediately practiced the contrary, just as if it had been a common sermon; for the vendue opened, and they began to buy extravagantly, notwithstanding, his cautions and their own fear of taxes. I found the good man had thoroughly studied

my almanacs, and digested all I had dropped on these topics during the course of five and twenty years. The frequent mention he made of me must have tired any one else, but my vanity was wonderfully delighted with it, though I was conscious that not a tenth part of the wisdom was my own, which he ascribed to me, but rather the gleanings I had made of the sense of all ages and nations. However, I resolved to be the better for the echo of it; and though I had at first determined to buy stuff for a new coat, I went away resolved to wear my old one a little longer. Reader, if thou wilt do the same, thy profit will be as great as mine. I am, as ever, thine to serve thee,

Richard Saunders[7]
July 7, 1757

★ *Meaning and Understanding*

1. What questions did the people ask of Father Abraham at the "vendue"?

2. What are Father Abraham's views on taxes? What does he mean when he says, "We are taxed twice as much by our idleness, three times as much by our pride, and four times as much by our folly"?

3. Father Abraham is particularly rough on leisure—idleness or sloth, as he calls it. Which of his comments provide the most memorable attacks on wasting time?

4. What is Father Abraham's advice for accumulating wealth?

5. What is the overall effect of Father Abraham's advice on the people at the sale? How do you know?

★ *Techniques and Strategies*

1. What is the purpose of the introduction to the vendue at which Father Abraham speaks? Why does Franklin choose a narrative framework for this selection?

2. Franklin uses *aphorisms* throughout the piece. What is an aphorism? Why does he use them? How does the device contribute to his purpose?

3. Who is Franklin's intended audience? How do you know? What does the letter format tell you about the intended audience?

4. What does the last paragraph contribute to the selection? What humorous results does Franklin achieve?

---

[7]Richard Saunders is the name used for the editor of The English *Apollo Angliccunus*, once again showing Franklin's debt to English sources.

5. Father Abraham is an invented figure who quotes the various maxims that "Richard Saunders," a.k.a. Poor Richard (Franklin himself) had written in his almanacs for twenty-five years. Why did Franklin choose such a strategy?

★ *Speaking of Values*

1. What is your reaction to the aphorism, "God helps those who help themselves"? How is the statement true? Not true? What examples can you point to to support your view?

2. Poor Richard says, "There are no gains without pains." Must all advances be accompanied by pain, do you think? Why? How has our century applied this aphorism to exercise and bodybuilding? How do you think Franklin would react to this restatement of his idea?

3. What is your view of the definition of leisure as "time for doing something useful"? How do Americans today define leisure? How would Franklin react to today's values regarding leisure?

4. What values do today's Americans hold toward debtors and creditors? Provide instances from your experience to support your opinion.

5. How is Franklin's view of attaining wealth consistent or at odds with what we believe today?

★ *Values Conversation*

Form groups to consider what the class thinks is the way to wealth in today's society. Consider all of Franklin's advice as you draw up your own list of suggestions and recommendations for achieving wealth.

★ *Writing about Values*

1. Write your own essay called "The Way to Wealth" in which you lay out your own formula for financial success. Argue against or in favor of any of Franklin's points, if you wish.

2. Create a series of your own aphorisms about leisure, work, laziness, wealth, and (or) frugality.

3. Write a letter to Benjamin Franklin in his guise as Poor Richard to explain how American values today would accept or challenge the points he makes here.

William Zinsser

The Road to Timbuktu: Why I Travel

William Zinsser was born in New York in 1922. He was educated at Princeton and has enjoyed a long and distinguished career as a college professor, notably at Yale University. In addition, he has written a number of books including *Paths of Resistance* (1988) and *Worlds of Childhood* (1990). In this essay he investigates the joys of travel.

———— ★ ————

The exotic travel bug that I caught as a G.I. in North Africa during World War II has never passed out of my system. I still feel its familiar tug and find myself getting out maps and applying for visas to faraway countries. Most recently the tug was to Laos. I've been clipping articles about Laos forever, picturing myself in the old royal capital of Luang Prabang, and earlier this year my wife put me out of my misery and said, "Let's go." Whatever journey I might think up, she has never regarded it as unthinkable, starting in 1954, when I persuaded her to get married and take a wedding trip across the heart of Africa, where few honeymooners had gone before.

"Why Laos?" friends asked, hearing about our latest trip. It was the same old question—"Why Burma?" "Why Yemen?" "Why Timbuktu?"—and I could only tell them it was the same old urge. But what *was* that urge? What impulse had driven me to seek out all those remote places? I've often asked myself that question, looking back in astonishment at bold decisions made with perfect confidence and risks routinely taken. Nothing in my early life suggested such a bent. I had a sheltered boyhood and was a cautious boy.

Norman Lewis, the great English travel writer, completing a memoir of his own at the age of eighty-seven, told me he had just realized he must have been born with a gene for adventurousness; otherwise he wouldn't have done so many things that struck him as normal conduct when he was young that now seem to have been unnecessarily foolish. I didn't get Lewis's gene: his indifference to comfort and safety and planning. I don't want to camp out in the mountains of New Guinea or the jungles of Brazil. I always want to know where I'll be spending the night, and I want it to be in a decent hotel with plumbing that works. In all my travels, I've only slept outside once, rolled up in a blanket on the Sahara. I'm not that kind of born traveler.

4   Nor am I the kind of traveler who wants to see everything there is to see. There are vast portions of the world I have absolutely no interest in seeing. Just the thought of visiting Norway, Sweden, Denmark, and Finland brings me close to narcolepsy, and my apathy extends in a broad swath across Estonia, Latvia, Lithuania, Germany, Poland, Central Europe, Russia, and all former Soviet states. I'd like to be parachuted into some of their cities to look at the architecture and the art: Cracow, Prague, Budapest, St. Petersburg. But then I'd like to be airlifted back out. No steppes or black forests, please. No peasant blouses.

5   Cold weather is obviously a factor here. Not only do I hate to be cold; I like to watch people going about their lives, and in the northern countries they stay indoors, keeping warm and keeping their homes famously tidy. My travel bug activates itself at the warm latitudes— at sunbaked Mediterranean ports where life spills untidily into the streets—and it follows the rising thermometer south through Africa and east to Egypt and the Levant and Arabia and India and Asia.

6   So what gene *did* I get? Plain curiosity must be somewhere in my DNA. I want to know what it feels like to actually be in a place that I've always heard about, to be part of its daily atmosphere and rhythm. I don't need to see every famous sight, every last mosque and museum; art is all around me, wherever I look—intricately woven baskets in an Asian market, elegant pottery in an African village, ornate silver jewelry on tribal women. I marvel at how broadly the artistic gene has been distributed: at the human ability to make ordinary objects of extraordinary beauty. I marvel at the beauty of the people themselves, especially women and children. I marvel at the infinite varieties of religious experience: the countless forms that faith can take, the endless thanking and beseeching and propitiating of gods through worship and song and dance. These are some of the common miracles I go in search of.

7   That still doesn't explain why I've been so drawn to the exotic. On a simple level the answer begins with language. Many of my destinations first came calling with their sound: Mombasa, Tahiti, Samoa, Rangoon, Bali, Macassar, Timbuktu. The name was reason enough to go. Often they also carried some strong association with the popular culture of my boyhood—the books and movies I grew up on. The Africa I wanted to cross with my bride was first put into my head by H. Rider Haggard's *King Solomon's Mines*. My Arabia was first shaped by chivalrous biographies of T. E. Lawrence, my Bangkok by *Anna and the King of Siam*, my India by *Gunga Din*, my Khartoum by *Four Feathers*, my South Seas by *Mutiny on the Bounty*. Most of it was romantic junk— a fantasy grafted by white writers onto the darker societies—and I swallowed it whole as historical truth. I was a product of my guileless times. World War II would put an end to that credulous era for me and

for the seven million other American boys it sent overseas to discover what the world was really like.

On a deeper level, I suspect that my yen has some roots in my life-long effort to wriggle out of the privileged WASP world I was born into. I snipped the umbilical cord by leaving Princeton to enlist in the army. I had no ambition to be an officer, and the army humored me in that democratic whim. Waking up one morning in North Africa was the wake-up call of my life. I was intoxicated by the otherness of the Arab world. Nobody from my world had ever traveled there or even mentioned the Arabs. Our world ended with England and Europe, Greece and Rome; everything else was terra incognita.   8

I don't mean that I came home from the war and renounced West-ern civilization; London and Paris and Rome are on my short list of fa-vorite cities. But Fez is also on that list—the "other" still exerts its pull; it was Luang Prabang that called me in 1996, not the Loire or the Lake Dis-trict. That gene is one that I have no trouble identifying. The central per-versity of my life is that I've never wanted to be doing what everyone else was doing. Something in me wants to take the road to Timbuktu—the road I wasn't expected to take. Something in me enjoys being the first person I know to visit Laos.   9

Of all my departures from an expected path, the pivotal one was my decision not to go into the family shellac business, William Zinsser & Co., though it had been on the same Manhattan block for more than a century and I was the fourth William Zinsser and only son, but to be-come a newspaperman. That decision enabled me to be a traveler. Most of my seemingly capricious jaunts were grounded in my vocation as a journalist. I've used writing to give myself an interesting life and a continuing education. I've persuaded editors to send me to places I wanted to see, or I've sent myself on stories I wanted to write that I thought editors would want to buy.   10

Often those stories grew out of some special interest or affection of mine. It was my love of music, not my love of travel, that took me to Shanghai and Venice for the two articles I'm most glad to have written—on the jazzmen Dwike Mitchell and Willie Ruff—and also took me to Brazil. I was sent there by a magazine to look for the roots of American jazz in Bahia, the Brazilian province largely populated by descendants of slaves brought from West Africa to work the Portuguese sugar plan-tations. What qualified me to go looking for those roots was that I knew jazz and had traveled in Africa, where the beat was born.   11

I therefore also travel to write: to bring back the news and to vali-date my experience. (Writers tend to think that no story has really hap-pened until they write about it.) The act of writing organizes how I spend my time when I arrive in a place. It gives me information, con-centrates my thoughts, and opens doors I wouldn't otherwise be al-lowed to knock on.   12

13   If I hadn't interviewed the governor of Fiji, Sir Ronald Garvey, I wouldn't have been invited to a formal dinner at the governor's mansion and played the cork game. Sir Ronald had invented the game to while away the long island nights. After dinner we were all deployed around a large table, and each of us was given a string with a cork attached to it. Lady Garvey brought several bath towels and piled them in the middle of the table to form a thick padded surface. Someone else arrived with the lid of an enormous silver soup tureen. Lady Garvey gave the lid to a brigadier, whose tunic gleamed with medals, and told him to grasp it firmly. The aide-de-camp, she said, was going to turn over a pack of cards. Every time a jack came up, we were to pull our string. Meanwhile the brigadier would slam down the silver lid and try to trap as many corks as he could.

14   Flip, flip, flip, flip went the cards. Oooooooh went the players when the jack came up. BOOOOOM! went the silver lid when it crashed down onto the towels, the table quivering under the blow. "Who got caught?" Lady Garvey asked, lifting the lid to find three corks nestled there, the others having flown away. She marked the three victims on her scoring pad and the game went on. And on and on. Flip, flip, flip, flip. Oooooooh. BOOOOOM! The faces around the table became a blur of British smiles and teeth. We were doomed to play the cork game forever. That long-ago evening still reverberates in my eardrums when I think of the ebbing power of the British Empire during my lifetime as a traveler. No other event could have given me such a vivid picture of Great Britain's outmoded colonial class trying to keep itself amused in the tropics. It wasn't just a dinner party; I was in on the end of a long historical process.

15   That, on the deepest level, is why I travel: to make a connection with what has gone before. I'm after the emotional moment. Most people, if asked to name the most emotional moment of their life, might recall some personal or family event: a birth, a wedding, a death. My three most emotional moments took place far from home. One was the day World War II ended. I happened to be visiting Siena with three other G.I.s, and we were the only American soldiers in town. When church bells began to toll the news, the townspeople hurried down to the great square where the Sienese have celebrated every important event since the Middle Ages. Noticing us in the crowd, they carried us around the square and through the streets.

16   My second most emotional moment took place at the Shanghai Conservatory of Music, where two black American musicians, the pianist Dwike Mitchell and the French-horn player Willie Ruff, were introducing live jazz to China. Ruff, who had taught himself Chinese, was explaining improvisation to three hundred music students and professors who didn't know what improvisation was and couldn't imagine that it was possible. The Chinese don't even have a word for *improvisa-*

tion of this kind. As Mitchell demonstrated, giving a series of elegant new lives to a short piano piece by one of the Chinese students, the room erupted in wonder and disbelief.

Ruff also provided my third moment—the richest one of all—when 17 he went to Venice to play Gregorian chants on his French horn in St. Mark's cathedral, at night, to test its amazing acoustics, which greatly influenced the Venetian school of music. For two hours, he and I and a sacristan were the only people in the cavernous church as darkness slowly fell over its interior and Ruff was left playing by the light of a single candle.

On all three occasions I was connected to immense historical, so- 18 cial, and cultural currents. In Siena I was connected to everyone in that jubilant city and to everyone else who had waited since 1939 for the end of World War II or had died to make it possible. In Shanghai I was connected to the ancient power of music to bridge the widest kind of cultural gulf: West and East, African and Asian, oral and written. In Venice I was connected to chants that had been played and sung in the liturgy of St. Mark's since it opened in 1067.

Dozens of other moments that were almost as resonant come back 19 to me. Watching a camel caravan materialize out of the desert carrying salt to Timbuktu, I was connected to all the caravans that ever crossed the Sahara. Watching the French explorer Eric de Bisschop sail away from Tahiti on a small bamboo raft bound for Chile, I was connected to all the sailors since the earliest Polynesians who have set out across the Pacific. Climbing to Robert Louis Stevenson's grave on a mountaintop in Samoa, watching an old Balinese drummer teach a temple dance to a five-year-old girl by placing her feet on his feet, meeting a Vietnamese poet in Hanoi who showed me a poem of healing reconciliation that he had written and left at the Vietnam Memorial in Washington, I was moved by mystical bonds and continuities that I could only have felt by leaving home and putting myself in their path. Such moments have caught me by surprise with their beauty and their grace and have stayed with me ever since.

★ *Meaning and Understanding*

1. How does Zinsser explain his impulse to seek out remote places? How was "waking up one morning in North Africa" the "wake-up call" (paragraph 8) of the writer's life?

2. How does Zinsser differ from Norman Lewis, whom he dubs the "great English travel writer" (paragraph 3)?

3. How does the writer link his past to his inclination toward traveling to exotic places?

4. Why didn't the writer work for the family business?

5. How does language enter the writer's interest in exotic places? His career as a writer? How do books and movies affect his love of travel?

★ *Techniques and Strategies*

1. What is the writer's thesis?

2. How does the title of the essay strike you? Why, of all the places named in the essay, does the writer choose "Timbuktu" for his title?

3. What is the purpose of the narrative about formal dinner at the governor's mansion in Fiji? What point does it help Zinsser make?

4. The writer offers a number of reasons for his love of travel and supports them with numerous examples. What reasons does he give? Which examples do you find most memorable?

5. What effect does the writer create by citing the names of so many people?

★ *Speaking of Values*

1. What qualities of character does the writer reveal about himself? What can you determine about his values? What is your reaction to the way he feels about travel?

2. In what ways is travel an important element on our culture today? Why do people today like to travel? What challenges would prevent people from traveling?

3. Why is the writer not interested in traveling to some places—for instance, Norway, Sweden, or Denmark? What does he say about the possibility of traveling to these places? What do these choices reveal about him?

4. What does the writer mean when he says he likes seeing life spill "untidily into the streets" (paragraph 5)? How is this an important element for the world traveler?

5. How is the idea of being "connected to immense historical, social, and cultural currents" (paragraph 18) important to the writer? Do you believe that these issues are important in traveling? Or should simply relaxation and pleasure be the primary goal? Why do you believe as you do?

★ *Values Conversation*

How do members of the class feel about travel? Form groups to discuss the issue. What rewards has travel brought to you or someone you know? What problems have you faced being a traveler?

★ *Writing about Values*

1. Write an essay called "Why I Travel" or an essay called "Why I Do Not Travel."

2. Write an essay about a vacation you took—with your family, your friends, or on your own—and indicate how what you observed went beyond simply "the experience of something new."

3. Write an essay in which you offer tips to people who choose exotic lands as travel destinations.

Mari Evans

When in Rome

Mari Evans was born in Toledo, Ohio in 1923 and received her education
at Toledo University. Her first book was *I Am a Black Woman* (1968). For
many years she was writer in residence at Indiana University. She is a
poet, an editor, a playwright, and the producer of PBS's award-winning
series *The Black Experience*. In this poem she shows the basic humorous
clash between classes.

———— ★ ————

Marrie dear
the box is full...
take
whatever you like
5   to eat...

       (an egg
       or soup
       ...there ain't no meat.)

there's endive there
10   and
cottage cheese...

       (whew! if I had some
       black-eyed peas...)

there's sardines
15   on the shelves
and such...
but
don't
get my anchovies...
20   they cost
too much!

       (me get the
       anchovies indeed!
       what she think, she got—
25   a bird to feed?)

there's plenty in there
to fill you up...

(yes'm. just the
sight's
enough!   30
Hope I lives till I get
home
I'm tired of eatin'
what they eats in Rome...)

★ Meaning and Understanding

1. What is Evans's point in this poem?

2. Who are the two speakers?

3. What is the relation of the speakers to each other? How do they feel about each other?

4. What is their topic of conversation?

5. What does the first speaker offer to Marrie?

★ Techniques and Strategies

1. Apart from the poem, what does the phrase "When in Rome" mean? It is only the first part of a famous saying. What is the full saying?

2. What does the title mean in the context of this poem? How is the title ironic? How has the poet put an original stamp on the familiar saying? What larger issue is she implying?

3. How does the grammatical structure of the sentences help you identify who each of the speakers is? Why is the first speaker so concerned about Marrie getting the anchovies?

4. Why does the poet place the second speaker's words in parentheses?

5. How does the poet achieve humorous effects in the poem?

★ Speaking of Values

1. On one level, the poem is about differing tastes in food. What values does each woman imply about her lifestyle through the food preferences identified in the poem? How does the choice of foods named by both speakers help you identify their character and background?

2. Which of the two speakers does the poet want us to side with? How do you know? Has she in fact made one of the two characters more appealing than the other? How do you feel about the two speakers? Why?

3. What attitude toward the woman who works for her does the first speaker convey? Would you call her solicitous, condescending, generous, thoughtful, insensitive? Why? What attitude to workers in general do the first speaker's words suggest? How do you feel about the kind of relation suggested in the poem?

★ *Values Conversation*

Form groups to discuss the values that the poet is trying to impart about the relations between rich and poor, employers and workers, whites and blacks.

★ *Writing about Values*

1. Write an essay called "When in Rome" in which you tell about a time you had to follow social or cultural or economic rules established by someone else, rules that you found different from those you valued.

2. Write an essay or poem about a conversation between "Marrie" and someone in her family in which she recounts the conversation she had with her employer about having something to eat.

Marcus Mabry

Living in Two Worlds

Marcus Mabry was born into a poor New Jersey family in 1967. Educated at Stanford University, he served as the *Newsweek* State Department correspondent and currently works for the magazine's Paris bureau. In this essay he contrasts life at Stanford University with his life at home.

──────── ★ ────────

A round, green cardboard sign hangs from a string proclaiming, "We built a proud new feeling," the slogan of a local supermarket. It is a souvenir from one of my brother's last jobs. In addition to being a bagger, he's worked at a fast-food restaurant, a gas station, a garage and a textile factory. Now, in the icy clutches of the Northeastern winter, he is unemployed. He will soon be a father. He is 19 years old.

In mid-December I was at Stanford, among the palm trees and weighty chores of academe. And all I wanted to do was get out. I joined the rest of the undergrads in a chorus of excitement, singing the praises of Christmas break. No classes, no midterms, no finals…and no freshmen! (I'm a resident assistant.) Awesome! I was looking forward to escaping. I never gave a thought to what I was escaping to.

Once I got home to New Jersey, reality returned. My dreaded freshmen had been replaced by unemployed relatives; badgering professors had been replaced by hard-working single mothers, and cold classrooms by dilapidated bedrooms and kitchens. The room in which the "proud new feeling" sign hung contained the belongings of myself, my mom and my brother. But for these two weeks it was mine. They slept downstairs on couches.

Most students who travel between the universes of poverty and affluence during breaks experience similar conditions, as well as the guilt, the helplessness and, sometimes, the embarrassment associated with them. Our friends are willing to listen, but most of them are unable to imagine the pain of the impoverished lives that we see every six months. Each time I return home I feel further away from the realities of poverty in America and more ashamed that they are allowed to persist. What frightens me most is not that the American socioeconomic system permits poverty to continue, but that by participating in that system I share some of the blame.

Last year I lived in an on-campus apartment, with a (relatively) modern bathroom, kitchen and two bedrooms. Using summer earnings,

I added some expensive prints, a potted palm and some other plants, making the place look like the more-than-humble abode of a New York City Yuppie. I gave dinner parties, even a *soirée française*.

6   For my roommate, a doctor's son, this kind of life was nothing extraordinary. But my mom was struggling to provide a life for herself and my brother. In addition to working 24-hour-a-day cases as a practical nurse, she was trying to ensure that my brother would graduate from high school and have a decent life. She knew that she had to compete for his attention with drugs and other potentially dangerous things that can look attractive to a young man when he sees no better future.

7   Living in my grandmother's house this Christmas break restored all the forgotten, and the never acknowledged, guilt. I had gone to boarding school on a full scholarship since the ninth grade, so being away from poverty was not new. But my own growing affluence has increased my distance. My friends say that I should not feel guilty: what could I do substantially for my family at this age, they ask. Even though I know that education is the right thing to do, I can't help but feel, sometimes, that I have it too good. There is no reason that I deserve security and warmth, while my brother has to cope with potential unemployment and prejudice. I, too, encounter prejudice, but it is softened by my status as a student in an affluent and intellectual community.

8   More than my sense of guilt, my sense of helplessness increases each time I return home. As my success leads me further away for longer periods of time, poverty becomes harder to conceptualize and feels that much more oppressive when I visit with it. The first night of break, I lay in our bedroom, on a couch that let out into a bed that took up the whole room, except for a space heater. It was a little hard to sleep because the springs from the couch stuck through at inconvenient spots. But it would have been impossible to sleep anyway because of the groans coming from my grandmother's room next door. Only in her early 60s, she suffers from many chronic diseases and couldn't help but moan, then pray aloud, then moan, then pray aloud.

9   This wrenching of my heart was interrupted by the 3 A.M. entry of a relative who had been allowed to stay at the house despite rowdy behavior and threats toward the family in the past. As he came into the house, he slammed the door, and his heavy steps shook the second floor as he stomped into my grandmother's room to take his place, at the foot of her bed. There he slept, without blankets on a bare mattress. This was the first night. Later in the vacation, a Christmas turkey and a Christmas ham were stolen from my aunt's refrigerator on Christmas Eve. We think the thief was a relative. My mom and I decided not to exchange gifts that year because it just didn't seem festive.

10   A few days after New Year's I returned to California. The Northeast was soon hit by a blizzard. They were there, and I was here. That

was the way it had to be, for now. I haven't forgotten; the ache of knowing their suffering is always there. It has to be kept deep down, or I can't find the logic in studying and partying while people, my people, are being killed by poverty. Ironically, success drives me away from those I most want to help by getting in education.

Somewhere in the midst of all that misery, my family has built, within me, "a proud feeling." As I travel between the two worlds it becomes harder to remember just how proud I should be—not just because of where I have come from and where I am going, but because of where they are. The fact that they survive in the world in which they live is something to be very proud of, indeed. It inspires within me a sense of tenacity and accomplishment that I hope every college graduate will someday possess.   11

★ Meaning and Understanding

1. What do we learn of the writer's brother at the start of the essay? How does the brother compare in situation to other of Mabry's relatives?

2. What are Mabry's living conditions like at Stanford?

3. What happens on the first night of school break? What happens at 3 A.M.?

4. What happens to the Christmas turkey and ham?

5. Why does Mabry feel particular pride in his family?

★ Techniques and Strategies

1. How does the title capture the essence of the writer's topic?

2. What is the thesis of the essay?

3. Where does the writer use concrete sensory detail to best advantage?

4. How does the "round, green, cardboard sign" (paragraph 1) serve the writer's purpose? In what way is it symbolic?

5. How does the writer use comparison and contrast to advance his point?

★ Speaking of Values

1. Why does Mabry feel guilt? Is this an understandable or justifiable emotion, given the circumstances? Does he in fact, as he fears, "have it too good"? Why or why not? What would he have to do to feel not guilty? How do you think you would feel under the circumstances?

2. How long has the writer lived away from home this way? In what ways might this contribute to his discomfort? In what ways does living away from home and then returning heighten the differences between the two lives people lead?

3. What contrasts do you notice between the world of your college environment and the world of being a student? Do you or your friends share any of Mabry's feelings? Which? Why?

4. How do you account for the theft of the turkey and ham? What could drive relatives to steal from each other?

5. The writer acknowledges the irony that his education and successes drive him further and further from the poverty-stricken people he wants to help. Do you fault him for abandoning his family to go to school? Why or why not? What conflicting values of American life and family come into play here? What does Mabry mean when he says in paragraph 10 "That was the way it had to be, for now"? What does the "for now" in that statement imply to you?

★ Values Conversation

Mabry implies that by participating in a system that permits poverty to continue we share some of the blame for that poverty. Form groups to discuss the issue. What do group members see as their responsibility, if any, for the state of poverty in America today?

★ Writing about Values

1. Write an essay called "My Two Worlds" in which you contrast two dramatically different elements of your current and (or) past life.

2. Do research about the realities of poverty in your neighborhood, city, or state today and the ways the government is attempting (or not attempting) to do anything about it.

3. Write an essay in which you discuss the way a family member or friend "changed" when he or she experienced financial success.

Dorothy Parker

The Standard of Living

Dorothy Parker (1893–1967) was a prolific writer and the subject of a recent film, *Mrs. Parker and the Vicious Circle,* about her life as a member of the Algonquin Round Table, a group of writers who met regularly at the famous New York hotel. Parker wrote many works, including *Laments for the Living* (1930) and *Not So Deep a Well* (1936). In this short story she examines the values of two office workers.

──────── ★ ────────

Annabel and Midge came out of the tea room with the arrogant slow gait of the leisured, for their Saturday afternoon stretched ahead of them. They had lunched, as was their wont, on sugar, starches, oils, and butterfats. Usually they ate sandwiches of spongy new white bread greased with butter and mayonnaise; they ate thick wedges of cake lying wet beneath ice cream and whipped cream and melted chocolate gritty with nuts. As alternates, they ate patties, sweating beads of inferior oil, containing bits of bland meat bogged in pale, stiffening sauce; they ate pastries, limber under rigid icing, filled with an indeterminate yellow sweet stuff, not still solid, not yet liquid, like salve that has been left in the sun. They chose no other sort of food, nor did they consider it. And their skin was like the petals of wood anemones, and their bellies were as flat and their flanks as lean as those of young Indian braves.

Annabel and Midge had been best friends almost from the day that Midge had found a job as stenographer with the firm that employed Annabel. By now, Annabel, two years longer in the stenographic department, had worked up to the wages of eighteen dollars and fifty cents a week; Midge was still at sixteen dollars. Each girl lived at home with her family and paid half her salary to its support.

The girls sat side by side at their desks, they lunched together every noon, together they set out for home at the end of the day's work. Many of their evenings and most of their Sundays were passed in each other's company. Often they were joined by two young men, but there was no steadiness to any such quartet; the two young men would give place, unlamented, to two other young men, and lament would have been inappropriate, really, since the newcomers were scarcely distinguishable from their predecessors. Invariably the girls spent the fine idle hours of their hot-weather Saturday afternoons together. Constant use had not worn ragged the fabric of their friendship.

4   They looked alike, though the resemblance did not lie in their features. It was in the shape of their bodies, their movements, their style,
and their adornments. Annabel and Midge did, and completely, all
that young office workers are besought not to do. They painted their
lips and their nails, they darkened their lashes and lightened their
hair, and scent seemed to shimmer from them. They wore thin, bright
dresses, tight over their breasts and high on their legs, and tilted slip-
pers, fancifully strapped. They looked conspicuous and cheap and
charming.

5   Now, as they walked across to Fifth Avenue with their skirts
swirled by the hot wind, they received audible admiration. Young men
grouped lethargically about newsstands awarded them murmurs, exclamations, even—the ultimate tribute—whistles. Annabel and Midge
passed without the condescension of hurrying their pace; they held
their heads higher and set their feet with exquisite precision, as if they
stepped over the necks of peasants.

6   Always the girls went to walk on Fifth Avenue on their free afternoons, for it was the ideal ground for their favorite game. The game
could be played anywhere, and indeed, was, but the great shop windows stimulated the two players to their best form.

7   Annabel had invented the game; or rather she had evolved it from
an old one. Basically, it was no more than the ancient sport of what-
would-you-do-if-you-had-a-million-dollars? But Annabel had drawn a
new set of rules for it, had narrowed it, pointed it, made it stricter. Like
all games, it was the more absorbing for being more difficult.

8   Annabel's version went like this: You must suppose that somebody
dies and leaves you a million dollars, cool. But there is a condition to
the bequest. It is stated in the will that you must spend every nickel of
the money on yourself.

9   There lay the hazard of the game. If, when playing it, you forgot
and listed among your expenditures the rental of a new apartment for
your family, for example, you lost your turn to the other player. It was
astonishing how many—and some of them among the experts, too—
would forfeit all their innings by such slips.

10   It was essential, of course, that it be played in passionate seriousness. Each purchase must be carefully considered and, if necessary,
supported by argument. There was no zest to playing wildly. Once Annabel had introduced the game to Sylvia, another girl who worked in
the office. She explained the rules to Sylvia and then offered her the
gambit "What would be the first thing you'd do?" Sylvia had not
shown the decency of even a second of hesitation. "Well," she said, "the
first thing I'd do, I'd go out and hire somebody to shoot Mrs. Gary Coo-
per, and then..." So it is to be seen that she was no fun.

11   But Annabel and Midge were surely born to be comrades, for
Midge played the game like a master from the moment she learned it.

It was she who added the touches that made the whole thing cozier. According to Midge's innovations, the eccentric who died and left you the money was not anybody you loved, or, for the matter of that, anybody you even knew. It was somebody who had seen you somewhere and had thought, "That girl ought to have lots of nice things. I'm going to leave her a million dollars when I die." And the death was to be neither untimely nor painful. Your benefactor, full of years and comfortably ready to depart, was to slip softly away during sleep and go right to heaven. These embroideries permitted Annabel and Midge to play their game in the luxury of peaceful consciences.

Midge played with a seriousness that was not only proper but extreme. The single strain on the girls' friendship had followed an announcement once made by Annabel that the first thing she would buy with her million dollars would be a silver-fox coat. It was as if she had struck Midge across the mouth. When Midge recovered her breath, she cried that she couldn't imagine how Annabel could do such a thing— silver-fox coats were common! Annabel defended her taste with the retort that they were not common, either. Midge then said that they were so. She added that everybody had a silver-fox coat. She went on, with perhaps a slight loss of head, to declare that she herself wouldn't be caught dead in silver fox. 12

For the next few days, though the girls saw each other as constantly, their conversation was careful and infrequent, and they did not once play their game. Then one morning, as soon as Annabel entered the office, she came to Midge and said that she had changed her mind. She would not buy a silver-fox coat with any part of her million dollars. Immediately on receiving the legacy, she would select a coat of mink. 13

Midge smiled and her eyes shone. "I think," she said, "you're doing absolutely the right thing." 14

Now, as they walked along Fifth Avenue, they played the game anew. It was one of those days with which September is repeatedly cursed; hot and glaring, with slivers of dust in the wind. People drooped and shambled, but the girls carried themselves tall and walked a straight line, as befitted young heiresses on their afternoon promenade. There was no longer need for them to start the game at its formal opening. Annabel went direct to the heart of it. 15

"All right," she said. "So you've got this million dollars. So what would be the first thing you'd do?" 16

"Well, the first thing I'd do," Midge said, "I'd get a mink coat." But she said it mechanically, as if she were giving the memorized answer to an expected question. 17

"Yes," Annabel said, "I think you ought to. The terribly dark kind of mink." But she, too, spoke as if by rote. It was too hot; fur, no matter how dark and sleek and supple, was horrid to the thoughts. 18

19   They stepped along in silence for a while. Then Midge's eye was caught by a shop window. Cool, lovely gleamings were there set off by chaste and elegant darkness.

20   "No," Midge said, "I take it back. I wouldn't get a mink coat the first thing. Know what I'd do? I'd get a string of pearls. Real pearls."

21   Annabel's eyes turned to follow Midge's.

22   "Yes," she said, slowly, "I think that's kind of a good idea. And it would make sense, too. Because you can wear pearls with anything."

23   Together they went over to the shop window and stood pressed against it. It contained but one object—a double row of great, even pearls clasped by a deep emerald around a little pink velvet throat.

24   "What do you suppose they cost?" Annabel said.

25   "Gee, I don't know," Midge said. "Plenty, I guess."

26   "Like a thousand dollars?" Annabel said.

27   "Oh, I guess like more," Midge said. "On account of the emerald."

28   "Well, like ten thousand dollars?" Annabel said.

29   "Gee, I wouldn't even know," Midge said.

30   The devil nudged Annabel in the ribs, "Dare you to go in and price them," she said.

31   "Like fun!" Midge said.

32   "Dare you," Annabel said.

33   "Why, a store like this wouldn't even be open this afternoon," Midge said.

34   "Yes, it is so, too," Annabel said. "People just came out. And there's a doorman on. Dare you."

35   "Well," Midge said. "But you've got to come too."

36   They tendered thanks, icily, to the doorman for ushering them into the shop. It was cool and quiet, a broad, gracious room with paneled walls and soft carpet. But the girls wore expressions of bitter disdain, as if they stood in a sty.

37   A slim, immaculate clerk came to them and bowed. His neat face showed no astonishment at their appearance.

38   "Good afternoon," he said. He implied that he would never forget it if they would grant him the favor of accepting his soft-spoken greeting.

39   "Good afternoon," Annabel and Midge said together, and in like freezing accents.

40   "Is there something—?" the clerk said.

41   "Oh, we're just looking," Annabel said. It was as if she flung the words down from a dais.

42   The clerk bowed.

43   "My friend and myself merely happened to be passing," Midge said, and stopped, seeming to listen to the phrase. "My friend here and myself," she went on, "merely happened to be wondering how much are those pearls you've got in your window."

"Ah, yes," the clerk said. "The double rope. That is two hundred and fifty thousand dollars, Madam."   44

"I see," Midge said.   45

The clerk bowed. "An exceptionally beautiful necklace," he said. "Would you care to look at it?"   46

"No, thank you," Annabel said.   47

"My friend and myself merely happened to be passing," Midge said.   48

They turned to go; to go, from their manner, where the tumbrel[1] awaited them. The clerk sprang ahead and opened the door. He bowed as they swept by him.   49

The girls went on along the Avenue and disdain was still on their faces.   50

"Honestly!" Annabel said. "Can you imagine a thing like that?"   51

"Two hundred and fifty thousand dollars!" Midge said. "That's a quarter of a million dollars right there!"   52

"He's got his nerve!" Annabel said.   53

They walked on. Slowly the disdain went, slowly and completely as if drained from them, and with it went the regal carriage and tread. Their shoulders dropped and they dragged their feet; they bumped against each other, without notice or apology, and caromed away again. They were silent and their eyes were cloudy.   54

Suddenly Midge straightened her back, flung her head high, and spoke, clear and strong.   55

"Listen, Annabel," she said. "Look. Suppose there was this terribly rich person, see? You don't know this person, but this person has seen you somewhere and wants to do something for you. Well, it's a terribly old person, see? And so this person dies, just like going to sleep, and leaves you ten million dollars. Now, what would be the first thing you'd do?"   56

★ Meaning and Understanding

1. What kinds of jobs do Midge and Annabel hold? How do the two women resemble each other?

2. What game do they play as they walk along Fifth Avenue? How do the "great shop windows" stimulate them "to their best form"?

3. What version of the game did Annabel create? What touches did Midge add to make the "whole thing cozier"? Who is the "better" player?

---

[1]A cart used during the French Revolution to take convicted aristocracy to their execution.

4. Why is Sylvia, the other coworker, indecent and "no fun"? What is wrong with Sylvia's first act in the game?

5. How do the women's attitudes change after the clerk quotes the price of the necklace?

★ *Techniques and Strategies*

1. What is the theme of this story? What point is Parker attempting to make?

2. What details best contribute to your understanding of what the characters Annabelle and Midge look like and how they behave?

3. How has Parker used dialogue skillfully here? What is the significance of repeated lines like "My friend and myself merely happened to be passing"?

4. What is the significance of the title? Parker is known for her biting wit and cynical views: how does the title reflect those judgments? In what ways is it ironical?

5. Parker's use of figurative language enlivens the story. Which similes and metaphors do you find memorable? Comment particularly on the phrase "where the tumbrel awaited them." What is a tumbrel? What cynically humorous dimension does the figure add to the story?

★ *Speaking of Values*

1. Parker says the women looked alike not in their features but "in the shape of their bodies, their movements, their style, and their adornments"—the point being that they conformed exactly to the day's stylistic requirements of dress and appearance. Parker says the girls "looked conspicuous and cheap and charming." Would you agree with her assessment? Why or why not?

2. In what ways do people today resemble each other because of the demands of style? What is your opinion of people who look alike because they adhere strictly to group values about dress and appearance?

3. Why does Parker go into such detail about what the women eat? What do choices of foods tell you about people's values? What point about the women's values do the food choices make here?

4. What does the story imply about the value of material objects? What is your view of a necklace for $250,000?

5. What point is Parker making about the standard of living in general? What do the women's salaries and how they must use their money

have to do with their view of economics? In the final moments of the story, Midge recasts the game by changing its parameters. Why? What advice would you give the two women?

★ *Values Conversation*

Form groups and characterize the values of the two characters in the story, Annabel and Midge. How do their values compare and contrast with the values of working men and women today?

★ *Writing about Values*

1. Write a letter to Annabel and Midge telling them about the standard of living you think they need to learn about.

2. Write an essay in which you discuss one or more persons you know whom you would characterize as "slaves to fashion." Describe each individual and why you think of them this way and then try to identify the differences between them.

3. Play the game and write an essay in which you explain what you would do with a million dollars—or ten million dollars.

Jerome Charyn

Faces on the Wall

Jerome Charyn is a professor of English who was born in New York City in 1937. He is an editor and the author of more than fifteen books, including *The Man Who Grew Younger* (1967). In this essay he writes about the effects of movies on his life.

★ ───────

1   I can say without melodrama, or malice, that Hollywood ruined my life. It's left me in a state of constant adolescence, searching for a kind of love that was invented by Louis B. Mayer and his brother moguls at Paramount and Columbia and Twentieth Century-Fox.

2   I've hungered for dream women, like Rita Hayworth, whose message has always been that love is a deadly thing, a system of divine punishment. Whatever she might say or do, Rita couldn't care less. She was so powerful she could perform the most erotic dance by simply taking off her gloves (in *Gilda*). And just when you thought you had her, fixed forever on the screen, she said good-bye to Hollywood and you and ran off with Aly Khan.

3   But it wasn't only Rita.

4   Someone must have sneaked me into a moviehouse while I was still in the cradle, because my earliest imaginings and adventures have come from the screen. While I sucked on a baby bottle I remembered Gene Tierney's oriental eyes. She was in *Belle Starr,* and I was only three. I didn't care about the six-gun strapped to her leg. I didn't care about Dana Andrews or Randolph Scott. They were only flies buzzing around Belle. I cared about her cheekbones, the hollows in her face, the essential beauty she had. It was painful to look at Gene. She stunned you like no other star. Later I would love Dietrich and Garbo and the young Mary Astor (until she cut her hair for Humphrey Bogart in *The Maltese Falcon*). But that was when I had a sense of *history* and could shovel back and forth in movie time and consider myself a fan. But when I discovered Belle Starr's face, it wasn't in some stinking retrospective. I had no idea what films were. I saw her face and suffered.

5   I've been suffering ever since. At fifty, still a boy somehow, I walk into a moviehouse close to midnight and watch Kevin Costner and Sean Young in *No Way Out,* a rather implausible remake of *The Big Clock,* with the Pentagon and a "masked" Soviet spy in place of a New York publishing empire (what's really missing is Charles Laughton's

face). The projector breaks down during a seduction scene in the back seat of a limo. Sean Young disappears from the theater's wall. The audience begins to riot. The images return with no sound track. And we're stuck in spooky silence. It doesn't take a genius to understand how much we depend on the little noises that surround a film—the rustle of a skirt, the opening of a door, the romantic leitmotiv more than the babble, which we can live without. We cannot bear absolute silence in a moviehouse; the shadows on the wall stop reassuring us, even in Technicolor; the faces *feel* sepulchral.

The sound returns, and I can watch Kevin Costner and Sean Young   6 (the beautiful android from *Blade Runner*) in my usual hibernation at the movies. The heartbeat slows. I'm like a bat with folded wings. Costner's conventional handsomeness soothes the blood. He's easy to look at. A star. But Sean Young dies a third of the way through the film. And we move from romance to a convoluted manhunt. I carry around all the illogic of a disappointed child. I want her to rise from the dead and return to Kevin Costner. Of course she doesn't. It's Hollywood in its seventh generation, not Dalí or Buñuel.

Still, I get up from my seat with the same exhilaration I often feel at   7 the end of a movie, as if I've been through a period of profound rest, no matter what maneuvers and machinations are on the screen. Those thirty-foot faces always hold my eye.

Movie time has its own logic and laws, related to little else in our   8 lives. I don't mean by this that watching a movie is more "authentic" than reading a book or attending the theater or making love. We dream our way through all these events, involved with the crazy continuum of present, future, and past, which never really figured in the safe mechanics of Sir Isaac Newton, the greatest scientist who ever lived. Sir Isaac believed that the universe was a magnificent but tight machine where "the whole future depends strictly upon the whole past."

Our own century, the century of Hollywood and Hitler, has pushed   9 us further and further away from Newton's corner. The wildness and randomness we've discovered in the universe, we've also discovered in ourselves. And not even Louis B. Mayer and his mother's famous chicken soup (dispensed at the MGM commissary for thirty-five cents a bowl) could keep this randomness out of films. He could nourish his stars on the MGM lots, groom them, reinvent their lives and their looks, but he couldn't control their faces on the moviehouse wall. Those faces had a darker message than any one L.B. subscribed to. They had their own wild resonance. They scared as much as they delighted. The simplest screen was much bigger (and darker) than any of the movie moguls. The studios could tyrannize the content of a film, declare a land of happy endings, but they weren't sitting with you in the dark. They could control Joan Crawford, but not the hysteria hidden behind those big eyes, or the ruby mouth that could almost suck you into the screen. The stars were very strange creatures. They had the power to hypnotize whole generations in ways that Sir Isaac couldn't have guessed. The stars were like the doubles of our own irrational, perverse selves. In matters of Hollywood, our feelings were often mixed: we were tender and murderous toward the stars. They were like a demonic parent-child, lover and stranger, and we were *always* involved in some sort of incestuous relationship with them, with those faces (and bodies) on the wall.

10   If I read *The Sound and the Fury* or *Middlemarch*, I'm filled with the aromas of either book, with past readings and relationships to the characters, with a whole continent of language and scenes, but the books don't frighten me. I can enter into their dream songs, and leave at my own will. But if I'm watching *Casablanca* on the wall, I'll let my eye slip past the phony details, the studio-bound streets, the laughable sense of a fabricated city, and drift into that dream of Humphrey Bogart and Rick's Café Américain, which exists outside any laws of physics, like the eternal dream of Hollywood itself, a little dopey, but with a power we can't resist. I don't crave popcorn while Bogart lisps. I'm a ghost "on the wrong side of the celluloid," almost as immaterial as those figures I'm watching, involved in their ghostly dance. I'm Bogart and Ingrid and the pianoplayer Sam and Paul Henreid's perennial wooden face. We lend ourselves, give up boundaries in the dark that we'd never dare give to a lover. We are ghosts absorbing other ghosts, cannibals sitting in a chair. . . .

11   I can remember the moviehouse where I saw *They Died with Their Boots On*. The RKO Chester. It was part of a special treat. I'd gone with my uncle and my older brother. It was at night. And I was barely five. It was the first time I could link a particular movie to a particular palace, and therefore it's my first memory as a moviegoer, sadder than seeing Gene Tierney as Belle Starr, because I can't recollect the circumstances surrounding her face. *Boots* starred Errol Flynn. It was about Custer's Last Stand. I couldn't have known who Custer was. I hadn't even graduated from kindergarten. But I remember horses' hoofs, Custer's mustache, his coat of animal hair, and Chief Crazy Horse (Anthony Quinn).

12   I've never seen the film again. But I haven't forgotten that call to death as Custer rides to meet the Sioux. It didn't matter that I was in short pants. I understood the vocabulary of this film. It was as if I'd been a moviegoer all my life. My uncle and brother were held in the suspense of the story, even though they must have heard of Little Bighorn. They were older, wiser, more schooled in the American way. But I could read faces on a wall. And I saw something amiss in Errol Flynn's eyebrows, in that dark knit of his face. I shivered in my seat and pondered the enigma of those side balconies with boxed-off chairs

that never made sense in a moviehouse, because you had to observe a film at such a deep angle all the action seemed to curve away from you, to fall right out of your grasp. I counted my fingers. I combed my hair with a pencil. Anything, anything rather than watch the massacre I felt was coming. I didn't want Errol to die. He had long hair, like a girl. He was much prettier than his screen wife, Olivia de Havilland. This was her last film with Errol. She was always a nub of virtue around his neck, whether the film was about Robin Hood, Custer, or Captain Blood. But I wasn't a film historian at five. I was crapping in my pants at the RKO Chester, and I couldn't keep my eyes off Errol Flynn.

Custer dying with all his men depressed me for months. It wasn't   13
that I had discovered death at the movies. There was polio and other diseases. A neighbor falling off the fire escape. Bombings in Europe that my brother had talked about. But screen dying is like no other dying in the world. I'd gotten used to Custer's long hair. I belonged with the Seventh Cavalry. There was almost a religious conversion in the dark. I'd become whatever Custer was. And when he died, the loss was just too great.

★ Meaning and Understanding

1. What is the topic of this piece?

2. How, according to Charyn, did Hollywood ruin his life?

3. What happened during the writer's viewing of the film *No Way Out*? Why was Charyn "depressed for months" after seeing Custer dying on the screen?

4. How, according to Charyn, has our century grown further and further away from Sir Isaac Newton's corner?

5. Who was Louis B. Mayer? Why couldn't he keep randomness out of films?

★ Techniques and Strategies

1. What is Charyn's thesis in this selection?

2. Why does the writer dwell on the very early experiences he had watching movies? Could a three-year-old appreciate all that the writer identifies from those youthful experiences? Why or why not?

3. The writer uses an informal, colloquial style here. Why? What is his purpose in this piece? What is your reaction to the writing style? Identify some colloquial expressions that contribute to the character of the piece.

4. How effective are the examples of films in supporting the points Charyn wants to make?

5. Why does Charyn use parenthetical expressions often? What does he achieve with this technique?

★ *Speaking of Values*

1. Charyn states that Louis B. Mayer and other movie moguls invented a kind of love. Do you agree that Hollywood and the movies define our notion of love? Why or why not? In what other ways does Hollywood affect our values as Americans?

2. What kinds of actors are the dream-men and dream-women presented to us by Hollywood today? What does our recognition and support of these actors say about American values?

3. Why might you agree or disagree with Charyn that "the wildness and randomness we've discovered in the Universe, we've also discovered in ourselves" and that these elements appear in the movies?

4. Why and how are the relations moviegoers have with stars "incestuous"? Do you agree with the observation? Why or why not?

5. How does Charyn compare books and movies? What is the essence of the difference, according to him? Do you agree with the suggestion? Why or why not?

6. Why might you agree or disagree that "screen dying is like no other dying in the world" (paragraph 13)?

★ *Values Conversation*

Films are a strong element of American culture. What needs or desires are actually satisfied by the culture of movie going? Form groups to discuss the hold movies have on our minds and imagination. How do the movies become shapers of our values? How do they simply reflect our values? Give examples from your own experiences.

★ *Writing about Values*

1. Write an essay in which you discuss your most memorable movie experience and how it affected you.

2. Write an essay about how Hollywood influences our view of some element in American culture—heroism, love, sex, family life, politics, or education, for example.

3. Which film stars today best capture what Americans value in people? Write an essay to explain what one or two of these stars projects and identify films that best illustrate your point.

Charles McGrath

Giving Saturday Morning Some Slack

Born in 1947, Charles McGrath graduated from Yale University. He spent more than two decades on the staff of the *New Yorker.* Currently he is the editor of the *New York Times Book Review.* In this essay he writes about how Saturday morning television programs for children require a fresh perspective—not from the educational but from the leisure point of view.

★

1   Remember Saturday morning? The expectancy, the blissfulness, the sense of utter freedom? The most sublime moment was the first—the instant when, unprodded by either alarm clock or parental summons, you emerged into consciousness and experienced an almost physical sense of release, a floating up from the mattress, as you realized that you didn't have to go to school. And the rest of the day—of the whole weekend—then seemed to spread out limitlessly from the edge of the bedcovers, a blank and beckoning horizon.

2   You could do absolutely anything you chose. You could turn over, tunnel under the pillow and go back to sleep. You could just lie there for a while, woolgathering and listening to Dad's snores rumble from down the hall. You could get up and play with your slot cars or your electric train. You could check on the gerbils, in hopes that they might be mating again. You could build a model plane, snuffling in deep, head-jolting whiffs of Testor's glue. You could even read—that was not unheard of back then.

3   But what you chose to do, of course, was watch TV. You sprang up and, still in your pj's, went to the kitchen and fixed yourself a bowl of Froot Loops or Lucky Charms, which in violation of the first commandment of the household—no food in the living room!—you carried boldly over the forbidden threshold and set on top of the Magnavox. You turned on your favorite show and then curled up on the sofa or stretched out on the carpet in front, and with any luck you remained there, motionless, for hours. If, as the critics used to complain, TV is a drug, then no opium den was ever sweeter. On a good Saturday morning, one when Mom wasn't too cranky, you got to stay in your pajamas until noon.

In those days, of course, television was largely unregulated. No one, not even Mom, was paying much attention to what or how much we watched. In recent years, children's programming has been endlessly scrutinized, and thanks in large part to parental lobbying groups, it has come under more vigilant Federal controls. The newest set of regulations was supposed to go into effect this fall, requiring that stations devote at least three hours a week—most of them on Saturday, presumably—to educational programming for children under 16. So far, compliance has been spotty at best. Like those that preceded them, the new regulations are vague and unenforceable. No one can agree on what constitutes educational television, and the burden of policing falls not on the Government but on viewers, who are expected to keep tabs on their local stations. The stations claim, not unreasonably, that their hands are tied by the networks, which these days supply almost all the programming. The networks, meanwhile, have for the most part done little more than tinker with the existing shows and declare that they fit the bill. Disney's *101 Dalmatians,* for example, turns out to teach friendship and responsibility, and *N.B.A. Inside Stuff,* professional basketball's show for children, is said to impart "life lessons." 4

This is actually not as dumb as it sounds. *All* TV imparts life lessons of a sort—if only lessons in how greedy or manipulative or boring television producers can be. And what we take away from the experience of watching television is more than what the programmers have put there. Watching television, even if you watch it alone, is also a social experience, and it's often a ritual. Part of the magic of the old Saturday-morning drill had almost nothing to do with content, or with anything that could be regulated. The magic was in the safeness and the sameness—the reassuring security—of the ritual itself. 5

What you watched, if you grew up in the 50's or early 60's, was not the parade of otherworldly characters that nowadays lurches forth—robots and superheroes mostly, so poorly animated that their dialogue and their expressionless mouths are forever out of sync and that Captain America, for example, walks as stiffly as if he had just had a hip replacement. In those days, what you watched, most likely, was a Saturday-morning program that originated at your local station. It featured an adult figure, either clownish or avuncular, depending on local custom, and perhaps a puppet or two or a dimwitted visitor, whose job it was to fill with patter the intervals between the showing of vintage cartoons, doled out as sparingly as if they were some rare elixir—which indeed they were. 6

In Boston, where I grew up, we had *Boomtown,* with Rex Trailer, a handsome singing cowboy, and his faithful, if none-too-bright, sidekick, the sombreroed and serape-clad Pablo. (I was astonished to discover once, when my father took me to one of Rex's "personal 7 appearances," that Pablo was not really Mexican and that he also had extremely bad breath.) The show began with a film clip of Rex galloping to the studio on his handsome palomino, Goldrush—galloping from where was never entirely clear; New Hampshire, perhaps—but the rest, except for the cartoons, was broadcast live. Rex did rope tricks and was occasionally persuaded to take out his guitar, or his "git-fiddle," as he called it, and sing. (One of his tunes, I seem to recall, had a chorus that consisted of the word "hoofbeats," repeated over and over.) Once in a while a visitor dropped by to talk about fire safety or disease prevention.

8   It was all a little boring and overearnest, and in retrospect it's amazing that *Boomtown* lasted as long as it did, from 1956 to 1976. (Pablo died years ago, but Rex, I was happy to learn recently while trolling through the Internet, has prospered in the new business of video résumés.) Yet the very dullness and predictability was an essential and soothing part of Saturday morning; it slowed time down, after a fashion, and helped stretch out those precious hours into a drowsy prelunch eternity—a kind of Keatsian daze in which the antics of Popeye and Bluto and Elmer and Woody never staled, no matter how many times we'd seen them before.

9   Had we known it, we never would have watched, but *Boomtown* was, by today's standards at least, highly "educational." And oddly enough, this show and others like it were in part done in through the efforts of Action for Children's Television and other lobbying groups dedicated to reforming children's programming and reducing its dependency on commercials.

10   Still, today's Saturday-morning fare, though much maligned, is in a number of essential ways no worse than what we watched as kids. Some of it, in fact, is little altered: the whole inspired Looney Tunes gang (Bugs, Porky, Daffy, Sylvester, Tweety et al.) still turn up; the Lucky Charms leprechaun, ageless and ever-twinkly, still boasts about how many marshmallows his product contains; Franken Berry, Count Chocula, Cocoa Puffs—they're still being hawked, too, the latter newly enhanced with an infusion of Hershey's chocolate. Barbie's still around, of course, and so are those various creatures—dolls, ponies, mermaids, trolls—with long manes in need of curling and brushing. Dolls that urinate have not gone out of fashion, and neither have weapons-laden space vehicles (batteries not included).

11   There are even some cartoons on now that are better and more sophisticated than anything we ever watched: the darkly ironic *Ren and Stimpy,* for example, or *Men in Black* (where the cheesiness of the animation actually contributes to the humor) or, my favorite, the improbable "Pinky and the Brain," about a pair of lab mice that, as the result of an accident at Acme Labs, have been transformed into, on the one hand, an airhead rodent with a high-pitched North London accent and,

on the other, a macrocephalic mad-scientist mouse with plans to take over the world. These shows, like the better prime-time cartoons—*The Simpsons* and *King of the Hill*—successfully talk to kids and adults both. They sometimes seem to operate on two simultaneous planes of reference, in fact, and they pay children the great compliment of not dumbing everything down for them. Or maybe they merely recognize that children know more than we think, or wish, they did.

But where the Saturday-morning TV of today differs enormously from the TV most of us watched is in the virtual absence (except in shows like *Captain Kangaroo,* for very young children) of adult figures—of the Rexes and Pablos, those benign gatekeepers, or emissaries from the real world, who while seeming to share our delight in cartoons, our near reverence for them, also reminded us of the importance of brushing our teeth and crossing at crosswalks. Grown-ups turn up on Saturday morning now as either idiots, like the crazed geek who does comic spots on *Disney's 1 Saturday Morning,* or meanies, like the crotchety, incompetent teachers and principals on the cartoons *Recess* and *Pepper Ann.* 12

Saturday-morning TV, moreover, is nothing like as sweetly languorous as it used to be. Where a show like *Boomtown* used to come on at 6:30 or 7 and stay on the air for several hours, the new programs come, one after the other, at half-hour intervals, further punctuated by promos and advertisements for shows coming up later, and most of these shows leap on the screen with MTV-like logo sequences and rock-inspired theme songs and then lurch from commercial to commercial in short, hyperactive bursts. Many of the newer shows—*The X-Men* and *The New Adventures of Voltron,* for example—are inspired by comic books, and with their lantern-jawed, steroidal heroes, stilted dialogue and creaky plots, they employ an aggressive, hard-edged freeze-frame style in which there is seldom a quiet or reflective moment. The violence in these shows, of which there's a fair amount, isn't realistic, exactly—the bad guys tend to be rendered unconscious rather than outright killed or maimed—but neither is it as surreally goofy as the violence in a Road Runner or Tweety and Sylvester episode, say, where bombs and missiles and explosives of every kind go off with thrilling frequency, blowing cats and coyotes sky high and wreaking amazing, if temporary, disfigurement (popping eyeballs, missing digits, smoking ears, anvil-shaped heads) without causing any harm at all. 13

In the end, the effect of the new, hyper Saturday-morning style, whether deliberate or not, is to make time pass faster and to do away with the old sensation of endlessness, of moments hardly ticking by. As an experiment, on a recent Saturday I watched children's TV for five hours straight, from 7 to noon. (Don't try this at home, parents, without medical supervision.) I was bored much of the time, yet when I closed my eyes and tried to doze, I was invariably jarred awake by some new 14 sound effect or other. But I was astonished by how quickly the hours flew. It was Saturday afternoon before I knew it.

15   The kids may not mind, however, or even notice, for how many of them get to enjoy the full five-hour orgy anymore? We wake them up before dawn for the long drive to the hockey rink, and then there's band practice, ballet lessons, the math tutor and, if there's time, that play date we penciled in a few weeks ago and that we can confirm now on the car phone on the way to the orthodontist.

16   Many kids today, if they watch Saturday-morning TV at all, watch it the way grown-ups watch *Today* or *Good Morning America*—on the run, in snatches, while hastily swallowing a vitamin pill. And on those mornings, increasingly rare, when we parents yield to temptation—when, in response to that gentle tugging on our foot or to the tiny hand clamped over our nose, we say, "Mommy and Daddy are tired right now, why don't you turn on TV for a little while?"—we are afterward undone with guilt, certain that we have cost them at least 20 points on the SATs. For grown-ups as well as children, Saturday morning is quickly becoming a thing of the past, just another slot in the overful datebook of our lives.

17   In the grand scheme of things, this may not be the worst fate that has befallen our civilization, but it's regrettable nonetheless. We all of us need some down time, and children especially. There is actually something to be said for doing nothing and for learning how to be bored. There is even more to be said for escapism, for stepping out of time. And this is where children's TV has truly let us down: not in its shameless huckstering or in its shying away from "educational content," whatever that is. The problem is that the sustained quality of the daydreaming it offers is so seldom worth waking up for. Children's TV doesn't need fewer cartoons; it needs better cartoons, better drawn and with better characters. It needs narrative, which is not the same as an action plot. It needs modulation and variety. And it needs, every now and then, the voice of an adult—if for no other reason than to gently remind children that they can't stay in their pajamas forever.

★ *Meaning and Understanding*

1. What were some of the things one could do as a child on Saturday mornings in the past? What does McGrath say that most youngsters chose to do?

2. What new television regulations does McGrath refer to? Why has compliance "been spotty at best" (paragraph 4)? How have the networks "tinkered" with existing shows to make them fit the regulations?

3. What was the "magic of the old Saturday-morning drill" (paragraph 5)?

4. What were the characteristics of Saturday morning programming for someone who grew up in the 1950s and 1960s?

5. How does today's programming resemble Saturday morning fare of fifty years ago? In what important ways, according to the writer, do they differ?

★ *Techniques and Strategies*

1. What is the thesis of this essay?

2. What is the effect of starting the essay with a question? How do the reminiscences that follow set up the basic premise of the essay?

3. How does the writer use comparison and contrast strategies in this piece? In what ways are they essential to the point he's trying to make?

4. Why does McGrath make so many references to specific programs? How do they contribute to his thesis?

5. What is your reaction to the repetition of the words "It needs" as sentence openers in the last paragraph? Why has McGrath chosen such a strategy?

★ *Speaking of Values*

1. Why does the writer value the Saturday mornings he spent as a child? What is he trying to indicate about the importance of how children fill their time? Do you agree with his point? Why or why not?

2. McGrath says, "*All* TV imparts life lessons of a sort.... And what we take away from the experience of watching television is more than what the programmers have put there" (paragraph 5). Why might you agree or disagree with this point? How do your own experiences support or challenge his observation?

3. Safeness and sameness—these elements McGrath finds important in children's programming. Do you agree with this point of view? Why or why not? Why does he approve of dullness and predictability in children's shows? Do you think he has a point here? Why or why not?

4. Why does McGrath say that adult figures, now missing from Saturday morning programming, are important? Why might you agree or disagree with his point?

5. What, according to McGrath, is "the effect of the new, hyper Saturday-morning style" (paragraph 14)? Why might you agree or disagree with him?

6. McGrath implies that parents feel guilty for encouraging kids to watch Saturday morning TV. Why do they feel guilty? Should they, do you think? Why or why not?

★ Values Conversation

McGrath takes a lonely side in the argument about children's programming by arguing that weak educational content and shameless huckstering are not what disappoints about television but that the "sustained quality of the day-dreaming it offers is so seldom worth waking up for" (paragraph 17). Form groups to discuss the qualities of children's television that you think Americans should value. Report your group's findings to the rest of the class.

★ Writing about Values

1. Write an essay about how you spent your Saturday mornings when you were younger.

2. Write an essay in which you argue for the kind of Saturday morning television programming that the networks should aim for.

3. Watch some Saturday morning children's television; then write a letter to one of the networks about what you have seen, what strengths you have observed, and what recommendations you would make for improved programming.

Hank Aaron

When Baseball Mattered

Born in 1934, Hall-of-Famer Henry (Hank) Aaron is baseball's all-time home run leader and an executive in the Atlanta Braves organization. In this essay from the *New York Times,* he looks back to a time when baseball was considered America's essential sport and men like Jackie Robinson were role models for America's youth.

———— ★ ————

Jackie Robinson meant everything to me. 1

Before I was a teen-ager, I was telling my father that I was going to 2 be a ballplayer, and he was telling me "Ain't no colored ballplayers." Then Jackie broke into the Brooklyn Dodgers lineup in 1947, and Daddy never said that again. When the Dodgers played an exhibition game in Mobile, Ala., on their way north the next spring, Daddy even came to the game with me. A black man in a major-league uniform: that was something my father had to see for himself.

Jackie not only showed me and my generation what we could do, 3 he also showed us how to do it. By watching him, we knew that we would have to swallow an awful lot of pride to make it in the big leagues. We knew of the hatred and cruelty Jackie had to quietly endure from the fans and the press and the anti-integrationist teams like the Cardinals and the Phillies and even from his teammates. We also knew that he didn't subject himself to all that for personal benefit. Why would he choose to get spiked and cursed at and spat on for his own account?

Jackie was a college football hero, a handsome, intelligent, talented 4 guy with a lot going for him. He didn't need that kind of humiliation. And it certainly wasn't in his nature to suffer it silently. But he had to. Not for himself, but for me and all the young black kids like me. When Jackie Robinson loosened his fist and turned the other cheek, he was taking the blows for the love and future of his people.

Now, 50 years later, people are saying that Jackie Robinson was an 5 icon, a pioneer, a hero. But that's all they want to do: *say* it.

Nobody wants to be like Jackie. Everybody wants to be like Mike. 6 They want to be like Deion, like Junior.

That's O.K. Sports stars are going to be role models in any genera- 7 tion. I'm sure Jackie would be pleased to see how well black athletes are doing these days, how mainstream they've become. I'm sure he would be proud of all the money they're making. But I suspect he'd want to shake some of them until the dollar signs fell from their eyes so they could once again see straight.

8   Jackie Robinson was about leadership. When I was a rookie with the Braves and we came north with the Dodgers after spring training, I sat in the corner of Jackie's hotel room, thumbing through magazines, as he and his black teammates—Roy Campanella, Don Newcombe, Junior Gilliam and Joe Black—played cards and went over strategy: what to do if a fight broke out on the field; if a pitcher threw at them; if somebody called one of them "nigger."

9   In his later years, after blacks were secure in the game, Jackie let go of his forbearance and fought back. In the quest to integrate baseball, it was time for pride to take over from meekness. And Jackie made sure that younger blacks like myself were soldiers in the struggle.

10   When I look back at the statistics of the late 1950's and 60's and see the extent to which black players dominated the National League (the American League was somewhat slower to integrate), I know why that was. We were on a mission. And, although Willie Mays, Ernie Banks, Frank Robinson, Willie Stargell, Lou Brock, Bob Gibson and I were trying to make our marks individually, we understood that we were on a collective mission. Jackie Robinson demonstrated to us that, for a black player in our day and age, true success could not be an individual thing.

11   To players today, however, that's exactly what it is. The potential is certainly there, perhaps more than at any time since Jackie came along, for today's stars to have a real impact on their communities. Imagine what could be accomplished if the players, both black and white, were to really dedicate themselves—not just their money, although that would certainly help—to camps and counseling centers and baseball programs in the inner city.

12   Some of the players have their own charitable foundations, and I applaud them for that. (I believe Dave Winfield, for instance, is very sincere.) But as often as not these good works are really publicity stunts. They're engineered by agents, who are acting in the interest of the player's image—in other words, his marketability. Players these days don't do anything without an agent leading them every step of the way (with his hand out). The agent, of course, could care less about Jackie Robinson.

13   The result is that today's players have lost all concept of history. Their collective mission is greed. Nothing else means much of anything to them. As a group, there's no discernible social conscience among them; certainly no sense of self-sacrifice, which is what Jackie Robinson's legacy is based on. It's a sick feeling, and one of the reasons I've been moving further and further away from the game.

The players today think that they're making $10 million a year because they have talent and people want to give them money. They have no clue what Jackie went through on their behalf, or Larry Doby or Monte Irvin or Don Newcombe, or even, to a lesser extent, the players of my generation. People wonder where the heroes have gone. Where there is no conscience, there are no heroes.

The saddest thing about all of this is that baseball was once the standard for our country. Jackie Robinson helped blaze the trail for the civil rights movement that followed. The group that succeeded Jackie—my contemporaries—did the same sort of work in the segregated minor leagues of the South. Baseball publicly pressed the issue of integration; in a symbolic way, it was our civil rights laboratory.

It is tragic to me that baseball has fallen so far behind basketball and even football in terms of racial leadership. People question whether baseball is still the national pastime, and I have to wonder, too. It is certainly not the national standard it once was.

The upside of this is that baseball, and baseball only, has Jackie Robinson. Here's hoping that on the 50th anniversary of Jackie's historic breakthrough, baseball will honor him in a way that really matters. It could start more youth programs, give tickets to kids who can't afford them, become a social presence in the cities it depends on. It could hire more black umpires, more black doctors, more black concessionaries, more back executives

It could hire a black commissioner.

You want a name? How about Colin Powell? He's a great American, a man more popular, maybe, than the President. I'm not out there pushing his candidacy, but I think he could be great for baseball. He would restore some social relevance to the game. He would do honor to Jackie Robinson's name.

It would be even more meaningful, perhaps if some of Jackie's descendants—today's players—committed themselves this year to honoring his name, in act as well as rhetoric.

Jackie's spirit is watching. I know that he would be bitterly disappointed if he saw the way today's black players have abandoned the struggle, but he would be happy for their success nonetheless. And I have no doubt that he'd do it all over again for them.

★ Meaning and Understanding

1. When did Jackie Robinson break into the Dodgers' lineup? What was significant about the event?

2. What does Aaron say that Robinson showed a generation of black ballplayers?

3. For successful ballplayers, why does Aaron say that Robinson would "want to shake some of them until the dollar signs fell from their eyes" (paragraph 7)?

4. Why does the writer say that contemporary players have lost a sense of history? What is their mission?

5. How does Aaron hope that Robinson's name will be honored?

★ Techniques and Strategies

1. What is the thesis of the essay?

2. How does the writer's own association with the sport of baseball contribute to the effectiveness of the essay?

3. What do the names of the sports figures the writer notes lend to the essay? How do the names affect Aaron's argument?

4. What does the title mean? What contrast does the title establish? How has Aaron built upon this contrast in the essay?

5. What is the effect of the one-sentence paragraph at the opening of the essay? Toward the end of the essay?

★ Speaking of Values

1. Why, according to Aaron, did Robinson withstand the early humiliations of playing baseball? What personal values does this suggest about the man? What other people that you know of chose personal sacrifice for a larger good? Do you consider such people brave, foolish, stubborn, unrealistic trailblazers? Why?

2. Aaron objects to commercialism in baseball. Why might you agree or disagree with him? What other areas of American culture, if any, do you find infused with commercialism? What does commercialism say about our values system?

3. Why should athletes have a social conscience or a sense of self-sacrifice? How much does race contribute to your view? What values does Aaron suggest about sports and athletic competition with his observations on conscience and sacrifice?

4. Was Robinson right, do you think, in behaving meekly at first and then turning to pride? Why or why not?

5. Do you agree that baseball has fallen behind football and basketball in terms of racial leadership? Why or why not?

★ *Values Conversation*

The writer states, "Baseball publicly pressed the issue of integration; in a symbolic way, it was our civil rights laboratory" (paragraph 15). Break into groups and discuss whether you agree with this statement and why. How can a national sport have such an effect upon a culture? What other sports serve as civil rights laboratories? What other leisure or entertainment activities have served in a similar way?

★ *Writing about Values*

1. Write an essay about your views of baseball's role in American society.

2. Write an argumentative essay in which you support or challenge the high salaries of your favorite sports figures or celebrities.

3. Write an essay in which you discuss the role of professional sports in providing opportunities for blacks and other minorities.

David Stout

The Sadness of the Hunter

David Stout was born in Erie, Pennsylvania in 1942. He has an M.A. from
SUNY, Buffalo. He has worked for many years as a newspaperman and
was city editor of the *New York Times*. He also wrote the mystery novel
Carolina Skeletons (1988). In this essay he reflects on shooting a deer.

★

1   So much has written about the joy of hunting and so little about the
sadness, the sadness that fills the silence after the echo of the shot has
died away.

2   If the hunter is skilled, or lucky, he has just killed something. In a
moment he may feel joy. But first he must pass through another emotion, one akin to grief. He must pull the trigger to get there. Nothing
could be more appropriate, for grief is supposed to be linked to death.

3   Hunting is going on in many places, and with it the conflict in the
heart of the hunter. Hunters use the word "harvest" again and again.
Hunters speak of harvesting deer or ducks or grouse or rabbits. There
is a paradox at work here, for the hunter knows better than his non-
hunting friends that pork chops and drumsticks do not grow on trees.

4   "I don't know any hunter who hasn't felt a sense of sadness after
he's shot a deer," said David C. Foster, editor of *Gray's Sporting Journal,*
a decidedly upscale hunting and fishing magazine, who is himself an
enthusiastic hunter.

5   Why do it, then? It is not enough to speak of loving the outdoors,
or the camaraderie, or the challenge. No, there is some kind of blood
communion between the hunter and that which he kills.

6   "It takes courage to kill an animal as beautiful as a deer," another
hunter, Ed Van Put of Sullivan County, N.Y., said. Then he mused: Was
courage the right word? For him it was. "It takes something extra to pull
the trigger," said Mr. Van Put, who monitors fish in lakes and streams for
the New York State Department of Environmental Conservation.

7   Many non-hunters find such talk absurd, or horrible. Many of
them wouldn't think of killing wild game yet think nothing of buying
meat at the supermarket. There are those who don't eat meat but do eat
fish, as though sure that the flopping in a net or boat is merely reflex,
not desperation, and that the writhing creature's unblinking eye be-
trays no more emotion than it will later, staring up from a bed of
chopped ice.

A longtime hunter may be sad at the sight of a giant tree, toppled 8
in its old age by rot or wind or lightning. This is death too. Such
thoughts grow with age, as the hunter's own years add to his knowledge about the frailty of life, and they lead in many directions.

Even if the hunter has a sound compass—some bedrock beliefs 9
about his place in the world, in which all time is borrowed—he will
wander around and around, returning only to a question: What life is
so precious that it should not be taken?

I remember hearing in my boyhood talk about whether it was less 10
noble to kill a doe than a buck; whether it was all right to hunt just for
trophy heads, antlers or tusks, or whether a decent hunter always ate
what he shot (not that he needed to). I found myself wrestling with
those questions too much. So I took a timid retreat, closeting my own
12-gauge shotgun and trying to shut away some emotions, which still
emerge from time to time out of some dark forest of memory.

It is reassuring to find that men who still hunt are stalked by these 11
emotions too. "There *is* a momentary feeling of sadness that you had to
take a life in pursuit of what you're doing," Jack Samson, the retired
editor of *Field and Stream* magazine, said the other day from his home in
Santa Fe, New Mexico, as he reflected on a lifetime of hunting big game
and small.

Nelson Bryant, a retired outdoors columnist for the *New York Times*, 12
said that he had never shot anything "without a sense of sadness, very
brief, but it's there... whether a duck or deer or whatever, it was something alive."

When pressed on just why they hunt if it brings such sadness, 13
hunters fumble with words. Mr. Van Put responded with, "It's something that man has done forever." Mr. Bryant tried to articulate his
thoughts and said finally, "It's inexplicable."

Inexplicable or not, the lure of hunting is also irresistible, at least 14
for some. *Field and Stream* is celebrating its 100th anniversary and has a
circulation of about two million, mostly middle class, according to a
managing editor, Slaton L. White.

The recent survey for the Interior Department Fish and Wildlife 15
Service showed that about 75 percent of Americans approve of hunting, 22 percent disapprove. Hugh Vickery, an agency spokesman, said
the money hunters contribute for conservation efforts is essential and
totaled some $700 million in 1994 through license fees and taxes on fire-
arms and ammunition.

There were 15.3 million licensed hunters in the United States in 1994, 16
down from the 1982 peak of 16 million. Mr. Vickery said the survey
found that dwindling open space was the main reason for the decline.

But perhaps there are other reasons, at least for a few. Mr. Bryant 17
said he knew of some men who stopped hunting as they got older, not

because they grew infirm but because they grew more keenly aware of the finality of all life.

18   And a personal note on why I gave up hunting. I was not squeamish, say, about slitting the belly of freshly killed rabbit and dumping the steaming gut onto the damp leaves on a chill November day. But I cannot forget the day when I was 13 and shot at a big rusty fox squirrel three times before it came tumbling down from the tree, bouncing off limbs as it fell, then trying to crawl away.

19   And this hunter who would not remain a hunter grabbed the animal by its tail, dragging it to a clearing to finish it off with the gun butt. Then he stood still in the dusk, listening to a chain saw in the distance and waiting for his sadness to go away. He has been waiting for 10 years.

★ Meaning and Understanding

1. What is the main point of the essay?

2. What does harvesting mean to hunters?

3. How do some hunters explain why they like this sport and why they do it? What do nonhunters find absurd or horrible, according to Stout?

4. What boyhood talk does Stout recall about hunting? What did he do as a result of the questions that arose?

5. Why does Stout say, "the lure of hunting is also irresistible" (paragraph 14)? How does he support that contention?

6. Why is the writer still remembering the scene with the squirrel that he notes at the end of the essay?

7. How is it possible there could be a "blood communion between the hunter and that which he kills" (paragraph 5)?

★ Techniques and Strategies

1. Where does Stout use statistics to support his point?

2. Why does he draw quotations from other sources? Which quotations do you find most effective? What are the credentials of the people Stout quotes? Why is the recounting of the situation regarding the squirrel at the end so effective?

3. In what way is the essay an argument opposing the sport of hunting? In what way is the essay an argument in favor of hunting? Do you find that these opposing elements strengthen or weaken the piece? Why?

4. What does the personal narrative at the end contribute to the essay? Why has Stout chosen to end the essay on such a deeply personal note?

5. Who is the audience for this essay? How do you know?

★ Speaking of Values

1. Many of the hunters cited here project a sense of values about hunting. What are those values? Do you find them convincing? Why or why not?

2. How do you account for the sadness of the hunter? If hunting brings them sadness, why do the hunters continue to hunt?

3. How do you account for the popularity of hunting and the fact that three-fourths of those surveyed approved of hunting?

4. What relation does the writer establish between hunting and eating meat and fish purchased from a supermarket? Do you find the point convincing? Why or why not? Is it hypocritical to oppose hunting for sport and still to be a meat eater? Why or why not?

5. Why might a hunter—or anyone else, for that matter—feel sad at the sight of a tree felled by natural causes?

★ Values Conversation

Form groups to discuss your views on hunting for sport. Comment on the values implicit in people who chose one side or the other in this debate. Report your findings to the class.

★ Writing about Values

1. Write an essay about a hunting or fishing experience of your own or of one of your friends or family members; explore what you can of the feelings of the hunter on the hunt.

2. Write an argument either advocating or opposing hunting for sport.

3. Many people oppose the death (or sacrifice) of animals in medical and scientific experimentation. Others argue that the benefits outweigh the advantages in animal research. What is your view on the issue? Present both sides of the argument carefully and then move to explain and support your own position.

Values in Review

1. Several of the writers in this chapter present their views on leisure activities in the United States and find in them special significance as indicators of cultural values and mores. Select two or more of the selections here and write an essay about what their views of leisure tell you about values in our country today.

2. Benjamin Franklin, Marcus Mabry, Mari Evans, and Dorothy Parker in their own ways investigate wealth, its absence, and class in their various contributions to this chapter. Drawing on the issues emerging from their selections and from your own observations, write an essay about wealth in America.

3. More and more, media and technology have an increasing hold on America's leisure time, and writers Jerome Charyn and Charles McGrath deal with the joys and complexities of small segments in our media entertainment world. Consider some of the ideas emerging from their essays and write a paper about the relation between media and entertainment in American society today. Once again, keep the issue of values to the forefront. What do the relations among media, wealth, and entertainment tell you of what Americans value?

Chapter 11

Individual and Community

White America

Factions

Immigrants

Superman

Self-reliance

Third culture of the borderlands

The values gap

"I celebrate myself"

James Webb

In Defense of Joe Six-Pack

Born in 1946 in St. Joseph, Missouri, James Webb was a Marine infantry officer in Vietnam and a former Secretary of the Navy. His best-known work, *Fields of Fire* (1978), is an important examination of the effects of combat on soldiers in Vietnam. In this essay, he examines affirmative action in the context of "white Americans."

———— ★ ————

1   Those who debate the impact of affirmative action and other social programs are fond of making distinctions among white Americans along professional and geographic lines while avoiding the tinderbox of ethnic distinctions among whites. But differences among white ethnic groups are huge, fed by cultural tradition, the time and geography of migrations to the country, and—not insignificantly—the tendency of white Americans to discriminate against other whites in favor of their own class and culture.

2   In 1974, when affirmative action was in its infancy, the University of Chicago's National Opinion Research Center published a landmark study, dividing American whites into seventeen ethnic and religious backgrounds and scoring them by educational attainment and family income. Contrary to prevailing mythology, the vaunted White Anglo Saxon Protestants were even then not at the top.

3   The highest WASP group—the Episcopalians—ranked only sixth, behind American Jews, then Irish, Italian, German, and Polish Catholics. WASPs—principally the descendants of those who had settled the Midwest and the South—constituted the bottom eight groups, and ten of the bottom twelve. Educational attainment and income levels did not vary geographically, as for instance among white Baptists (who scored the lowest overall) living in Arkansas or California, a further indication that these differences are culturally rather than geographically based.

4   Family income among white cultures in the NORC study varied by almost $5,000 dollars, from the Jewish high of $13,340 to the Baptist low of $8,693. By comparison, in the 1970 census the variance in family income between whites taken as a whole and blacks was only $3,600. In addition, white Baptists averaged only 10.7 years of education, which was almost four years less than American Jews and at the same level of black Americans in 1970. This means that, even prior to the major affirmative action programs, there was a greater variation within "white

America" than there was between "white America" and black America, and the whites at the bottom were in approximately the same situation as blacks.

These same less-advantaged white cultures by and large did the most to lay out the infrastructure of this country, quite often suffering educational and professional regression as they tamed the wilderness, built the towns, roads, and schools, and initiated a democratic way of life that later white cultures were able to take advantage of without paying the price of pioneering. Today they have the least, socioeconomically, to show for these contributions. And if one would care to check a map, they are from the areas now evincing the greatest resistance to government practices.

It would be folly to assume that affirmative action has done anything but exacerbate these disparities. The increased stratification and economic polarization in American life since 1974 is well documented. In the technological age, with the shrinking of the industrial base, the decrease in quality of public education, and the tendency of those who "have" to protect their own and to utilize greater assets to prepare them for the future, the divergence in both expectation and reward among our citizens has grown rather than disappeared. The middle class has shrunk from 65 percent of the population in 1970 to less than 50 percent today. Its share of aggregate household income declined by 5 percent from 1968 to 1993, while the top 5 million households increased their incomes by up to 10 percent a year. A similar rift has occurred in the black culture, with dramatic declines at the bottom and significant gains among the top 5 percent.

Because America's current elites are somewhat heterogeneous and in part the product of an academically based meritocracy, they have increasingly deluded themselves regarding both the depth of this schism and the validity of their own advantages. The prevailing attitude has been to ridicule whites who have the audacity to complain about their reduced status, and to sneer at every aspect of the "redneck" way of life. In addition to rationalizing policies that hold the working-class male back from advancement in the name of an amorphous past wrong from which he himself did not benefit, the elites take great sport in debasing the man they love to call "Joe Six-Pack."

And what does "Joe Six-Pack" make of this?

He sees a president and a slew of other key luminaries who excused themselves from the dirty work of society when they were younger, feeling not remorse but "vindication" for having left him or perhaps his father to fight a war while they went on to graduate school and solidified careers.

He sees a governmental system that seems bent on belittling the basis of his existence, and has established a set of laws and regulations that often keep him from competing. His ever-more-isolated leaders have mandated an "equal opportunity" bureaucracy in the military, government, and even industry that closely resembles the Soviet "political cadre" structure whose sole function is to report "political incorrectness" and to encourage the promotion of literally everyone but him and his kind.

11   He sees the meaning of words like "fairness" cynically inverted in the name of "diversity," while groups who claim to have been disadvantage by old practices, and even those who have only just arrived in the country, are immediately moved ahead of him for no reason other than his race. In one of the bitterest ironies, he is required to pay tax dollars to finance special training for recent immigrants even as he himself is held back from fair competition and the "equal opportunity" bureaucracies keep him from receiving similar training, gaining employment, or securing a promotion.

12   He sees cultural rites buttressed by centuries of tradition—particularly the right to use firearms and pass that skill to future generations—attacked because many who make the laws do not understand the difference between his way of life and that of criminals who are blowing people away on the streets of urban America.

13   He watched the Democratic Party, once a champion of the worker-producer, abandon him in favor of special interests who define their advancement mostly through the extent of his own demise. To him "diversity" is a code word used to exclude him—but seldom better-situated whites—no matter the extent of his qualifications and no matter the obstacles he has had to overcome. The Republican Party, to which he swung in the last election, has embraced him on certain social issues, but has yet to support policies that would override the tendency of elites to simply protect their own rather than reverse the travails of affirmative action and the collapse of public education.

14   Finally, he sees the people who erected and continue to enforce such injustices blatantly wheedling and maneuvering themselves and their children out of the casualty radius of their own policies. A smaller percentage of whites in academia and the professions is acceptable, so long as their children make it. The public school system is self-destructing, but their children go to private schools and receive special preparatory classes to elevate college board scores. International peacekeeping is a lofty goal, so long as their children are not on the firing line. Continuous scrutiny is given to minority percentages in employment, but little or none is applied to how or why one white applicant was chosen over another.

15   Faced as he is with such barriers, it is difficult to fault him for deciding that those who make their living running the government or commenting on it are at minimum guilty of ignorance, arrogance, and self-interest. And it is not hyperbole to say that the prospect of a class

war is genuine among the very people who traditionally have been the strongest supporters of the American system.

★ Meaning and Understanding

1. Why, according to Webb, are ethnic distinctions among whites important in considering affirmative action programs? Why might you agree or disagree with him?

2. How does the NORC study convince the writer that "there was greater variation within 'white America' than there was between 'white America' and black America" (paragraph 4)? Does the study convince you? Why or why not?

3. Who is Joe Six-Pack?

4. What is the main point of this selection?

5. What is the "'redneck way of life" referred to in paragraph 7?

★ Techniques and Strategies

1. Who is the intended audience for this selection? What is the tone? How do you know?

2. Analyze the tinderbox metaphor in the opening sentence. How does it work to help you understand Webb's point?

3. Where does the writer come closest to stating the thesis of the essay?

4. What does the Joe Six-Pack metaphor bring to mind? What does the writer suggest by its use? Why is it particularly powerful in the title? What is your reaction to the label "Joe Six-Pack": Do you find it accurate, endearing, degrading, humorous, or something else? Why?

5. What is the impact of the statistics that Webb provides in paragraph 6? Why does he use statistics from as long ago as 1970? Does doing so in any way weaken his argument? Why or why not?

★ Speaking of Values

1. How and where do you think "ethnic discrimination" exists in America? Provide examples to support your point.

2. What exactly is Webb defending in this essay?

3. Do you agree with Webb that affirmative action policies have led to the cynical "inversion" of words like "fairness" (paragraph 11)? Why or why not?

4. Webb suggests that neither the Democratic Party nor the Republican Party satisfies the political needs of Joe Six-Pack. What reasons does he give for this position? Do you agree? Why or why not?

5. Webb asserts that affirmative action has exacerbated disparities. Do you agree or disagree with his assertion? Why?

★ Values Conversation

Webb argues that society and politics have overlooked the white American male in general in favor of policies supporting ethnic and racial minorities and ignoring the values in a "redneck" way of life. Form groups to discuss his position. Do you agree with it? Why or why not? What steps would you take to correct any problems you see? What consequences might result from your proposed corrective measures?

★ Writing about Values

1. Write an essay defending or challenging affirmative action policies in our country.

2. Look again at the reasons that Webb gives for the alienation of Joe Six-Pack. Write a paper in which you argue either that Joe is justified in feeling the way he does or is not justified. Be sure to give concrete examples and illustrations to help support your points.

3. Write an essay that explores the status of the white American female— the wife or girlfriend or mother or sister of "Joe Six-Pack."

Walt Whitman

Song of Myself

Born on Long Island, Walt Whitman (1819–1892) came into prominence as a poet with the publication of *Leaves of Grass* in 1855, which embraced the entirety and optimism of the American spirit in the years prior to the Civil War. In this excerpt from "Song of Myself," a poem in *Leaves of Grass,* Whitman declares, "I celebrate myself . . . ."

1

I celebrate myself, and sing myself,
And what I assume you shall assume,
For every atom belonging to me as good belongs to you.

I loafe and invite my soul,
I lean and loafe at my ease observing a spear of summer grass.   5

My tongue, every atom of my blood, form'd from this soil,
    this air,
Born here of parents born here from parents the same, and
    their parents the same,
I, now thirty-seven years old in perfect health begin,
Hoping to cease not till death.

Creeds and schools in abeyance,   10
Retiring back a while sufficed at what they are, but never
    forgotten,
I harbor for good or bad, I permit to speak at every hazard,
Nature without check with original energy.

2

Houses and rooms are full of perfumes, the shelves are
    crowded with perfumes,
I breathe the fragrance myself and know it and like it,   15
The distillation would intoxicate me also, but I shall not let it.

The atmosphere is not a perfume, it has no taste of the
    distillation, it is odorless,

It is for my mouth forever, I am in love with it,
I will go to the bank by the wood and become undisguised
        and naked,
20   I am mad for it to be in contact with me.
The smoke of my own breath,
Echoes, ripples, buzz'd whispers, love-root, silk-thread, crotch
        and vine,
My respiration and inspiration, the beating of my heart, the
        passing of blood and air through my lungs,
The sniff of green leaves and dry leaves, and of the shore and
        dark-color'd sea-rocks, and of hay in the barn,
25   The sound of the belch'd words of my voice loos'd to the
        eddies of the wind,
A few light kisses, a few embraces, a reaching around of arms,
The play of shine and shade on the trees as the supple
        boughs wag,
The delight alone or in the rush of the streets, or along the
        fields and hill-sides
The feeling of health, the full-noon trill, the song of me rising
        from bed and meeting the sun.

30   Have you reckon'd a thousand acres much? have you reckon'd
        the earth much?
Have you practis'd so long to learn to read?
Have you felt so proud to get at the meaning of poems?

Stop this day and night with me and you shall possess the
        origin of all poems,
You shall possess the good of the earth and sun, (there are
        millions of suns left,)
35   You shall no longer take things at second or third hand, nor
        look through the eyes of the dead, nor feed on the
        spectres in books,
You shall not look through my eyes either, nor take things
        from me,
You shall listen to all sides and filter them from your self.

3

I have heard what the talkers were talking, the talk of the
        beginning and the end,
But I do not talk of the beginning or the end.

40   There was never any more inception than there is now,
Nor any more youth or age than there is now,

And will never be any more perfection than there is now,
Nor any more heaven or hell than there is now.

Urge, and urge, and urge,
Always the procreant urge of the world.

Out of the dimness opposite equals advance, always substance
and increase, always sex,
Always a knit of identity, always distinction, always a breed
of life.

To elaborate is no avail, learn'd and unlearn'd feel that it is so.

Sure as the most certain sure, plumb in the uprights, well
entretied, braced in the beams,
Stout as a horse, affectionate, haughty, electrical,
I and this mystery, here we stand.

Clear and sweet is my soul, and clear and sweet is all that is not
my soul.

Lack one lacks both, and the unseen is proved by the seen,
Till that becomes unseen, and receives proof in its turn.

Showing the best and dividing it from the worst age
vexes age,
Knowing the perfect fitness and equanimity of things, while
they discuss I am silent, and go bathe and admire myself.

Welcome is every organ and attribute of me, and of any man
hearty and clean,
Not an inch, nor a particle of an inch is vile, and none shall be
less familiar than the rest.

I am satisfied—I see, dance, laugh, sing;
As the hugging and loving bed-fellow sleeps at my side
through the night, and withdraws at the peep of the day
with stealthy tread,
Leaving me baskets cover'd with white towels swelling the
house with their plenty,
Shall I postpone my acceptation and realization and scream at
my eyes,
That they turn from gazing after and down the road,
And forthwith cipher and show me to a cent,
Exactly the value of one and exactly the value of two, and
which is ahead?

4

Trippers and askers surround me,
People I meet, the effect upon me of my early life or the ward
      and city I live in, or the nation,
The latest dates, discoveries, inventions, societies, authors old
      and new,
My dinner, dress, associates, looks, compliments, dues,
70   The real or fancied indifference of some man or woman I love,
The sickness of one of my folks or of myself, or ill-doing or
      loss or lack of money, or depressions or exaltations,
Battles, the horrors of fratricidal war, the fever of doubtful
      news, the fitful events;
These come to me days and nights and go from me again,
But they are not the Me myself.

75   Apart from the pulling and hauling stands what I am,
Stands amused, complacent, compassionating, idle, unitary,
Looks down, is erect, or bends an arm on an impalpable
      certain rest,
Looking with side-curved head curious what will come next,
Both in and out of the game and watching and wondering at it.

80   Backward I see in my own days where I sweated through fog
      with linguists and contenders,
I have no mockings or arguments, I witness and wait.

★ Meaning and Understanding

1. What does Whitman mean in line 1 when he says "I celebrate myself, and sing myself"?

2. Where is the poet inviting his soul to or what is he inviting it to do?

3. What does Whitman mean by "original energy" in line 13?

4. What seems to be the main point of these stanzas?

5. What does the poet mean in line 33 when he says "Stop this day and night with me and you shall possess the origin of all poems"? Does the idea of "poems" mean something in particular to Whitman? What do you think it is?

★ Techniques and Strategies

1. Look at the individual lines of this poem. Why do you think the poet made them so long?

2. If we accept that the "I" of the poem is the poet himself, then who is the "You" he seems to be addressing?

3. One of Whitman's characteristic poetic techniques is *cataloguing:* he simply lists a series of examples, such as actions, objects, or images. Where does he use the technique here? How effective is it?

4. Lines 8 and 9 read: "I, now thirty-seven years old in perfect health begin,/Hoping to cease not till death." Why does the poet tell us his age? What is he about to "begin"?

5. How would you describe the language of the poem? Which images do you find most vivid? Why?

★ *Speaking of Values*

1. What relation between the individual and the larger society does Whitman imply here?

2. The poet celebrates himself. Does this seem egotistical to you? Is egotism necessarily a bad thing? What is the difference between egotism and individualism?

3. How should a person today celebrate himself or herself, do you think? Is this a valid goal for people in today's society? Why or why not?

★ *Values Conversation*

Form groups and reread stanza 2 with particular attention to lines 30–32. In your groups answer the four questions Whitman raises there. What do your answers tell you about your attitudes and priorities? How do they compare to Whitman's?

★ *Writing about Values*

1. Write an essay called "I Celebrate Myself."

2. "Song of Myself" attempts to define the relation of the poet to the larger community of which he is a part. Using this poem as a model, write a poem or essay to express your sense of what you are in relation to the larger society.

3. Write an analysis of this selection with particular attention to Whitman's voice as a poet. What values does he imply about poets and poetry?

Jules Feiffer

The Minsk Theory of Krypton

Jules Feiffer was born in 1929 in the Bronx, New York. Long a cartoonist for the *Village Voice,* he is also a playwright and screenwriter. Among Feiffer's better-known works are the play *Little Murders* (1967), for which he also wrote the screenplay, and *Carnal Knowledge* (1971). In this essay he investigates the creation of the Superman character for comic books in the 1930s.

——————— ★ ———————

Up in the sky! It's a bird! It's a plane! It's . . . Superman!

1   Oh, he was a giant back then. And he may have been a touch innocent, even primitive, but he was unique. One of a kind. And he was like an early New Dealer; he fought on behalf of the helpless and oppressed. This was over a half-century and four wars ago.

2   Hard to imagine today, when we suffer a glut of outlandishly costumed, steroidally muscled superheroes, whose bloodlust and paranoia differ only in degree from that of the militia movement. In 1935, life was simpler, more idealistic. There were merely the Depression and Hitler to contend with. The times were pre-angst, pre-noir, pre-self-awareness. Horatio Alger still lived, very much so in the heart of Jerry Siegel, grown up poor and Jewish in the American heartland. Siegel felt destined to make it, and make it big. His medium was the funny papers.

3   His first collaboration with Joe Shuster, his lifelong partner, was a comic strip for their school paper at Glenville High, just outside of Cleveland: "Goober, The Mighty," a crude mix of "Popeye" and "Tarzan." E. C. Segar's Popeye was, at that time, the strongest man in newsprint, and although cartoony and not exactly super, bullets *had* bounced off his chest. Tarzan, on the other hand, was a realistically rendered adventure strip, with blocks of text set below the illustrations. The artist was the excellent Harold Foster, who later was to give us "Prince Valiant."

4   Tarzan's origin bears striking parallels to Superman's. A shipwrecked son of an English lord, the baby Tarzan is washed up on African shores to be rescued and raised by nurturing apes who teach him their ways, inspiring him to protect the helpless by fighting lions, tigers, white hunters and savage tribesmen with scary headdresses.

5   Jerry Siegel's earliest approach to a super-character was in a highschool fanzine, run off on a mimeograph. It was called "The Reign of

the Superman," but this fellow had nothing to do with the Man of Steel. He was a villain, honoring the tradition, still intact, that presents Evil as smarter, cleverer and stronger than Good. Good prevails only at the last moment, through tenacity and dumb luck. Your local Cineplex is, no doubt, showing recent examples of the genre.

But one summer night in 1934, tossing and turning in bed, Jerry   6
Siegel conjured up a switcheroo. What if his superman was not a villain but a hero? In a world sick with the Depression, violent crime, the threat of fascism and war, Americans seemed in dire need of a neo-Nietzschean hero who used his powers to rescue, not subjugate.

The bare bones of plot came in a rush. In a far-off galaxy, a planet   7
(call it Krypton) explodes. The single survivor is an infant, shot aloft in a space capsule by his scientist father. The baby Superman crash-lands, not on African shores like Tarzan but in the American Midwest, where he is rescued and raised not by nurturing apes like Tarzan but by the kindly Kents. They teach him the American way and inspire him to go off, not in a leopard skin like Tarzan but in cape and leotard, to protect the helpless against not lions and tigers but crooks, mad scientists, dictators and natural disasters.

Siegel wrote and revised and handed the scripts to Shuster, who   8
drew it in comic-book format intended for newspaper syndication. Syndicated adventure strips were in their heyday: "Flash Gordon," "Terry and the Pirates," "Dick Tracy," "Wash Tubbs"...an odd American art form, trapping the reader's eye with its blatant immediacy, vulgar and elegant at the same time. Daily strips ran large on the comics pages, five or six columns, a visual and narrative treat. Today's minimally drawn, miniaturized strips don't begin to suggest their charm and influence.

"The Superman" was rejected, revised, rejected again. Siegel flirted   9
with another, more experienced illustrator, but after more than a year of frustration returned to the neophyte Joe Shuster. With little training as an artist, Shuster sought models, got the agile Siegel to leap about as the Man of Steel and looked for a model for the girl reporter. The pretty girl he hired as Lois Lane later became Mrs. Jerry Siegel.

Comic books finally gave Superman a home. By 1937, Siegel and   10
Shuster were writing and drawing a batch of features for the Detective Comics line of National Allied Publishing (later to be known as DC Comics): "Slam Bradley," "Federal Men," "Radio Squad," "Spy," all freely borrowed from successful newspaper strips. The Action Comics line was looking for a lead feature for its first issue. "The Superman," rejected for syndication, was cut up, reframed and laid out into comic-book format. One look and it was clear that it was in the right place. The rest is history.

Comic books, until then a small-time enterprise, took off like a   11
space shot from Krypton, with Superman carrying most of the weight

on his shoulders. For their efforts, Siegel and Shuster got less, far less, than was due them. To make it into print, they were forced to sign over their copyright to the publisher. Instead of royalties, they were put on page rates, splitting $10 a page. Even when the rate went up, it was never more than a bad joke. Money arguments led to fights, led to lawyers, led to lawsuits that Siegel and Shuster lost. By 1948, the game was played out. The creators were fired from their creation. Their fate constitutes the dark side of the Superman legend. Years later, after the Man of Steel came under new ownership, a gaggle of pugnacious cartoonists prevailed upon management to make amends. By that time, in 1975, it was all but too late for Siegel and Shuster, but not for their families who at long last have become Superman's heirs.

12   Sixty years on, why do we care? In the mid-50's, in "Seduction of the Innocent," the noted psychiatrist Frederic Wertham wrote: "I have known many adults who have treasured ... the books they read as children. I have never come across any adult or adolescent ... who would ever dream of keeping ... '[comic] books' for any sentimental or other reason." Today, Wertham is forgotten while Superman still reigns. Original art of the 30's, 40's and 50's sells for tens of thousands of dollars.

13   A high price for nostalgia, or is something else at work here? What is the significance of it all? You need to look back on that hot summer night in Cleveland when Jerry Siegel, unable to sleep, hit upon a vision. There he was, a first-generation Jewish boy of Russian stock, planted in the Midwest during the birth of native American fascism, the rise of anti-Semitism, the radio broadcasts of Father Coughlin. Siegel, an uncertain young man of ambition and drive, was not like the kids he went to school with. If he was at all like me (another Jewish boy in a different place at roughly the same time), he sensed the difference, his otherness. We were aliens.

14   We didn't choose to be mild-mannered, bespectacled and self-effacing. We chose to be bigger, stronger, blue-eyed and sought-after by blond cheerleaders. *Their* cheerleaders. We chose to be *them*.

15   Superman was the ultimate assimilationist fantasy. The mild manners and glasses that signified a class of nerdy Clark Kents was, in no way, our real truth. Underneath the schmucky facade there lived Men of Steel! Jerry Siegel's accomplishment was to chronicle the smart Jewish boy's American dream. Acknowledge that, and you can better understand the symbolic meaning of the planet Krypton. It wasn't Krypton that Superman really came from; it was the planet Minsk or Lodz or Vilna or Warsaw.

16   And when the Depression ended, and the war as well, when the United States rocketed into a cold-war world of affluence and paranoia, the otherness and alienation of Siegel's poetic construct spread outward, beyond Jews and other minorities, to the blond, blue-eyed hunks that we envied and wished to be. America cloned itself into a

country made up of millions of Clark Kents. And day after day, you could hear them muttering to themselves: "I'm not really like this. If they only knew my real identity."

Siegel Man knew.　　　17

★ *Meaning and Understanding*

1. What was Jerry Siegel's medium for success?

2. How do Superman's origins compare with Tarzan's? How do you account for the similarities?

3. How did Siegel change the character of his early Superman hero? What role did Joe Shuster play?

4. What does Feiffer mean by the statement, "The creators were fired from their creation"?

5. What do you think is the main point of this essay?

6. What is the significance of comic books to the main point as Feiffer presents them in this essay?

7. What is an "assimilationist fantasy" (paragraph 15)?

★ *Techniques and Strategies*

1. Look at the very first line of the essay. Why does it begin with the word "Oh"?

2. Why does Feiffer give us a brief history of Siegel's career as the creator of Superman?

3. Why is it relevant for us to know that the original model for Lois Lane eventually married Siegel?

4. Why does Feiffer end the essay by referring to Siegel as "Siegel Man"? What is the effect of the three-word last paragraph as the conclusion of the essay?

5. What is the significance of the title? What is Minsk? Krypton? How does the title capture the essence of Feiffer's thesis?

6. The writer uses a variety of comparison and contrast strategies to make important points. Where do you find the use of comparison and contrast most effective?

★ *Speaking of Values*

1. In what way does Feiffer suggest that Jerry Siegel was a "typical" American?

2. Feiffer remarks that we operate in a tradition that "presents Evil as smarter, cleverer and stronger than Good." What do you think he means by this? Do you agree or disagree with this observation? Why?

3. Feiffer draws an analogy between Superman as an alien and himself and Jerry Siegel as aliens. Discuss the analogy and explain how it helps illuminate the question of individual identity and community. How did being an outsider help both Feiffer and Siegel? What value is there in being an outsider today?

4. Why did "the otherness and alienation of Siegel's poetic construct spread outward" after the end of World War II (paragraph 16)? What does he mean that "America cloned itself into a country made up of millions of Clark Kents"? Are we still such a nation? How do you know?

5. If, as Feiffer says, young men like him did not "choose to be mild-mannered, bespectacled and self-effacing" (paragraph 14), then why were they?

★ *Values Conversation*

We all have a vision of ourselves that may be different from who we seem to be to outward appearances. Form groups and pair off within each group. List the characteristics that you think define who your partner is. Then list the characteristics that you think define your "real" inner self. Compare your findings and discuss.

★ *Writing about Values*

1. Choose a favorite comic book and write a paper to analyze the reasons for its popularity. Be sure to think about the underlying associations that readers may make and why they might or might not identify with the main characters.

2. See the video versions of any one (or more) of the modern-day Superman films and write a paper on what they say about American values. How does Superman represent in these films the "ultimate assimilationist fantasy"?

3. Feiffer refers in paragraph 15 to "the smart Jewish boy's American dream." Is the American dream different for different ethnic groups? What do you think? Write a paper analyzing this issue and be sure to include your own version of the American dream.

Ralph Waldo Emerson

Self-Reliance

Born in Boston, Ralph Waldo Emerson (1803–1882) expressed in his writing the early nineteenth-century American optimism. He supported and made famous the philosophical movement known as Transcendentalism. From the pulpit and through the essay, Emerson influenced the important writers and thinkers of his time. In this essay Emerson highlights what many see as the defining element of the American character—self-reliance.

—————— ★ ——————

"Ne te quaesiveris extra."[1]

"Man is his own star; and the soul that can
Render an honest and a perfect man,
Commands all light, all influence, all fate;
Nothing to him falls early or too late.
Our acts our angels are, or good or ill,
Our fatal shadows that walk by us still."
  Epilogue to Beaumont and Fletcher's *Honest Man's Fortune*[2]

Cast the bantling on the rocks,
Suckle him with the she-wolf's teat;
Wintered with the hawk and fox,
Power and speed be hands and feet.[3]

I read the other day some verses written by an eminent painter[4] which were original and not conventional. The soul always hears an admonition in such lines, let the subject be what it may. The sentiment they instil is of more value than any thought they may contain. To believe your own thought, to believe that what is true for you in your private heart, is true for all men,—that is genius. Speak your latent conviction and it shall be the universal sense; for the inmost in due time becomes the outmost,—and our first thought is rendered back to us by the trumpets of the Last Judgment. Familiar as the voice of the mind is to each,

1

---

[1]Latin for "Do not seek outside yourself."

[2]Elizabethan playwrights Francis Beaumont (1584–1616) and John Fletcher (1579–1625) wrote *Honest Man's Fortune* (1647).

[3]These are Emerson's own words.

[4]Probably a reference to Washington Allston (1779–1843), American poet and painter.

the highest merit we ascribe to Moses, Plato, and Milton, is that they set at naught books and traditions, and spoke not what men wrote but what they thought. A man should learn to detect and watch that gleam of light which flashes across his mind from within, more than the lustre of the firmament of bards and sages. Yet he dismisses without notice his thought, because it is his. In every work of genius we recognize our own rejected thoughts: they come back to us with a certain alienated majesty. Great works of art have no more affecting lesson for us than this. They teach us to abide by our spontaneous impression with good-humored inflexibility then most when the whole cry of voices is on the other side. Else, to-morrow a stranger will say with masterly good sense precisely what we have thought and felt all the time, and we shall be forced to take with shame our own opinion from another.

2   There is a time in every man's education when he arrives at the conviction that envy is ignorance; that imitation is suicide; that he must take himself for better, for worse, as his portion; that though the wide universe is full of good, no kernel of nourishing corn can come to him but through his toil bestowed on that plot of ground which is given to him to till. The power which resides in him is new in nature, and none but he knows what that is which he can do, nor does he know until he has tried. Not for nothing one face, one character, one fact makes much impression on him, and another none. This sculpture in the memory is not without preestablished harmony. The eye was placed where one ray should fall, that it might testify of that particular ray. We but half express ourselves, and are ashamed of that divine idea which each of us represents. It may be safely trusted as proportionate and of good is-sues, so it be faithfully imparted, but God will not have his work made manifest by cowards. A man is relieved and gay when he has put his heart into his work and done his best; but what he has said or done oth-erwise, shall give him no peace. It is a deliverance which does not de-liver. In the attempt his genius deserts him; no muse befriends; no invention, no hope.

3   Trust thyself: every heart vibrates to that iron string. Accept the place the divine Providence has found for you; the society of your con-temporaries, the connexion of events. Great men have always done so and confided themselves childlike to the genius of their age, betraying their perception that the absolutely trustworthy was seated at their heart, working through their hands, predominating in all their being. And we are now men, and must accept in the highest mind the same transcendent destiny; and not minors and invalids in a protected cor-ner, not cowards fleeing before a revolution, but guides, redeemers, and benefactors, obeying the Almighty effort, and advancing on Chaos and the Dark.

4   What pretty oracles nature yields us on this text in the face and be-havior of children, babes and even brutes. That divided and rebel

mind, that distrust of a sentiment because our arithmetic has computed the strength and means opposed to our purpose, these have not. Their mind being whole, their eye is as yet unconquered, and when we look in their faces, we are disconcerted. Infancy conforms to nobody: all conform to it, so that one babe commonly makes four or five out of the adults who prattle and play to it. So God has armed youth and puberty and manhood no less with its own piquancy and charm, and made it enviable and gracious and its claims not to be put by, if it will stand by itself. Do not think the youth has no force because he cannot speak to you and me. Hark! in the next room his voice is sufficiently clear and emphatic. It seems he knows how to speak to his contemporaries. Bashful or bold, then, he will know how to make us seniors very unnecessary.

The nonchalance of boys who are sure of a dinner, and would disdain as much as a lord to do or say aught to conciliate one, is the healthy attitude of human nature. A boy is in the parlour what the pit[5] is in the playhouse; independent, irresponsible, looking out from his corner on such people and facts as pass by, he tries and sentences them on their merits, in the swift summary way of boys, as good, bad, interesting, silly, eloquent, troublesome. He cumbers himself never about consequences, about interests: he gives an independent, genuine verdict. You must court him: he does not court you. But the man is, as it were, clapped into jail by his consciousness. As soon as he has once acted or spoken with eclat, he is a committed person, watched by the sympathy or the hatred of hundreds whose affections must now enter into his account. There is no Lethe[6] for this. Ah, that he could pass again into his neutrality! Who can thus avoid all pledges, and having observed, observe again from the same unaffected, unbiassed, unbribable, unaffrighted innocence, must always be formidable. He would utter opinions on all passing affairs, which being seen to be not private but necessary, would sink like darts into the ear of men, and put them in fear.

These are the voices which we hear in solitude, but they grow faint and inaudible as we enter into the world. Society everywhere is in conspiracy against the manhood of every one of its members. Society is a joint-stock company in which the members agree for the better securing of his bread to each shareholder, to surrender the liberty and culture of the eater. The virtue in most request is conformity. Self-reliance is its aversion. It loves not realities and creators, but names and customs.

Whoso would be a man must be a nonconformist. He who would gather immortal palms must not be hindered by the name of goodness, but must explore if it be goodness. Nothing is at last sacred but the integrity of your own mind. Absolve you to yourself, and you shall have

5

6

7

---

[5]In Elizabethan theaters patrons in the inexpensive seats were rowdy and wild.
[6]River of Forgetfulness in Greek mythology.

the suffrage of the world. I remember an answer which when quite young I was prompted to make to a valued adviser who was wont to importune me with the dear old doctrines of the church. On my saying, What have I to do with the sacredness of traditions, if I live wholly from within? my friend suggested—"But these impulses may be from below, not from above." I replied, "They do not seem to me to be such; but if I am the Devil's child, I will live then from the Devil." No law can be sacred to me but that of my nature. Good and bad are but names very readily transferable to that or this; the only right is what is after my constitution, the only wrong what is against it. A man is to carry himself in the presence of all opposition as if everything were titular and ephemeral but he I am ashamed to think how easily we capitulate to badges and names, to large societies and dead institutions. Every decent and well-spoken individual affects and sways me more than is right. I ought to go upright and vital, and speak the rude truth in all ways. If malice and vanity wear the coat of philanthropy, shall that pass? If an angry bigot assumes this bountiful cause of Abolition, and comes to me with his last news from Barbadoes,[7] why should I not say to him, "Go love thy infant; love thy wood-chopper: be good-natured and modest: have that grace; and never varnish your hard, uncharitable ambition with this incredible tenderness for black folk a thousand miles off. Thy love afar is spite at home." Rough and graceless would be such greeting, but truth is handsomer than the affectation of love. Your goodness must have some edge to it—else it is none. The doctrine of hatred must be preached as the counteraction of the doctrine of love when that pules and whines. I shun father and mother and wife and brother, when my genius calls me. I would write on the lintels of the door-post, *Whim*. I hope it is somewhat better than whim at last, but we cannot spend the day in explanation. Expect me not to show cause why I seek or why I exclude company. Then, again, do not tell me, as a good man did to-day, of my obligation to put all poor men in good situations. Are they *my* poor? I tell thee, thou foolish philanthropist, that I grudge the dollar, the dime, the cent I give to such men as do not belong to me and to whom I do not belong. There is a class of persons to whom by all spiritual affinity I am bought and sold; for them I will go to prison, if need be; but your miscellaneous popular charities; the education at college of fools; the building of meeting-houses to the vain end to which many now stand; alms to sots; and the thousandfold Relief Societies;—though I confess with shame I sometimes succumb and give the dollar, it is a wicked dollar which by and by I shall have the manhood to withhold.

8   Virtues are in the popular estimate rather the exception than the rule. There is the man *and* his virtues. Men do what is called a good ac-

[7]In 1834 the island of Barbados in the British West Indies abolished slavery.

tion, as some piece of courage or charity, much as they would pay a fine in expiation of daily non-appearance on parade. Their works are done as an apology or extenuation of their living in the world,—as invalids and the insane pay a high board. Their virtues are penances. I do not wish to expiate, but to live. My life is for itself and not for a spectacle. I much prefer that it should be of a lower strain, so it be genuine and equal, than that it should be glittering and unsteady. I wish it to be sound and sweet, and not to need diet and bleeding. I ask primary evidence that you are a man, and refuse this appeal from the man to his actions. I know that for myself it makes no difference whether I do or forbear those actions which are reckoned excellent. I cannot consent to pay for a privilege where I have intrinsic right. Few and mean as my gifts may be, I actually am, and do not need for my own assurance or the assurance of my fellows any secondary testimony.

What I must do, is all that concerns me, not what the people think.   9
This rule, equally arduous in actual and in intellectual life, may serve for the whole distinction between greatness and meanness. It is the harder, because you will always find those who think they know what is your duty better than you know it. It is easy in the world to live after the world's opinion; it is easy in solitude to live after our own; but the great man is he who in the midst of the crowd keeps with perfect sweetness the independence of solitude.

The objection to conforming to usages that have become dead to   10
you, is, that it scatters your force. It loses your time and blurs the impression of your character. If you maintain a dead church, contribute to a dead Bible-Society, vote with a great party either for the Government or against it, spread your table like base housekeepers,—under all these screens, I have difficulty to detect the precise man you are. And, of course, so much force is withdrawn from your proper life. But do your work, and I shall know you. Do your work, and you shall reinforce yourself. A man must consider what a blindman's-bluff is this game of conformity. If I know your sect, I anticipate your argument. I hear a preacher announce for his text and topic the expediency of one of the institutions of his church. Do I not know beforehand that not possibly can he say a new and spontaneous word? Do I not know that with all this ostentation of examining the grounds of the institution, he will do no such thing? Do I not know that he is pledged to himself not to look but at one side,—the permitted side, not as a man, but as a parish minister? He is a retained attorney, and these airs of the bench are the emptiest affectation. Well, most men have bound their eyes with one or another handkerchief, and attached themselves to some one of these communities of opinion. This conformity makes them not false in a few particulars, authors of a few lies, but false in all particulars. Their every truth is not quite true. Their two is not the real two, their four not the real four: so that every word they say chagrins us, and we know not

where to begin to set them right. Meantime nature is not slow to equip us in the prison-uniform of the party to which we adhere. We come to wear one cut of face and figure, and acquire by degrees the gentlest asinine expression. There is a mortifying experience in particular which does not fail to wreck itself also in the general history; I mean "the foolish face of praise,"[8] the forced smile which we put on in company where we do not feel at ease in answer to conversation which does not interest us. The muscles, not spontaneously moved, but moved by a low usurping wilfulness, grow tight about the outline of the face with the most disagreeable sensation.

11   For nonconformity the world whips you with its displeasure. And therefore a man must know how to estimate a sour face. The bystanders look askance on him in the public street or in the friend's parlor. If this aversation had its origin in contempt and resistance like his own, he might well go home with a sad countenance; but the sour faces of the multitude, like their sweet faces, have no deep cause, but are put on and off as the wind blows, and a newspaper directs. Yet is the discontent of the multitude more formidable than that of the senate and the college. It is easy enough for a firm man who knows the world to brook the rage of the cultivated classes. Their rage is decorous and prudent, for they are timid as being very vulnerable themselves. But when to their feminine rage the indignation of the people is added, when the ignorant and the poor are aroused, when the unintelligent brute force that lies at the bottom of society is made to growl and mow, it needs the habit of magnanimity and religion to treat it godlike as a trifle of no concernment.

12   The other terror that scares us from self-trust is our consistency; a reverence for our past act or word, because the eyes of others have no other data for computing our orbit than our past acts, and we are loath to disappoint them.

13   But why should you keep your head over your shoulder? Why drag about this corpse of your memory, lest you contradict somewhat you have stated in this or that public place? Suppose you should contradict yourself; what then? It seems to be a rule of wisdom never to rely on your memory alone, scarcely even in acts of pure memory, but to bring the past for judgment into the thousand-eyed present, and live ever in a new day. In your metaphysics you have denied personality to the Deity: yet when the devout motions of the soul come, yield to them heart and life, though they should clothe God with shape and color. Leave your theory as Joseph his coat in the hand of the harlot,[9] and flee.

14   A foolish consistency is the hobgoblin of little minds, adored by little statesmen and philosophers and divines. With consistency a great

[8]From Alexander Pope's, *Epistle to Dr. Arbuthnot*, l. 212.
[9]See Genesis 39:12.

soul has simply nothing to do. He may as well concern himself with his shadow on the wall. Speak what you think now in hard words, and to-morrow speak what to-morrow thinks in hard words again, though it contradict every thing you said to-day.—'Ah, so you shall be sure to be misunderstood.'—Is it so bad then to be misunderstood? Pythagoras was misunderstood, and Socrates, and Jesus, and Luther, and Coperni-cus, and Galileo, and Newton, and every pure and wise spirit that ever took flesh. To be great is to be misunderstood.

I suppose no man can violate his nature. All the sallies of his will are rounded in by the last of his being as the inequalities of Andes and Himmaleh are insignificant in the curve of the sphere. Nor does it mat-ter how you gauge and try him. A character is like an acrostic or Alex-andrian stanza;[10]—read it forward, backward, or across, it still spells the same thing. In this pleasing contrite wood-life which God allows me, let me record day by day my honest thought without prospect or retrospect, and, I cannot doubt, it will be found symmetrical, though I mean it not, and see it not. My book should smell of pines and resound with the hum of insects. The swallow over my window should inter-weave that thread or straw he carried in his bill into my web also. We pass for what we are. Character teaches above our wills. Men imagine that they communicate their virtue or vice only by overt actions and do not see that virtue or vice emit a breath every moment.

There will be an agreement in whatever variety of actions, so they be each honest and natural in their hour. For of one will, the actions will be harmonious, however unlike they seem. These varieties are lost sight of at a little distance, at a little height of thought. One tendency unites them all. The voyage of the best ship is a zigzag line of a hun-dred tacks. See the line from a sufficient distance, and it straightens it-self to the average tendency. Your genuine action will explain itself and will explain your other genuine actions. Your conformity explains nothing. Act singly, and what you have already done singly, will justify you now. Greatness appeals to the future. If I can be firm enough to-day to do right and scorn eyes, I must have done so much right before, as to defend me now. Be it how it will, do right now. Always scorn ap-pearances, and you always may. The force of character is cumulative. All the foregone days of virtue work their health into this. What makes the majesty of the heroes of the senate and the field, which so fills the imagination? The consciousness of a train of great days and victories behind. They shed an united light on the advancing actor. He is at-tended as by a visible escort of angels. That is it which throws thunder into Chatham's voice, and dignity into Washington's port, and Amer-ica into Adams's eye. Honor is venerable to us because it is no ephem-eris. It is always ancient virtue. We worship it to-day, because it is not

[10]Palindrome, or statement that reads the same forward and backward.

of to-day. We love it and pay it homage, because it is not a trap for our love and homage, but is self-dependent, self-derived, and therefore of an old immaculate pedigree, even if shown in a young person.

17   I hope in these days we have heard the last of conformity and consistency. Let the words be gazetted and ridiculous henceforward. Instead of the gong for dinner, let us hear a whistle from the Spartan fife. Let us never bow and apologize more. A great man is coming to eat at my house. I do not wish to please him: I wish that he should wish to please me. I will stand here for humanity, and though I would make it kind, I would make it true. Let us affront and reprimand the smooth mediocrity and squalid contentment of the times, and hurt in the face of custom, and trade, and office, the fact which is the upshot of all history, that there is a great responsible Thinker and Actor working wherever a man works; that a true man belongs to no other time or place, but is the centre of things. Where he is, there is nature. He measures you, and all men, and all events. Ordinarily every body in society reminds us of somewhat else or of some other person. Character, reality, reminds you of nothing else; it takes place of the whole creation. The man must be so much that he must make all circumstances indifferent. Every true man is a cause, a country, and an age; requires infinite spaces and numbers and time fully to accomplish his design;—and posterity seem to follow his steps as a train of clients. A man Caesar is born, and for ages after, we have a Roman Empire. Christ is born, and millions of minds so grow and cleave to his genius, that he is confounded with virtue and the possible of man. An institution is the lengthened shadow of one man; as, Monachism, of the Hermit Antony; the Reformation, of Luther; Quakerism of Fox; Methodism, of Wesley; Abolition, of Clarkson. Scipio, Milton called "the height of Rome;" and all history resolves itself very easily into the biography of a few stout and earnest persons.

18   Let a man then know his worth, and keep things under his feet. Let him not peep or steal, or skulk up and down with the air of a charity-boy, a bastard, or an interloper, in the world which exists for him. But the man in the street finding no worth in himself which corresponds to the force which built a tower or sculptured a marble god, feels poor when he looks on these. To him a palace, a statue, or a costly book have an alien and forbidding air, much like a gay equipage, and seem to say like that, "Who are you, sir?" Yet they all are his, suitors for his notice, petitioners to his faculties that they will come out and take possession. The picture waits for my verdict: it is not to command me, but I am to settle its claims to praise. That popular fable of the sot who was picked up dead drunk in the street, carried to the duke's house, washed and dressed and laid in the duke's bed, and, on his waking, treated with all obsequious ceremony like the duke, and assured that he had been insane, owes its popularity to the fact, that it symbolizes so well the state

of man, who is in the world a sort of sot, but now and then wakes up, exercises his reason, and finds himself a true prince.

Our reading is mendicant and sycophantic. In history, our imagina-   19
tion plays us false. Kingdom and lordship, power and estate are a gaudier vocabulary than private John and Edward in a small house and common day's work: but the things of life are the same to both: the sum total of both is the same. Why all this deference to Alfred, and Scanderbeg, and Gustavus? Suppose they were virtuous: did they wear out virtue? As great a stake depends on your private act to-day, as followed their public and renowned steps. When private men shall act with original views, the lustre will be transferred from the actions of kings to those of gentlemen.

The world has been instructed by its kings, who have so magne-   20
tized the eyes of nations. It has been caught by this colossal symbol the mutual reverence that is due from man to man. The joyful loyalty with which men have everywhere suffered the king, the noble, or the great proprietor to walk among them by a law of his own, make his own scale of men and things, and reverse theirs, pay for benefits not with money but with honor, and represent the Law in his person, was the hieroglyphic by which they obscurely signified their consciousness of their own right and comeliness, the right of every man.

The magnetism which all original action exerts is explained when   21
we inquire the reason of self-trust. Who is the Trustee? What is the aboriginal Self on which a universal reliance may be grounded? What is the nature and power of that science-baffling star, without parallax, without calculable elements, which shoots a ray of beauty even into trivial and impure actions, if the least mark of independence appear? The inquiry leads us to that source, at once the essence of genius, of virtue, and of life, which we call Spontaneity or Instinct. We denote this primary wisdom as Intuition, whilst all later teachings are tuitions. In that deep force, the last fact behind which analysis cannot go, all things find their common origin. For the sense of being which in calm hours rises, we know not how, in the soul, is not diverse from things, from space, from light, from time, from man, but one with them, and proceeds obviously from the same source whence their life and being also proceed. We first share the life by which things exist, and afterwards see them as appearances in nature, and forget that we have shared their cause. Here is the fountain of action and of thought. Here are the lungs of that inspiration which giveth man wisdom, and which cannot be denied without impiety and atheism. We lie in the lap of immense intelligence, which makes us receivers of its truth and organs of its activity. When we discern justice, when we discern truth, we do nothing of ourselves, but allow a passage to its beams. If we ask whence this comes, if we seek to pry into the soul that causes, all philosophy is at fault. Its presence or its absence is all we can affirm. Every man discriminates

between the voluntary acts of his mind, and his involuntary perceptions, and knows that to his involuntary perceptions a perfect faith is due. He may err in the expression of them, but he knows that these things are so, like day and night, not to be disputed. My wilful actions and acquisitions are but roving;—the idlest reverie, the faintest native emotion, command my curiosity and respect. Thoughtless people contradict as readily the statement of perceptions as of opinions, or rather much more readily; for, they do not distinguish between perception and notion. They fancy that I choose to see this or that thing. But perception is not whimsical, but fatal. If I see a trait, my children will see it after me, and in course of time, all mankind,—although it may chance that no one has seen it before me. For my perception of it is as much a fact as the sun.

22   The relations of the soul to the divine spirit are so pure that it is profane to seek to interpose helps. It must be that when God speaketh, he should communicate not one thing, but all things; should fill the world with his voice; should scatter forth light, nature, time, souls, from the centre of the present thought; and new date and new create the whole. Whenever a mind is simple, and receives a divine wisdom, old things pass away,—means, teachers, texts, temples fall; it lives now and absorbs past and future into the present hour. All things are made sacred by relation to it,—one as much as another. All things are dissolved to their centre by their cause, and in the universal miracle petty and particular miracles disappear. If, therefore, a man claims to know and speak of God, and carries you backward to the phraseology of some old mouldered nation in another country, in another world, believe him not. Is the acorn better than the oak which is its fullness and completion? Is the parent better than the child into whom he has cast his ripened being? Whence then this worship of the past? The centuries are conspirators against the sanity and authority of the soul. Time and space are but physiological colors which the eye makes, but the soul is light; where it is, is day; where it was, is night; and history is an impertinence and an injury, if it be anything more than a cheerful apologue or parable of my being and becoming.

23   Man is timid and apologetic; he is no longer upright; he dares not say 'I think,' 'I am,' but quotes some saint or sage. He is ashamed before the blade of grass or the blowing rose. These roses under my window make no reference to former roses or to better ones; they are for what they are; they exist with God to-day. There is no time to them. There is simply the rose; it is perfect in every moment of its existence. Before a leaf-bud has burst, its whole life acts; in the full-blown flower, there is no more; in the leafless root, there is no less. Its nature is satisfied, and it satisfies nature, in all moments alike. But man postpones or remembers; he does not live in the present, but with reverted eye laments the past, or, heedless of the riches that surround him, stands on

tiptoe to foresee the future. He cannot be happy and strong until he too lives with nature in the present, above time.

This should be plain enough. Yet see what strong intellects dare not yet hear God himself, unless he speak the phraseology of I know not what David, or Jeremiah, or Paul. We shall not always set so great a price on a few texts, on a few lives. We are like children who repeat by rote the sentences of grandames and tutors, and, as they grow older, of the men of talents and character they chance to see,—painfully recollecting the exact words they spoke; afterwards, when they come into the point of view which those had who uttered these sayings, they understand them, and are willing to let the words go; for, at any time, they can use words as good, when occasion comes. If we live truly, we shall see truly. It is as easy for the strong man to be strong, as it is for the weak to be weak. When we have new perception, we shall gladly disburden the memory of its hoarded treasures as old rubbish. When a man lives with God, his voice shall be as sweet as the murmur of the brook and the rustle of the corn.

And now at last the highest truth on this subject remains unsaid; probably, cannot be said; for all that we say is the far off remembering of the intuition. That thought, by what I can now nearest approach to say it, is this. When good is near you, when you have life in yourself, it is not by any known or accustomed way; you shall not discern the footprints of any other; you shall not see the face of man; you shall not hear any name;—the way, the thought, the good shall be wholly strange and new. It shall exclude example and experience. You take the way from man, not to man. All persons that ever existed are its forgotten ministers. Fear and hope are alike beneath it. There is somewhat low even in hope. In the hour of vision, there is nothing that can be called gratitude, nor properly joy. The soul raised over passion beholds identity and eternal causation, perceives the self-existence of Truth and Right, and calms itself with knowing that all things go well. Vast spaces of nature, the Atlantic Ocean, the South Sea,—long intervals of time, years, centuries,—are of no account. This which I think and feel underlay every former state of life and circumstances, as it does underlie my present, and what is called life, and what is called death.

Life only avails, not the having lived. Power ceases in the instant of repose; it resides in the moment of transition from a past to a new state, in the shooting of the gulf, in the darting to an aim. This one fact the world hates, that the soul *becomes;* for, that forever degrades the past, turns all riches to poverty, all reputation to a shame, confounds the saint with the rogue, shoves Jesus and Judas equally aside. Why then do we prate of self-reliance? Inasmuch as the soul is present, there will be power not confident but agent. To talk of reliance, is a poor external way of speaking. Speak rather of that which relies, because it works and is. Who has more obedience than I, masters me, though he should not raise his finger. Round him I must revolve by the gravitation of spirits. We fancy it rhetoric when we speak of eminent virtue. We do not yet see that virtue is Height, and that a man or a company of men plastic and permeable to principles, by the law of nature must over-power and ride all cities, nations, kings, rich men, poets, who are not.

27   This is the ultimate fact which we so quickly reach on this as on ev-ery topic, the resolution of all into the ever blessed ONE. Self-existence is the attribute of the Supreme Cause, and it constitutes the measure of good by the degree in which it enters into all lower forms. All things real are so by so much virtue as they contain. Commerce, husbandry, hunting, whaling, war, eloquence, personal weight, are somewhat, and engage my respect as examples of its presence and impure action. I see the same law working in nature for conservation and growth. Power is in nature the essential measure of right. Nature suffers nothing to re-main in her kingdoms which cannot help itself. The genesis and matu-ration of a planet, its poise and orbit, the bended tree recovering itself from the strong wind, the vital resources of every animal and vegeta-ble, are demonstrations of the self-sufficing, and therefore self-relying soul.

28   Thus all concentrates; let us not rove; let us sit at home with the cause. Let us stun and astonish the intruding rabble of men and books and institutions by a simple declaration of the divine fact. Bid the in-vaders take the shoes from off their feet, for God is here within. Let our simplicity judge them, and our docility to our own law demonstrate the poverty of nature and fortune beside our native riches.

29   But now we are a mob. Man does not stand in awe of man, nor is his genius admonished to stay at home, to put itself in communication with the internal ocean, but it goes abroad to beg a cup of water of the urns of other men. We must go alone. I like the silent church before the service begins, better than any preaching. How far off, how cool, how chaste the persons look, begirt each one with a precinct or sanctuary. So let us always sit. Why should we assume the faults of our friend, or wife, or father, or child, because they sit around our hearth, or are said to have the same blood? All men have my blood, and I have all men's. Not for that will I adopt their petulance or folly, even to the extent of being ashamed of it. But your isolation must not be mechanical, but spiritual, that is, must be elevation. At times the whole world seems to be in conspiracy to importune you with emphatic trifles. Friend, client, child, sickness, fear, want, charity, all knock at once at thy closet door and say,—"Come out unto us." But keep thy state; come not into their confusion. The power men possess to annoy me, I give them by a weak curiosity. No man can come near me but through my act. "What we love that we have, but by desire we bereave ourselves of the love."

30   If we cannot at once rise to the sanctities of obedience and faith, let us at least resist our temptations; let us enter into the state of war, and

wake Thor and Woden,[11] courage and constancy, in our Saxon breasts. This is to be done in our smooth times by speaking the truth. Check this lying hospitality and lying affection. Live no longer to the expectation of these deceived and deceiving people with whom we converse. Say to them, O father, O mother, O wife, O brother, O friend, I have lived with you after appearances hitherto. Henceforward I am the truth's. Be it known unto you that henceforward I obey no law less than the eternal law. I will have no covenants but proximities. I shall endeavor to nourish my parents, to support my family, to be the chaste husband of one wife,—but these relations I must fill after a new and unprecedented way. I appeal from your customs. I must be myself. I cannot break myself any longer for you, or you. If you can love me for what I am, we shall be the happier. If you cannot, I will still seek to deserve that you should. I will not hide my tastes or aversions. I will so trust that what is deep is holy, that I will do strongly before the sun and moon whatever inly rejoices me, and the heart appoints. If you are noble, I will love you; if you are not, I will not hurt you and myself by hypocritical attentions. If you are true, but not in the same truth with me, cleave to your companions; I will seek my own. I do this not selfishly, but humbly and truly. It is alike your interest and mine and all men's, however long we have dwelt in lies, to live in truth. Does this sound harsh to-day? You will soon love what is dictated by your nature as well as mine, and if we follow the truth, it will bring us out safe at last.—But so you may give these friends pain. Yes, but I cannot sell my liberty and my power, to save their sensibility. Besides, all persons have their moments of reason when they look out into the region of absolute truth; then will they justify me and do the same thing.

The populace think that your rejection of popular standards is a rejection of all standard, and mere antinomianism, and the bold sensualist will use the name of philosophy to gild his crimes. But the law of consciousness abides. There are two confessionals, in one or the other of which we must be shriven. You may fulfil your round of duties by clearing yourself in the *direct,* or, in the *reflex* way. Consider whether you have satisfied your relations to father, mother, cousin, neighbor, town, cat, and dog; whether any of these can upbraid you. But I may also neglect this reflex standard, and absolve me to myself. I have my own stern claims and perfect circle. It denies the name of duty to many offices that are called duties. But if I can discharge its debts, it enables me to dispense with the popular code. If any one imagines that this law is lax, let him keep its commandment one day.   31

And truly it demands something godlike in him who has cast off the common motives of humanity, and has ventured to trust himself for a taskmaster. High be his heart, faithful his will, clear his sight, that he   32

---

[11]Thor and Woden (Odin) are powerful gods of Norse mythology.

may in good earnest be doctrine, society, law to himself, that a simple purpose may be to him as strong as iron necessity is to others.

33   If any man consider the present aspects of what is called by distinction *society*, he will see the need of these ethics. The sinew and heart of man seem to be drawn out, and we are become timorous desponding whimperers. We are afraid of truth, afraid of fortune, afraid of death, and afraid of each other. Our age yields no great and perfect persons. We want men and women who shall renovate life and our social state, but we see that most natures are insolvent, cannot satisfy their own wants, have an ambition out of all proportion to their practical force, and do lean and beg day and night continually. Our housekeeping is mendicant, our arts, our occupations, our marriages, our religion we have not chosen, but society has chosen for us. We are parlor soldiers. We shun the rugged battle of fate, where strength is born.

34   If our young men miscarry in their first enterprizes, they lose all heart. If the young merchant fails, men say he is *ruined*. If the finest genius studies at one of our colleges, and is not installed in an office within one year afterwards in the cities or suburbs of Boston or New York, it seems to his friends and to himself that he is right in being disheartened and in complaining the rest of his life. A sturdy lad from New Hampshire or Vermont, who in turn tries all the professions, who *teams it, farms it, peddles,* keeps a school, preaches, edits a newspaper, goes to Congress, buys a township, and so forth, in successive years, and always, like a cat, falls on his feet, is worth a hundred of these city dolls. He walks abreast with his days, and feels no shame in not 'studying a profession,' for he does not postpone his life, but lives already. He has not one chance, but a hundred chances. Let a Stoic open the resources of man, and tell men they are not leaning willows, but can and must detach themselves; that with the exercise of self-trust, new powers shall appear; that a man is the word made flesh,[12] born to shed healing to the nations, that he should be ashamed of our compassion, and that the moment he acts from himself, tossing the laws, the books, idolatries, and customs out of the window, we pity him no more but thank and revere him,—and that teacher shall restore the life of man to splendor, and make his name dear to all History.

35   It is easy to see that a greater self-reliance must work a revolution in all the offices and relations of men; in their religion; in their education; in their pursuits; their modes of living; their association; in their property; in their speculative views.

36   1. In what prayers do men allow themselves! That which they call a holy office, is not so much as brave and manly. Prayer looks abroad and asks for some foreign addition to come through some foreign virtue, and loses itself in endless mazes of natural and supernatural, and

[12]See John 1:14.

mediatorial and miraculous. Prayer that craves a particular commodity,—
any thing less than all good,—is vicious. Prayer is the contemplation of
the facts of life from the highest point of view. It is the soliloquy of a beholding and jubilant soul. It is the spirit of God pronouncing his works
good.[13] But prayer as a means to effect a private end, is meanness and
theft. It supposes dualism and not unity in nature and consciousness.
As soon as the man is at one with God, he will not beg. He will then see
prayer in all action. The prayer of the farmer kneeling in his field to
weed it, the prayer of the rower kneeling with the stroke of his oar, are
true prayers heard throughout nature, though for cheap ends. Car-
atach, in Fletcher's Bonduca, when admonished to inquire the mind of
the god Audate, replies,—

"His hidden meaning lies in our endeavors,
Our valors are our best gods."

Another sort of false prayers are our regrets. Discontent is the want
of self-reliance: it is infirmity of will. Regret calamities, if you can
thereby help the sufferer; if not, attend your own work, and already the
evil begins to be repaired. Our sympathy is just as base. We come to
them who weep foolishly, and sit down and cry for company, instead of
imparting to them truth and health in rough electric shocks, putting
them once more in communication with their own reason. The secret of
fortune is joy in our hands. Welcome evermore to gods and men is the
self-helping man. For him all doors are flung wide: him all tongues
greet, all honors crown, all eyes follow with desire. Our love goes out
to him and embraces him, because he did not need it. We solicitously
and apologetically caress and celebrate him, because he held on his
way and scorned our disapprobation. The gods love him because men
hated him. "To the persevering mortal," said Zoroaster, "the blessed
Immortals are swift."

As men's prayers are a disease of the will, so are their creeds a disease of the intellect. They say with those foolish Israelites, "Let not God
speak to us, lest we die. Speak thou, speak any man with us, and we will
obey."[14] Everywhere I am hindered of meeting God in my brother, because he has shut his own temple doors, and recites fables merely of his
brother's, or his brother's brother's God. Every new mind is a new classification. If it prove a mind of uncommon activity and power, a Locke,
a Lavoisier, a Hutton, a Bentham, a Fourier, it imposes its classification
on other men, and lo! a new system. In proportion to the depth of the
thought, and so to the number of the objects it touches and brings
within reach of the pupil, is his complacency. But chiefly is this apparent

37

38

[13]Genesis 1:31.
[14]See Exodus 20:19.

in creeds and churches, which are also classifications of some powerful mind acting on the elemental thought of Duty, and man's relation to the Highest. Such is Calvinism, Quakerism, Swedenborgianism. The pupil takes the same delight in subordinating every thing to the new terminology, as a girl who has just learned botany in seeing a new earth and new seasons thereby. It will happen for a time, that the pupil will find his intellectual power has grown by the study of his master's mind. But in all unbalanced minds, the classification is idolized, passes for the end, and not for a speedily exhaustible means, so that the walls of the system blend to their eye in the remote horizon with the walls of the universe; the luminaries of heaven seem to them hung on the arch their master built. They cannot imagine how you aliens have any right to see,—how you can see; "It must be somehow that you stole the light from us." They do not yet perceive, that light, unsystematic, indomitable, will break into any cabin, even into theirs. Let them chirp awhile and call it their own. If they are honest and do well, presently their neat new pinfold will be too strait and low, will crack, will lean, will rot and vanish, and the immortal light, all young and joyful, million-orbed, million-colored, will beam over the universe as on the first morning.

39   2. It is for want of self-culture that the superstition of Travelling, whose idols are Italy, England, Egypt, retains its fascination for all educated Americans. They who made England, Italy, or Greece venerable in the imagination, did so by sticking fast where they were, like an axis of the earth. In manly hours, we feel that duty is our place. The soul is no traveller: the wise man stays at home, and when his necessities, his duties, on any occasion call him from his house, or into foreign lands, he is at home still, and shall make men sensible by the expression of his countenance, that he goes the missionary of wisdom and virtue, and visits cities and men like a sovereign, and not like an interloper or a valet.

40   I have no churlish objection to the circumnavigation of the globe, for the purposes of art, of study, and benevolence, so that the man is first domesticated, or does not go abroad with the hope of finding somewhat greater than he knows. He who travels to be amused, or to get somewhat which he does not carry, travels away from himself, and grows old even in youth among old things. In Thebes, in Palmyra, his will and mind have become old and dilapidated as they. He carries ruins to ruins.

41   Travelling is a fool's paradise. Our first journeys discover to us the indifference of places. At home I dream that at Naples, at Rome, I can be intoxicated with beauty, and lose my sadness. I pack my trunk, embrace my friends, embark on the sea, and at last wake up in Naples, and there beside me is the stern Fact, the sad self, unrelenting, identical, that I fled from. I seek the Vatican, and the palaces. I affect to be intoxicated with sights and suggestions, but I am not intoxicated. My giant goes with me wherever I go.

3. But the rage of travelling is a symptom of a deeper unsoundness   42
affecting the whole intellectual action. The intellect is vagabond, and
our system of education fosters restlessness. Our minds travel when
our bodies are forced to stay at home. We imitate; and what is imitation
but the travelling of the mind? Our houses are built with foreign taste;
our shelves are garnished with foreign ornaments; our opinions, our
tastes, our faculties, lean, and follow the Past and the Distant. The soul
created the arts wherever they have flourished. It was in his own mind
that the artist sought his model. It was an application of his own
thought to the thing to be done and the conditions to be observed. And
why need we copy the Doric or the Gothic model? Beauty, convenience, grandeur of thought, and quaint expression are as near to us as
to any, and if the American artist will study with hope and love the precise thing to be done by him, considering the climate, the soil, the
length of the day, the wants of the people, the habit and form of the
government, he will create a house in which all these will find themselves fitted, and taste and sentiment will be satisfied also.

Insist on yourself; never imitate. Your own gift you can present ev-   43
ery moment with the cumulative force of a whole life's cultivation; but
of the adopted talent of another, you have only an extemporaneous,
half possession. That which each can do best, none but his Maker can
teach him. No man yet knows what it is, nor can, till that person has ex-
hibited it. Where is the master who could have taught Shakspeare?
Where is the master who could have instructed Franklin, or Washington, or Bacon, or Newton? Every great man is a unique. The Scipionism
of Scipio is precisely that part he could not borrow. Shakspeare will
never be made by the study of Shakspeare. Do that which is assigned
you, and you cannot hope too much or dare too much. There is at this
moment for you an utterance brave and grand as that of the colossal
chisel of Phidias, or trowel of the Egyptians, or the pen of Moses, or
Dante, but different from all these. Not possibly will the soul all rich, all
eloquent, with thousand-cloven tongue, deign to repeat itself; but if
you can hear what these patriarchs say, surely you can reply to them in
the same pitch of voice: for the ear and the tongue are two organs of
one nature. Abide in the simple and noble regions of thy life, obey thy
heart, and thou shalt reproduce the Foreworld again.

4. As our Religion, our Education, our Art look abroad, so does   44
our spirit of society. All men plume themselves on the improvement of
society, and no man improves.

Society never advances. It recedes as fast on one side as it gains on   45
the other. It undergoes continual changes: it is barbarous, it is civilized,
it is christianized, it is rich, it is scientific; but this change is not amelio-
ration. For every thing that is given, something is taken. Society acquires new arts and loses old instincts. What a contrast between the
well-clad, reading, writing, thinking American, with a watch, a pencil,

and a bill of exchange in his pocket, and the naked New Zealander, whose property is a club, a spear, a mat, and an undivided twentieth of a shed to sleep under. But compare the health of the two men, and you shall see that the white man has lost his aboriginal strength. If the traveller tell us truly, strike the savage with a broad axe, and in a day or two the flesh shall unite and heal as if you struck the blow into soft pitch, and the same blow shall send the white to his grave.

46   The civilized man has built a coach, but has lost the use of his feet. He is supported on crutches, but lacks so much support of muscle. He has a fine Geneva watch, but he fails of the skill to tell the hour by the sun. A Greenwich nautical almanac he has, and so being sure of the information when he wants it, the man in the street does not know a star in the sky. The solstice he does not observe; the equinox he knows as little; and the whole bright calendar of the year is without a dial in his mind. His note-books impair his memory; his libraries overload his wit; the insurance office increases the number of accidents; and it may be a question whether machinery does not encumber; whether we have not lost by refinement some energy, by a christianity entrenched in establishments and forms, some vigor of wild virtue. For every stoic was a stoic; but in Christendom where is the Christian?

47   There is no more deviation in the moral standard than in the standard of height or bulk. No greater men are now than ever were. A singular equality may be observed between the great men of the first and of the last ages; nor can all the science, art, religion and philosophy of the nineteenth century avail to educate greater men than Plutarch's heroes, three or four and twenty centuries ago. Not in time is the race progressive. Phocion, Socrates, Anaxagoras, Diogenes, are great men, but they leave no class. He who is really of their class will not be called by their name, but will be his own man, and, in his turn the founder of a sect. The arts and inventions of each period are only its costume, and do not invigorate men. The harm of the improved machinery may compensate its good. Hudson and Behring accomplished so much in their fishing-boats, as to astonish Parry and Franklin, whose equipment exhausted the resources of science and art. Galileo, with an opera-glass, discovered a more splendid series of celestial phenomena than any one since. Columbus found the New World in an undecked boat. It is curious to see the periodical disuse and perishing of means and machinery which were introduced with loud laudation, a few years or centuries before. The great genius returns to essential man. We reckoned the improvements of the art of war among the triumphs of science, and yet Napoleon conquered Europe by the Bivouac, which consisted of falling back on naked valor, and disencumbering it of all aids. The Emperor held it impossible to make a perfect army, says Las Cases, "without abolishing our arms, magazines, commissaries, and carriages, until in imitation of the Roman custom, the soldier should

receive his supply of corn, grind it in his hand-mill, and bake his bread himself."

Society is a wave. The wave moves onward, but the water of which it is composed, does not. The same particle does not rise from the valley to the ridge. Its unity is only phenomenal. The persons who make up a nation to-day, next year die, and their experience with them. 48

And so the reliance on Property, including the reliance on governments which protect it, is the want of self-reliance. Men have looked away from themselves and at things so long, that they have come to esteem the religious, learned, and civil institutions, as guards of property, and they deprecate assaults on these, because they feel them to be assaults on property. They measure their esteem of each other, by what each has, and not by what each is. But a cultivated man becomes ashamed of his property, out of new respect for his nature. Especially he hates what he has, if he see that it is accidental,—came to him by inheritance, or gift, or crime; then he feels that it is not having; it does not belong to him, has no root in him, and merely lies there, because no revolution or no robber takes it away. But that which a man is, does always by necessity acquire, and what the man acquires is living property, which does not wait the beck of rulers, or mobs, or revolutions, or fire, or storm, or bankruptcies, but perpetually renews itself wherever the man breathes. "Thy lot or portion of life," said the Caliph Ali, "is seeking after thee; therefore be at rest from seeking after it." Our dependence on these foreign goods leads us to our slavish respect for numbers. The political parties meet in numerous conventions; the greater the concourse, and with each new uproar of announcement, The delegation from Essex! The Democrats from New Hampshire! The Whigs of Maine! the young patriot feels himself stronger than before by a new thousand of eyes and arms. In like manner the reformers summon conventions, and vote and resolve in multitude. Not so, O friends! will the God deign to enter and inhabit you, but by a method precisely the reverse. It is only as a man puts off all foreign support, and stands alone, that I see him to be strong and to prevail. He is weaker by every recruit to his banner. Is not a man better than a town? Ask nothing of men, and in the endless mutation, thou only firm column must presently appear the upholder of all that surrounds thee. He who knows that power is inborn, that he is weak because he has looked for good out of him and elsewhere, and so perceiving, throws himself unhesitatingly on his thought, instantly rights himself, stands in the erect position, commands his limbs, works miracles; just as a man who stands on his feet is stronger than a man who stands on his head. 49

So use all that is called Fortune. Most men gamble with her, and gain all, and lose all, as her wheel rolls. But do thou leave as unlawful these winnings, and deal with Cause and Effect, the chancellors of God. In the Will work and acquire, and thou hast chained the wheel of 50

Chance, and shalt sit hereafter out of fear from her rotations. A political victory, a rise of rents, the recovery of your sick, or the return of your absent friend, or some other favorable event, raises your spirits, and you think good days are preparing for you. Do not believe it. Nothing can bring you peace but yourself. Nothing can bring you peace but the triumph of principles.

★ Meaning and Understanding

1. Emerson proclaims "Trust thyself" (paragraph 3). What reasons does he give for that advice? Why does he remind readers of "great men" and the "nonchalance of boys" in this context?

2. How does Emerson define "genius"? Do you agree with his definition? Why or why not?

3. In what way is society "in conspiracy against the manhood of every one of its members" (paragraph 6)?

4. Why does the writer attack "foolish philanthropies"? How is the attack consistent with the main point of the essay?

5. How, according to Emerson, does our consistency scare us from our self-trust (paragraph 12)?

6. What does Emerson see as the relation between the soul and the divine spirit (paragraphs 22–24)?

★ Techniques and Strategies

1. "Self-Reliance" begins with three epigraphs. What is an epigraph and what purpose do these three serve?

2. Like other of Emerson's essays, "Self-Reliance" contains many *aphorisms*. What is an aphorism? Identify the aphorisms that you find most memorable. Why do you think the writer chooses an aphoristic style?

3. The essay contains many allusions to writers and philosophers, contemporary figures, political leaders, and geographical locations. What is Emerson's purpose in using so many allusions? What does this tell you about the nature of his audience?

4. How do the title and opening paragraph or two help establish the point of the essay? How does the last paragraph serve as a fitting conclusion to the essay?

5. Emerson has a reputation as a brilliant stylist. How do you account for this reputation? What writing techniques and strategies—imagery and

figurative language, syntax, vocabulary, for example—contribute to his stature as an essayist?

★ *Speaking of Values*

1. Emerson's fundamental point here is, as the title proclaims, self-reliance and its essential role in American society. What is your view of self-reliance? How important is it in today's society, when we accent group power and politics? Under what circumstances is self-reliance important? How does one achieve it?

2. Do you agree with the writer that "For non-conformity the world whips you with its displeasure"? In what ways are nonconformity and self-reliance essentially two sides to the same coin? Can one exist without the other? How? Explain your response.

3. Emerson sees society as an enemy of self-reliance. Why might you agree or disagree with him? How does contemporary society work against self-reliance? How does society enhance self-reliance?

4. Why does Emerson call traveling—a great preoccupation of today's society, keep in mind—"a fool's paradise"? Why might you agree or disagree with him?

5. Many people would argue that consistency is a virtue; yet, as you have seen, Emerson condemns it in what is perhaps one of the most famous of his aphorisms (paragraph 14, line 1). What are your views on consistency? What are society's views? What does Emerson have to contribute to the discussion?

★ *Values Conversation*

Form groups and discuss the last two sentences of the essay: "Nothing can bring you peace but yourself. Nothing can bring you peace but the triumph of principles." How accurate are these statements for the modern world? In what ways are the sentences only catchy aphorisms? In what ways are they truly guidelines for moral living? Report back to the entire class the findings of each group.

★ *Writing about Values*

1. Write an essay in which you define "self-reliance." explaining your own meaning of the term. Or, if you choose, define "nonconformity."

2. Choose any aphorism from this essay and write a paper discussing its significance to you and (or) today's society. Feel free to challenge or

endorse Emerson's idea. Be sure to use illustrations and examples to support your argument.

3. Write a narrative essay in which you show a moment in which you practiced self-reliance or nonconformity to your advantage.

Bret Harte

The Outcasts of Poker Flat

Born in Albany, New York, Bret Harte (1839–1902) taught school and mined for gold in California. By 1868, however, he had launched a career as a journalist and had begun to publish short stories and verses in the *Overland Monthly,* which he himself founded. "The Outcasts of Poker Flat" helped establish the Western tale as a literary genre; in it Harte explores the expression of human character put to the test by catastrophe.

──────── ★ ────────

As Mr. John Oakhurst, gambler, stepped into the main street of Poker Flat on the morning of the 23d of November, 1850, he was conscious of a change in its moral atmosphere since the preceding night. Two or three men, conversing earnestly together, ceased as he approached, and exchanged significant glances. There was a Sabbath lull in the air, which, in a settlement unused to Sabbath influences, looked ominous. 1

Mr. Oakhurst's calm, handsome face betrayed small concern in these indications. Whether he was conscious of any predisposing cause was another question. "I reckon they're after somebody," he reflected: "likely it's me." He returned to his pocket the handkerchief with which he had been wiping away the red dust of Poker Flat from his neat boots, and quietly discharged his mind of any further conjecture. 2

In point of fact, Poker Flat was "after somebody." It had lately suffered the loss of several thousand dollars, two valuable horses, and a prominent citizen. It was experiencing a spasm of virtuous reaction, quite as lawless and ungovernable as any of the acts that had provoked it. A secret committee had determined to rid the town of all improper persons. This was done permanently in regard to two men who were then hanging from the boughs of a sycamore in the gulch, and temporarily in the banishment of certain other objectionable characters. I regret to say that some of these were ladies. It is but due to the sex, however, to state that their impropriety was professional, and it was only in such easily established standards of evil that Poker Flat ventured to sit in judgment. 3

Mr. Oakhurst was right in supposing that he was included in this category. A few of the committee had urged hanging him as a possible example and a sure method of reimbursing themselves from his pockets of the sums he had won from them. "It's agin justice," said Jim Wheeler, "to let this yer young man from Roaring Camp—an entire 4 stranger—carry away our money." But a crude sentiment of equity residing in the breasts of those who had been fortunate enough to win from Mr. Oakhurst overruled this narrower local prejudice.

5   Mr. Oakhurst received his sentence with philosophic calmness, none the less coolly that he was aware of the hesitation of his judges. He was too much of a gambler not to accept fate. With him life was at best an uncertain game, and he recognized the usual percentage in favor of the dealer.

6   A body of armed men accompanied the deported wickedness of Poker Flat to the outskirts of the settlement. Besides Mr. Oakhurst, who was known to be a coolly desperate man, and for whose intimidation the armed escort was intended, the expatriated party consisted of a young woman familiarly known as "The Duchess"; another who had won the title of "Mother Shipton"; and "Uncle Billy," a suspected sluice-robber and confirmed drunkard. The cavalcade provoked no comments from the spectators, nor was any word uttered by the escort. Only when the gulch which marked the uttermost limit of Poker Flat was reached, the leader spoke briefly and to the point. The exiles were forbidden to return at the peril of their lives.

7   As the escort disappeared, their pent-up feelings found vent in a few hysterical tears from the Duchess, some bad language from Mother Shipton, and a Parthian volley of expletives from Uncle Billy. The philosophic Oakhurst alone remained silent. He listened calmly to Mother Shipton's desire to cut somebody's heart out, to the repeated statements of the Duchess that she would die in the road, and to the alarming oaths that seemed to be bumped out of Uncle Billy as he rode forward. With the easy good humor characteristic of his class, he insisted upon exchanging his own riding-horse, "Five-spot," for the sorry mule which the Duchess rode. But even this act did not draw the party into any closer sympathy. The young woman readjusted her somewhat draggled plumes with a feeble, faded coquetry; Mother Shipton eyed the possessor of "Five-spot" with malevolence, and Uncle Billy included the whole party in one sweeping anathema.

8   The road to Sandy Bar—a camp that, not having as yet experienced the regenerating influences of Poker Flat, consequently seemed to offer some invitation to the emigrants—lay over a steep mountain range. It was distant a day's severe travel. In that advanced season the party soon passed out of the moist, temperate regions of the foothills into the dry, cold, bracing air of the Sierras. The trail was narrow and difficult. At noon the Duchess, rolling out of her saddle upon the ground, declared her intention of going no farther, and the party halted.

9   The spot was singularly wild and impressive. A wooded amphitheater surrounded on three sides by precipitous cliffs of naked granite, sloped gently toward the crest of another precipice that overlooked the valley. It was, undoubtedly, the most suitable spot for a camp, had

camping been advisable. But Mr. Oakhurst knew that scarcely half the journey to Sandy Bar was accomplished, and the party were not equipped or provisioned for delay. This fact he pointed out to his companions curtly, with a philosophic commentary on the folly of "throwing up their hand before the game was played out." But they were furnished with liquor, which in this emergency stood them in place of food, fuel, rest and prescience. In spite of his remonstrances, it was not long before they were more or less under its influence. Uncle Billy passed rapidly from a bellicose state into one of stupor, the Duchess became maudlin, and Mother Shipton snored. Mr. Oakhurst alone remained erect, leaning against a rock, calmly surveying them.

Mr. Oakhurst did not drink. It interfered with a profession which   10
required coolness, impassiveness, and presence of mind, and, in his own language, he "couldn't afford it." As he gazed at his recumbent fellow exiles, the loneliness begotten of his pariah trade, his habits of life, his very vices, for the first time seriously oppressed him. He bestirred himself in dusting his black clothes, washing his hands and face, and other acts characteristic of his studiously neat habits, and for a moment forgot his annoyance. The thought of deserting his weaker and more pitiable companions never perhaps occurred to him. Yet he could not help feeling the want of that excitement which, singularly enough, was most conducive to that calm equanimity for which he was notorious. He looked at the gloomy walls that rose a thousand feet sheer above the circling pines around him, at the sky ominously clouded, at the valley below already deepening into shadow; and, doing so, suddenly he heard his own name called.

A horseman slowly ascended the trail. In the fresh, open face of the   11
newcomer Mr. Oakhurst recognized Tom Simson, otherwise known as "The Innocent," of Sandy Bar. He had met him some months before over a "little game," and had, with perfect equanimity, won the entire fortune—amounting to some forty dollars—of that guileless youth. After the game was finished, Mr. Oakhurst drew the youthful speculator behind the door and thus addressed him: "Tommy, you're a good little man, but you can't gamble worth a cent. Don't try it over again." He then handed him his money back, pushed him gently from the room, and so made a devoted slave of Tom Simson.

There was a remembrance of this in his boyish and enthusiastic greet-   12
ing of Mr. Oakhurst. He had started, he said, to go to Poker Flat to seek his fortune. "Alone?" No, not exactly alone; in fact (a giggle), he had run away with Piney Woods. Didn't Mr. Oakhurst remember Piney? She that used to wait on the table at the Temperance House? They had been engaged a long time, but old Jake Woods had objected, and so they had run away, and were going to Poker Flat to be married, and

here they were. And they were tired out, and how lucky it was they had found a place to camp, and company. All this the Innocent delivered rapidly, while Piney, a stout, comely damsel of fifteen, emerged from behind the pine tree, where she had been blushing unseen, and rode to the side of her lover.

13   Mr. Oakhurst seldom troubled himself with sentiment, still less with propriety; but he had a vague idea that the situation was not fortunate. He retained, however, his presence of mind sufficiently to kick Uncle Billy, who was about to say something, and Uncle Billy was sober enough to recognize in Mr. Oakhurst's kick a superior power that would not bear trifling. He then endeavored to dissuade Tom Simson from delaying further, but in vain. He even pointed out the fact that there was no provision, nor means of making a camp. But, unluckily, the Innocent met this objection by assuring the party that he was provided with an extra mule loaded with provisions, and by the discovery of a rude attempt at a log house near the trail. "Piney can stay with Mrs. Oakhurst," said the Innocent, pointing to the Duchess, "and I can shift for myself."

14   Nothing but Mr. Oakhurst's admonishing foot saved Uncle Billy from bursting into a roar of laughter. As it was, he felt compelled to retire up the cañon until he could recover his gravity. There he confided the joke to the tall pine trees, with many slaps of his leg, contortions of his face, and the usual profanity. But when he returned to the party, he found them seated by a fire—for the air had grown strangely chill and the sky overcast—in apparently amiable conversation. Piney was actually talking in an impulsive girlish fashion to the Duchess, who was listening with an interest and animation she had not shown for many days. The Innocent was holding forth, apparently with equal effect, to Mr. Oakhurst and Mother Shipton, who was actually relaxing into amiability. "Is this yer a d—d picnic?" said Uncle Billy, with inward scorn, as he surveyed the sylvan group, the glancing firelight, and the tethered animals in the foreground. Suddenly an idea mingled with the alcoholic fumes that disturbed his brain. It was apparently of a jocular nature, for he felt impelled to slap his leg again and cram his fist into his mouth.

15   As the shadows crept slowly up the mountain, a slight breeze rocked the tops of the pine trees and moaned through their long and gloomy aisles. The ruined cabin, patched and covered with pine boughs, was set apart for the ladies. As the lovers parted, they unaffectedly exchanged a kiss, so honest and sincere that it might have been heard above the swaying pines. The frail Duchess and the malevolent Mother Shipton were probably too stunned to remark upon this last evidence of simplicity, and so turned without a word to the hut. The fire was replenished, the men lay down before the door, and in a few minutes were asleep.

Mr. Oakhurst was a light sleeper. Toward morning he awoke be-   16
numbed and cold. As he stirred the dying fire, the wind, which was
now blowing strongly, brought to his cheek that which caused the
blood to leave it—snow!

He started to his feet with the intention of awakening the sleepers   17
for there was no time to lose. But turning to where Uncle Billy had been
lying, he found him gone. A suspicion leaped to his brain, and a curse
to his lips. He ran to the spot where the mules had been tethered—they
were no longer there. The tracks were already rapidly disappearing in
the snow.

The momentary excitement brought Mr. Oakhurst back to the fire   18
with his usual calm. He did not waken the sleepers. The Innocent slum-
bered peacefully, with a smile on his good-humored, freckled face; the
virgin Piney slept beside her frailer sisters as sweetly as though attended by celestial guardians; and Mr. Oakhurst, drawing his blanket
over his shoulders, stroked his mustaches and waited for the dawn. It
came slowly in a whirling mist of snowflakes that dazzled and confused the eye. What could be seen of the landscape appeared magically
changed. He looked over the valley, and summed up the present and
future in two words, "Snowed in!"

A careful inventory of the provisions, which, fortunately for the   19
party, had been stored within the hut, and so escaped the felonious fingers of Uncle Billy, disclosed the fact that with care and prudence they
might last ten days longer. "That is," said Mr. Oakhurst *sotto voce* to the
Innocent, "if you're willing to board us. If you ain't—and perhaps
you'd better not—you can wait till Uncle Billy gets back with provisions." For some occult reason, Mr. Oakhurst could not bring himself to
disclose Uncle Billy's rascality, and so offered the hypothesis that he
had wandered from the camp and had accidentally stampeded the animals. He dropped a warning to the Duchess and Mother Shipton, who,
of course, knew the facts of their associate's defection. "They'll find out
the truth about us *all* when they find out anything," he added significantly, "and there's no good frightening them now."

Tom Simson not only put all his worldly store at the disposal of Mr.   20
Oakhurst, but seemed to enjoy the prospect of their enforced seclusion.
"We'll have a good camp for a week, and then the snow'll melt, and
we'll all go back together." The cheerful gayety of the young man and
Mr. Oakhurst's calm infected the others. The Innocent, with the aid of
pine boughs, extemporized a thatch for the roofless cabin, and the
Duchess directed Piney in the rearrangement of the interior with a taste
and tact that opened the blue eyes of that provincial maiden to their full-
est extent. "I reckon now you're used to fine things at Poker Flat," said
Piney. The Duchess turned away sharply to conceal something that reddened her cheeks through their professional tint, and Mother Shipton
requested Piney not to "chatter." But when Mr. Oakhurst returned

from a weary search for the trail, he heard the sound of happy laughter echoed from the rocks. He stopped in some alarm, and his thoughts first naturally reverted to the whiskey, which he had prudently cached. "And yet it don't somehow sound like whiskey," said the gambler. It was not until he caught sight of the blazing fire through the still blinding storm, and the group around it, that he settled to the conviction that it was "square fun."

21   Whether Mr. Oakhurst had cached his cards with the whiskey as something debarred the free access of the community, I cannot say. It was certain that, in Mother Shipton's words, he "didn't say 'cards' once" during that evening. Haply the time was beguiled by an accordion, produced somewhat ostentatiously by Tom Simson from his pack. Notwithstanding some difficulties attending the manipulation of this instrument, Piney Woods managed to pluck several reluctant melodies from its keys, to an accompaniment by the Innocent on a pair of bone castanets. But the crowning festivity of the evening was reached in a rude camp-meeting hymn, which the lovers, joining hands, sang with great earnestness and vociferation. I fear that a certain defiant tone and Covenanter's swing to its chorus, rather than any devotional quality, caused it speedily to infect the others, who at last joined in the refrain:—

> "I'm proud to live in the service of the Lord,
> And I'm bound to die in his army."

The pines rocked, the storm eddied and whirled above the miserable group, and the flames of their altar leaped heavenward, as if in token of the vow.

22   At midnight the storm abated, the rolling clouds parted, and the stars glittered keenly above the sleeping camp. Mr. Oakhurst, whose professional habits had enabled him to live on the smallest possible amount of sleep, in dividing the watch with Tom Simson somehow managed to take upon himself the greater part of that duty. He excused himself to the Innocent by saying that he had "often been a week without sleep." "Doing what?" asked Tom. "Poker!" replied Oakhurst sententiously. "When a man gets a streak of luck—nigger-luck—he don't get tired. The luck gives in first. Luck," continued the gambler reflectively, "is a mightly queer thing. All you know about it for certain is that it's bound to change. And it's finding out when it's going to change that makes you. We've had a streak of bad luck since we left Poker Flat—you come along, and, slap, you get into it, too. If you can hold your cards right along you're all right. For," added the gambler, with cheerful irrelevance—

> "'I'm proud to live in the service of the Lord,
> And I'm bound to die in his army.'"

The third day came, and the sun, looking through the white-   23
curtained valley, saw the outcasts divide their slowly decreasing store
of provisions for the morning meal. It was one of the peculiarities of
that mountain climate that its rays diffused a kindly warmth over the
wintry landscape, as if in regretful commiseration of the past. But it revealed drift on drift of snow piled high around the hut—a hopeless,
uncharted trackless sea of white lying below the rocky shores to which
the castaways still clung. Through the marvelously clear air the smoke
of the pastoral village of Poker Flat rose miles away. Mother Shipton
saw it, and from a remote pinnacle of her rocky fastness hurled in that
direction a final malediction. It was her last vituperative attempt, and
perhaps for that reason was invested with a certain degree of sublimity.
It did her good, she privately informed the Duchess. "Just you go out
there and cuss, and see." She then set herself to the task of amusing
"the child," as she and the Duchess were pleased to call Piney. Piney
was no chicken, but it was a soothing and original theory of the pair
thus to account for the fact that she didn't swear and wasn't improper.

When night crept up again through the gorges, the reedy notes of   24
the accordion rose and fell in fitful spasms and long-drawn gasps by
the flickering camp-fire. But music failed to fill entirely the aching void
left by insufficient food, and a new diversion was proposed by Piney,—
story telling. Neither Mr. Oakhurst nor his female companions caring
to relate their personal experiences, this plan would have failed too,
but for the Innocent. Some months before he had chanced upon a stray
copy of Mr. Pope's ingenious translation of the Iliad. He now proposed
to narrate the principal incidents of that poem—having thoroughly
mastered the argument and fairly forgotten the words—in the current
vernacular of Sandy Bar. And so for the rest of that night the Homeric
demigods again walked the earth. Trojan bully and wily Greek wres-
tled in the winds, and the great pines in the cañon seemed to bow to the
wrath of the son of Peleus. Mr. Oakhurst listened with quiet satisfaction. Most especially was he interested in the fate of "Ash-heels," as the
Innocent persisted in denominating the "swift-footed Achilles."

So, with small food and much of Homer and the accordion, a week   25
passed over the heads of the outcasts. The sun again forsook them, and
again from leaden skies the snowflakes were sifted over the land. Day by
day closer around them drew the snowy circle, until at last they looked
from their prison over drifted walls of dazzling white, that towered
twenty feet above their heads. It became more and more difficult to re-
plenish their fires, even from the fallen trees beside them, now half hidden in the drifts. And yet no one complained. The lovers turned from the
dreary prospect and looked into each other's eyes, and were happy. Mr.
Oakhurst settled himself coolly to the losing game before him. The
Duchess, more cheerful than she had been, assumed the care of Piney.
Only Mother Shipton—once the strongest of the party—seemed to

sicken and fade. At midnight on the tenth day she called Oakhurst to her side. "I'm going," she said, in a voice of querulous weakness, "but don't say anything about it. Don't waken the kids. Take the bundle from under my head, and open it." Mr. Oakhurst did so. It contained Mother Shipton's rations for the last week, untouched. "Give 'em to the child," she said, pointing to the sleeping Piney. "You've starved yourself," said the gambler. "That's what they call it," said the woman querulously, as she lay down again, and turning her face to the wall, passed quietly away.

26   The accordion and the bones were put aside that day, and Homer was forgotten. When the body of Mother Shipton had been committed to the snow, Mr. Oakhurst took the Innocent aside, and showed him a pair of snow-shoes, which he had fashioned from the old pack-saddle. "There's one chance in a hundred to save her yet," he said, pointing to Piney, "but it's there," he added, pointing toward Poker Flat. "If you can reach there in two days, she's safe." "And you?" asked Tom Simson. "I'll stay here," was the curt reply.

27   The lovers parted with a long embrace. "You are not going, too?" said the Duchess, as she saw Mr. Oakhurst apparently waiting to accompany him. "As far as the cañon," he replied. He turned suddenly and kissed the Duchess, leaving her pallid face aflame, and her trembling limbs rigid with amazement.

28   Night came, but not Mr. Oakhurst. It brought the storm again and the whirling snow. Then the Duchess, feeding the fire, found that some one had quietly piled beside the hut enough fuel to last a few days longer. The tears rose to her eyes, but she hid them from Piney.

29   The women slept but little. In the morning, looking into each other's faces, they read their fate. Neither spoke, but Piney, accepting the position of the stronger, drew near and placed her arm around the Duchess's waist. They kept this attitude for the rest of the day. That night the storm reached its greatest fury, and, rending asunder the protecting vines, invaded the very hut.

30   Toward morning they found themselves unable to feed the fire, which gradually died away. As the embers slowly blackened, the Duchess crept closer to Piney, and broke the silence of many hours: "Piney, can you pray?" "No, dear," said Piney simply. The Duchess, without knowing exactly why, felt relieved, and, putting her head upon Piney's shoulder, spoke no more. And so reclining, the younger and purer pillowing the head of her soiled sister upon her virgin breast, they fell asleep.

31   The wind lulled as if it feared to waken them. Feathery drifts of snow, shaken from the long pine boughs, flew like white winged birds, and settled about them as they slept. The moon through the rifted clouds looked down upon what had been the camp. But all human stain, all trace of earthly travail, was hidden beneath the spotless mantle mercifully flung from above.

They slept all that day and the next, nor did they waken when   32
voices and footsteps broke the silence of the camp. And when pitying
fingers brushed the snow from their wan faces, you could scarcely have
told from the equal peace that dwelt upon them which was she that
had sinned. Even the law of Poker Flat recognized this, and turned
away, leaving them still locked in each other's arms.

But at the head of the gulch, on one of the largest pine trees, they   33
found the deuce of clubs pinned to the bark with a bowie-knife. It bore
the following, written in pencil in a firm hand:—

BENEATH THIS TREE

LIES THE BODY

OF

JOHN OAKHURST

WHO STRUCK A STREAK OF BAD LUCK

ON THE 23D OF NOVEMBER 1850,

AND

HANDED IN HIS CHECKS

ON THE 7TH OF DECEMBER 1850

And pulseless and cold, with a derringer by his side and a bullet in his
heart, though still calm as in life, beneath the snow lay he who was at
once the strongest and yet the weakest of the outcasts of Poker Flat.

★ Meaning and Understanding

1. Why was Poker Flat in fact "after somebody"? What had the town
   lost? What was the purpose of the secret committee?

2. Who were the people cast out of Poker Flat—particularly Oakhurst,
   "The Duchess," and Mother Shipton?

3. Where are the outcasts headed? Why? Where does the group stop
   when the Duchess insists on going no further? Why does Oakhurst admonish them?

4. Who is the newcomer, Tom Simson? Why is he called "The Innocent"?
   Who accompanies him?

5. Why did "Uncle Billy" run away with the mules? How do his actions
   affect the group's destiny?

★ Techniques and Strategies

1. What do you think is Harte's theme in this story? What point is he trying to make?

2. Irony and cynicism characterize Harte's style. Find examples to illustrate these stylistic qualities. How effective are they in the telling of the tale?

3. Are the dialogue and diction among the characters what you would expect from people like these? Why or why not?

4. Why do you think Harte informs us of the specific date of the action in the first paragraph?

5. Explain the title, "The Outcasts of Poker Flat." Defend Harte's choice of it as the title for the story. How are the characters outcasts? How are the characters not outcasts? What significance do you find in the name of the town itself?

★ Speaking of Values

1. Of what "crimes" were the outcasts guilty? What kind of justice would you say prevails in Poker Flat? What positive and (or) negative values do you see in this kind of justice?

2. Some critics see Harte's characters here as overly sympathetic and sentimental portrayals of crooks, vagabonds, and pariahs. Why might you agree or disagree with that point of view?

3. Which characters would you say undergo a transformation amid the adversity they meet in the story? What transforms them? What other incidents of adversity do you know of from your reading or experience that have had an ennobling effect on people?

4. What does the story say about the value of community and cooperation? Why is it important that the group of misfits projects this value?

5. In the final analysis, who would you see are the moral people in the tale: the townspeople of Poker Flat or the group of misfits banished from the town? Why?

★ Values Conversation

Form groups to discuss the relation between individualism and community values. Using Harte's story as a springboard, weigh the relative merits in each. Consider Uncle Billy—who no doubt survived by individualism—against the remaining group—who did not survive despite their strong sense of community. When should we act as individuals? When should we act for the good of the group?

★ *Writing about Values*

1. Have you ever been in a difficult or life-threatening position along with other people? Write a paper describing the event. Be sure to comment on any changes that occurred in the way that people acted, or dealt with one another, or felt.

2. Choose another work you may be familiar with that deals with a person or group of people in an extreme situation—*Lord of the Flies,* "To Build a Fire," *Titanic, Alive,* and so on. Write a paper comparing and contrasting the work with the characters and events in "The Outcasts of Poker Flat."

3. Write a paper to explain why Harte calls Oakhurst "at once the strongest and yet the weakest of the outcasts of Poker Flat."

Marjorie Miller
and Ricardo Chavira

A Unique Culture Grows in the Desert

Marjorie Miller and Ricardo Chavira were staff writers for the *San Diego Union* when this article appeared in 1983. In it they examine the blending of Mexican and U.S. cultures along the common border of the two nations.

———— ★ ————

1 Highway 80, a blacktop ribbon of road through scrub brush and hill after rugged hill, unfolds to the south toward Douglas. The windswept Arizona highway leads to the 1,900-mile border where Mexico and the United States stand face to face in a barren land.

2   At the border, the highway joins a trio of narrow Mexican highways that also traverse the arid geography.

3   But there are more than lonesome roads among the scrub brush. These Mexican and American highways form a network that connects far-apart towns and cities from San Diego to Brownsville, Texas; from Tijuana to Matamoros, Tamaulipas.

4   It is in these remote border cities, far from national capitals, that the United States and Mexico not only meet but merge to form a new society.

5   It is a society of people like Elsa Vega and Celia Díaz, both of whom grew up south of the border, but now live north. It is people like Barney Thompson and William Arens, who married women from Tijuana but live in San Diego.

6   It is Robert Bracker, whose father built a store in Nogales, Arizona to serve Mexican customers, or Pablo Hourani, who lives in Bonita and commutes south daily to run his family clothing business. Or Leobardo Estrada of Los Angeles, the grandson of Mexican immigrants whose family still extends south to Tijuana.

7   At the border, a wealthy technological superpower meets a developing agricultural nation; a predominantly Anglo-Protestant people encounters a society of *mestizos,* Indians, and Spanish Catholics.

8   Here on the border a 200-year-old, upstart culture meets one with roots that predate Christ. Together they meld into a new, third culture of the borderlands that blurs the very border from which it was born.

734

This barren land has been fertile ground after all, fertile for a cul- 9
ture that has flourished in part because of its isolation. The border culture has had room to grow in the desert.

It has grown in Mexican cities like Mexicali, where the land once 10
belonged to American developers, and in Tijuana, which was so isolated that until the 1940s Tijuanans had to pass through the United
States to visit their mainland.

It has grown in American cities like Laredo and Calexico, where 11
the mainstream is a Hispanic majority.

The culture of the borderlands is a binational world where Mexi- 12
cans are becoming more Americanized and where Americans are becoming more Mexicanized. It is an area, sometimes hundreds of miles
wide, where families, businesses, languages, and values from the two
countries often are entwined as tightly as the chain link fence that attempts to separate them.

While not all of the cities and the 7 million people who live along 13
the U.S.-Mexico boundary belong to the binational culture, there is a
border society that is distinct from Mexico and the United States.

In parts, the border culture reaches as far north as Santa Barbara 14
and San Antonio, Texas, as far south as La Paz in Baja California Sur,
and Chihuahua City, Chihuahua.

In a few instances, the borderlands culture crops up like an island 15
far from the international boundary, such as in Chicago—where Mexican immigrants have converted old neighborhoods into replicas of border communities.

By and large, the culture clings to the area along the U.S.-Mexico 16
border, where people might live in one country and work or go to
school in another.

It is where Americans and Mexicans intermarry and have children 17
who are dual citizens for the first 18 years of their lives, until they must
choose one country or the other.

It is a region where the people speak English and Spanish and of- 18
ten a third language, Spanglish, that is a hybrid of the two.

And it is a society where certain businesses exist simply because 19
the border exists—businesses like currency exchange houses, import-
export brokerage firms, and drive-through Mexican car insurance
agencies—and where businessmen must learn to operate in two cultures so that after years of doing so they become bicultural.

The border society is made up of towns and cities that experience in- 20
ternational issues, like illegal immigration, as local problems. Pollution,
sewage, and natural disasters affect Mexican and American border cities
equally, because such problems do not respect an international boundary.

Society on the border is united by footbridge, ferry and bus; by bi- 21
lingual radio and television; by millions of people who legally cross the

border hundreds of times each year, and by countless others who cross illegally.

22   It is a society in which the local economies on each side of the border often are more attached to one another than to the mother country's.

23   It is a society that is slightly scorned by both Mexico and the United States for its unconventional behavior.

24   Even some of the cities have blended. Take Calexico and Mexicali—on opposite sides of the border, but both named by the Colorado Land River Co. from the words California and Mexico. And cities such as Columbus, New Mexico, and its neighbor Palomas, Chihuahua, that have merged in other ways, helping to sustain each other.

25   Many Columbus residents have family in Palomas, while nearly half of Columbus' schoolchildren are from the border's other side. Columbus provides the Mexican town with ambulance and fire services. Mexicans commonly use the hospital on the U.S. side, the only one in the area.

26   On the other hand, Palomas is still the place where Columbus residents go to eat bargain-priced steak dinners and drink hearty Mexican beer. And despite Mexico's ailing economy, Columbus still relies on Mexican shoppers to spend money in the U.S. town.

27   But this binational blend is not spread evenly along the boundary. The border society is not homogeneous.

28   The border region is the wealthiest in Mexico, but one of the poorest regions of the United States.

29   Its people are a mix of pioneers who have called the frontier home for generations, and a generation of new settlers who arrived yesterday from Ohio or Oaxaca, from Michigan or Michoacan.

30   There are people living along the boundary line who are so oblivious to the new, third culture that they might be nearer the Canadian border. There are fourth, fifth, sixth cultures, such as that of the Kickapoo Indians in Texas, the Chinese of Mexicali, the Filipinos of San Ysidro, that exist under the umbrella of the border society. And there are differences between urban and rural people, the rich and poor, Texans and Californians.

31   In fact, those who are totally immersed in the border culture are a minority. Far greater are the numbers who dip in and out, whose cross-border experience might be limited to occasional shopping or dining in the other country, whose cross-cultural experience might be limited to Mexicans seeing an American movie or to San Diegans living next door to a family whose mother tongue is Spanish.

32   Some might be touched by the border only because they work with Americans or employ a Mexican. But inevitably, bits and pieces of the culture rub off—exposure to another language or lifestyle, a conversion from dollars to pesos or kilometers to miles, a sketchy knowledge of the history of another country, a familiarity with its holidays and traditions.

While some people who live in the border culture embrace it as a   33
positive and inevitable change, others are hostile toward it for fear it
will degrade their own culture.

The history of the border begins with such antagonism.   34

After a two-year war between Mexico and the United States, the   35
present-day border was drawn up, which cost Mexico nearly half its
territory. Mutual hate and distrust poisoned relations, and for years after the conquest Americans and Mexicans launched cross-border raids
against each other.

Mexico later decided to put up the only barrier it had—people—to   36
prevent Americans from capturing more land by simply moving onto
it. The government in the 1930s made it a national policy to entice Mexicans to move north—ironically, by offering them access to cheap
American goods.

More recently, Mexicans in the interior have chastised those north-   37
ern Mexicans for becoming too Americanized and too dependent on
American goods.

Today, many Mexicans see the cultural encroachment of the United   38
State in Mexico as a further "occupation" of their country. Many Americans, on the other hand, fear that Mexicans are slowly reconquering
the Southwest with *their* cultural encroachment.

Just as the border is not homogeneous, neither is it completely   39
unified.

Conflicts, clashes and contradictions have developed out of the in-   40
teraction between two such diverse peoples: Mexicans and Americans.

On both sides of the border, there is the necessary mutual depen-   41
dence of neighbors. But respect and friendship often have combined
with resentment and racism to form a love-hate relationship.

There is suspicion and scorn on both sides.   42

Americans who value speed and efficiency often huff if Mexican   43
goods break down or service is slow; Mexicans, on the other hand,
sometimes turn up their noses at Americans whom they feel are rush-
ing through life too fast to appreciate living it.

Many Mexicans are envious of American wealth while, at the same   44
time, they are put off by the individualism, egotism, and selfishness
that they believe goes with it. They are offended by American haughti-
ness and bluntness.

A mythology has evolved on both sides that leads Americans to be-   45
lieve all Mexican police will demand a bribe or throw them in jail, and
Mexicans to believe that U.S. businessmen always are honest and that
U.S. authorities always will deal with them fairly.

U.S. police along the border patrol America's underbelly. It is 1,900   46
miles of largely unprotected boundary that is vulnerable to anyone determined enough to enter or to bring something into the country.

47   Even in an era of sophisticated electronic surveillance, millions of people and billions of dollars of narcotics find their way north, while stolen cars, high-tech equipment, and top-secret defense documents flow south. It is that permeability that scares Americans.

48   Mexicans, meanwhile, have heard horror stories about discrimination in the United States and for that reason some are wary of going north.

49   Americans continue to picture the Mexican border as replete with good-time towns of sleazy, honky-tonk bars where anything is for sale for the right price. Some of that does exist, yet Americans played a large role in the creation of that Mexico in the '20s and '30s during Prohibition.

50   While spending their dollars for fun, Americans developed a double standard, frowning on Mexico for being "that kind of place."

51   Mexicans invoked their own double standard, profiting from the indulgence while disapproving of Americans for acting as they would not act at home.

52   Misconceptions and misunderstandings about border life still exist, but they are not unique to the border. They exist away from the border—in Mexico City and Washington, D.C., among other places.

53   For all that border residents criticize each other, however, they are becoming more tolerant of each other and more alike.

54   U.S. border residents who do business in Mexico learn to temper some of their American straightforwardness with a little Mexican graciousness. Mexican businessmen learn to speed up their timetables to meet Americans' habits, so that a 2 P.M. lunch in Tijuana becomes a noon lunch in San Diego.

55   American hostesses who invite guests from south of the border learn to time their evenings accordingly, because one never knows how long it will take to cross the border.

56   Many border Mexicans want their children schooled in the United States to learn English, but send them to Catholic schools to make sure they preserve traditional values of family, religion, and respect.

57   A few Americans send their children south to learn proper Spanish.

58   Tastes have changed along the U.S. border.

59   From California to Texas, tacos and burritos have become as American as apple pie—so American, in fact, that the way they are prepared is foreign to many Mexicans from the interior.

60   While Mexican restaurants are just now becoming an expensive fad in New York, rare is the shopping mall or hotel center along the border without at least one Mexican restaurant—fast-food or fancy.

61   And products from both countries intermingle easily on supermarket shelves for people whose tastes include chilies and Idaho potatoes, tortillas and grits.

Some holidays are heartily celebrated on both sides of the border. 62
In the United States, Cinco de Mayo has become the St. Patrick's Day of
the Southwest. Border Mexicans have become attuned to American
holidays such as July Fourth, Labor Day, and Memorial Day, if only because they mean added business over long weekends.

U.S. sports teams in the borderlands are vigorously supported by 63
thousands of Mexican fans. While Mexicans head north to see football
and baseball, Americans head south for bullfights, cockfights, and jai
alai.

For residents of the binational society, the border is united by co- 64
operation among peoples through charity and neighborliness, among
businesses through joint ventures, and governments through joint
projects.

Despite the rugged terrain of scrub brush and fear, the border is not 65
a barrier but a network of relationships and opportunities: The people
who straddle the boundary guarantee that the border society will continue to grow in the desert.

★ Meaning and Understanding

1. What, according to the writers, is the significance of the fact that Highway 80 joins with "a trio of Mexican highways"?

2. What is the "new, third culture of the borderlands" referred to in paragraph 8? How does it blur the culture "from which it was born"? Why
   is the border society "slightly scorned by both Mexico and the United
   States" (paragraph 23)?

3. What are some of the border cities, both Mexican and American, in
   which the new culture has grown? What are some distinguishing features of the border culture? How have some cities blended?

4. In paragraph 47 the authors suggest that there is a "permeability" about
   the border that "scares Americans." What do they mean by "permeability" and in what way is it frightening to Americans?

5. What mythology has evolved that leads to certain expectations by
   Americans and Mexicans? Why do you think this mythology has come
   to pass? How, in fact, have Mexicans and Americans learned to become more tolerant of each other?

★ Techniques and Strategies

1. In paragraphs 5 and 6 the authors provide a short catalogue of border
   residents. What is their purpose for doing so?

2. The essay is made up of a number of relatively short sentences and paragraphs. How does this technique contribute to your understanding of the main point?

3. What is the tone of this essay? Who is the intended audience? How do you know?

4. Why do the authors provide a brief history of the border beginning with paragraph 34?

5. What is the thesis of the essay?

★ Speaking of Values

1. This essay speaks to the issue of cultural values. What are cultural values and how are they determined and developed? Should cultural values be maintained at all costs? Why or why not?

2. Is there a distinct American culture? If so, how would you define it? If not, then what exists in its place?

3. Many people are children of mixed heritage. How does mixed heritage affect one's understanding of culture? One's cultural identity?

4. Some people argue that border cultures exist not only at true junctures of countries but also between neighborhoods within our cities and states. Would you agree with this position? Why or why not? How may two cultures living in one city create a border culture? What similarities and differences do you see between such border cultures and the ones introduced in this piece?

5. What do Miller and Chavira suggest by the statement in paragraph 28 that "the border region is the wealthiest in Mexico, but one of the poorest regions of the United States"?

★ Values Conversation

Form groups and discuss the advantages and disadvantages you see in mixing cultures. How are the two groups enriched? Challenged? What mixed cultures have you observed?

★ Writing about Values

1. Imagine what life in a border culture would be like and write an essay about your experiences on one day. Try to indicate the strengths and hardships you would face.

2. Consult a map and select a town that is on the U.S. border with Mexico or Canada. Then do some library research on that town to discover the ways in which the two cultures accommodate themselves to one another. Write a paper reporting on the results of your research.

3. Write a paper called "Border: Barrier or Opportunity" in which you present your views on the issues raised in this selection.

Melissa Healy

Fighting to Fill
the Values Gap

Melissa Healy is a staff writer for the *Los Angeles Times,* in which this
piece appeared in 1996. Healy explores what people say is the moral decline in America, their suspicion of political leaders who promise redress,
and how individual citizens are taking the matters in their own hands.

1   "Values? *Values???*" asks 37-year-old Lila Robinson, her pitch rising as
she warms to her subject. "I've been waiting for someone to ask me
about this for years! Hold on a sec, let me get my soapbox!"

2   For Robinson, proof of the nation's moral slide is everywhere. She
is irked by the kids who tromp down the grass as they cut across the
lawn of her family's new home in Brunswick, Ohio. She gets even more
steamed when she dares not chastise the teenage trespassers for fear
trouble might ensue.

3   She fumes over a kid punching loaves of bread in the supermarket
and over his mother spewing expletives when a stranger suggests he
stop. She smolders over a sister's divorce and the fact that the parents
play their children off one another.

4   Yet she has little use for politicians and activists who patter on
about family values and seek to legislate common virtues, such as civility, compassion, respect and responsibility. She suspects that they
would like to curtail some of the freedoms she cherishes.

5   Robinson, a "bleeding-heart liberal who realizes the government
can't do it all," prefers to take matters into her own hands. Acknowledging candidly that "some of the things I did when I was single and
crazed were wrong," she is determined to teach her children to avoid
her mistakes—without denying that she made them.

6   Robinson's worries—as well as her response—put her on the front
lines of a social movement that has millions of foot soldiers but few, if any,
field marshals. Convinced that the nation is suffering from a values decline of crisis proportions, more and more Americans are fighting back.

7   Some have embraced legislative remedies ranging from tightening
up divorce laws to restricting welfare benefits. Others, like Robinson,
are wary of government intervention and believe that the answer lies
within communities, families and individuals—including themselves.

742

At home, she and others are making more time for their children   8
by returning to family meals or turning off the TV. Others are reaching
out to neighbors to organize fathers' groups or plan new school curricula designed to teach good character.

While many still tend to blame others for society's ills, a sizable mi-   9
nority says it is willing to change its behavior and accept some limits
on civil liberties for the common good. Thus, moved by concern for
plunging social standards, they agree to make their kids wear uniforms
to public school, or they embrace technologies that would black out unwanted TV programs at home.

"There's a growing sense that we stand at a cultural crossroads,"   10
said Thomas Lickona, an education professor at the State University of
New York, Cortland, and a leader of the character education movement. "Either we reverse the current trends or continue the slide and
go down the tubes."

For many Americans, particularly baby boomers now entering   11
middle age, the values movement is an attempt to synthesize the best
elements of the "do-your-own-thing" philosophy of the 1960s and '70s
with the social stability of an earlier era.

"We're having a debate now we simply couldn't have 15 years   12
ago," said William Galston, 50, a public administration professor at the
University of Maryland and a former domestic policy advisor to President Clinton. "I don't think we're going to end up back in the 1950s,
but I don't think we're going to remain tied to the kind of revolt against
the 1950s. We are looking for a new balance."

Amitai Etzioni, a George Washington University professor, leads   13
the "communitarian" movement that helped launch the current debate. He asserts that when Americans limit their behavior for the good
of the community, they do not feel as if they have made sacrifices or
forfeited freedoms. They feel as if their personal choices have helped
build a more cohesive, supportive community.

"Today, everybody's free to do anything, but it's not what they   14
want," Etzioni said. "It's not liberating; it's not freedom." The debate
over values and what to do about them, he adds, "is a clear indication
we're groping for new ways to come together and, yes, impose some
requirements on ourselves."

Mention the V-word across the country and you will hear the hiss and   15
bubble of a thousand stories boiling over the top. Some come from the TV
news or the headlines, but most originate in their tellers' backyards,
schools and workplaces. Stories of friends on welfare getting pregnant
again, of whole college classes conspiring to cheat on a test. Stories of parents worried sick that nice clothes may mark their children for violence.

The stories reflect a powerful feeling among Americans that the na-   16
tion's sense of right and wrong—its moral compass—is dangerously

out of kilter. "It just seems like not many people have morals," said Myorka Cummings, a 24-year-old homemaker in Marshalltown, Iowa. "They don't seem to care about their neighbor. They'd just as soon rob him as come over and say hi."

17   Americans, notes pollster Peter Hart, "look at all the basics of our society and see them going in a direction they're uncomfortable with. They look at schools and they see violence. That scares them. They look at the media and they see [TV] programs they find unacceptable and that go beyond bounds of public decency. They look at athletic fields and see behavior they do not consider good sportsmanship. They look at the institution of family and marriage and they see breakups."

18   In a Los Angeles Times Poll conducted nationwide April 13–16, 78% of respondents said they were dissatisfied with today's moral values. Of that group, 47% identified family issues such as divorce, working parents and undisciplined children as the main causes. Another 34% blamed a breakdown in personal responsibility and community involvement.

19   The anxieties cross lines of race, age, gender, income and region. They spread well beyond the political bounds of religious conservatives, who have dominated debate on family values for much of the past decade.

20   Charles Dewane, a 27-year-old unmarried father in Detroit, says he "is trying to go the right way—the straight and narrow." He is engaged to the mother of his child, he says, and he takes an active role in his care.

21   As he sees it, the trouble with society is "punk parents raising kids, not giving their kids any values or morals." A self-described member of "a lost education generation," he has decided to do better by 8-month-old Charles Dewane Jr.

22   Although Dewane, who installs heating and cooling systems, has not attended church in years, he plans to send his son to parochial school because "people who send their kids to Catholic schools give a damn."

23   Marsha "Pat" Maliszewski, 49, is a mother of two and until recently a marketing representative for a small computer firm. She quit her job this spring to devote herself full time to organizing a community-wide forum on "character" in Battle Creek, Mich. The wife of a police officer, she hears a daily litany of stories attesting to a moral slide in her city of 35,000.

24   Maybe, she concluded, if she could bring together liberals and conservatives, teachers and church people, artists and bank tellers and corporate leaders from the town's largest employer, Kellogg Co., they could talk about common values. Maybe they could even forge a consensus on how those values could be reinforced in everyday life.

25   As a result, Battle Creek will have its first countywide community meeting on character and ethics June 18–21. The planned sessions, at

which almost three dozen community leaders will be trained in ethical decision-making, have drawn an enthusiastic crowd of all stripes. "We're on fire out here," said Maliszewski, who hopes the forum will result in programs in schools, churches, workplaces and athletic fields.

The seed was planted when she attended a lecture on teaching chil- 26
dren good character. It prompted her to examine the daily compromises and white lies that had chipped away at her own sense of right and wrong. Now, she says, "it is time to walk the walk," and she is determined to take her ethics mission statewide.

For the nearly 63 million Americans with children at home, the 27
values debate is both especially urgent and difficult. The bulk of those parents grew up in the 1960s, '70s or '80s, when younger Americans embraced freedom of expression and self-actualization with near-religious fervor.

Today, divorce rates have doubled since 1960, crime rates are soar- 28
ing, educational standards are slipping and civic debate is increasingly uncivil. And these children of a rebellious age are asking themselves if perhaps too many people have chosen to do their own thing. They suspect that their rebellion, while rooting out some of the 1950s' ugliest prejudices and loosening some of its most constricting mores, also might have damaged some of society's basic institutions and erected little to replace them.

"Basically I feel I'm very openminded, very liberal," says Emalie 29
Mobarekeh, 45, a mother of two and part-time middle-school teacher in Sarasota, Fla. But groups that she has supported, like the American Civil Liberties Union, "keep wanting to push the norms of society further and further.

"I think, how much more are people going to take and say OK to? 30
And I'm not a right-winger! They say you've got to accept this—say, gay girls and homosexuals adopting kids. All this deviation from the norm? I don't know. It bothers me after a while."

Now with children at home, parents like her are painfully aware of 31
their responsibility to impart a sense not only of what is wrong with society but of what is right and wrong for individuals. And for children of the nonjudgmental 1960s and 1970s that often is a wrenching adjustment.

"We've engaged in a generation-long experiment, testing the limits 32
of individual freedom and its social consequences," said Galston, the University of Maryland professor. "My sense is that a lot of people about my age are reassessing the balance that our generation struck in its youth and are looking for a new balance. . . . They've discovered that the values and practices and ways of thinking they embraced when young turned out to be a double-edged sword and that raising children calls upon us to reconsider lots of things."

As a result, polls today indicate a surprising willingness among 33
Americans to disapprove of other people's personal decisions that they

believe have hurt society. Half of Americans, for instance, say they believe that it is always or almost always wrong for a woman to have a child out of wedlock, and 46% say they believe that it is always or almost always wrong to have sex outside of marriage.

34   The conflicting themes of freedom and order are one of democracy's perennial tensions, and demographers argue that surging tides of social conservatism recur at regular intervals in the American body politic. Making the latest outbreak of soul-searching noteworthy are the extreme demographic and societal spikes that have prompted it—a rise in violent crime, a surge in divorce and single-parent families, a stubborn drug problem.

35   Stephen Carter, 41, who teaches law and ethics at Yale University, says there is another factor that makes the current round of moral fretting unique:

36   "This is the first era in our public's history where people feel queasy about discussing publicly notions of right and wrong." In the wake of the 1960s and '70s, he adds, "some people feel incorrectly that public discussion of right and wrong is a threat to individual freedom. It's not. They fear that because they think that if most people are against something, they want to make it illegal. But that's not the point of moral conversation. Only in America do we think that talking about right and wrong means we want to legislate it."

37   While the impulse to legislate morality is a powerful theme in American society, it is counterbalanced by an equally powerful mistrust of the government and of politicians as arbiters of the nation's values. The result, a deep ambivalence about the values debate, helps explain Americans' fitful efforts to effect legislative changes that address the problems they see.

38   The Times Poll dramatically illustrates the conflicts and contradictions that shade Americans' views about public values.

39   A 57% majority, for instance, says that "too many people have lifestyles and beliefs which are harmful to themselves and society," and that those are a greater danger than intolerance for other people's lifestyles and beliefs.

40   Cast the question in terms of government intervention, however, and majority support quickly evaporates.

41   The poll asked people to identify which annoyed them more: government intrusion into citizens' private lives or government's protecting activities that flout traditional family values. A slim majority of 52% found government intrusion the greater irritant, while 36% said they are more annoyed by government protection of activities that run counter to "family values."

42   Part of the public's ambivalence about legislative remedies appears to reflect the fact that few Americans blame themselves for having contributed to the social ills they bemoan. As a result, say pollsters, they

are reluctant to embrace government interventions that could crimp their own freedoms along with those of the people they blame for the values breakdown.

The Times Poll suggested that only 11% of respondents say they   43
believe that their own behavior has contributed to the moral problems the nation faces. Similarly, 96% say they believe that they are doing an excellent or good job teaching their children about morals and values. But those numbers don't square with their perception of how others are behaving: 93% say that parents are not taking enough responsibility for teaching their children moral values.

For all of Americans' qualms about government intrusion, an   44
overwhelming majority expect government to do *something* to support families.

In a January poll conducted as part of the University of Texas' Na-   45
tional Issues Convention, 92% said they would like government to strengthen families and family values with benefits such as child care and preschool. Increasingly, Americans are looking to their public schools to teach and reinforce civic and personal virtues with character education. And large majorities have supported legislation that would give parents the V-chip to limit their children's TV and computer expo-sure to sex and violence.

American parents, says Sen. Joseph I. Lieberman (D-Conn.), "want   46
help" from the government. At a minimum, he adds, "they want to feel that we [politicians] get it, that we understand what they're going through—that there's a values problem in this country, and that we're going to do what we can to put ourselves on their side."

Americans such as Agnes Shelton, 32, a homemaker from Greene-   47
ville, Tenn., echo that sense:

"It's hard to say where the government should start at. If they   48
would even honor families being together instead of separate" it would be an improvement.

But how much help Americans want, Lieberman adds, "is not yet   49
clear." Inside Congress, he says, "we're hesitant to go too far."

Nevertheless, the perceived values crisis has become a potent elec-   50
toral issue for politicians across the spectrum. Four years ago, Republican Vice President Dan Quayle ignited acrimonious debate when he criticized television's Murphy Brown, an unmarried woman, for having a child.

These days, Clinton regularly makes the same point, decrying out-   51
of-wedlock births and popular entertainment that glamorizes sex and single parenthood. He exhorts Americans to teach virtue in public schools, to stay together as families, to be better parents and to "over-come the notion that self-gratification is more important than our obli-gation to others."

And Clinton appears to have met with some success in laying   52
claim to issues that traditionally have belonged to Republicans. The

Times Poll found that 39% of respondents say they believe that Democrats have the best ideas for handling family values and morality, while 37% favor Republicans' views.

53   Many Americans appear willing to let politicians take the debate much further than it has gone in decades. They are urging state and national legislators to pass laws addressing what most see as the cause of declining values today—the breakdown of the family:

- In several states, legislatures are debating restrictions on the rights of couples with children to divorce.
- Congress has proposed to cut off welfare payments to women who bear additional children out of wedlock, and many states are proceeding with experimental programs to do so.
- States have adopted aggressive programs to track down divorced spouses who do not pay child support.
- Many politicians say they are determined to get rid of the marriage penalty that is a byproduct of the federal income tax system. Some propose offering stay-at-home spouses tax breaks.

54   On the home front, the debate over the nation's moral standards is less public and less clamorous. But when parents take steps to act on their convictions at home, their actions may well have the greatest impact, for it is here that most Americans agree that children learn their values.

55   While Americans remain reluctant to subject their own behavior to criticism or limitations, many are wrestling with personal decisions that they know have broader social consequences. And many, moved by the conviction that public virtue must begin in private, are making decisions they might not have made in the prevailing climate of a decade ago.

56   Thus when parents stay together for the sake of their children, when they attend school meetings about curriculum changes, when an unmarried woman decides not to have a baby on her own, or a man decides that an office assignment should not take precedence over his daughter's soccer tournament, each—wittingly or not—has taken a stand in a debate over personal and public values.

57   Americans have always made personal choices with powerful public consequences. In the current ferment over values, however, many are explicitly considering broader social concerns as factors in their personal decisions.

58   That is the kind of decision Mike Rademacher, a farmer in Longmont, Colo., and his wife, Vicki, made some years ago. Parents of children who are now 14 and 7, the Rademachers decided that Vicki should quit her job as a secretary, sacrificing an income that in many

FIGURE 11.1 *Result of the Times Poll on Moral Values*

An overwhelming majority of Americans say they are dissatisfied with the nation's moral values these days. They cite the breakdown of the family unit as one of the top reasons for their discontent. Therefore, it is not surprising that many agree that it is better to raise children in a house where there are two parents and that divorce should be made more difficult to obtain.

Satisfied or dissatisfied?

Would you say you are satisfied or dissat-isfied with moral values these days?

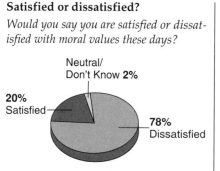

Neutral/
Don't Know **2%**

20%
Satisfied

78%
Dissatisfied

Why they're dissatisfied

Why are you dissatisfied with the nation's moral values? (among respondents who say they are dissatisfied; two answers accepted; net answers shown)

Breakdown in family	47%
Lack of community involvement	34
Crime	12
Too much sex/violence in movies/TV	11
Lack of religion	5
Schools not strict enough/ should teach civics	5

Parents' role

Do you agree or disagree with the following statement: "Parents today are not taking enough responsibility for teaching their kids moral values?"

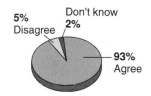

Don't know
2%
5%
Disagree

93%
Agree

Two-parent families

Do you agree or disagree with the following statement: "It's always best for children to be raised in a home where a married man and woman are living together as father and mother?"

Agree	71%
Disagree	28
Don't know	1

Poll also found...

42% believe divorce should be more difficult to obtain (9% say easier).

83% believe the way TV shows depict sex tends to encourage immorality.

91% of parents have rules limiting what the children can watch or listen to.*

Source: *Los Angeles Times* Poll.

Note: Numbers may not add up to 100% where more than one response was accepted or not all answer categories are shown.

*Parents with children under 18 responded to this question.

years outstripped her husband's, so that the children would have a parent available at any time.

59   "Parental involvement is the backbone of our society, and that's been lost" in an economy in which a second income is often necessary to "afford the basics or buy the extras," said Mike Rademacher, one of several Times Poll respondents who discussed his views with a reporter. "It was our decision that raising our family was more important than the monetary value" of Vicki's income.

60   It is a choice, he says, that he would like to see more parents make, although he sees no role for government in prodding such decisions. "It'd be good for everybody," he said, "especially the kids."

61   To many experts, the public policy debates that swirl around the values issues are bellwethers of a larger movement: Americans, they say, appear ready to forfeit some measure of their cherished freedoms in the interest of restoring a lost sense of community.

62   The search for that new balance point may be hinted at in the Times Poll. Asked if they would be willing to abridge civil liberties—such as censoring television—to improve the nation's moral climate, 17% said they would not and more than twice as many—35%—said they would.

63   As Americans experiment with new ways to restore their sense of lost community and family values, some see a corner turned.

64   Brenda Clark, principal of Azalea Elementary School in St. Petersburg, Fla., has struggled to improve the quality of teaching and to restore a sense of accountability among students and teachers. Her latest bid to improve the learning environment involves mandatory uniforms for kids starting in September. She has been heartened by the reaction.

65   "I think people are saying, 'Enough! We've had enough of this! Let's get back to what is right and good,'" she said. "I think we've hit bottom and are heading back."

★ *Meaning and Understanding*

1. What evidence does Lisa Robinson offer as proof of the "nation's moral slide"?

2. How, according to the writer, are many Americans fighting "a values decline of crisis proportions"?

3. What is the "values movement" mentioned in paragraph 11?

4. Why is the values debate "especially urgent and difficult" for Americans with children?

5. Why is the public ambivalent about legislative remedies? What, according to Healy, do a majority of Americans expect government to do to support families? Why, in this context, do some Americans support forfeiting some of their freedoms?

6. What do you think is the main point of this essay?

★ *Techniques and Strategies*

1. Look at the first paragraph. In what way does the statement by Lila Robinson set the stage for the rest of the essay?

2. In paragraphs 10–14, Healy presents some observations from college professors. And in paragraphs 20–24 we hear from an unmarried father and a mother of two. In what way do these comments help you understand the point Healy is trying to make?

3. Where does Healy use transitions effectively to make the ideas in the selection cohere?

4. Where do you find the use of data or expert testimony most effective? Least effective? Why?

5. Who is the intended audience for this piece? How can you tell?

★ *Speaking of Values*

1. Do you believe, on the evidence of this article and from your own experience, that a values decline in America has reached a stage of crisis? Why? How does our current society compare with earlier ones in regard to values, do you think?

2. In your opinion should the government legislate morality? Can it? Why do you think so? When has government tried to do so? What results have we seen as a result?

3. In paragraph 30 one citizen complains about "all this deviation from the norm." Who determines social norms? Under what circumstances should Americans follow these norms? Challenge them?

4. Healy suggests in this essay that many Americans harbor "a powerful mistrust of the government and of politicians as arbiters of the nation's values." Do you agree? Why or why not? Why are some people mistrustful of the government and of politicians? Do they have reason to be? Explain.

5. Healy quotes a Yale law professor who asserts: "This is the first era in our public's history where people feel queasy about discussing publicly notions of right and wrong." Do you agree with this statement? Why or why not? Why would people be reluctant to discuss right and wrong in public?

6. Do you agree with Healy that "public virtue must begin in private"? Why or why not?

★ *Values Conversation*

Form groups and consider all the individual rights you surrender even on a daily basis for the good of the larger community. Discuss how you feel about your sacrifice. In other words, how much do you lose and how much do you gain by doing so?

★ Writing about Values

1. Eighteenth-century philosopher Jean-Jacques Rousseau posited the idea that people voluntarily give up their "natural freedoms" in order to formulate laws so that they might live together in civilized societies. Are there any laws you can think of which seem unnecessary to you? That is, are there behaviors people would or would not practice even if there were no laws concerning them? Write a paper identifying these laws and the behaviors they relate to and discuss why you think the laws are not necessary.

2. Write a process paper explaining to parents how to rear their children in an appropriate moral framework. Draw on your own family experiences and, if you like, on external sources as well—books, articles, discussions with experts.

3. Many of the people interviewed in Healy's article believe that America is engaged in some kind of "moral slide." Do you agree that our society is less moral than it used to be? Write a paper discussing this issue. Be sure that you make an attempt to define what you mean by a "moral society." Also, you might wish to take a look at certain TV shows—Happy Days, The Waltons, and so on—to consider how the media help us view the past in a moral context.

Lucie Prinz

Say Something:
They're Only Children

Lucie Prinz is a staff editor at the *Atlantic*. Born in 1931, she attended the University of Chicago. She is a cowriter with Victor Weisskopf of *The Joy of Insight*. In this essay she examines the role adults should play in disciplining children.

———— ★ ————

I was sitting on the subway a few weeks ago when I looked up and saw a baby, just a little less than a year old, swinging from the overhead bar. She was flanked by two young teenage girls who thought this was a great way to entertain their little sister. As the train began to move, I could visualize the baby flying across the car. Without really thinking, I said to the girls, "Hey, that's not a good idea. That baby is going to get hurt. You better sit down with her on the seat." The kids gave me one of those "Who do you think you are?" looks they reserve for meddling adults, but they took the baby off the bar and sat down.

I was suddenly struck by the silence in the subway car. The normal hum of conversation had vanished. My fellow passengers, who had witnessed my encounter with the kids, were now engrossed in their newspapers and books or staring at something fascinating on the subway-tunnel wall. The car was not very crowded, and everyone had seen that endangered baby just as clearly as I had, but they had chosen not to get involved. Although most of them now avoided eye contact with me, a few treated me to the kind of disdain reserved for troublemakers. Could it be that my fellow passengers didn't care about that baby? Or were they just afraid to interfere?

We've all heard the old African saying "It takes a whole village to raise a child." Americans have adopted it, and I understand why. It expresses some things that we can all easily accept: family values, shared responsibility, community spirit. But do we really believe in it as a guiding principle for our lives? When we repeat it, are we pledging ourselves to carry out its imperative? I don't think so.

Americans are known for generosity. We're ready to rescue the suffering children of the world. We send food to Ethiopia after our television screens show us little kids with huge eyes and distended bellies. We help the victims of floods, and we fund agencies to take care of refugees and abandoned children. We are the nation that invented the poster child and the telethon. These nameless suffering children touch our hearts—but they do not touch our lives.

5   The same adults who are profoundly moved by the plight of children they will never know seem to be willing to ignore the children they encounter every day, even if it is obvious that these children are in trouble or that they need a little adult guidance. I've watched adults actually move away from children they see approaching. I'm not talking about hostile, swaggering gangs of teenage boys—although even some of them are just exhibiting the high that comes with that first surge of testosterone. I'm talking about the ordinary, harmless children we all come in contact with every day on the streets of our cities, towns, and, yes, villages.

6   I'm keeping score, counting the number of times I find myself the only person in a crowd who dares to interact with a child she doesn't know.

7   A few days after the swinging-baby incident I was waiting on a crowded subway platform when someone pushed me from behind. I turned to see three teenage girls, giggling, ebullient, and so eager to get on the train just pulling into the station that they were shoving. Again I reacted without thinking. "Stop pushing—we'll all get on," I said. After a few murmured remarks along the lines of "Get lost, lady," they stopped. So did the conversation around me. Eyes swiveled away. I felt a collective intake of breath. Disapproval hung in the air, but mainly I sensed fear.

8   Seconds later the train doors opened, and we all stepped in. The woman who dropped into the seat next to me said. "Wow, that was a brave thing to do." When I suggested that it was no such thing, she said, "Well, you can't be too careful these days." That's just it, I thought. You *can* be too careful.

9   In both these encounters I treated harmless children as if they were indeed harmless. They may have been foolish, thoughtless, rambunctious, rude, or annoying. But the only one in any danger was that baby swinging on the bar.

10   I live in a big city. I know that there are violent armed children, hopeless and desperate kids out there. There is no way that I can attack the serious urban problems we all hear about on the evening news. But I am convinced that we can contribute to the larger solutions by refusing to recoil from kids just because they are acting like kids. A lost child who encounters fear instead of concern is twice lost. By responding to these children we may begin to build a village where they will flourish and adults can live without fear.

★ Meaning and Understanding

1. Under what circumstances does the writer address the two teenage girls with the baby?

2. Why do some of Prinz's fellow passengers treat her with "disdain." What does "disdain" mean and why did they treat her this way?

3. What does she say to the "giggling, ebullient" girls on the subway platform? Why?

4. Each time Prinz addresses young people, the adults around her seem to be uncomfortable. Why do you think this is?

5. What do you think is the main point of this essay?

★ Techniques and Strategies

1. What is the tone of this selection? Who is the intended audience? How do you know?

2. How does narration serve the purposes of the essay?

3. How do comparison and contrast as rhetorical techniques serve the larger purposes of the essay?

4. The essay directs an argument to readers and also intends to persuade them to take some action. Has Prinz convinced you to act now in a certain way when you see "children" acting badly? Why or why not?

5. How do the title and subtitle of the essay contribute to its goal of persuasion?

★ Speaking of Values

1. Prinz cites the African adage that "It takes a whole village to raise a child." Hillary Rodham Clinton wrote a book called *It Takes a Village.* What do you understand the saying to mean? Whose responsibility is it to rear a child?

2. What kind of person does Prinz appear to be? Do you agree with the woman in the train who believes Prinz is brave? Or do you think people who watch her admonishing children who misbehave appropriately disdain Prinz? Why or why not?

3. How can Prinz be so sure that the "harmless" children she refers too are "indeed harmless"?

4. What does she mean in paragraph 8 when she remarks that "you *can* be too careful"? The usual expression is "You *can't* be too careful." Why might you agree or disagree with Prinz's version?

5. What can you infer from this essay about Prinz's idea of what "community" ought to be? Do you agree with that idea? Why or why not? Do strangers, in fact, have a responsibility to children whom they don't

know but who might benefit from an adult's observation of their behavior?

★ *Values Conversation*

Prinz comments that we as a nation do not really adhere to the idea behind the saying "It takes a whole village to raise a child." Form groups to discuss this observation. Do you agree with her? What would it take for a "village" (define it in your groups) to bring up a child appropriately?

★ *Writing about Values*

1. Write a paper about the time an unknown adult reprimanded or corrected you or someone you know in public.

2. Write a paper called "Saying Nothing" in which you point out the value and consequences of not interfering in actions you observe among strangers.

3. Write a paper in which you classify what you see as appropriate times for speaking up when you observe someone else's behavior.

James Madison

The Federalist, Number 10

Born in Virginia, James Madison (1751–1836) was the fourth president of the United States. Favoring a strong constitutional government, along with John Jay and Alexander Hamilton he published a series of essays explaining various important aspects of the new Constitution to the American public. *The Federalist, Number 10* is one of the most famous of these essays, and focuses on how to deal with factions.

───────── ★ ─────────

To the People of the State of New York.

Among the numerous advantages promised by a well constructed Union, none deserves to be more accurately developed than its tendency to break and control the violence of faction. The friend of popular governments, never finds himself so much alarmed for their character and fate, as when he contemplates their propensity to this dangerous vice. He will not fail therefore to set a due value on any plan which, without violating the principles to which he is attached, provides a proper cure for it. The instability, injustice and confusion introduced into the public councils, have in truth been the mortal diseases under which popular governments have every where perished; as they continue to be the favorite and fruitful topics from which the adversaries to liberty derive their most specious declamations. The valuable improvements made by the American Constitutions on the popular models, both ancient and modern, cannot certainly be too much admired; but it would be an unwarrantable partiality, to contend that they have as effectually obviated the danger on this side as was wished and expected. Complaints are every where heard from our most considerate and virtuous citizens, equally the friends of public and private faith, and of public and personal liberty; that our governments are too unstable; that the public good is disregarded in the conflicts of rival parties; and that measures are too often decided, not according to the rules of justice, and the rights of the minor party; but by the superior force of an interested and overbearing majority. However anxiously we may wish that these complaints had no foundation, the evidence of known facts will not permit us to deny that they are in some degree true. It will be found indeed, on a candid review of our situation, that some of the distresses under which we labor, have been erroneously charged on the operation of our governments; but it will be found, at the same time, that other causes will not alone account for many of our heaviest misfortunes; and particularly, for that prevailing and increasing distrust of public engagements, and alarm for private rights, which are echoed from one end of the continent to the other. These must be chiefly, if not wholly, effects of the unsteadiness and injustice, with which a factious spirit has tainted our public administrations.

2   By a faction I understand a number of citizens, whether amounting to a majority or minority of the whole, who are united and actuated by some common impulse of passions or of interest, adverse to the rights of other citizens, or to the permanent and aggregate interests of the community.

3   There are two methods of curing the mischiefs of faction: the one, by removing its causes; the other, by controling its effects.

4   There are again two methods of removing the causes of faction: the one by destroying the liberty which is essential to its existence; the other, by giving to every citizen the same opinions, the same passions, and the same interests.

5   It could never be more truly said than of the first remedy, that it is worse than the disease. Liberty is to faction, what air is to fire, an aliment without which it instantly expires. But it could not be a less folly to abolish liberty, which is essential to political life, because it nourishes faction, than it would be to wish the annihilation of air, which is essential to animal life, because it imports to fire its destructive agency.

6   The second expedient is as impracticable, as the first would be unwise. As long as the reason of man continues fallible, and he is at liberty to exercise it, different opinions will be formed. As long as the connection subsists between his reason and his self-love, his opinions and his passions will have a reciprocal influence on each other; and the former will be objects to which the latter will attach themselves. The diversity in the faculties of men from which the rights of property originate, is not less an insuperable obstacle to a uniformity of interests. The protection of these faculties is the first object of Government. From the protection of different and unequal faculties of acquiring property, the possession of different degrees and kinds of property immediately results: and from the influence of these on the sentiments and views of the respective proprietors, ensues a division of the society into different interests and parties.

7   The latent causes of faction are thus sown in the nature of man; and we see them every where brought into different degrees of activity, according to the different circumstances of civil society. A zeal for different opinions concerning religion, concerning Government and many other points, as well of speculation as of practice; an attachment to different leaders ambitiously contending for pre-eminence and power; or to persons of other description whose fortunes have been interesting to the human passions, have in turn divided mankind into parties, in-

flamed them with mutual animosity, and rendered them much more disposed to vex and oppress each other, than to cooperate for their common good. So strong is this propensity of mankind to fall into mutual animosities, that where no substantial occasion presents itself, the most frivolous and fanciful distinctions have been sufficient to kindle their unfriendly passions, and excite their most violent conflicts. But the most common and durable source of factions, has been the various and unequal distribution of property. Those who hold, and those who are without property, have ever formed distinct interests in society. Those who are creditors, and those who are debtors, fall under a like discrimination. A landed interest, a manufacturing interest, a mercantile interest, a monied interest, with many lesser interests, grow up of necessity in civilized nations, and divide them into different classes, actuated by different sentiments and views. The regulation of these various and interfering interests forms the principal task of modern Legislation, and involves the spirit of party and faction in the necessary and ordinary operations of Government.

No man is allowed to be a judge in his own cause; because his interest would certainly bias his judgment, and, not improbably, corrupt his integrity. With equal, nay with greater reason, a body of men, are unfit to be both judges and parties, at the same time; yet, what are many of the most important acts of legislation, but so many judicial determinations, not indeed concerning the rights of single persons, but concerning the rights of large bodies of citizens; and what are the different classes of legislators, but advocates and parties to the causes which they determine? Is a law proposed concerning private debts? It is a question to which the creditors are parties on one side, and the debtors on the other. Justice ought to hold the balance between them. Yet the parties are and must be themselves the judges; and the most numerous party, or, in other words, the most powerful faction must be expected to prevail. Shall domestic manufactures be encouraged, and in what degree, by restrictions on foreign manufactures? are questions which would be differently decided by the landed and the manufacturing classes; and probably by neither, with a sole regard to justice and the public good. The apportionment of taxes on the various descriptions of property, is an act which seems to require the most exact impartiality; yet, there is perhaps no legislative act in which greater opportunity and temptation are given to a predominant party, to trample on the rules of justice. Every shilling with which they overburden the inferior number, is a shilling saved to their own pockets.

It is in vain to say, that enlightened statesmen will be able to adjust these clashing interests, and render them all subservient to the public good. Enlightened statesmen will not always be at the helm: Nor, in many cases, can such an adjustment be made at all, without taking into view indirect and remote considerations, which will rarely prevail over the immediate interest which one party may find in disregarding the rights of another, or the good of the whole.

10   The inference to which we are brought, is, that the *causes* of faction cannot be removed; and that relief is only to be sought in means of controling its *effects*.

11   If a faction consists of less than a majority, relief is supplied by the republican principle, which enables the majority to defeat its sinister views by regular vote: It may clog the administration, it may convulse the society; but it will be unable to execute and mask its violence under the forms of the Constitution. When a majority is included in a faction, the form of popular government on the other hand enables it to sacrifice to its ruling passion or interest, both the public good and the rights of other citizens. To secure the public good, and private rights, against the danger of such a faction, and at the same time to preserve the spirit and the form of popular government, is then the great object to which our enquiries are directed: Let me add that it is the great desideratum, by which alone this form of government can be rescued from the opprobrium under which it has so long labored, and be deliberate to the esteem and adoption of mankind.

12   By what means is this object attainable? Evidently by one of two only. Either the existence of the same passion or interest in a majority at the same time, must be prevented; or the majority, having such co-existent passion or interest, must be rendered, by their number and local situation, unable to concert and carry into effect schemes of oppression. If the impulse and the opportunity be suffered to coincide, we well know that neither moral nor religious motives can be relied on as an adequate control. They are not found to be such on the injustice and violence of individuals, and lose their efficacy in proportion to the number combined together; that is, in proportion as their efficacy becomes needful.

13   From this view of the subject, it may be concluded, that a pure Democracy, by which I mean, a Society, consisting of a small number of citizens, who assemble and administer the Government in person, can admit of no cure for the mischiefs of faction. A common passion or interest will, in almost every case, be felt by a majority of the whole; a communication and concert results from the form of Government itself; and there is nothing to check the inducements to sacrifice the weaker party, or an obnoxious individual. Hence it is, that such Democracies have ever been spectacles of turbulence and contention; have ever been found incompatible with personal security, or the rights of property; and have in general been as short in their lives, as they have been violent in their deaths. Theoretic politicians, who have patronized this species of Government, have erroneously supposed, that by reducing mankind to a perfect equality in their political rights, they would, at the same time, be perfectly equalized and assimilated in their possessions, their opinions, and their passions.

A Republic, by which I mean a Government in which the scheme of   14
representation takes place, opens a different prospect, and promises the
cure for which we are seeking. Let us examine the points in which it
varies from pure Democracy, and we shall comprehend both the nature
of the cure, and the efficacy which it must derive from the Union.

The two great points of difference between a Democracy and a Re-   15
public are, first, the delegation of the Government, in the latter, to a
small number of citizens elected by the rest: secondly, the greater number of citizens, and greater sphere of country, over which the latter may
be extended.

The effect of the first difference is, on the one hand to refine and en-   16
large the public views, by passing them through the medium of a chosen body of citizens, whose wisdom may best discern the true interest
of their country, and whose patriotism and love of justice, will be least
likely to sacrifice it to temporary or partial considerations. Under such
a regulation, it may well happen that the public voice pronounced by
the representatives of the people, will be more consonant to the public
good, than if pronounced by the people themselves convened for the
purpose. On the other hand, the effect may be inverted. Men of factious
tempers, of local prejudices, or of sinister designs, may by intrigue, by
corruption or by other means, first obtain the suffrages, and then betray the interests of the people. The question resulting is, whether small
or extensive Republics are most favorable to the election of proper
guardians of the public weal: and it is clearly decided in favor of the
latter by two obvious considerations.

In the first place it is to be remarked that however small the Repub-   17
lic may be, the Representatives must be raised to a certain number, in
order to guard against the cabals of a few; and that however large it
may be, they must be limited to a certain number, in order to guard
against the confusion of a multitude. Hence the number of Representatives in the two cases, not being in proportion to that of the Constitu-
ents, and being proportionally greatest in the small Republic, it follows,
that if the proportion of fit characters, be not less, in the large than in
the small Republic, the former will present a greater option, and consequently a greater probability of a fit choice.

In the next place, as each Representative will be chosen by a greater   18
number of citizens in the large than in the small Republic, it will be
more difficult for unworthy candidates to practise with success the vicious arts, by which elections are too often carried; and the suffrages of
the people being more free, will be more likely to centre on men who
possess the most attractive merit, and the most diffusive and established characters.

It must be confessed, that in this, as in most other cases, there is a   19
mean, on both sides of which inconveniences will be found to lie. By enlarging too much the number of electors, you render the representative

too little acquainted with all their local circumstances and lesser interests; as by reducing it too much, you render him unduly attached to these, and too little fit to comprehend and pursue great and national objects. The Federal Constitution forms a happy combination in this respect, the great and aggregate interests being referred to the national, the local and particular, to the state legislatures.

20   The other point of difference is, the greater number of citizens and extent of territory which may be brought within the compass of Republican, than of Democratic Government; and it is this circumstance principally which renders factious combinations less to be dreaded in the former, than in the latter. The smaller the society, the fewer probably will be the distinct parties and interests composing it; the fewer the distinct parties and interests, the more frequently will a majority be found of the same party; and the smaller the number of individuals composing a majority, and the smaller the compass within which they are placed, the more easily will they concert and execute their plans of oppression. Extend the sphere, and you take in a greater variety of parties and interests; you make it less probable that a majority of the whole will have a common motive to invade the rights of other citizens; or if such a common motive exists, it will be more difficult for all who feel it to discover their own strength, and to act in unison with each other. Besides other impediments, it may be remarked, that where there is a consciousness of unjust or dishonorable purposes, communication is always checked by distrust, in proportion to the number whose concurrence is necessary.

21   Hence it clearly appears, that the same advantage, which a Republic has over a Democracy, in controling the effects of faction, is enjoyed by a large over a small Republic—is enjoyed by the Union over the States composing it. Does this advantage consist in the substitution of Representatives, whose enlightened views and virtuous sentiments render them superior to local prejudices, and to schemes of injustice? It will not be denied, that the Representation of the Union will be most likely to possess these requisite endowments. Does it consist in the greater security afforded by a greater variety of parties, against the event of any one party being able to outnumber and oppress the rest? In an equal degree does the encreased variety of parties, comprised within the Union, encrease this security? Does it, in fine, consist in the greater obstacles opposed to the concert and accomplishment of the secret wishes of an unjust and interested majority? Here, again, the extent of the Union gives it the most palpable advantage.

22   The influence of factious leaders may kindle a flame within their particular States, but will be unable to spread a general conflagration through the other States: a religious sect, may degenerate into a political faction in a part of the Confederacy: but the variety of sects dispersed over the entire face of it, must secure the national Councils against any danger from that source: a rage for paper money, for an abolition of

debts, for an equal division of property, or for any other improper or wicked project, will be less apt to pervade the whole body of the Union, than a particular member of it; in the same proportion as such a malady is more likely to taint a particular county or district, than an entire State.

In the extent and proper structure of the Union, therefore, we be- 23
hold a Republican remedy for the diseases most incident to Republican Government. And according to the degree of pleasure and pride, we feel in being Republicans, ought to be our zeal in cherishing the spirit, and supporting the character of Federalists.

★ *Meaning and Understanding*

1. In paragraph 1, what is the meaning of "faction" as Madison uses it?

2. What are the two methods Madison proposes for curing the "mischiefs" of factions?

3. What two ways are there for removing the causes of faction? Why does Madison reject both of them?

4. Does he convince you, in fact, that we cannot control the causes of faction, only its effects? Why or why not?

5. What distinction does Madison make between a democracy and a republic?

6. What is Madison's view of how to control the effects of faction? Why does he put so much stock in the "extent of the Union"?

★ *Techniques and Strategies*

1. Who is the intended audience for this selection? How do you know?

2. What is Madison's thesis here?

3. In formal argumentative terms, this Federalist paper is an extended syllogism. What is a syllogism? What are the major and minor premises here? How effective is Madison as a writer of argument? Does he leave you convinced of the rightness of his point? Why or why not?

4. What are the connotations here for the word "mischiefs," which Madison repeats throughout the essay?

5. What does this analogy from paragraph 5 mean: "Liberty is to faction, as air is to fire, an aliment without which it instantly expires."

6. Madison draws on a variety of rhetorical strategies to strengthen his argument. How does he use comparison and contrast, definition, and process analysis to advance his point?

7. Many people consider Madison as one of the greatest essayists of the early Republic. Why might you agree or disagree with this assessment? How does the structure of this essay show a master's hand?

★ *Speaking of Values*

1. What are the advantages of a democracy over a republic? The disadvantages? Which does Madison favor? Which do you favor? Why?

2. The idea of faction in our age often appears as "minority rights" within the broader context of "majority rules." How do you think Madison would react to this evolution of the idea of faction? What is your reaction to it? Has the society managed to control dangerous factions? Should it?

3. How would you characterize Madison's attitude toward the "public"? Why might you agree or disagree with his interpretation?

4. Madison seems to favor a large republic over a small one. Why might you agree or disagree with him? Some people think that our government has grown too large to be effective? What is your reaction to that assertion?

5. Madison's anxieties seem to stem from a fear of the violence of faction. Does factionalism invariably turn to violence? Can factions exist without violence? Why do you believe as you do?

★ *Values Conversation*

Form groups and discuss the following statement from Madison's essay: "The latent causes of faction are thus sown in the nature of man; and we see them every where wrought into different degrees of activity, according to the different circumstances of civil society." Why might you agree or disagree with him? How accurate is his view for our world today? What examples can you propose to prove him right? Wrong?

★ *Writing about Values*

1. Madison writes, "Men of factious tempers, of local prejudices, or of sinister designs, may by intrigue, by corruption or by other means, first obtain the suffrages [i.e., voters' support], and then betray the interests of the people." Write an essay in which you argue for or against that position as it applies to today's American society.

2. The central tension in all societies that attempt to uphold the principles of liberty is that between the individual and the larger society, represented by government. Write a paper in which you analyze this

tension between the individual and government. Be sure to provide appropriate examples and illustrations to support your argument.

3. Madison argues that "the most common and durable source of factions, has been the various and unequal distribution of property." Write an essay in which you consider the role of property ownership in a republic like ours.

Values in Review

1. Marjorie Miller and Ricardo Chavira, Linda Chavez, and Jules Feiffer all reexamine the issue of immigrants assimilating into American culture. Write a paper in which you explain the perspectives these writers present and then compare and contrast their views.

2. The rights, responsibilities, and obligations of the individual in relation to the larger society is a theme explored in various ways by Ralph Waldo Emerson, Walt Whitman, and Bret Harte. Write a paper in which you compare and contrast their views. Be sure to consider the following: What does the fact that each of these writers was alive in the nineteenth century tell you about attitudes toward individual prerogatives during that time? How does the genre each employs affect or influence your understanding of his point of view? Is there anything peculiarly American about their perspectives? If so, what is it?

3. Melissa Healy and Lucie Prinz both raise questions about the appropriateness of individual initiative in a free society. Write a paper in which you analyze their respective points of view using James Madison's *Federalist, Number 10* as a guide. Consider carefully what Madison has to say about "faction" and how his "solution" has relevance to both Healy and Prinz.

AMERICAN VALUES

Focus on *The Pursuit of Happiness*

The writers in this section shape a landscape of America's pursuit of happiness and the attendant values that lead us down some paths and away from others. Through this pursuit we demonstrate another feature of the nation's character. What do the selections here tell you about America or American society as we live out Jefferson's assurance of the third inalienable night? Write an essay about the pursuit of happiness: draw on the readings presented in the four chapters here, your own personal experience, and (or) what you have read or observed in America today.

Credits

★

Pages 26–29: Gregory Curtis, "Leave Ozzie and Harriet Alone" from the *New York Times Magazine* (January 19, 1997). Copyright © 1997 by The New York Times Company. Reprinted with the permission of the *New York Times*.

Pages 32–34: Randall Williams, "Daddy Tucked the Blanket" from the *New York Times* (June 10, 1975). Copyright © 1975 by The New York Times Company. Reprinted with the permission of the the the *New York Times*.

Pages 37–43: Ruth Gay, "Floors: The Bronx—Then" from *Unfinished People: East European Jews in America*. Originally published in *The American Scholar* (Summer 1995). Copyright © 1995, 1996 by Ruth Gay. Reprinted with the permission of W. W. Norton & Company, Inc.

Pages 47–51: David Blankenhorn, Chapter 7 "The Deadbeat Dad" from *Fatherless America: Confronting Our Most Urgent Social Problem*. Copyright © 1995 by the Institute for American Values. Reprinted with the permission of Basic Books, a subsidiary of Perseus Books Group, LLC.

Pages 53–58: E. B. White, "Once More to the Lake" from *One Man's Meat* (New York: Harper & Brothers, 1941). Copyright © 1941 by E. B. White. Copyright renewed © 1998 by Joel White. Reprinted with the permission of Tilbury House, Publishers, Gardiner, Maine.

Pages 61–68: Alice Walker, "Everyday Use" from *In Love & Trouble: Stories of Black Women*. Copyright © 1973 by Alice Walker. Reprinted with the permission of Harcourt Brace & Company.

Pages 71–73: Mel Lazarus, "Angry Fathers" from the *New York Times Magazine* (May 28, 1995). Copyright © 1995 by The New York Times Company. Reprinted with the permission of the *New York Times*.

Pages 76–80: Judith S. Wallerstein, Ph.D. and Sandra Blakeslee, "The Children of Divorce" (editors' title; originally titled, and excerpted from, "The Nature of Divorce") from *Second Chances: Men, Women and Children a Decade after Divorce*. Copyright © 1989 by Judith S. Wallerstein and Sandra Blakeslee. Reprinted with the permission of Ticknor & Fields/Houghton Mifflin Company. All rights reserved.

Page 83: Langston Hughes, "Mother to Son" from *The Collected Poems of Langston Hughes,* edited by Arnold Rampersad and David Roessel. Copyright 1926 by Alfred A. Knopf, Inc., renewed 1954 by Langston Hughes. Reprinted with the permission of Alfred A. Knopf, Inc.

Pages 88–94: Toni Cade Bambara, "The Lesson" from *Gorilla, My Love.* Copyright © 1972 by Toni Cade Bambara. Reprinted with the permission of Random House, Inc.

Pages 97–102: Robert Coles, "A Lesson from History: On Courage" from *The Moral Intelligence of Children*. Copyright © 1997 by Robert Coles. Reprinted with the permission of Random House, Inc.

Index of Authors
and Titles

———————— ★ ————————